"Andreas Köstenberger is a first-rate New Testament scholar, and his commentary has much to commend it. One of its major strengths is the topical presentation of the theology of the Letters to Timothy and Titus, which goes far beyond what one would expect in an average commentary. Pastors and teachers will greatly benefit from this fine exegetical and theological tool."

Armin D. Baum, *Professor für Neues Testament und Prorektor für Forschung, Freie Hochschule für Theologie, Giessen, Germany*

"Too often scholars impose preexisting theological grids on Scripture rather than inductively surfacing its themes. By stark contrast, Köstenberger is to be commended for his careful biblical-theological method: in a readable way, exegeting the text sequentially and then topically and I believe very thoroughly cataloguing the many themes that arise from this study. I know no other major attempt to catalogue the theology of the Pastoral Epistles in this way. He respectfully engages a range of authors and views, both contemporary and historic, while offering valuable intertextual observations and insights into soteriology, mission, eschatology, ethics, suffering, and numerous other areas."

Craig S. Keener, *F. M. and Ada Thompson Professor of Biblical Studies, Asbury Theological Seminary*

"While there are a number of good commentaries on the Pastoral Epistles, there are few that cover all the bases: scholarly, theological, pastoral, insightful, practical, and encouraging. But Andreas Köstenberger's new volume is all of these. It is now my go-to commentary on these important books and is sure to be the standard resource for pastors and scholars in generations to come."

Michael J. Kruger, *president and professor of New Testament, Reformed Theological Seminary, Charlotte, NC*

"The architects of the new commentary series have of their own accord set for themselves an 'ambitious project': an ocean of biblical scholarship to be navigated, the theologies of individual biblical writers to be distilled as canonical unity and diversity are negotiated, and all of this to be rendered in a way that is useful and accessible for those engaged in the teaching and preaching ministries of the church. Andreas Köstenberger's early contribution to this project is an admirable example of how to manage these challenges. His engagement with the important scholarship is thorough, judicious, and remains on task; his reconstruction of the biblical writer's theology is well executed, creatively insightful, and shaped to communicate clearly its importance and relevance to his audience. This commentary makes a contribution both to scholarship and to the church's mission, a resource that will enrich the messages and messengers who support and sustain our experience of Christian existence. As a biblical scholar and a parish priest, I most heartily recommend this book."

Philip H. Towner, *director and dean of the Nida Institute for Biblical Scholarship at American Bible Society; assistant rector, St. Ignatius of Antioch Episcopal Church, NYC*

"Andreas Köstenberger has given us a thorough exposition conversant with the latest scholarship on the Letters to Timothy and Titus. This is followed by a treatment of key theological themes in the letters. The combination of these two elements will make this a very useful resource."

Ray Van Neste, *professor of Biblical Studies and director of the Ryan Center for Biblical Studies at Union University*

"First and Second Timothy and Titus have fallen on hard times in much scholarship due to skepticism regarding their author. This commentary demonstrates the coherence, distinctive structure, literary flow, cultural connections, and theological themes found in each epistle. It also relates their teaching and admonition to the other New Testament writings, showing that the Pastoral Epistles, profoundly Pauline, are no island. The wonderful result is a commentary with scholarly ballast, literary grace, doctrinal insight, and spiritual sensitivity. It is informed by deep exegesis but does not get bogged down in technicalities. Full footnotes offer running commentary on discussion in many quarters over many decades. This should become a first go-to resource for advanced students in their research and for pastors concerned to do full justice to these writings in their ministerial labors and exposition of the Scriptures."

Robert W. Yarbrough, *professor of New Testament, Covenant Theological Seminary*

1–2 TIMOTHY & TITUS

1–2 TIMOTHY & TITUS

Evangelical Biblical Theology Commentary

General Editors
T. Desmond Alexander, Thomas R. Schreiner,
Andreas J. Köstenberger

Assistant Editors
James M. Hamilton, Kenneth A. Mathews,
Terry L. Wilder

Andreas J. Köstenberger

1–2 Timothy & Titus
Evangelical Biblical Theology Commentary

Lexham Academic, an imprint of Lexham Press
1313 Commercial St., Bellingham, WA 98225
LexhamPress.com

ISBN 9781683594314
Library of Congress Control Number 2020942291

General Editors: T. Desmond Alexander, Thomas R. Schreiner,
Andreas J. Köstenberger
Assistant Editors: James M. Hamilton, Kenneth A. Mathews, Terry L. Wilder

25 26 27 28 29 30 31 / IN / 12 11 10 9 8 7 6 5 4 3

CONTENTS

GENERAL EDITORS' PREFACE

In recent years biblical theology has seen a remarkable resurgence. Whereas, in 1970, Brevard Childs wrote *Biblical Theology in Crisis*, the quest for the Bible's own theology has witnessed increasing vitality since Childs prematurely decried the demise of the movement. Nowhere has this been truer than in evangelical circles. It could be argued that evangelicals, with their commitment to biblical inerrancy and inspiration, are perfectly positioned to explore the Bible's unified message. At the same time, as D. A. Carson has aptly noted, perhaps the greatest challenge faced by biblical theologians is how to handle the Bible's manifest diversity and how to navigate the tension between its unity and diversity in a way that does justice to both.[1]

What is biblical theology? And how is biblical theology different from related disciplines such as systematic theology? These two exceedingly important questions must be answered by anyone who would make a significant contribution to the discipline. Regarding the first question, the most basic answer might assert that biblical theology, in essence, is *the theology of the Bible*, that is, the theology expressed by the respective writers of the various biblical books *on their own terms* and *in their own historical contexts*. Biblical theology is the attempt to understand and embrace *the interpretive perspective of the biblical authors*. What is more, biblical theology is the theology of the *entire* Bible, an exercise in *whole-Bible theology*. For this reason biblical theology is not just a modern academic discipline; its roots are found already in the use of earlier

[1] D. A. Carson, "New Testament Theology," in *DLNT*, 810.

Old Testament portions in later Old Testament writings and in the use of the Old Testament in the New.

Biblical theology thus involves a close study of *the use of the Old Testament in the Old Testament* (that is, the use of, say, Deuteronomy by Jeremiah, or of the Pentateuch by Isaiah). Biblical theology also entails the investigation of *the use of the Old Testament in the New*, both in terms of individual passages and in terms of larger Christological or soteriological themes. Biblical theology may proceed *book by book*, trace *central themes* in Scripture, or seek to place the contributions of individual biblical writers within the framework of the Bible's larger overarching *metanarrative*, that is, the Bible's developing story from Genesis through Revelation at whose core is *salvation* or *redemptive history*, the account of God's dealings with humanity and his people Israel and the church from creation to new creation.

In this quest for the Bible's own theology, we will be helped by the inquiries of those who have gone before us in the *history of the church*. While we can profitably study the efforts of interpreters over the entire sweep of the history of biblical interpretation since patristic times, we can also benefit from the labors of scholars since J. P. Gabler, whose programmatic inaugural address at the University of Altdorf, Germany, in 1787 marks the inception of the discipline in modern times. Gabler's address bore the title "On the Correct Distinction between Dogmatic and Biblical Theology and the Right Definition of Their Goals."[2] While few (if any) within evangelicalism would fully identify with Gabler's program, the proper distinction between dogmatic and biblical theology (that is, between biblical and systematic theology) continues to be an important issue to be adjudicated by practitioners of both disciplines, and especially biblical theology. We have already defined biblical theology as whole-Bible theology, describing the theology of the various biblical books *on their own terms* and *in their own historical contexts*. Systematic theology, by contrast, is more topically oriented and focused on contemporary contextualization. While there are different ways in which the relationship between biblical and systematic theology can be construed, maintaining a proper

[2] The original Latin title was *Oratio de iusto discrimine theologiae biblicae et dogmaticae regundisque recte utriusque finibus*.

distinction between the two disciplines arguably continues to be vital if both are to achieve their objectives.

The present set of volumes constitutes an ambitious project, seeking to explore the theology of the Bible in considerable depth, spanning both Testaments. Authors come from a variety of backgrounds and perspectives, though all affirm the inerrancy and inspiration of Scripture. United in their high view of Scripture and in their belief in the underlying unity of Scripture, which is ultimately grounded in the unity of God himself, each author explores the contribution of a given book or group of books to the theology of Scripture as a whole. While conceived as stand-alone volumes, each volume thus also makes a contribution to the larger whole. All volumes provide a discussion of introductory matters, including the historical setting and the literary structure of a given book of Scripture. Also included is an exegetical treatment of all the relevant passages in succinct commentary-style format. The biblical theology approach of the series will also inform and play a role in the commentary proper. The commentator permits a discussion between the commentary proper and the biblical theology it reflects by a series of cross-references.

The major contribution of each volume, however, is a thorough discussion of the most important themes of the biblical book in relation to the canon as a whole. This format allows each contributor to ground biblical theology, as is proper, in an appropriate appraisal of the relevant historical and literary features of a particular book in Scripture while at the same time focusing on its major theological contribution to the entire Christian canon in the context of the larger salvation-historical metanarrative of Scripture. Within this overall format, there will be room for each individual contributor to explore the major themes of his or her particular corpus in the way he or she sees most appropriate for the material under consideration. For some books of the Bible, it may be best to have these theological themes set out in advance of the exegetical commentary. For other books it may be better to explain the theological themes after the commentary. Consequently, each contributor has the freedom to order these sections as best suits the biblical material under consideration so that the discussion of biblical-theological themes may precede or follow the exegetical commentary.

This format, in itself, would already be a valuable contribution to biblical theology. But other series try to accomplish a survey of the Bible's theology as well. What distinguishes the present series is its orientation toward Christian proclamation. This is the Evangelical Biblical Theology Commentary series! As a result, the ultimate purpose of this set of volumes is not exclusively, or even primarily, academic. Rather, we seek to relate biblical theology to our own lives and to the life of the church. Our desire is to equip those in Christian ministry who are called by God to preach and teach the precious truths of Scripture to their congregations, both in North America and in a global context.

The base translation for the Evangelical Biblical Theology Commentary series is the Christian Standard Bible (CSB). The CSB places equal value on faithfulness to the original languages and readability for a modern audience. The contributors, however, have the liberty to differ with the CSB as they comment on the biblical text. In the CSB, OT passages that are quoted in the NT are set in boldface type.

We hope and pray that the forty volumes of this series, once completed, will bear witness to the unity in diversity of the canon of Scripture as they probe the individual contributions of each of its sixty-six books. The authors and editors are united in their desire that in so doing the series will magnify the name of Christ and bring glory to the triune God who revealed himself in Scripture so that everyone who calls on the name of the Lord will be saved—to the glory of God the Father and his Son, the Lord Jesus Christ, under the illumination of the Holy Spirit, and for the good of his church. To God alone be the glory: *soli Deo gloria.*

DEDICATION

To all faithful pastors, elders, and deacons:
"so that you will know how people ought to conduct
themselves in God's household,
which is the church of the living God,
the pillar and foundation of the truth.
And most certainly, the mystery of godliness is great:
He was manifested in the flesh,
vindicated in the Spirit,
seen by angels,
proclaimed among the nations,
believed on in the world,
taken up in glory."
—1 Tim 3:14–16 CSB

ACKNOWLEDGMENTS

The present commentary continues a twenty-five-year-long quest to properly interpret and faithfully live out Paul's letters to Timothy and Titus. In fact, my engagement with these letters reaches back even further to the time when I was converted to Christ in my native Vienna, Austria, in 1983 and listened to a sermon series on 1–2 Timothy by Hans Finzel at the Vienna International Chapel. I am grateful for the mentors in the faith God provided for me since that time until today and for the opportunity to pass on what I have learned from them to others (2 Tim 2:2).

The letters to Timothy and Titus contain vital teaching on many subjects, not least the role of men and women in the church and the related topic of requirements for church leaders. The first book I coedited, *Women in the Church*—originally published in 1995, now in its third edition—addresses these vital issues, with particular focus on 1 Tim 2:9–15. Subsequently, I wrote an expository commentary on 1–2 Timothy and Titus for the revised Expositor's Bible Commentary (published in 2006). The present commentary builds on this earlier effort with a special focus on the biblical-theological dimension of these letters.

I am grateful to my student Chuck Bumgardner for his competent research assistance for this volume, in particular with regard to the biblical-theological exposition §§1 and 2 (originally one section), and portions of §3, as well as for his tireless bibliographic work. Chuck is a capable scholar in his own right and is sure to make a significant contribution to the study of the letters to Timothy and Titus, both in his Ph.D. dissertation and otherwise. Thanks are also due Dave Phillips for his research assistance with parts of §§4 and 5. It is a joy to mentor students like these!

This commentary is not written merely for fellow academicians but also—even primarily—for practitioners in the pulpit, the classroom, and the local and global church. Few scriptural books are as loaded with applicable insights and directions as the letters to Timothy and Titus. It is my hope and prayer that perusing this commentary will not merely result in greater scriptural knowledge but in more faithful practice of the principles enunciated in those letters. I have certainly learned a great deal from working on this volume, in particular with regard to the biblical-theological contribution they make to the NT and biblical canon.

Last but not least, I'd like to express my love and gratitude to my wife Margaret and to my four children—one a college graduate, two currently in college, and one starting high school. I thank God for you! I'd gladly exchange all the books and articles I've written for being your husband, Margaret, and, children, for being your dad. Paul urged Timothy, "Pay close attention to your life and your teaching; persevere in these things, for in doing this you will save [i.e., help preserve from error] both yourself and your hearers" (1 Tim 4:16). Toward this end, I dedicate this book to all pastors, elders, and deacons. May you be faithful in shepherding God's flock!

LIST OF ABBREVIATIONS

Journals, Series, and Reference Works

AB	Anchor Bible
ABD	*Anchor Bible Dictionary*
ACCS	Ancient Christian Commentary on Scripture
AnBib	Analecta Biblica
ANRW	*Aufstieg und Niedergang der römischen Welt*
ANTC	Abingdon New Testament Commentaries
ASE	*Annali di storia dell' esegesi*
AzTh	Arbeiten zur Theologie
BBR	*Bulletin for Biblical Research*
BBRSup	Bulletin for Biblical Research Supplement
BDAG	Bauer, W., F. W. Danker, W. F. Arndt, and F. W. Gingrich. *Greek-English Lexicon of the New Testament and Other Early Christian Literature*. 3rd ed. Chicago, 2000
BDF	Blass, F., A. Debrunner, and R. W. Funk, *A Greek Grammar of the New Testament and Other Early Christian Literature*. Chicago, 1961
BECNT	Baker Exegetical Commentary on the New Testament
BETL	Bibliotheca Ephemeridum Theologicarum Lovaniensium
BGU	*Berliner griechische Urkunden*
Bib	*Biblica*
BibInt	*Biblical Interpretation*

BIS	Biblical Interpretation Series
BK	*Bibel und Kirche*
BNTC	Black's New Testament Commentaries
BR	*Biblical Research*
BSac	*Bibliotheca Sacra*
BT	*The Bible Translator*
BTB	*Biblical Theology Bulletin*
BTZ	*Berliner Theologische Zeitschrift*
BZ	*Biblische Zeitschrift*
BZAW	Beihefte zur Zeitschrift für die alttestamentliche Wissenschaft
BZNW	Beihefte zur Zeitschrift für die neutestamentliche Wissenschaft
CBQ	*Catholic Biblical Quarterly*
CBQMS	Catholic Biblical Quarterly Monograph Series
Colloq	*Colloquium*
ConBNT	Coniectanea Biblica: New Testament Series
CP	*Classical Philology*
CSB	Christian Standard Bible
CTR	*Criswell Theological Review*
DBSJ	*Detroit Baptist Seminary Journal*
DJG	*Dictionary of Jesus and the Gospels.* 2nd edition. Edited by J. B. Green, J. K. Brown, and N. Perrin. Downers Grove, 2013.
DLNT	*Dictionary of the Later New Testament and Its Developments.* Edited by R. P. Martin and P. H. Davis. Downers Grove, 1997.
DNTB	*Dictionary of New Testament Background.* Edited by C. A. Evans and S. E. Porter. Downers Grove, 2000.
DPL	*Dictionary of Paul and His Letters.* Edited by G. F. Hawthorne, R. P. Martin, and D. G. Reid. Downers Grove, 1993.
EBC	Expositor's Bible Commentary
EBib	*Etudes bibliques*
ECC	Eerdmans Critical Commentary
ECL	Early Christianity and Its Literature
EDNT	*Exegetical Dictionary of the New Testament.* Edited by H. Balz and G. Schneider. ET. Grand Rapids, 1990–1993

EKKNT	Evangelisch-katholischer Kommentar zum Neuen Testament
EstBib	*Estudios bíblicos*
ESV	English Standard Version
ETL	*Ephemerides Theologiae Lovanienses*
ETS	Evangelical Theological Society
EuroJTh	*European Journal of Theology*
EvQ	*Evangelical Quarterly*
ExAud	*Ex Auditu*
Exp	*The Expositor*
ExpTim	*Expository Times*
FCNTECW	Feminist Companion to the New Testament and Early Christian Writings
FilNeot	*Filologia neotestamentaria*
FoiVie	*Foi et Vie*
HNT	Handbuch zum Neuen Testament
HorBT	*Horizons in Biblical Theology*
HThKNT	Herders Theologischer Kommentar zum Neuen Testament
HUCA	*Hebrew Union College Annual*
HUT	Hermeneutische Untersuchungen zur Theologie
IBS	*Irish Biblical Studies*
ICC	International Critical Commentary
IKZ	*Internationale kirchliche Zeitschrift*
Int	*Interpretation*
IVPNTC	IVP New Testament Commentary
JAC	*Jahrbuch für Antike und Christentum*
JBL	*Journal of Biblical Literature*
JBMW	*Journal for Biblical Manhood and Womanhood*
JETh	*Jahrbuch für evangelikale Theologie*
JETS	*Journal of the Evangelical Theological Society*
JGRChJ	*Journal of Greco-Roman Christianity and Judaism*
JJS	*Journal of Jewish Studies*
JOTT	*Journal of Translation and Textlinguistics*
JPS	Jewish Publication Society
JR	*Journal of Religion*
JRA	*Journal of Roman Archaeology*
JRelS	*Journal of Religious Studies*
JSNT	*Journal for the Study of the New Testament*

JSNTSup	Journal for the Study of the New Testament: Supplement Series
JSOT	*Journal for the Study of the Old Testament*
JSP	*Journal for the Study of the Pseudepigrapha*
JTS	*Journal of Theological Studies*
KBW	Katholisches Bibelwerk
KJV	King James Version
L&N	Lou, Johannes P., and Eugene A. Nida, eds. *Greek-English Lexicon of the New Testament: Based on Semantic Domains.* 2nd ed. New York: United Bible Societies, 1989
LCL	Loeb Classical Library
LEC	Library of Early Christianity
LNTS	Library of New Testament Studies
LS	*Louvain Studies*
LSJ	Liddell, H. G., R. Scott, and H. S. Jones, *Greek-English Lexicon*. 9th ed. with revised supplement. Oxford, 1996
LTP	*Laval théologique et philosophique*
LTQ	*Lexington Theological Quarterly*
LTT	Letters to Timothy and Titus
LXX	Septuagint
MM	Moulton, J. H., and G. Milligan, *The Vocabulary of the Greek Testament*. London, 1930. Reprint, Peabody, MA, 1997
NAC	New American Commentary
NASB	New American Standard Bible
NCBC	New Century Bible Commentary
NDBT	*New Dictionary of Biblical Theology: Exploring the Unity and Diversity of Scripture*. Edited by T. D. Alexander, B. S. Rosner, D. A. Carson, and G. Goldsworthy. Downers Grove, 2000
Neot	*Neotestamentica*
NewDocs	*New Documents Illustrating Early Christianity*. Edited by G. H. R. Horsley and S. Llewelyn. North Ryde, N.S.W., 1981–
N.F.	Neue Folge
NIB	*The New Interpreter's Bible*
NIBCNT	New International Biblical Commentary New Testament

NIBCOT	New International Biblical Commentary Old Testament
NICNT	New International Commentary on the New Testament
NIDNTT	*New International Dictionary of New Testament Theology*. Edited by C. Brown. 4 vols. Grand Rapids, 1975–1978
NIDNTTE	*New International Dictionary of New Testament Theology and Exegesis*. Edited by M. Silva. 5 vols. Grand Rapids, 2014
NIGTC	New International Greek Testament Commentary
NIV	New International Version
NKJV	New King James Version
NLT	New Living Translation
NovT	*Novum Testamentum*
NovTSup	Supplements to Novum Testamentum
NPNF1	*Nicene and Post-Nicene Fathers*, Series 1
NRSV	New Revised Standard Version
NS	New Series
NSBT	New Studies in Biblical Theology
NT	New Testament
NTAbh	Neutestamentliche Abhandlungen
NTL	New Testament Library
NTOA	Novum Testamentum et Orbis Antiquus
NTS	*New Testament Studies*
OT	Old Testament
PBI	Pontifical Biblical Institute
PE	Pastoral epistles
PL	Patrologia Latina
PNTC	Pillar New Testament Commentary
PRSt	*Perspectives in Religious Studies*
QD	Quaestiones Disputatae
RB	*Revue biblique*
ResQ	*Restoration Quarterly*
RevExp	*Review and Expositor*
RevScRel	*Revue de sciences religieuses*
RGRW	Religions in the Graeco-Roman World
RHPR	*Revue d'histoire et de philosophie religieuses*
RNT	Regensburger Neues Testament

RTR	*Reformed Theological Review*
SBET	*Scottish Bulletin of Evangelical Theology*
SBL	Society of Biblical Literature
SBLDS	Society of Biblical Literature Dissertation Series
SBLMS	Society of Biblical Literature Monograph Series
SBLSP	Society of Biblical Literature Seminar Papers Series
SBS	Stuttgarter Bibelstudien
ScrB	*Scripture Bulletin*
SEÅ	*Svensk exegetisk årsbok*
SJLA	Studies in Judaism in Late Antiquity
SJT	*Scottish Journal of Theology*
SNTS	Society for New Testament Studies
SNTSMS	Society for New Testament Studies Monograph Series
SNTSU	Studien zum Neuen Testament und seiner Umwelt
SP	Sacra Pagina
ST	*Studia Theologica*
StBibLit	Studies in Biblical Literature (Lang)
Str-B	Strack, H. L., and P. Billerbeck, *Kommentar zum Neuen Testament aus Talmud und Midrasch*. 6 vols. Munich, 1922–1961
SUNT	Studien zur Umwelt des Neuen Testaments
TD	*Theology Digest*
TDNT	*Theological Dictionary of the New Testament*. Edited by G. Kittel and G. Friedrich. Translated by G. W. Bromiley. 10 vols. Grand Rapids, 1964–1976
TGST	Tesi Gregoriana, Serie Teologia
Them	*Themelios*
THNTC	Two Horizons New Testament Commentary
TJ	*Trinity Journal*
TLNT	*Theological Lexicon of the New Testament*. C. Spicq. Translated and edited by J. D. Ernest. 3 vols. Peabody, MA, 1994
TLZ	*Theologische Literaturzeitung*
TNTC	Tyndale New Testament Commentaries

TQ	*Theologische Quartalschrift*
TynBul	*Tyndale Bulletin*
TZ	*Theologische Zeitschrift*
VC	*Vigiliae Christianae*
VE	*Vox Evangelica*
WBC	Word Biblical Commentary
WTJ	*Westminster Theological Journal*
WUNT	Wissenschaftliche Untersuchungen zum Neuen Testament
ZECNT	Zondervan Exegetical Commentary on the New Testament
ZNW	*Zeitschrift für die neutestamentliche Wissenschaft*
ZTK	*Zeitschrift für Theologie und Kirche*
ZWT	*Zeitschrift für wissenschaftliche Theologie*

Apocrypha and Septuagint

Sir	Sirach
Bar	Baruch
1–2 Macc	1–2 Maccabees

Old Testament Pseudepigrapha

Let. Aris.	Letter of Aristeas
4 Macc.	4 Maccabees
Sib. Or.	Sibylline Oracles
Sib. Or. frag.	Sibylline Oracles fragments
T. Jud.	Testament of Judah
T. Reu.	Testament of Reuben

Qumran

DSS	Dead Sea Scrolls
1QS	Community Rule
CD	Damascus Document

Targumic Texts

Tg. Ps.-J.	Targum Pseudo-Jonathan

Rabbinic Works

b.	Babylonian Talmud
B. Bat.	Baba Batra
Ber.	Berakot
m.	Mishnah
Mek. Ex.	Mekilta Exodus

Apostolic Fathers

Barn.	Barnabas
1–2 Clem.	1–2 Clement
Did.	Didache
Diogn.	Diognetus
Ignatius of Antioch	
Ign. *Eph.*	*To the Ephesians*
Ign. *Magn.*	*To the Magnesians*
Ign. *Phld.*	*To the Philadelphians*
Ign. *Pol.*	*To Polycarp*
Ign. *Smyrn.*	*To the Smyrnaeans*
Ign. *Trall.*	*To the Trallians*
Pol. *Phil.*	Polycarp, *To the Philippians*

New Testament Apocrypha and Pseudepigrapha

Apos. Con.	Apostolic Constitutions and Canons

Classical and Ancient Christian Writings

Athenagoras, *Leg.*	*Legatio pro Christianis*
Callimachus, *Hymn.*	*Hymns*
Cassius Dio, *Hist.*	*Roman History*
Cicero, *Quint. fratr.*	*Epistulae ad Quintum fratrem*
Clement, *Exc.*	*Excerpts from Theodotus*
Strom.	*Miscellanies*
Demosthenes, *Halon.*	*On the Halonnesus*
Neaer.	*Against Neaera*
Epictetus, *Diatr.*	*Diatribai (Dissertationes)*
Ench.	*Enchiridion*

Epiphanius, *Pan.*	*Refutation of All Heresies*
Eusebius, *Dem. ev.*	*Demonstration of the Gospel*
Hist. eccl.	*Ecclesiastical History*
Heraclitus, *Ep.*	*Epistles*
Hippocrates, *Vet. med.*	*Ancient Medicine*
Epid.	*Epidemiae*
Irenaeus, *Haer.*	*Against Heresies*
Jerome, *Comm. Tit.*	*Commentary on Titus*
Vir. ill.	*De viris illustribus*
Josephus, *Ant.*	*Antiquities of the Jews*
J.W.	*Jewish Wars*
Justin, *1 Apol.*	*First Apology*
Juvenal, *Sat.*	*Satires*
Lucian, *Philops.*	*The Lover of Lies*
Tim.	*Timon*
Origen, *Cels.*	*Against Celsus*
Ovid, *Am.*	*Amores*
Philo, *Alleg. Interp.*	*Allegorical Interpretation*
Creation	*On the Creation of the World*
Drunkenness	*On Drunkenness*
Embassy	*On the Embassy to Gaius*
Flaccus	*Against Flaccus*
Hypothetica	*Hypothetica (Apology for the Jews)*
Moses	*On the Life of Moses*
Spec. Laws	*On the Special Laws*
Philodemus, *Rhet.*	*Volumina rhetorica*
Plato, *Gorg.*	*Gorgias*
Phaedr.	*Phaedrus*
Resp.	*Respublica (Republic)*
Pliny the Elder, *Nat.*	*Natural History*
Pliny the Younger,	
Ep.	*Letters*
Plutarch, *Aem.*	*Aemilius Paullus*
Cat. Min.	*Cato the Younger*
Is. Os.	*De Iside et Osiride*
Lys.	*Lysander*
Mor.	*Moralia*
Num.	*Numa*
Quaest. conv.	*Quaestionum convivalum*
Polybius, *Hist.*	*Histories*

Ps.-Phoc.	Pseudo-Phocylides
Ps.-Sophocles	Pseudo-Sophocles
Seneca, *Helv.*	*Ad Helviam*
Strabo, *Geogr.*	*Geography*
Tacitus, *Ann.*	*Annals*
Tertullian, *An.*	*The Soul*
Apol.	*Apology*
Bapt.	*Baptism*
Praescr.	*Prescription against Heretics*
Theophilius, *Autol.*	*To Autolycus*

INTRODUCTION

Paul's letters to Timothy and Titus (LTT), his apostolic delegates,[1] form a vital part of the Pauline corpus. While many in recent years have questioned Pauline authorship, there is good reason to believe these letters culminate Paul's apostolic ministry, seeking to perpetuate his legacy and to ensure the continuity of faithful gospel ministry for subsequent generations. While Paul's earlier letters, with the exception of Philemon, are directed to local congregations and address a variety of specific issues, the LTT primarily aim to equip individuals who were dispatched by the apostle to establish and maintain proper church governance in conjunction with the false teaching in Ephesus and Crete, respectively.[2] While it's virtually impossible to determine whether 1 Timothy or Titus was written first, Paul's second letter to Timothy, the most personal of the three, was probably written last, constituting Paul's final appeal to his longtime coworker and protégé. The letter constitutes a moving tribute to the passion and

[1] See, e.g., W. D. Mounce, *Pastoral Epistles*, WBC 46 (Nashville: Nelson, 2000), lxxxviii: "Timothy and Titus stand outside the church structure. They are not bishops or elders. . . . They are itinerant, apostolic delegates sent with Paul's authority to deal with local problems. . . . Timothy and Titus are never told to rely on their institutional position in the local church for authority; rather they rely on the authority of Paul and the gospel." Similarly, T. R. Schreiner, "Overseeing and Serving the Church in the Pastoral and General Epistles," in *Shepherding God's Flock: Biblical Leadership in the New Testament and Beyond*, ed. B. L. Merkle and T. R. Schreiner (Grand Rapids: Kregel, 2014), 99: "Timothy and Titus were not pastors/overseers/elders. They were temporary delegates for the churches."

[2] In addition, the plurals "you" in 1 Tim 6:21; 2 Tim 4:22; and Titus 3:15 suggest that Timothy and Titus were to share the contents of the letters with their respective congregations.

intensity for preaching the gospel that fueled Paul's ministry until his final hour.

In studying the LTT, it will be vital to adopt a balanced interpretive approach that investigates in depth the matrix of the historical setting, literary character, and theological message of each letter.[3] Rather than assuming that the settings are identical, we'll attempt to determine the background of each letter individually. With regard to literary and linguistic matters, we'll aim to analyze the genre, literary structure, and meaning of key terms in their ancient context, in conversation with other modern interpreters of the letters.[4] Since the historical setting and literary structure set the stage for interpreting the theological message of a given book, and since conventional commentaries cover exegetical matters in some detail, the primary focus of this commentary will be on significant theological themes featured in these letters, such as mission, salvation, the church as God's household, the life of faith, and the end times, and on relating the LTT to the rest of the canon, particularly the OT, the other Pauline letters, Luke-Acts, and the other NT letters.

For those committed to the authority of Scripture, it's hardly necessary to underscore the relevance of these letters for the

---

[3] See A. J. Köstenberger and R. D. Patterson, *Invitation to Biblical Interpretation: Exploring the Hermeneutical Triad of History, Literature, and Theology* (Grand Rapids: Kregel, 2012).

[4] Although many insightful works on the LTT were produced before the twentieth century, I have chosen in this commentary to limit myself largely to literature produced in the last century, which in turn often takes into account earlier treatments. For those interested in engaging earlier writers, an excellent starting point is P. Gorday, *Colossians, 1–2 Thessalonians, 1–2 Timothy, Titus, Philemon*, ACCS (Downers Grove: InterVarsity, 2000). The outstanding "History of Interpretation" in L. T. Johnson, *The First and Second Letters to Timothy*, AB 35A (Garden City, NY: Doubleday, 2001), 20–54, surveys the gamut of interpreters and interpretive approaches of those letters across the entire sweep of church history. Although there are far too many earlier works—even in English translation—to list here, a few may be profitably noted: John Chrysostom, "Homilies on the Epistles of St. Paul the Apostle to Timothy, Titus, and Philemon," in *NPNF1* 13, ed. P. Schaff (1899; repr. Grand Rapids: Eerdmans, 1956); Theodore of Mopsuestia, *Commentary on the Minor Pauline Epistles*, trans. R. A. Greer, SBL Writings from the Greco-Roman World 26 (Atlanta: SBL, 2010), 525–772; Thomas Aquinas, *Commentaries on St. Paul's Epistles to Timothy, Titus, and Philemon*, trans. C. Baer (South Bend, IN: St. Augustine, 2008); Martin Luther, *Lectures on Titus, Philemon, and Hebrews*, Luther's Works 29 (St. Louis: Concordia, 1968); John Calvin, *1 & 2 Timothy & Titus* (1556, 1549; repr., Wheaton: Crossway, 1998).

church today.[5] While Paul's instructions are firmly embedded in their first-century context, many of the issues addressed in these letters transcend the original occasion and are of perennial value in guiding the governance of local congregations and the lives of individual believers. It is precisely the intricate interweaving of intimate personal details and abiding ecclesiastical realities that roots these letters so firmly in Paul's relationship with his recipients.[6] In modern times scholars have often noted differences in wording and subject matter between Paul's earlier letters and the LTT, relegating the latter to the post-apostolic period. More likely, as will be argued in greater detail below, they constitute the culmination of Paul's apostolic ministry and theological thought at a time when the aged apostle was seeking to pass on his legacy. Together with his other canonical letters, the LTT therefore provide a rich and indispensable contribution to Pauline and biblical theology.[7]

---

[5] Cf. K. P. Donfried, "Rethinking Scholarly Approaches to 1 Timothy," in *1 Timothy Reconsidered*, ed. K. P. Donfried, Colloquium Oecumenicum Paulinum 18 (Leuven: Peeters, 2008), 156: "A serious pastoral problem that only emerged at the end of the last century is that the radically corrective approach has effectively led to the disenfranchisement of these letters in much of mainline Protestantism since they have, for all intents and purposes, been moved to the edge or out of the canon, a process facilitated by much of feminist biblical scholarship." Cf. M. M. Jacobs, "On 1 Timothy 2:9–15: Why Still Interpret 'Irredeemable' Biblical Texts?," *Scriptura* 88 (2005): 85–100, who says this passage reveals "the darker side of the Bible" which at times "rouses acute anger" but may "become a therapeutic exercise, a turning-point and thereby a starting-point for going ahead in a very different way" (p. 99); and G. West, "Taming Texts of Terror: Reading (Against) the Gender Grain of 1 Timothy," *Scriptura* 86 (2004): 160–73.

[6] See also the interesting observation by R. Wall: "Moreover, the different social locations of the Pastoral Epistles—the urban and urbane Ephesus of Timothy and the uncivilized Crete of Titus (cf. 1:12)—create something of a cultural merism such that readers might accept the similar instructions of both letters as providing guidance for every congregation. The credentials for leaders, the household codes, and the pastoral instructions and exhortations in both letters, directed to disparate places, suggest that the claims of Paul's gospel and his instructions to congregations and their leaders do not change from place to place." R. W. Wall, with R. B. Steele, *1 and 2 Timothy and Titus*, THNTC (Grand Rapids: Eerdmans, 2012), 332.

[7] Unfortunately, however, the LTT are often excluded from Pauline theologies: see, e.g., J. D. G. Dunn, *The Theology of Paul the Apostle* (Grand Rapids: Eerdmans, 2006); U. Schnelle, *Apostle Paul: His Life and Theology*, trans. M. E. Boring (Grand Rapids: Baker, 2005); but cf. F. J. Matera, *God's Saving Grace: A Pauline Theology* (Grand Rapids: Eerdmans, 2012); H. Ridderbos, *Paul: An Outline of His Theology*, trans. J. R. De Witt (Grand Rapids: Eerdmans, 1975); T. R. Schreiner, *Paul, Apostle of God's Glory*

I. Author and Date

The LTT form an integral part of the fabric of early Christian history.[8] Supplementing Acts, they provide instructions regarding congregational leadership and other important matters related to governing and administering the local church. Most likely they were the last letters Paul wrote during his long missionary career toward the end of his apostolic ministry. As early as in the Muratorian Fragment (ca. AD 180), the special character of these letters is recognized, and they are acknowledged as being concerned with "the regulation of ecclesiastical discipline."[9] The often used designation "Pastoral Epistles" dates back to D. N. Berdot, who called Titus a "Pastoral Epistle" in 1703, and P. Anton of Halle, who in 1726 delivered a series of lectures on the LTT entitled "The Pastoral Epistles."[10] The eighteenth-century phrase has an antecedent in T. Aquinas, who called 1 Timothy "a rule, so to speak, for pastors" (*quasi pastoralis regula*).[11] Nevertheless, as we'll see shortly, the label "Pastorals" is not without its drawbacks.

---

in Christ: A Pauline Theology (Downers Grove: InterVarsity, 2006). For a survey of different approaches to biblical theology, see A. J. Köstenberger, "The Present and Future of Biblical Theology," *Them* 37 (2012): 445–64.

[8] For a survey of relevant introductory matters, see A. J. Köstenberger, S. L. Kellum, and C. L. Quarles, *The Cradle, the Cross, and the Crown: An Introduction to the New Testament*, 2nd ed. (Nashville: B&H Academic, 2016), chap. 15. For an expository commentary, see A. J. Köstenberger, "1–2 Timothy, Titus," in *Expositor's Bible Commentary*, vol. 12: *Ephesians-Philemon*, rev. ed. (Grand Rapids: Zondervan, 2006), 487–625.

[9] Cf. L. T. Johnson, *Letters to Paul's Delegates: 1 Timothy, 2 Timothy, Titus*, The NT in Context (Valley Forge, PA: Trinity Press International, 1996), 3; G. W. Knight, *Commentary on the Pastoral Epistles*, NIGTC (Grand Rapids: Eerdmans, 1992), 3. See further the discussion under Canonicity below.

[10] P. Anton, *Exegetische Abhandlung der Pastoralbriefe S. Pauli an Timotheum und Titum*, ed. J. A. Maier (Halle, 1753–55); D. N. Berdot, *Exercitatio theologica exegetica in epistulam Pauli ad Titum* (Halle, 1703), 3–4.

[11] J. D. Quinn, *The Letter to Titus*, AB 35 (Garden City, NY: Doubleday, 1990), 1, with reference to T. Aquinas, *Commentariea* 2.184D; *Super I Epistolam ad Timotheum, lectio ii in 1:3* (Turin: Marietti, 1929). Johnson, *First and Second Letters to Timothy*, 13n3, also notes that Abraham Scultetus used the term *pastoralis* in the mid-seventeenth century (see also p. 35 regarding Aquinas).

A. Relationship among the Letters

The LTT are often treated as a distinct, self-referential corpus.[12] In fact, 1 and 2 Timothy share the same recipient, and all three letters were written to Paul's apostolic delegates in Ephesus and Crete, respectively, in order to provide instructions on how to continue Paul's mission work in a given locale under his overall jurisdiction. All three letters were most likely written toward the end of Paul's life and ministry subsequent to his ten other letters included in the NT canon. There are also some similarities in the descriptions of the opponents in these letters, particularly 1 and 2 Timothy.[13] What is more, there is an indisputable broad congruence in conceptuality—even specific vocabulary—and subject matter among the three letters.[14]

For example, 1 Timothy and Titus share the following topics in common:

1 Timothy	Titus	Topic
2:1–2	3:1–2	Civic authorities
3:1–13	1:5–9	Church officers
5:1–6:2	2:1–15	Conduct in God's household*
*This includes specific instructions to slaves: 1 Tim 6:1–2; Titus 2:9–10.		

Similarly, 1 and 2 Timothy share several points of contact:

[12] See especially P. Trummer, "Corpus Paulinum—Corpus Pastorale: Zur Ortung der Paulustradition in den Pastoralbriefen," in *Paulus in den neutestamentlichen Spätschriften: Zur Paulusrezeption im Neuen Testament*, ed. K. Kertelge, QD 89 (Freiburg: Herder, 1981), 122–45. See also G. Häfner, "Das Corpus Pastorale als literarisches Konstrukt," *TQ* 187 (2007): 258–73.

[13] E.g., the word "myth" (μῦθος) is used in all three letters; see the discussion under Historical Context below. D. T. Thornton, *Hostility in the House of God: An Investigation of the Opponents in 1 and 2 Timothy*, BBRSup 15 (Winona Lake, IN: Eisenbrauns, 2016), limits his investigation to 1 and 2 Timothy because he believes the opponents are different from those in Titus; Herzer, "Juden—Christen—Gnostiker: Zur Gegnerproblematik der Pastoralbriefe," *BTZ* 25 (2008): 143–68 believes three different kinds of opponents are in view. See also Herzer, "Abschied vom Konsens? Die Pseudepigraphie der Pastoralbriefe als Herausforderung an die neutestamentliche Wissenschaft," *TLZ* 129 (2004): 1267–82, arguing for the pseudonymity of all three letters.

[14] See chart 71, "Similarities between the Pastoral Epistles," in L. Kierspel, *Charts on the Life, Letters, and Theology of Paul* (Grand Rapids: Kregel, 2012), 133–35; see also pp. 234–35.

1 Timothy	2 Timothy	Topic
1:12–16	1:8–15	Personal recollection
1:18; 4:14; 6:13	1:6; 4:1	Personal commission
1:3–7; 4:1–3; 6:4, 20	2:14, 16, 23; 3:1–5; 4:1–4	Warning against false teaching*
*Cf. J. D. G. Dunn, "The First and Second Letters to Timothy and the Letter to Titus: Introduction, Commentary, and Reflections," in *NIB* 11:776–77.		

At the same time, each of these letters has its own original setting, which requires that introductory matters such as recipient, date, purpose, and occasion be adjudicated individually and each letter be read and interpreted in its own right.[15] Also, technically Timothy and Titus were apostolic delegates, not local pastors. For these and other reasons, viewing 1 and 2 Timothy and Titus as a self-contained corpus ("The Pastoral Epistles") is of limited value.[16] This is the case also because such a procedure sets off these epistles from the other ten Pauline letters rather than viewing them as part

[15] Notably, proponents of authenticity and proponents of pseudonymity alike argue against corpus reading. Among those favoring authenticity while opposing a corpus reading are R. Fuchs, *Unerwartete Unterschiede: Müssen wir unsere Ansichten über "die" Pastoralbriefe revidieren?* (Wuppertal: R. Brockhaus, 2003; see the summary on pp. 222–26); and M. Prior, *Paul the Letter-Writer and the Second Letter to Timothy*, JSNTSup 23 (Sheffield: JSOT, 1989). Another strong proponent of reading the letters separately is L. T. Johnson, *First and Second Letters to Timothy*; Johnson, *Letters to Paul's Delegates*. Among those advocating pseudonymity and opposing a corpus reading of these letters are B. Ehrman, *Forgery and Counterforgery: The Use of Literary Deceit in Early Christian Polemic* (Oxford: Oxford University Press, 2013); J. Herzer, "Rearranging the 'House of God': A New Perspective on the Pastoral Epistles," in Empsychoi Logoi—*Religious Innovations in Antiquity: Studies in Honour of Pieter Willem van der Horst*, ed. A. Houtman, A. de Jong, and M. Misset-van de Weg (Leiden: Brill, 2008), 547–66; and J. Murphy O'Connor, "2 Timothy Contrasted with 1 Timothy and Titus," *RB* 98 (1991): 403–18.

[16] See P. H. Towner, *The Letters to Timothy and Titus*, NICNT (Grand Rapids: Eerdmans, 2006), 88–89, who believes it's time to say farewell to the nomenclature "Pastoral Epistles" because it serves as a "restraining device" from studying the letters individually. Towner opposes the tendency to "corpus read" the three letters and to treat them as an indivisible unit. At the same time he recognizes that they form a "cluster" in light of their commonalities. Similarly, Johnson, *First and Second Letters to Timothy*, 63–64; and Thornton, *Hostility in the House of God*, 5, who concurs that "it is best to set aside this sobriquet" since these documents "do not constitute a primer on church polity, and there is little to suggest that the first addressees should be thought of as pastors." However, Thornton's substitute, "Pauline Delegates" (PD; p. 6), is problematic as well, since texts such as the LTT cannot easily be thought of as "delegates."

of the Pauline body of writings at large. What is more, treating 1 and 2 Timothy and Titus as part of the larger Pauline letter collection is in keeping with patristic evidence and early canonical lists (see Canonicity below).

An investigation of the relationship among the three letters calls for judiciousness and balance. Two extremes should be avoided: (1) treating the three letters as completely separate without acknowledging points of contact among them (e.g., same recipient in 1 and 2 Timothy; both Timothy and Titus are Paul's apostolic delegates; the false teachers share some common characteristics); and (2) collapsing the boundaries between 1 Timothy, 2 Timothy, and Titus as distinct letters to the extent that their individuality is insufficiently recognized. In the end it seems best to engage the three letters not as a corpus but as a "cluster," being sensitive to both the things that bind them together and the things that make them distinct. The present commentary therefore avoids speaking of "The Pastoral Epistles" while pointing out connections between two or all three of these letters as appropriate.

While caution is called for in designating the three letters as a separate corpus apart from the other NT Pauline letters, the similarities in language and content, not to mention explicit attribution of all three letters to Paul, do seem to indicate common authorship.[17] Keeping 1 and 2 Timothy and Titus distinct from one another and yet viewing them as related and as part of the larger Pauline letter collection has the advantage of placing these letters within the larger Pauline theological orbit and historical chronology and of showing affinities as well as differences in relation to the other ten canonical Pauline letters. This will be particularly helpful in the biblical-theological exposition of major themes in 1, 2 Timothy and Titus later on in this volume.

[17] Against W. A. Richards, *Difference and Distance in Post-Pauline Christianity: An Epistolary Analysis of the Pastorals*, StBibLit 44 (New York: P. Lang, 2002), who claims the three letters are post-Pauline and manifest differences in Christianity toward the end of the first century. But see the critique by I. H. Marshall, "Pastoral Epistles in Recent Study," in *Entrusted with the Gospel: Paul's Theology in the Pastoral Epistles*, ed. A. J. Köstenberger and T. L. Wilder (Nashville: B&H, 2010), 284–85, who objects that Richards has taken too little account of the resemblances between the letters, particularly given that "the theologies expressed in these letters and the way in which they are presented are recognizably the same" (p. 285).

B. Role of Timothy and Titus

Timothy and Titus are often viewed as pastors of local congregations. However, as mentioned, their role is not actually that of permanent, resident pastor of a church. Rather, these men serve as Paul's apostolic delegates who are temporarily assigned to their present location in order to deal with particular problems that have arisen in their respective churches and require special attention (§1.3).[18] For this reason Paul's correspondence with Timothy and Titus doesn't merely contain advice to younger ministers. It records Paul's instructions to his special delegates toward the close of the apostolic era at a time when the aging apostle feels a keen responsibility to ensure the orderly transition from the apostolic to the post-apostolic period.[19] Toward that end the LTT provide authoritative and relevant apostolic guidance not only for the original recipients but also for the governance of the church at any place and time.

NT REFERENCES TO TIMOTHY OUTSIDE 1–2 TIMOTHY

"Paul went on to Derbe and Lystra, where there was a disciple named **Timothy**, the son of a believing Jewish woman, but his father was a Greek. The brothers and sisters at Lystra and Iconium spoke highly of him. Paul wanted **Timothy** to go with him; so he took him and circumcised him because of the Jews who were in those places, since they all knew that his father was a Greek." (Acts 16:1–3)

---

[18] See G. D. Fee, *1 and 2 Timothy, Titus*, NIBCNT 13 (Peabody, MA: Hendrickson, 1988), 21.

[19] Advocates of pseudonymity place the letters at a later point in the Pauline trajectory. See, e.g., J. W. Aageson, "The Pastoral Epistles, Apostolic Authority, and the Development of the Pauline Scriptures," in *The Pauline Canon*, ed. S. E. Porter, Pauline Studies 1 (Leiden: Brill, 2004), 5–26, who contends that the LTT present Paul as the "defender of correct doctrine and the recipient of divine authority" (p. 11); Aageson, *Paul, the Pastoral Epistles, and the Early Church* (Peabody, MA: Hendrickson, 2008); M. Y. MacDonald, *The Pauline Churches: A Socio-Historical Study of Institutionalism in the Pauline and Deutero-Pauline Writings*, SNTSMS 60 (Cambridge: Cambridge University Press, 1988). M. C. de Boer, "Images of Paul in the Post-Apostolic Period," *CBQ* 42 (1980): 359–80 believes the LTT are part of the post-Pauline trajectory and present Paul as the paradigmatic apostle to the nations who brought the gospel to the whole world and suffered as the redeemed prosecutor and authoritative teacher of the church (p. 370). R. F. Collins, "The Image of Paul in the Pastorals," *LTP* 31 (1975): 147–73 contends that the LTT contain traces of an emerging Pauline hagiography and are characterized by "Pauline reductionism," presenting him as *the* apostle, norm for church doctrine and practice, and as *the* model for Christians to emulate.

NT REFERENCES TO TIMOTHY OUTSIDE 1–2 TIMOTHY (continued)

"But when the Jews from Thessalonica found out that the word of God had been proclaimed by Paul at Berea, they came there too, agitating and upsetting the crowds. Then the brothers and sisters immediately sent Paul away to go to the coast, but Silas and **Timothy** stayed on there. Those who escorted Paul brought him as far as Athens, and after receiving instructions for Silas and **Timothy** to come to him as quickly as possible, they departed." (Acts 17:13–15)
"When Silas and **Timothy** arrived [in Corinth] from Macedonia, Paul devoted himself to preaching the word and testified to the Jews that Jesus is the Messiah." (Acts 18:5)
"After these events [in Ephesus], Paul resolved by the Spirit to pass through Macedonia and Achaia and go to Jerusalem. 'After I've been there,' he said, 'it is necessary for me to see Rome as well.' After sending to Macedonia two of those who assisted him, **Timothy** and Erastus, he himself stayed in Asia for a while." (Acts 19:21–22)
"[Paul] was accompanied by Sopater son of Pyrrhus from Berea, Aristarchus and Secundus from Thessalonica, Gaius from Derbe, **Timothy**, and Tychicus and Trophimus from the province of Asia." (Acts 20:4)
"**Timothy**, my coworker, and Lucius, Jason, and Sosipater, my fellow countrymen, greet you." (Rom 16:21)
"This is why I have sent **Timothy** to you. He is my dearly loved and faithful child in the Lord. He will remind you about my ways in Christ Jesus, just as I teach everywhere in every church." (1 Cor 4:17)
"If **Timothy** comes [to Corinth], see that he has nothing to fear while with you, because he is doing the Lord's work, just as I am. So let no one look down on him. Send him on his way in peace so that he can come to me, because I am expecting him with the brothers." (1 Cor 16:10–11)
"Paul, an apostle of Christ Jesus by the will of God, and **Timothy** our brother: To the church of God at Corinth, with all the saints who are throughout Achaia." (2 Cor 1:1–2)
"For the Son of God, Jesus Christ, whom we proclaimed among you—Silvanus, **Timothy**, and I—did not become 'Yes and no.' On the contrary, in him it is always 'Yes.'" (2 Cor 1:19)
"Paul and **Timothy**, servants of Christ Jesus: To all the saints in Christ Jesus who are in Philippi, including the overseers and deacons." (Phil 1:1)

NT REFERENCES TO TIMOTHY OUTSIDE 1–2 TIMOTHY (continued)

"Now I hope in the Lord Jesus to send **Timothy** to you soon so that I too may be encouraged by news about you. For I have no one else like-minded who will genuinely care about your interests; all seek their own interests, not those of Jesus Christ. But you know his proven character, because he has served with me in the gospel ministry like a son with a father. Therefore, I hope to send him as soon as I see how things go with me. I am confident in the Lord that I myself will also come soon." (Phil 2:19–24)
"Paul, an apostle of Christ Jesus by God's will, and **Timothy** our brother: To the saints in Christ at Colossae, who are faithful brothers and sisters." (Col 1:1)
"Paul, Silvanus, and **Timothy**: To the church of the Thessalonians in God the Father and the Lord Jesus Christ." (1 Thess 1:1)
"Therefore, when we could no longer stand it, we thought it was better to be left alone in Athens. And we sent **Timothy**, our brother and God's coworker in the gospel of Christ, [to Thessalonica] to strengthen and encourage you concerning your faith, so that no one will be shaken by these afflictions. . . . But now **Timothy** has come to us from you and brought us good news about your faith and love. He reported that you always have good memories of us and that you long to see us, as we also long to see you." (1 Thess 3:1–3a, 6)
"Paul, Silvanus, and **Timothy**: To the church of the Thessalonians in God our Father and the Lord Jesus Christ." (2 Thess 1:1)
"Paul, a prisoner of Christ Jesus, and **Timothy** our brother: To Philemon our dear friend and coworker, to Apphia our sister, to Archippus our fellow soldier, and to the church that meets in your home." (Phlm 1–2)
"Brothers and sisters, I urge you to receive this message of exhortation, for I have written to you briefly. Be aware that our brother **Timothy** has been released. If he comes soon enough, he will be with me when I see you." (Heb 13:22–23)

NT REFERENCES TO TITUS OUTSIDE THE LETTER TO TITUS

"When I came to Troas to preach the gospel of Christ, even though the Lord opened a door for me, I had no rest in my spirit because I did not find my brother **Titus**. Instead, I said good-bye to them and left for Macedonia." (2 Cor 2:12–13)
"In fact, when we came into Macedonia, we had no rest. Instead, we were troubled in every way: conflicts on the outside, fears within. But God, who comforts the downcast, comforted us by the arrival of **Titus**, and not only by his arrival, but also by the comfort he received from you." (2 Cor 7:5–7)

NT REFERENCES TO TITUS OUTSIDE THE LETTER TO TITUS (continued)

"In addition to our own comfort, we rejoiced even more over the joy **Titus** had, because his spirit was refreshed by all of you. For if I have made any boast to him about you, I have not been disappointed; but as I have spoken everything to you in truth, so our boasting to **Titus** has also turned out to be the truth. And his affection toward you is even greater as he remembers the obedience of all of you, and how you received him with fear and trembling." (2 Cor 7:13b–15)
"So we urged **Titus** that just as he had begun, so he should also complete among you this act of grace. . . . Thanks be to God, who put the same concern for you into the heart of **Titus**. For he welcomed our appeal and, being very diligent, went out to you by his own choice. . . . As for **Titus**, he is my partner and coworker for you; as for our brothers, they are the messengers of the churches, the glory of Christ." (2 Cor 8:6, 16–17, 23)
"Did I take advantage of you by any of those I sent you? I urged **Titus** to go, and I sent the brother with him. **Titus** didn't take advantage of you, did he? Didn't we walk in the same spirit and in the same footsteps?" (2 Cor 12:17–18)
"Then after fourteen years I went up again to Jerusalem with Barnabas, taking **Titus** along also. I went up according to a revelation and presented to them the gospel I preach among the Gentiles, but privately to those recognized as leaders. I wanted to be sure I was not running, and had not been running, in vain. But not even **Titus**, who was with me, was compelled to be circumcised, even though he was a Greek." (Gal 2:1–3)
"Make every effort to come to me soon, because Demas has deserted me, since he loved this present world, and has gone to Thessalonica. Crescens has gone to Galatia, **Titus** to Dalmatia." (2 Tim 4:9–10)

C. Order of the Letters

Most likely, 1 Timothy and Titus were written following Paul's release from his first Roman imprisonment but prior to a second, more severe Roman imprisonment during which Paul composed 2 Timothy (see Pauline Chronology below). It's unknown whether Paul wrote 1 Timothy or Titus first.[20] In the canon the order is 1 Timothy–2 Timothy–Titus, even though the actual chronological order of writing was almost certainly 1 Timothy–Titus–2 Timothy

[20] See Mounce, *Pastoral Epistles*, lxi, who adds, "It is not possible to determine whether Paul wrote 1 Timothy or Titus first. All that I am comfortable saying is that the similarity of language between 1 Timothy and Titus may suggest that they were written at approximately the same time" (p. lxii).

or Titus–1 Timothy–2 Timothy.[21] In this volume the canonical order will be followed, and 2 Timothy be discussed prior to Titus and in conjunction with 1 Timothy, since 1 and 2 Timothy share a common recipient and overlap in other respects as well.[22]

D. Canonicity

In all probability, Paul's letters to Timothy were known to Polycarp (ca. 117), who may have cited 1 Tim 6:7, 10 (*Phil.* 4.1).[23] The first unmistakable patristic attestations are found in Athenagoras (*Leg.* 37.1; ca. 180) and Theophilus (*Autol.* 3.14; later 2nd c.), both of whom cite 1 Tim 2:1–2 and allude to other passages. Irenaeus (*Haer.* 1.preface; 1.23.4; 2.14.7; 3.1.1; ca. 130–200) cites the letters and identifies Paul as their author.[24] Clement of Alexandria (ca. 150–215) notes that some Gnostics who perceive themselves to be

---

[21] Mounce (ibid., lxii) notes that the Muratorian Canon (ca. AD 180) has the order Titus–1 Timothy–2 Timothy, presumably so as to place 2 Timothy last as Paul's final letter. J. D. Quinn (*Letter to Titus*, 19–20) seeks to make a case for the priority of Titus (cf. W. G. Doty, "The Classification of Epistolary Literature," *CBQ* 31 [1969]: 192–98). I. H. Marshall, *Pastoral Epistles*, ICC (Edinburgh: T&T Clark, 1999), 92 hypothesizes that 2 Timothy came first and 1 Timothy and Titus were written by someone other than Paul after his death. Similarly, Johnson (*Letters to Paul's Delegates*) deals first with 2 Timothy and then with 1 Timothy and Titus. See also M. Engelmann, *Unzertrennliche Drillinge? Motivsemantische Untersuchungen zum literarischen Verhältnis der Pastoralbriefe*, BZNW 192 (Berlin: de Gruyter, 2012), who argues that 1 Timothy was written last and that the author had already received the two other letters as part of the Pauline tradition.

[22] The earliest extant manuscript containing portions of Titus is the John Rylands fragment (𝔓[32]; 3rd c.) which contains parts of 1:11–15 and 2:3-8. E. Gathergood ("Papyrus 32 Titus as a Multi-text Codex: A New Reconstruction," *NTS* 59 [2013]: 588–606) offers a reconstruction suggesting that this fragment was part of a multitext codex and that Titus was preceded by at least one other book (possibly 1 Timothy) and may have been part of a collection of thirteen or fourteen Pauline epistles.

[23] See the discussion in Marshall, *Pastoral Epistles*, 3–8 (including the tables on pp. 4–5). Note also P. Hartog, *Polycarp and the New Testament: The Occasion, Rhetoric, Theme and Unity of the Epistle to the Philippians and Its Allusions to New Testament Literature*, WUNT 134 (Tübingen: Mohr Siebeck, 2002), 178–79. On the reception of the LTT in the Apostolic Fathers, see *The Reception of the New Testament in the Apostolic Fathers*, ed. A. F. Gregory and C. M. Tuckett (Oxford/New York: Oxford University Press, 2006), 151 (*1 Clement*), 170–72 (Ignatius), 215–18 (Polycarp), 288–89 (*2 Clement*).

[24] Cf. Gathergood, "Papyrus 32," 598, who also discusses the Muratorian fragment and other Fathers such as Tertullian, Theophilus, and Clement of Alexandria.

the targets of the denunciation of 1 Tim 6:20–21 reject Paul's letters to Timothy (*Strom.* 2.11).

The Muratorian Fragment (ca. AD 180) includes all three letters in the Pauline corpus. The relevant portion reads as follows:

> [Paul also wrote] out of affection and love one [epistle] to Philemon, *one [epistle] to Titus, and two [epistles] to Timothy*; and these are held sacred in the esteem of the Church catholic for the regulation of ecclesiastical discipline. There is current also [a letter] to the Laodiceans, [and] another to the Alexandrians, [both] forged in Paul's name to [further] the heresy of Marcion, and several others which cannot be received into the catholic Church—for it is not fitting that gall be mixed with honey. (Lines 59–67; emphasis added)

This important early document (not so much a canonical list as a kind of introduction to the NT that provides historical information as well as theological reflection) affirms the Pauline authorship of the LTT along with that of Paul's other NT letters and distinguishes them from several known spurious letters "forged in Paul's name."[25]

Subsequently, all three letters became part of the established NT canon of the church, and Paul's authorship of 1–2 Timothy and Titus was not seriously questioned for well over a millennium and a half.[26] Marshall's overall assessment of the patristic evidence regarding the LTT is noteworthy especially since he does not affirm Pauline authorship: "It can be concluded that the PE were known to Christian writers from early in the second century

[25] See text and discussion in E. J. Schnabel, "The Muratorian Fragment: The State of Research," *JETS* 57 (2014): 231–64. See also S. E. Porter, "Paul and the Pauline Letter Collection," in *Paul and the Second Century*, ed. M. F. Bird and J. R. Dodson, LNTS 412, T&T Clark Library of Biblical Studies (New York: T&T Clark, 2011), 19–36, who discusses the Pauline letter collection with reference to 𝔓[46], Marcion's canon, the Muratorian fragment, and six collection theories, including the personal involvement theory (whether by Paul himself, Timothy, or Luke).

[26] See D. Guthrie (*The Pastoral Epistles*, TNTC, rev. ed. [Grand Rapids: Eerdmans, 1990], 19–20) and W. G. Kümmel (*Introduction to the New Testament*, trans. H. C. Kee, 2nd ed. [Nashville: Abingdon, 1975], 370), who point out that from the end of the second century the LTT were regarded as unquestionably Pauline and attested as strongly as most of the other Pauline letters.

and that there is no evidence of rejection of them by any writers except for Marcion."[27]

E. Authenticity

It was only in the late eighteenth century that the authenticity of Paul's correspondence with Timothy and Titus began to be challenged.[28] A number of commentators claim these letters constitute an instance of pseudonymous writing in which a later follower attributes his work to his revered teacher in order to perpetuate his teaching and influence,[29] possibly including some

[27] Marshall, *Pastoral Epistles*, 8. For possible early citations and allusions to the LTT, see C. Looks, *Das Anvertraute bewahren: Die Rezeption der Pastoralbriefe im 2. Jahrhundert*, Münchner theologische Beiträge (Munich: H. Utz, 1999); note especially the helpful summary table on pp. 481–90.

[28] See J. van Nes, "On the Origin of the Pastorals' Authenticity Criticism: A 'New' Perspective," *NTS* 62 (2016): 315–20 (319), who notes that E. Evanson alleged Titus's pseudonymity in his work *The Dissonance of the Four Generally Received Evangelists and the Evidence of Their Respective Authenticity Examined* (Ipswich: Jermyn, 1792), 267–69. See also T. L. Wilder, "Does the Bible Contain Forgeries?," in *In Defense of the Bible: A Comprehensive Apologetic for the Authority of Scripture*, ed. S. B. Cowan and T. L. Wilder (Nashville: B&H, 2013), 177. A classic defense is J. D. James, *The Genuineness and Authorship of the Pastoral Epistles* (London: Longmans, Green & Co., 1906). For a brief survey of the history of scholarship, see R. F. Collins, *Letters That Paul Did Not Write* (Wilmington, DE: M. Glazier, 1988), 89–90, who names as the earliest challengers of the authenticity of the letters J. Schmidt (1804), F. Schleiermacher (1807), J. G. Eichhorn (1812), F. C. Baur (1835), and H. Holtzmann (1885). See also E. J. Schnabel, "Paul, Timothy, and Titus: The Assumption of a Pseudonymous Author and of Pseudonymous Recipients in the Light of Literary, Theological, and Historical Evidence," in *Do Historical Matters Matter to Faith?*, ed. J. K. Hoffmeier and D. R. Magary (Wheaton: Crossway, 2012), 383–84, whose list is identical to Collins's; and E. E. Ellis, "Pastoral Letters," *DPL*, 659. Cf. N. Brox, "Lukas als Verfasser der Pastoralbriefe," *JAC* 13 (1970): 63, who notes that H. A. Schott (*Isagoge historico-critica in libros Novi Foederis sacros* [Jena, 1830]) was the first to posit Lukan authorship on the assumption of the LTT's inauthenticity. For a helpful chart summarizing arguments for and against Pauline authorship, see chart 72, "Authorship of the Pastoral Epistles," in Kierspel, *Charts on the Life, Letters, and Theology of Paul*, 136.

[29] E.g., L. R. Donelson, *Pseudepigraphy and Ethical Argument in the Pastoral Epistles*, HUT 22 (Tübingen: Mohr-Siebeck, 1986), who maintains that the writing of pseudepigrapha was an essential part of the process of defining and establishing the boundaries of the apostolic faith by which Paul was reclaimed for the orthodox position against the false teachers. Similarly, N. Brox, *Falsche Verfasserangaben: Zur Erklärung der frühchristlichen Pseudepigraphie* (Stuttgart: KBW, 1975; see further discussion below). See the thorough survey and adjudication in T. L. Wilder,

authentic material.[30] At a first glance this contention may appear surprising since all three letters open with the unequivocal attribution, "Paul, an apostle of Christ Jesus," or a similar phrase (1 Tim 1:1; 2 Tim 1:1; Titus 1:1). It's difficult to imagine someone other than Paul writing these letters and falsely attributing them to the apostle without deceptive intent,[31] and the church accepting them into the NT canon on the mistaken notion that they were Pauline.[32]

"Pseudonymity and the New Testament," in *Interpreting the New Testament: Essays on Methods and Issues*, ed. D. A. Black and D. S. Dockery (Nashville: B&H, 2001), 296–335; Wilder, *Pseudonymity, the New Testament, and Deception: An Inquiry into Intention and Reception* (Lanham, MD: University Press of America, 2004); and Wilder, "Pseudonymity, the New Testament, and the Pastoral Epistles," in *Entrusted with the Gospel*, 28–51. Cf. D. A. Carson, "Pseudonymity and Pseudepigraphy," *DNTB*, 856–64.

[30] E.g., P. N. Harrison, *The Problem of the Pastoral Epistles* (London: Oxford University Press, 1921). Cf. J. van Nes, "The Problem of the Pastoral Epistles: An Important Hypothesis Reconsidered," in *Paul and Pseudepigraphy*, ed. S. E. Porter and G. P. Fewster, Pauline Studies 8 (Leiden: Brill, 2013), 153–69, who chastises modern writers such as Ehrman and Dunn for giving Harrison's theory an undeserved pass in their works and for failing to take note of the severe criticism Harrison's statistical data have received over the past ninety years. Cf. A. E. Bird, "The Authorship of the Pastoral Epistles: Quantifying Literary Style," *RTR* 56 (1997): 118–37. See also J. D. Miller, *The Pastoral Letters as Composite Documents*, SNTSMS 93 (Cambridge: Cambridge University Press, 1997), who argues that the LTT are a disparate anthology of Pauline fragments supplemented by paraenetic material compiled by a later follower of the apostle. Many works arguing for pseudonymous authorship will provide a fairly standard list of objections to authentic authorship; see recently J. D. G. Dunn, *Neither Jew nor Greek: A Contested Identity*, Christianity in the Making 3 (Grand Rapids: Eerdmans, 2015), 85–89.

[31] See, e.g., D. G. Meade, *Pseudonymity and Canon: An Investigation into the Relationship of Authorship and Authority in Jewish and Earliest Christian Tradition*, WUNT 39 (Tübingen: Mohr-Siebeck, 1986), who proposes that a later author wrote the LTT in Paul's name in order to affirm the significance of Pauline tradition and that the early church was unconcerned with deceptive pseudonymity in the first century and hardened in its rejection of it only at a later point in time. But see A. D. Baum, *Pseudepigraphie und literarische Fälschung im frühen Christentum. Mit ausgewählten Quellentexten samt deutscher Übersetzung*, WUNT 2/138 (Tübingen: Mohr-Siebeck, 2001); and Wilder, *Pseudonymity, the New Testament, and Deception*.

[32] Contra C. B. Ansberry, C. A. Strine, E. W. Klink III, and D. Lincicum, "Pseudepigraphy and the Canon," in C. M. Hays and C. B. Ansberry, eds., *Evangelical Faith and the Challenge of Historical Criticism* (London: SPCK/Grand Rapids: Baker, 2013), esp. 154, who contend that evangelicals ought to develop new models of understanding that "make sense of pseudepigraphical compositions that may at some level have an intention to deceive, but still function as canonical Scripture"

There are essentially three options: (1) Paul wrote 1–2 Timothy and Titus to Timothy and Titus as asserted in the letter openings (authenticity); (2) 1–2 Timothy and Titus were written in Paul's name by a later author who expected his readers to be aware of the literary device of pseudonymity (transparent fiction); (3) 1–2 Timothy and Titus were written in Paul's name by a later author who forged the letter (forgery).[33] As will be argued below, the available evidence supports authenticity, while pseudonymity or allonymity is problematic for a number of reasons.[34] In adjudicating the issue, several questions arise. Was pseudonymous letter-writing an acceptable first-century practice and, if so, was this practice devoid of deceptive intent?[35] Would the church have knowingly accepted pseudonymous letters into the canon? Is pseudonymity more plausible than authenticity?[36]

The evidence suggests that pseudonymity was exceedingly rare in the case of ancient letters,[37] a genre which by its nature

---

(p. 154). But see the review by D. A. Carson, *BBR* 25 (2015): 437–39, who calls "the effrontery" of the volume "jaw-dropping," in particular the argument that "unless one agrees with all the authors' skeptical conclusions, one is not actually engaging in honest historical criticism" (p. 439).

[33] Schnabel, "Paul, Timothy, and Titus," 386. These are general options, and variations are certainly possible. For example, some might consider 2 Timothy to be authentic and 1 Timothy and Titus to be pseudonymous or vice versa. Also, among those who consider the LTT to be authentic, some favor Paul's use of an amanuensis, especially Luke (see further the discussion below).

[34] Allonymity or allepigraphy (the view that the LTT were written "under another name" without deceptive intent) is advocated by Marshall, *Pastoral Epistles*, 83–84. For a thorough assessment of literary, theological, and historical arguments advanced in favor of pseudonymity, see Schnabel, "Paul, Timothy, and Titus," 383–403. See also the discussion "Are the Pastoral Epistles Forgeries?" in Wilder, "Does the Bible Contain Forgeries?," 172–77.

[35] For a forceful argument against this contention, see E. E. Ellis, "Pseudonymity and Canonicity of New Testament Documents," in *Worship, Theology and Ministry in the Early Church*, ed. M. J. Wilkins and T. Page, JSNTSup 87 (Sheffield: JSOT Press, 1992), 212–24; cf. Wilder, *Pseudonymity, the New Testament, and Deception.*

[36] For a still valuable discussion of these issues, see D. Guthrie, *New Testament Introduction*, 2nd ed. (Downers Grove: InterVarsity, 1990), 607–49, 1011–28. From the standpoint of likely pseudonymity, see D. A. Hagner, *The New Testament: A Historical and Theological Introduction* (Grand Rapids: Baker, 2012), 614–26, who considers language and style; church organization; theology and ethics; nature of opposition; picture of Paul; and personal history of Paul.

[37] R. Bauckham notes the rarity of apocryphal or pseudepigraphical apostolic letters in relation to other genres and conjectures that the reason for this "may

entails interpersonal communication.[38] Not only is there little evidence for the common acceptance of pseudonymous letters during the apostolic period, but there seems to have been considerable concern that letters might have been forged (2 Thess 2:2: "a letter supposedly from us").[39] Consequently, Paul in his earlier letters repeatedly refers to his own distinctive hand (1 Cor 16:21; Gal 6:11; Col 4:18; 2 Thess 3:17; Phlm 19), though admittedly the LTT do not include such an *autographon*. Later, Tertullian (ca. 160–225) reports that an Asian presbyter was removed from office for forging a letter in Paul's name (*Bapt.* 17). Both 3 Corinthians and the Epistle to the Laodiceans are transparent attempts to fill in a perceived gap in canonical revelation (see 1 Cor 5:9; 2 Cor 2:4; 7:8; Col 4:16).[40] Serapion, bishop of Antioch (d. 211), pointedly distinguishes between apostolic writings and those that "falsely bear their names" (*pseudepigrapha*; cited in Eusebius, *Hist. eccl.* 6.12.3). In light of this evidence, it is unlikely that the early church would have knowingly accepted pseudonymous letters into the Christian canon.[41]

---

well have been the sheer difficulty of using a pseudepigraphical letter to perform the same functions as an authentic letter." He concludes that "among the letters surveyed there is no really good example of a pseudepigraphical letter that achieves didactic relevance by the generality of its contents" ("Pseudo-Apostolic Letters," *JBL* 107 [1988]: 487).

[38] The labels "epistle" and "letter" for the Epistle of Jeremiah and the Letter of Aristeas are misleading because neither writing is properly a letter: the former is a homily, the latter an account of the circumstances surrounding the translation of the Hebrew Scriptures into Greek (Bauckham ["Pseudo-Apostolic Letters," 478] considers it "misclassified" and a "dedicated treatise"). Bauckham also discusses several didactic letters such as 1 Enoch 92–105; Epistle of Jeremiah; Baruch; and 2 Baruch 78–87. See Wilder, "Does the Bible Contain Forgeries?," 167.

[39] Wilder, "Does the Bible Contain Forgeries?," 170.

[40] Bauckham ("Pseudo-Apostolic Letters," 485) calls the Epistle to the Laodiceans "a remarkably incompetent attempt to fill the gap . . . nothing but a patchwork of Pauline sentences and phrases from other letters, mainly Philippians." Third Corinthians is part of the late second-century Acts of Paul.

[41] See, e.g., T. D. Lea, "The Early Christian View of Pseudepigraphic Writings," *JETS* 27 (1984): 65–75. This is true despite Metzger's conclusion that "since the use of the literary form of pseudepigraphy need not be regarded as necessarily involving fraudulent intent, it cannot be argued that the character of inspiration excludes the possibility of pseudepigraphy among the canonical writings" ("Literary Forgeries and Canonical Pseudepigrapha," *JBL* 91 [1972]: 22). See especially J. Duff, "A Reconsideration of Pseudepigraphy in Early Christianity" (Ph.D. dissertation, Oxford University, 1998), who concludes (1) that the value of a text was closely linked to its true authorship; (2) that pseudonymity was generally

Another factor to consider is the significant number of *historical particularities* featured in these letters. While it's possible that a later imitator of Paul fabricated these pieces of information to lend greater verisimilitude to his writing, there seems to be no compelling reason these references couldn't reflect actual circumstances in Paul's life and ministry.[42] Some object that the historical details in the LTT cannot be easily fitted into the chronology in Acts. This is true, but they can be accommodated without much difficulty at a later time toward the end of Paul's career (see Pauline Chronology

---

viewed as a deceitful practice; and (3) that texts thought to be pseudonymous were marginalized. Duff also points out that the question of pseudonymity is important for interpretation because one will interpret the LTT differently if one views them as second-century forgeries rather than first-century authentic compositions. Against J. D. G. Dunn, "The Problem of Pseudonymity," in *The Living Word*, 2nd ed. (Minneapolis: Fortress, 2009), 53–68, who claims that authoritative tradition was not regarded as fixed and static but as living tradition which continued to be reworked. According to Dunn, the criterion for acceptability was not authorship by the one to whom a given piece of writing was overtly attributed but continuity and coherence of the newer expression of a living tradition with preceding ones (Dunn cites Matthew's and Luke's use of Mark and the Chronicler's use of Samuel–Kings as canonical examples). In this vein Dunn views the LTT as "appropriate and authentic reexpression of the Pauline heritage and tradition," which the church acknowledged as such based on the "Jewish understanding and practice of tradition as a living force" (pp. 67–68). However, one looks in vain for confirmation of this understanding of the LTT in the patristic writings.

[42] Contra Bauckham ("Pseudo-Apostolic Letters," 492), who believes the author of the LTT "has thought himself into situations in Paul's ministry and . . . has filled out whatever historical information was available to him with historical fiction." Bauckham even ventures the conjecture that Timothy might have written 1–2 Timothy himself (p. 494). Also against Dunn ("Problem of Pseudonymity," 66), who believes Paul was "the fountainhead of the Pastorals' tradition" and that 1–2 Timothy and Titus reexpress for a later situation "the voice of the Pauline tradition for a new day"; and N. Brox ("Zu den persönlichen Notizen der Pastoralbriefe," *BZ* 13 [1969]: 76–94), who believes the personal references constitute "typical situations in the ecclesiastical office, which are historicized and attributed to Paul." See also Brox, *Falsche Verfasserangaben*, where Brox claims that pseudonymity is an instance of a noble lie which was justifiable for defending the Pauline heritage; and Ehrman, *Forgery and Counterforgery*, who considers most Christian literature of the first 400 years of the Christian era, including a good portion of the NT, to have been forged and thus inauthentic. Cf. J. Luttenberger, *Prophetenmantel oder Bücherfutteral? Die persönlichen Notizen in den Pastoralbriefen im Licht antiker Epistolographie und literarischer Pseudepigraphie*, Arbeiten zur Bibel und ihrer Geschichte 40 (Leipzig: Evangelische Verlagsanstalt, 2012), who suggests 2 Timothy and Titus may be authentic while 1 Timothy may be a literary supplement to these two letters.

below).[43] In fact, the notion of pseudonymous authorship is rendered less plausible because it would likely entail a pseudonymous readership as well (double pseudonymity), not to mention the inauthenticity of the plethora of historical details in these letters. Consistency would seem to demand that pseudonymity envelop a given letter in its totality (which seems difficult to sustain in the case of the LTT).[44] While one might make a case for using "Paul" as the author if the letters are situated firmly in the stream of Pauline tradition, it's another thing altogether to fabricate historical particularities and to posit false recipients.[45]

One piece of evidence often adduced by those questioning the Pauline authorship of 1–2 Timothy and Titus is *differences in style and vocabulary when compared with other Pauline letters* (see discussion of Vocabulary below under Literary Analysis and Structure).[46] The LTT feature words not used elsewhere in Paul's undisputed writings,[47] while characteristic Pauline terminology is lacking.[48]

---

[43] Wilder, "Does the Bible Contain Forgeries?," 176.

[44] Thornton, *Hostility in the House of God*, 11–12, contends that "whether doubly authentic or doubly pseudonymous, the destination of both letters was most likely Ephesus" (following P. Trebilco, *The Early Christians in Ephesus from Paul to Ignatius*, WUNT 166 [Tübingen: Mohr-Siebeck, 2004], 209). He adds: "While I agree with Trebilco's conclusion, I acknowledge the fact that he and other proponents of the pseudonymous position are open to the criticism of inconsistency here: the letters were *not really* written by the Apostle Paul to his delegate, Timothy, but the letters *were actually* sent to Ephesus" (p. 12n13).

[45] See on this Schnabel, "Paul, Timothy, and Titus," 396–97.

[46] See Marshall, *Pastoral Epistles*, 60–61; Mounce, *Pastoral Epistles*, xcix–cxviii; Ben Witherington III, *Letters and Homilies for Hellenized Christians*, vol. 1: *A Socio-Rhetorical Commentary on Titus, 1–2 Timothy and 1–3 John* (Downers Grove: InterVarsity, 2006), 54–62 (see also pp. 68–72 on the rhetorical character and substance of the PE and pp. 72–75 for "a cautionary word"); and Schnabel, "Paul, Timothy, and Titus," 386–91, who points out that "the notion that an author has a consistent style is a romantic notion of the modern Western world" and asserts that "it is the occasion that determines the style adopted" (p. 389). Similarly, A. W. Pitts, "Style and Pseudonymity in Pauline Scholarship: A Register Based Configuration," in *Paul and Pseudepigraphy*, 113, who avers, "Studies in the Pastoral letters famously employ several (mainly) linguistic criteria to detect shifts in style on the typically unargued assumption that a shift in style necessarily entails a shift in authorship," and goes on to question that "unargued assumption" on the basis of "theoretical and field research in sociolinguistics."

[47] E.g., εὐσέβεια ("godliness"), σώφρων ("self-controlled"), and ἐπιφάνεια in the place of παρουσία ("coming," referring to Christ's return).

[48] E.g., ἐλευθερία ("freedom"), σάρξ ("flesh," in contrast to "Spirit"), σταυρός ("cross"), and δικαιοσύνη θεοῦ ("righteousness of God"). Cf. the list in Marshall,

What is more, the LTT include a large number of unique words (*hapax legomena*) not found elsewhere in the NT.[49] There are also differences in sentence length, word order, and the use of conjunctions and particles.[50] However, establishing authorship on the basis of stylistic differences is fraught with difficulty and remains notoriously inconclusive.[51] Not only is there a difference between public letters sent to congregations and personal correspondence addressed to individuals,[52] Paul's desire to preserve his apostolic legacy would adequately account for the emphasis on church leadership and the faithful passing on of apostolic tradition in these letters (§7.3).[53] What's more, while Paul's earlier letters owe

Pastoral Epistles, 104–6, who discusses themes that some have alleged are missing from or are less prominent in the LTT: (1) the fatherhood of God; (2) the power and witness of the Spirit; (3) union with Jesus Christ and spiritual resurrection from death in sin; and (4) freedom from the law; and the discussion in Mounce, *Pastoral Epistles*, lxxxviii–xcvii (including the chart on p. xc).

[49] E.g., ἀνδραποδιστής ("slave-trader") and ἐπίορκος ("perjurer," both in 1 Tim 1:10); and ἀφθορία ("integrity," Titus 2:7). See Guthrie, *New Testament Introduction*, 619, who puts the number at 175; Harrison, *Problem of the Pastoral Epistles*, whose count is 176; and Mounce, *Pastoral Epistles*, xcix–cxviii, who provides an extensive analysis of the data as well as a critique of Harrison's work. Kierspel, *Charts on the Life, Letters, and Theology of Paul*, 156, says there are 175 NT *hapax legomena* and 131 additional words not found in the other Pauline letters. See also the lexical data (including special vocabulary) provided in A. Köstenberger and R. Bouchoc, *The Book Study Concordance* (Nashville: B&H Academic, 2003), 1172–234.

[50] See the literature cited in Schnabel, "Paul, Timothy, and Titus," 387nn14–15.

[51] For an incisive treatment, see B. M. Metzger, "A Reconsideration of Certain Arguments against the Pauline Authorship of the Pastoral Epistles," *ExpTim* 70 (1958): 91–94 (see especially the four questions on p. 93). See also Wilder, "Does the Bible Contain Forgeries?," 173: "Stylistic arguments tend to be quite subjective and unimpressive. . . . Furthermore, the Pastoral Epistles are simply too brief to determine with accuracy the writing habits of a particular author"; and the similar assessment by Schnabel, "Paul, Timothy, and Titus," 387–88. See also A. D. Baum, "Semantic Variation within the *Corpus Paulinum*: Linguistic Considerations Concerning the Richer Vocabulary of the Pastoral Epistles," *TynBul* 59 (2008): 271–92 (including an extensive word list), who shows that 1–2 Timothy and Titus feature "a much higher percentage of distinctive words than the rest of the Pauline letters" (p. 277).

[52] See esp. Prior, *Paul the Letter-Writer and the Second Letter to Timothy*; Prior, "Revisiting the Pastoral Epistles," *ScrB* 31 (2001): 2–19, who raises the fact of coauthorship in most of Paul's letters (p. 14); and Johnson, *First and Second Letters to Timothy*, 55–99.

[53] In addition, Paul may have employed amanuenses, as he did at other occasions (e.g., Rom 16:22). See Ellis, "Pastoral Letters," 663–64; R. N. Longenecker, "Ancient

more to conceptual orality, regularly featuring parentheses and anacolutha (syntactical inconsistencies), the LTT are closer to conceptual writing, which suggests that "their author has expressed himself more carefully and probably had more time at his disposal than the author . . . of the other ten Paulines."[54]

In addition, it is often claimed that the *church structure* in the LTT reflects the church in the early second century rather than the first, most notably as set forth by Ignatius of Antioch (ca. 35–110), who advocates a monarchial episcopate and a three-tiered ecclesiastical hierarchy (see *Eph.* 2.2; *Magn.* 3.1; *Trall.* 2.2; 3.1).[55] For this reason, the LTT are said to exhibit a form of "early Catholicism."[56] However, the LTT hardly fit this description. Paul and Barnabas appointed elders in the churches they established as early as AD 50 (Acts 14:23; see 11:30; 15:2; 20:28–31; 21:18), and the terms "overseer" (ἐπίσκοπος) and "elder" (πρεσβύτερος) are used interchangeably with

---

Amanuenses and the Pauline Epistles," in *New Dimensions in New Testament Study*, ed. R. N. Longenecker and M. C. Tenney (Grand Rapids: Zondervan, 1974), 281–97; E. R. Richards, *The Secretary in the Letters of Paul*, WUNT 2/42 (Tübingen: Mohr-Siebeck, 1991); Richards, *Paul and First-Century Letter Writing: Secretaries, Composition and Collection* (Downers Grove: InterVarsity, 2004); Schnabel, "Paul, Timothy, and Titus," 390; and Witherington, *Letters and Homilies for Hellenized Christians*, 67–68, who maintains that Luke served as amanuensis, esp. of 2 Timothy (cf. 2 Tim 4:11).

[54] Baum, "Semantic Variation," 290, with reference to M. Reiser, "Paulus als Stilist," *SEÅ* 66 (2001): 151–65. But see the summary and critique by Marshall, "Pastoral Epistles in Recent Study," 291–92, who objects that the synonyms advanced by Baum aren't close enough and that the vocabulary in the LTT "indicates a process of thought different from that of the other letters" (p. 292). Marshall also notes that Baum's hypothesis doesn't account for the smaller number of particles in the LTT when compared with the undisputed Pauline letters (p. 292). See also Yarbrough's summary of Schlatter's assessment, who attributes new vocabulary to new controversies and situations that had arisen in the church (R. W. Yarbrough, "Schlatter on the Pastorals: Mission in the Academy," in *New Testament Theology in Light of the Church's Mission: Essays in Honor of I. Howard Marshall*, ed. J. C. Laansma, G. R. Osborne, and R. F. Van Neste [Eugene, OR: Wipf & Stock, 2011], 307–8).

[55] See Mounce (*Pastoral Epistles*, lxxxvi–lxxxviii, 186–92), who cites Polycarp, Clement, Clement of Alexandria, and Irenaeus as referring to a two-tiered structure, using ἐπίσκοπος and πρεσβύτερος interchangeably.

[56] See, e.g., E. Käsemann, "Paul and Early Catholicism," in *New Testament Questions of Today*, trans. W. J. Montague (Philadelphia: Fortress, 1969), 237–50.

reference to the same office (Titus 1:5, 7; see Acts 20:17, 28).[57] Paul's instruction to Titus to "appoint elders in every town" (Titus 1:5) is therefore hardly novel. What's more, the fact that Titus is to appoint elders in *every* town also speaks against the presence of a monarchial episcopate at the time of writing.[58] Elsewhere, Paul addresses one of his letters to the "overseers and deacons" at Philippi (Phil 1:1), which coheres well with the two-tiered structure presupposed in 1 Timothy. Finally, the emphasis on qualifications for overseers and deacons in 1 Timothy and Titus speaks decisively in favor of a first-century date because a second-century writer would almost certainly have expected his readers already to be familiar with this pattern.[59]

Proponents of pseudonymity also maintain that there are insurmountable *theological and conceptual differences* between Paul's earlier letters and the LTT.[60] Some argue that references to the gospel as "sound teaching," "the faith," or "the truth" (1 Tim 1:10, 19; 3:9, 13; 4:1, 6; 6:3, 10; 2 Tim 1:13; 4:3; Titus 1:9, 13; 2:1) reflect a later point in time when the body of Christian teaching had shifted from a dynamic expression of faith in Christ to a fixed set of creedal beliefs. However, there's no reason Paul toward the end of his life shouldn't look at the gospel as a precious stewardship to be passed on to the next generation of leaders. What's more, there are some indications that Paul even earlier viewed the gospel in similar terms (e.g., Rom 16:17; 1 Cor 4:17; 11:2; 15:1–3). Others contend that the references to "godliness" (εὐσέβεια) in the LTT indicate a more advanced stage subsequent to Paul's martyrdom. However, it's much more likely that Paul here upholds a virtue that was highly valued in the surrounding Greco-Roman culture in the belief that it was "truly attainable only in Christ."[61] Similar arguments can be made with regard to references to both God and

---

[57] B. L. Merkle, *The Elder and Overseer: One Office in the Early Church*, StBibLit 57 (New York: P. Lang, 2003). F. M. Young ("On ἐπίσκοπος and πρεσβύτερος," *JTS* 45 [1994]: 142–48) ventures the "admittedly tentative" hypothesis that the origins of ἐπίσκοπος and πρεσβύτερος are distinct. However, her interpretation of the LTT in light of Ignatius (died ca. 110) rather than vice versa is of doubtful merit.

[58] Wilder, "Does the Bible Contain Forgeries?," 174.

[59] See A. J. Köstenberger, "Church Government," in *The Encyclopedia of Christian Civilization*, vol. 1: *A–D*, ed. G. T. Kurian (Oxford: Blackwell, 2011), 543–51.

[60] See Schnabel, "Paul, Timothy, and Titus," 391–96.

[61] Towner, *Letters to Timothy and Titus*, 174.

Christ as Savior (§3.3), to the church as "God's household" (§4.1), and to "epiphany" (ἐπιφάνεια) language (§§3.2, 6.6).[62]

The theology of the LTT is not identical in form to that of Paul's other letters, but it can plausibly be viewed as complementary rather than contradictory and as no less Pauline than the earlier undisputed letters (see Pauline Chronology below).[63] As E. Schnabel contends,

> The absence of Pauline theological themes from the Pastoral Epistles (e.g., the cross, the Holy Spirit, the flesh/spirit dichotomy) does not prove inauthenticity. There is no reason why Paul should mention the whole range of basic theological topics in all of his letters, particularly in letters to coworkers who know his theology. It is only if it could be shown that the theology of the Pastoral Epistles *contradicts* Paul's undisputed letters that we would have a serious problem.[64]

In light of this set of historical, literary, and theological considerations, the conclusion seems reasonable that the LTT "are much more akin to the accepted letters of Paul than they are to the known pseudonymous documents that circulated in the early church."[65] This is not to deny that there are legitimate differences

---

[62] Schnabel, "Paul, Timothy, and Titus," 393–95. See, e.g., D. C. Verner, *The Household of God: The Social World of the Pastoral Epistles*, SBLDS 71 (Chico, CA: Scholars Press, 1983), who argues that the metaphor of the "household of God" is used to enforce the traditional patriarchal structure of the household within the church in response to the charge that the church is subverting the political structures of the state; and D. G. Horrell, "From ἀδελφοί to οἶκος θεοῦ: Social Transformation in Pauline Christianity," *JBL* 120 (2001): 293–311, who contends that whereas Paul addresses believers as "brothers," the pseudo-Pauline letters use the model of a hierarchically structured household.

[63] Another possible reason for alleging pseudonymity is that the chronology of the LTT seems to be incompatible with Acts.

[64] Schnabel, "Paul, Timothy, and Titus," 392.

[65] D. A. Carson and D. J. Moo, *An Introduction to the New Testament*, 2nd ed. (Grand Rapids: Zondervan, 2005), 563. Similarly, D. Guthrie, "The Development of the Idea of Canonical Pseudepigrapha in New Testament Criticism," *VE* 1 (1962): 43–59. See already the similar assessment by Schlatter, who "reads the PE as an artifact of Paul's finals [*sic*] years of apostolic ministry based on linguistic, literary, and concrete historical considerations" (Yarbrough's summary: "Schlatter on the Pastorals," 309).

between Paul's earlier undisputed letters and the LTT. Clearly the LTT are written at a later juncture in the history and mission of the early church and aim to contextualize the Christian message in the midst of a unique set of circumstances. This is the genuine insight underlying pseudonymity proposals. However, there seems to be no compelling evidence to push the LTT beyond Paul's lifetime into the post-Pauline period. Historically, literarily, and theologically, these three letters fit at least as comfortably toward the end of Paul's ministry as they do in the period following his death.[66]

F. Pauline Chronology

At what point in his ministry did Paul write the LTT? A brief survey of Pauline chronology will help set the stage for adjudicating this question.[67] Paul hailed from "the thriving commercial and

---

One further argument is mentioned by G. D. Fee ("Reflections on Church Order in the Pastoral Epistles, with Further Reflection on the Hermeneutics of *Ad Hoc* Documents," *JETS* 28 [1985]: 141): the lack of a satisfactory answer to the question, "Why three letters? That is, given 1 Timothy, why did a pseudepigrapher write Titus, and given 1 Timothy and Titus and their concerns, why 2 Timothy at all?" Similarly, T. Manabu, "Der zweite Timotheus als letzter Gefangenschaftsbrief," *Kwansei Gakuin University Humanities Review* 11 (2006): 2.

J. D. Quinn and W. C. Wacker, *The First and Second Letters to Timothy*, ECC (Grand Rapids: Eerdmans, 2000), 20, respond by pointing to the genre of letter collections, maintaining that the LTT "as a collection would have been received and read not as individual letters from the Paul of history but as a 'characterization' of the great apostle and his teaching for the new generation." Manabu ("Der zweite Timotheus," 2) also draws attention to the fact that 2 Timothy never refers to 1 Timothy, which would be curious if the three letters were intended as a letter collection (he cites 1–2 Peter and 1–2 Thessalonians as contrasting examples; cf. 2 Pet 3:1; 2 Thess 2:2).

[66] Cf. P. H. Towner, "Pauline Theology or Pauline Tradition in the Pastoral Epistles: The Question of Method," *TynBul* 46 (1995): 287–314.

[67] For helpful discussions setting the general framework, see Köstenberger, Kellum, and Quarles, *The Cradle, the Cross, and the Crown*, chap. 9; and C. L. Quarles, *Illustrated Life of Paul* (Nashville: B&H Academic, 2014). For a detailed discussion of the question of chronology in relation to Acts, see C. S. Keener, *Acts: An Exegetical Commentary*, vol. 3: *15:1–23:35* (Grand Rapids: Baker, 2014), 3023–26. Keener favors the traditional view of a second Pauline imprisonment and of the events mentioned in the LTT subsequent to those referenced in the book of Acts. A rather idiosyncratic set of proposals comes from B. Adamczewski, *Heirs of the Reunited Church: The History of the Pauline Mission in Paul's Letters, in the So-Called Pastoral Letters, and in the Pseudo-Titus Narrative of Acts* (Frankfurt: Peter Lang, 2010), who claims the LTT develop in an ethopoeic way the information contained about Timothy and Titus in the other letters of Paul and the book of Acts,

intellectual center" of Tarsus of Cilicia (Acts 9:11; 21:39; 22:3).[68] He studied under the eminent first-century Jewish rabbi Gamaliel I (Acts 22:3; see 5:34–39) and zealously persecuted the early Christians (Acts 7:56–8:3; 9:1–2; 1 Cor 15:9; Phil 3:6). An encounter with the risen Christ on the road to Damascus (Acts 9:1–9; 22:6–10; 26:12–18) caused a radical reorientation of Paul's life and a paradigm shift in his thinking. Up until that moment Paul had considered Jesus to be a messianic pretender cursed by God; now he recognized him as the Messiah sent by God (Gal 3:10–14; 2 Cor 5:21). With this the church's most committed nemesis (see 1 Tim 1:15–17) became its most fervent propagator.

After a quiet period of preparation (Gal 1:21–24), Barnabas recruited Paul to participate in the early church's mission to the Gentiles (Acts 11:25–26). Paul quickly rose to assume a leadership role and gathered a group of coworkers including Timothy and Titus. While assuming responsibility for the churches he established, Paul delegated certain tasks to his trusted associates.[69] This became a necessity especially toward the end of Paul's life, which was characterized by imprisonments (Acts 24:22–27; 28:11–31; 2 Cor 11:23; Eph 6:20; Phil 1:14; 2 Tim 1:8), ailments (Gal 4:13–15; 2 Cor 12:7–10), and advancing age.[70] If Paul is the author of the LTT, the setting of these writings, as mentioned, is most likely his desire to ensure continuity between the apostolic and the post-apostolic period, to pass on the message of the Christian faith, and to provide sound principles for church governance.[71]

---

presenting Titus as a model Gentile Christian (p. 74) and Timothy as a model Jewish Christian (p. 75) and implying that Paul died in AD 49 (p. 82).

[68] R. N. Longenecker, *The Ministry and Message of Paul* (Grand Rapids: Zondervan, 1971), 24.

[69] See M. M. Mitchell, "New Testament Envoys in the Context of Greco-Roman Diplomatic and Epistolary Conventions: The Example of Timothy and Titus," *JBL* 111 (1992): 641–62, who focuses on 1 Thessalonians 3 and 2 Corinthians 7; and "The Role of Paul's Delegates" in Johnson, *First and Second Letters to Timothy*, 94–96.

[70] See A. J. Malherbe, "*Paulus Senex*," *ResQ* 36 (1994): 197–207.

[71] Regarding the appropriateness of speaking of first-century "orthodoxy," see A. J. Köstenberger and M. J. Kruger, *The Heresy of Orthodoxy: How Contemporary Culture's Fascination with Diversity Has Reshaped Our Understanding of Early Christianity* (Wheaton: Crossway, 2010). Cf. J.-D. Dubois, "Les pastorales, la gnose et l'hérésie," *FoiVie* 34 (1995): 41–48, who argues that it's best to situate the LTT on a Pauline trajectory halfway between the Corinthian controversies and the Gnostic movements known to Irenaeus.

There are essentially three possibilities as to when the LTT were written:[72] (1) during Acts;[73] (2) after the end of Acts;[74] or (3) after Paul's death.[75] Dating the letters to the years covered in Acts was common in the early centuries of the church and into the nineteenth century.[76] The view was rejected not on the basis of contrary evidence but in favor of inauthenticity and non-Pauline authorship (pseudonymity).[77] In light of the difficulties of

---

[72] For a survey, see S. E. Porter, "Pauline Chronology and the Question of Pseudonymity of the Pastoral Epistles," in *Paul and Pseudepigraphy*, 65–88, who concludes that "there is and can be no final and definitive solution to the issue of Pauline authorship and pseudepigraphy of the Pastoral Epistles on the basis of Pauline chronology" (p. 88). Porter believes 2 Timothy was probably written from a Roman imprisonment, most likely during one of the missionary journeys recorded in Acts. For a tentative reconstruction, see Ellis, "Pastoral Letters," 661–62; cf. Köstenberger, "1–2 Timothy, Titus," 596–98. For a comparison, see chart 73, "Locating the Pastoral Epistles within Paul's Ministry," in Kierspel, *Charts on the Life, Letters, and Theology of Paul*, 137, 235.

[73] See, e.g., J. van Bruggen, *Die geschichtliche Einordnung der Pastoralbriefe* (Wuppertal: R. Brockhaus, 1981); R. Fuchs, "Eine vierte Missionsreise des Paulus im Osten? Zur Datierung des ersten Timotheosbriefs und des Titusbriefs," *JETh* 25 (2011): 33–58; Fuchs, *Unerwartete Unterschiede*, 5–30; B. Reicke, "Chronologie der Pastoralbriefe," *TLZ* 101 (1976): 81–96; D. A. deSilva, *An Introduction to the New Testament: Contexts, Methods & Ministry Formation* (Downers Grove: InterVarsity, 2004), 734–35; Towner, *Letters to Timothy and Titus*, 10–15; Towner, *1–2 Timothy & Titus*, IVPNTC 14 (Downers Grove: InterVarsity, 1994), 14–20; P. Walker, "Revisiting the Pastoral Epistles: Part I," *EuroJTh* 21 (2012): 4–16; Walker, "Revisiting the Pastoral Epistles: Part II," *EuroJTh* 21 (2012): 120–32.

[74] See, e.g., Ellis, "Pastoral Letters," 661–62; Fee, *1 and 2 Timothy, Titus*, 3–4; Keener, *Acts*, 3:2023–26; J. B. Lightfoot, "The Date of the Pastoral Epistles," in *Biblical Essays* (London: Macmillan, 1893), 399–410; and J. B. Polhill, *Paul and His Letters* (Nashville: B&H, 1999), 405.

[75] See, e.g., R. I. Pervo, *The Making of Paul: Constructions of the Apostle in Early Christianity* (Minneapolis: Fortress, 2010); Quinn and Wacker, *Letters to Timothy*, 1–23; and the discussion of pseudonymity above. See also R. Riesner, who believes Luke served as the redactor of the LTT which serve as "a kind of third volume to Luke-Acts" ("The Pastoral Epistles and Paul in Spain [2 Timothy 4:16–18]," in *Rastreando Los Origenes: Lengua y exegesis en el Nuevo Testamento*, ed. J. M. G. Perez [Madrid: Ediciones Encuentro/CEU Ediciones/Fundacion San Justino, 2011], 316–35). Riesner believes "Luke redacted 2 Timothy right after the apostle's death as his spiritual testament using personal memories and even some written Pauline material" (p. 334). As Yarbrough points out, "No one suggests, of course, that the PE might precede the undoubted Pauline letters" ("Schlatter on the Pastorals," 307n36).

[76] Kierspel, *Charts on the Life, Letters, and Theology of Paul*, 235.

[77] Van Bruggen, *Geschichtliche Einordnung*, 21.

accommodating the information contained in the LTT within the Acts chronology, postulating a date after the end of Acts may be the "simplest solution,"[78] but this, too, is not without its difficulties. First, the ministry locations mentioned in the LTT may presuppose ministry in the East, such as Ephesus (1 Tim 3:14–15), Troas (2 Tim 4:13), and Miletus (2 Tim 4:20), a region Paul had left after the third missionary journey and didn't expect to revisit (cf. Acts 20:25). Second, Paul speaks of Timothy's "youth" in 1 Timothy 4:12, which may point to an earlier date. Third, the detailed instructions regarding church order and qualifications for church leaders in 1 Timothy and Titus suggest a time when the church was still being established. In addition, it's possible to accommodate the information included in the LTT within the Acts chronology. J. van Brugge, followed by R. Fuchs and P. Towner, suggests Paul may have interrupted his three-year ministry in Ephesus on his third missionary journey (Acts 19; cf. 20:31) and embarked on an "interim journey" to Macedonia (1 Tim 1:3) and Crete (Titus 1:5) during that time.[79]

Nevertheless, on balance it seems that a date after the end of Acts but prior to Paul's death is preferred.[80] Any reconstruction

---

[78] Polhill, *Paul and His Letters*, 405.

[79] Van Bruggen, *Geschichtliche Einordnung*, 91–96; Fuchs, "Vierte Missionsreise des Paulus im Osten?," 33–58; Fuchs, *Unerwartete Unterschiede*, 5–30; Towner, *Letters to Timothy and Titus*, 10–15; Towner, *1–2 Timothy & Titus*, 14–20. See also Walker, "Revisiting the Pastoral Epistles: Part I"; Walker, "Revisiting the Pastoral Epistles: Part II," who proposes that Paul wrote 1 Timothy and Titus in the period between September AD 55 and January AD 57 when he left Ephesus and went into Macedonia and Illyricum before wintering in Corinth (Acts 20:1–3; Rom 15:19) and that he wrote 2 Timothy when arriving in Rome in March AD 60 (Acts 28:14) prior to writing his other "prison epistles," Colossians, Ephesians, Philemon, and Philippians. Cf. Walker, *In the Steps of Paul* (Oxford: Lion, 2008), 12–13, which stipulates AD 56 as the date for 1 Timothy and Titus (both prior to Romans!) and early AD 60 as the date for 2 Timothy. Walker essentially reiterated his proposal in "1 Timothy and Titus: Reimagining the Connections (with Other Pauline Letters)," a paper presented at the annual meeting of the ETS in Atlanta, Georgia (November 18, 2015).

[80] See the discussion by J. M. G. Barclay, "The Last Years of Paul: What Are the Issues?," in *The Last Years of Paul: Essays from the Tarragona Conference, June 2013*, ed. Armand Puig i Tàrrech, John M. G. Barclay, and Jörg Frey, WUNT 352 (Tübingen: Mohr-Siebeck, 2015), 1–14. But note his proposal that Paul's ministry ended not in "triumph and success" but in "disappointment and failure" (pp. 11, 14) and that Paul was convicted and martyred as early as AD 62 for *seditio* or *maiestas* in relation to the

within Acts is essentially an argument from silence (though to some extent this is the case for every type of chronological reconstruction), and it's far from certain that Luke would have omitted reference to such an "interim journey" to Macedonia and Crete in his account of Paul's whereabouts in Acts. On the other hand, if such a journey took place after Acts, its noninclusion in Acts would be plausible if Luke chose to end his account with Paul's arrival in Rome. While Paul in Romans envisioned traveling west, not east (Rom 15:24, 28), and while Acts reports that Paul didn't expect to visit Ephesus again following his "Ephesian farewell" (Acts 20:25), this doesn't rule out subsequent travels to the Aegean region; Paul's plans were known to change (see, e.g., 2 Cor 1:16–24; 1 Thess 2:18).

Most likely, therefore, Paul engaged in a second Aegean ministry after his release from his first Roman imprisonment, which may have occurred in AD 62 (Acts 28).[81] He wrote the first letter to Timothy from Macedonia (1 Tim 1:3) sometime after the year 62 but before 65 or 66 (the likely date of his second Roman imprisonment, issuing in his martyrdom under Nero who died in 68).[82] Timothy, who was at

---

Roman emperor (p. 13; see also H. Omerzu, *Der Prozess des Paulus: Eine exegetische und rechtshistorische Untersuchung der Apostelgeschichte* [Berlin: de Gruyter, 2002], 508). If so, of course Paul didn't write 2 Timothy. If so, too, Paul's expectation in Phil 1:19–26 and Phlm 22 that he would shortly be released proved unfounded. One wonders if this "deliberately provocative" proposal (Barclay's own words, p. 14) is in fact the best reading of the evidence. See, e.g., Eusebius, *Hist. eccl.* 2.25.5; Jerome, *Vir. ill.* 5.9–10 and other ancient and patristic evidence adduced by V. Marotta, "St. Paul's Death: Roman Citizenship and *summa supplicia*," in *Last Years of Paul*, 259.

[81] Cf. A. Scriba, "Von Korinth nach Rom. Die Chronologie der letzten Jahre des Paulus," in *Das Ende des Paulus. Historische, theologische und literargeschichtliche Aspekte*, ed. F. W. Horn (Berlin: de Gruyter, 2001), 157–73, who argues that a date of AD 59 or 60 for Paul's arrival in Rome is most likely. See also R. Riesner, "Paul's Trial and End according to Second Timothy, *1 Clement*, the Canon Muratori, and the Apocryphal Acts," in *Last Years of Paul*, 395, who cites relevant evidence and concludes that "according to the most probable chronological reconstruction, the apostle was in captivity in Rome from 60 to 62" (with reference to Riesner, *Paul's Early Period: Chronology, Mission Strategy, Theology* [Grand Rapids: Eerdmans, 1998], 218–28); see Riesner, "Paul's Trial," 406, citing other scholars holding this view in n. 93.

[82] See Köstenberger, Kellum, and Quarles, *Cradle, the Cross, and the Crown*, 394–95. Thornton, *Hostility in the House of God*, 11 (following M. Gill, *Jesus as Mediator: Politics and Polemic in 1 Timothy 2:1–7* [New York: P. Lang, 2008, 71–78]), posits a range of ca. AD 64–100 for the writing of both 1 and 2 Timothy." However, this range seems too restrictive on the front end since composition earlier in the AD 60s prior to AD 64 seems like a real possibility in the case of 1 Timothy; also, a date in or close to AD 100 seems highly unlikely.

that time stationed in Ephesus, needed counsel on how to deal with false teachers in the Ephesian church, which provided the occasion for Paul to issue a series of instructions.[83] Paul likely wrote the letter to Titus either between 1 and 2 Timothy or prior to 1 Timothy from an unknown location (possibly Macedonia or Achaia).[84] He probably wrote 2 Timothy from Rome subsequent to 1 Timothy and Titus during his second, more severe imprisonment in 65 or 66.[85]

Date(s)	Event(s) in Paul's Last Years
59/60	Arrival in Rome, two-year imprisonment/house arrest, writes "prison epistles" (Ephesians, Philippians, Colossians, Philemon; cf. Acts 28:11–31)
62	Release from first Roman imprisonment
62–65	Second Aegean ministry (cf. 2 Tim 4:9–18), possible trip to Spain (cf. Rom 15:24, 28),* writes 1 Timothy from Macedonia and Titus from an unknown location

[83] So Johnson (*Letters to Paul's Delegates*, 106–7, 168), who calls this the *mandata principis* ("commandments of the ruler") letter, citing several ancient parallels.

[84] So Quarles, *Illustrated Life of Paul*, 259. For a more detailed discussion, see introduction to Titus below.

[85] For theories that Luke wrote or redacted the LTT or served as Paul's amanuensis, see §7.3 below. For an attempted reconstruction of Paul's last two years, see Riesner, "Paul's Trial," 406–8. However, Riesner's reconstruction is highly conjectural if not often implausible; Herzer rightly assigns it to the "genre" of *Vermutungswissenschaft* ("guesswork"; M. Hengel's term). See Jens Herzer, "The Mission and the End of Paul between Strategy and Reality: A Response to Rainer Reiser," in *The Last Years of Paul: Essays from the Tarragona Conference, June 2013*, ed. J. Barclay et al., Wissenschaftliche Untersuchungen zum Neuen Testament (Tubigen: Mohr Siebeck, 2015), 411–31 (with reference to the classic essay [originally an SNTS presidential address] by M. Hengel, "Aufgaben der neutestamentlichen Wissenschaft," *NTS* 40 [1994]: 321–57, esp. 334).

Date(s)	Event(s) in Paul's Last Years (continued)
65/66/67	Second Roman imprisonment; writes 2 Timothy from Rome, martyrdom (beheaded by the sword)**
68	Death of Nero

*On the question of whether Paul ever realized his goal of evangelizing Spain, see the essays by Barclay, Puig i Tàrrech, and Karakolis in *Last Years of Paul*. See also discussion in the commentary at Titus 1:5 below.

** See Tertullian, *Praescr.* 36; Eusebius, *Hist. eccl.* 3.1.3. Tradition commemorates Paul's death on June 29. See Barclay, "Last Years of Paul," 7–8, with reference to H. W. Tajra, *The Martyrdom of St. Paul* (Tübingen: Mohr-Siebeck, 1994); D. L. Eastman, *Paul, the Martyr: The Cult of the Apostle in the Latin West* (Atlanta: SBL, 2011); and H. G. Thümmel, *Die Memorien für Petrus und Paulus in Rom: Die archäologischen Denkmäler und die literarische Tradition* (Berlin: de Gruyter, 1999). Cf. Tacitus, *Ann.* 15.41.3, who states that the fire of Rome broke out on July 19, AD 64. On the manner of Paul's death and the circumstances surrounding it, see esp. Marotta, "St. Paul's Death"; and J. G. Cook, "Roman Penalties Regarding Roman Citizens Convicted of Heavy Charges in I CE," in *Last Years of Paul*, 271–303 (see esp. pp. 298–99 detailing other known executions under Nero). As Riesner, "Paul's Trial," 407, documents, scholars date Paul's martyrdom anywhere between AD 62 and 68 (he himself favors 63/64); the exception is R. Penna, who proposes AD 58 (R. Penna, "The Death of Paul in the Year 58," in *Last Years of Paul*, 533–52).

As J. M. G. Barclay points out, the available sources provide a fascinating set of portrayals of the apostle's final years.[86] Luke depicts Paul as the triumphant, albeit persecuted, messenger of the gospel, who preaches the gospel of God's kingdom unhindered for two whole years (Acts 28:31). Second Timothy, which I believe Paul wrote himself (though Barclay considers the letter pseudonymous), casts Paul as a "lonely hero, but a heroic figure nonetheless," who in "this last will and testament . . . . announces the fulfillment of his task," not unlike Jesus himself (2 Tim 4:7; cf. John 17:4; 19:30), and who thus is able to point to his apostolic teaching, conduct, and suffering as an example for others to follow (2 Tim 3:10–11).[87] For Clement of Rome, Paul is an example of endurance who "taught righteousness to the whole world" (1 Clem. 5:7).

[86] Barclay, "Last Years of Paul," 7.

[87] Ibid.

Finally, the Martyrdom of Paul, the conclusion of the Acts of Paul, casts the apostle as the quintessential martyr.[88]

Internal Evidence in the Letters to Timothy and Titus: Toward an Integration with Pauline Chronology

Internal Evidence	Comments
"As I urged you when I went to Macedonia, remain in Ephesus." (1 Tim 1:3)	The most natural reading is that Paul wrote 1 Timothy from Macedonia.
"I write these things to you, hoping to come to you soon. But if I should be delayed . . ." (1 Tim 3:14–15a)	
"Until I come, give your attention to public reading, exhortation, teaching." (1 Tim 4:13)	
"So don't be ashamed of the testimony about our Lord, or of me his prisoner. . . . May the Lord grant mercy to the household of Onesiphorus, because he often refreshed me and was not ashamed of my chains." (2 Tim 1:8a, 16)	A literal understanding of "prisoner" and "chains" suggests Paul is in prison when writing 2 Timothy.
"For I am already being poured out as a drink offering, and the time for my departure is close. I have fought the good fight, I have finished the race, I have kept the faith. There is reserved for me the crown of righteousness, which the Lord, the righteous Judge, will give me on that day." (2 Tim 4:6–8)	At the time of writing 2 Timothy, Paul believes he is nearing the end of his life.
"Crescens has gone to Galatia, Titus to Dalmatia." (2 Tim 4:10b)	

[88] Barclay (ibid., 7–9) notes the striking diversity of these portraits (though we should note that they aren't necessarily contradictory) and argues that these sources attest to the emergence of "the Paul of faith" (p. 9). Cf. M. de Boer, "Images of Paul in the Post-Apostolic Period," *CBQ* 42 (1980): 359–80; R. Pervo, *The Making of Paul: Constructions of the Apostle in Early Christianity* (Minneapolis: Fortress, 2010).

Internal Evidence in the Letters to Timothy and Titus: Toward an Integration with Pauline Chronology (continued)

"I left Trophimus sick at Miletus." (2 Tim 4:20b)	Trophimus accompanies Paul on his third missionary journey (Acts 20:4, 15) and arrives with him in Jerusalem (Acts 21:29).
"Make every effort to come before winter." (2 Tim 4:21)	
"The reason I left you in Crete . . ." (Titus 1:5)	"Left you in Crete" may, but need not necessarily, imply that Paul went with Titus to Crete and left him there. No mission to Crete is mentioned in Acts (though see the reference to sailing along the south side of Crete and to Cretan cities in Acts 27:7–8, 12).
"Appoint elders [πρεσβύτερος] in every town . . . an overseer [ἐπίσκοπος] . . . must be . . ." (Titus 1:5, 7)	The terms "elder" and "overseer" are used interchangeably (cf. Acts 20:17, 28), which differs from the three-tiered ecclesiastical hierarchy mentioned in the second-century letters of Ignatius.
"Make every effort to come to me in Nicopolis, because I have decided to spend the winter there." (Titus 3:12)	

II. Historical Context

A. The Nature of the False Teachings

Paul's concern in his LTT isn't primarily to *describe* the respective type of false teaching—with which his apostolic delegates would have been thoroughly familiar—but to *refute* it.[89] The nature of the false teaching combated in these letters must therefore be largely inferred from the apostle's remarks.[90] What's more, while there are doubtless similarities between the opponents in the LTT, it shouldn't be assumed at the outset that they're identical.[91]

Broadly speaking, the false teachers in both locales (Ephesus and Crete) are said to display a tendency toward acrimony and speculation (1 Tim 1:4, 6; 6:4, 20; 2 Tim 2:14, 16, 23; Titus 1:10;

---

[89] For programmatic methodological considerations, see K. Berger, "Die implizit-en Gegner: Zur Methode des Erschließens von 'Gegnern' in neutestamentlichen Texten," in *Kirche: Festschrift für Günther Bornkamm zum 75. Geburtstag*, ed. D. Lührmann and G. Strecker (Tübingen: Mohr-Siebeck, 1980), 373–400. See also R. J. Karris, "The Background and Significance of the Polemic of the Pastoral Epistles," *JBL* 92 (1973): 549–64; and O. Skarsaune, "Heresy and the Pastoral Epistles," *Them* 20/1 (1994): 9–14; H. T. Ong, "Is There a Heresy in the Pastorals? A Sociolinguistic Analysis of 1 and 2 Timothy via the Ethnography of Communication Theory," *Paul and Gnosis*, ed. S. E. Porter and D. I. Yoon, Pauline Studies 9 (Leiden: Brill, 2016), 119–38.

[90] See the discussion under the next heading below. See also Thornton, *Hostility in the House of God*, who helpfully isolates explicit and implicit passages dealing with Timothy's opponents in 1 and 2 Timothy. According to Thornton, explicit passages include 1 Tim 1:3–7; 1:18–20; 4:1–5; 6:2b–5, 20–21a; 2 Tim 2:14–26; 3:1–9; and 4:1–5. Implicit passages include 1 Tim 1:8–11; 2:9–15; 4:6–10; 5:9–16; 6:6–10; and 2 Tim 2:8–13.

[91] So Thornton, *Hostility in the House of God*, 7, who limits the scope of his investigation to the letters to Timothy; cf. Towner, *1–2 Timothy & Titus*, 22. See also Herzer, "Juden—Christen—Gnostiker," who argues, over against the tendency to blend the various heretical elements into some kind of Jewish-Christian Gnosticism, that a specific, distinctive group of opponents stands behind each letter; and J. L. Sumney, "Studying Paul's Opponents: Advances and Challenges," in *Paul and His Opponents*, ed. S. E. Porter, Pauline Studies 2 (Leiden: Brill, 2005), 48–50, who after a careful investigation of Paul's opponents in all of his letters (including the LTT) suggests that while variety existed among Paul's opponents, broad anti-Pauline movements can be discerned involving opponents portrayed in multiple canonical letters. Others, such as J. B. Lightfoot ("Additional Note on the Heresy Combated in the Pastoral Epistles," in *Biblical Essays*, 411–18), assume the same false teaching in all three letters. For a list of those who treat the opponents in Ephesus and Crete as one and the same, see Thornton, *Hostility in the House of God*, 6n34.

3:9), deceptiveness (1 Tim 4:1–3; 2 Tim 3:6–9, 13; Titus 1:10–13), immorality (1 Tim 1:19–20; 2 Tim 2:22; 3:3–4; Titus 1:15), and greed (1 Tim 6:5; 2 Tim 3:2, 4; Titus 1:11).[92] They evince an interest in myths and genealogies (1 Tim 1:4; 4:7; 2 Tim 4:4; Titus 1:14; 3:9)[93] and use the law (1 Tim 1:7; Titus 1:10, 14; 3:9), though the "circumcision party" is mentioned only in Titus 1:10.[94]

Characteristics of the False Teachers and Their Teaching in the Letters to Timothy and Titus*

Characteristic	1 Timothy	2 Timothy	Titus
The false teaching seems to have arisen **within** the church.	1:3; 6:2; cf. 1:20	2:14; 4:2; cf. 2:17–18	1:13; 3:10
The false teaching involves an interest in **myths** and **genealogies.**	1:4; 4:7	4:4	1:14; 3:9

[92] Many scholars argue that the polemic in the LTT consists of stock characterizations. See the discussion under the next heading below.

[93] The "Jewish myths" in view may have reference to Second Temple Jewish works related to the Law such as Jubilees, Pseudo-Philo, and the Genesis Apocryphon. The first-century Greek geographer Strabo writes that "the things that are ancient and false and monstrous are called myths, but history wishes for the truth" (*Geogr.* 11.5.3), and Philo frequently contrasts myths and truth (see the discussion and source references in Spicq, *Les épîtres pastorales*, 93–96; Spicq, "μύθος," *TLNT* 2:529–30). "Myth" thus stands in contrast with the Christian message which is grounded in historical reality (cf. Titus 1:3). "Genealogies" probably has a broader referent than OT stylized genealogies such as Genesis 5 or 1 Chr 1:1–9:44 (though passages such as Genesis 5 may possibly be in view; personal conversation with P. Gentry). See F. J. A. Hort, *Judaistic Christianity: A Course of Lectures* (New York: Macmillan, 1894), 135–38, with reference to Polybius, *Hist.* 9.1.1–5; 9.2.1–2, who speaks of "myths and genealogies" and writes that in his day many "historians . . . attract a variety of readers by entering upon all the various branches of history" and that the "curious reader is attracted by the genealogical style"; see also Philo, *Moses* 2.8.

[94] As D. T. Thornton ("Hostility in the House of God: An 'Interested' Investigation of the Opponents in 1 and 2 Timothy" [Ph.D. thesis, University of Otago, 2014)], 8) notes, this may suggest that the opponents in Crete are Jewish while those in Ephesus are not. Ignatius (died ca. 110) likewise warns his readers not to be "led astray by strange doctrines or by old fables which are profitless" (*Magn.* 8.1; cf. *Pol.* 3.1; *Smyrn.* 6.2), linking these teachings with Judaism (cf. *Magn.* 9.1; 10.3; *Phld.* 6.1) involving the proper interpretation of the OT Scriptures (*Phld.* 8.2). Cf. S. Westerholm, "The Law and the 'Just Man' (1 Tim 1, 3–11)," *ST* 36 (1982): 82. I will discuss the opponents for each letter separately in the introductions to 1 Timothy, 2 Timothy, and Titus below.

Characteristics of the False Teachers and Their Teaching in the Letters to Timothy and Titus (continued)

The false teaching involves use of the **Law of Moses.**	1:7		1:10, 14; 3:9
In Ephesus at least, the false teaching involves **ascetic** elements such as the prohibition of marriage and eating certain foods.	4:1–5		
In Ephesus at least, the false teachers taught that the **resurrection** had already taken place.	Cf. 1:19–20	2:17–18	
The false teachers tended toward **acrimony** and **speculation.**	1:4, 6; 6:4, 20	2:14, 16, 23	1:10; 3:9
The false teachers tended toward **deceptiveness.**	4:1–3	3:6–9, 13	1:10–13
The false teachers tended toward **immorality.**	1:19–20	2:22; 3:3–4	1:15
The false teachers tended toward **greed.**	6:5	3:2, 4	1:11
*This comparison chart is simply designed to surface initial data and doesn't imply that the opponents in Ephesus and Crete are identical. See also Köstenberger, "1–2 Timothy, Titus," 491–92; Köstenberger, Kellum, and Quarles, *Cradle, the Cross, and the Crown*, 645–46.			

B. The Polemic against the False Teachers

Paul denounces the various permutations of the false teachings in strong language as "fruitless discussion" (1 Tim 1:6), "godless myths and old wives' tales" (1 Tim 4:7 NIV), "irreverent and empty speech" (1 Tim 6:20), "foolish and stupid arguments" (2 Tim 2:23 NIV), and "foolish debates" (Titus 3:9). This polemic serves to caution believers against associating with the false teachers.[95] The

[95] See Karris, "Background and Significance of the Polemic," 548–64, who argues that the purpose of the polemic is to bolster the author's authority. L. T. Johnson, "II Timothy and the Polemic against False Teachers: A Reexamination," *JRelS* 6–7 (1978): 1–26, against Karris, contends that there was no need to bolster the author's authority, since the letters are addressed to Paul's apostolic delegates. L. K. Pietersen, "Despicable Deviants: Labelling Theory and the Polemic of the Pastorals," *Sociology of Religion* 58 (1997): 343–52; Pietersen, *The Polemic of the Pastorals: A Sociological*

opponents also serve as a foil for what Timothy and Titus must avoid in shepherding God's flock.[96]

It's sometimes argued that the author of the LTT denounces his opponents and accentuates institutional authority while Paul in his undisputed letters engages his opponents theologically.[97] However, this is a false dichotomy, because there are times when Paul strongly denounces his opponents in his earlier letters as well (e.g., Rom 2:8; 1 Cor 16:22; Gal 1:8–9; Phil 3:18–19; 2 Thess 3:6, 14) or appeals to his teaching without further elaboration (e.g., Rom 16:17; Gal 1:8–9; 2 Thess 3:6).

What's more, the LTT are written to coworkers who hardly need to be told what the false teaching is they're combating.[98] Most likely, the polemic against the false teachers in the LTT, therefore, serves the purpose of providing a foil for Paul's coworkers, exhorting them to avoid emulating the false teachers' example. This suggests the opponents are real rather than imagined.[99] We'll explore the opponents in Ephesus and Crete in greater detail in the introductions to the individual letters below.

Examination of the Development of Pauline Christianity, JSNTSup 264 (New York: T&T Clark, 2004), contends the LTT resemble a status degradation ceremony by which "previously influential insiders . . . are transformed into outsiders" (*Polemic*, p. 1), arguing that the polemic in these letters is aimed at marginalizing the opponents' influence. G. Häfner, "Die Gegner in den Pastoralbriefen und die Paulusakten," *ZNW* 92 (2001): 64–77 assesses the proposal that the LTT are directed against traditions and their tradents that come to literary expression in the *Acts of Paul and Thecla*.

[96] This is the central thesis of Johnson, "II Timothy and the Polemic against False Teachers."

[97] E.g., N. Brox, *Die Pastoralbriefe* (1969; repr., RNT, Regensburg: F. Pustet, 1989), 39–42.

[98] Schnabel, "Paul, Timothy, and Titus," 395, with reference to Mounce, *Pastoral Epistles*, xcvii.

[99] Contra M. Bjelland Kartzow, *Gossip and Gender: Othering of Speech in the Pastoral Epistles*, BZNW 164 (Berlin: de Gruyter, 2009), who contends that the false teachers "represented modes of speech that were not to be found in real men" (p. 194) and that the author draws on the stereotype of gossip for the purpose of "undermin[ing] his opponents' masculinity" (p. 201).

Lexical Links in Descriptions of the False Teachers and Their Teaching among the Letters to Timothy and Titus

Reference	1 Timothy	2 Timothy	Titus
The teaching involves interest in genealogies (γενεαλογία).	1:4		3:9
The teaching involves myths (μῦθος).	1:4; 4:7	4:4	1:14
The false teachers have a seared or defiled conscience (συνείδησις).	1:5–6 (deviated from a good conscience); 1:19 (rejected a good conscience); 4:2 (consciences are seared); cf. 3:9		1:15 (consciences are defiled)
The false teachers are lovers of money (φιλαργυρία/φιλάργυρος).	6:10	3:2	
The false teachers are in opposition to the faith (πίστις).	1:19 (rejected the faith); 4:1 (departed from the faith); 6:10 (wandered away from the faith); 6:21 (deviated from the faith); cf. 1:4	3:8 (worthless in regard to the faith)	1:13 (not sound in the faith)
The false teachers are disobedient (ἀπειθής).		3:2	1:16
The false teachers engage in empty talk (ματαιολογία); they are empty talkers (ματαιολόγος).	1:6		1:10
The false teachers are slanderers (βλασφημία/βλάσφημος).	6:4	3:2	

Lexical Links in Descriptions of the False Teachers and Their Teaching among the Letters to Timothy and Titus (continued)

Reference	1 Timothy	2 Timothy	Titus
The false teachers stir up controversy (ζήτησις/ ἐκζήτησις).	1:4; 6:4	2:23	3:9
The false teachers engage in word battles (λογομαχία/λογομαχέω).	6:4	2:14	
The false teachers stand against the truth (ἀλήθεια).	6:5 (deprived of the truth; cf. 4:3)	2:18 (deviated from the truth); 2:25 (needed knowledge of the truth); 3:7 (never able to come to knowledge of the truth); 3:8 (resisted the truth); 4:4 (turned away from hearing truth)	1:14 (rejected the truth)
The false teachers reject sound teaching (ὑγιαίνω).	6:3 (cf. 1:10)	4:3	1:13 (cf. 1:9; 2:1)
The false teaching is opposed to godliness (εὐσέβεια).	6:3, 5 (cf. 4:7; 6:11)	3:5	
The false teaching involves quarrels (μάχη).		2:23	3:9
The false teaching is irreverent (βέβηλος).	4:7; 6:20	2:16	
The false teachers are evil (πονηρός).		3:13	
The false teachers are wicked and engage in wickedness (κακός).	6:10		1:12

Lexical Links in Descriptions of the False Teachers and Their Teaching among the Letters to Timothy and Titus (continued)

Reference	1 Timothy	2 Timothy	Titus
The false teachers are disqualified (ἀδόκιμος) as to faith or good deeds.		3:8	1:16 Less direct connections
The false teachers have fallen into the snare (παγίς) of the devil (διάβολος), and elders must have a good reputation lest they do the same.	3:7 (cf. 4:1)	2:26	
The false teachers engage in foolish talk (κενοφωνία) which the man of God must shun.	6:20	2:16	

C. The Social Setting of the Letters to Timothy and Titus

The overall understanding of the social setting of the LTT has a significant bearing on how the letters are read and interpreted.[100]

[100] See esp. the summary of scholarship on the social setting of the LTT by M. Harding, *What Are They Saying about the Pastoral Epistles?* (Mahwah, NJ: Paulist, 2001), 46–65. Harding himself holds to double pseudonymity: see Harding, *Tradition and Rhetoric in the Pastoral Epistles*, StBibLit 3 (New York: P. Lang, 1998). See also Marshall, "Pastoral Epistles in Recent Study," 286–87. For summaries and assessments, see S. C. Barton, "Social-Scientific Approaches to Paul," *DPL*, 892–900; Barton, "Social Setting of Early Non-Pauline Christianity," *DLNT* 1102–11; Barton, "Historical Criticism and Social-Scientific Perspectives in New Testament Study," in *Hearing the New Testament: Strategies for Interpretation*, ed. J. B. Green (Grand Rapids: Eerdmans, 1995), 61–89; Barton, "Social-Scientific Criticism," in *Handbook to Exegesis of the New Testament*, ed. S. E. Porter, NT Tools and Studies 25 (Leiden: Brill, 1997), 277–89; K. Berding, "The Hermeneutical Framework of Social-Scientific Criticism: How Much Can Evangelicals Get Involved?," *EvQ* 75 (2005): 3–22; T. E. Best, "The Sociological Study of the New Testament: Promise and Peril of a New Discipline," *SJT* 36 (1983): 181–94; "Social-Scientific Criticism," in C. L. Blomberg with J. F. Merkley, *A Handbook of New Testament Exegesis* (Grand Rapids: Baker, 2010), 85–92; J. D. Dvorak, "John H. Elliott's Social-Scientific Criticism," *TJ* 28 (2007): 251–78;

In this regard, scholarship in the last few decades has sought to understand the social institutions, the ancient household, the socio-economic background of first-century Christians, and the institutionalization of the first-century church, moving from description to explanation.[101]

With regard to social setting, E. A. Judge emphasizes the household as the social context in which Christianity was propagated and in which believers gathered.[102] He observes that the NT writers use household terminology to depict believers' relationships to one another and to God. Judge also notes the affinity between early Christian communities and Greco-Roman voluntary religious associations. While voluntary associations were more democratic,

---

D. G. Horrell, "Social Sciences Studying Formative Christian Phenomena: A Creative Movement," in *Handbook of Early Christianity: Social Science Approaches*, ed. A. J. Blasi, J. Duhaime, and P.-A. Turcotte (Walnut Creek, CA: AltaMira, 2002), 3–28; Horrell, "Whither Social-Scientific Approaches to New Testament Interpretation? Reflections on Contested Methodologies and the Future," in *After the First Urban Christians: The Social-Scientific Study of Pauline Christianity Twenty-Five Years Later*, ed. T. D. Still and D. G. Horrell (London/New York: T&T Clark, 2009), 6–20; M. R. Mulholland Jr., "Sociological Criticism," in *Interpreting the New Testament: Essays on Methods and Issues*, ed. D. A. Black and D. S. Dockery (Nashville: B&H, 2001), 170–86; T. E. Schmidt, "Sociology and New Testament Exegesis," in *Introducing New Testament Interpretation*, ed. S. McKnight (Grand Rapids: Baker, 1989), 115–32; D. A. deSilva, "Embodying the Word: Social-Scientific Interpretation of the New Testament," in *The Face of New Testament Studies: A Survey of Recent Research*, ed. S. McKnight and G. R. Osborne (Grand Rapids: Baker, 2004), 118–29; and D. J. Tidball, "On Wooing a Crocodile: An Historical Survey of the Relationship between Sociology and New Testament Studies," *VE* 15 (1985): 95–109.

[101] Best, "Sociological Study of the NT," 185. Moving from least to most speculative, methods encompass social description, sociological clarification, and sociological analysis. See Schmidt, "Sociology and NT Exegesis," 117–21, developed further in Blomberg and Merkley, *Handbook of NT Exegesis*, 86–90. For a treatment of some of the most pertinent issues involved, see D. A. deSilva, *Honor, Patronage, Kinship and Purity: Unlocking New Testament Culture* (Downers Grove: InterVarsity, 2000). See also J. H. Neyrey and E. C. Stewart, eds., *The Social World of the New Testament: Insights and Models* (Peabody, MA: Hendrickson, 2008).

[102] E. A. Judge, *The Social Pattern of Christian Groups in the First Groups in the First Century: Some Prolegomena to the Study of New Testament Ideas of Social Obligation* (London: Tyndale, 1960). For an extended discussion and appreciation of the pioneering work of Judge (as well as of G. Theissen and W. Meeks) see N. T. Wright, *Paul and His Recent Interpreters: Some Contemporary Debates* (Minneapolis: Fortress, 2015), 229–43 (but note that Wright does not discuss the LTT). See also the tribute to Judge paid by B. W. Winter, *Divine Honours for the Caesars: The First Christians' Responses* (Grand Rapids: Eerdmans, 2015), ix–x.

the household was strongly hierarchical, which, according to Judge, explains why there is a tension between fraternity and hierarchy in Paul's letters. Judge also detects a heightened sensitivity to public opinion in the LTT.

With regard to the "household of God" metaphor (§4.1), many believe it reflects an accommodationist stance toward the surrounding Greco-Roman culture, perhaps in response to the charge that the early Christians were seeking to subvert society. D. Balch, in his seminal monograph on the *Haustafel* in 1 Pet 2:13–3:8, agrees with Judge that the Romans saw women and slaves involved in cults as potentially subversive. He argues that the NT house tables are not signs of a diminishing eschatological outlook but a response to Greco-Roman expectations that citizens accept prevailing cultural norms.[103] D. Balch and C. Osiek contend that the household management *topos* in the LTT conveys the author's acculturation to the current patriarchal social conventions of the cities and towns of the empire.[104]

Building on Balch's work, D. Verner maintains that the church, when accused of subverting the political structures of the state, promoted the metaphor of the church as the "household of God" in order to enforce the traditional patriarchal structure of the household within local Christian congregations.[105] According to Verner, this was done both to ensure the church's survival and to enhance its effective witness. Likewise, the church's leadership was limited to qualified, older, well-to-do male householders while women were forbidden to teach and slaves were commanded to obey their masters. No longer were leadership ministries charismatically driven, but offices were entered through the laying on of hands by the current leadership.

In his seminal commentary M. Dibelius proposed the influential theory that the LTT reflect "bourgeois Christianity" (*bürgerliches Christentum*).[106] At a time when eschatological expectation had

---

[103] D. L. Balch, *Let Wives Be Submissive: The Domestic Code in 1 Peter*, SBLMS 26 (Chico, CA: Scholars Press, 1981).

[104] D. L. Balch and C. Osiek, *Families in the New Testament World: Households and House Churches* (Louisville: John Knox, 1997).

[105] D. C. Verner, *The Household of God: The Social World of the Pastoral Epistles*, SBLDS 71 (Chico, CA: Scholars Press, 1983).

[106] M. Dibelius, *Die Pastoralbriefe*, HNT 13, 2nd ed. (Tübingen: J. C. B. Mohr, 1931); rev. M. Dibelius and H. Conzelmann, *The Pastoral Epistles*, Hermeneia, trans. P. Buttolph and A. Yarbro (Philadelphia: Fortress, 1972).

largely waned, the author of these letters promoted "good citizenship" which would situate the church well in the surrounding Greco-Roman culture in which it was embedded and would ensure its survival. According to Dibelius, this bourgeois ethos converged with the social status of the emergent middle class which constituted the majority among the recipients of the LTT. Dibelius's proposal elicited a considerable number of responses, many of which were negative.[107]

E. A. Judge rejected the notion that Christians were emerging from the poorer classes only at a later date, arguing that the socially pretentious were in the majority in urban Christian communities early on.[108] R. Schwarz, in the first full-fledged analysis of Dibelius's theory, maintains that the LTT aren't accommodationist so as to promote conventional social expectations but because the false teachers were failing to promote these values.[109] Rather than resulting from fading eschatological expectations, the ethical exhortations in these letters are grounded in an eschatological outlook. In a later study, P. Towner argues, similar to Verner, that the goal of the ethical stance adopted by the author was effective evangelistic outreach.[110]

A series of studies is devoted to the role of the wealthy and the LTT. W. Countryman contends that the early church reflected the entire social spectrum of urban society.[111] While the wealthy were expected to help poor church members, this potentially led to their insubordination to church leaders because, in keeping with Greco-Roman societal norms, they expected an influential and honored role in religious associations in return for their benefaction. In response, the LTT attempt to balance exhortations to the rich to help the poor with efforts to preserve legitimate church leadership. One such strategy involved co-opting wealthy male householders into the ranks of church leaders as long as they were qualified.

---

[107] For a brief summary and assessment, see D. W. Pao, "Let No One Despise Your Youth: Church and the World in the Pastoral Epistles," *JETS* 57 (2014): 743–44.

[108] Judge, *Social Pattern of Christian Groups*.

[109] R. Schwarz, *Bürgerliches Christentum im Neuen Testament?* (Klosterneuburg: Österreichisches Katholisches Bibelwerk, 1983).

[110] P. H. Towner, *The Goal of Our Instruction: The Structure of Theology and Ethics in the Pastoral Epistles*, JSNTSup 34 (Sheffield: JSOT, 1989).

[111] L. W. Countryman, *The Rich Christian in the Church of the Early Empire: Contradictions and Accommodations* (New York/Toronto: E. Mellen, 1980).

R. Kidd, in interaction with Countryman and Verner, maintains that the solution wasn't to co-opt wealthy benefactors into the ranks of church leadership but to tell them not to expect favors in return for their benefaction.[112] Thus the LTT aren't accommodating themselves to the prevailing culture but possess a countercultural dimension. Kidd concurs with Judge that the recipients of these letters aren't socially ascendant as Dibelius maintained but that Christian congregations included some well-to-do members from the beginning. Also, according to Kidd, similar to R. Schwarz, an eschatological outlook still underlies the ethical exhortations in the LTT.

Much research has been devoted to the question of institutionalization. E. Käsemann, in an influential essay, speaks of the "early Catholicism" reflected in these letters.[113] Käsemann's work contrasts charismatically driven ministry in letters such as 1 Corinthians with later institutionalized ministry, which he finds in the LTT. This emphasis on institutionalization, says Käsemann, is the result of the waning of eschatological expectation and charismatic enthusiasm. Others, such as M. MacDonald, distinguish multiple stages of development. In each case a certain type of institutionalization takes place: first, community-building (undisputed Paulines); then, community-stabilizing (Prison Epistles); and finally, community-protecting (1–2 Timothy, Titus).[114]

S. Barton discusses the question of gendered church order (see esp. 1 Tim 2:8–15).[115] He contends, first, that Christians were the heirs of traditions in Israel that tied ministry to ritual purity. Women, who incurred ritual impurity through menstruation, were thus disqualified from serving in the priesthood, which was reserved strictly for men (the Levites). Second, in the Mediterranean world social space was divided up into public and private space, with the male representing political leadership roles and the female being assigned primary space in the household (see, e.g., Philo, *Spec. Laws* 3.169–70). Charismatic authority, as well as

---

[112] R. M. Kidd, *Wealth and Beneficence in the Pastoral Epistles: A "Bourgeois" Form of Early Christianity?*, SBLDS 122 (Atlanta: Scholars Press, 1990).

[113] Käsemann, "Paul and Early Catholicism."

[114] M. Y. MacDonald, *The Pauline Churches: A Socio-Historical Study of Institutionalism in the Pauline and Deutero-Pauline Writings*, SNTSMS 60 (Cambridge: Cambridge University Press, 1988).

[115] Barton, "Social Setting of Early Non-Pauline Christianity," 1105–6. Notice, however, that Barton assigns the LTT to the post-Pauline period.

apocalyptic or early Gnostic influences, may have disturbed this gendered ordering of space. The gendered church order in the LTT may thus have served the purpose of protecting the church against disintegration and of maintaining a credible witness in society at large.

Finally, numerous studies have been devoted to ancient honor and shame cultures.[116] As D. Pao aptly sums up, "Recent studies on the cultural framework of the ancient Mediterranean world have emphasized the importance of honor and shame as pivotal values in the structuring of both social networks within individual political units as well as perceived ideological values that provide coherence to a group."[117] Pao himself, in an important study, applies social-scientific insights to the study of one particular text in the LTT: the reference to Timothy's youth in 1 Tim 4:12. Pao draws attention to the "rich set of vocabulary that expresses the cultural value of honor and shame" in the letter and shows that this terminology is applied not only to Timothy but also to elders, widows, slaves, and even God himself.[118] Pao concludes that in a challenge to prevailing cultural mores, "Without denying the need to respect the elders, Paul denies that the youthful should be ignored as being insignificant and irrelevant in the gospel ministry simply because of their age."[119]

While these kinds of studies have doubtless shed considerable light on the social setting of the LTT, most of the research is predicated on pseudonymity, which assigns these letters to the post-Pauline period. Also, one must guard against reductionism (i.e., the tendency to explain biblical phenomena *solely* or *primarily* on the basis of social factors) and anachronism (i.e., one must ensure a

[116] See, e.g., B. J. Malina, *Christian Origins and Cultural Anthropology: Practical Models for Biblical Interpretation* (Atlanta: John Knox, 1986); V. H. Matthews and D. C. Benjamin, eds., *Honor and Shame in the World of the Bible*, Semeia 68 (Atlanta: Scholars Press, 1996); more broadly, deSilva, *Honor, Patronage, Kinship and Purity*. For important caveats regarding the appropriation of honor and shame research in NT studies see Pao, "Let No One Despise Your Youth," 746 (see also the bibliographic references to the application of such research to the study of specific NT books or corpora in ibid., 746n19).

[117] Pao, "Let No One Despise Your Youth," 745.

[118] Timothy: 4:12; widows: 5:3, 7; elders: 5:17, 20; slaves: 6:1; God: 1:17; 6:16.

[119] Pao, "Let No One Despise Your Youth," 750.

given model of analysis is appropriate to the time frame studied).[120] On the positive side, these studies take seriously the Greco-Roman embeddedness of the letters which seems to be reflected in their distinctive vocabulary and conceptualities, such as those related to the household, Christian virtues, good citizenship, and the ordering of the church with regard to authority, qualifications, and gender. Those who maintain Pauline authorship of the LTT, however, will discern a closer affinity with the other Pauline NT letters. They will stress continuity with OT paradigms, practices, and principles and look at the salvation-historical trajectory represented in these letters at the transition from the apostolic to the post-apostolic period (§§2.7; 7.1).[121]

III. Literary Analysis and Structure

A. Genre

In light of the common issues presented by all three letters, I'll provide an initial joint treatment at this point of this volume.[122] In general terms the LTT conform to the standard format of the ancient letter, including an opening salutation, a body with features such as thanksgiving and the main content, and a closing greeting.[123] Beyond this, 1 Timothy and Titus, as well as 2 Timothy (though see further below), are often identified as exemplars of the paraenetic or hortatory letter, which contains a series of exhortations to its recipients.

---

[120] See, e.g., Barton, "Social-Scientific Approaches to Paul," 894; Berding, "Hermeneutical Framework of Social-Scientific Criticism," 12–19; Dvorak, "John H. Elliott's Social-Scientific Criticism," 277–78; Mulholland, "Sociological Criticism," 179; deSilva, "Embodying the Word," 126–28; and Schmidt, "Sociology and NT Exegesis," 128–30.

[121] Note that I'm not arguing for the embeddedness of the LTT in OT substructures *to the exclusion of* contextualization with the Greco-Roman world. I believe this is not an either-or but rather a both-and proposition. However, in light of the tendency by some to focus unilaterally on the Greco-Roman background, the recognition of the OT substructure provides a much-needed counterweight.

[122] In addition to technical and semitechnical commentaries, which usually discuss genre, see D. A. Aune, "The Pastoral Letters: 1 and 2 Timothy and Titus," in *The Blackwell Companion to the New Testament* (Chichester, UK: Wiley-Blackwell, 2010), 551–63.

[123] For helpful comparisons of structural elements in the Pauline letters, see chart 42, "Formal Structural Components of Paul's Letters," in Kierspel, *Charts on the Life, Letters, and Theology of Paul*, 84.

That said, 2 Timothy is often considered a special case. Since it is Paul's last recorded letter—written from a second and much more severe Roman imprisonment with Paul's martyrdom apparently imminent—it seems to some to take on the character of a last testament in certain respects, similar to 2 Peter,[124] though in light of some important differences, it may be best to classify 2 Timothy as a personal paraenetic letter.[125]

S. Martin, regarding 2 Timothy as pseudonymous, argues that the letter is Paul's testament much like Deuteronomy is the testament of Moses, in the sense that both books present a prominent figure as passing on their authority to their successor and summarizing their teaching.[126] Martin draws attention to the references to Moses in 2 Tim 2:19 and 3:8–9, in both cases in the context of Moses's authority being challenged (similar to Timothy's). He also compares Moses's laying on of hands on Joshua with Paul's laying on of hands on Timothy (Num 27:18–23; Deut 34:9; 2 Tim 1:6; cf. 1 Tim 4:14). Martin further adduces the designations "servant of the Lord" and "man of God," both used for Timothy, as evocative of Moses and views the exhortation to "be strong" (2 Tim 2:1) in light of Deuteronomy 31. The parallels Martin notes are

[124] Cf. T. Simeon. See M. D. Mathews, "The Genre of 2 Peter: A Comparison with Jewish and Early Christian Testaments," *BBR* 21 (2011): 51–64. See also the discussion in G. S. MaGee, "Paul's Response to the Shame and Pain of Imprisonment in 2 Timothy," *BSac* 165 (2008): 338–53, who explores Paul's imprisonment in historical context, in particular with regard to the pain and shame associated with it; Manabu, "Der zweite Timotheus als letzter Gefangenschaftsbrief," who adduces parallels to other Pauline Prison Epistles (Ephesians, Philippians, Colossians, and Philemon); and Marshall, *Pastoral Epistles*, 12–13.

[125] See esp. C. A. Smith, *Timothy's Task and Paul's Prospect: A New Reading of 2 Timothy* (Sheffield: Sheffield Phoenix, 2006), esp. 75–89; S. K. Stowers, *Letter Writing in Greco-Roman Antiquity*, LEC (Philadelphia: Westminster, 1986), 95–96; and Thornton, "Hostility in the House of God," 20–23, citing Johnson, *First and Second Letters to Timothy*, 321–24.

[126] S. C. Martin, *Pauli Testamentum: 2 Timothy and the Last Words of Moses*, TGST 18 (Rome: Pontificia Università Gregoriana, 1999). Compare and contrast C. A. Smith, "A Study of 2 Timothy 4:1–8: The Contribution of Epistolary Analysis and Rhetorical Criticism," *TynBul* 57 (2006): 151–54, who analyzes 2 Tim 4:1–8 as a charge containing five elements: (1) a command (first person); (2) an addressee (second person); (3) a declaration of authority; (4) a command; and (5) a depiction of the results of obedience or disobedience. Smith argues that Paul is expecting his release and that the primary purpose of Paul's command is to encourage Timothy.

highly suggestive, even though they don't prove pseudonymous authorship or establish the genre of 2 Timothy as a last testament (§7.1.3).[127]

What's more, the LTT aren't merely letters written by one individual to another for the purpose of conveying exhortation and information. As T. D. Gordon observes, "The Pastoral Epistles are the only New Testament writings that are expressly written with the purpose of providing instructions for ordering churches at the close of the apostolic era."[128] He continues,

> The very apostle who had established churches and provided for their continued oversight, doctrinal purity, and worship, now gives instructions to his co-workers [*sic*] regarding the organization of churches in subsequent generations. The norms and principles he himself had observed in the ordering of his churches, Paul makes explicit to his colleagues so that they, too, might order their churches correctly.[129]

For this reason the genre of these letters is inextricably bound up with the historical life-setting of Paul's ministry as set forth in Acts and Paul's earlier letters. Hermeneutically the important implication from this understanding of the genre of the LTT is that these "letters contain norms that are especially germane to the issues of life in the church, the 'household of God'" (see 1 Tim 3:14–15).[130] As Gordon observes, "The instructions in these letters, far from being primarily of local significance, are significant wherever there is concern for the proper ordering of God's house. Indeed, as instructions given to post-apostolic ministers, the instructions contained in the Pastoral Epistles are particularly germane to other post-apostolic churches."[131]

---

[127] See the brief critique by Marshall, "Pastoral Epistles in Recent Study," 285–86 from whom some of the above summary is drawn. Also strained is Martin's drawing of parallels between Moses's three roles as prophet, lawgiver, and suffering intercessor, and Paul's alleged three similar roles.

[128] T. D. Gordon, "A Certain Kind of Letter: The Genre of 1 Timothy," in *Women in the Church: A Fresh Analysis of 1 Timothy 2:9–15*, ed. A. J. Köstenberger, T. R. Schreiner, and H. S. Baldwin (Grand Rapids: Baker, 1995), 59.

[129] Ibid. Gordon provides a specific list of such instructions on pp. 59–60.

[130] Ibid., 60.

[131] Ibid.

B. Literary Integrity

Writing in 2004, R. Van Neste summarized the state of scholarship on the LTT in this way: "Until recently, one of the widely accepted tenets of modern scholarship regarding the Pastoral Epistles was that they lacked any significant, careful order or structure."[132] This is not limited to liberal critics; even an otherwise conservative commentator such as D. Guthrie writes, "There is a lack of studied order, some subjects being treated more than once in the same letter without apparent premeditation. . . . These letters are, therefore, far removed from literary exercises."[133] A. T. Hanson, an opponent of the Pauline authorship of the LTT, maintains, "The Pastorals are made up of a miscellaneous collection of material. They have no unifying theme; there is no development of thought."[134]

However, more recently the pendulum has largely swung away from such assessments. Against those who argue against the literary unity and integrity of the LTT, Van Neste demonstrates that there is "evidence of a high level of cohesion in each of the Pastoral Epistles" and that "all three letters show evidence of care in their design."[135] I. H. Marshall also observes that "there is a growing body of evidence that the Pastoral Epistles are not a conglomerate of miscellaneous ideas roughly thrown together with no clear plan, purpose or structure. On the contrary, they demonstrate signs of a coherent structure and of theological competence."[136] In light of assessments such as these, it appears that

---

[132] R. Van Neste, *Cohesion and Structure in the Pastoral Epistles*, JSNTSup 280 (New York: T&T Clark, 2004), 1. See also Van Neste, "Cohesion and Structure in the Pastoral Epistles," in *Entrusted with the Gospel*, 84–104.

[133] Guthrie, *Pastoral Epistles*, 18.

[134] A. T. Hanson, *The Pastoral Epistles* (Grand Rapids: Eerdmans, 1982), 42. But see R. Van Neste, "Structure and Cohesion in Titus: Problems and Method," *BT* 53 (2002): 118–33, who finds that the concerted focus on behavior and doctrine, the use of transitional devices, and the use of repetitions indicate a considerable degree of cohesion in Titus.

[135] Van Neste, *Cohesion and Structure*, 285, against Miller, *Pastoral Letters as Composite Documents*. See also J. T. Reed, "Cohesive Ties in 1 Timothy: In Defence of the Epistle's Unity," *Neot* 26 (1992): 131–47; Reed, "Discourse Features in New Testament Letters: With Special Reference to the Structure of 1 Timothy," *JOTT* 6 (1993): 228–52, who applies Halliday and Hasan's theory of cohesive ties to 1 Timothy and finds the letter to be cohesive, centering on the person of Timothy and the problem of heretical teachings.

[136] I. H. Marshall, "The Christology of Luke-Acts and the Pastoral Epistles," in *Crossing Boundaries: Essays in Biblical Interpretation in Honor of Michael D. Goulder*,

the literary integrity and coherence of the LTT has been largely vindicated.

C. Vocabulary

In terms of total word length, 1 Timothy is the longest and Titus the shortest epistle among the LTT.[137] Taken together, Paul's letters to Timothy comprise almost a thousand words (994, to be exact) while his letter to Titus is 291 words in length (or less than a third the total length of Paul's correspondence with Timothy).

Word Statistics

	1 Timothy	2 Timothy	Titus
Number of words	538	456	291
Number of words occurring 10+ times	25	20	9
Words occurring once	342	310	212

The distinctive vocabulary is remarkably consistent in the LTT.[138] Frequent vocabulary, as might be expected, includes the words for God, Lord, Jesus, Christ, and Savior, attesting to the thoroughly theological, Christological, and soteriological nature of these letters. In addition, there is a pronounced emphasis on words related to teaching as well as to works and piety.[139]

Frequency Rank	1 Timothy	2 Timothy	Titus
1.	θεός ("God"; 22)	κύριος ("Lord"; 16)	θεός ("God"; 13)
2.	πίστις ("faith"; 19)	θεός ("God"; 13)	ἔργον ("work"; 8)
3.	καλός ("good"; 16)	Ἰησοῦς ("Jesus"; 13)	πίστις ("faith"; 6)
4.	Χριστός ("Christ"; 15)	Χριστός ("Christ"; 13)	σωτήρ ("Savior"; 6)

ed. S. E. Porter, P. Joyce, and D. E. Orton (Leiden: Brill, 1994), 171.

[137] Statistics are drawn from Köstenberger and Bouchoc, *Book Study Concordance*, 1172–235.

[138] The chart below doesn't include articles, pronouns, conjunctions, and prepositions.

[139] In addition to the occurrences of individual words, it's also beneficial to study the use of words within the context of semantic domains. A helpful tool in this regard is J. P. Louw and E. A. Nida, *Greek-English Lexicon of the New Testament Based on Semantic Domains*, 2 vols. (New York: United Bible Societies, 1988, 1989).

Frequency Rank	1 Timothy	2 Timothy	Titus
5.	Ἰησοῦς ("Jesus"; 14)	πίστις ("faith"; 8)	ἄνθρωπος ("person"; 5)
6.	πιστός ("faithful"; 11)	λόγος ("word/ speech"; 7)	καλός ("good"; 5)
7.	ἄνθρωπος ("person"; 10)	ἀλήθεια ("truth"; 6)	λόγος ("word/ speech"; 5)
8.	γυνή ("woman/wife"; 9)	δίδωμι ("give"; 6)	ἀγαθός ("good"; 5)
9.	διδασκαλία ("teaching"; 8)	ἔργον ("work"; 6)	διδασκαλία ("teaching"; 4)
10.	εὐσέβεια ("god-liness"; 8)	ἄνθρωπος ("person"; 5)	Ἰησοῦς ("Jesus"; 4)
(tie)	λόγος ("word/ speech"; 8)		ὑγιαίνω ("sound"; 4)
(tie)	χήρα ("widow"; 8)		χάρις ("grace"; 4)
(tie)			Χριστός ("Christ"; 4)

D. Use of Preformed Traditions

Distinct from, but related to, the questions of authenticity, literary integrity, and distinctive vocabulary is the use of preformed traditions in the LTT. Possible instances include the "trustworthy sayings"; confessional, hymnic, or creedal statements; vice lists; and evident connections with the OT.[140]

E. Ellis categorizes possible preformed traditions by their identifying markers: (1) "faithful is the saying"; (2) "knowing that/ know this"; (3) "these things teach/command/exhort/guard"; and miscellaneous other markers.[141] By Ellis's estimation, as much as 35 percent of 1 and 2 Timothy and Titus consist of preformed material: 41 percent of 1 Timothy; 16 percent of 2 Timothy; and 46 percent of Titus. According to Ellis, this use of preformed material by the author of these letters has important implications for the question of authorship. In the end, "the role of an amanuensis may

[140] In addition, proponents of the fragment theory of authorship (such as Miller, *Pastoral Letters as Composite Documents*) argue for authentic Pauline "preformed material" included in the LTT, but see the discussion under the previous heading above.

[141] E. E. Ellis, "Traditions in the Pastoral Epistles," in *Early Jewish and Christian Exegesis*, ed. C. A. Evans and W. F. Stinespring (Atlanta: Scholars Press, 1987), 237–53.

be less important than the effect of non-Pauline preformed traditions on the literary expression and formation of the letters."[142] Ellis conjectures that while in Rome or Caesarea and after writing his other canonical epistles, Paul "apparently found traditions, especially some with a soteriological and church-order idiom and emphasis reminiscent of the Jerusalem church."[143] Upon return from his post-Roman-imprisonment Western mission, he found the churches he planted in disarray and sent letters, "or better, virtual manuals of traditions and commentary," to coworkers who would mediate them to their congregations.[144] Ellis concludes, "By this means Paul can give his personal communications to Timothy and Titus and at the same time provide them with an apostolic authorization for their teachings."[145]

More recently, M. Yarbrough, presupposing Pauline authorship, identified three principal types of preformed material in 1 Timothy—creedal, confessional, and hymnic—that serve to "strengthen literary cohesion, provide rhetorical leverage, and present theological directives that combat counter-mission doctrine in the letter."[146] Yarbrough posited eight basic criteria for identifying such preformed traditions. Under "structure" he lists (1) formulaic introductions and conclusions and (2) self-contained texts. Under "content" he identifies (3) an emphasis on early orthodoxy; (4) an emphasis on paraenesis; and (5) parallels with external passages. Under "style" he lists (6) poetic characteristics; (7) uncommon vocabulary; and (8) unusual syntactical structure.[147] This yields the following twelve instances of preformed material in 1 Timothy (excluding OT usage): 1:8–10, 15a–b, 17; 2:5–6a; 3:1, 16; 4:8, 9–10b; 5:24–25; 6:7, 10a, and 11–16. Yarbrough concludes that about 20 percent of 1 Timothy consists of preformed material, about half of Ellis's total.[148] Yarbrough's list includes three "trustworthy sayings" (1:15a–b; 3:1; 4:8), a vice list (1:8–10), four creedal, confessional, or

[142] Ibid., 250.

[143] Ibid., 252.

[144] Ibid.

[145] Ibid., 253.

[146] M. M. Yarbrough, *Paul's Utilization of Preformed Traditions in 1 Timothy: An Evaluation of the Apostle's Literary, Rhetorical, and Theological Tactics*, LNTS 417 (London/New York: T&T Clark, 2009), 143.

[147] Ibid., chap. 2 and app. 1.

[148] Ibid., 142. Yarbrough attributes the difference to Ellis's broader set of criteria which led him to include passages such as 1 Tim 2:9–15; 3:2–13; and 4:1–5.

hymnic portions (1:17; 2:5–6a; 3:16; 4:9–10b), a final charge including a closing benediction (6:11–16), and other sayings (5:24–25; 6:7, 10a).[149]

Preformed Traditions in 1 Timothy

Trustworthy Sayings	Vice List	Creedal, Confessional, or Hymnic Material	Final Charge with Closing Benediction	Other Sayings
1 Tim 1:15a–b	1 Tim 1:8–10	1 Tim 1:17	1 Tim 6:11–16	1 Tim 5:24–25
1 Tim 3:1		1 Tim 2:5–6a		1 Tim 6:7
1 Tim 4:8		1 Tim 3:16		1 Tim 6:10a
		1 Tim 4:9–10b		

While various concerns have been raised with Yarbrough's study, especially by proponents of pseudonymity, on the whole his criteria and identification of passages are sound.[150] One need not agree with all of his larger structural proposals (including various macro- and micro-chiasms, see discussion below) to affirm his overall conclusion that the author of 1 Timothy used a variety of preformed material in his letter, which lends his writing literary cohesion, rhetorical force, and a unifying message *vis-à-vis* the false teachers. Yarbrough's work needs to be supplemented with a closer study of the use of the OT in 1 Timothy and with studies of the use of preformed material in 2 Timothy and Titus.[151] In addition, note should be taken of several helpful studies on individual categories

---

Yarbrough also notes that his figure is more in line statistically with Paul's use of the OT which he puts at about 25 percent.

[149] These categories are mine, not Yarbrough's.

[150] There may be minor quibbles with Yarbrough's assessment, such as why he doesn't include 1 Tim 6:8 among preformed material or why he does include 1 Tim 4:9–10b as a separate saying in addition to 1 Tim 4:8. For reviews, see J. R. Asher, *CBQ* 73 (2011): 409–10; and A. B. Huizenga, *JR* 91 (2011): 81–83. See also the cautionary note struck in Mounce, *Pastoral Epistles*, xcv: "It is certainly the case that the author of the PE uses traditional material . . . ; however, I am not convinced that the author uses as much as is often stated, and Paul is capable of stating theological truths in hymnic form."

[151] See below. See also A. Merz, *Die fiktive Selbstauslegung des Paulus: Intertextuelle Studien zur Intention und Rezeption der Pastoralbriefe*, NTOA 52 (Göttingen: Vandenhoeck & Ruprecht, 2004), who investigates how the author of the LTT (whom she assumes to be pseudonymous) refers to and draws on previous Pauline letters. Merz argues that the author of the LTT, writing with deceptive intent, sought to impose a reinterpretation of the existing Pauline epistles (case in point: the role of

of preformed tradition, such as the "trustworthy sayings" (§2.6),[152] confessional, hymnic, or creedal statements,[153] virtue and vice lists (§6.3),[154] and OT usage (§7.1).[155]

Regarding preformed traditions in 2 Timothy and Titus, Ellis identifies the following likely candidates: 2 Tim 1:9–10; 2:11–13; 2:19–21; 3:1–5; Titus 2:11–14; and 3:3–7. These can be categorized under the following rubrics: (possibly) hymnic confessions (2 Tim 1:9–10; Titus 3:3–7); other hymns (2 Tim 2:11–13; Titus 2:11–14); OT commentary (2 Tim 2:19–21); and vice lists/prophecy (2 Tim 3:1–5).[156]

---

women, including their secondary status in creation, their priority in sin, and their salvation through childbearing).

[152] See esp. R. A. Campbell, "Identifying the Faithful Sayings in the Pastoral Epistles," *JSNT* 54 (1994): 73–86; G. W. Knight, *The Faithful Sayings in the Pastoral Letters* (Kampen: Kok, 1968); and the excurses in Marshall, *Pastoral Epistles*, 326–30; Mounce, *Pastoral Epistles*, 48–49; and J. Roloff, *Der erste Brief an Timotheus*, EKKNT 15 [Zurich: Benziger, 1988], 88–90.

[153] See S. E. Fowl, *The Story of Christ in the Ethics of Paul: An Analysis of the Function of the Hymnic Material in the Pauline Corpus*, JSNTSup 36 (Sheffield: Sheffield Academic Press, 1990); W. H. Gloer, "Homologies and Hymns in the New Testament: Form, Content, and Criteria for Identification," *PRSt* 11 (1984): 115–32; R. P. Martin, "Some Reflections on New Testament Hymns," in *Christ the Lord: Studies in Christology Presented to Donald Guthrie*, ed. H. H. Rowdon (Grand Rapids: Eerdmans, 1982), 37–49; and J. T. Sanders, *The New Testament Christological Hymns: Their Historical Religious Background* (Cambridge: Cambridge University Press, 1971).

[154] See J. D. Charles, "Vice and Virtue Lists," *DNTB*, 1252–57, who notes that the LTT "contain the densest usage of ethical lists in the NT" (p. 1255); cf. C. G. Kruse, "Virtues and Vices," *DPL*, 962–63; D. G. Reid, "Virtues and Vices," *DLNT*, 1190–94. R. F. Collins, "How Not to Behave in the Household of God," *LS* 35 (2011): 7–31, counts eight vice catalogs in these letters—five in 1 Timothy, one in 2 Timothy, and two in Titus—and notes that only two of the vices mentioned in these letters refer to human sexuality. See also A. Hock, "Equipping the Successors of the Apostles: A Comparative Study of the Ethical Catalogues in Paul's Pastoral Letters (1 Tim 1:9–10; 6:4–5; 2 Tim 3:2–4; Ti 3:3)," *EstBíb* 64 (2006): 85–98; R. López, "A Study of Pauline Passages with Vice Lists," *BSac* 168 (2011): 301–16; and N. J. McEleney, "The Vice Lists in the Pastoral Epistles," *CBQ* 36 (1974): 203–19. Older treatments include B. S. Easton, "New Testament Ethical Lists," *JBL* 51 (1932): 1–12; E. Kamlah, *Die Form der katalogischen Paränese im Neuen Testament*, WUNT 7 (Tübingen: Mohr-Siebeck, 1964); A. Vögtle, *Die Tugend- und Lasterkataloge exegetisch, religions- und formgeschichtlich untersucht* (Münster: W. Aschendorff, 1936); and S. Wibbing, *Die Tugend- und Lasterkataloge im Neuen Testament und ihre Traditionsgeschichte unter besonderer Berücksichtigung der Qumran-Texte* (Berlin: A. Töpelmann, 1959).

[155] See esp. P. H. Towner, "1–2 Timothy and Titus," in *Commentary on the New Testament Use of the Old Testament*, ed. G. K. Beale and D. A. Carson (Grand Rapids: Baker, 2007), 891–918.

[156] E. E. Ellis, "The Origin and Composition of the Pastoral Epistles," in *History and Interpretation in New Testament Perspective*, BIS 54 (Leiden: Brill, 2001), 79–82.

Possible relevant marks for identification include introductory formulas (2 Tim 2:11; 3:1), contextual dislocation or an unusual syntactical structure (2 Tim 1:9–10; 2:11–13; Titus 2:11–14; 3:3–7), emphasis on early orthodoxy (2 Tim 1:9–10; 2:11–13; Titus 2:11–14; 3:3–7), paraenesis (2 Tim 2:19; 3:1–5; Titus 2:11–14; 3:3–7), poetic characteristics (2 Tim 1:9–10; 2:11–13; Titus 2:11–14; 3:3–7), and uncommon vocabulary (Titus 2:11–14).

Preformed Traditions in 2 Timothy and Titus

Hymnic Confessions	Other Hymns	OT Commentary	Vice List/ Transmitted Prophecy
2 Tim 1:9–10	2 Tim 2:11–13	2 Tim 2:19–21	2 Tim 3:1–5
Titus 3:3–7	Titus 2:11–14		

The confession in 2 Tim 1:9–10 extols God's salvation in and through the appearing of Jesus Christ and is woven into Paul's testimony. The remarkable trinitarian confession in Titus 3:3–7 (couched in terms of a "trustworthy saying," v. 8), similarly refers to the goodness and lovingkindness of "God our Savior" which appeared in "Jesus Christ our Savior" and was accompanied by the "washing of regeneration and renewal by the Holy Spirit."

The possible preformed tradition in 2 Tim 2:11–13 is a "trustworthy saying," while Titus 2:11–14, like the hymnic confessions mentioned above, speaks of the appearing of God's grace, providing salvation in Christ, and the hope of "the appearing of the glory of our great God and Savior, Jesus Christ." Second Timothy 2:19–21 constitutes an OT commentary or midrash, while 2 Tim 3:1–5 may convey a prophecy regarding mounting end-time apostasy in the form of a vice list.

On the whole, the use of preformed traditions in the LTT is undeniable and rather frequent. This constitutes an often overlooked element in the debate regarding the authenticity of these letters. On the one hand, the use of preformed material alleviates the contrast between 1 and 2 Timothy and Titus and Paul's undisputed letters. At the same time it should be acknowledged that the use of preformed material can be accommodated under the rubric of either authenticity or pseudonymity.

Other possible preformed traditions may be found in 2 Tim 2:4–6 (proverbs), 8 (cf. Rom 1:3–4); 4:1 (baptismal language?), 18 (doxology); and Titus 1:15 (tradition).

EXPOSITION OF 1 TIMOTHY

Occasion and Purpose

The occasion for 1 Timothy is stated at the outset of the letter as follows: "As I urged you when I went to Macedonia, remain in Ephesus so that you may command certain people not to teach false doctrine" (1 Tim 1:3–4; see vv. 18–20).[1] The question is whether this occasion constitutes the purpose for the letter in its entirety or Paul has other purposes besides instructing Timothy on how to deal with these false teachers. Contrary to those who emphasize the *ad hoc* nature of the LTT, it is likely that Paul's purpose is broader than merely dealing with the opponents.[2]

---

[1] Note that Ephesus was the third largest city in the Roman Empire (smaller only than Rome and Alexandria), boasting a population of 200,000–250,000. Cf. P. Trebilco, *The Early Christians in Ephesus from Paul to Ignatius*, WUNT 166 (Tübingen: Mohr-Siebeck, 2004), 17.

[2] G. W. Knight, "The Scriptures Were Written for Our Instruction," *JETS* 39 (1996): 3–13; contra G. D. Fee, "Reflections on Church Order in the Pastoral Epistles, with Further Reflection on the Hermeneutics of *Ad Hoc* Documents," *JETS* 28 (1985): 141–51; Fee, *1 and 2 Timothy, Titus*, NIBCNT 13 (Peabody, MA: Hendrickson, 1988), 5–14, who claims that "the whole of 1 Timothy . . . is dominated by this singular concern" of refuting the false teachers and that "the whole of chs. 2–3 is best understood as instruction vis-à-vis the behavior and attitudes" of the false teachers ("Reflections," 142–43). See also the critique by A. J. Köstenberger ("1–2 Timothy, Titus," in *Expositor's Bible Commentary*, vol. 12: *Ephesians–Philemon*, rev. ed. [Grand Rapids: Zondervan, 2005], 514), who observes that Fee unduly diminishes the structural markers in 2:1 and 3:15–16 that set off chaps. 2 and 3 from chaps. 1 and 4–6, respectively (see the further interaction under the heading "Reflections"; Köstenberger, "1-2 Timothy, Titus," 520). See also F. A. Tomlinson, "The Purpose

While chapters 1 and 4–6 are concerned primarily with the challenge of the false teachers, chapters 2–3 focus on general ecclesiastical matters. This is indicated by the phrase introducing 2:1–3:16 ("First of all, then"; 1 Tim 2:1), which suggests the beginning of a new unit,[3] as well as the closing words of the same unit: "But if I should be delayed, *I have written so that you will know how people ought to conduct themselves in God's household, which is the church of the living God, the pillar and foundation of the truth*" (1 Tim 3:15; emphasis added). This solemn affirmation, as well as the following hymn in 1 Tim 3:16, suggests that Paul's instructions in this letter possess abiding relevance for the church rather than being limited to the specific occasion.

Also, in keeping with the genre of these letters, Paul's apostolic office (1 Tim 1:1; 2 Tim 1:1; Titus 1:1) requires that his letters be applicable to the church as a whole, transcending the scope of any one local congregation. As Paul writes elsewhere, the church, "God's household," is "built on the foundation of the apostles and prophets, with Christ Jesus himself as the cornerstone" (Eph 2:20). For this reason, the LTT should be considered foundational documents for the church, not merely *ad hoc* instructions dealing with local circumstances that lack lasting implications for the church overall.[4]

Following the confession in 1 Tim 3:16, Paul returns to the matter of false teachers (4:1). Yet even where the apostle addresses local circumstances requiring resolution, such as principles for the care of needy widows (5:3–16) or sinning elders (5:17–25), the truths and principles Paul enunciates as an apostle are true and therefore binding—not merely for Timothy and the church of Ephesus at the time of writing but also for every church, "the church of the living God, the pillar and foundation of the truth" (3:15).[5] For this reason Paul's purpose for writing 1 Timothy is *both*

---

and Stewardship Theme within the Pastoral Epistles," in *Entrusted with the Gospel: Paul's Theology in the Pastoral Epistles*, ed. A. J. Köstenberger and T. L. Wilder (Nashville: B&H, 2010), esp. 52–53.

[3] The verb παρακαλέω ("I urge"), which is found in 1 Tim 2:1, is used regularly by Paul in transitioning to the "business portion" of a letter (1 Cor 1:19; 2 Cor 2:8; 6:1; Eph 4:1; 1 Thess 4:1; Phlm 10).

[4] See the discussion of genre in III. A. of the introduction.

[5] See A. J. Köstenberger, "Women in the Church: A Response to Kevin Giles," *EvQ* 73 (2001): 205–24; in response to K. Giles, "A Critique of the 'Novel' Contemporary Interpretation of 1 Timothy 2:9–15 Given in the Book, *Women in the Church*. Parts I and II," *EvQ* 72 (2000): 151–67, 195–215.

to instruct Timothy on how to deal with false teachers *and* to provide guidelines on a variety of matters of perennial significance for the church.[6]

The Opponents

In keeping with Paul's prediction (Acts 20:28–31), the opposition in Ephesus may have arisen from within the church's ranks rather than having invaded it from the outside.[7] It is even possible, if not likely, that some of the false teachers were former or current elders.[8] Alternatively, the scenario envisaged by Paul in his farewell to the Ephesian elders in Acts 20 may have materialized at a later time.[9]

In dealing with these false teachers, Timothy finds himself confronted with ascetic elements such as the prohibition of marriage[10]

---

[6] This raises the issue of hermeneutical consistency. If an interpreter were to relativize Paul's instructions regarding women in church leadership in 1 Tim 2:11–15, he or she, to be consistent, would need to view Paul's instructions on qualifications for church leaders in 1 Tim 3:1–12 as relative and nonbinding for the church as well. See W. D. Mounce, *Pastoral Epistles*, WBC 46 (Nashville: Nelson, 2000), 185. See also Col 4:16.

[7] See 1 Tim 1:3; 6:2; 2 Tim 2:14; 4:2; Titus 1:13; 3:10; cf. 1 Tim 1:20; 2 Tim 2:17–18.

[8] So Fee, *1 and 2 Timothy, Titus*, 7–9.

[9] D. T. Thornton, "Hostility in the House of God: An 'Interested' Investigation of the Opponents in 1 and 2 Timothy" (Ph.D. thesis, University of Otago, 2015), 56–57.

[10] The practice of forbidding marriage is found in both Judaism (especially among the Essenes; see Philo, *Hypothetica* 380) and later Gnosticism (Irenaeus, *Haer.* 1.24.2). Even Paul at times extols the advantages of celibacy (1 Cor 7:1–7), though he never forbids marriage; to the contrary, he highly extols it (e.g., Eph 5:21–33). See P. H. Towner, *1–2 Timothy & Titus*, IVPNTC 14 (Downers Grove: InterVarsity, 1994), 25, who argues that perhaps there was a "growing suspicion that marriage belonged to the old order which had passed away, or that the model for living in the resurrection age was to be found in descriptions of life before the fall into sin."

See also R. B. Hays, *1 Corinthians*, Interpretation (Louisville: Westminster John Knox, 1997), 114, who comments with regard to 1 Cor 7:1–7,

> This sort of [sexual] asceticism was "in the air" in ancient Mediterranean culture. The Stoic and Cynic philosophical schools . . . debated whether a philosopher should marry or whether the unmarried state was more conducive to the pursuit of wisdom. In Greek popular religion, virginity and sexual purity were often associated with those set aside for the service of the gods, particularly for women who were prophets—the priestess of the oracle at Delphi, for example. In Paul's day, even Judaism, which classically had celebrated procreation as the duty of everyone, developed ascetic movements such as the Essenes and the Therapeutae

and of certain foods (1 Tim 4:1–5; cf. Titus 1:15; see also Col 2:8, 18–23), as well as with the teaching that the resurrection has already taken place (1 Tim 1:19–20; cf. 2 Tim 2:17–18; see also 1 Cor 15:12, 34).[11] What Paul apparently opposes is teachings and practices that may have been motivated in part by an unduly narrow application of the Mosaic law and in part by a form of Greek dualism[12] that misunderstood the Christian teaching on the nature of believers' resurrection.[13]

---

about whom Philo of Alexandria wrote glowingly. . . . Sexual abstinence was widely viewed as a means to personal wholeness and religious power.

Though the LTT were written against ascetic practices, they were subsequently reinterpreted to justify the asceticism that characterized much of the early church, a practice documented in E. A. Clark, *Reading Renunciation: Asceticism and Scripture in Early Christianity* (Princeton, NJ: Princeton University Press, 1999), 353–70. These exegetical maneuvers may suggest ways the opponents in Ephesus justified their teaching in a Pauline church.

[11] See P. H. Towner, "Gnosis and Realized Eschatology in Ephesus (of the Pastoral Epistles) and the Corinthian Enthusiasm," *JSNT* 31 (1987): 95–124, who argues that Paul's teachings on "eventual dissolution of certain social distinctions and barriers within the New Community" (e.g., Gal 3:28; 1 Cor 12:13; Col 3:11) were apparently claimed in the present day. Cf. D. A. Mappes, "The Heresy Paul Opposed in 1 Timothy," *BSac* 156 (1999): 452–58.

[12] Many describe the false teaching in terms of Gnosticism. E. E. Ellis speaks of "Judaism crossed with Gnosticism" ("Pastoral Letters," *DPL* 663, with reference to Lightfoot; cf. Ignatius [died ca. 110], *Magn.* 8–11; *Trall.* 9). G. W. Knight describes the false teaching as a "Gnosticizing form of Jewish Christianity" (*Commentary on the Pastoral Epistles*, NIGTC [Grand Rapids: Eerdmans, 1992], 27–28). Mounce labels it as "a form of aberrant Judaism with Hellenistic/Gnostic tendencies" (*Pastoral Epistles*, lxix–lxxvi). R. F. Collins calls it "Jewish proto-Gnosticism" (*Letters That Paul Did Not Write* [Wilmington, DE: M. Glazier, 1988], 100, referring to A. T. Hanson and M. Dibelius). See also J. Roloff, "Der Kampf gegen die Irrlehrer. Wie geht man miteinander um?," *BK* 46 (1991): 114–20; and T. Söding, "*Mysterium fidei*: Zur Auseinandersetzung mit der 'Gnosis' in den Pastoralbriefen," *IKZ* 26 (1997): 502–24.

Against this phalanx of scholars, however, it's doubtful that proto-Gnosticism stands behind the false teaching. See esp. the analysis by Thornton, *Hostility in the House of God*, 24–25, 38, 62–70, 86–87, 257–59. I. H. Marshall ("Identifying the Opposition," in *Pastoral Epistles*, ICC [Edinburgh: T&T Clark, 1999], 46–51) posits a combination of Jewish, Christian, and ascetic elements. Similarly, Towner ("Gnosis and Realized Eschatology in Ephesus," 114) contends that "gnosis in the Pastorals seems to lack the salvific power that was associated with it in later Gnosticism." Mounce notes that while some (e.g., A. T. Hanson, *Pastoral Epistles*, NCBC [Grand Rapids: Eerdmans, 1982], 25) adduce a connection between "(endless) genealogies" (γενεαλογίαις [ἀπεράντοις]) in 1 Tim 1:4 and Titus 3:9 and the progression of aeonic emanations characteristic of Gnostic teaching, there are no examples of γενεαλογία being used by Gnostics to describe this phenomenon (*Pastoral Epistles*, lxx).

[13] So S. Westerholm, "The Law and the 'Just Man' (1 Tim 1, 3–11)," *ST* 36 (1982): 82. Cf. the overview of scholarly opinions from the Reformation onward by E. E. Ellis, "Paul and His Opponents: Trends in the Research," in *Christianity, Judaism and Other Greco-Roman Cults: Studies for Morton Smith at Sixty*, vol. 1: *New Testament*,

J. Sumney observes, "The central issue that causes the author to reject these opponents is their interpretation of the Law, an interpretation that requires Gentile Christians to adopt the Torah's dietary laws. They impose stricter regulations about marriage than 1 Timothy thinks is proper, but this does not necessarily mean they think the material world is evil."[14] As Thornton notes, what links the opponents in 1 and 2 Timothy seems to be their overrealized view of the resurrection (see esp. 2 Tim 2:18), which may also lead them to reject marriage and childbearing as belonging to a bygone era (1 Tim 2:15; 4:3).[15]

Structure

W. D. Mounce divides 1 Timothy as follows:

I. Salutation (1:1–2)
II. The Ephesian problem (1:3–20)
III. Correction of improper conduct in the Ephesian church (2:1–4:5)
IV. Personal notes to Timothy (4:6–16)
V. How Timothy is to relate to different groups in the church (5:1–6:2a)
VI. Final instructions (6:2b–21).[16]

---

ed. J. Neusner, SJLA 12 (Leiden: Brill, 1975), 264–98, who views the false teachers as "'teachers of the law' who engage in disputes about it and, in haggadic fashion, expound Jewish 'fables' . . . and genealogies" (p. 297). According to Ellis, the opponents are pneumatics and promote "a perverse asceticism that issues, perhaps, in a subtle licentiousness" (p. 297).

[14] J. L. Sumney, "Studying Paul's Opponents: Advances and Challenges," in *Paul and His Opponents*, ed. S. E. Porter, Pauline Studies 2 (Leiden: Brill, 2005), 42.

[15] See esp. Thornton, *Hostility in the House of God.*

[16] Mounce, *Pastoral Epistles*, cxxxv (note that the numbering is off in that Mounce has 2 II.s and 2 IV.s). Similarly, D. Guthrie (*The Pastoral Epistles*, TNTC, rev. ed. [Grand Rapids: Eerdmans, 1990], 63–64) has these major divisions: I. 1:1–20; II. 2:1–4:16; III. 5:1–6:2; IV. 6:3–21. Even fewer units are discerned by T. Lea and H. P. Griffin Jr. (*1, 2 Timothy, Titus*, NAC [Nashville: B&H, 1992], 17), who divide the letter into I. 1:1–2; II. 1:3–20; and III. 2:1–6:21.

On the whole, this outline is sound, especially in drawing a line of demarcation between 1:20 and 2:1[17] and in identifying 5:1–6:2a as a separate literary unit. However, it seems preferable to view 3:16 as concluding Paul's instructions that began in 2:1 and to regard 4:1 as starting a new major unit with reference to the last days.[18] If so, the discussion of the literary plan of 1 Timothy may proceed as follows:[19]

---

[17] Against P. H. Towner (*The Letters to Timothy and Titus*, NICNT [Grand Rapids: Eerdmans, 2006], ix), who keeps 1:3–3:16 as a single unit and gives insufficient attention to the markers "first of all" and "then" at 2:1. But Towner (unlike Mounce) rightly discerns a break between 3:16 and 4:1 (ibid., x).

[18] See the interaction with G. D. Fee, "Reflections on Church Order," 145 in Köstenberger, "1–2 Timothy, Titus," 504, 509–10.

[19] See Köstenberger, "1–2 Timothy, Titus," 497. Cf. the proposed structure by Marshall (*Pastoral Epistles*, 30), who divides the letter between 1:3–3:16 and 4:1–6:21a. Thornton, "Hostility in the House of God," 19, structures the letter with special focus on the opponents:

The Problem of the Opponents and Timothy's Task of Correction: Part 1 (1:3–20)

The House of God: Orderly Worship and Qualified Leaders (2:1–3:13)

The Problem of the Opponents and Timothy's Task of Correction: Part 2 (3:14–4:16)

The House of God: Ministering to Different Groups (5:1–6:2a)

The Problem of the Opponents and Timothy's Task of Correction: Part 3 (6:2b–21a)

Note that Thornton's outline is virtually identical to Yarbrough's (see the next note), except that Thornton doesn't use the word "chiasm" but simply refers to "a noteworthy pattern of oscillation" (p. 19).

Structurally speaking, we may note as well the clear *inclusio* of ἑτεροδιδασκαλέω in 1:3 and 6:3. As well, R. F. Collins suggests that the doxologies of 1 Tim 1:17 and 6:15–16 "form a loose inclusio that encompasses the core of the document" and "are the theological bookends that provide a framework for [1 Timothy's community] regulations" (*1 and 2 Timothy and Titus: A Commentary*, NTL [Louisville: Westminster John Knox, 2002]), 45; cf. R. Van Neste, *Cohesion and Structure in the Pastoral Epistles*, JSNTSup 280 (New York: T&T Clark, 2004), 136–41. These two parallels, among others, point to the possibility of 1:3–20 and 6:2b–21 acting as an *inclusio* for the entire letter; see C. O. Hetzler, "Our Savior and King: Theology Proper in 1 Timothy" (Ph.D. diss., The Southern Baptist Theological Seminary, 2008), 55–56 with further references.

I. Opening (1:1–2)

II. Personal Charge (1:3–20)
  A. The Challenge of the False Teachers (1:3–11)
  B. Paul's Testimony (1:12–17)
  C. Exhortation to Timothy (1:18–20)

III. Congregational Matters: Promoting Unity and Order in God's Household, Qualifications for Church Officers (2:1–3:16)
  A. On Prayer (2:1–8)
  B. Regarding Women (2:9–15)
  C. Qualifications for Leaders (3:1–13)
    1. Overseers (3:1–7)
    2. Deacons (3:8–13)
  D. Purpose of Paul's Letter and Concluding Confession (3:14–16)

IV. Further Charges (4:1–6:2a)
  A. Latter-day Apostasy (4:1–5)
  B. Being a Good Servant of Jesus Christ (4:6–16)
  C. Further Congregational Matters: Dealing with Different Age Groups, Widows, Elders, and Slaves (5:1–6:2a)
    1. Relating to Older and Younger Men, Older and Younger Women (5:1–2)
    2. Ministering to Widows (5:3–16)
    3. Dealing with Elders (5:17–25)
    4. Instructions for Slaves (6:1–2a)

V. Extended Final Exhortation (6:2b–19)

VI. Closing (6:20–21)[20]

---

[20] Note also M. M. Yarbrough, *Paul's Utilization of Preformed Traditions in 1 Timothy: An Evaluation of the Apostle's Literary, Rhetorical, and Theological Tactics*, LNTS 417 (London/New York: T&T Clark, 2009), 158 and app. 4, who proposes the following chiasm:

(A) Timothy and the False Teachers (1:3–20)
  (B) Church Order for Various Groups (2:1–3:13)
    (C) Timothy and the False Teachers (3:14–4:16)
  (B′) Church Order for Various Groups (5:1–6:2)
(A′) Timothy and the False Teachers (6:3–21a)

He posits another chiasm for the central unit (p. 152):

(A) The Christological Hymn (3:14–16)
  (B) The Prophecy of False Doctrine (4:1–5)

Paul's first letter to Timothy immediately turns to the subject at hand: the need for Timothy to "instruct certain people not to teach false doctrine" in the church at Ephesus (1:3–4). The customary thanksgiving follows after initial comments regarding these false teachers, which is in fact a thanksgiving to God for Paul's own conversion since he himself at one point persecuted the church of God (1:12–17). At the end of the first chapter, Paul mentions two of these false teachers by name, Hymenaeus and Alexander (1:20).

Paul then transitions ("First of all, then," 2:1) to a section where he sets forth instructions for the church, in keeping with his purpose: "I write these things to you, hoping to come to you soon. But if I should be delayed, I have written so that you will know how people ought to conduct themselves in God's household, which is the church of the living God, the pillar and foundation of the truth" (3:14–15). As mentioned, this suggests that 2:1–3:16 constitutes a separate unit devoted to positive instructions for Timothy on how to govern the church, including directions on prayer (2:1–8), women's roles (2:9–15), and qualifications for church leaders (3:1–13). The unit concludes with the "mystery of godliness," possibly drawing on a liturgical piece (3:16).

Chapter 4 opens with the dramatic phrase, "Now the Spirit explicitly says" (4:1), setting the work of the false teachers in an end-time context during which matters will move from bad to worse. In this context Timothy must set himself apart by giving close attention to his personal life and doctrine, preserving both himself and his hearers (4:11–16).[21] Additional instructions are given regarding the care of widows (5:3–16), dealing with elders, including those who sinned (5:17–25), the proper conduct of Christian slaves (6:1–2), and the rich (6:3–10, 17–19). Timothy, for his part, must guard what has been entrusted to him, as Paul's final charge makes clear (6:11–16, 20–21).[22]

(B′) The Charge to Minister (4:6–10)

(A′) Timothy's Ordination Affirmed (4:11–16)

[21] R. A. Gibson, "The Literary Coherence of 1 Timothy," *RTR* 55 (1996): 53–66, believes he detects a chiasm in 1 Timothy, with 4:6 ("If you point these things out to the brothers and sisters, you will be a good servant of Christ Jesus, nourished by the words of the faith and the good teaching that you have followed") at the center. Since 2:1–10 has no parallel in Gibson's structure, he proposes that this passage contains "theological first principles that inform the whole letter." However, the macro-chiasm Gibson proposes is unconvincing, and a linear structure is more likely.

[22] P. G. Bush, "A Note on the Structure of 1 Timothy," *NTS* 36 (1990): 152–56, finds an *inclusio* in 1:12–20 and 6:11–16, 20–21.

Commentary

I. Opening (1:1–2)

[1] Paul, an apostle of Christ Jesus by the command of God our Savior and of Christ Jesus our hope:

[2] To Timothy, my true son in the faith.

Grace, mercy, and peace from God the Father and Christ Jesus our Lord.

1:1 The letter opening follows the standard pattern for first-century salutations: sender-recipient-greeting. Paul's self-reference, "an apostle of Christ Jesus by the *command* of God our Savior" (cf. Titus 1:3), slightly modifies his customary "by the *will* of God" (see 1 Corinthians, 2 Corinthians, Ephesians, Colossians, 2 Timothy). He may use "command" rather than "will" to allude to the fact that Timothy, too, is under orders (v. 18). Paul's apostolic consciousness (cf. 1 Cor 15:8–10) led him to view his ministry as grounded in the will and command of God rather than in mere human appointment (Acts 9:1–31; Gal 1:1). Consequently, Timothy and the readers of the letter should receive it as an authoritative apostolic missive.[23] Paul's apostolic calling involves the worldwide proclamation of the good news of salvation in Jesus Christ (Rom 16:26).

The phrase "God our Savior" brings together the Jewish and Hellenistic contexts interfacing in the present letter (cf. 2:3; §3.3).[24] The OT frequently speaks of God as Savior.[25] In the first century

---

[23] On the character of 1 Tim 1:1–20, see L. T. Johnson, "First Timothy 1,1–20: The Shape of the Struggle," in *1 Timothy Reconsidered*, ed. K. P. Donfried, Colloquium Oecumenicum Paulinum 18 (Leuven: Peeters, 2008), 25–26, who writes that "the personal and filial language Paul addresses to Timothy, the identification of the would-be teachers, and the recollection both of Paul's and Timothy's call to ministry, make this passage an appropriate introduction to the specific *mandata* that Paul begins to enumerate in 2,1."

[24] In the present context, the passage may echo Ps 65:5, which speaks of the "God of our salvation, the hope of all the ends of the earth" (ὁ θεὸς ὁ σωτὴρ ἡμῶν ἡ ἐλπὶς πάντων τῶν περάτων τῆς γῆς; cf. 1 Tim 1:1: θεοῦ σωτῆρος ἡμῶν καὶ Χριστοῦ Ἰησοῦ τῆς ἐλπίδος ἡμῶν). Towner understands Ps 65:5 as a "reference to God as the hope of *Israel*" (*Letters to Timothy and Titus*, 98), while Wieland argues for "some continuity between what God is and does for Israel and what he can be for all" (*The Significance of Salvation: A Study of Salvation Language in the Pastoral Epistles* [Milton Keynes, UK: Paternoster, 2006], 25). See also K. Salisbury, "Paul's First Letter to Timothy: An Example of Missional Contextualization," *Colloq* 44 (2012): 89.

[25] See, e.g., 2 Sam 22:3; Ps 106:21; Isa 43:3, 11; 45:15, 21; 49:26; 60:16; 63:8. OT language is also reflected in Luke 1:47.

"Savior" was a title regularly attributed to rulers, including Roman emperors such as Nero (AD 54–68).[26] Paul, by contrast, maintains that the Christian God, and he alone, is "our Savior" (including himself within the purview of salvation), rejecting competing claims by contemporaneous savior figures. "God our Savior" is linked with "Christ Jesus our hope."[27] In NT terms hope is much more than a vague wish; it is a confident expectation of the fulfillment of God's promises.[28] In the present passage Paul may refer to the expectation of Christ's second coming (Titus 2:13), eternal life (Titus 1:2; 3:7), or both.

1:2 This is the first of only four instances in the letters to Timothy where Timothy is mentioned by name (cf. v. 18; 6:20; 2 Tim 1:2).[29] Paul tenderly refers to Timothy as his "true (γνήσιος) son in the faith" (Titus 1:4; Phil 4:3; 2 Cor 8:8; cf. 1 Cor 4:17). The cognate adverb is used in Phil 2:20, where Paul announces his intention to send Timothy to the Philippians and writes, "For I have no one else like-minded who will *genuinely* (γνησίως) care about your interests." The expression "true son" could, but need not necessarily, imply that Paul led Timothy to faith in Christ (cf. 2 Tim 1:5; 3:15). In Acts 16:1–2, upon his initial encounter with Paul (AD 49–50), Timothy is already referred to as "a disciple" (μαθητής), though it's possible that Timothy had contact with Paul at an earlier occasion, such as Paul's first visit to Lystra (Acts 14:8–20). Most likely, "true son in the faith" means Timothy genuinely reproduces Paul's own spiritual characteristics as a natural son would reflect the natural characteristics of his father.

Paul's first letter to Timothy was written about fifteen years after Paul's initial encounter with Timothy. If Timothy was a young man in his mid-twenties when he first met the apostle, he would have been about forty years of age at the time of writing (cf. the reference to Timothy's "youth" in 1 Tim 4:12). The apostle would have been in his late fifties or early sixties. The respective designations "apostle . . . son" therefore indicate both the different degrees of authority (nowhere is Timothy called "brother") and the affectionate relationship between these two men of God. As his life and ministry draw to

---

[26] See W. Foerster, "σωτήρ," *TDNT* 7:1003–21.

[27] Jesus is called "our Lord" in v. 2; cf. Col 1:27.

[28] Heb 11:1: "reality"; 1 Pet 1:3: "living hope."

[29] For a short study of the patristic reception of the references to Timothy in Acts and Paul's letters including the LTT, see M. Meiser, "Timothy in Acts: Patristic Reception," *Annali di Storia dell'Esegesi* 32 (2015): 325–32.

a close, Paul seeks to preserve his legacy through his adoptive son in the faith. The phrase "true son" thus legitimizes Timothy as Paul's rightful successor in the church (cf. Titus 1:4) without imposing on their relationship a tight formal doctrine of apostolic succession as later became characteristic of Roman Catholic dogma (§1.3). "The faith," a common expression in the LTT, refers to the Christian faith and the body of teaching it encompasses.[30]

The blessing "grace, mercy, and peace" (cf. 2 Tim 1:2; 2 John 1:3) takes the place of the more common "grace and peace." "Grace" (χάρις) corresponds to the Greek word for "greeting" (χαίρειν), yet Paul uses it in the distinctly Christian sense of "God's unmerited favor." "Mercy" (ἔλεος, which may echo the Hebrew *hesed*, "loving-kindness") is added here as well as in 2 Timothy, possibly reflecting the difficult nature of Timothy's assignment. Note that later in the letter it's implied that Timothy wasn't awarded the respect due him owing to his relative youth (1 Tim 4:12) and that in the second letter Paul seems to intimate that Timothy is timid and needs encouragement (2 Tim 1:7). Mercy also features prominently later in the chapter when Paul recites his own testimony (vv. 13, 16). "Peace" (εἰρήνη) corresponds to the Hebrew *shalôm*, expressing the notion of a wholesome relationship with God and others. The final phrase "from God the Father and Christ Jesus our Lord" points to the source of all blessings (cf. 2 Tim 1:2; Titus 1:4). The threefold reference to Christ Jesus in the opening greeting attests to the strong Christological focus of the letter.[31]

In biblical-theological terms, the letter opening sounds the foundational theme of Paul's apostleship (v. 1) and his vital connection with Timothy, his apostolic delegate and "son in the faith" (v. 2). It also starts out with the central affirmation that God is "our Savior" and Jesus Christ "our hope" (v. 1). "God the Father" and "Christ Jesus our Lord" are also featured in parallel fashion in the following verse (v. 2). In this way the themes of mission, salvation, and theology/Christology are inextricably intertwined, as they will continue to be in the remainder of the letter and the LTT.

---

[30] Cf. 1 Tim 1:4, 5, 14, 19; 2:7, 15; 3:9, 13; 4:1, 6, 12; 5:8, 12; 6:10, 11, 12, 21; 2 Tim 1:5, 13; 2:18, 22; 3:8, 10, 15; 4:7; Titus 1:1, 4, 13; 2:2, 10; 3:15.

[31] Compare the reference to God as "God our Savior" (v. 1) and "God the Father" (v. 2) and the lack of reference to the Spirit in the opening greeting.

II. Personal Charge (1:3–20)

A. The Challenge of the False Teachers (1:3–11)

[3] As I urged you when I went to Macedonia, remain in Ephesus so that you may instruct certain people not to teach false doctrine [4] or to pay attention to myths and endless genealogies. These promote empty speculations rather than God's plan, which operates by faith. [5] Now the goal of our instruction is love that comes from a pure heart, a good conscience, and a sincere faith. [6] Some have departed from these and turned aside to fruitless discussion. [7] They want to be teachers of the law, although they don't understand what they are saying or what they are insisting on. [8] But we know that the law is good, provided one uses it legitimately. [9] We know that the law is not meant for a righteous person, but for the lawless and rebellious, for the ungodly and sinful, for the unholy and irreverent, for those who kill their fathers and mothers, for murderers, [10] for the sexually immoral and homosexuals, for slave traders, liars, perjurers, and for whatever else is contrary to the sound teaching [11] that conforms to the gospel concerning the glory of the blessed God, which was entrusted to me.

Relation to Surrounding Context

Immediately after the opening in vv. 1–2, Paul gets to the occasion for writing. The fact that he progresses straight from the opening to the occasion without further delay and without the customary opening pleasantries, thanksgiving, and/or prayer conveys a sense of considerable urgency on the part of the apostle. Certain men are teaching false doctrine (v. 3); the goal of Paul's instruction is in jeopardy (v. 5); some alleged teachers of the law have veered from the heart of the saving gospel message and turned to fruitless discussions about the minutiae of the Mosaic law (vv. 6–7; cf. v. 11). Paul thus gets straight to the point: these people who are at cross-purposes with Paul's gospel must be told to stop.

Structure

Verses 3–4 plainly state the occasion for the letter. Verses 5–7 enunciate the purpose of Paul's instruction and how the opponents, self-styled "teachers of the law," fall short. Verses 8–11 then contain an aside elaborating on the false teachers' improper use of the law in contrast to "sound teaching" in keeping with the "gospel concerning the glory of the blessed God" with which Paul had been entrusted.

1:3 The occasion for writing is stated at the outset: the challenge of the false teachers.[32] Rather than engage in opening pleasantries, Paul is "all business" (cf. Titus 1:5), conveying a sense of urgency in addressing the problem (note the term "urged," παρακαλέω; cf. 2:1; 5:1; 6:2). He recalls the time when Timothy and he parted ways, Paul moving on to Macedonia and Timothy remaining in Ephesus, at which time the task of purging the church from false teachers fell to Timothy.[33] The rendering "instruct" (παραγγέλλω) is a bit weak; the term is better understood as "command" by virtue of Paul's delegated apostolic authority.[34]

"Certain people" is Paul's customary way of referring to the opponents in this letter (cf. vv. 6, 19; 4:1; 5:15, 24; 6:3, 10, 21).[35] The effect of this designation is to establish a clear distinction between the false teachers and the propagators of the true gospel (Paul and Timothy).[36] While the reference is generic, the named teachers in 1–2 Timothy are all men (1 Tim 1:20; 2 Tim 2:17). Paul likely didn't know the name of every single individual who perpetrated false

---

[32] The opening phrase in v. 3, "As [καθώς] I urged you," lacks an apodosis and is syntactically ambiguous, though the meaning is clear enough. See Towner, *Letters to Timothy and Titus*, 106. Cf. Marshall, *Pastoral Epistles*, 362–63.

[33] M. Dibelius and H. Conzelmann, *The Pastoral Epistles*, Hermeneia, trans. P. Buttolph and A. Yarbro (Philadelphia: Fortress, 1972), 15, believe the natural inference is that Paul was in Ephesus with Timothy; but see the critique in Mounce, *Pastoral Epistles*, 16–18. Timothy would have been familiar with Ephesus and Macedonia from his previous evangelistic work with Paul. On ancient Ephesus, see Trebilco, *Early Christians in Ephesus*, who provides a comprehensive history of the development of Christianity in the city of Ephesus from AD 35 to 110.

[34] Cf. 1 Cor 7:10; 11:17; 1 Thess 4:11; 2 Thess 3:4, 6, 10, 12; 1 Tim 4:11; 5:7; 6:13, 17. Thornton, *Hostility in the House of God*, 34–36, has an interesting discussion on whether Paul's telling Timothy to "command" the false teachers means they had at one time been members in good standing in the Ephesian church and were therefore still expected to submit to apostolic authority. In any case it would seem that these men needed to be told authoritatively to stop propagating their false message in the environs of the Ephesian church.

[35] Cf. the use of indefinite pronouns to refer to Paul's opponents in his undisputed letters: 1 Cor 15:12; 2 Cor 10:12; Gal 1:7; 2:12; Phil 1:15.

[36] Cf. Marshall, *Pastoral Epistles*, 365. The indefinite reference to the opponents allows any sympathizers in the congregations to change their allegiance back to the true gospel in a face-saving manner (B. Fiore, *The Pastoral Epistles: 1 Timothy, 2 Timothy, Titus*, SP 17 [Collegeville, MN: Liturgical Press, 2007], 117–18) while depicting "the troublemakers as shadowy figures with an indistinct past" obscuring "their actual numbers and influence" (J. M. Bassler, *1 Timothy, 2 Timothy, Titus*, ANTC [Nashville: Abingdon, 1996], 38).

doctrine in Ephesus; in any case, he was less concerned with the specific *individuals* than with preserving the purity of the Christian *message.*

The term "teach false doctrine" (one word in the original, ἑτεροδιδασκαλεῖν; lit. "other-teach," i.e., teach a message other than the apostolic gospel) forms an *inclusio* with 6:3 (the term's only other NT use) and may have been coined by Paul.[37] Together with "teachers of the law" (νομοδιδάσκαλοι) in v. 7, the designation identifies the opponents as *teachers* (cf. the contrast with "sound teaching" in v. 10 and "the gospel" in v. 11). Similar to his earlier charge that the Judaizers preached a "different gospel" (Gal 1:6; cf. 2 Cor 11:4), the apostle is concerned that the gospel be preserved from anything that detracts from its truth or dilutes its saving power (cf. Rom 1:16–17).[38]

1:4 The false teachers didn't merely dabble in alternatives to the apostolic gospel; they were strongly devoted (προσέχειν) to their teaching.[39] The reference to "myths and endless geneal-

---

[37] "Teach *false* doctrine" seems to imply the existence of a standard body of Christian teaching (cf. Gal 1:6–9: "a different gospel," "another gospel," "a gospel contrary to what we have preached to you," "a gospel contrary to what you received"; Jude 3: "the faith that was delivered to the saints once for all": see esp. A. J. Köstenberger and M. J. Kruger, *The Heresy of Orthodoxy: How Contemporary Culture's Fascination with Diversity Has Reshaped Our Understanding of Early Christianity* (Wheaton: Crossway, 2010). Contra F. Wisse, "*Heterodidaskalia*: Accounting for Diversity in Early Christian Texts," in *The Changing Face of Judaism, Christianity, and Other Greco-Roman Religions in Antiquity*, Studien zu den Jüdischen Schriften aus hellenistisch-römischer Zeit 2, ed. I. H. Henderson and G. S. Oegema (Gütersloh: Gütersloher Verlagshaus, 2006), 265–79, who places the LTT in the post-Pauline period and claims that "heterodoxy preceded orthodoxy" (p. 277); and K. Zamfir, *Men and Women in the Household of God: A Contextual Approach to Roles and Ministries in the Pastoral Epistles*, NTOA/SUNT 103 (Göttingen: Vandenhoeck & Ruprecht, 2013), 170–71, who contends that we shouldn't label the opponents "heretics" because we lack independent primary sources delineating their teaching.

[38] This "preservation theme" pervades the LTT (§3.5.7). See A. J. Köstenberger, "Ascertaining Women's God-Ordained Roles: An Interpretation of 1 Timothy 2:15," *BBR* 7 (1997): 107–44, esp. 130–32.

[39] The particle μηδέ conjoins the two actions ἑτεροδιδασκαλεῖν and προσέχειν. The term προσέχειν conveys strong control or influence in all of its instances in the LTT, whether exerted by deviant or demonically inspired teaching (1 Tim 4:1; Titus 1:14), Scripture (1 Tim 4:13), or wine (1 Tim 3:8).

ogies" most likely alludes to the teachers' use of the law.[40] Later, "pointless and silly myths"—in context, asceticism such as the prohibition of marriage and abstinence from certain foods—are contrasted with "the faith and the good teaching" (1 Tim 4:6–7). In 2 Tim 4:4 "myths" are contrasted with "the truth," suggesting that these "myths" were dangerous first and foremost because they deviated from the gospel. In 2 Pet 1:16 the contrast is between "cleverly contrived myths" and apostolic eyewitness testimony. "Myths," therefore, most likely understood as speculative interpretations of the Mosaic law—note the presence of genealogies in the book of Genesis—are the antithesis of the truth of the gospel and stunt growth in true godliness.

The genealogies aren't only mythical; they're "endless" (ἀπέραντος). This means most likely not so much that they're literally infinite (Job 36:26 LXX; 3 Macc. 2:9) as that they're of a highly conjectural and irrelevant nature: they're both pointless

[40] Cf. Titus 1:14: "Jewish myths." The expression "genealogies and myths" was used by Hellenistic writers to disparage a certain mode of writing history (F. H. Colson, "'Myths and Genealogies': A Note on the Polemic of the Pastoral Epistles," *JTS* 19 [1918]: 265–71. According to Colson, the phrase should be understood in connection with the teaching of histories in Greco-Roman grammatical schools where the teaching of literature, especially poetry, was important and where there were those who devoted themselves to the "elucidation of allusions, and the accumulation of knowledge real and supposed as to the personages and things mentioned in the poems." "Myth" was used to describe the legendary material in narrating events in such histories while "genealogies" pertained to people. Both terms were "accepted and leading terms in the technical talk or jargon of a large literary or dilettante public which made great account of such studies," though another portion of the public looked askance at these studies and considered them as useless and time wasting. The second-century BC historian Polybius, for example, contrasted his plain account of history with those who dealt in "matters concerning genealogies and myths" (*Hist.* 9.2.1). In essence, such a practice was tantamount to a preoccupation with the inane and trivial. Perhaps Paul is borrowing from this kind of polemic. Colson argues that the LTT may be directed against a frivolous intellectualism that concerned itself with the trivia of the Torah, attacking "a somewhat conceited pseudo-Hellenic Judaism" (p. 269). Colson does recognize, however, that the issue in view does seem to be more serious than mere intellectual dilettantism in light of passages such as Titus 1:11 or 2 Tim 3:6–7. There's little to be said for the thesis that the author of 1 Tim 1:3–7 perceived Matthew 1–2 (in particular, Matthew's narration of the virgin birth) as a combination of genealogy, myth, and midrash, as is suggested by B. T. Viviano, "The Genres of Matthew 1–2: Light from 1 Timothy 1:4," *RB* 97 (1990): 31–53.

and fruitless.[41] The result is empty speculations (ἐκζητήσεις; cf. 6:4; 2 Tim 2:23) rather than believers growing in their faith. The only other NT occurrence of "genealogy" (γενεαλογία), Titus 3:9, references "foolish debates, genealogies, quarrels, and disputes *about the law*," connoting the teaching's likely Jewish background.[42] That said, the false teachers may have been individuals who approached the Hebrew Scriptures from a philosophical and allegorical, rather than proper historical, vantage point.

"God's plan (οἰκονομίαν θεοῦ), which operates by faith" is reminiscent of the reference to the "stewardship" with which Paul was entrusted by God, especially in some of Paul's later letters (1 Cor 9:17; Eph 1:10; 3:2, 9; Col 1:25; cf. 2 Tim 1:9–10). Thus, stewardship of what has been entrusted to Paul by God in keeping with God's redemptive arrangement stands in marked contrast to empty speculations about supposed myths.[43] "Faith" (πίστις) here most likely refers to the believer's ongoing trust relationship with God, in contrast to pointless human speculation. The term is used differently in this verse than in v. 2, where, as mentioned, it most likely conveys the notion of the Christian faith and the body of teaching it encompasses. The term is one of the central concepts in this letter and in Paul's correspondence with Timothy and Titus as a whole.[44] There is a close relationship between "the faith" and the gospel Paul preaches, which highlights God's grace in Jesus Christ apart from any human contribution.

1:5 Rather than promote endless genealogies and empty speculations, Paul's instruction has a more practical purpose: "Now the goal of our instruction is love."[45] The word "goal" (τέλος) indicates

---

[41] Cf. Thornton, *Hostility in the House of God*, 38.

[42] As Thornton (ibid.) notes, the term is found frequently in contemporaneous and subsequent literature (e.g., Philo, *Moses* 2.47; Josephus, *Ant*. 11.71; Plutarch, *Num*. 18.4; Irenaeus, *Haer*. 1. Preface 1; Eusebius, *Hist. eccl*. 1.7), referring to a lineage of ancestors.

[43] On the stewardship theme in the LTT, see esp. Tomlinson, "The Purpose and Stewardship Theme within the Pastoral Epistles," 52–83. See also G. A. Couser, "God and Christian Existence in the Pastoral Epistles: Toward Theological Method and Meaning," *NovT* 42 (2000): 262–83, who contends the author contrasts God's redemptive arrangement with the false teaching.

[44] See the list of references above.

[45] R. Fuchs, "Ist 'die Agape das Ziel der Unterweisung' (1. Tim 1,5)? Zum unterschiedlichen Gebrauch des ἀγαπ- und des φιλ- Wortstammes in den Schreiben an Timotheus und Titus," *JETh* 18 (2004): 93–125, draws attention to the different

the desired end toward which his proclamation of the gospel is directed (Rom 6:22; 10:4; 1 Pet 1:9); the controversies engendered by the false teachers have the opposite effect: fruitless discussion (v. 6) and never-ending controversy. "Instruction" (παραγγελία) refers to the general charge or commission assigned to Timothy (cf. vv. 3, 18).[46] "Love" (ἀγάπη), regularly in the LTT coupled with "faith" (πίστις; see below), is conceived as the practical outworking of faith in Christ. The preacher's goal is not merely faith but faith's expression in acts of love.[47]

The triad of "pure heart" (2 Tim 2:22; cf. 1 Pet 1:22), "clear conscience" (1 Tim 3:9), and "sincere faith" (2 Tim 1:5) enunciates a set of biblical convictions: (1) love is at the heart of God's commands (Matt 22:37–40; Rom 13:8–10; Gal 5:14); (2) purity of heart is more important than external acts of obedience (Matt 5:8; Mark 7:15 par.; Rom 14:17; cf. 2 Tim 2:22; Pss 24:4; 51:10); and (3) heartfelt sincerity is essential for pleasing God (Mark 7:6–7).[48] Thus, "Timothy cannot achieve the τέλος of his commission apart from the proclamation of the apostolic gospel, which includes a call for

---

use of the ἀγαπ- and φιλ- word groups in the LTT. He contends that the letters to Timothy (using ἀγαπ- vocabulary) are more Hellenistic-Jewish in nature and presuppose previous exposure to biblical and early Christian language, while the letter to Titus (using φιλ- language) is written to newly baptized Greco-Roman Christians on Crete who lack such a background. This is part of Fuchs's larger concern that interpreters not level the distinctions between the letters traditionally grouped together as "the Pastoral Epistles."

[46] L. T. Johnson, *The First and Second Letters to Timothy*, AB 35A (Garden City, NY: Doubleday, 2001), 164.

[47] See the discussion in Thornton, *Hostility in the House of God*, 40–42.

[48] Faith and love are regularly juxtaposed in the LTT as key Christian virtues (1:14; 2:15; 4:12; 6:11; 2 Tim 1:13; 2:22; 3:10; Titus 2:2). See the excursus on the πίστις word group in Marshall, *Pastoral Epistles*, 213–17; Marshall, "Faith and Works in the Pastoral Epistles," *SNTSU-A* 9 (1984): 203–18. Note also the close conceptual parallel Titus 2:14, which ties believers' cleansing to the performance of good works. With regard to conscience, the term is common not only in the LTT but also in Paul's other letters (esp. in 1–2 Corinthians). See also the excursus in Marshall on συνείδησις in the LTT (*Pastoral Epistles*, 217–27), which is concerned to show that the concept of conscience in the LTT is consistent with that in the undisputed Pauline letters, over against critical scholars who contend they're incompatible; and the excursus in Towner, *Letters to Timothy and Titus*, 117–19 ("Conscience in the Letters to Timothy and Titus"). On conscience in Paul's writings, see J. M. Gundry-Volf, "Conscience," *DPL*, 153–56; M. E. Thrall, "The Pauline Use of ΣΥΝΕΙΔΗΣΙΣ," *NTS* 14 (1967): 118–25.

repentance and faith."[49] By contrast, the false teachers' motives were impure (1 Tim 6:9–10), their consciences defiled (v. 19; 4:2), their faith shipwrecked (v. 19; but see commentary below), and their work resulted in division, destruction, and doom (6:9–10).

1:6 Those (the plural indefinite τινες marks a shift back to the opponents) who have "departed" (ἀστοχήσαντες; cf. 2 Tim 2:18) from the faith and "turned aside" (ἐξετράπησαν, elsewhere only in 5:15; 6:20; 2 Tim 4:4; Heb 12:13)[50] to "fruitless discussion"[51] (ματαιολογία, a NT *hapax legomenon*; cf. 1 Tim 6:20; 2 Tim 2:16; Titus 1:10) are people who engage in "contradictions from what is falsely called knowledge" (1 Tim 6:20). Like Hymenaeus, Alexander, and Philetus, these individuals "have departed from the truth, saying that the resurrection has already taken place" (2 Tim 2:17–18; cf. 1 Tim 1:19–20).[52]

The characterization of the false teachers as those who stray from the right, straight path is predicated upon the biblical understanding of the righteous man who conducts his life in integrity and honor without straying to the right or to the left (e.g., Prov 4:18, 25–27). Unlike Timothy, who is to pursue the goal of love (v. 5), these false teachers miss the mark. In the absence of true conversion, they're incapable of expressing love that arises out of genuine faith. Their rejection of the gospel (vv. 3–4) has rendered them incapable of compelling gospel proclamation and reduced them to empty speech entirely lacking in transformative power.[53]

1:7–11 Verse 7 describes the false teachers in some more detail. The verses that follow (vv. 8–11) represent an aside, followed by another aside (vv. 12–17), while vv. 18–20 resume the

---

[49] Thornton, *Hostility in the House of God*, 43. As Thornton rightly notes, adducing the parallel 2 Tim 1:5, "sincere faith" is "one that stands the test of time. Where the opponents have deviated, those with authentic faith will endure."

[50] Turning away from the faith is referred to in Paul's letters to Timothy by a variety of Greek terms: "reject" (ἀποθέομαι; 1:19); "depart from" (ἀφίστημι; 4:1); "turn away" (ἐκτρέπομαι; 5:15); "deviate" or "wander away" (ἀστοχέω; 1:6; 6:10); and "turn away" (ἀποστρέφω; 2 Tim 4:4).

[51] See P. G. R. de Villiers, "Empty Talk in 1 Timothy in the Light of Its Graeco-Roman Context," *Acta Patristica et Byzantina* 14 (2003): 152, who argues that the similarities between 1 Tim 1:6 and Greco-Roman texts "reflect a widespread concern in Graeco-Roman times about the necessity of practicing what one preaches."

[52] For a cogent textual study of the opponents in the letters to Timothy, see Thornton, *Hostility in the House of God*.

[53] Cf. Eph 5:6; Col 2:8; and de Villiers, "Empty Talk in 1 Timothy," 144–45.

argument of vv. 3–7. The first aside elaborates on the false teachers' misuse of the law; it's not that they use the *wrong* text but that they *misuse* the *right* text.[54] The second aside presents Paul as the model of a sinner saved by grace in contrast to the false teachers. This shows that Paul isn't exalting himself above his opponents because he's superior to them. It's solely his acceptance of God's gracious offer of salvation and forgiveness in Christ that sets him apart from the false teachers.

In v. 7 Paul challenges the claims exerted by the would-be "teachers of the law" (νομοδιδάσκαλοι).[55] (While the term "teachers of the law" and the use of the OT Scriptures may suggest the teachers were Jewish, this does not necessarily follow.[56]) In any case, despite their confident demeanor (διαβεβαιοῦνται; cf. Titus 3:8), the opponents understand neither the law's true purpose (v. 8) nor its intended audience (vv. 9–10).[57] In fact, their use of the law as a standard for Christian living is incompatible with sound doctrine that conforms to the "gospel concerning the glory of the blessed God" (v. 11; cf. 6:3; 2 Tim 1:13; 4:3; Titus 1:9; 2:1).

The phrase introducing the assertion, "But we know" (Οἴδαμεν δέ), in v. 8 serves "to introduce a statement which the writer can assume will be generally acceptable to those whom he is addressing or whom he has in mind."[58] Conversely, the false teachers are

---

[54] Thornton, *Hostility in the House of God*, 89.

[55] The term occurs elsewhere in the NT only in Luke 5:17 (paired with the Pharisees) and in Acts 5:34 (with reference to Paul's teacher Gamaliel); see also Rom 2:20–21. Later instances of νομοδιδάσκαλος include Clement, *Exc.* 1.5.5; Irenaeus, *Haer.* 1.1.5; and Eusebius, *Hist. eccl.* 1.8.

[56] See, e.g., E. Schlarb, *Die gesunde Lehre: Häresie und Wahrheit im Spiegel der Pastoralbriefe* (Marburg: N. G. Elwert, 1990), 91, who contends that these individuals' *desire* to be teachers of the law may suggest that they were in fact non-Jews. Zamfir. *Men and Women in the Household of God*, 177n60, argues that by that time "Scripture had become the common ground of Christians of any (previous) religious background." See also Thornton, *Hostility in the House of God*, 89–99.

[57] The theme of the false teachers' ignorance is found also in 6:4, 20; 2 Tim 2:23; Titus 1:15; 3:9; cf. 2 Tim 3:7, to be contrasted with the reference to Timothy's understanding (νοέω) in 2 Tim 2:7. The double negative (μήτε . . . μήτε, elsewhere in Paul only in 2 Thess 2:2) further accentuates the false teachers' ignorance (Marshall, *Pastoral Epistles*, 373).

[58] C. E. B. Cranfield, "Changes of Person and Number in Paul's Epistles," in *Paul and Paulinism*, ed. M. D. Hooker and S. G. Wilson (London: S.P.C.K., 1982), 285. Cf. Knight, *Pastoral Epistles*, 80: "used by Paul to indicate that what he says is . . . commonly known, believed, and accepted."

out of step with this broad Christian consensus.[59] With this Paul turns to the opponents' misuse of the law (νόμος, i.e., the Mosaic law; cf., e.g., Rom 5:20; Gal 3:19).[60] As Paul observes, the law (νόμος) itself is good (καλός) if used properly (νομίμως, "lawfully"; cf. 2 Tim 2:5: "according to the rules"), that is, in keeping with its God-intended purposes,[61] a wordplay in the original Greek.

What this means is that the law is not self-interpreting; rather, it needs to be rightly understood and applied. What is at issue, therefore, is not the intrinsic value of the law itself but its results in the lives of those to whom it is addressed (or not addressed). As Paul proceeds to clarify, then, contrary to what the opponents taught, the law isn't actually addressed to "the righteous" (i.e., "right-living" believers;[62] cf. vv. 15–16) but rather aims to convict the unrighteous (to restrain sin?; cf. Gal 3:23–4:7). But if the law was given to restrain sin, and believers have been set free from sin, in their case the law's purpose has already been fulfilled.[63]

---

[59] Towner, *Letters to Timothy and Titus*, 122.

[60] Note that elsewhere in the LTT Paul calls for the public reading of Scripture (1 Tim 4:13) and affirms the relevance of OT principles for believers (1 Tim 5:18; cf. Deut 25:4). For helpful studies on Paul and the law, see D. J. Moo, "'Law,' 'Works of the Law,' and Legalism in Paul," *WTJ* 45 (1983): 75–90; T. R. Schreiner, *The Law and Its Fulfillment: A Pauline Theology of Law* (Grand Rapids: Baker, 1993), 33–40; and S. Westerholm, *Perspectives Old and New on Paul: The "Lutheran" Paul and His Critics* (Grand Rapids: Eerdmans, 2004), 297–340. For an argument that the present passage stands in harmony with Paul's teaching on the role of the law in Romans, see D. T. Thornton, "Sin Seizing an Opportunity through the Commandments: The Law in 1 Tim 1:8–11 and Rom 6–8," *HorBT* 36 (2014): 142–58.

[61] Cf. Westerholm, "The Law and the 'Just Man,'" 82: suggests rendering the term "in line with its intended purpose."

[62] Westerholm (ibid., 84): "the *Christian* as right-living person" (emphasis original). The term δίκαιος seems to be used here primarily with regard to a believer's righteous way of life without heavy doctrinal content (along the lines of "justification by faith"), though regeneration and inner transformation is most likely presupposed. See the discussion in Thornton, *Hostility in the House of God*, 94–95; cf. Thornton, "Sin Seizing an Opportunity," 142–58.

[63] This argument is consistent with Paul's teaching on the law's purpose (see esp. Rom 7:7, 12–14, 16) and its ramifications for believers (Gal 5:14, 22–23; Rom 8:3–4; 13:8–10) in his earlier letters. In his biblical-theological treatment of Paul and the law, B. S. Rosner (*Paul and the Law: Keeping the Commandments of God*, NSBT 31 [Downers Grove: InterVarsity, 2013], 73–76) considers 1 Tim 1:8–10 to be one of the "key instances of Paul's negative critique of the law," indicating that as used "lawfully"—i.e., "as a legal code to punish sin," "with the force of law," "as law"—the Mosaic law is decidedly not for believers ("the righteous"). This is not to

What follows is a catalog of vices or sinners, listed here in six groups of two or three each (with groups four–six echoing commandments five–nine, see below), plus a final overall phrase:[64]

- lawless (ἀνόμοις; cf. Luke 22:37 = Isa 53:12; Acts 2:23) and rebellious (ἀνυποτάκτοις, "unsubjected"; Titus 1:6, 10; cf. Heb 2:8): people behaving as if there were no law,[65] i.e., insubordinate people refusing to be subject to a higher authority (subordination is stressed in 2:11; 3:4; Titus 2:5, 9; 3:1);
- ungodly (ἀσεβέσι; Rom 4:5; 5:6; 1 Pet 4:18; 2 Pet 2:5–6; 3:7; Jude 4, 15) and sinful (ἁμαρτωλοῖς; Rom 5:8, 19; Heb 7:26; 12:3; Jas 4:8; 5:20; 1 Pet 4:18; Jude 15), i.e., unsaved and separated from God;
- unholy (ἀνοσίοις; 2 Tim 3:2; cf. 2 Macc 7:34; 8:32; 3 Macc 2:2; 5:8; 4 Macc 12:11; Wis 12:4) and irreverent (βεβήλοις; 4:7; 6:20; 2 Tim 2:16; Heb 12:16): profane as opposed to sacred, devoid of holiness (cf. Lev 10:10 LXX);[66]
- those who kill their fathers and mothers (πατρολῴαις, μητρολῴαις), murderers (ἀνδροφόνοις): all three words are NT *hapax legomena*,[67] echoing the **fifth and sixth commandments**;

---

say that Paul here indicates that the law is of no use whatsoever for Christians—that question is not addressed in the present passage; in fact, other references in the LTT (e.g., 1 Tim 5:18 quoting Deut 25:4) indicate that the law is indeed useful in certain ways. It is to say, however, that Christians do not need the strictures of the law to "tell them what not to do." For a critique of the contention by scholars such as H. Räisänen (*Paul and the Law* [Philadelphia: Fortress, 1983], 206) and Bassler (*1 Timothy, 2 Timothy, Titus*, 41) that the stance taken toward the law in the present passage is un-Pauline see Thornton, "Sin Seizing an Opportunity."

[64] J. D. Quinn and W. C. Wacker, *The First and Second Letters to Timothy*, ECC (Grand Rapids: Eerdmans, 2000), 95, following N. J. McEleney, "The Vice Lists in the Pastoral Epistles," *CBQ* 36 (1974): 204–10, see here four pairs connected with "and" plus six single terms, composing an unholy "Decalogue." For other vice lists in Paul's writings, see Rom 1:29–31; 1 Cor 5:11; 6:9–10; Gal 5:19–21; and 2 Tim 3:2–4. Of the sins in the present list, only "sexually immoral/adulterers" and "perverts" are found in an earlier list (1 Cor 6:9). Rabbinic Judaism produced no such lists (but see 1QS 4:9–11). See McEleney, "Vice Lists," 203–19.

[65] Cf. Marshall, *Pastoral Epistles*, 379.

[66] Thornton, "Hostility in the House of God," 96, notes that βέβηλος is the only word in the vice list that is used elsewhere in the LTT repeatedly with clear reference to the opponents (1 Tim 4:7; 6:20; 2 Tim 2:16).

[67] Cf. Plato, *Phaedr.* 114A, where all three terms are found (the first with the alternate spelling πατραλοίας).

- sexually immoral/adulterers (πόρνοις; 1 Cor 5:9–11; 6:9; Eph 5:5; Heb 12:16; 13:4; Rev 21:8; 22:15) and homosexuals (NASB, CSB; ἀρσενοκοίταις; first time in Greek in 1 Cor 6:9; cf. Rom 1:27): echoing the **seventh commandment**;
- slave traders (CSB) or kidnappers (NASB; ἀνδραποδισταῖς), liars (ψεύσταις; John 8:44, 55; Rom 3:4; Titus 1:12; 1 John 1:10; 2:4, 22; 4:20; 5:10; cf. Lev 19:11 LXX), perjurers (ἐπιόρκοις; cf. Zech 5:3 LXX; a person swearing an oath and subsequently breaking it):[68] echoing the **eighth and ninth commandments**; and, as an overall catchphrase,
- whatever else is contrary (ἀντίκειμαι, "to be opposed") to the sound teaching (ὑγιαινούσῃ διδασκαλίᾳ; 2 Tim 4:3; Titus 1:9; 2:1; for similar summary statements, see Rom 13:9; Gal 5:21), an unmistakable way of associating the opponents with the vices enumerated in this list.[69]

Within these pairs or expressions of three, the respective offenses are roughly the same. For example, both "sexually immoral/adulterers" and "homosexuals" refer to sexual sin. It appears that Paul's list, after three initial general pairs (conveying the notion of godlessness, which may in some general sense be related to the first four commandments), follows the second half of the Ten Commandments (Exod 20:12–16; Deut 5:16–21), specifically numbers five to nine. Paul employs strong language, perhaps to highlight the degree of evil prevalent in the pagan world and the need for the law on the part of those who have not heard the gospel (see Rom 1:21–32). Most expressions are self-explanatory, but two call for special comment.

---

[68] See J. T. Fitzgerald, "The Problem of Perjury in Greek Context: Prolegomena to an Exegesis of Matthew 5:33; 1 Timothy 1:10; and *Didache* 2.3," in *The Social World of the First Century: Essays in Honor of Wayne A. Meeks*, ed. L. M. White and O. L. Yarbrough (Minneapolis: Fortress, 1995), 156–77, who adduces the parallel in *Did.* 2.3: "You shall neither swear false oaths nor break those that you take."

[69] The term "sound" (ὑγιαίνω) constitutes a medical metaphor referring to the "healthy" nature of teaching found in the gospel (v. 11) in contrast to the false teachers' "unhealthy" interest (6:4) in strange doctrines that will "spread like gangrene" (2 Tim 2:17; similar to cancer). The metaphor is not found in Paul's earlier writings. Cf. A. J. Malherbe, "Medical Imagery in the Pastoral Epistles," in *Texts and Testaments: Critical Essays on the Bible and Early Church Fathers*, ed. W. E. March (San Antonio: Trinity University Press, 1980), 19–35.

The first expression requiring discussion is "homosexuals" (ἀρσενοκοίταις; cf. 1 Cor 6:9). The meaning of the word is reflected in its etymology, which is literally "ones who lie or sleep with men," that is, those who engage in homosexual acts.[70] The term, a new coinage, probably echoes the prohibition of homosexuality in the Levitical code (Lev 18:22; 20:13 LXX).[71] Some have argued that the term is restricted to male prostitution or pederasty[72] or refers merely to homosexual acts, not to "celibate" homosexual relationships (i.e., refraining from sexual intercourse).[73] The NT teaching, they maintain, pertains only to the negative dehumanizing pattern of homosexuality prevalent in first-century Hellenistic culture and doesn't apply to consensual nonexploitative homosexual relationships today.

However, ἀρσενοκοίται is a broad term that is not limited to specific instances of homosexual activity such as male prostitution or pederasty.[74] The OT equivalent, likewise, "lying with a male," is

---

[70] Hence the NASB's "homosexuals"; CSB's and NIV's "men who have sex with men"; and NLT's "those who . . . practice homosexuality."

[71] D. F. Wright, "Homosexuals or Prostitutes? The Meaning of ἀρσενοκοῖται (1 Cor. 6:9, 1 Tim. 1:10)," *VC* 38 (1984): 125–53; Wright, "Translating ἀρσενοκοῖται (1 Cor. 6:9; 1 Tim. 1:10)," *VC* 41 (1987): 396–98.

[72] Male prostitution is understood to be in view by, e.g., J. Boswell, *Christianity, Social Tolerance, and Homosexuality: Gay People in Western Europe from the Beginning of the Christian Era to the Fourteenth Century* (Chicago: University of Chicago Press, 1980). Understanding ἀρσενοκοίταις to indicate pederasty are, e.g., J. V. Brownson, *Bible, Gender, Sexuality: Reframing the Church's Debate on Same-Sex Relationships* (Grand Rapids: Eerdmans, 2013), 274–75; R. Scroggs, *The New Testament and Homosexuality* (Philadelphia: Fortress, 1983), 99–122. M. Vines (*God and the Gay Christian* [New York: Convergent, 2014], 123–26) sees this as a possibility.

[73] An important early work arguing this understanding is D. S. Bailey, *Homosexuality and the Western Christian Tradition* (London: Longmans, Green, 1955).

[74] The observations of J. D. G. Dunn, *The Theology of Paul the Apostle* (Grand Rapids: Eerdmans, 2006), 122n103, on the use of ἀρσενοκοίταις in 1 Cor 6:9 have implications for the hypothesis of pederasty here: (1) "had Paul wished to be so specific, the term 'pederast' (*paiderastēs*) itself lay close to hand"; and (2) limiting Paul's critique in Rom 1:26–27 to pederasty "ignores the fact that the condemnation implies a similarity in the desire (*orexis*) of the male partners for each other (1.27) and includes lesbian relationships (1.26)." See the thorough treatment of this term in R. A. J. Gagnon, *The Bible and Homosexual Practice: Texts and Hermeneutics* (Nashville: Abingdon, 2001), 312–36, with its use in 1 Tim 1:10 discussed on pp. 332–36; note as well the briefer summary treatment in J. B. De Young, *Homosexuality:*

all encompassing and relates to "every kind of male-male intercourse."[75] In fact, the Hebrew Scriptures prohibit every type of homosexual intercourse (including consensual sex), not merely male prostitution or intercourse with youths. Also, while Paul focuses on homosexual acts, he would hardly have considered "celibate" homosexual relationships legitimate, since this would have exchanged a man's "natural" function for an "unnatural" one (Rom 1:26–27; cf. 1 Cor 6:9–10).[76]

Second, the term "slave trader" or "kidnapper" (ἀνδραποδισταῖς; cf. 2 Cor 11:26) presupposes the common first-century practice of slave trading. It's possible that Paul uses the term in a derivative sense here, referring to the false teachers who "kidnapped" members of God's household by deceiving them through an illegitimate use of the Mosaic law.[77] In fact, the expression served as a stereotype for contempt of one's opponents in the ancient

---

Contemporary Claims Examined in Light of the Bible and Other Ancient Literature and Law (Grand Rapids: Kregel, 2000), 175–204. See also S. D. Fortson III and R. G. Grams, *Unchanging Witness: The Consistent Christian Teaching on Homosexuality in Scripture and Tradition* (Nashville: B&H Academic, 2016), 294–98.

[75] G. J. Wenham, "The Old Testament Attitude to Homosexuality," *ExpTim* 102 (1991): 362.

[76] See also the perceptive interaction by C. L. Quarles, "Apples and Oranges? Why I Have Not Changed My Mind on Homosexuality," *Between the Times* (blog), June 6, 2014, accessed 28 August 2014, http://betweenthetimes.com/index.php/2014/06/06/apples-and-oranges-why-i-have-not-changed-my-mind-on-homosexuality.

[77] J. A. Harrill, "The Vice of Slave Dealers in Greco-Roman Society: The Use of a Topos in 1 Timothy 1:10," *JBL* 118 (1999): 122: "He [the author of 1 Timothy] saw the leaders of the heretical group (or groups) functioning as 'slave dealers' who steal family members from their rightful parents and household, and who sell them to an alien group marked by corruption." S. H. Geiger, "Distinction of Terms—the Slave Trade in Imperial Rome: 1 Timothy 1:9–11," *Wisconsin Lutheran Quarterly* 106 (2009): 49–51 adduces parallels in Philo (*Spec. Laws* 4.14, 17) and Strabo (*Geogr.* 14.5.2) and argues that "kidnapper" may be the basic idea (citing J. Bodel, "*Caveat emptor*: Towards a Study of Roman Slave-Traders," *JRA* 18 [2005]: 181–95). He also notes the Vulgate translation *plagiariis*, which means "kidnapper" (the English term "plagiarism" reflects the underlying notion of stealing). Cf. LSJ 128: "*slave-dealer* or *kidnapper* . . . : metaph., . . . *one who sells* his own *independence*."

world.[78] There's also evidence that Jewish rabbis interpreted the seventh commandment with reference to slave trading.[79]

The vice list in vv. 9–10 leads to Paul's discussion of the "grace of our Lord" Christ Jesus who "came into the world to save sinners" (vv. 14–15). Paul himself had previously been among those whose actions were condemned by the law, but now he has been granted mercy. This holds out hope for the false teachers if they repent and stop their misuse of the Mosaic law. In v. 11, "gospel concerning the glory" renders the phrase "gospel of glory," reflecting Semitic style (cf. Titus 2:13; Eph 1:17). The characterization of God as "blessed" in v. 11 recurs in 6:15.[80] The phrase "was entrusted" is found in various other Pauline letters as well (Rom 3:2; Gal 2:7; 2 Thess 1:10) and echoes earlier references to his stewardship from God (cf. vv. 1, 14). In the face of errant teaching, the stewardship takes on added solemnity, significance, and urgency.

Against the backdrop of references to "God's plan, which operates by faith" (v. 4) and the "gospel concerning the glory of the blessed God, which was entrusted to me" (v. 11), this section (vv. 3–11) has introduced the occasion for the writing of the letter: the threat of the false teachers (see esp. v. 3). The reference to "faith" in v. 4 and the sustained discussion of the role of the law later in the passage (vv. 7–10) suggest that the bone of contention was the opponents' misunderstanding and misrepresentation of the gospel message, similar to the way in which the Judaizers in Galatians drew Paul's ire and dismay (cf. Gal 1:6). Later Paul will set the emergence of the false teachers within the purview of the last days (1 Tim 4:1–5) and use them as a foil for his exhortation of Timothy to pursue godly Christian virtues (1 Tim 4:6–16).

Bridge

In this passage, and in fact the entire letter, Paul exhibits great zeal for keeping the church free from error, and in particular legalism that threatens the purity of the Christian gospel of salvation

---

[78] Cf. Cicero, *Quint. fratr.* 1.2.6; Plutarch, *Mor.* 632F; Heraclitus, *Ep.* 7; cf. Quinn and Wacker, *Letters to Timothy*, 88–89.

[79] *Mek. Ex.* 20:15 (77b); 21:16 (87b). Str-B 1:810–12 deduce from this that the author of the LTT had rabbinic training.

[80] See B. W. Winter, *Divine Honours for the Caesars: The First Christians' Responses* (Grand Rapids: Eerdmans, 2015), 163, who cites Epicurean parallels.

by grace through faith apart from works. For the false teachers in his day, scrupulous attention to the minutiae of the Jewish law was essential and salvation apart from obligation to the observance of a plethora of rules unthinkable. But the Christian gospel is one of sheer grace because it is based on what Christ has done on the cross, unaided by any of us. For this reason grateful acceptance of Jesus's substitutionary sacrifice, not self-effort, is the proper response. Even in our day where the gospel is subverted in perhaps more subtle ways, we must be vigilant to preserve the notion that salvation is by grace alone and firmly resist the intrusion of any contradictory message into the church.

B. Paul's Testimony (1:12–17)

> 12 I give thanks to Christ Jesus our Lord who has strength-
> ened me, because he considered me faithful, appointing me
> to the ministry — 13 even though I was formerly a blasphemer,
> a persecutor, and an arrogant man. But I received mercy be-
> cause I acted out of ignorance in unbelief, 14 and the grace of
> our Lord overflowed, along with the faith and love that are
> in Christ Jesus. 15 This saying is trustworthy and deserving of
> full acceptance: "Christ Jesus came into the world to save sin-
> ners"—and I am the worst of them. 16 But I received mercy
> for this reason, so that in me, the worst of them, Christ Jesus
> might demonstrate his extraordinary patience as an example
> to those who would believe in him for eternal life. 17 Now to
> the King eternal, immortal, invisible, the only God, be honor
> and glory forever and ever. Amen.

Relation to Surrounding Context

The thanksgiving that was omitted following the letter opening (vv. 1–2) now ensues following the statement and elaboration on the letter's purpose (vv. 3–11). In fact, vv. 12–17 represent an aside coming on the heels of the earlier aside in vv. 8–11, with vv. 18–20 then resuming the argument of vv. 3–7. Following the first aside on the false teachers' misuse of the law, this second aside contrasts Paul with the false teachers as a model of a sinner saved by grace. This exhibits Paul's humility in awareness that only God's grace separates him from his opponents.

Structure

Paul's testimony is framed in terms of a thanksgiving (v. 12). As indicated by em-dashes in the CSB, vv. 13–15 constitute a parenthesis containing a threefold confession of Paul's past as a blasphemer, persecutor, and arrogant man, as well as an acknowledgment of God's grace toward the apostle illustrated by a "trustworthy saying." "But I received mercy" at the beginning of v. 16 then resumes the identical assertion in v. 13, elaborating on the purpose of God's mercy toward Paul: the demonstration of his patience toward those who believe and are saved. Verse 17 fittingly concludes the thanksgiving/testimony with a benediction/"amen."

1:12–14 Paul's testimony makes clear that only God's grace set Paul apart from his opponents. In contrast to Paul's second letter to Timothy where the thanksgiving section centers on Timothy (2 Tim 1:3–7), the focus of Paul's thanksgiving in the present letter is on himself as a model of a sinner saved by grace. The reason for this may be that Paul's first letter to Timothy is of a more public nature while 2 Timothy is more personal. Here, therefore, Paul holds himself up as the prototypical forgiven sinner in contrast to the false teachers while in 2 Timothy he assures Timothy of his prayers and affection as his life draws to a close.

In turning from the topic of law in vv. 8–11 to his own experience,[81] Paul maintains that what the law was unable to do, Christ did: through grace and by faith, Paul was not only shown mercy, patience, and forgiveness, but he was also put into service. The language of this intensely personal section bears an uncanny Pauline imprint. In the present case the apostle's testimony is framed by an epistolary thanksgiving, with χάριν ἔχω (see also 2 Tim 1:3; Luke 17:9;

[81] See the discussion of connections between 1:8–11 and 1:12–17 in Van Neste, *Cohesion and Structure*, 78–81. The false teachers are characterized as opposed to healthy teaching (1:3, 10) and thus precisely as the kinds of people for whom the law was given (1:8–10), while Paul's gospel (1:11)—as exemplified in his conversion (1:12–16) and encapsulated in the trustworthy saying (1:15)—stands as healthy teaching over against what the false teachers taught. Also, in 1:8–11 Paul points out that the law is not for the righteous but for sinners (note esp. ἁμαρτωλός, v. 9); then, in 1:12–17, he shows by way of both testimony and tradition that it is precisely sinners (ἁμαρτωλός, v. 15) whom Jesus came to save. Paul also contrasts himself with the false teachers in terms of their respective lack of understanding: they desire to be teachers of the law without understanding (μὴ νοοῦντες) what they are asserting, having rejected the faith (πίστις; 1:19); while Paul's acting in ignorance (ἀγνοῶν ἐποίησα) was met with God's mercy while he was yet in unbelief (ἀπιστία; cf. Marshall, *Pastoral Epistles*, 394; Towner, *Letters to Timothy and Titus*, 141).

Heb 12:28) taking the place of the more familiar εὐχαριστέω (Rom 1:4; 1 Cor 1:4, 14; 14:18; Eph 1:16; Phil 1:3; Col 1:3, 12; 3:17).[82]

More commonly Paul directs his thanks to *God*; here the apostle gives thanks to *Christ*, "who has strengthened" him (ἐνδυναμώσαντί με, v. 12; cf. 2 Tim 2:1; 4:17; Eph 6:10; Phil 4:13: ἐνδυναμοῦντί με). The expression "faithful" or "trustworthy" is part of an extended wordplay in the Greek: Paul was *entrusted* (ἐπιστεύθην) with the gospel (v. 11) and was considered *trustworthy* (πιστόν; v. 12); even though he acted in *unbelief* (ἀπιστίᾳ; v. 13), God's grace came to him with *faith* (πίστεως; v. 14; see also vv. 15–16, 19; cf. 1 Cor 4:2; 7:25); and the saying that Jesus came into the world to save sinners is *trustworthy* (πιστός; v. 15). The term "appointing me to the ministry" (θέμενος) in v. 12 is the same as in 2 Cor 5:19.

As in Gal 1:13–16 and 1 Cor 15:9–10, Paul's perspective on his conversion and call to ministry as acts of divine grace elicits a vivid memory of the past. The reference to Paul's appointment to service—possibly in contrast with the false teachers who merely *want* to be teachers of the law—is reminiscent of his encounter with the risen Christ on the road to Damascus (Acts 9; 22; 26). There Jesus confronted Paul—who had zealously persecuted the church—with the question, "Saul, Saul, why are you persecuting me?" (Acts 9:4). Later Paul frequently recalled the way in which the appearance of the risen Christ had changed the direction of his life.

Describing himself in triadic negative fashion, Paul states that he was formerly (1) a blasphemer (βλάσφημος): he had denied that Jesus was the Messiah and thus rejected the salvation-historical purposes of God (Acts 6:11; cf. 1:20; 6:1; Titus 2:5); he was (2) a persecutor (διώκτης; cf. 1 Cor 15:9; Gal 1:13, 23; Phil 3:6); and (3) an arrogant man (ὑβριστής; cf. Rom 1:30).[83] Unlike his renowned and widely respected teacher, Gamaliel I, who had counseled

[82] Within a framework of pseudonymity, K. Zamfir, "Thanksgiving as Instrument of Legitimation in 1 Timothy 1,12–17," *Studia Universitatis Babeş-Bolyai, Theologia Catholica Latina* 44 (2009): 3–14 contends that the author of the letter is concerned to legitimize contemporary church leaders ("Timothy") by grounding their ministry in the succession of Paul. Similarly, M. Wolter, "Paulus, der bekehrte Gottesfeind: Zum Verständnis von 1. Tim 1:13," *NovT* 31 (1989): 48–66 holds that the pseudonymous author here seeks to invoke Paul's appointment to preach the gospel as a conversion experience.

[83] The term διώκτης is first attested in the NT (the sole reference is found in 1 Tim 1:13). See *NIDNTTE* 1:750.

moderation (cf. Acts 5:34–39), Paul (then Saul) mercilessly tracked down Christians as far as Damascus to the north (Acts 8:3; 9:1–2; though God showed him mercy; cf. 1 Cor 7:25; 2 Cor 4:1). This is why Paul regarded himself "the least of the apostles" (1 Cor 15:9) who was not even worthy of being called an apostle.

Nevertheless, God, in Jesus Christ, extended to Paul overflowing[84] grace (ὑπερεπλεόνασεν; NASB: "more than abundant"; cf. Rom 5:20; 6:1), faith(fulness?), and love.[85] The triad "grace, faith, and love" in v. 14[86] offsets the threefold description of Paul as a former blasphemer, persecutor, and arrogant man in v. 13. Not only was Paul forgiven; he was strengthened (v. 12; cf. Phil 4:13), considered faithful (cf. 1 Cor 7:25), and appointed to the ministry. It is difficult to imagine anyone forging this moving and genuine testimony (e.g. Gal 1:11–24; Phil 3:1–11), just as it is hard to see how a later "admirer" of Paul could have called him "the worst of [sinners]" (vv. 15–16).

When stating that he was shown mercy because he acted out of ignorance in unbelief, Paul draws on the OT distinction between unwitting and deliberate sin (Num 15:22–31; Lev 4:13; 5:18; 22:14; cf. Acts 3:17; 13:27; 17:30; Heb 9:7). In Romans the apostle described the Jewish rejection of Jesus in similar terms (3:3; 11:20, 23). The false teachers, by contrast, are said to have deliberately rejected the faith (v. 19; 2 Tim 2:17–18; cf. 1 Tim 1:5–6; 6:21), which places them in a category different from Paul (though, as mentioned, not beyond the pale of forgiveness).[87]

---

[84] Πλεονάζω, "abound," occurs nine times in the NT, eight of which are in Paul (e.g., Rom 5:20; 6:1; 2 Cor 4:15; 8:15), and ὑπέρ- compounds are a trademark of Paul (see, e.g., ὑπερνικάω, "more than conquerors," in Rom 8:37; ὑπερεπερισσεύω, "knows no bounds," in Rom 5:20 and 2 Cor 7:4; ὑπερυψόω, "exalted to the highest place," in Phil 2:9; and ὑπεραυξάνω, "growing more and more," in 2 Thess 1:3).

[85] Towner rightly views the sense of "faith and love" here as equivalent to their sense in Gal 5:6 ("faith working through love") as a "summary of Christian existence. . . . Together the two terms encompass the vertical relationship of trust in God and the horizontal outworking of this in service to others" (*Letters to Timothy and Titus*, 142).

[86] Mounce, *Pastoral Epistles*, 54: "Faith and love complete the triad begun by grace."

[87] Marshall, *Pastoral Epistles*, 394. See also ibid., 411: "ἀπωθέομαι conveys a picture of deliberate rejection of the voice of the conscience, i.e. refusal to listen to it; ἥν must refer only to συνείδησιν and not to πίστιν." Similarly, BDAG 126, s.v. ἀπωθέω.

1 Timothy 1:15–16

Moving on to 1:15–16, it's interesting to note the following broad parallelism between vv. 12–14 and vv. 15–16:[88]

The work of Christ	"I give thanks to Christ Jesus our Lord who has strengthened me, because He considered me faithful, appointing me to the ministry." (1:12)	"This saying is trustworthy and deserving of full acceptance: 'Christ Jesus came into the world to save sinners." (1:15ab)
Reference to Paul's sin	"Even though I was formerly a blasphemer, a persecutor, and an arrogant man." (1:13a)	"And I am the worst of them." (1:15c)
The provision of mercy	"But I received mercy because I acted out of ignorance in unbelief." (1:13b)	"But I received mercy." (1:16a)
Culmination	"And the grace of our Lord overflowed, along with the faith and love that are in Christ Jesus." (personal, 1:14)	"For this reason, so that in me, the worst of them, Christ Jesus might demonstrate his extraordinary patience as an example to those who would believe in him for eternal life." (beyond personal to general, 1:16b)

1:15–16 Verse 15 contains the first of five "trustworthy sayings" (πιστὸς ὁ λόγος) in the LTT: "Christ Jesus came into the world to save sinners" (§2.6).[89] "Came into the world" seems to imply preexistence and incarnation as well as indicating the primary purpose of Jesus's mission.[90] The fact that this saying is soteriological

[88] Knight, *Pastoral Epistles*, 92–93. In each subsection Paul moves from a reference to Christ's work (1:12, 15ab), to his own sin (1:13a, 15c), to his reception of mercy (ἀλλά [. . .] ἠλεήθην; 1:13b, 16a); the subsections culminate contrastively with a look back (1:13b–14) and a look forward (1:16b).

[89] For other "trustworthy sayings" in the LTT, see 3:1; 4:8; 2 Tim 2:11–13; and Titus 3:8. Cf. Campbell, "Identifying the Faithful Sayings," 73–86, who argues that the formula always introduces the saying; Knight, *The Faithful Sayings in the Pastoral Letters*, Baker Biblical Monographs (Grand Rapids: Baker, 1979).

[90] Dibelius and Conzelmann aver that "the expression 'he came into the world' (ἦλθεν εἰς τὸν κόσμον) by no means contains the conception of preexistence" (*Pastoral Epistles*, 29). However, as Knight rightly notes, preexistence and incarnation would seem to be necessary implications when early Christians spoke of Christ, given the way the language is used in other NT writings (*Faithful Sayings*, 36–37).

in nature may suggest that the false teaching likewise pertained to salvation.[91] The saying is reminiscent of Jesus's statement in Luke 19:10: "For the Son of Man has come to seek and to save the lost." While in Pharisaic Judaism—Paul's tradition—"sinner" referred to those who didn't scrupulously keep the law, especially Gentiles (cf. Gal 2:15), here—as typically in Paul—"sinner" is a universal term encompassing Paul as well as the rest of humanity.[92]

Not only this, but Paul called himself "the worst of sinners" (note the present tense "I am" and the emphasis on "worst" in the original). While some consider the statement hyperbolic, exaggerating Paul's consciousness of guilt, his conscience was deeply seared by his past persecution of the church. Thus it's possible that Paul honestly believed himself to be literally the worst of sinners. If so, his conversion from persecutor of the church to fervent propagator of the gospel serves as a characteristic pattern of God's merciful dealings with people.[93]

In his own case Paul draws particular attention to Christ's patience (μακροθυμία; cf. 2 Tim 3:10; 4:2); Timothy would need the same in dealing with the false teachers (2 Tim 2:24–26). In fact, Paul regards himself as a prototypical example (ὑποτύπωσις) of Christ's patience (cf. 2 Tim 1:13). The nature of Paul's conversion is such that God accepted him in Christ "apart from adherence to Jewish ritual or moral requirements,"[94] which may provide a model of conversion contrary to the teaching of the opponents who seem to have stressed the importance of observing the law. Both Paul and Peter refer to God's patience and kindness waiting for people

---

[91] Towner suggests that "the fundamental nature of that redemptive event [i.e., of 1:15] was . . . apparently being redefined by the false teachers or by the community under their influence" (*Letters to Timothy and Titus*, 134–35).

[92] See M. F. Bird, "Sin, Sinner," *DJG* 2nd ed., 863–68, esp. 864–65.

[93] See A. D. Clarke, "'Be Imitators of Me': Paul's Model of Leadership," *TynBul* 49 (1998): 354–55. Others, such as K. Löning, "'Von ihnen bin ich der Erste' (1 Tim 1,15): Paulus als soteriologische Schlüsselfigur in den Pastoralbriefen," in *Neutestamentliche Exegese im 21. Jahrhundert: Grenzüberschreitungen. Für Joachim Gnilka*, ed. T. Schmeller (Freiburg: Herder, 2008), 131–50, claim that the pseudonymous author of the LTT, writing at the turn of the second century AD, sought to transport Paul literarily into the present ("literarisch *vergegenwärtigt*") in order to relate Paul's special apostolic role to the universal soteriological role of believers).

[94] Towner, *Letters to Timothy and Titus*, 151.

to repent.[95] "Eternal life," common in John (e.g. 3:15–16; 11:26), occurs in the LTT also in 4:8; 6:12; 2 Tim 1:10; Titus 1:2; 3:7 (cf. 1 Tim 6:19). The phrase refers to "life in the age to come," already ours in Christ but fully realized at his "appearing" (cf. 6:12–15; 2 Tim 4:6–8; Titus 2:13–14).[96]

1:17 Paul concludes his testimony with a brief prayer and doxology, consisting of (1) an address to the recipient ("to the King eternal ['King of the ages'], immortal, invisible, the only God");[97] (2) an ascription of praiseworthy attributes ("be honor and glory"); and (3) a solemn affirmation of the truth ("forever and ever. Amen"; cf. Rev 1:6; 4:11; 5:12–13; 7:12). The doxology has a liturgical ring to it and may echo synagogue worship.

God's eternal kingship is commonly referred to in the OT (esp. Jer 10:10; cf. Pss 10:16; 74:12). The term "immortal" is a Jewish import from Greek philosophy (Wis 12:1; Philo [120 times]). "Invisible" casts God as incapable of being depicted in visual images (Exod 20:4–5; Col 1:15; Heb 11:27; cf. John 1:18; 5:37; 6:46; 1 John 4:20). Note that both "immortal" and "invisible," as well as "only," recur in the doxology at the end of the letter (1 Tim 6:15–16).

"Only God" (see Jude 25; cf. John 5:44; 17:3) expresses the monotheism characteristic of both Judaism and Christianity (cf. Deut 6:4; Rom 3:29–30; 16:27; 1 Cor 8:4–5; Gal 3:20; Eph 4:5–6). This affirmation of a belief in one God stands in sharp contrast with the polytheism of the Greco-Roman world. With Paul we may legitimately marvel that the transcendent, glorious God has come into the world to save sinners in the person of the Lord Jesus Christ.

In biblical-theological terms, vv. 12–17, in form of a thanksgiving, feature Paul as an example of God's grace and mercy. In this regard it's no coincidence that the first "trustworthy saying" in the LTT centers around the theme of salvation: "Christ Jesus came into the world to save sinners." In many ways the saying encapsulates the central message of the LTT, that of salvation in Christ. What's more, it does so here in an introductory way, in conjunction with none other than the apostle Paul himself, in contradistinction to the false teachers (vv. 3–11, 18–20). Thus the apostolic

---

[95] Pauline and Petrine references to repentance include Rom 2:4; 3:25–26; 9:22–23; 1 Pet 3:20; 2 Pet 3:9, 15. The theme is already found in the OT (Num 14:18; Joel 2:13).

[96] See Mounce, *Pastoral Epistles*, 59: "a sharing of the eschatological age here and now in anticipation of life in the eschaton."

[97] See the helpful discussion on God as King in Hetzler, "Our Savior and King," 27–45.

mission and salvation in Christ are asserted as the foundational and central affirmations underlying the theology of the LTT.

Bridge

Paul's testimony presents him as a paradigmatic sinner saved by grace and put into God's service of preaching the gospel. The only thing that separates him from the unsaved is that by God's grace he was responsive to God's mercy and patience. This is an important reminder for all believers not to exalt themselves above others who are not (yet) saved and to keep a humble disposition that turns reception of God's grace into an opportunity for grateful service and gospel proclamation in word and deed. What's more, if Paul, the "worst of sinners" who blasphemed God by denying Christ and persecuted the church in arrogance, was not beyond the pale of God's salvation, there is hope for any sinner because God is a gracious, loving, and forgiving God.

C. Exhortation to Timothy (1:18–20)

> [18]Timothy, my son, I am giving you this instruction in keeping with the prophecies previously made about you, so that by recalling them you may fight the good fight, [19]having faith and a good conscience. Some have rejected these and have shipwrecked their faith. [20]Among them are Hymenaeus and Alexander, whom I have delivered to Satan, so that they may be taught not to blaspheme.

Relation to Surrounding Context

After a series of asides, Paul now resumes his instruction of Timothy from vv. 3–7. While at the outset the apostle referred vaguely to "certain people" who perpetrated false teaching, he now proceeds to identify two of these individuals by name: Hymenaeus and Alexander (v. 20). He encourages Timothy by mentioning him, too, by name; by calling him his "son"; and by reminding him of "the prophecies previously made about" him (v. 18), contrasting him with the false teachers (v. 19).

Structure

Following the benediction concluding with an emphatic "amen" in the preceding unit, the present section opens with a direct address to Timothy, similar to v. 3 above (though here Timothy is addressed by name, just as the false teachers are named in v. 20). In this way Timothy is presented as a model follower of

Paul and the gospel, while the false teachers by way of typology represent those who oppose the gospel and are ultimately inspired by Satan himself (v. 20).

1:18–20 Following the digression of vv. 8–17, the opening section concludes with an exhortation to Timothy and an identification of two false teachers by name, Hymenaeus and Alexander. With this Paul resumes the argument of vv. 3–7; "this instruction" probably refers to παραγγελία in v. 5, which in turn refers to vv. 3–4.[98] "Timothy, my son" recalls the opening greeting in v. 2. Turning to a somber and serious subject, Paul reassures Timothy of his filial relationship and continues to write in a tone conveying fatherly affection. The exhortation concludes Paul's personal charge to Timothy that began with a unit on the false teachers and the apostle's personal testimony. In the preceding verses Paul contrasted the gospel of God's grace in Christ with the speculative teachings of the self-appointed teachers of the law who threatened the spiritual health of the congregation Timothy served.

Before moving on to specific instructions on how to order the life of the church (2:1–3:16), Paul reminds Timothy of "the prophecies previously made about you,"[99] a reference to the recognition of Timothy's gifts for ministry and God's appointment and its prophetic announcement to the congregation in the public laying on of hands (see at 4:14; 2 Tim 1:6; cf. Acts 13:1–3). Paul exhorts Timothy to "fight the good fight" of faith (cf. 6:12; 2 Tim 2:3–4; of Paul: 2 Cor 10:3–4; cf. 2 Tim 4:7; 1 Cor 9:7), challenging him to maintain faith and a good conscience (cf. v. 5).[100]

---

[98] Quinn and Wacker, *Letters to Timothy*, 147.

[99] For a discussion of the syntactical issues involved in this phrase, see Marshall, *Pastoral Epistles*, 409.

[100] An interesting parallel to Paul's language here is found in 4 Macc 9:24: "Fight the sacred and noble fight for true religion." See also the use of military metaphors in Rom 13:12; 1 Cor 9:7; 2 Cor 6:7; 10:3–5; 1 Thess 5:8; Eph 6:10–17; and Phil 2:25. On the difference between Paul's use of military and athletic metaphors, see V. C. Pfitzner, *Paul and the Agōn Motif* (Leiden: Brill, 1967), 158. Seesengood argues that in using the metaphorical language of slave, athlete, and soldier here and elsewhere in the LTT, Paul is not engaging three different metaphors but three subordinate elements of a single metaphor, that of a gladiator. R. P. Seesengood, "Contending for the Faith in Paul's Absence: Combat Sports and Gladiators in the Disputed Pauline Epistles," *LTQ* 41 (2006): 87–118.

While Timothy is cast in the role of soldier (στρατεύω, v. 18; cf. 2 Tim 2:4; the phrase "by recalling them" refers to the just-mentioned prophecies), "some" (τινες) have willfully rejected (ἀπωθέω; cf. Acts 7:27, 39; 13:46; Rom 11:1–2) a good conscience (cf. vv. 5–6; the relative pronoun ἥν is feminine singular and refers to the immediate antecedent, ἀγαθὴν συνείδησιν).[101] In so doing, they have "shipwrecked" (ναυαγέω) the faith (perhaps more likely than the CSB's "their faith")[102]—a potent metaphor in Ephesus, one of the major seaports in Asia Minor (cf. 2 Cor 11:25; Acts 27:27–44).[103]

After several instances of the vague indefinite pronoun "some" (τινες; cf. vv. 3, 19), the explicit identification of two teachers by name ("Among them are Hymenaeus and Alexander") in v. 20 comes as somewhat of a surprise, even shock.[104] Similar to the (perhaps jarring) identification of Euodia and Syntyche in Phil 4:2–3, Paul doesn't hesitate to single out individuals who pose a threat to the unity of the congregation by name (though Euodia and Syntyche's argument was probably much less severe than the threat posed by Hymenaeus and Alexander). Hymenaeus is paired with Philetus in 2 Tim 2:18 as saying the resurrection has already

---

[101] This is more likely than the CSB's "these," implying that the antecedents are both "the faith" and "good conscience." The NLT makes this explicit: "For some people have deliberately violated their consciences." See also the NRSV: "By rejecting conscience."

[102] Since the phrase "concerning the faith" in its two other occurrences in the letters to Timothy refers to "the faith" in an objective sense as to its content rather than to personal faith (cf. 1 Tim 6:21; 2 Tim 3:8), it's likely that in the present instance, too, "the faith" rather than the false teachers' personal faith is in view. So rightly the NIV; cf. the literal translation "concerning faith" in the KJV (similarly, NKJV); and the more common (but less likely) rendering "their faith" not only in the CSB but also in the ESV, NASB, and most other versions. See further the discussion in Thornton, *Hostility in the House of God*, 51–52.

[103] Note that the shipwreck isn't merely the result of gradual, unwitting drifting but of conscious rejection. Today we might say the false teachers have caused a "train wreck" with regard to the faith; they have caused a head-on collision with the apostolic gospel. Cf. Mounce, *Pastoral Epistles*, 67.

[104] Fee (*1 and 2 Timothy, Titus*, 59) speculates that Hymenaeus and Alexander were "almost certainly leaders, therefore probably elders." It does appear from 2 Tim 2:18 that Hymenaeus was a teacher, but whether he was an elder in the church is almost impossible to determine. Other speculations include that Paul only names the persons whom he knew by name or that he names the persons whose error was most egregious.

taken place; Alexander may be "the coppersmith" mentioned in 2 Tim 4:14–15.[105]

"Delivering" a person to Satan may constitute a semitechnical term for removing a person from the church—the sphere of the Spirit—and placing them back into the world—the sphere of Satan's operation.[106] The purpose of such a procedure is that of correction (παιδεύω, cf. 2 Tim 2:25; Titus 2:12). Paul's resolve to purge the congregation from false teaching underscores the need for church leaders to be committed to exercising proper church discipline (cf. 1 Cor 5:3–5; 2 Thess 3:14–15; Titus 3:10–11). Perhaps Paul here subtly urges Timothy to move ahead with excommunicating the false teachers. In any case he wants to send an unequivocal message.

Paul has handed these men over to Satan (v. 20; cf. 5:15) to "be taught not to blaspheme."[107] Earlier, the apostle had handed over to Satan a man in the church at Corinth who had his father's wife (presumably his stepmother: 1 Cor 5:5; cf. Rom 1:24, 26, 28). Most likely this refers not to final condemnation but to the last resort of allowing people to experience Satan's wrath so they may be purged from their sin (cf. 2 Tim 2:25–26).[108] The passage is reminiscent of the disciplinary procedure stipulated by Jesus, that if a person "doesn't pay attention even to the church, let him be like a Gentile and a tax collector to you" (Matt 18:15–17; cf. Titus 3:10–11).

The juxtaposition between Timothy and Paul in v. 18 and the false teachers and Satan in v. 20 presents the axis of good and evil pervading this letter and the LTT in their entirety. In this way the apostolic mission, including Paul's apostolic delegates, are shown

---

[105] Though Ephesus was a large city, and there were doubtless numerous individuals named Alexander.

[106] The likely theological antecedent is Job 2:6 LXX where the Lord tells Satan, "Behold, I deliver him to you." Just as in the present instance, God uses Satan as his instrument to accomplish his purpose. Cf. S. Page, "Satan: God's Servant," *JETS* 50 (2007): 449–65, esp. 452. See also D. T. Thornton, "Satan as Adversary and Ally in the Process of Ecclesial Discipline: The Use of the Prologue to Job in 1 Corinthians 5:5 and 1 Timothy 1:20," *TynBul* 66 (2015): 148–50.

[107] The charge of blasphemy (note that Paul himself was formerly a blasphemer, v. 13) may constitute an oblique reference to the false teaching alluded to elsewhere in Paul's letters to Timothy. Blasphemy probably refers to misrepresentation of the Christian faith (Marshall, *Pastoral Epistles*, 415).

[108] In this sense Paul, Timothy, and God, with Satan as his instrument, are said to work toward the possible conversion of the false teachers. Cf. Thornton, *Hostility in the House of God*, 53–55.

to be opposed by none other than Satan—who uses the false teachers as his instruments—as a sign that the end times have already dawned. This casts the shadow of an eschatological framework on the remainder of the letter, including its ecclesiology, which will unfold in chapters 2–3 on the basis of the characterization of the "church of the living God" as God's household and as a pillar and foundation of the truth (1 Tim 3:15).

Bridge

Paul here invokes the strong bond Timothy shares with him as his spiritual "son" in the faith, urging him to "fight the good fight, having faith and a good conscience" (v. 19). In a potent metaphor in his own day, Paul contrasts Timothy with the false teachers who have "shipwrecked their faith" (v. 19). This is a form of spiritual bankruptcy; whatever faith there was has now vanished. We, too, should sustain a strong spiritual bond with our mentors in the faith and "fight the good fight" armed with faith and a good conscience.

III. Congregational Matters: Promoting Unity and Order in God's Household, Qualifications for Church Officers (2:1–3:16)

The main purpose for the present section is given in 3:14–15: "I write these things to you, hoping to come to you soon. But if I should be delayed, I have written so that you will know how people ought to act in God's household, which is the church of the living God, the pillar and foundation of the truth." The solemn descriptive terms used for the church in this passage speak decisively against the suggestion that these instructions are of value solely for first-century Ephesus. While the letter may be occasioned by the false teachers (1:3–4, 18–20), Paul's purpose for writing is broader; chapters 2 and 3 contain positive guidelines for church leadership, particularly a list of qualifications for church leaders, in an effort to promote unity and order in the church. Hermeneutical consistency demands that the injunctions regarding women in chapter 2 be awarded the same normative status as the stipulations in chapter 3.[109]

---

[109] Some argue that dealing with false teachers was Paul's sole purpose in writing 1 Timothy and thus interpret 1 Tim 2:12 as narrowly concerned to prohibit

A. On Prayer (2:1–8)

[1]First of all, then, I urge that petitions, prayers, intercessions, and thanksgivings be made for everyone, [2]for kings and
all those who are in authority, so that we may lead a tranquil
and quiet life in all godliness and dignity. [3]This is good, and it
pleases God our Savior, [4]who wants everyone to be saved and
to come to the knowledge of the truth.

[5]For there is one God and one mediator between God and
humanity, the man Christ Jesus, [6]who gave himself as a ransom for all, a testimony at the proper time.

[7]For this I was appointed a herald, an apostle (I am telling
the truth; I am not lying), and a teacher of the Gentiles in faith
and truth.

[8]Therefore, I want the men in every place to pray, lifting
up holy hands without anger or argument.

Relation to Surrounding Context

Paul's preceding remarks in chapter 1 state the occasion for writing and contain Paul's testimony as a sinner saved by grace called to proclaim the gospel. Both Paul and Timothy his protégé are set against the false teachers, self-styled teachers of the Jewish law who have shipwrecked the faith. In this new section, which extends all the way to 3:16, Paul instructs Timothy as to proper conduct in God's household of faith. This includes prayer for the governing authorities and careful selection and appointment of church leaders. The emphasis on the universality of salvation may respond polemically to a (Jewish?) exclusivism on the part of the false teachers in the Ephesian church.

---

women from teaching false doctrine in the Ephesian church. See, e.g., Fee, *1 and 2 Timothy, Titus*, passim; Fee, "Issues in Evangelical Hermeneutics, Part III: The Great Watershed—Intentionality and Particularity/Eternality: 1 Timothy 2:8–15 as a Test Case," *Crux* 26 (1990): 31–37; Fee, "Reflections on Church Order in the Pastoral Epistles," 141–51. However, structurally Paul's instructions in 1 Timothy 2–3 seem to point in the opposite direction; 1 Tim 2:12 is part of a section in the letter that includes instructions to "the household of God," "the church of the living God," "a pillar and foundation of truth" (3:14–15), which is relevant for people "in every place" (2:8), not merely first-century Ephesus. Paul's appeal to creation order with Adam and Eve in v. 13 also gives the passage a universal sense. See the interaction with Fee in A. J. Köstenberger, "'Biblical Hermeneutics: Basic Principles and Questions of Gender' by Roger Nicole and 'Hermeneutics and the Gender Debate' by Gordon D. Fee," *JBMW* 10, no. 1 (Spring 2005): 88–95; "1–2 Timothy, Titus," 504.

Structure

"First of all, then, I urge" in v. 1 marks a shift in focus from a concern with the false teachers to a series of more positive instructions for proper conduct in God's household, the church (cf. 3:14–15). Verses 1–2a state Paul's command (prayer for the governing authorities); v. 2b enunciates the desired result (believers being able to live a tranquil and quiet life); vv. 3–4 affirm the rightness of Paul's command in light of the fact that God wants everyone to be saved; vv. 5–6 follow up with a Christian confession; v. 7 states Paul's threefold calling as herald, apostle, and teacher; and v. 8, by way of possible *inclusio*, urges men to be unified in prayer.

2:1 With the transition "First of all, then, I urge," Paul turns to the business at hand—that is, congregational prayer (vv. 1–8) and church leadership (2:9–3:13).[110] It makes sense that Paul starts with this particular command, as political stability is vital for providing a conducive environment for proclaiming the gospel. This, in turn, points to the foundational nature of the mission theme in the LTT.[111] The command to pray for those in authority, while often neglected today, is hardly limited to first-century Ephesus.[112] If prayer for political rulers could be urged when an emperor as cruel as Nero was on the throne, it's difficult to imagine a scenario in which believers are exempt from this responsibility. Similar to

[110] M. M. Mitchell, "Corrective Composition, Corrective Exegesis: The Teaching on Prayer in 1 Tim 2,1–15," in *1 Timothy Reconsidered*, ed. K. P. Donfried, Colloquium Oecumenicum Paulinum 18 (Leuven: Peeters, 2008), 41–62, building on the work of A. Merz, *Die fiktive Selbstauslegung des Paulus: Intertextuelle Studien zur Intention und Rezeption der Pastoralbriefe*, NTOA 52 (Göttingen: Vandenhoeck & Ruprecht, 2004), argues that the pseudonymous author of 1 Timothy engaged in "corrective composition" to demonstrate that Paul was not against prayer for emperors and rulers. However, the simpler reading—that Paul himself urged prayer for emperors and rulers in this passage—comports better with Pauline passages such as Rom 13:1–7, which also happens to support the authenticity of 1 Timothy (see discussion of pseudonymity in the introduction above).

[111] See esp. C. E. Ho, "Mission in the Pastoral Epistles," in *Entrusted with the Gospel*, 241–67.

[112] At the same time, it's not implausible to wonder whether Paul's encouragement was given at least in part to counteract the lack of corporate prayer (Marshall, *Pastoral Epistles*, 417). Marshall also points out that the emphasis on the universality of the gospel and on Paul's role is striking, suggesting that "the false teachers, who stressed Jewish myths and genealogies and apparently also the law, were not enthusiastic for the Gentile mission" (pp. 416–17).

Christians in the second half of the first century, believers today should take positive action toward those in authority, such as engaging in intercessory prayer for them, rather than taking an adversarial or antagonistic stance.

As in 1:3, Paul opens his exhortation with the term παρακαλέω ("I urge"), a verb Paul used regularly when transitioning to the "business portion" of a letter (1 Cor 1:10; 2 Cor 2:8; 6:1; Eph 4:8; Phil 4:1; 1 Thess 4:1; Phlm 10). The terms "then" (οὖν) and "first of all" (πρῶτον, reversed in the CSB) indicate that Paul is now progressing past preliminaries and moving on to the main body of his letter. "Then" loosely connects the following section with the preceding remarks;[113] "first of all" could imply a series of exhortations but, more likely, conveys the sense "above all" or "especially," since the phrase is never followed by "second," etc. (cf. 5:4; Rom 1:8; 3:2; 1 Tim 5:4).

The apostle's initial instruction relates to prayers offered for "all [kinds of] people" (cf. vv. 4, 6), particularly those in authority.[114] By urging intercession for these rulers, Paul affirms that they have ultimately been appointed under God's sovereign providence.[115] Submission to governing authorities represents standard NT teaching (e.g., Rom 13:1–7; 1 Pet 2:13–17; Titus 3:1–2).[116] Where

---

[113] See J. K. Heckert, *Discourse Function of Conjoiners in the Pastoral Epistles* (Dallas: SIL International, 1996), who understands οὖν in 2:1 as continuative/resumptive rather than inferential because he sees most of chapter 1 as a digression from the initial directive given to Timothy in 1:3. Others see the digression as limited to 1:19b–20 (S. H. Levinsohn, "Some Notes on the Information Structure and Discourse Features of 1 Timothy," rev. ed. [Dallas: SIL International, 2011], 10; Marshall, *Pastoral Epistles*, 418). M. Gill, *Jesus as Mediator: Politics and Polemic in 1 Timothy 2:1–7* (New York: Peter Lang, 2008), 138, sees οὖν as both inferential (reaching back to the charges in 1:3 and 1:18) and transitional (facilitating movement into "a new, but connected, discussion surrounding the activities of his readership"). See also Van Neste, *Cohesion and Structure*, 82–83.

[114] The offering of prayer for authorities is built on Jewish precedent, as attested by references in (1) the OT (Ezra 6:10); (2) Second Temple literature (1 Macc 7:33; *Let. Aris.* 44–45); (3) and later Jewish writings (Josephus, *J.W.* 2.196; *m. 'Abot* 3:2).

[115] L. Oberlinner, *Die Pastoralbriefe: Erster Timotheusbrief*, HThKNT XI.2/1 (Freiburg: Herder, 1994), 68.

[116] It's unnecessary to argue, as M. Tsuji, "Die Intertextualität von 1 Tim 2,1–3/Tit 3,1–2," in *Neutestamentliche Exegese im Dialog: Hermeneutik—Wirkungsgeschichte—Matthäusevangelium: Festschrift für Ulrich Luz zum 70. Geburtstag*, ed. P. Lampe, M. Mayordomo, and M. Sato (Neukirchener-Vluyn: Neukirchener, 2008), 99–110, does, that a pseudonymous author drew on Paul's

those in power engage in ungodly conduct, intercession for them is an instance of loving one's enemies and of praying for those who persecute believers, in keeping with Jesus's command (Matt 5:44 par. Luke 6:27–28).

In speaking of prayer, Paul employs a series of four expressions (of a total of seven found in the NT), describing the different elements of which prayer may consist (the order may be incidental): "petitions" (δεήσεις) for God to meet specific needs; "prayers" in general (προσευχάς); "intercessions" (ἐντεύξεις), that is, earnest, urgent, and bold appeals for divine action on others' behalf (cf. ἐντυγχάνω in Rom 8:27, 34; 11:2); and "thanksgivings" (εὐχαριστίας; cf. 1 Tim 4:3–4; see also Phil 4:6, on which see further below).

All four terms are plural, indicating the variety and frequency of prayers addressed to God. The term "thanksgiving" recurs in 4:3–4 (cf. "intercession" in v. 5). Paul himself regularly offers up "petitions" (2 Tim 1:3). The first two types of prayers, "petitions" and "prayers," are uttered by godly widows in 5:5. The close parallel Phil 4:6 features three of the four terms ("intercession" is replaced by "requests," αἰτήματα). "For everyone" probably means "for all kinds of people" and is said in v. 2 (note the repeated ὑπέρ, "for") to include governmental authorities.

Thanksgiving (εὐχαριστία) is commonly connected with petition in Paul:

- "Don't worry about anything, but in everything, through prayer (προσευχή) and petition (δέησις) with thanksgiving (εὐχαριστία), present your requests to God" (Phil 4:6).
- "Devote yourselves to prayer (προσευχή), stay alert in it with thanksgiving (εὐχαριστία)" (Col 4:2).

The closest parallel in the present letter is 1 Tim 4:4–5, where Paul writes with regard to those who forbid marriage and urge abstinence from certain foods that "everything created by God is good, and nothing is to be rejected if it is received with *thanksgiving* (εὐχαριστίας), since it is sanctified by the word of God and by *prayer*" (ἐντεύξεως; emphasis added).

---

teaching in Romans 13 to legitimize his teaching regarding the necessity of submission to church leaders. More likely, the author of 1 Tim 2:1–3, Titus 3:1–2, and Rom 13:1–7 was one and the same (Paul), who in his respective letters made appropriate application of the general principle of submission to authority.

In fact, when thanksgiving is enjoined in conjunction with prayer (Phil 4:6; Col 4:2; 1 Tim 2:1; 4:4–5), it pertains not merely to the person or item prayed about but is offered in recognition of God's role as the Creator and in anticipation of his answers to prayers uttered in keeping with his good design. As Pao notes,

> When petition is grounded in thanksgiving, God and not self-interest becomes the focus. On the other hand, thanksgiving without petition proclaims God to be the Creator without trusting that he indeed is one who is able to provide for his people. In the Pauline epistles, petitions are often found precisely in the thanksgiving paragraphs that introduce the epistles. The two cannot be separated in the Pauline model of prayer.[117]

2:2 "Kings" (βασιλέων) in the original context refers to the Roman emperor (most likely Nero). Beyond this, "all those who are in authority" (πάντων τῶν ἐν ὑπεροχῇ ὄντων) are included, such as provincial governors or other local government officials (i.e., the city clerk; Acts 19:35; cf. 1 Pet 2:13–17; Titus 3:1).[118] The primary purpose of prayer adduced by Paul is "so that we may lead[119] a tranquil and quiet life in all godliness and dignity," which "pleases God our Savior, who wants everyone to be saved and to come to the knowledge of the truth" (vv. 2–4; see further below).[120] What

---

[117] D. W. Pao, *Thanksgiving: An Investigation of a Pauline Theme*, NSBT 13 (Downers Grove: InterVarsity, 2002), 36–37. Similarly, Marshall observes, "The assumption is that, when praying, the congregation remembers with gratitude how former prayers have been answered and therefore prays with all the more confidence" (*Pastoral Epistles*, 419–20). See also C. Spicq: "In their request, they can already express their gratitude for the expected answer" (*TLNT* 2:9). Spicq contrasts ἔντευξις-related "misadventures of human justice" from the papyri—negligent officials, a backed-up bureaucracy—with the confident expectation of God's answer.

[118] Prayer on behalf of the emperor was common in the larger culture: see the overview in Gill, *Jesus as Mediator*, 141–44. Prayer *to* the emperor was also common at various times, but that practice is clearly not enjoined in the NT.

[119] Διάγω ("lead (life)"/"live") is also found in Titus 3:3.

[120] By implication this seems to include the rulers themselves. Contra, e.g., K. Zamfir, *Men and Women in the Household of God: A Contextual Approach to Roles and Ministries in the Pastoral Epistles*, NTOA 103 (Göttingen: Vandenhoeck & Ruprecht, 2013), 147n43. That the conversion of rulers is in mind is suggested by (1) the fact that rulers are a subset of "everyone" (v. 1b); the asyndeton between ὑπὲρ

Paul seeks to promote, then, is favorable conditions for continued gospel proclamation.[121] Again, this is standard Pauline teaching (cf. 1 Thess 4:11–12; 2 Thess 3:10–12).[122]

The term ἤρεμος ("tranquil") occurs only here in the NT; ἡσύχιον can mean either "quiet" or "silent" depending on context (it means "quiet" here; see esp. 2 Thess 3:12; 1 Pet 3:4). As Paul's ministry illustrates, this doesn't mean freedom from affliction (see,

---

πάντων ἀνθρώπων and ὑπὲρ βασιλέων may suggest a generic-specific relationship (see S. H. Levinsohn, *Discourse Features of New Testament Greek* [2nd ed.; Dallas: SIL International, 2000], 118–19); (2) the structural parallel between ὑπὲρ πάντων ἀνθρώπων and ὑπὲρ βασιλέων καὶ πάντων τῶν ἐν ὑπεροχῇ ὄντων (vv. 1b–2a), which suggests that if salvation of "everyone" is in view, the salvation of "kings and all . . . those in authority" is in view as well; (3) Paul's recognition, as recorded by Luke, that he was commissioned to bear the name of Jesus before kings (Acts 9:15) and his explicit desire for their conversion (e.g., Acts 26:26–29). In connection with this passage, Wall speaks of "a Christian mission that boldly evangelizes the surrounding pagan culture from top to bottom" and avers that "prayers for the emperor's personal safety and political wisdom were ultimately offered to God in prospect of his salvation" (R. W. Wall, with R. B. Steele, *1 and 2 Timothy and Titus*, THNTC [Grand Rapids: Eerdmans, 2012], 81). See also J. P. Dickson, *Mission-Commitment in Ancient Judaism and in the Pauline Communities: The Shape, Extent, and Background of Early Christian Mission*, WUNT 2/159 (Tübingen: Mohr-Siebeck, 2003), 216–19.

[121] Cf. Tertullian, *Apol.* 32 (PL 1, 508–9): "There is also another and a greater necessity for our offering prayer in behalf of the emperors, nay, for the complete stability of the empire, and for Roman interests in general." See also Tertullian, *Apol.* 39 (PL 1, 532): "We pray, too, for the emperors, for their ministers and for all in authority, for the welfare of the world, for the prevalence of peace, for the delay of the final consummation."

[122] Cf. Marshall, *Pastoral Epistles*, 423: "The effective leadership of the State will maintain an environment conducive to witness." Wainwright notes that "the idea . . . of the *pax Romana* as providential circumstances for the spread of the gospel" is "as old as Origen [*Cels.* 2.30] and Eusebius [*Dem. ev.* 3.7, 30–35]" and that "the connection of political peace with the spread of the gospel was maintained by the classical Protestant Reformers" ("Praying for Kings," 121). This missionary motivation stands over against the *christliche Bürgerlichkeit* proposal of Dibelius and Conzelmann; the "quiet and peaceable existence" of v. 2 is not an end in itself. Rather, praying for a tranquil existence—one not disturbed by turbulent circumstances, particularly those specifically brought against Christians—furthers the goal of praying for the salvation of all people because it allows freedom to express the Christian faith in observable ways. As Towner notes, "Prayer for the tranquil setting is prayer for an ideal set of social circumstances in which Christians might give unfettered expression to their faith in observable living. . . . The church is to pray for the salvation of 'all,' and it participates in that mission by making God present in society in its genuine expression of the new life for all to see" (*Letters to Timothy and Titus*, 170).

e.g., the attacks on Paul in Corinth, Acts 18:12–18, or the Ephesian riots, Acts 19:23–41; cf. 2 Tim 1:8; 3:12), but a life lived under the overall protection of the civil authorities, which provided a measure of tranquility that allowed Paul to engage in continued, even extensive, gospel ministry (e.g., Phil 1:12–14; cf. Jer 29:7).

Over half of the occurrences of "godliness" (εὐσέβεια) in the NT are found in 1 Timothy (§5.1.3).[123] Paul uses this expression in contrast to the conduct exhibited by his opponents. For example, the "mystery of godliness" consists in the apostolic confession of Christ (3:16). Rather than engage in ascetic practices like the false teachers, Timothy must train himself to be godly (4:7–8), being content rather than motivated by greed (6:3, 5–6, 11). Knowledge of the truth leads to godliness (Titus 1:1). The opponents, for their part, have a "form of godliness" while "denying its power." "Dignity" (σεμνότης) recurs in 3:4 with regard to overseers and in Titus 2:7 with regard to Titus (the adjective σεμνός is found in Phil 4:8; 1 Tim 3:8, 11; Titus 2:2).[124]

2:3 After directing Timothy to encourage prayer for the governing authorities for the purpose of gospel proclamation in vv. 1–2, Paul elaborates on elements of this injunction in vv. 3–7 before briefly returning to his original exhortation in v. 8. It is possible, if not likely, that in this section Paul is combating an elitism and exclusivism espoused by the false teachers.[125] It's also possible that vv. 5–6 correspond to vv. 3–4 in the following manner:

---

[123] On the term "godliness" (εὐσέβεια) in the LTT, see W. Foerster, "Εὐσέβεια in den Pastoralbriefen," *NTS* 5 (1958–59): 213–18; J. J. Wainwright, "Εὐσέβεια: Syncretism or Conservative Contextualization?" *EvQ* 65 (1993): 211–24; and the excursus in Marshall, *Pastoral Epistles*, 135–44. Marshall concludes that the expression "functions to describe the life (noun), or the manner of life (adverb) which is true Christianity" (p. 143).

[124] M. Silva, "σεμνός, σεμνότης," *NIDNTTE* 4:283. See also Towner: "Paul's use of the adjective σεμνός . . . calls for attention to the way Christians project themselves in public" (*Letters to Timothy and Titus*, 175).

[125] See the characterization of the opponents' soteriology in Fee, *1 and 2 Timothy, Titus*, 61–62; Marshall, *Pastoral Epistles*, 420, 425–26; and Mounce, *Pastoral Epistles*, 75–76.

[3] It pleases God our Savior,	[5] For there is one God
[4a] who wants everyone to be saved	and one mediator between God and humanity, the man Christ Jesus, [6a] who gave himself as a ransom for all,
[4b] and to come to the knowledge of the truth.	[6b] a testimony at the proper time*

*See J. D. Quinn, "Jesus as Savior and Only Mediator (1 Tim 2:3–6): Linguistic Paradigms of Acculturation," in *Fede e cultura alla luce della Bibbia. Atti della Sessione plenaria 1979 della Pontificia Commissione Biblica* (Torino: Editricelle Di Ci, 1981), 253, who calls vv. 5–6 a "confession-acclamation" and asserts that the "acclamation form is already a signal that behind the previous, carefully framed theological principle on the unqualified universality of the divine offer of salvation, there stood Christian public worship, in which a believing community spontaneously responded in awe at and gratitude for the stupendous benefits that they had experienced from the regal, divine power at work in their midst" (ibid., with reference to Spicq and Murphy-O'Connor).

First, Paul observes that praying for those in authority is good and pleases God.[126] We can infer from v. 4 that such prayer includes requests for the salvation of these individuals, though in light of the purpose statement in v. 2, proper governance may be in view as well.[127] This, in turn, is part of the overarching mission theme in the LTT.[128] As in the opening verse, God is identified as "our Savior" ("our Savior-God"). In the following verses Paul elaborates on his rationale for praying for the governing authorities (assumed to be unbelievers).

2:4 "Everyone" (more literally, "all people," πάντας ἀνθρώπους, so the ESV, NIV), fronted in the original Greek for emphasis, suggests that the scope of God's saving activity is universal, including pagans as well as Jews (cf. Acts 22:15; Rom 11:32; 1 Cor 12:13; Gal

[126] Towner (*Letters to Timothy and Titus*, 176) proposes that the language of v. 3 "reflects the statement found several times in Deuteronomy that affirms certain practices as in accordance with the law and thus pleasing to God: 'Do what is pleasing and good in the Lord's sight' (Deut 6:18)" (cf. Deut 12:25, 28; 13:19; 21:9). The term ἀπόδεκτος ("acceptable") may bring to mind the use of this expression in Leviticus to describe "acceptable" sacrifices (cf. Rom 15:16; Phil 4:18; 1 Pet 2:5).

[127] See discussion at 2:2 above.

[128] See esp. Ho, "Mission in the Pastoral Epistles" and §1 in the Biblical-Theological Exposition below.

3:28; Col 3:11).[129] Salvation is here equated with coming to a full knowledge of the truth (ἐπίγνωσις ἀληθείας, 2 Tim 2:25; 3:7; Titus 1:1; cf. Heb 10:26; John 10:9; 14:6; 17:3); elsewhere the church is called "the pillar and foundation of the truth" (3:15), and "truth" is contrasted with false teaching (4:3; 2 Tim 3:7–8; 4:3–4). Such salvation requires repentance (2 Tim 2:25). The false teachers and their followers, however, are "always learning but never able to come to a knowledge of the truth" (2 Tim 3:7), while Paul's calling centers on building up "the faith of God's elect and their knowledge of the truth that leads to godliness" (Titus 1:1).

2:5–6 Paul continues to elaborate on his command in vv. 1–2 by specifying the nature of the gospel that is to be proclaimed in terms of monotheism, unique sacrificial intercession, and mission.[130] The following affirmation may draw on a Christian confession ("a testimony at the proper time").[131] The existence of one God (monotheism) was affirmed by Judaism (Deut 6:4),[132] with

---

[129] Alternatively, σωθῆναι in v. 4 may mean "preserved" or "kept from harm," as it most likely does in v. 15 and in 4:16 (see discussion below). See J. Reumann, "How Do We Interpret 1 Timothy 2:1–5 (and Related Passages)?," in *The One Mediator, the Saints, and Mary*, Lutherans and Catholics in Dialogue 8 (Minneapolis: Augsburg Fortress, 1992), 154, who further adduces 4:10; Matt 14:30; John 11:12; 12:27 for the "weaker" sense of the verb.

[130] See Quinn, "Jesus as Savior and Only Mediator," 258.

[131] M. M. Yarbrough, *Paul's Utilization of Preformed Traditions in 1 Timothy: An Evaluation of the Apostle's Literary, Rhetorical, and Theological Tactics*, LNTS 417 (London: T&T Clark, 2009), 79–86. The present statement is called a "hymnic-type confession" by E. E. Ellis, "Traditions in the Pastoral Epistles," in *Early Jewish and Christian Exegesis*, ed. C. A. Evans and W. F. Stinespring (Atlanta: Scholars Press, 1987), 246. In the Gospels, Jesus's death is said to be "in the place of" (ἀντί; Mark 10:45) or "for" (ὑπέρ; Luke 22:19) others; elsewhere in Paul, it is said to be "for" (ὑπέρ; 1 Cor 11:24) others. The present passage combines both notions (ἀντίλυτρον, ὑπέρ).

[132] The phrase doesn't match Deut 6:4 LXX (κύριος ὁ θεὸς ἡμῶν κύριος εἷς ἐστιν) precisely, but R. J. Bauckham notes that the usual form of an allusion to the *Shema* in the Second Temple period was εἷς θεός (ἐστι), citing Sib. Or. 3:11; Sib. Or. frag. 1:7, 32; Josephus, *Ant.* 4.201; Ps.-Sophocles; Philo, *Creation* 171; *Spec. Laws* 1.30 ("Biblical Theology and the Problems of Monotheism," in *Out of Egypt: Biblical Theology and Biblical Interpretation*, ed. M. Healy, K. Möller, R. Parry, and C. Bartholomew [Grand Rapids: Zondervan, 2004], 219). G. S. MaGee, "Paul's Gospel, the Law, and God's Universal Reign in Rom 3:31," *JETS* 57 (2014): 348 points out that "the *Shema* enjoys an unparalleled role in shaping Israel's faith and practice." This can be seen also in the summary of the law in the "royal law" of Leviticus by Jesus, Paul, and James (Matt 22:39; Mark 12:31; Rom 13:8–10; Gal 5:14; Jas 2:8). Cf. J. H. Tigay,

important implications for Gentiles (cf. Acts 17:23–31; Rom 1:12; 3:30; 1 Cor 8:6; Gal 3:20).[133] However, first-century Jews frequently defined their salvation-historical privilege in narrow, nationalistic terms.[134] This ethnic presumption was strongly opposed by Jesus and the early church, including Peter (1 Pet 2:4–10, though not without initial struggles: cf. Acts 10:9–23; Gal 2:11–14), Paul (Romans, Galatians, Eph 2:11–22), and John (e.g., 10:16; 11:51–52; 12:32).[135] Since there are other monotheistic religions besides Christianity, Paul goes on to emphasize that there is only one mediator between God and humanity, "the man Christ Jesus, who gave himself as a ransom for all."

Just as there's only one God, there's also only one mediator (μεσίτης) between God and the human race, "the man Christ Jesus" (cf. John 14:6b).[136] The letter to the Hebrews presents Jesus as the

---

Deuteronomy, JPS Torah Commentary (Philadelphia: Jewish Publication Society, 1996), 76; N. T. Wright, *The Climax of the Covenant: Christ and the Law in Pauline Theology* (Minneapolis: Fortress, 1992), 95; N. Lamm, *The Shema: Spirituality and Law in Judaism* (Philadelphia: Jewish Publication Society, 1998), 9–11.

[133] MaGee, "Paul's Gospel, the Law, and God's Universal Reign," 348, points out that even though most Jews conceived of the *Shema* as setting Israel apart from the other nations, there was also precedent for viewing the *Shema*'s scope more broadly (cf. esp. Zech 14:9; see also Pss 66:8; 96; 117; Isa 2:2; 56:7; 66:18–20; Zech 2:11; 8:22–23; 14:16; Mal 1:11). See Lamm, *Shema*, 31–32; Tigay, *Deuteronomy*, 76; C. J. H. Wright, *Deuteronomy*, NIBCOT (Peabody, MA: Hendrickson, 1996), 97. Cf. C. Bruno, *"God Is One": The Function of* Eis ho Theos *as a Ground for Gentile Inclusion in Paul's Letters*, LNTS 497 (New York: Bloomsbury T&T Clark, 2013), 42–61, 139–44, who argues that Paul in Rom 3:20 is viewing Deut 6:4 through the lens of Zech 14:9 (p. 199). In this vein God's law serves to promote the recognition of God's righteous reign over the entire earth among all people without distinction.

[134] For a discussion of the tension between God's universal claim over all of humanity and his particular care for Israel in rabbinic texts, see N. A. Dahl, *Studies in Paul: Theology for the Early Christian Mission* (Minneapolis: Augsburg, 1977), 182–88; J. D. G. Dunn, *Romans 1–8*, WBC 38A (Nashville: Thomas Nelson, 1988), 188. See also K. H. Tan, "The *Shema* and Early Christianity," *TynBul* 59 (2008): 191–95; Wright, *Climax of the Covenant*, 2, 154–55, 170–71.

[135] Cf. the astute observation by Towner: "In Paul's missiology, the formula 'God is one' yields the logical corollary, 'therefore all have access to his salvation, both Jews and Gentiles'" (*Letters to Timothy and Titus*, 180). This, of course, is regularly affirmed by Paul in his earlier writings (e.g., Rom 1:16; Gal 3:28).

[136] A. Oepke, "μεσίτης, κτλ.," *TDNT* 611–15; M. Silva, "μεσίτης, κτλ.," *NIDNTTE* 3:285. Note the repetition of the word εἷς ("one") in v. 5. Note also that in this confession, which moves from θεός to ἄνθρωπος, the Christological attribute stressed is Christ's humanity (εἷς γὰρ θεός, εἷς καὶ μεσίτης θεοῦ καὶ ἀνθρώπων, ἄνθρωπος Χριστὸς

mediator of a new covenant that replaces the old covenant mediated by Moses (Heb 8:6; 9:15; 12:24; cf. Gal 3:19–20).[137] Jesus supersedes all other intermediaries, whether angels (Col 2:18; Heb 2:2), Moses (Gal 3:19; Heb 3:1–6), Jewish high priests (Heb 8:6, 9, 15; 9:15; 12:24), or other religious figures.[138] The "mediator" concept is further described as a "ransom" (ἀντίλυτρον, see ἀπολύτρωσις in Rom 3:24; 8:23; 1 Cor 1:30; Col 1:14) paid through Jesus's death (cf. Titus 2:14: λυτρόω).[139] This presupposes universal human sinfulness (cf. Romans 1–3). The reference to Jesus's humanity stresses both his identification with humankind and his status as the man/human *par excellence* who alone was able to provide redemption from sin (see Paul's Adam/Christ theology in Rom 5:12–21; 1 Cor 15:21–22, 45–49).

The expression echoes Jesus's statement that he would give his life as a ransom "for many" (Semitic style; cf. Matt 20:28 =

Ἰησοῦς). As Marshall aptly notes, "The insistence in I Timothy 2:5 that Christ Jesus was human" is "a point that there was no need to emphasize if he was not already thought of as divine" (*New Testament Theology* [Downers Grove: InterVarsity, 2004], 409). A. T. Hanson, *Studies in the Pastoral Epistles* (London: S.P.C.K., 1968), 57–58, is among those who argue that the word μεσίτης ("mediator") originally came from Job 9:33 LXX where Job laments, "I wish there were our mediator and reprover and one to hear the case between us both." While Job complained that God was not a man and therefore he couldn't plead his case before him, the passage in 1 Timothy emphasizes that the mediator whose absence Job deplored had now appeared in Christ Jesus. For a helpful monograph that takes its point of departure from the present verse, see S. O. Stout, *The "Man Christ Jesus": The Humanity of Jesus in the Teaching of the Apostle Paul* (Eugene, OR: Wipf & Stock, 2011).

[137] Cf. J. Jeremias, "πολλοί," *TDNT* 6:543–44. See the discussion in Quinn, "Jesus as Savior and Only Mediator," 254–55.

[138] For the possible anti-Roman polemic (Jesus is the mediator, not the Roman emperor), see Gill, *Jesus as Mediator*.

[139] For discussions of NT terms involving "ransom" or "redemption," see J. C. Edwards, *The Ransom Logion in Mark and Matthew: Its Reception and Its Significance for the Study of the Gospels*, WUNT 2/327 (Tübingen: Mohr-Siebeck, 2012); D. Hill, *Greek Words and Hebrew Meanings*, SNTSMS 5 (Cambridge: Cambridge University Press, 1967), 49–81; I. H. Marshall, "The Development of the Concept of Redemption in the New Testament," in *Reconciliation and Hope*, ed. R. Banks (Grand Rapids: Eerdmans, 1974), 153–69; and L. Morris, *The Apostolic Preaching of the Cross* (Grand Rapids: Eerdmans, 1955), 9–59. See also W. A. Grudem, *Systematic Theology: An Introduction to Biblical Doctrine* (Grand Rapids: Zondervan, 1994), 580–81 (including critique of the "ransom to Satan" theory held by Origen and others).

Mark 10:45: λύτρον).[140] Here the ransom is said to be "for all" (ὑπὲρ πάντων; cf. 2 Cor 5:14–15; Titus 2:11; 1 John 2:2). Jesus gave his life in exchange for (ἀντί) and on behalf of others (ὑπέρ; cf. vv. 1 and 2).[141] "Ransom" involves payment and deliverance from bondage (cf. Titus 2:14).[142] Jesus died so that others might live—including some of those who hold positions of authority. "A testimony *at the proper time*"[143] in the context of vv. 5–7 may refer to Christ's own bearing of witness in giving himself (cf. 6:13; John 18:37; Rom 3:21–30; 5:8) and/or to Paul's testifying by way of preaching (cf. 1 Cor 1:6; 2 Thess 1:10).[144] The exact same phrase "at the [or his] proper time" (καιροῖς ἰδίοις) is found at 6:15 (cf. Titus 1:3), underscoring God's sovereign providence in human history (cf. Gal 4:4; 6:9).

2:7 Before returning to the subject of prayer (for a similar transitional statement see 1:11), Paul affirms that it is the proclamation of the gospel (as explained in vv. 5–6) that is his calling. He has already made clear that he was entrusted with the gospel (1:11) and appointed for service (1:12). Here he asserts that he was made a herald (κῆρυξ, cf. 2 Tim 1:11; 2 Peter 2:5), an apostle (ἀπόστολος, Paul's customary self-designation), and a teacher (διδάσκαλος, cf. 2 Tim 1:11; 4:3) of the Gentiles—the same threefold description as

---

[140] See also Jesus's words at the institution of the Lord's Supper on the night he was betrayed (Mark 14:22–24; cf. 1 Cor 11:24–25). The Matthean/Markan "ransom saying" may, in turn, echo Isa 53:11. For further discussion, see Edwards, *Ransom Logion in Mark and Matthew*, esp. pp. 6–10, 138–58.

[141] As Harris notes, "In 1Ti 2:6 ὑπέρ gains a substitutionary sense under the influence of the ἀντι- in ἀντίλυτρον and the ἀντι of Mk 10:45." M. J. Harris, *Prepositions and Theology in the Greek New Testament: An Essential Reference Resource for Exegesis* (Grand Rapids: Zondervan, 2012), 215; cf. R. E. Davies, "Christ in Our Place: The Contribution of the Prepositions," *TynBul* 21 (1970): 81–90; M. Silva, "ὑπέρ," *NIDNTTE* 4:555. Note also the related uses of ὑπέρ in John 11:50; Rom 5:6, 8; 1 Cor 5:14–15; Gal 3:13; 1 Thess 5:10. A ransom (ἀντίλυτρον), of course, entails the notion of substitution.

[142] J. C. Edwards, "Reading the Ransom Logion in 1 Tim 2,6 and Titus 2,14 with Isa 42,6–7; 49:6–8," *Bib* 90 (2009): 264–66, who argues that the author of 1 Tim 2:6 and Titus 2:14 exhibits a pattern of reading the "ransom saying" in light of Isa 42:6–7 and 49:6–8 (adducing *Barn*. 14.6).

[143] Note that the phrase in the Greek is actually plural: καιροῖς ἰδίοις, though it is universally translated in the singular in the major English translations.

[144] See the discussion in R. D. Balge, "Exegetical Brief: 1 Timothy 2:6—'The Testimony Given in Its Proper Time,'" *Wisconsin Lutheran Quarterly* 98 (2001): 291–92. Quinn ("Jesus as Savior and Only Mediator," 257), with reference to v. 7, argues that "a testimony at the proper time" refers to the apostolic witness.

in 2 Tim 1:11—in faith and truth (cf. Acts 9:15; Romans 9–11; 2 Cor 5:18, 20; 6:1; Gal 2:7; Eph 3:7–9; Col 1:25–27).

"Herald" (NASB, "preacher"), "apostle," and "teacher" describe distinct but partially overlapping roles. For example, "apostle" includes evangelistic proclamation ("herald") and teaching. Paul may use all three terms here and in 2 Tim 1:11 to present himself as a model for Timothy (see 1:16, 18; cf. 2 Tim 4:7) who likewise is exhorted to "preach the word" (κηρύσσω, 2 Tim 4:2) and to teach (διδάσκω, 1 Tim 4:11; 6:2; 2 Tim 2:2), though the term "apostle" is reserved for Paul.[145]

Heralds, proclaiming various kinds of messages and news, were a common feature in the ancient world; Paul's message was the good news of salvation in Jesus Christ (§1.4).[146] "Teacher *of the Gentiles*" again stresses the universal scope of the gospel message and shuts the door on Jewish exclusivism (cf. "everyone" in vv. 4 and 6). The phrase "I am telling the truth, I am not lying" (ἀλήθειαν λέγω οὐ ψεύδομαι, virtually identical to Paul's solemn affirmation in Rom 9:1: Ἀλήθειαν λέγω ἐν Χριστῷ, οὐ ψεύδομαι; cf. 2 Cor 11:31; Gal 1:20) adds further solemnity to Paul's summary of his own calling. It is also possible that the apostle's authority was challenged by some in Ephesus (cf. 2 Cor 10:10).

Concluding our discussion of 2:1–7, Paul's first major instruction to Timothy in the body of this letter, we may register the following biblical-theological observations.

1. The passage attests to the foundational nature of the mission theme in the LTT (§1). Paul's underlying concern here is to promote the kind of peaceful environment that lends itself to the expeditious and unhindered proclamation of the gospel.
2. Most likely in contrast to the false teachers, and in keeping with his mission calling to the Gentiles, Paul contends that the gospel should be proclaimed to all (i.e., by implication, not only to Jews). In this way he sets himself against any

---

[145] On Paul's role as a teacher within the context of first-century Greco-Roman education, see F. M. Young, *The Theology of the Pastoral Letters*, New Testament Theology (Cambridge: Cambridge University Press, 1994), 89.

[146] See esp. N. T. Wright, "Paul's Western Missionary Project: Jerusalem, Rome, Spain in Historical and Theological Perspectives," in *The Last Years of Paul: Essays from the Tarragona Conference, June 2013*, ed. A. Puig i Tàrrech, J. M. G. Barclay, and J. Frey, WUNT 352 (Tübingen: Mohr-Siebeck, 2015), 60.

elitist or exclusivistic conception of Christianity that may have been propagated by the opponents.

3. Paul invokes the fact that God is one—the central Jewish confession—to advance his argument that there's only one way of salvation for all. He goes on to argue that Jesus—assumed to be divine, but human as well, and thus able to act as a mediator—is the only mediator between God and humanity by virtue of the ransom he paid for human sin.
4. In this way Paul invokes theology, Christology, and soteriology to drive home a missiological point. Rather than being a theologian advocating mission, Paul, the missionary, engages in theological reasoning to refute defective theological, Christological, and soteriological views held by his opponents, first and foremost because he considered them to have a detrimental effect on the cause of his Gentile mission which extended to all.[147]

2:8 Paul now moves past his first main topic, the offering of various kinds of prayer (vv. 1–2), to the second related injunction (οὖν, "therefore," here and in v. 1, there translated "then"). He wants the men in the congregation to unite in prayer (προσεύχεσθαι; cf. v. 1 and 5:5) without any hint of anger or argument. Just as Jews prized ritual purity, NT believers were to pray with their hands cleansed from any spiritual defilement or impurity (ὁσίους χεῖρας, "holy hands").[148] The plural (τοὺς ἄνδρας, "[the] men") points to a plurality of men leading the congregation in prayer and worship (cf. v. 12; 3:2, 5; 4:11–16; 5:17).[149]

---

[147] On the formative influence of Paul's missionary calling on his theology, see I. H. Marshall, *New Testament Theology: Many Witnesses, One Gospel* (Downers Grove: InterVarsity, 2004), 34: "New Testament theology is essentially missionary theology"; and T. R. Schreiner, *Paul: Apostle of God's Glory in Christ* (Downers Grove: InterVarsity, 2006), esp. chaps. 2–4, who contends that Paul was fundamentally a missionary who understood his mission in theological terms.

[148] Technically, "holy" (ὅσιος) can modify either the action of "lifting" the hands or the "hands" themselves. S. E. Porter, "1 Timothy 2:8: Holy Hands or Holy Raising?," in S. E. Porter, *Linguistic Analysis of the Greek New Testament: Studies in Tools, Methods, and Practice* (Grand Rapids: Baker, 2015), 339–46, argues for the former ("men lifting [their] hands in holiness"), but the meaning of the passage is not significantly affected whichever option is chosen.

[149] G. J. Stiekes, "Liturgy in the Pastoral Epistles," *Artistic Theologian* 2 (2013): 45–46, argues against Fee that Paul has men *in particular* in mind as "taking leadership in prayer among the people of God." He does not see Paul as restricting women

1 Timothy 2:8

The immediate point of reference of "in every place" (ἐν παντὶ τόπῳ) is most likely the various house churches making up the Ephesian church, though ultimately the scope is universal (cf. 1 Cor 1:2; 2 Cor 2:14; 1 Thess 1:8; cf. Mal 1:11 LXX; §1).[150] The lifting up of hands in prayer was practiced in OT times and is attested in Second Temple Jewish, Greco-Roman, and Christian literature.[151] By this time "lifting up hands" in prayer may have become a figurative expression similar to "wash[ing] the saints' feet" (5:10). In a congregation devoted to prayer, there must be neither anger (ὀργή; cf. Eph 4:31; Col 3:8) nor argument (διαλογίσμος; cf. Phil 2:14). Paul's teaching here echoes that of Jesus (Matt 5:22–24; cf. 6:14–15; 18:21–35; Mark 11:25).

Paul's concern, similar to Jesus's, is the removal of barriers for the purpose of effective prayer (1 Cor 7:5; Eph 4:26–27; cf. 1 Pet 3:7). His main emphasis is on the word "holy" (ὁσίους; cf. Titus 1:8; Heb 7:26). The picture Paul paints is that of a church submitted to authority and united in prayer for the salvation of all. If there's unity (v. 8), and if there's order (vv. 9–15), the church's mission will be able to proceed without hindrance or disruption.

Bridge

While Christians aren't normally in positions of government themselves, they're not therefore to completely disengage from the political process. At a minimum they're to pray for those in authority so that the environment will be stable and conducive

---

from prayer but does note that "even when women pray in 1 Cor 11:5, 13 the issue is raised over the symbols of their submissiveness to authority."

[150] E. Ferguson, "Τόπος in 1 Timothy 2:8," *ResQ* 33 (1991): 65–73, surveys the Jewish and early Christian usage of the phrase ἐν παντὶ τόπῳ and concludes that 1 Tim 2:8 should be understood as a reference to "men leading in prayer 'in the Christian assemblies'" (p. 73).

[151] C. Pearson surveys relevant OT texts (Gen 14:22; Deut 32:40; 1 Kgs 8:22ff; Ezra 9:5; Neh 8:6; Pss 28:2; 44:20; 63:4; 88:9; 134:2; 141:2; Lam 1:17; 2:19; 3:41–42) and argues that the practice of "lifting hands in prayer" in the OT is virtually always associated with lament, conveying dependence on God, but Pearson doesn't adequately define "lament," and it's not clear that the passages he discusses bear out his conclusion. C. Pearson, "Lifting Holy Hands? Comparing Contemporary Practice with Biblical Injunctions and Descriptions," *Journal of the Grace Evangelical Society* 21 (2008): 65–76; Pearson, "'Lifting Holy Hands': Nuance, Nuisance, or Error? A Biblical Theology of the Practice of Lifting Hands in Worship," *Artistic Theologian* 2 (2013): 26–36.

for gospel propagation. If this was true in the days of Emperor Nero, who in a bout of madness set Rome on fire and blamed the Christians, resulting in untold suffering and martyrdom, it's certainly true in our day. On the premise that there's one God and Savior and one mediator between God and humans, the Lord Jesus Christ, men ought to lead the church in a spirit of unity and gospel centeredness. Paul will next elaborate on the role of women in the church.

B. Regarding Women (2:9–15)[152]

> [9] Also, the women are to dress themselves in modest clothing, with decency and good sense, not with elaborate hairstyles, gold, pearls, or expensive apparel, [10] but with good works, as is proper for women who profess to worship God. [11] A woman is to learn quietly with full submission. [12] I do not allow a woman to teach or to have authority over a man; instead, she is to remain quiet. [13] For Adam was formed first, then Eve. [14] And Adam was not deceived, but the woman was deceived and transgressed. [15] But she will be saved through childbearing, if they continue in faith, love, and holiness, with good sense.

Relation to Surrounding Context

In the context of his instructions for proper conduct in God's household which span 2:1–3:16, Paul moves from believing prayer for the governing authorities to proper leadership in the congregation. Verse 8 has already highlighted the apostle's concern that the church be free from contention. This concern continues to be in view as he now addresses the proper role of women in the church. The following unit (3:1–7) will then address proper qualifications for (male) church leaders, followed by a section on (male and female) deacons (3:8–13) and a concluding section (3:14–16).

Structure

The opening "Also" connects this section with the previous injunction regarding men engaging in unified prayer. This is now the equivalent injunction regarding women, suggesting that unity

---

[152] For the massive literature on this passage, see the research bibliography in A. J. Köstenberger and T. R. Schreiner, eds., *Women in the Church: An Analysis and Application of 1 Timothy 2:9–15*, 3rd ed. (Wheaton: Crossway, 2016), 363-406.

and freedom from contention is again the overriding concern. At first the focus is on modest dress, accompanied by good works, revealing a godly inner disposition (vv. 9–10). This same disposition is then urged with regard to women learning in the gathered assembly. As in vv. 9–10, so also in vv. 11–12 proper conduct is contrasted with improper conduct. Paul's command is supported with reference to creation order (v. 13) and the fall (v. 14). The unit closes with a reference to women's devotion to their God-given calling and continuance in faith, love, and holiness (v. 15).

2:9–10 Paul now moves on to address women's proper decorum with regard to attire and activities in the local church.[153] With regard to the former (2:9–10), women are to dress modestly; with regard to the latter (2:11–15), they must not teach or exercise

---

[153] For the Ephesian background, see esp. S. M. Baugh, "A Foreign World: Ephesus in the First Century," in *Women in the Church*, 3rd ed., 27–66; Baugh, "The Apostle among the Amazons," *WTJ* 56 (1994): 153–71. For a discussion of the Roman background, see R. Berg, "Wearing Wealth: *Mundus Muliebris* and *Ornatus* as Status Markers for Women in Imperial Rome," in *Women, Wealth and Power in the Roman Empire*, ed. P. Setälä, R. Berg, R. Hälikkä, M. Keltanen, J. Pölönen, and V. Vuolanto, Acta Instituti Romani Finlandiae 25 (Rome: Institutum Romanum Finlandiae, 2002), 15–73; B. W. Winter, "The 'New' Roman Wife and 1 Timothy 2:9–15: The Search for a *Sitz im Leben*," *TynBul* 51 (2000): 285–94; more broadly Winter, *Roman Wives, Roman Widows: The Appearance of New Women and the Pauline Communities* (Grand Rapids: Eerdmans, 2003). See also F. R. Ames and J. D. Miller, "Prayer and Syncretism in 1 Timothy," *ResQ* 52 (2010): 65–80, who contend that vv. 9–10 are concerned with eliminating Artemisian syncretism. Rather than emulating the elaborate adornment of Artemisian women, Christian women in Ephesus are to pray in modest attire, trusting God. G. G. Hoag, "Decorum and Deeds in 1 Timothy 2:9–10 in Light of *Ephesiaca* by Xenophon of Ephesus," *ExAud* 27 (2011): 134–60, explores the passage against the backdrop of a document he dates to about AD 50; see also Hoag, *Wealth in Ancient Ephesus and the First Letter to Timothy: Fresh Insights from* Ephesiaca *by Xenophon of Ephesus*, BBRSup 11 (Winona Lake, IN: Eisenbrauns, 2015), with reference to 2:9–15; 3:1–13; 6:1–2a; 6:2b–10; and 6:17–19. A helpful survey including judicious interaction is provided by Thornton, *Hostility in the House of God*, 99–103 (see, e.g., his critique of P. B. Payne, "Libertarian Women in Ephesus: Response to D. J. Moo's Article, '1 Timothy 2:11–15: Meaning and Significance,'" *TJ* 2 [1981]: 185–90, on pp. 130–32). For a comparison between the *Haustafeln* in Ephesians and Colossians and similar passages in the LTT from a pseudonymous vantage point see B. Fiore, "Household Rules at Ephesus: Good News, Bad News, No News," in *Early Christianity and Classical Culture: Comparative Studies in Honor of Abraham J. Malherbe*, ed. J. T. Fitzgerald, T. H. Olbricht, and L. M. White, NovTSup 110 (Leiden: Brill 2003), 600–604 (but note that he thinks the passage is addressed to husbands and wives).

authority over men. The striking parallel in 1 Pet 3:1–6 (esp. vv. 2–4) makes clear that the injunction in vv. 9–10 isn't unique to Paul but represents standard apostolic teaching.[154] Paul uses the term ὡσαύτως ("also") elsewhere in the LTT to mark the transition between addressing different groups of people (3:8, 11; Titus 2:3, 6). In all likelihood the phrase "in every place" is implied from the previous verse, indicating the universal applicability of Paul's commands (cf. 3:15). The predicate "are to" is implied from the previous verse as well (βούλομαι, v. 8).

What do Paul's directives concerning men in v. 8 and his instructions concerning women in vv. 9–10 share in common? The common element is most likely the idea of holiness. Men are to pray in a holy manner, that is, in a contention-free spirit. Women, likewise, are to exhibit holiness, not only at prayer (προσεύχεσθαι, "to pray," like the other terms mentioned in the previous paragraph, may be implied from the preceding verse),[155] but in their

---

[154] See the exploration of the ancient Greco-Roman background in A. J. Batten, "Neither Gold nor Braided Hair (1 Timothy 2.9; 1 Peter 3.3): Adornment, Gender and Honour in Antiquity," *NTS* 55 (2009): 484–501, in particular regarding the way in which women's adornment may have had economic and social status implications. However, Batten doesn't consider biblical-theological factors, such as Paul's stated rationale in vv. 13–14, which skews her analysis of 1 Tim 2:9 as being exclusively a function of social and economic forces (see esp. p. 499). See also the investigation by A. B. Huizenga, "Epitomizing Virtue: Clothing the Christian Woman's Body," in *Christian Body, Christian Self: Concepts of Early Christian Personhood*, ed. C. K. Rothschild and T. W. Thompson, WUNT 284 (Tübingen: Mohr-Siebeck, 2011), 261–81, who discusses 1 Tim 2:9–10 (which she considers post-Pauline) against the backdrop of Greek paraenetic texts on the topic of women's apparel (hairstyle, clothing, jewelry, cosmetics, perfumes and oils, food and drink, bathing) and argues that three issues stand behind references to specific items of adornment: (1) uneasiness with ostentatious display of wealth; (2) the perception of women as weaker and more likely to act on sexual desires than men; (3) the notion that adornment is gendered as feminine and relates to the female physical body. As well, S. E. Hylen, *A Modest Apostle: Thecla and the History of Women in the Early Church* (Oxford: Oxford University Press, 2015), 45–49, suggests that the injunction on women's adornment doesn't indicate that an actual problem existed in that regard but simply served as "prescriptive rhetoric" to criticize the opponents' viewpoints. However, the parallel she adduces in Livy's *History* is inexact, and the simplest reading of 1 Tim 2:9–10 suggests that Paul did understand female modesty to be a live issue in the Ephesian church.

[155] Contra K. L. Cukrowski, "An Exegetical Note on the Ellipsis in 1 Timothy 2:9," in *Transmission and Reception: New Testament Text-Critical and Exegetical Studies*, Texts and Studies: Contributions to Biblical and Patristic Literature, Third

entire lives. Their "dress," as it were, ought to be good works. "Dress . . . in modest clothing" translates the more literal "adorn themselves with modest deportment" (καταστολή; only here in the NT; cf. Isa 61:3 LXX; Josephus, *J.W.* 2.126), which, while primarily referring to dress, also includes modest attitude (cf. Epictetus, *Diatr.* 2.10.15). "Modest" (κόσμιος) occurs with reference to male overseers in 3:2 ("respectable"; κοσμέω occurs in 1 Pet 3:5; used figuratively in Titus 2:10).

The term "decency" (αἰδοῦς) is unique in the NT (Josephus, *Ant.* 2.50–52, refers to Joseph challenging Potiphar's wife to chastity); "good sense" (σωφροσύνης) recurs in v. 15 (cf. Acts 26:25). "Good sense," in the sense of self-control, was one of the four Greek primary virtues, conveying self-mastery with regard to bodily passions.[156] Modesty in dress and conduct was commonly viewed as an important virtue for Christian women (1 Pet 3:1–6), as were good works (5:10; Acts 9:36; Rom 16:6, 12). In all likelihood Paul's remarks are hyperbolic and thus shouldn't be interpreted as absolute prohibition of braids, jewelry, or nice clothes. Paul's primary purpose was to promote a focus on women's inner beauty and godly character rather than on their external appearance. The dual principle is that Paul "is prohibiting not only extravagant and ostentatious adornment but also clothing that is seductive and enticing."[157]

Modesty with regard to a woman's external appearance and a focus on her inward character stands in contrast with the pagan practice of dressing up for public festivals in a woman's finest garments. The decadent, extravagant styles of fashion in Rome, with the empress serving as the prime role model, quickly spread to the

---

Series 4, ed. J. W. Childers and D. C. Parker (Piscataway, NJ: Gorgias, 2006), 232–38, who suggests that only the verb βούλομαι should be supplied. See K. Zamfir and J. Verheyden. "Text-Critical and Intertextual Remarks on 1 Tim 2:8–10," *NovT* 50 (2008): 376–406, who argue that both options are possible and that the present passage represents a relecture (rereading) of 1 Cor 11:4–15, particularly vv. 4–5, 7a.

[156] The importance of the term σωφροσύνη for the interpretation of vv. 9–15 is stressed, and the ancient Greek philosophical background explored, by A. J. Malherbe, "The *Virtus Feminarum* in 1 Timothy 2:9–15," in *Renewing Tradition: Studies in Texts and Contexts in Honor of James W. Thompson*, ed. M. W. Hamilton, T. H. Olbricht, and J. Peterson, Princeton Theological Monograph Series 65 (Eugene, OR: Pickwick, 2007), 45–65.

[157] T. R. Schreiner, "An Interpretation of 1 Timothy 2:9–15: A Dialogue with Scholarship," in *Women in the Church*, 3rd ed., 185. See the discussion on pp. 178–86.

rest of the Greco-Roman world and found eager followers among women everywhere who copied the elaborate hairstyles and fashion trends promulgated in the empire's capital.[158] According to Paul, however, Christian women ought to take a different approach. They should express their spirituality in modest attire that doesn't betray a preoccupation with their physical appearance or indulge in self-centered vanity but expresses devotion toward God and humility toward others.

"Worship God" renders the noun θεοσέβεια, a NT *hapax* and virtual synonym of εὐσέβεια.[159] The expression is also found in the LXX in the sense of "fear of God" or "godliness" (Gen 20:11; Job 28:28; cf. Bar 5:4; Sir 1:24; 4 Macc. 7:6, 22) and the church fathers, where it is variously rendered "piety," "religion," or "reverence" (*2* Clem. 20.4; Diogn. 1; 3.3; 4.5). Women's focus in expressing their Christian religion should be on good works (2 Tim 2:21; 3:17; Titus 3:1; cf. Matt 5:16 and v. 15 below).[160] Rather than being unduly preoccupied with what women may *not* do (vv. 11–12), churches ought rather to focus on what they *should* do in practicing their Christian faith (vv. 9–10, 15).[161] This is in keeping with the importance of proving one's faith by one's deeds (Jas 2:14–17). Examples of such women in the book of Acts include Dorcas (Acts 9:36), Lydia (Acts 16:14), and Priscilla (Acts 18:1–3, 26).[162]

---

[158] See Baugh, "Foreign World," 57–58; Winter, *Roman Wives*, 97–109. See also Thornton, *Hostility in the House of God*, 106, who provides representative quotes by Epictetus: "Immediately, after they are fourteen, women are called 'ladies' by men. And so when they see that they have nothing else but only to be the bedfellows of men, they begin to beautify themselves, and put all their hopes in that" (*Ench*. 40); Seneca, who said the "new Roman women" were wearing dresses that were so revealing that removing them "exposed no greater nakedness" (*Helv*. 16.5); and Juvenal: "There is nothing that a woman will not permit herself to do, nothing that she deems shameful, when she encircles her neck with green emeralds, and fastens huge pearls to her elongated ears" (*Sat*. 6.458–59).

[159] Θεοσέβεια and εὐσέβεια are paralleled in Philo, *Creation* 154–55. It is difficult to determine why the less common term is used here; perhaps it is simply a matter of stylistic variation.

[160] "Good works" (ἔργα ἀγαθά/καλά) terminology is found in the NT almost exclusively in the LTT (5:10, 25; 6:18; Titus 2:7, 14; 3:8, 14; although see Eph 2:10; cf. Acts 9:36).

[161] The word πρέπω ("proper") in v. 10 means "suitable" or "appropriate": cf. Titus 2:1; see also 1 Cor 11:13; Eph 5:3.

[162] Hoag, "Decorum and Deeds in 1 Timothy 2:9–10," 158–59.

2:11–12 In this important passage, Paul prohibits women from teaching, understood as "the authoritative and public transmission of tradition about Christ and the Scripture," which is usually a function of the elders or overseers (§4.3.1).[163] "A woman" refers to women generically (cf. "women" in vv. 9–10 and v. 15 and the generic reference to "men" in v. 8).[164] "Learn quietly" contrasts with "teach," while "full submission" corresponds to "have authority over a man":

[11] A woman is to *learn quietly* with *full submission*.	[12] I do not allow a woman to *teach* or to *have authority* over a man.

Women should not be put in positions of ultimate leadership over the church and serve as elders or pastor-teachers.[165] That they don't aspire to roles God doesn't intend for them to hold is part of women's proper modesty (cf. vv. 9–10). In fact, the first woman

---

[163] Schreiner, "Dialogue," 192–93. Cf. the summary by K. Zamfir, "Women Teaching—Spiritually Washing the Feet of the Saints? The Early Christian Reception of 1 Timothy 2:11–12," *Annali di Storia dell'Esegesi* 32 (2015): 358: "According to ancient cultural conventions, women may not speak in public and wield authority over men. . . . Women teaching men reverse this normal relationship. In 1 Timothy, too, women who teach in public, moreover, teach men, exercise illegitimate authority, regardless of the content of their teaching. Such activity is prohibited." In her survey of patristic interpreters, Zamfir finds that the concern was women's "teaching in itself, not its content" (p. 378). K. L. Waters, "Saved through Childbearing: Virtues as Children in 1 Timothy 2:11–15," *JBL* 123 (2004): 703–35, argues unconvincingly that vv. 11–15 represent an allegory in which certain virtues are depicted as children of Ephesian women who will be saved. J. Hübner, "Revisiting the Clarity of Scripture in 1 Timothy 2:12," *JETS* 59 (2016): 99–117, argues, equally unconvincingly, that the passage is unclear and thus inapplicable. However, one presumes the passage was clear to Timothy, its original recipient, and it is clear to many (esp. in the non-Western world) today. That said, there are, of course, areas of contemporary application that may be adjudicated in a variety of ways.

[164] F. J. Long, "A Wife in Relation to a Husband: Greek Discourse Pragmatic and Cultural Evidence for Interpreting 1 Tim 2:11–15," *Journal of Inductive Bible Studies* 2, no. 2 (2015): 6–43, implausibly contends that the reference is limited to husband-and-wife relationships. Arguably, the reference in v. 8 is to men in general, not merely to husbands; likewise, the reference in vv. 9–10 is to women in general, not merely to wives (see discussion above). Long's gloss of v. 14 as referring to "the wife" (p. 39) is unpersuasive as well. Thus his critique of A. J. Köstenberger, "A Complex Sentence: The Syntax of 1 Timothy 2:12," in *Women in the Church*, 2nd ed., 53–84, is invalid (p. 40).

[165] For a biblical-theological treatment of this subject, see A. J. and M. E. Köstenberger, *God's Design for Man and Woman: A Biblical-Theological Survey* (Wheaton: Crossway, 2014), chap. 6.

yielded to the temptation of stepping outside her God-given role, which precipitated the fall (v. 14). It has at times been alleged that the prohibition is due to local or cultural factors, whether women's lack of education, their assertiveness in aspiring to political and/or ecclesiastical offices, or various other factors. However, background research hasn't confirmed this, and the explicit rationale for vv. 11–12 stated in vv. 13–14 strongly suggests otherwise.[166]

The context (vv. 9–10) requires that "a woman" here refers to women in general, not merely wives (after all, it's not only *married* women who should observe propriety in dress and external appearance but *all* women). The present prohibition for women not to teach or have authority over men therefore applies to *all* women rather than merely to *wives* in relation to their husbands (in which case one would also expect a qualifier such as "their own," ἴδιος).

The emphasis in the injunction "A woman is to learn" (μανθανέτω, cf. 5:4; 2 Tim 3:14; Titus 3:14) is not on learning as such but on learning *in a certain manner*—"quietly with full submission" (cf. 1 Cor 14:35). This injunction, while sounding strange to modern ears, is entirely in keeping with the role of women in ancient Jewish and Greco-Roman culture. It stands in contrast with Paul's description of sensual young widows who roam idly from house to house (5:13) and of weak-willed women who are "always learning but never able to come to a knowledge of the truth" (2 Tim 3:7). It's also in line with his concern that people "not be unfruitful" (Titus 3:14). Also, the command to "learn" implies that Christian doctrine is taught in the congregation (see comments on διδάσκειν in v. 12 below; see also 3:2; 5:17).

The term ἡσυχία (variously translated "silence," "quietly," or "quietness") probably doesn't convey absolute silence here (as in Acts 22:2; cf. Luke 14:4) but rather corresponds to the "quiet," peaceful life mentioned in v. 2 (ἡσύχιον; cf. 1 Thess 4:11; 2 Thess 3:12). The parallel 1 Pet 3:4, which commends a "gentle and quiet spirit," hardly envisions women literally being silent at all times.

---

[166] See Baugh, "Foreign World"; see also S. J. Friesen, "Ephesian Women and Men in Public Religious Office in the Roman Period," in *100 Jahre Österreichische Forschungen in Ephesos. Akten des Symposions Wien 1995*, ed. H. Friesinger, F. Krinzinger, B. Brandt, and K. R. Krierer (Wien: Österreichische Akademie der Wissenschaften, 1999), 107–13; E. A. Judge, "§2 A Woman's Behaviour," *NewDocs* 6:18–23; and R. A. Kearsley, "§3 Women in Public Life," *NewDocs* 6:24–27.

"Quietly" here therefore conveys submissiveness to Christian teachers in contrast to rebellion against authority (note the parallel "with full submission"). Just as Paul elsewhere calls wives to submit to their husbands at home (e.g., Eph 5:22), he here extends the principle to the church, understood as God's "household" (cf. 3:4–5, 12, 15), where women are called to submit to the teaching and ruling authority of the church's male leadership (§4.3.2).

The verb "permit" (ἐπιτρέπω; cf. 1 Cor 14:34; 16:7) is roughly equivalent to βούλομαι (used in v. 8 and implied in v. 9) and may be used alternatively here for the sake of stylistic variation. The expression conveys Paul's apostolic authority (1:1; v. 7; cf. 1 Cor 14:34) and is used elsewhere in the NT with regard to a person in authority granting permission for another person to speak (Acts 21:39–40; 26:1). The references to the divine order of creation and its violation at the fall in vv. 13–14 ground vv. 11–12 in universal rather than merely cultural norms.[167]

"Teaching" (διδάσκειν) is elsewhere in the LTT an integral part of the role assigned to Paul's apostolic delegates and the overseers/elders of the church (3:2; 4:11; 5:17; cf. 1 Cor 12:28–29; Eph 4:11; Jas 3:1). The teaching in view in v. 12, therefore, is "the public transmission of authoritative material (cf. 1 Tim. 4:13, 16; 6:2; 2 Tim. 4:2; Titus 2:7)."[168] Teaching also entails refuting false teaching (1:3, 10; 4:1; 6:3; 2 Tim 4:3; Titus 1:9, 11) and passing on apostolic teaching to successive generations (2 Tim 1:12, 14; 2:2). The directive that women not teach men pertains to situations where women would be teaching men by preaching to a congregation including both men and women.

"Exercise (or have) authority" (αὐθεντεῖν) in the present context is tantamount to being in charge of and responsible for a church in its entirety by holding the office of overseer/elder (see 3:4–5; 5:17).[169] The contrast with "full submission" (see v. 11 above)

---

[167] This is insufficiently recognized by J. G. Stackhouse Jr., *Partners in Christ: A Conservative Case for Egalitarianism* (Downers Grove: InterVarsity, 2015), rev. and exp. ed. of *Finally Feminist? A Pragmatic Christian Understanding of Gender*, Acadia Studies in Bible and Theology (Grand Rapids: Baker, 2005), who claims that, as in the case of slavery, the NT teaching on gender affirms the status quo but only temporarily.

[168] Schreiner, "Dialogue," 193.

[169] Regarding αὐθεντεῖν, see esp. the extensive treatment by A. Wolters, "The Meaning of ΑΥΘΕΝΤΕΩ," in *Women in the Church*, 3rd ed., 67–117, who shows

and the parallel structure with the term "teaching" make clear that the expression αὐθεντεῖν has no necessary negative connotation.[170] Paul's use of functional terminology ("teach," "exercise authority") makes reference to those in the church who exercise these functions by virtue of holding a certain office (i.e., overseer/elder/pastor-teacher; cf. 3:2, 4–5; 5:17; Acts 20:17, 28; Eph 4:11).

The phrase "over a man" (ἀνδρός, like γυναικί used generically) most likely qualifies "have authority over." Women are not to occupy positions in the church that involve permanent ruling functions over men; these are reserved for males. At the same time, nothing said here keeps women from ministering to other women (Titus 2:3–5) or children (Eph 6:4; 2 Tim 1:5; 3:14–15; cf. Acts 16:1). Neither does the passage rule out the private instruction of men by women together with their husbands (Acts 18:25-26) or their participation in the church's decision making on an informal or advisory basis.

Finally, the phrase "instead, she is to remain quiet" (set off by the strong contrastive term ἀλλά, untranslated in the NIV) reinforces Paul's directive for women to accept their proper role (here,

---

that the evidence strongly supports a nonpejorative and noningressive rendering of αὐθεντεῖν as "exercising authority over" in v. 12; see also Wolters, "A Semantic Study of αὐθέντης and Its Derivatives," *JBMW* 11 (2006): 44–65; Wolters, "Αὐθέντης and Its Cognates in Biblical Greek," *JETS* 52 (2009): 719–29; Wolters, "An Early Parallel of αὐθεντεῖν in 1 Tim 2:12," *JETS* 54 (2011): 673–84; and H. S. Baldwin, "A Difficult Word: αὐθεντέω in 1 Timothy 2:12," in *Women in the Church*, 2nd ed., 39–51, who notes that the only pre-Pauline instances of the term are Philodemus, *Rhet.* 133.14 ("those in authority" [1st c. BC]) and *BGU* 1208.38 ("exercised authority" [27 BC]). The understanding advocated here stands against recent treatments such as J. Hübner, "Revisiting αὐθεντέω in 1 Timothy 2:12: What Does the Extant Data Really Show?," *Journal for the Study of Paul and His Letters* 4 (2015): 41–70; C. L. Westfall, "The Meaning of αὐθεντέω in 1 Timothy 2.12," *JGRChJ* 10 (2014): 138–73.

[170] Regarding the syntax of v. 12, see esp. A. J. Köstenberger, "A Complex Sentence: The Syntax of 1 Timothy 2:12," in *Women in the Church*, 3rd ed., 119–63. For the history of the debate see Köstenberger, "A Complex Sentence: The Syntax of 1 Timothy 2:12," in *Women in the Church*, 2nd ed., 53–84; Köstenberger, "Syntactical Background Studies to 1 Timothy 2:12 in the New Testament and Extrabiblical Greek Literature," in *Discourse Analysis and Other Topics in Biblical Greek*, ed. S. E. Porter and D. A. Carson (Sheffield: JSOT, 1995), 156–79; the challenge by P. B. Payne, "1 Tim 2.12 and the Use of *oude* to Combine Two Elements to Express a Single Idea," *NTS* 54 (2008): 235–53; and the surrejoinder by Köstenberger, "The Syntax of 1 Timothy 2:12: A Rejoinder to Philip B. Payne," *JBMW* 14 (2009): 37–40. See also T. R. Schreiner, "Review of P. B. Payne, *Man and Woman, One in Christ*," *JBMW* 15 (2010): 43–44.

not to teach or exercise authority over men) without agitation or disruption. Women should refrain from exercising authoritative public teaching functions and be silent in this regard. Similarly, in 1 Cor 14:26–35 women are told not to participate in the evaluation of prophecy, while it was earlier assumed that they would pray or prophesy during public worship (1 Cor 11:5).

2:13–14 Paul's rationale (causal γάρ) for this prohibition is twofold, invoking both Genesis 2 and 3 (§7.1.4).[171] Positively, the apostle points to the order of creation: Adam, the man, was created first, then Eve, the woman (v. 13; cf. 1 Cor 11:8–9).[172] The term "formed" (πλάσσω) confirms that the reference is to the Genesis account (cf. Gen 2:7, 15, 19 LXX). As commonly understood in Jewish thought, primogeniture (being the firstborn) entails certain privileges. This is true all the more with regard to "first creation."[173] The principle Paul adduces is supported by a close reading of the Genesis fall narrative, where Adam, not Eve, is held responsible for the fall (Gen 3:9), an indication of his ultimate responsibility for the human couple (cf. Rom 5:12–19).

Negatively, Paul was concerned that people in the church avoid the scenario that had precipitated the fall where Satan

---

[171] "For" (γάρ) gives the reason for Paul's command in v. 12 (v. 14 provides a second reason linked with "and," καί). Efforts to diminish the force of γάρ here and to downgrade it to a mere illustration or example fail to convince, since elsewhere in the LTT γάρ following a command almost invariably denotes the reason for that command (4:7–8, 16; 5:4, 11, 15, 18; 2 Tim 1:6–7; 2:7, 16; 3:5–6; 4:3, 5–6, 9–10; 4:11, 15; Titus 3:1–3, 9, 12; the only exceptions are 1 Tim 3:13 and 2 Tim 2:11). See D. K. Huttar, "Causal γάρ in 1 Timothy 2:13: A Response to Linda L. Belleville," *JBMW* 11 (2006): 30–33; and Schreiner, "Dialogue," 212–18. See also G. J. Stiekes, "The Fall of Eve in Paul" (Ph.D. diss., Southeastern Baptist Theological Seminary, 2016), esp. his coverage of Second Temple Jewish literature in chap. 3 and his study of references to Eve in Paul's writings in chap. 4.

[172] See B. L. Merkle, "Paul's Arguments from Creation in 1 Corinthians 11:8–9 and 1 Timothy 2:13–14: An Apparent Inconsistency Answered," *JETS* 49 (2006): 527–48.

[173] Contra W. J. Webb, *Slaves, Women & Homosexuals: Exploring the Hermeneutics of Cultural Analysis* (Downers Grove: InterVarsity, 2001), 134–45, who contends that Paul's rationale in v. 13 is merely cultural. For helpful responses, see W. Grudem, "Should We Move Beyond the New Testament to a Better Ethic?," *JETS* 47 (2004): 327–28; B. Reaoch, *Women, Slaves, and the Gender Debate: A Complementarian Response to the Redemptive-Movement Hermeneutic* (Phillipsburg: P&R, 2012); and T. R. Schreiner. "William J. Webb's *Slaves, Women and Homosexuals:* A Review Article," *The Southern Baptist Journal of Theology* 6, no. 1 (2002): 46–65.

deceived the woman.[174] The role reversal had been complete: rather than God being in authority over the man, who was in authority over the woman, who were in authority over the animal world (including the serpent), the pattern prevailing at the fall was the exact opposite: the serpent tempted and deceived the woman, who exerted leadership over the man, and both rebelled against God and transgressed his command. Both positively and negatively, therefore, Paul directs that the man, not the woman, function in roles of ultimate leadership and responsibility for the church.

In v. 14 the apostle in all likelihood observes that, according to the Genesis fall narrative, Eve was the first target of deception (cf. 2 Cor 11:3), with disastrous results, rather than suggesting that Eve was more gullible than Adam or that Adam was never deceived.[175] Less likely, the term "first" from v. 13 is to be implied in v. 14 as well ("And Adam was not deceived *first*"). If so, Paul's point would be that Adam wasn't the *first* to be deceived, suggesting that the woman by herself, apart from her husband, was in a more vulnerable position in dealing with Satan's temptation. That said, it's more likely that Paul's comment, "And Adam was *not* deceived" (v. 14), is to be taken at face value.

The fact that Paul is rooting his directive in the order of creation rather than providing a cultural rationale strongly suggests that vv. 11–12 are permanently applicable.[176] The fact that Paul

[174] The shift from ἀπατάω (cf. Eph 5:6; Jas 1:26) in the case of Adam to ἐξαπατάω (cf. Rom 7:11; 16:18; 1 Cor 3:18; 2 Cor 11:3; 2 Thess 2:3) in the case of Eve is probably merely stylistic (cf. Gen 3:13, ἀπατάω).

[175] For a study of other texts addressing Eve's deception by the serpent, see Hanson, *Studies in the Pastoral Epistles*, 65–77, 129–30, who discusses 4 Macc 18:6–8; Philo; Jewish apocryphal literature; 2 Cor 11:1–3, 14; the Protevangelium of James; and rabbinic evidence. On Jewish views concerning Eve and childbirth as they relate to 1 Tim 2:13–15, see S. Y.-W. Chan, "1 Timothy 2:13–15 in the Light of Views Concerning Eve and Childbirth in Early Judaism" (Ph.D. diss., Dallas Theological Seminary, 2006). In particular, see chap. 3 on the portrayal of Eve in early Judaism. See also M. Korpel and J. de Moor, *Adam, Eve, and the Devil: A New Beginning*, Hebrew Bible Monographs 65 (Sheffield: Sheffield Phoenix, 2014).

[176] R. W. Wall, "1 Timothy 2:9–15 Reconsidered (Again)," *BBR* 14 (2004): 81–103, argues that the intent behind the passage is theological and missionary rather than ontological and sociological, encouraging women to witness to the surrounding culture by their modesty, good works, and submission to male teachers, not because their female gender made them second class, more susceptible to deception, or better suited for the domestic sphere (p. 83). This, however, is too dichotomous a way

grounds his command in the order of creation, not only the fall, also contradicts the argument that female submission to male leadership in the church is solely a result of the fall.[177] This is clearly not how Paul read the creation narrative (cf. 1 Cor 11:8–9). In applying and extending God's order of creation to the church and in attempting to avoid the negative consequences of the fall, Paul places ultimate responsibility for teaching and exercising authority in the church on qualified men (see 3:1–7 below). For this reason, women are not to listen to the opponents whose false teaching subverted sound doctrine but instead are to learn from qualified and duly appointed teachers in the church.

2:15 The first woman didn't adhere to her proper domain and consequently fell into sin. How will women in the church age avoid succumbing to the same fate? They'll be preserved from Satan if they adhere to their God-given role focused on their family and home (with "childbearing" constituting a figure of speech called synecdoche, in which the part, "childbearing," stands for the whole, "being devoted to a woman's domestic sphere"; cf. 5:14: "to marry, have children, manage their households").[178] The word rendered "saved" (σῴζω) is here better rendered "preserved" in light of Paul's concern that believers be kept safe from the devil and the false teachers (cf. 5:15). In this vein Timothy will help preserve his listeners if he pays close attention to his life and teaching

---

of putting things and unduly diminishes the abiding nature of Paul's rationale in vv. 13–14. A similar argument is set forth by R. G. Gruenler, "The Mission-Lifestyle Setting of 1 Tim 2:8–15," *JETS* 41 (1998): 215–38.

[177] As is commonly held by evangelical feminists: see, e.g., S. J. Grenz with D. M. Kjesbo, *Women in the Church: A Biblical Theology of Women in Ministry* (Downers Grove: InterVarsity, 1995), 165: "Egalitarians, in contrast, argue that it [women's subordination] is a result of the Fall."

[178] On women's condition in first-century Ephesus with regard to physical childbirth, see Baugh, "Foreign World," 54–55. Baugh notes that the reference to women's preservation in childbirth "would have caught the attention of every Ephesian" in light of the fact that "young women faced significant dangers in childbirth, particularly where diet, health problems, and the rudimentary medical skills of the time made pregnancy and childbirth a very real threat to the lives of both mother and baby" (p. 55). Baugh mentions a document that relates a mother's deep relief that her daughter "escaped" (ἐκφεύγω) the ordeal of childbirth (S. R. Llewelyn, *NewDocs* 9:57–58). Note also in this connection M. Hubbard, "Kept Safe through Childbearing: Maternal Mortality, Justification by Faith, and the Social Setting of 1 Timothy 2:15," *JETS* 55 (2012): 743–62.

(4:16). The false teachers, on the other hand, are a tool of Satan attempting to deceive those in the church at Ephesus.[179]

With regard to Paul's instructions for men and women thus far (vv. 8–15), v. 15 brings a sense of closure. While the apostle doesn't want women to teach or exercise authority over men (which would amount to overstepping their God-given boundaries), he urges them to devote themselves to their domestic role (which is how they'll be preserved from the devil, unlike Eve who overstepped her God-given boundaries and consequently was deceived).[180] This preservation, in turn, depends on women's continuance in faith, love, and holiness, with "good sense" (σωφροσύνη, an *inclusio* with v. 9, "good sense"; see above). Paul's teaching shouldn't be misconstrued as *confining* women to the home; it aims at delineating women's proper *focus*, not *exclusive* sphere of involvement. What's more, if "childbearing" is an idiom for a woman's focus on her family and home, v. 15 is more directly applicable to single women as well.

In biblical-theological terms, this section of the letter proceeds on the notion of the importance of unity and order in God's household, the church (§4.1). Men are to be united in prayer (v. 8), and women are to excel in good works and modesty and submit to male teaching and leadership in the church, devoting themselves to their domestic and familial calling (vv. 9–15). Importantly, Paul grounds his teaching in this section in the foundational teaching on God's design for man and woman in Genesis 1–2 and, negatively, in the scenario at the fall (Genesis 3). This underscores the unity of Scripture and the essential continuity between the God-ordained order in the natural household and the corresponding order in God's household, the church (cf. 1 Tim 3:2, 4–5, and 15 below).

---

[179] See Köstenberger, "Ascertaining Women's God-Ordained Roles," 107–44, followed by C. Smith, *God's Good Design: What the Bible Really Says about Men and Women* (Kingsford, NSW, Australia: Matthias Media, 2012), 37–40.

[180] Contra Hubbard ("Kept Safe through Childbearing," 743–62), who argues that the passage means "God will be faithful to those who are faithful, and he will keep you safe even through this harrowing ordeal of childbirth." However, Hubbard makes too little of the spiritual preservation theme in the LTT that extends beyond mere physical preservation. For further interaction, see Köstenberger and Köstenberger, *God's Design for Man and Woman*, 218–19n40. Also contra C. R. Hutson, "'Saved through Childbearing': The Jewish Context of 1 Timothy 2:15," *NovT* 56 (2014): 392–410, who similarly interprets the passage against the backdrop of Jewish traditions about why women die in childbirth.

Bridge

Paul's command in v. 12 that women not teach or exercise authority over men in the church runs counter to a strong egalitarian emphasis in Western culture. And yet it is of a timeless nature in that it is grounded in God's design for man and woman at creation and supported by the scenario at the fall where the woman usurped the man's leadership and the man abdicated his leadership role with disastrous results.[181] Far from being an isolated passage, the present unit is part of a pervasive biblical pattern of male leadership and male-female partnership.[182] God's design for man and woman is one of dignity, respect, and partnership, and its application in our day calls for great wisdom and discernment.[183]

C. Qualifications for Church Leaders (3:1–13)

Candidates for overseer (male only) must meet certain qualifications (3:1–7), as do candidates for deacon (male or female, 3:8–13; see discussion below; §4.3.2). The following initial observations will provide a general framework for the more detailed commentary to follow.

1. The qualifications for church leaders are general in nature (see, e.g., v. 1: "anyone"; v. 15: "people"). While occasioned by the presence of false teachers in the church at Ephesus (1:3–4), Paul's directives are broadly relevant and not limited to the original occasion.
2. The qualifications for church leaders don't differ substantially from Greco-Roman ideals of a virtuous person. The type of person qualified to lead the church would thus command respect from people in the surrounding pagan culture.

---

[181] Contra Derek Tidball and Dianne Tidball, *The Message of Women: Creation, Grace and Gender*, The Bible Speaks Today (Downers Grove: InterVarsity, 2012), 249–68, who argue the passage is culturally relative and "was never meant as a fixed principle" (p. 268).

[182] See Köstenberger and Köstenberger, *God's Design for Man and Woman*. Contra Tidball and Tidball, *Message of Women*.

[183] See Köstenberger and Köstenberger, *God's Design for Man and Woman*, chap. 8: "God's Design Lived Out Today."

3. The standards set for church leaders are reasonable and attainable. The underlying idea is personal integrity and maturity, not perfection. In fact, many of the same qualities are encouraged for all believers.
4. The qualifications primarily relate to character and conduct. The reason for this may be that godliness and sound teaching go hand in hand, while false teaching will inevitably result in an ungodly way of life.
5. Timothy's task as an apostolic delegate, unlike that of Titus (Titus 1:5), is not the first-time appointment of elders (cf. Acts 20:17–38). Rather, he is to ensure that elders meet proper qualifications and replace any errant elders with properly qualified ones. Paul has already hinted that two false teachers should be excommunicated (whether elders or not). Later, he refers to charges against sinning elders (5:19–20) and urges Timothy not to be hasty in appointing church leaders (raising the specter that this may have happened previously; 5:22).
6. The division between chapters 2 and 3 obscures the integral relationship between them. Just as the "trustworthy saying" in 1:15 doesn't start a new unit but continues the discussion in vv. 12–14, the saying in 3:1 continues the discussion of proper and improper church leadership in 2:12–15 (see esp. the prohibition of women from teaching or exercising authority over men in 2:12 and the requirement that overseers be faithful husbands in 3:2).
7. The terms ἐπίσκοπος and διάκονος are variously translated "bishop"/"deacon" (KJV), "supervisor"/"helper," or otherwise.[184] While not reflecting the hierarchical pattern that emerged in the second century, the roles do refer to the formal church offices of overseer/elder and deacon.
8. Paul stipulates two offices, overseer/elder and deacon, that confer on the officeholders official standing and, in the case of overseer/elder, ruling and teaching authority. New Testament ministry is not only charismatic—that is, a function of spiritual gifting—within the framework of the

[184] L. T. Johnson, *Letters to Paul's Delegates: 1 Timothy, 2 Timothy, Titus*, The NT in Context (Valley Forge, PA: Trinity Press International, 1996), 142–43, 151.

NT teaching of the priesthood of all believers, certain qualified men are assigned an authoritative office (ἐπισκοπή, 3:1) in the church.

9. There are no stipulations of term limits. Elders may have served indefinitely unless they were removed for doctrinal error or moral failure or excused themselves for some other reason (such as moving away from the area or poor health). The role of deacons, on the other hand, may have been more contingent on concrete needs in the local church.

1. Overseers (3:1–7)

[1]This saying is trustworthy: "If anyone aspires to be an overseer, he desires a noble work." [2]An overseer, therefore, must be above reproach, the husband of one wife, self-controlled, sensible, respectable, hospitable, able to teach, [3]not an excessive drinker, not a bully but gentle, not quarrelsome, not greedy. [4]He must manage his own household competently and have his children under control with all dignity. [5](If anyone does not know how to manage his own household, how will he take care of God's church?) [6]He must not be a new convert, or he might become conceited and incur the same condemnation as the devil. [7]Furthermore, he must have a good reputation among outsiders, so that he does not fall into disgrace and the devil's trap.

Relation to Surrounding Context

The unit starts with the second "trustworthy saying" in this letter (cf. 1:15). That said, there's no major shift in subject matter from the previous chapter. The topic continues to be proper conduct in God's household (vv. 5, 15) and now, specifically, proper qualifications for church leaders. These are particularly important in light of the presence of false teachers (cf. 1:3), who may have arisen from within the church and in some cases, at least, may still have awaited censure by Timothy (cf. 5:17–25). In some cases this may have resulted from appointing church leaders prematurely (v. 6; cf. 5:22). The qualifications are largely congruent with the similar list in Titus 1:6–9. The assumption that overseers be male (see the "husband of one wife" requirement in v. 2; cf. Titus 1:6) is consistent with the previous injunction that women not teach or exercise authority over men in the church (2:12).

Structure

The unit is introduced by an affirmation in the form of a "trustworthy saying" regarding overseers (v. 1). This is followed by a list of qualifications, both positive and negative (vv. 2–7), including a parenthetical statement regarding the overseer's household management in v. 5. Specifically, Paul first lists seven positive traits (v. 2), followed by four negative ones (v. 3), and then elaborates on three final qualifications in greater detail, in each case supplying a rationale (vv. 4–7). A possible *inclusio* is supplied by the opening requirement that an overseer be "above reproach" and the concluding stipulation that he "have a good reputation among outsiders."

3:1 After issuing instructions concerning prayer and the proper roles of men and women in the church, Paul now stipulates specific requirements for church leaders.[185] In the original context this meets Timothy's need for guidance in giving direction to the church at Ephesus. Beyond this, as the general nature of vv. 1 ("anyone") and 15 ("how people ought to [act]") makes clear, Paul's directions transcend the immediate occasion. At this critical juncture, the apostle sets forth qualifications for church leaders that possess continuing validity for the church.[186]

Paul transitions into the new subsection with another "trustworthy saying" (πιστὸς ὁ λόγος; cf. 1:15): "If anyone aspires to be [NASB "aspires to the office of"] an overseer, he desires a noble work."[187] "Aspires" (ὀρέγεται) recurs in 6:10 with reference to the

---

[185] For a helpful survey, see D. A. Mappes, "Moral Virtues Associated with Eldership," *BSac* 160 (2003): 202–18, who argues that some of the qualifications are designed to contrast true and false teachers and discusses the list of qualifications within the larger context of the power of the personal example in the LTT. Mappes also compares elder qualifications in 1 Tim 3:1–6 with Greco-Roman lists of virtues and vices (pp. 207–12). See also J. K. Goodrich, "Overseers as Stewards and the Qualifications for Leadership in the Pastoral Epistles," *ZNW* 14 (2013): 77–97; and B. A. Paschke, "The *cura morum* of the Roman Censors as Historical Background for the Bishop and Deacon Lists of the Pastoral Epistles," *ZNW* 98 (2007): 105–19, who investigates the *cura morum* ("care of manners") practiced by Roman censors investigating the private life of candidates for the Roman senate.

[186] Cf. B. L. Merkle, "Are the Qualifications for Elders or Overseers Negotiable?," *BSac* 171 (2014): 172–88.

[187] Some have argued, unconvincingly, that the "trustworthy saying" is the confession at the end of the chapter (3:16–18). Others, equally unconvincingly, have contended that the saying is found at the end of chap. 2. See Knight, *Faithful Sayings*, 52–55.

false teachers' love of money (elsewhere in the NT only in Heb 11:16). Such an aspiration is a noble pursuit (lit., "a good work"; καλοῦ ἔργου).[188] Interestingly, Paul does not mention a divine call to the ministry as a requirement here but instead speaks of an aspiration or desire (cf. 1 Pet 5:2).

The terms "overseer" (ἐπίσκοπος) and "elder" (πρεσβύτερος) refer to one and the same office in the LTT and elsewhere in the NT (Titus 1:5, 7; cf. Acts 20:17, 28).[189] In v. 1 the word ἐπισκοπή (cf. Acts 1:20) is used to denote the "office of overseer" (cf. Luke 19:44; Acts 1:20; 1 Pet 2:12). In v. 2 ἐπίσκοπος refers to the person serving in such a role (cf. Acts 20:28; Phil 1:1; Titus 1:7; 1 Pet 2:25; regarding πρεσβύτερος, see esp. 5:1–2, 17, 19; Titus 1:5; 1 Pet 5:1, 5; Jas 5:14). In the LXX the expression designates someone in charge of a given operation (Num 4:16). The Qumran equivalent was the *mebaqqer* (1QS 6:12, 20; CD 9:18–19, 22; 13:6–7). The term πρεσβύτερος is Jewish in origin, generally signifying seniority, whereas ἐπίσκοπος is of Greek provenance, indicating a person's superintending role.[190]

In keeping with his customary pattern (Acts 14:23), Paul instructed Titus likewise to "appoint elders in every town" (Titus 1:5). The two-tiered leadership structure—overseers/elders and deacons—found in the present passage corresponds to the two offices attested in the church at Philippi (Phil 1:1). Presumably,

---

[188] The church fathers are replete with admonitions to seek the service, but not honor, involved in this role; cf. Gorday, ed., *Colossians, 1–2 Thessalonians, 1–2 Timothy, Philemon*, 168–69. For other references to "good works" in the singular see 2 Tim 2:21; 3:17; Titus 1:17; 3:1; for references in the plural, see 1 Tim 2:10; 5:10, 25; 6:18; Titus 2:7, 14; 3:8, 14.

[189] See B. L. Merkle, *The Elder and Overseer: One Office in the Early Church*, StBibLit 57 (New York: Peter Lang, 2003); T. R. Schreiner, "Overseeing and Serving the Church in the Pastoral and General Epistles," in *Shepherding God's Flock: Biblical Leadership in the New Testament and Beyond*, ed. B. L. Merkle and T. R. Schreiner (Grand Rapids: Kregel, 2014), 100–101. As J. R. W. Stott, *Guard the Truth: The Message of 1 Timothy & Titus*, The Bible Speaks Today (Downers Grove: InterVarsity, 1996), 90, rightly notes, it's anachronistic to translate ἐπίσκοπος as "bishop" because "the development of the 'monarchial episcopate' (a single bishop presiding over a college of presbyters) cannot be dated earlier than Ignatius of Syrian Antioch, c. AD 110)."

[190] For a helpful study (including a critique of J. Jeremias), see J. P. Meier, "*Presbyteros* in the Pastoral Epistles," *CBQ* 35 (1973): 323–45. Meier discusses 1 Tim 5:1–2; 5:17, 19; Titus 1:5–7; and 1 Tim 4:14.

overseers/elders made up the "council of elders" (πρεσβυτέριον) mentioned in 1 Tim 4:14. The survey below lays out the basic framework for church leadership set forth in the LTT and Paul's other NT letters.

Two-Tiered Structure: 1 Timothy **3:1–12; Philippians 1:1**

First Tier: Overseers/Elders/Shepherds
(cf. Eph 4:11: pastor-teacher)

Composed of:

A plurality of men[191]

Plurality: 1 Tim 4:14: "council of elders"; plural in Phil 1:1; Titus 1:5; Acts 20:17, 29; 1 Pet 5:1–2

Men: 1 Tim 2:12: not a woman; 1 Tim 3:2 = Titus 1:6: faithful husband

Synonymous terms:

Titus 1:5–7: "appoint *elders* . . . an *overseer*" (same qualifications as those for *overseers* in 1 Tim 3:1–7)

Acts 20:17, 28: "the *elders* of the church . . . Be on guard . . . for all the flock of which the Holy Spirit has appointed you as *overseers*, to *shepherd* the church of God . . ."

1 Pet 5:1–3: "I exhort the *elders* among you as a fellow *elder* . . . *Shepherd* God's flock among you, not *overseeing* out of compulsion but willingly . . . being examples to the flock"

Terminology:

"Overseer" refers to the function of giving oversight to the church

"Elder" refers to life stage/experience and commensurate status in community

"Shepherd" (pastor) is a metaphor for personal care for members of the church

Function:

Ruling (all, jointly) and teaching (some)

---

[191] The singular reference to "overseer" in v. 2 is generic. Thus it may well have a plurality of elders in view, esp. in conjunction with the plural references to elders/overseers elsewhere in the NT. This is true despite the fact that in v. 8 "deacons" is found in the plural, joined with the conjunction "likewise."

1 Tim 3:2: "able to teach"
1 Tim 5:17: "elders who are good leaders . . . especially those who work hard at preaching and teaching"
Titus 1:9: "to encourage with sound teaching and to refute those who contradict it"
1 Thess 5:12: "give recognition to those who labor among you and lead you (ESV: "are over you") in the Lord and admonish you"

Summary:
The biblical pattern is for a group of elders to give joint oversight to a local congregation, with one or several pastors being primarily devoted to teaching and providing pastoral care.

Second Tier: Deacons

Composed of:
Male (1 Tim 3:8–10, 12) and
Female deacons (1 Tim 3:11; Rom 16:1: Phoebe)

Function:
Term means "servant"
"Able to teach" not a requirement
Nonruling, nonteaching function

Summary:
Deacons assist those who give oversight to the church by helping meet a variety of needs in the local church.

3:2 The overseer/elder/pastor bears ultimate responsibility for the church before God (cf. v. 15; 5:17). According to the instructions in the previous chapter on women's roles (esp. v. 12), the office is limited to men. This is confirmed by the "husband of one wife" requirement in the present verse.[192] What are the qualifications for this honorable office?[193] First, an overseer must be

[192] For a survey of patristic interpretations of the "husband of one wife" requirement, see D. G. Hunter, "'A Man of One Wife': Patristic Interpretations of 1 Timothy 3:2, 3:12, and Titus 1:6 and the Making of Christian Priesthood," *Annali di storia dell'esegesi* 32 (2015): 333–52. Hunter observes that the requirement merged in the patristic period with conceptions of the priestly identity of church leaders.

[193] As Schreiner, "Overseeing and Serving," 102, rightly notes, the list is representative rather than exhaustive.

"above reproach" (ἀνεπίλημπτον; cf. Titus 1:7: ἀνέγκλητος).[194] Just like Daniel in OT times (see Dan 6:4), this person must be a man of integrity against whom no legitimate charge can be brought. He must be a mature individual with solid, proven character. This, in fact, is Paul's desire for all believers (5:7), not just church leaders, and applies to Timothy as well (6:14). In addition, "above reproach" may serve as an umbrella term for all the following characteristics.

The requirement of being, literally, a "one-wife-type-of-husband" resembles that of the Roman *univira* (a "one-husband-type-of-wife").[195] This term conveying marital fidelity initially applied to wives during their lifetime and later became an epithet husbands gave to their wives after they died, as is attested by numerous extant tombstone inscriptions. The understanding that this requirement was aimed at excluding polygamists is implausible because polygamy wasn't a widespread practice in the Greco-Roman world of the time. More likely Paul here excludes men with one or several concubines.[196] This common practice conflicted with biblical morals since sexual union with a concubine constituted adultery and amounted to polygamy. Most likely, therefore, "husband of one wife" represents an idiom for marital faithfulness (e.g., NIV: "faithful to his wife").[197]

This is further suggested by the parallel wording in 5:9, where a widow must have been "the wife of one husband" in order to be eligible for church support and where the equivalent phrase ἑνὸς ἀνδρὸς γυνή is used (cf. 1 Cor 7:2–5). In that case the issue is not polyandry (simultaneous marriage to multiple husbands) because Paul addresses women bereft of their husbands. It's inconceivable that Paul would first have encouraged younger widows to remarry only to disqualify them later because they had been married more than once. The same requirement obtains also for deacons (v. 12). It is in keeping with the prohibition of adultery in the Decalogue

[194] Note the *inclusio* between "above reproach" in v. 2 and "good reputation among outsiders" in v. 7.

[195] Cf. M. Lightman and W. Zeisel, "*Univira*: An Example of Continuity and Change in Roman Society," *Church History* 46 (1977): 19–32.

[196] A work attributed to Demosthenes is often cited in this regard: "Mistresses we keep for the sake of pleasure, concubines for the daily care of our persons, but wives to bear us legitimate children and to be faithful guardians of our households" (*Neaer.* 59.122; trans. DeWitt and DeWitt).

[197] See S. Page, "Marital Expectations of Church Leaders in the Pastoral Epistles," *JSNT* 50 (1993): 105–20, esp. 108–9 and 114n27.

(Exod 20:14; Deut 5:18). Marital fidelity was held in high regard in the Greco-Roman world; thus this quality would commend such men to people in their pagan surroundings.[198]

If this is correct, divorced (and remarried) men wouldn't necessarily be disqualified from serving as overseers or deacons, especially if the divorce was biblically legitimate (i.e., in cases of a wife's marital unfaithfulness, Matt 19:9; remarriage owing to the death of a spouse, Rom 7:2–3; or desertion by an unbelieving wife, 1 Cor 7:15–16). This might also be the case if the divorce occurred in the distant past (especially if the man wasn't a believer at the time) and if his present pattern and proven track record indicate marital faithfulness. Nevertheless, in conjunction with the requirement that overseers be "above reproach" (which includes community reputation), it may often be preferable not to appoint divorcees to the role of overseer, especially when other qualified candidates are available that have not been divorced.[199]

The requirement does also not apply to unmarried candidates, who would be required to practice sexual abstinence. In light of Paul's positive stance toward the gift of celibacy elsewhere in his writings, it's safe to assume that a man's singleness wouldn't have disqualified him from service as overseer/elder.[200] Nevertheless, the "husband of one wife" requirement assumes that a candidate for church office will normally be married. This, incidentally, ran counter to the teaching propagated by the false teachers in Timothy's day who were known to "forbid marriage" (4:3). In light of these considerations, the present statement "does not mean that bishops had to be married; it just commends marriage as something that is not at all inconsistent with the episcopal [pastoral] office."[201]

The overseer/elder must be self-controlled (νηφάλιον), which is required also of female deacons (v. 11; see below) and older women (Titus 2:2). He must also be sensible (NASB, "prudent";

[198] Ibid., 117–18.

[199] See A. J. Köstenberger with D. W. Jones, *God, Marriage, and Family: Rebuilding the Biblical Foundation*, 2nd ed. (Wheaton: Crossway, 2010), chap. 12.

[200] Contra R. F. Collins, *Accompanied by a Believing Wife: Ministry and Celibacy in the Earliest Christian Communities* (Collegeville, MN: Liturgical Press, 2013), 225: "The requirement that a leader of the Church be married only once means that he be married and that he remain faithful to his wife."

[201] J. Calvin, *1 & 2 Timothy & Titus* (1556; repr., Wheaton: Crossway, 1998), 54.

σώφρονα; cf. Titus 1:8), a quality likewise desired in older and younger men (Titus 2:2, 6), older and younger women (Titus 2:5; cf. 1 Tim 2:9, 15), and believers in general (Titus 2:12). He must be respectable (κόσμιον; cf. 1 Tim 2:9; vv. 4, 8), hospitable (φιλόξενον; cf. Titus 1:8; 1 Pet 4:9),[202] and able to teach (διδακτικόν; 2 Tim 2:24; contrast 1 Tim 2:12). Notably, "able to teach" is not included among the qualifications for deacons, which indicates that teaching—and the commensurate authority—is a special prerogative and responsibility of overseers (cf. Titus 1:9; 2:1–10).

3:3 To the seven positive traits of maturity listed in the previous verse, Paul adds four negative ones: (1) not an excessive drinker (μὴ πάροινον; cf. Titus 1:7; see also 1 Tim 3:8; Titus 2:3), a reference to moderation rather than total abstinence;[203] (2) not a bully (i.e., violent; μὴ πλήκτην; cf. Titus 1:7) but gentle (ἐπιεικῆ; cf. Phil 4:5; Titus 3:2; Jas 3:17; 1 Pet 2:18); (3) not quarrelsome (ἄμαχον; cf. Titus 3:2); (4) not greedy (lit., "a lover of money," ἀφιλάργυρον; cf. Heb 13:5; contrast 1 Tim 6:10; Luke 16:14; 2 Tim 3:2). By contrast the false teachers who are depicted by Paul as argumentative and motivated by financial gain exhibit at least some of these traits (6:4–5, 9–10). The compensation for overseers would have been modest, hence the need for contentment. Also, their position involves financial oversight, which requires integrity. For these reasons the possession of any of these negative characteristics—all of which apply to every believer, not just church leaders (cf., e.g., Eph 5:18; Titus 3:2; 1 Tim 6:10)—would disqualify someone from serving as overseer.

3:4–7 After listing these eleven traits in brief, Paul discusses three further qualifications in greater detail. The candidate for overseer must (1) manage his own household competently (v. 4:

---

[202] Note that "hospitality" may primarily relate to people opening their home to traveling believers, particularly teachers (3 John 5–8); see further the brief discussion at 1 Tim 5:9–10 below.

[203] On Paul's stance toward the drinking of wine, see A. Merkt, "Reading Paul and Drinking Wine," in *Asceticism and Exegesis in Early Christianity: The Reception of New Testament Texts in Ancient Ascetic Discourses*, NTOA/SUNT 101, ed. H.-U. Weidemann (Göttingen: Vandenhoeck & Ruprecht, 2014), 69–77, who contends that Paul advocated what later came to be called the principle of *discretio*, that is, one must take into account the particular situation and disposition of the person involved (p. 77). See also the discussion in H.-U. Weidemann, "Engelsgleiche, Abstinente—und ein moderater Weintrinker: Asketische Sinnproduktion als literarische Technik im Lukasevangelium und im 1. Timotheusbrief," in ibid., 60–63.

προϊστάμενον, "be in charge of, preside over"; cf. Rom 12:8; 1 Thess 5:12; 1 Tim 3:12; 5:17)[204] and have his children under control with all dignity (cf. Titus 1:6); (2) not be a new convert; and (3) have a good reputation with those outside the church.

In each case Paul gives a rationale. In the first instance he establishes an analogy between a man's natural household and God's "household," the church (v. 5; cf. v. 15). The argument is from the lesser to the greater: if such a man cannot manage (προστῆναι) his own family, how can he be expected to care for God's church? The implied answer is self-evident: he cannot. The requirement for church leaders to manage their own households competently excludes candidates who are capable leaders but whose private lives are in disarray. Also, as in the home, overseers must care for God's people gently rather than rule with an iron fist (in Luke 10:34–35, ἐπιμελέομαι, "care for," denotes the tender care exercised by the good Samaritan). "*God's* church" underscores the sacredness and solemn responsibility of caring for God's people. "Having children in submission" (ὑποταγή; with reference to women in 1 Tim 2:11) means that a man commands the respect (σεμνότης; elsewhere in the NT only in 2:2; Titus 2:7; cf. 1 Tim 3:12; Titus 1:6) of his children in the home and that he is able to institute God's order for the family in his home.

Second, Paul expresses concern that a candidate not be trapped by the devil, a concern that is part of the larger preservation theme in the LTT (vv. 6–7; cf. 2:14–15; 5:14–15; 2 Tim 2:26; §3.5.7). "New convert" (v. 6) comes from the Greek word for "newly planted" (νεόφυτος; in a literal sense in Job 14:9; Pss 128:3; 144:2; Isa 5:7). If drafted into service prematurely, such an untested individual will likely "become conceited" (τυφόομαι; cf. 6:4; 2 Tim 3:4) and fall into the same condemnation as the devil (v. 6). How much better it is to wait until his "airy ideas have been subdued."[205]

---

[204] J. H. Neyrey, "Teaching You in Public and from House to House (Acts 20.20): Unpacking a Cultural Stereotype," *JSNT* 26 (2003): 81–82, culls from ancient literature various "male duties in the private world of the household": controlling his children, arranging and providing dowries for wise marriages for his daughters, properly using patrimony, fulfilling funeral rites for parents, protecting the virtue and reputation of the women in the household, and overseeing slaves and servants in the household.

[205] Calvin, *1 & 2 Timothy & Titus*, 57.

Third, Paul requires of a candidate for overseer not only spiritual maturity and healthy relationships but also a good reputation (μαρτυρία, cf. Titus 1:13) with those outside the church. Otherwise, he will fall into disgrace (ὀνειδισμός)—an offense that should be caused only by the reproach of Christ borne for the sake of the gospel (cf. Rom 15:3; Heb 10:33; 11:26; 13:13)—and the devil's "trap" (παγίς; cf. 6:9: greed; 2 Tim 2:26: deception). However, "there is no need to multiply its [the world's] opportunities by unnecessary scandal, in addition to the necessary offense of the cross."[206]

Bridge

Historically this was the time when the aging apostle sought to make provision for the continuing administration of the Christian church. Clearly Paul thought the character of church leaders to be of primary significance. Also, Paul primarily focused on a man's character rather than external characteristics, in particular his marriage and leadership of his family. In short, such a man must be mature, command the respect of others, and exhibit self-control. The strategic importance of church leadership cannot be overestimated. In any age, people neglect this issue at their own peril and will likely pay a price for doing so.

2. Deacons (3:8–13)

As in the case of overseers, some general observations will put this section into perspective:

1. Structurally, ὡσαύτως ("likewise") in vv. 8 and 11 suggests that qualifications are given for two other types of individuals in addition to candidates for overseer. The way v. 11 is placed between vv. 8–10 and vv. 12–13 suggests one larger category, the office of deacon, with qualifications for male and female officeholders and a closing general statement pertaining to both. The two offices of elder and deacon are also mentioned in Phil 1:1.
2. By comparison with the qualifications for overseers, one notes the absence of terms related to teaching or ruling (most notably, "able to teach," see v. 2; see also v. 5b). This

[206] C. K. Barrett, *The Pastoral Epistles*, New Clarendon Bible (Oxford: Clarendon, 1963), 60.

suggests that, in keeping with the term διάκονος, "servant," deacons don't bear ultimate responsibility for the church. At the same time they, too, occupy a formal office that has particular requirements.

3. While not part of the ruling body of the church, deacons occupy an important role. This is indicated by the similarity between the qualifications for overseers and deacons. While Paul doesn't spell out the precise realm of service, deacons most likely are to render all kinds of practical and administrative help required to run a church, including benevolence, finances, physical maintenance, and a wide variety of other services and ministries.
4. Overseers/elders are in charge of the entire congregation (e.g., 5:17), including deacons, so that deacons should submit to overseers/elders just as all church members are to do.

Relation to Surrounding Context

The transition "likewise" indicates that Paul now moves on to a second church office, that of deacon. Again Paul lists a number of qualifications. While Paul didn't permit women to serve as overseers (2:12; cf. 3:2), he here stipulates qualifications for women deacons (the most likely understanding of v. 11). This underscores the biblical pattern of male leadership and male-female partnership.

Structure

As mentioned, v. 8 signals a second church office. Verses 8–10 are devoted to male deacons; v. 11 turns to women (whether deaconesses or deacons' wives, the former being more likely); v. 12 then returns to male deacons; and v. 13 rounds out the discussion by stating the rewards that come from serving well as a deacon.

> [8]Deacons, likewise, should be worthy of respect, not hypocritical, not drinking a lot of wine, not greedy for money, [9]holding the mystery of the faith with a clear conscience. [10]They must also be tested first; if they prove blameless, then they can serve as deacons. [11]Wives, too, must be worthy of respect, not slanderers, self-controlled, faithful in everything. [12]Deacons are to be husbands of one wife, managing their children and their own households competently. [13]For those who have served well as deacons acquire a good standing for themselves and great boldness in the faith that is in Christ Jesus.

3:8–10 Deacons (cf. Phil 1:1; not mentioned in Titus), "likewise" (cf. 2:9; v. 11; Titus 2:3, 6), must meet certain requirements. Positively, they are to be worthy of respect (σεμνός, cf. Phil 4:8; 1 Tim 3:11; Titus 2:2). Negatively, they should not be hypocritical (διλόγους; lit., "double-tongued," NASB); drink a lot of wine (cf. Titus 2:3); or be greedy (μὴ αἰσχροκερδεῖς; cf. Titus 1:7; 1 Pet 5:2). Rather, they must hold the "mystery [NIV: "deep truths"] of the faith" (cf. v. 16) with a clear conscience (cf. 1:5, 19), in marked contrast to the opponents (cf. 1:5–6, 19–20).

Like the candidates for the office of overseer (καί, "also"; translated in the NASB and CSB but not NIV), those who desire to serve as deacons must first be tested. If they pass this test (δοκιμάζω, only here in the LTT but sixteen times elsewhere in Paul) and prove blameless (ἀνέγκλητος, a synonym of ἀνεπίλημπτος, v. 2, required of overseers in Titus 1:6–7 and elsewhere in the NT only in 1 Cor 1:8; Col 1:22), they may serve (διακονέω; it's unclear whether the testing should be understood as formal or informal examination).

3:11 "Wives, too" (CSB) translates γυναῖκας, which can also mean "women [deacons]" or "deaconesses" (NIV, "the women"; NASB, "women"). The meanings "woman" (2:9, 10, 11, 12, 14) and "wife" (3:2, 12; 5:9; cf. Titus 1:6) are both found in this letter; context must decide. On the whole, "women deacons" is preferable, for the following reasons:

1. the absence of qualifications for overseers' wives;
2. the adverb ὡσαύτως ("too") indicating an office similar to that of male deacon;
3. the parallel sentence structure and characteristics in vv. 8 and 11;
4. the absence of a qualifier for γυναῖκας such as "their."[207]

[207] J. H. Stiefel, "Women Deacons in 1 Timothy: A Linguistic and Literary Look at 'Women Likewise . . .' (1 Tim 3.11)," *NTS* 41 (1995): 442–57. As Quinn and Wacker, *Letters to Timothy*, 286, rightly note, the conspicuous absence of any references to these women's family lives (such as children, marital faithfulness; cf. 5:9 for widows) renders it unlikely that these women are wives of male deacons who team up with them in diaconal ministry. This suggests that these women needn't be married. In the Ephesian context, since these women were free from childrearing and homemaking responsibilities (1 Tim 2:15; 5:14), they could devote themselves to Christian ministry in the local church (cf. 1 Cor 7:34). For this reason churches today should appoint male or female deacons on an individual basis rather than

The reason Paul didn't call these women "deaconesses" is that in his day the word διάκονος (plus the respective article to indicate gender) was still used for both males and females; the term *diakonissa* was coined only later (*Apos. Con.* 8.19, 20, 28).[208] Phoebe is called a διάκονος of the church at Cenchrea in Rom 16:1. Later (ca. AD 115), Pliny the Younger refers to two female deaconesses (*ministrae*) in Bithynia under Trajan's rule (*Ep.* 10.96.8).

Paul's reference to deaconesses coheres well with his earlier prohibition of women serving in teaching or ruling functions over men (2:12) and reference to male overseers in vv. 1–7. Since serving as a deacon doesn't involve teaching or ruling, both men and women are eligible to function in this capacity. The requirements for deaconesses are therefore similar to those for male deacons.

Positively, they should be worthy of respect (σεμνάς; cf. v. 8; Titus 2:2). Negatively, they should not be slanderers (διαβόλους; cf. v. 8; 2 Tim 3:3; Titus 2:3) but self-controlled (νηφαλίους; cf. vv. 2–3, 8; Titus 2:2) and faithful in everything (πιστὰς ἐν πᾶσιν; cf. 3:9; 5:16; 2 Tim 2:2; Titus 1:6; etc.). Compared to overseers, certain requirements are omitted with regard to male and female deacons: hospitable, able to teach, good reputation with outsiders, not a new convert. While the omission of "able to teach" is almost certainly significant, the lack the reference to the other requirements may merely be incidental. Also, in the case of women, there's no equivalent to "faithful husbands," perhaps because female deacons, as mentioned, weren't necessarily expected to be married.

3:12–13 The discussion of female deacons (or deacons' wives) is followed by additional comments regarding male deacons. Paul

---

married couples only, with husbands and wives serving jointly. (Of course, if both husband and wife are qualified, they may both be appointed to serve.) See also B. L. Blackburn, "The Identity of the 'Women' in 1 Timothy 3.11," in *Essays on Women in Earliest Christianity*, vol. 1, ed. C. D. Osburn (Joplin, MO: College Press, 1993), 303–19; J. Hübner, *A Case for Female Deacons* (Eugene, OR: Wipf & Stock, 2014); and G. R. Perry, "Phoebe of Cenchreae and 'Women' of Ephesus: 'Deacons' in the Earliest Churches," *Presbyterion* 36, no. 1 (2010): 32–33. For texts from early church commentators who speak of women deacons in 1 Tim 3:11, see K. Madigan and C. Osiek, eds., *Ordained Women in the Early Church: A Documentary History* (Baltimore: Johns Hopkins University Press, 2005), 19–21.

[208] Bjelland Kartzow, *Gossip and Gender*, 134, notes that "specifically feminine gender terms for 'women deacons/deaconesses' are not attested until the fourth century."

adds that such deacons, like overseers, must be "husbands of one wife" (i.e., faithful husbands; see on v. 2 above) who manage their children and households competently (cf. vv. 4–5). Paul closes his discussion on an encouraging note, adding that those who have served well acquire a good standing (βαθμὸν καλόν, only here in the NT)—that is, can expect to be recognized for their faithful service—and great boldness in the faith (cf. 2 Cor 3:12; 7:4; Phlm 8). These benefits, rather than financial gain, should be rewards for faithful service in the church.

Bridge

Discussions of deacons in the NT are comparatively rare; apart from the present passage we find references to deacons only in Phil 1:1 ("To all the saints . . . including the overseers and deacons") and Rom 16:1 ("our sister Phoebe, who is a servant of the church"), not to mention the precursors of the deacon office, the Seven, in Acts 6:1–6. While elders oversee, teach, and shepherd God's flock, deacons, both male and female, serve to meet a variety of practical needs in the church.

D. Purpose of Paul's Letter and Concluding Confession (3:14–16)

[14] I write these things to you, hoping to come to you soon.
[15] But if I should be delayed, I have written so that you will
know how people ought to conduct themselves in God's
household, which is the church of the living God, the pillar
and foundation of the truth. [16] And most certainly, the mystery of godliness is great:

He was manifested in the flesh,
vindicated in the Spirit,
seen by angels,
preached among the nations,
believed on in the world,
taken up in glory.

Relation to Surrounding Context

The function of the present unit is to provide closure to the unit that began at 2:1. As at previous occasions (see esp. 2:5–6), Paul in v. 16 draws on a Christian confession or liturgical piece to authorize and supplement his teaching. The hymn, which Paul titles "the mystery of godliness," marks the climax of the letter. Paul will continue to elaborate on the importance of godliness in the remainder of the letter (see esp. 4:7). Godliness also forms the subject of the next "trustworthy saying" (4:8–9).

Structure

"These things" in v. 14 most likely refers to the instructions in 2:1–3:13 regarding proper conduct in the church including qualifications for leadership. This is underscored in the programmatic statement in v. 15 indicating that the instructions aren't merely cultural. The hymn in v. 16 consists of three couplets linking earthly and heavenly realities (flesh/Spirit; angels/nations; world/glory) in the form of a chiasm. The first couplet shows Christ's work as accomplished; the second as being made known; the third as acknowledged.

3:14–16 This section concludes Paul's instructions to Timothy, which started with "First of all" in 2:1. "I write these things" thus most likely refers to the entirety of Paul's comments in chapters 2 and 3. The thrust of this first main section (2:1–3:16) is thus not exclusively negative (i.e., directed against the false teachers) but constructive. What's more, Paul's instructions aren't limited to the original context; instead, they set forth "how people ought to conduct themselves in God's household" (cf. 1 Thess 4:1), reaching from the apostolic era to people in the church today.

The unit ends with a statement summarizing the purpose of Paul's letter and a concluding hymn. The section is both the high point and the turning point of the letter. Paul announces his plan of an impending visit (4:13; though while his resolve was firm, it's unclear whether, and if so, when, he actually made the trip). In the meantime the present letter serves as a substitute for Paul's presence with Timothy in Ephesus (cf. 1 Cor 4:17–19; Phil 2:19, 24; 1 Thess 3:1–6; "I am writing these things to you" parallels 2 Cor 13:10).

To add force and solemnity to his apostolic directives, Paul concludes, first, with an explanatory clause describing "God's household" (οἴκῳ θεοῦ) as "the church of the living God" (ἐκκλησία θεοῦ ζῶντος; "living God" is an OT phrase, used fourteen times elsewhere in the NT) and as "the pillar and foundation of the truth" (στῦλος καὶ ἑδραίωμα τῆς ἀληθείας). Designating the Christian congregation as a "household" was a fitting epithet in a first-century

Greco-Roman context.[209] Similarly, "pillar and foundation" was an evocative building metaphor in booming Ephesus.[210]

Second, the apostle cites a confession (ὁμολογουμένως; NASB, "by common confession"), which he calls "the mystery of godliness" (regarding εὐσέβεια, see 2:2; cf. 4:7–8; 6:3, 5–6, 11).[211] Most likely the hymn consists of three couplets, each of which links earthly and heavenly realities (flesh/Spirit; angels/nations; world/glory) in form of a chiasm (AB-BA-AB). The first of the three couplets presents Christ's work as accomplished; the second shows it being made known; and the third depicts it as acknowledged.[212]

The hymn refers to Jesus's incarnation ("manifested in the flesh"; cf. John 1:14)[213] and resurrection ("vindicated in the Spirit";

---

[209] See K. Zamfir, "Is the ἐκκλησία a Household (of God)? Reassessing the Notion of οἶκος θεοῦ in 1 Tim 3.15," *NTS* 60 (2014): 511–28, esp. 526–28.

[210] On "pillar," στῦλος, see Gal 2:9; Rev 3:12; 10:1. "Foundation," ἑδραίωμα, occurs only here in the NT; cf. 1 Kgs 8:10–13. "Truth," ἀλήθεια, sets true believers apart from the false teachers: 2:4; 4:3; 6:5; etc.

[211] See W. Metzger, *Der Christushymnus 1. Timotheus 3,16: Fragment einer Homologie der paulinischen Gemeinden*, AzTh 62 (Stuttgart: Calwer, 1979), who contends that the passage represents preformed material incorporated by Paul or perhaps his amanuensis. See also P. Trebilco, "1 Timothy 3.16 as a Proto-Rule of Faith," in *Ears That Hear: Explorations in Theological Interpretation of the Bible*, ed. J. B. Green and T. Meadowcroft (Sheffield: Sheffield Phoenix, 2013), 170–90, who calls 1 Tim 3:16 a "proto-creed or proto-rule of faith" that was probably known to the readers (173n13). For a study of the underlying concept of μυστήριον in v. 16, see G. S. MaGee, "Uncovering the 'Mystery' in 1 Timothy 3," *TJ* 29 (2008): 247–65. MaGee concludes that the Christian conception of an eternal mystery once hidden but now revealed through the apostolic preaching of the gospel constitutes the backdrop of the Pauline conception of μυστήριον in the present passage. For a study of εὐσέβεια in v. 16 as indicating a different set of opponents in 1 Timothy and Titus/2 Timothy, respectively, see J. Herzer, "Das Geheimnis der Frömmigkeit (1 Tim 3,16)," *TQ* 187 (2007): 309–29. For a detailed analysis, see R. H. Gundry, "The Form, Meaning and Background of the Hymn Quoted in 1 Timothy 3:16," in *Apostolic History and the Gospel*, ed. W. W. Gasque and R. P. Martin (Exeter: Paternoster, 1970), 203–22. For an exposition, see D. J. MacLeod, "Christology in Six Lines: An Exposition of 1 Timothy 3:16," *BSac* 159 (2002): 334–48. For a discussion of translation issues, see D. C. Arichea, "Translating Hymnic Materials: Theology and Translation in 1 Timothy 3.16," *BT* 58 (2007): 179–85.

[212] Knight, *Pastoral Epistles*, 183. R. Lülsdorff, "Ἐκλεκτοί ἄγγελοι: Anmerkungen zu einer untergegangenen Amtsbezeichnung," *BZ* 36 (1992): 104–8 argues, unconvincingly, that the ἄγγελοι are human officeholders.

[213] Winter, *Divine Honours for the Caesars*, 72, notes the parallel in wording between the presence of Jesus as "manifested in the flesh" (ἐφανερώθη ἐν σαρκί) and

cf. Rom 1:4); Jesus as seen by angels (resurrection appearances?) and as the object of universal proclamation ("preached among the nations"; cf. Col 1:6, 23); the faith elicited by this proclamation ("believed on in the world"); and Jesus's ascension and exaltation ("taken up in glory"). The first and final lines provide the overall framework, while lines 2–5 fill out the confession, which is "great" (cf. Eph 5:32).[214]

In terms of its biblical-theological significance, chapter 3 makes a vital contribution to NT ecclesiology by specifying qualifications for church leaders as part of the LTT's overriding ecclesiological metaphor, God's household (§4.1). This set of instructions is embedded in the letter within the larger framework of Paul's apostolic mission (§1) and the teaching of God and Christ as Savior (§3.3). Grounded in God's foundational creation design for man and woman, this teaching is set within the larger framework of the activity of the false teachers (who, in turn, are instruments of Satan) in these "last days" (see 4:1–5 below).

Bridge

The unit provides eloquent expression of the high importance of the church in God's program. It is "God's household," "the church of the living God," "the pillar and foundation of the truth" (v. 15), brought into being through the incarnate, resurrected, and exalted Christ (v. 16). In this vein Paul's instructions in this letter take on great solemnity not only for the original recipients but for the church of any age. Thus we must give supreme attention to Paul's instructions today or risk being disobedient to God's Word and incurring the negative consequences resulting from such disobedience.

---

the reference to Claudius in an Oxyrhynchus papyrus announcing Claudius's death and Nero's succession as "god manifest" (ἐνφανὴς θεός; P. Oxy. 1021, lines 2–3).

[214] An alternative is presented by B. L. Martin, "1 Timothy 3:16: A New Perspective," *EvQ* 85 (2013): 105–20, who suggests that the six lines present, respectively, the roles of God (lines 1, 6), Christ (1), the Holy Spirit (2), angels (3), and humans (4 and 5) in saving sinners (cf. 1 Tim 1:15). See also F. Manns, "Judeo-Christian Context of 1 Tim 3:16," *TD* 29 (1981): 119–22, who suggests that the hymn uses Jewish numerical symbolism in portraying Jesus's career as recapitulating the six days of creation and effecting a new creation.

IV. Further Charges (4:1–6:2a)

A. Latter-day Apostasy (4:1–5)

[1] Now the Spirit explicitly says that in later times some will depart from the faith, paying attention to deceitful spirits and the teachings of demons, [2] through the hypocrisy of liars whose consciences are seared. [3] They forbid marriage and demand abstinence from foods that God created to be received with gratitude by those who believe and know the truth. [4] For everything created by God is good, and nothing is to be rejected if it is received with thanksgiving, [5] since it is sanctified by the word of God and by prayer.

Relation to Surrounding Context

The present unit, which is closely connected to 3:14–16 ("I write these things to you . . ."), marks a sharp transition from the first to the second half of the letter (cf. the similar dynamic in 2 Tim 3:1). This shift is characteristic of many Pauline letters, such as Ephesians and Colossians. After having laid out qualifications for church leaders, Paul now sets the church within the larger framework of an apostate culture that has turned its back on God and the devil's opposition, which is evinced by false teachers who disparage the goodness of God's creation (vv. 4–5). This resumes the argument at the end of chapter 1 (vv. 18–20); it also contrasts with the description of the church as "the pillar and foundation of the truth" in 3:15. In this way Timothy is set off against the false teachers and reminded that he must fulfill his calling in the midst of a hostile world that, in form of the opponents, has even sought to infiltrate the church itself.

Structure

The opening two verses declare that "later times" will be marked by false teachings inspired by deceitful spirits and demons. Verse 3 specifically states the false teaching as prohibition of marriage and abstinence from certain kinds of food. That both prohibitions apparently flowed from a kind of matter-spirit dualism that disparaged God's creation is made explicit in vv. 4–5 ("For").

4:1–2 After issuing a series of positive instructions, and on the heels of a purpose statement and common confession (3:14–16), Paul now returns to the opponents, picking up where he left off at the end of chap. 1 (δέ, "Now," translated in the NASB and CSB ["But"] but left untranslated in the NIV). In keeping with Paul's "inaugurated eschatology," in which the "present age" and the "age to come" overlap (§6), he states that the final apostasy envisaged for the end times is already looming on the horizon (cf. 2 Tim 3:1; Jude 17–18; 2 Pet 3:3; 1 John 4:1).[215] Returning to the challenge of the false teachers, Paul places them into the larger context of latter-day apostasy.

Discerning the Spirit's "explicit" (ῥητῶς, a NT *hapax*; cf. Josephus, *Ant.* 1.24; Justin, *1 Apol.* 35.10; 54.7; 63.11) voice in the present (λέγει, "says"), Paul asserts that the false teachers fulfill end-time prophecy (Matt 24:11 and par.; cf. Acts 20:29–30; 2 Thess 2:3; 2 Pet 2:1);[216] the proliferation of false teaching is a mark of "later times" (cf. 2 Tim 3:1: "last days").[217] The opponents are among those (τινες) who depart (ἀποστήσονταί; cf. Heb 3:12) from the faith (πίστις, regularly used in the LTT in an objective sense), paying attention to (προσέχω + dat.; cf. 1:4; 4:13) deceitful spirits

[215] Cf. J. D. G. Dunn, *The Theology of Paul the Apostle* (Grand Rapids: Eerdmans, 2006), 464.

[216] It is unclear whether the source of this "explicit" voice of the Spirit was special revelation, the Scriptures, or some other means. See the discussion in Towner, *Letters to Timothy and Titus*, 287, who notes the similar reference to Agabus's prophecy, "the Holy Spirit says" (Acts 21:11; see also 11:27–28) and to "what the Spirit says" in Revelation (2:7, 11, 17, 29; 3:6, 13, 22). Towner surmises, not implausibly, that the "whole phrase may be something of a Christian formula, with the now fully present Spirit occupying the gap experienced by the OT prophets who announced, 'Thus says the Lord.'" On the significance of the Holy Spirit in the theology of the LTT, see P. Trebilco, "The Significance and Relevance of the Spirit in the Pastoral Epistles," in *The Holy Spirit and Christian Origins: Essays in Honor of James D. G. Dunn*, ed. G. N. Stanton, B. W. Longenecker, and S. C. Barton (Grand Rapids: Eerdmans, 2004), 241–56. The reference to the "explicit" or "clear" voice of the Spirit provides an implicit contrast with the "deceitful spirits" mentioned later in v. 1.

[217] W. L. Lane, "1 Tim iv.1–3: An Instance of Over-Realized Eschatology?," *NTS* 11 (1964–65): 164–67, argues that the false teaching is also an instance of over-realized eschatology, a failure to distinguish the present era inaugurated by the resurrection of Jesus from the consummation at the yet-future resurrection; for more recent proponents of this view, see Trebilco, *Early Christians in Ephesus*, 214–22; Thornton, *Hostility in the House of God*, 213–24. See also P. H. Towner, "The Present Age in the Eschatology of the Pastoral Epistles," *NTS* 32 (1986): 427–48, where Towner argues that the LTT reflect a "balanced eschatological framework" with an "already/not yet conception of the nature of salvation" (p. 444).

and demonic teachings (see 1:20; 3:6–7; 5:15; cf. 1 Kgs 22:21–23; 1 Cor 10:21–22; 2 Cor 11:3, 13–15; 1 John 4:1).[218] Strong words indeed.[219]

In fact, these false teachers are hypocritical liars engaging in pretense.[220] Their actions *seem* spiritual, but they practice immorality (2 Tim 3:5), oblivious to the fact that "everyone who calls on the name of the Lord" must "turn away from wickedness" (2 Tim 2:19). Their consciences are seared as with a hot iron (κεκαυστηριασμένων, a "diabolical passive," implying Satan as the agent; 1 Tim 4:2; cf. Titus 1:15), having been branded (i.e., cauterized) by the devil, resulting in a loss of sensitivity, a powerful image in a culture where people were sometimes branded as punishment for certain crimes.[221] Rendered ineffective by a seared conscience, the opponents' lives and teachings bear the mark of Satan.[222]

4:3–5 Paul goes on to specify two particular related items of false teaching: (1) forbidding marriage (and presumably sexual activity altogether)[223] and (2) demanding abstinence (middle of ἀπέχω; cf. Rom 14:21) from certain foods.[224] Paul himself at times emphasized the advantages of singleness, allowed for temporary sexual abstinence (1 Cor 7:5), and fasted for religious reasons, but

---

[218] The words "spirits" and "demons" in 4:1 are likely synonymous (cf. Rev 16:14).

[219] At times these words are viewed as mere polemic. However, there's no good reason to doubt that the author genuinely believed his opponents' teachings were demonically inspired. So rightly D. J. Downs, "Early Catholicism and Apocalypticism in the Pastoral Epistles," *CBQ* 67 (2005): 657–58 and Towner, *Letters to Timothy and Titus*, 290.

[220] The noun ὑπόκρισις occurs elsewhere in Paul's writings only in Gal 2:13, there in the context of the Judaizing heresy (see also the Gospel references in Matt 23:28; Mark 12:15; Luke 12:1). The rare term ψευδολόγων (cf. Josephus, *Ant*. 8.410) draws special attention to the "false *words*" of Paul's opponents. Though unregenerate, these pretenders may claim to be believers in good standing in the church and even present themselves as teachers of the law so they can propagate their false doctrine. See Thornton, *Hostility in the House of God*, 59.

[221] Alternatively, being branded may designate ownership, or perhaps both aspects (loss of sensitivity and ownership) are in view. So, e.g., Collins, *1 and 2 Timothy and Titus*, 114.

[222] By contrast Paul extols the value of a good conscience (1:5, 19; 3:9; cf. 2 Tim 1:3).

[223] Cf. Marshall, *Pastoral Epistles*, 541.

[224] The original Greek is incomplete; literally, the sentence reads, "forbidding [people] to marry, to abstain from foods." Presumably a word such as "demand" (CSB) or "order" (NIV) is supposed to be implied in the second part of the sentence (a figure of speech called "zeugma" or "ellipsis"; cf. BDF §479.2).

he never *forbade* people to marry—which would have been considered odd by most people in the Jewish or Greco-Roman world of his day—or required them to abstain from food. Paul notes that what motivated the false teaching was a disparagement of the goodness of God's creation (Gen 1:31 LXX). Already in the garden, the devil questioned God's goodness (Gen 3:1). Earlier in the letter Paul invoked both God's order of creation and humanity's fall (1 Tim 2:13–14).

Some believe the inspiration for such doctrines may have been a Gnostic-style dualism that pitted spirit against matter and prized the former while denigrating the latter.[225] Such Greek thought may have blended with Jewish-style legalism that took its cue from OT food laws (cf. Col 2:21–23). However, primary documents supporting this kind of teaching are rather late, and it may be precarious to extrapolate earlier manifestations of a given teaching from later, more fully developed expressions of thought.[226] It may therefore be safer to surmise that what we find here is similar to what Paul encountered in the Corinthian context where overrealized eschatology led to disparagement of sexual activity for the sake of "higher" spiritual experience (1 Cor 15:12, 35; 2 Tim 2:18).[227]

Paul's response to the opponents' false teaching consists in a corrected interpretion of the Genesis account. According to Scripture, God created all there is and pronounced everything he made "good," so the created universe shouldn't be considered inferior or evil (Gen 1:20–21, 31; cf. Gen 1:29 LXX). Jesus himself declared all food clean (Mark 7:19; cf. Titus 1:15). The customary prayer of thanksgiving at meals commended the enjoyment of the

---

[225] B. Dehandschutter, "The History-of-Religions Background of 1 Timothy 4:4: 'Everything that God Has Created Is Good,'" in *The Creation of Heaven and Earth: Re-interpretations of Genesis 1 in the Context of Judaism, Ancient Philosophy, Christianity, and Modern Physics*, ed. G. H. van Kooten, Themes in Biblical Narrative: Jewish and Christian Traditions 8 (Leiden: Brill, 2005), 211–21, cites Irenaeus's denunciation of the "doctrine" of Satornil (Saturninus), who "said that to marry and get children comes from Satan. Most of his followers even abstain from animal food, misleading many by this false type of temperance" (*Haer.* I.24; see also Epiphanius, *Pan.* 45.2.1).

[226] D. R. Streett, *"They Went Out from Us": The Identity of the Opponents in 1 John*, BZNW 177 (Berlin: de Gruyter, 2011), 128. See further the detailed discussion in Thornton, *Hostility in the House of God*, 61–67.

[227] So esp. Towner, "Gnosis and Realized Eschatology," 99–100.

Creator's good gifts, which aren't only good but "sanctified" by the Word of God and prayer (cf. Jas 1:17; ἁγιάζω, "consecrated," is found with a similar sense in 1 Cor 7:14; contrast Rom 1:21).[228] In this way Scripture strongly rejects denial of one's human earthly, material existence in favor of a mere spiritual, otherworldly one.

Bridge

The disparagement of marriage and certain foods is not a true mark of godliness. As Paul wrote elsewhere, such practices "have indeed an appearance of wisdom in promoting self-made religion and asceticism and severity to the body, but they are of no value in stopping the indulgence of the flesh" (Col 2:23 ESV). In fact, these kinds of stipulations are demonically inspired. Likewise, today we must not be fooled by achievements of human self-effort, which may seem impressive on the outside but detract from the gospel of grace in Christ.

B. Being a Good Servant of Jesus Christ (4:6–16)

> 6 If you point these things out to the brothers and sisters,
> you will be a good servant of Christ Jesus, nourished by the
> words of the faith and the good teaching that you have fol-
> lowed. 7 But have nothing to do with pointless and silly myths.
> Rather, train yourself in godliness. 8 For the training of the
> body has limited benefit, but godliness is beneficial in every
> way, since it holds promise for the present life and also for
> the life to come. 9 This saying is trustworthy and deserves full
> acceptance. 10 For this reason we labor and strive, because we
> have put our hope in the living God, who is the Savior of all
> people, especially of those who believe.
>
> 11 Command and teach these things. 12 Don't let anyone
> despise your youth, but set an example for the believers in
> speech, in conduct, in love, in faith, and in purity. 13 Until I
> come, give your attention to public reading, exhortation, and
> teaching. 14 Do not neglect the gift that is in you; it was giv-

---

[228] See P. Trebilco, "The Goodness and Holiness of the Earth and the Whole Creation (1 Timothy 4.1–5)," in *Readings from the Perspective of the Earth*, ed. N. C. Habel (Sheffield: Sheffield Academic Press, 2000), 204–20, who argues that the present passage enunciates the principle of responsible custodianship implying limited and restricted use of creation. The word for "prayer" (ἔντευξις) denotes intercession and is part of the prayer vocabulary in the LTT along the more common terms δέησις, προσευκή, and εὐχαριστία (1 Tim 2:1).

> en to you through prophecy, with the laying on of hands by the council of elders. [15] Practice these things; be committed to them, so that your progress may be evident to all. [16] Pay close attention to your life and your teaching; persevere in these things, for in doing this you will save both yourself and your hearers.

Relation to Surrounding Context

The present unit includes the third "trustworthy saying" in this letter, affirming the benefits of true godliness, which far surpass any such benefits arising from bodily exercise (v. 8). Again Timothy serves as a model "good servant of Christ Jesus" (v. 6). Earlier Timothy had been reminded of the prophecies previously made about him (1:18); here he is exhorted not to "neglect the gift" of ministry bestowed on him by the council of elders at his ordination service (v. 14). Just as women will be preserved from falling into error by adhering to their God-ordained role (2:15), so by his exemplary conduct Timothy will preserve both himself and his entire congregation (v. 16; note the use of σῴζω in both passages as conveying divine preservation rather than spiritual salvation).

Structure

The unit shifts from the negative depiction of the "later times" in vv. 1–5 to a positive portrayal of Timothy as a "good servant of Christ Jesus" (v. 6). "These things" in v. 6 links the present unit to vv. 4–5 in the previous unit, while "these things" in v. 11 refers to v. 6. The present passage pivots on the "trustworthy saying" in v. 8. The remainder of the unit features a series of instructions for Timothy prior to Paul's anticipated visit (v. 13). Just as the requirements for church leaders in chapter 3, Timothy's actions are to flow from godly character and set the example for believers, despite his relative youth (v. 12).

4:6–8 After warning Timothy regarding the false teachers, Paul provides further instructions on how to be a good servant of Christ Jesus (διάκονος; this is the only nontechnical use of the term in the LTT; the NIV translates "minister," but the expression is probably generic: cf. Eph 6:21; Col 1:7; 4:7).[229] The second-person singular commands παραιτοῦ ("have nothing to do") and γύμναζε

[229] H. Dionson, "1 Timothy 4:6–16: Towards a Theology of Encouragement," *Asian Journal of Pentecostal Studies* 18, no. 2 (2015): 7–21, highlights the strong personal challenge and encouragement for Timothy in the passage.

("train") in v. 7 are the first such imperatives in the letter, marking a shift from instructions concerning the church as a whole to those specifically for Timothy.[230]

Positively, Timothy is to "point out" (pres. ptc. ὑποτιθέμενος, probably conveying means; in this sense only here in the NT) "these things" (in the immediate context, vv. 1–5, but ultimately the contents of the entire letter) to "the brothers and sisters" (ἀδελφοί, i.e., the members of his congregation; cf. 6:2; 2 Tim 4:21),[231] nourishing himself (pres. ptc. ἐντρεφόμενος, only here in the NT; cf. Epictetus, *Diatr.* 4.4.48) by the words of the faith and the good teaching he has followed (perf. ptc. παρηκολούθηκας probably has the intensified sense of "following closely": cf. 2 Tim 3:10; Luke 1:3). Similarly, God's servants of every age must continually nourish themselves spiritually so they can nurture the people in their congregation.[232] Thus the order is (1) closely following good teaching (παρηκολούθηκας), (2) continually nurturing oneself in the faith (ἐντρεφόμενος), and (3) instructing others accordingly (ὑποτιθέμενος).

Negatively (δέ; NASB and CSB, "but"; untranslated in the NIV), Timothy must have nothing to do with (παραιτέομαι; cf. 2 Tim 2:23; of persons, Titus 3:10) what Paul derogatorily calls "pointless and silly myths" (cf. on 1:4).[233] Rather, he must "train [himself]

---

[230] Van Neste, *Cohesion and Structure*, 47.

[231] Paul does seem to use at times the designation "the brothers"—ἀδελφοί with the article—to refer specifically to congregational leaders or missionary coworkers in contradistinction to the church as a whole (see esp. E. E. Ellis, "Paul and His Co-Workers," in *Prophecy and Hermeneutic in Early Christianity: New Testament Essays*, WUNT 1/18 [Tübingen: J. C. B. Mohr (Paul Siebeck), 1978], 13–22), and that may be the case in 1 Tim 4:6; if so, then the instruction here would be along the lines of that in 2 Tim 2:2, where Timothy is to pass along Paul's instruction to faithful men who will be able to teach others as well.

[232] In contrast to 2 Tim 1:5 and 3:15, which speak of Timothy's past upbringing, the present passage most likely refers to his current daily spiritual routine. See, e.g., Knight, *Pastoral Epistles*, 194; Marshall, *Pastoral Epistles*, 549; Towner, *Letters to Timothy and Titus*, 304. See also the NASB's "constantly nourished," rightly suggesting that the reference here extends beyond Timothy's infancy.

[233] See the discussion in Thornton, *Hostility in the House of God*, 134–36. On βέβηλος, see on 1:9 (see also 6:20; 2 Tim 2:16). "Silly" (γραώδης) is found only here in the NT. The term is found in philosophical discourse (e.g., Plato, *Resp.* 350E; *Gorg.* 527a; Epictetus, *Diatr.* 2.16.39). Later, both Irenaeus (*Haer.* 1.9.3.7) and Origen (*Cels.* 5.20.12) use the term with reference to their opponents. Bjelland Kartzow, *Gossip and Gender*, 138, claims that Paul is using the term as a rhetorical device "to undermine the masculinity, and hence the authority, of his opponents."

in godliness" (on εὐσέβεια, see on 2:2). The term "train," γυμνάζω, referring to physical exercise, is also applied to spiritual exercise in Hebrews (5:14; 12:11) and 2 Peter (2:14; see also Josephus, *Ant.* 6.185). Γυμνασία (athletic facilities) were an integral part of Hellenistic culture. Paul doesn't disparage physical exercise altogether: it has "limited benefit" (πρὸς ὀλίγον; i.e., only for this life, see below; better than NASB: "only of little profit"; cf. Heb 12:10; Jas 4:14). Spiritual exercise, however, yields rewards (ὠφέλιμος, NASB: "profitable," cf. 2 Tim 3:16; Titus 3:8) and holds promise (ἐπαγγελίαν ἔχουσα; cf. 2 Tim 1:1) for both the present life and the life to come (see further on vv. 9–10 below).[234]

Most likely, the contrast between physical exercise and training in godliness in v. 8 is triggered by the opponents who, as Paul just mentioned, taught abstinence from marriage or sex and certain foods (v. 3). Not only is their teaching "worldly" (NASB, v. 7), their focus is "bodily," pertaining merely to the physical realm. This sheds important light on the orientation of the false teachers. Most likely, they "advocated a *spiritual* experience that could be enjoyed presently in what they considered to be the *eternal* age" (cf. 2 Tim 2:18), yet Paul "underscores the fact that godliness is the true path of eschatological existence."[235] Paul's words remain relevant today in a world where many indulge in self-centered hedonism and egregious (or not-so-egregious) materialism. Just as women should refrain from obsessive attention to their outward appearance, donning elaborate hairstyles and jewelry (2:9–10), men should avoid undue preoccupation with "body-sculpting" in modern-day fitness centers.[236]

4:9–10 At this juncture Paul refers to yet another "trustworthy saying" (the third in this letter; cf. 1:15; 3:1; §2.6). As in 1:15, he adds, "deserves full acceptance" (ἀποδοχή, only found in 1 Timothy in the NT) as well as the further comment, "For this reason we labor and strive." There is some debate as to whether the saying is found in v. 8 or v. 10. While the latter is possible (v. 10 has greater theological weight), more likely the saying is found in

---

[234] "Promise" (ἐπαγγελία) terminology in Paul's letters includes Rom 4:13–20; 9:4–9; 2 Cor 1:20; 7:1; Gal 3:14–29; Eph 1:13; 2:12; 3:6.

[235] Thornton, *Hostility in the House of God*, 139 (emphasis original).

[236] See S. M. Baugh, "1 Timothy, 2 Timothy, Titus" in *1 & 2 Thessalonians, 1 & 2 Timothy, Titus*, by J. A. D. Weima and S. M. Baugh, *Zondervan Illustrated Bible Backgrounds Commentary*, ed. C. E. Arnold (Grand Rapids: Zondervan, 2001), 62–63.

v. 8: "The training of the body has a limited benefit, but godliness is beneficial in every way, since it holds promise for the present life and also for the life to come."

Verse 8 is favored by the majority of interpreters (though not translations) as the "trustworthy saying" mentioned in v. 9.[237] The following reasons have led many to believe the phrase refers to v. 8: (1) v. 8 has the form of a proverbial saying; (2) γυμνασία and σωματική are rare words; (3) only v. 8, but not v. 10, speaks of an action for which v. 9 seems to call; (4) v. 8a can be better explained as part of a saying. Most likely, it is directed against the false teachers.[238]

If so, Paul's affirmation in v. 10 further supports (γάρ) his contention that godliness holds promise for the life to come. This is the point of reference of "for this reason" in v. 10, further explicated in v. 10 as the grounds for the "labor" (κοπιάω; see 5:17; 2 Tim 2:6; cf. 1 Cor 15:10; Phil 2:16; Col 1:29) and "striving" (ἀγωνίζομαι; see esp. Col 1:29; see also 1 Cor 9:25; Col 4:12; 1 Tim 6:12; 2 Tim 4:7) of Paul and his coworkers: "because we have put our hope in the living God, who is the Savior of all people." On the designation "the living God" (cf. Rom 9:26; 2 Cor 3:3; 1 Thess 1:9: "you turned to God from idols to serve the living and true God"), see on 3:15 above.[239]

---

[237] See, e.g., Brox, *Pastoralbriefe*, 177; Johnson, *First and Second Letters to Timothy*, 250; Kelly, *Pastoral Epistles*, 101; Knight, *Pastoral Epistles*, 198; Walter Lock, *A Critical and Exegetical Commentary on the Pastoral Epistles*, ICC (Edinburg: T&T Clark, 1924), 51; Marshall, *Pastoral Epistles*, 554; Quinn and Wacker, *Letters to Timothy*, 376–77; and Towner, *Letters to Timothy and Titus*, 308–9. Commentators who believe the phrase points forward to v. 10 include Collins, *1 and 2 Timothy and Titus*, 126–27; Dibelius and Conzelmann, *Pastoral Epistles*, 68; Guthrie, *Pastoral Epistles*, 107; Mounce, *Pastoral Epistles*, 247; and J. Roloff, *Der erste Brief an Timotheus*, EKKNT 15 [Zurich: Benziger, 1988], 240.

[238] Thornton, *Hostility in the House of God*, 143; Towner, *Letters to Timothy and Titus*, 144–45.

[239] M. J. Goodwin, "The Pauline Background of the Living God as Interpretive Context for 1 Timothy 4.10," *JSNT* 61 (1996): 65–85, argues unconvincingly that "living God" in 1 Tim 4:10 reflects a post-Pauline oral tradition attested in the Acts of Paul. In addition, he argues, against Dibelius, that "living God" has missionary significance, adducing the use of the words κοπιάω, ἀγωνίζομαι (which are often used in Paul's letters in a missionary context), and σωτήρ. However, there's no good reason this would not also be true if 1 Timothy were written by Paul during his lifetime; in fact, much of the evidence adduced by Goodwin seems to favor this.

1 Timothy 4:9–10

God (the Father) is called "Savior" at the beginning of the letter (1:1) and again in 2:3 (cf. Titus 1:3; 2:10; 3:4). In the sense that God has provided salvation through Jesus's substitutionary atonement, he is the Savior of all. In another sense, however, God is more specifically the Savior of those who believe and accept his offer of salvation in Christ (on μάλιστα, "especially," see 5:8, 17; cf. 2 Tim 4:13; Titus 1:10).[240] In contrast to Greco-Roman culture, where "savior" referred to human benefactors (such as the Roman emperor), Paul maintains that God alone is the true benefactor of all people, including those in the pagan world with its false gods and rampant superstition.[241]

In a later work, Goodwin examines "living God" terminology in the OT and Hellenistic Judaism (where it is typically used in prayer, missionary appeal, and idol polemic) as well as in Paul's writings (1 Thess 1:9–10; 2 Cor 3:3; 6:16; Rom 9:25–26) and the "Pauline tradition" (Acts 14:15; 1 Tim 3:10; 4:10; Acts of Paul), arguing that the phrase has roots in Gentile conversion to Judaism. He finds that "Hellenistic Jews developed their own distinctive living God theology, adjusting the traditional biblical view of the living God to one that was more universalized. The living God was no longer simply the covenantal God of Israel, but also the universal lord of all people, active in the affairs of Gentiles as well as Jews." Goodwin, *Paul, Apostle of the Living God: Kerygma and Conversion in 2 Corinthians* (Harrisburg, PA: Trinity Press International, 2001), 84–85.

[240] See T. R. Schreiner, "'Problematic Texts' for Definite Atonement in the Pastoral and General Epistles," in *From Heaven He Came and Sought Her: Definite Atonement in Historical, Biblical, Theological, and Pastoral Perspective*, ed. D. Gibson and J. Gibson (Wheaton: Crossway, 2013), 382, who argues that μάλιστα in 1 Tim 4:10 means "especially" and that "1 Timothy 2:1–7, 4:10, and Titus 2:11 focus on salvation being accomplished for all without distinction, both Jews and Gentiles."

[241] See S. M. Baugh, "'Savior of All People': 1 Tim 4:10 in Context," *WTJ* 54 (1992): 331–40, who with reference to epigraphical material from ancient Ephesus, shows how σωτήρ was a common description of emperors or deities in Paul's day, contending that the passage doesn't directly relate to atonement or eternal salvation but to God's gracious benefaction to all humanity (p. 333); but see Schreiner, "Problematic Texts," 383–85. See also F. W. Danker, *Benefactor: Epigraphic Study of a Graeco-Roman and New Testament Semantic Field* (St. Louis: Clayton, 1982), 324–25; A. D. Nock, "*Sotēr* and *Euergetēs*," in *Essays on Religion and the Ancient World* (Cambridge, MA: Harvard University Press, 1972), 2:720–25; and standard reference works such as BDAG; LSJ; MM; and *TDNT* 7.1003–21. Winter, *Divine Honours for the Caesars*, 71, points out that the title in 1 Tim 4:10, "savior of all humankind" (σωτὴρ πάντων ἀνθρώπων), was also found on a statue of the Roman emperor Claudius (τὸν πάντων ἀνθρώπων σωτῆρα). Cf. E. M. Smallwood, *Documents Illustrating the Principates of Gaius, Claudius and Nero* (Cambridge: Cambridge University Press, 1967), no. 135, lines 21–22 (AD 52–53). Winter (ibid., 72) also cites a reference to Claudius as "truly our Savior" (ἀληθῶς σωτῆρος ἡμῶν; *Inscriptiones Graecae ad*

What's more, God the Father is "the Great Architect of the redemptive arrangement, the plan the opponents are attempting to redesign (1 Tim 1:4)."[242] The Father wants all people to be saved (1 Tim 2:3–4).[243] The Father also provides salvation for all people, especially those who believe (1 Tim 4:10).[244] And the Father saves the church and pours out his Holy Spirit through the Son

---

Res Romanas Pertinentes 1, 1118, lines 34–35; April 5, AD 54); and an Alexandrian coin referring to Nero as "the savior of the world" (ὁ σωτὴρ τῆς οἰκουμένης). Cf. A. Burnett, M. Amandry, and P. P. Ripollès, *Roman Provincial Coinage: From the Death of Caesar to the Death of Vitellius (44 B.C.–A.D. 69)* (London/Paris: British Museum Press/Bibliothèque nationale de France, 1998), no. 5271E (AD 62–63).

[242] Thornton, *Hostility in the House of God*, 144–45; cf. G. A. Couser, "The Sovereign Savior of 1 and 2 Timothy and Titus," in *Entrusted with the Gospel*, 107–24.

[243] Cf. Towner, *Letters to Timothy and Titus*, 302, who notes several connections between the present passage and 2:1–7. Kelly (*Pastoral Epistles*, 102) suggests that 4:10 is a reiteration of 2:4.

[244] T. C. Skeat, "'Especially the Parchments': A Note on 2 Tim 4:13," *JTS* 30 (1979): 173–77, repr. in *The Collected Biblical Writings of T. C. Skeat*, ed. J. K. Elliot, NovTSup 113 (Leiden: Brill, 2004), 262–66, proposed that in some cases the term μάλιστα might mean "that is" or "namely," as opposed to its standard meaning, "particularly" or "especially." However, while adopting this understanding in 1 Tim 4:10 would remove any hint of universalism (God is the Savior of all people, *that is*, of those who believe), Skeat's proposal, while adopted by some (e.g., Hanson, *Pastoral Epistles*, 92; Knight, *Pastoral Epistles*, 203–4; I. Howard Marshall, "Universal Grace and Atonement in the Pastoral Epistles," in *The Grace of God and the Will of Man*, ed. Clark Pinnock [Minneapolis: Bethany House, 1989], 55; Marshall, *Pastoral Epistles*, 556–57), fails to convince. See esp. the critique by V. S. Poythress, "The Meaning of μάλιστα in 2 Timothy 4:13 and Related Verses," *JTS* 53 (2002): 523–32; a similar—and apparently independent—treatment may be found in H. B. Kim, "The Interpretation of μάλιστα in 1 Timothy 5:17," *NovT* 46 (2004): 360–68. To sum up Poythress's case, (1) there is a Greek expression for "namely" or "that is" (τοῦτ' ἔστιν) used repeatedly in the NT (Matt 27:46; Mark 7:2; Acts 1:19; 19:4; Rom 7:18; 9:8; 10:6, 7, 8; Phlm 12; Heb 2:14; 7:5; 9:11; 10:20; 11:16; 13:15; 1 Pet 3:20) that would have unambiguously suited Paul's purposes if that is what he meant to say where he used μάλιστα; (2) Skeat's counterexamples are either ambiguous or invalid. In addition, Kim points out that (3) the major Greek lexicons have not adopted Skeat's readings. Skeat attempted to provide a surrejoinder, which likewise proved unconvincing (Elliot, ed., *Collected Biblical Writings of T. C. Skeat*, xxi–xxiii). One point of major importance for Skeat is that the standard rendering of μάλιστα in 1 Tim 4:10 as "especially" yields a nonsensical meaning for the verse; however, John's use of "Savior of the world" (ὁ σωτὴρ τοῦ κόσμου) in John 4:42 and 1 John 4:14 speaks against Skeat's contention.

(Titus 3:4–6). In fact, the entire plan of salvation originates with God the Father (1 Tim 3:16).[245]

4:11–12 "These things" most likely harks back to v. 6, which refers to Paul's instruction in response to the asceticism advocated by the false teachers. From his position of delegated apostolic authority, Timothy must not only teach but even command (παράγγελλε) acceptance of Paul's teaching (cf. 1:3; see also 5:7; 6:13, 17), although some apparently disparaged (καταφρονέω) Timothy's teaching on account of his relative youth (νεότης; cf. Mark 10:20 par. Luke 18:21; Acts 26:4; he may have been in his late thirties at the time of writing).[246] While people normally wouldn't consider this too young for pastors in our culture, leaders in the ancient world were typically older people who commanded respect in the community and possessed extensive life experience.[247] In the context of a culture that tends to prize the energy and enthusiasm of youth over the wisdom and experience of age, today's churches should learn from first-century practice and avoid putting young men in charge of congregations before they're ready (cf. "not . . .

---

[245] Trebilco, "1 Timothy 3.16 as a Proto-Rule of Faith," 183.

[246] Cf. similarly (though without reference to Timothy's age) 1 Cor 16:10–11: "If Timothy comes, see that he has nothing to fear while with you, because he is doing the Lord's work, just as I am. So let *no one look down on him*. Send him on his way in peace" (emphasis added; see also Titus 2:15b: "Let no one disregard you"). See esp. D. W. Pao, "Let No One Despise Your Youth: Church and the World in the Pastoral Epistles," *JETS* 54 (2014): 743–55, with reference to Pao, *Commentary on the Pastoral Epistles*, Brill Exegetical Commentary (Leiden: Brill, forthcoming). Pao notes the significance of the verb καταφρονέω in ancient honor-shame discourse (pp. 748–51; on the vocabulary of honor and shame, see pp. 746–47) and contends that Paul's instructions constitute a challenge to prevailing cultural mores. Pao (p. 747) notes that honor and shame language is also found in the remaining portions of 1 Timothy with reference to widows (1 Tim 5:3, 7), elders (1 Tim 5:17, 20), and slaves (1 Tim 6:1), not to mention Timothy (1 Tim 6:11, 14) and even God himself (1 Tim 6:16; cf. 1:17).

[247] See J. M. G. Barclay, "There Is Neither Old Nor Young? Early Christianity and Ancient Ideologies of Age," *NTS* 53 (2007): 225–41, who notes that demographics indicate that adults (ages 30 to 60) typically comprised no more than two generations, the "older" and the "younger." He also cites the parallel from Ignatius, *Magn.* 3:1: "Indeed, it is right for you also not to take advantage of the youthfulness of your bishop, but to give him all the respect due him." Regarding 1 Timothy as post-Pauline, Barclay argues that authentic Pauline churches were more charismatic in nature—"Spirit-led and age-blind" (p. 241)—but that later "the typical links between seniority, experience, and wisdom would naturally emerge" (ibid.).

a new convert" in 3:6).[248] Nevertheless, as D. Pao rightly notes, "Without denying the need to respect the elders, Paul denies that the youthful should be ignored as being insignificant and irrelevant in the gospel ministry simply because of their age."[249]

Paul counsels Timothy, his trusted apostolic delegate who has been nurtured in the faith from his youth, to counter his age liability by setting an example (τύπος; cf. Titus 2:7; Phil 3:17; 1 Thess 1:7; 1 Pet 5:3; Acts 20:18–21, 33–34). Specifically, Paul singles out five areas in which Timothy should strive to conduct himself in an exemplary manner: speech, conduct, love, faith, and purity (cf. 6:11; 2 Tim 2:22). "Speech" translates the word λόγος, which is rendered "preaching" in its closest parallel in the present letter (5:17). The connection is made explicit in 2 Tim 4:2: "Preach the word" (κήρυξον τὸν λόγον; cf. 2 Tim 4:15; 2:17).

Unlike the case of the false teachers, Timothy's life must not be divorced from his teaching. Rather, he should watch his life and teaching closely (v. 16; cf. 1 Cor 9:22). In this way he will be a great blessing to his congregation and help preserve it from all harm (v. 16). As mentioned, the qualifications for church leaders in chapter 3 likewise focus primarily on character and conduct (ἀναστροφή, cf. Gal 1:13). The vital connection between a leader's life and teaching is often insufficiently appreciated today. Another vital ingredient is love, the cardinal Christian virtue (1 Corinthians 13). Too often leaders who ought to set a godly example are competitive, opinionated, and selfish. Yet love is concerned with the

---

[248] Note, however, that this qualification is absent from the instructions regarding elders to Titus in Crete, a more recent church plant, where Paul's apostolic delegate may have had little choice but to appoint fairly recent converts. See Merkle, "Are the Qualifications for Elders or Overseers Negotiable?," 185–86.

[249] Pao, "Let No One Despise Your Youth," 750. As Pao notes, "The exact age of the youth is less important than the fact that they were not old" (p. 749, with reference to Barclay, "There Is Neither Old Nor Young," 234). This, then, constitutes a remarkable reversal: Timothy, who is young, is given authority over elders. This explains the need for Paul to exhort the church not to despise Timothy's youth, which would have undermined his ability to carry out Paul's directives. According to Pao, this reversal (he calls it "subversive stance," p. 751) is rooted in the redemptive plan of God and involves Timothy's setting an example and hoping in God. For an argument that the absence of this qualification in Titus doesn't make it optional, see M. S. Robertson, "Neophyte Pastors: Can Titus 1 Be Used to Justify Placing New Converts in the Office of Pastor?," *Southwestern Theological Journal* 57 (2014): 77–86.

well-being of others and instructs opponents with gentleness (2 Tim 2:24–25).

Timothy is to excel in two more areas: faith and purity. First, he should excel in faith. As Paul has stated at the outset, God's plan operates by faith that is sincere and issues from a pure heart (1:5; cf. 2 Tim 1:5), not empty speculations. Like love, faith is ultimately the gift of God (cf. Eph 2:8–9).[250] In contrast to the opponents who have "shipwrecked" whatever "faith" was theirs, Timothy must hold firmly to his faith (1:19; cf. 6:10, 21). Faith is also linked with a good conscience (1:5, 19). Second, Timothy should excel in purity. Purity of heart is essential for a church leader (as it is for every believer; cf. 2 Tim 2:22; and on 5:2 below). Only a pure heart can be the source of true love (cf. 1:5). Again, this purity of motive contrasts with the false teachers whose motives are anything but pure (cf. 5:9–10).[251]

The virtues held up in v. 12 comprise the sort of godliness Timothy should pursue. Like physical exercise, these virtues don't appear instantaneously. They must be cultivated by diligent practice over time. In Timothy's day as well as in ours, leaders in the church must lead by example (τύπος; cf. Titus 2:7; 1 Pet 5:3; 1 Cor 10:6).

4:13 "Until I come" refers to Paul's envisioned visit (cf. 3:14–15). In the interim the present letter contains the needed instructions for Timothy. Paul urges particular devotion to three matters in proper sequence.[252] First, parallel to synagogue practice, Timothy should be careful to observe the public reading of Scripture (ἀναγνώσει; cf. Acts 13:15; see also Luke 4:16–20; 2 Cor 3:14).[253] Though some had access to written materials in the first century (cf. 2 Tim 4:13), book production was costly and literacy

---

[250] Faith and love are also linked in 2:15; 6:11; 2 Tim 1:13; 2:22; 3:10; Titus 2:2; 3:15, yet only here does "love" precede "faith."

[251] Purity of heart is also extolled in the OT (e.g. Ps 24:3–4). Jesus called the pure in heart blessed in his Sermon on the Mount (Matt 5:8).

[252] Quinn and Wacker, *Letters to Timothy*, 390. Note the parallel wording and repetition of the article:

πρόσεχε τῇ ἀναγνώσει,
τῇ παρακλήσει,
τῇ διδασκαλίᾳ.

[253] D. Nässelqvist (*Public Reading in Early Christianity: Lectors, Manuscripts, and Sound in the Oral Delivery of John 1–4*, NovTSup 163 [Leiden: Brill, 2016], 115) suggests that the instruction of 4:13 doesn't necessitate that Timothy himself was

limited. Thus the public reading and exposition of Scripture were particularly important.[254] While this would have certainly included the OT writings, it may also have included the public reading of Paul's letters (cf. Col 4:16) and possibly other apostolic writings. Second, Timothy should be diligent in preaching (παρακλήσει; CSB and NASB, "exhortation"; cf. Acts 13:15; Heb 13:22; see also Rom 15:4; Heb 12:5) and, third, in teaching (διδασκαλία; see on 1:10; cf. v. 16; 5:17). The former most likely refers to the oral delivery of messages (sermons or homilies) in the context of congregational worship while the latter pertains to teaching as the continual task of sound doctrinal instruction.[255] After the text had been read aloud, therefore, exhortation would follow as Timothy laid the moral weight of the text upon his listeners in urging them toward proper living. This, in turn, would take place in the context of the larger body of apostolic Christian doctrine (cf. Acts 2:42; Eph 2:20).

4:14 Once again Paul reminds Timothy of his appointment to the ministry (cf. 1:18), in the present instance with specific reference to his ordination service (cf. 2 Tim 1:6). Timothy shouldn't neglect his gift but exercise it diligently. In context "gift" may refer to Timothy's empowerment for ministry, which in turn is given by the Holy Spirit.[256] Beyond this the principle holds true in general as well: rather than neglecting (ἀμελέω; cf. Matt 22:5; Heb 2:3; 8:9) their gift through complacency or worldliness, believers

---

personally performing any or all of the three tasks the verse enjoins, simply that he was responsible to see that they occurred.

[254] See P. H. Towner, "The Function of the Public Reading of Scripture in 1 Timothy 4:13 and in the Biblical Tradition," *Southern Baptist Journal of Theology* 7 (2003): 44–54, who argues that "Scripture" in the present context refers to the OT (p. 45) and that the public reading of Scripture assumes particular importance in crisis moments such as the emergence of heresy (p. 49; cf., e.g., Neh 8:7–8; Josiah in 2 Chr 34:18–19, 30). Towner proposes that "the deliberate public reading of Scripture . . . is one way of rehearsing the acts of God in behalf of his people and his creation and finding and renewing our identity-center in that story over and over again," "the public reminder of the story of faith, rehearsed regularly, both for its didactic/parenetic value, and for the way in which it underlined the identity of the present believers in Messiah in continuity with the past people of God" (p. 52). Cf. Stiekes, "Liturgy in the Pastoral Epistles," 46–49.

[255] Towner, "Function," 48; Spicq, *Les épîtres pastorales*, 515–16.

[256] Cf. Towner, *Letters to Timothy and Titus*, 322: "'the gift in Timothy' refers to his giftedness or empowerment for ministry (including the activities just listed), though admittedly the indwelling of the Holy Spirit (i.e., the gift of the Spirit) is not far from [his] mind."

should put it to use in the church for the common good. Gifts that are buried soon become "rusty and degenerate."[257] The NASB's "spiritual gift" (χαρίσμα) is potentially misleading since spiritual gifts aren't given only when someone is specifically set apart for ministry.

The laying on of hands as a sign of a patriarchal blessing (Gen 48:18) or for the purpose of appointing someone to a particular task (Moses of Joshua; Num 27:18–23) was a common OT practice as a "symbolic social or cultic action."[258] In the early church the custom signified authorization and occurred in the context of the appointment of elders (1 Tim 5:22), deacons (Acts 6:6), missionaries (Acts 13:3), and particular ministry such as healing (Acts 28:8; cf. 9:12, 17) or the impartation of other God-given gifts (Acts 8:17, 19; 19:6).[259]

Analogous to Joshua's succession of Moses, Paul looked to Timothy as his heir apparent (§7.1.3).[260] Paul is a link in the tradition, passing on what he received from others before him (1 Cor 15:3), and he wants Timothy to continue the chain of transmission (2 Tim 2:2). As Moses laid hands on "young" Joshua (Exod 33:11; Deut 34:9), Paul did on young Timothy (4:12, 14; cf. 5:22). And just as in Jewish life God's commandments were passed on from father

---

[257] Calvin, *1 & 2 Timothy & Titus*, 76–77.

[258] Towner, *Letters to Timothy and Titus*, 323.

[259] See the discussion in ibid., 323–24. See also R. A. Culpepper, "The Biblical Basis for Ordination," *RevExp* 78 (1981): 471–84. See also O. Hofius, "Die Ordination zum Amt der Kirche und die apostolische Sukzession nach dem Zeugnis der Pastoralbriefe," *ZTK* 107 (2010): 261–84; R. Schwarz, "Ordination durch Handauflegung in den Pastoralbriefen," *Studien zum Neuen Testament und seiner Umwelt* 35 (2010): 145–59; J. F. Tipei, *The Laying on of Hands in the New Testament: Its Significance, Techniques, and Effects* (Lanham, MD: University Press of America, 2009), esp. 262–71; and D. F. Wright, "Ordination," *Them* 10, no. 3 (1985): 5–9. A familial household context is suggested by J. D. Quinn, "Ordination in the Pastoral Epistles," *Communio* 8 (1981): 358–69. See also C. D. Robinson, "The Laying on of Hands, with Special Reference to the Reception of the Holy Spirit in the New Testament" (Ph.D. diss., Fuller Theological Seminary, 2008), who examines the laying on of hands in biblical, Jewish, Egyptian, Mesopotamian, and Greco-Roman literature and applies the understanding gleaned to the NT references to the laying on of hands to bestow the Holy Spirit.

[260] M. Warkentin, "The Laying on of Hands in 1 and 2 Timothy," in *Ordination: A Biblical-Historical View* (Grand Rapids: Eerdmans, 1982), 136–52 (though her proposal that every believer is "ordained" by virtue of receiving the Spirit at conversion is doubtful).

to son, so Paul imparted the gospel to his spiritual son in the faith (1:2; 4:6–8; 2 Tim 1:2, 14). Also like Joshua, Timothy must therefore be strong and courageous as he "strongly engages in battle" for the sake of faith (1:18; 6:12; 2 Tim 2:1, 3–4).[261]

"Council of elders" (better than the NASB's "presbytery") translates the Greek word πρεσβυτέριον, designating the board of elders, which is most likely the same group as that referred to in 5:17 as "the elders who direct the affairs of the church" (NIV; cf. Acts 20:17; see also Jas 5:14).[262] In its two Lucan references, the expression refers to the Jewish Sanhedrin (or "council of elders"; cf. Luke 22:66; Acts 22:5). This suggests that the early church patterned its leadership structure after that found in Judaism.[263]

4:15–16 Paul's comments bring this series of admonitions to a close. "Practice these things" (NIV, "be diligent"; NASB, "take pains") renders the rare term μελετάω (cf. Ps 1:2 LXX). The underlying idea is that of a heartfelt concern, underscored by the phrase "be committed to them" (NIV, "give yourself wholly to them"; lit., "be in them," cf. NASB). Paul is concerned that Timothy's personal progress (προκοπή; see esp. Phil 1:25; cf. Phil 1:12; 2 Pet 1:5–8) extends to both his life and teaching (διδασκαλία; see on vv. 12–13 above), not only for Timothy's sake but also for the sake of his congregation. By contrast Paul's opponents "progress" in the wrong direction (2 Tim 2:16; 3:9: προκόψουσιν). The notion of moral

---

[261] Cf. Martin, *Pauli Testamentum*, who argues that the author of 2 Timothy is attempting throughout the letter to stake out a claim to authority by multiple allusions to Moses, "the authority *par excellence* in Jewish estimation," specifically to Moses's final words in Deuteronomy (though he engages the Testament of Moses, Philo, Pseudo-Philo, and Josephus as well). For details see §2.7 below.

[262] J. P. Meier, "Πρεσβύτερος in the Pastoral Epistles," *CBQ* 35 (1973): 323–45.

[263] P. Beasley-Murray, "Ordination in the New Testament," in *Anyone for Ordination? A Contribution to the Debate on Ordination*, ed. P. Beasley-Murray (Turnbridge Wells: MARC, 1993), 1–13 observes that in 1 Tim 4:14 it is the body of elders laying hands on Timothy while in 2 Tim 1:6 it is Paul. Beasley-Murray suggests that Paul presided over Timothy's ordination similar to a rabbi who was ordained by his teacher with the assistance of two others (p. 9). J. C. Poirier, "Spirit-Gifted Callings in the Pauline Corpus, Part I: The Laying On of Hands," *Journal of Biblical and Pneumatological Research* 1 (2009): 83–99, proposes that the laying on of hands by the elders in 1 Tim 4:14 is an "identificational rite" (ordination) while the laying on of Paul's hands in 2 Tim 1:6 "involves a real transfer of a charism from Paul to Timothy" (p. 98).

progress (προκοπή) also featured prominently in Greek (esp. Stoic) philosophy.

The reference to Timothy's need to "pay close attention" to these matters (ἐπέχω; cf. Phil 2:16; giving something one's undivided attention, see Acts 3:5) and to "persevere" in them (ἐπιμένω; see esp. Col 1:23) underscores the strength of commitment and depth of devotion Paul expects from his foremost disciple. Literally speaking, Timothy "will save" (σώσεις) neither himself nor his hearers. Rather, by paying close attention to his life and teaching (in contrast to the opponents; cf. 1:4; v. 12), he will help *preserve* both himself (cf. Ezek 33:8) and his congregation from evil influences (for a similar use of σῴζω, see 2:15; NASB, "ensure salvation") and the false teaching of the opponents.

The biblical-theological contribution of chapter 4 consists primarily in its depiction of the false teachers and their activity as indicative of the arrival of the "last days" and their function in the letter as foil for Paul's exhortation to Timothy to help preserve believers and to pursue godly virtue. The apostolic mission, and the distinctive Christian teaching concerning God and Christ our Savior, are vitally at stake in a context where Satan and the false teachers are seeking to undermine the foundations of the mission and the gospel message. This is why Paul devotes great care to constructing a solid missiological, soteriological, theological, and ecclesiological foundation in this letter and in the LTT as a whole. In this way the church will be able to serve as a bulwark against the attacks of the false teachers.

Bridge

Casting Timothy as a model servant, the present passage provides an example for believers (and church leaders in particular) to follow in any age. By tying his relationship with Timothy to salvation-historical antecedents such as Moses and Joshua, Paul underscores the importance of mentoring, which he will develop further in his second letter to Timothy (see esp. 2 Tim 2:2; cf. 3:10–17). While often lacking in the contemporary church, such emphasis on mentoring the younger generation is vital and grounded in the precedent of Jesus's close mentoring of the Twelve as a main priority of his earthly ministry.

C. Further Congregational Matters: Dealing with Different Age Groups, Widows, Elders, and Slaves (5:1–6:2a)

After fortifying Timothy against the false teachers (4:1–5) and issuing general instructions on how to be a good servant of Jesus Christ (4:6–16), Paul now moves on to more specific directives on how to minister to different groups in the congregation, in keeping with the notion of the church as God's household (3:15; §4.1). After a general statement concerning ministry to older and younger men as well as older and younger women (5:1–2), Paul, following the conventional "summary-expansion" form (cf. Eph 5:21, expanded in 5:22–6:9), devotes significant attention to caring for widows (5:3–16). He concludes with instructions concerning elders (5:17–25) and slaves (6:1–2a; note the *inclusio* παρακάλει in 5:1 and 6:2b), all important members of "God's household," the church.

1. Relating to Older and Younger Men, Older and Younger Women (5:1–2)

> [1]Do not rebuke an older man, but exhort him as a father, younger men as brothers, [2]older women as mothers, and the younger women as sisters with all purity.

Relation to Surrounding Context

Having earlier spoken of the church as "God's household" (3:15; cf. 3:5), Paul now proceeds to provide brief specific instructions for relating to the various age groups, both male and female, in the church. After this he will focus on two additional groups in greater detail, namely widows and elders, in light of practical issues that need to be adjudicated in each case.

Structure

The structure is straightforward, moving from older to younger and from male to female, in keeping with the honor that was due in ancient culture to older persons and to men in a patriarchal society. Hence the pattern followed is (1) (a) older men; (b) younger men; (2) (a) older women; (b) younger women.

5:1–2 Crossing gender and generation lines in ministry calls for caution and care. Paul's instructions to Timothy on how to deal with various groups in the congregation are predicated upon the model of the church as God's household (3:15; cf. 6:2; §4.1.2). Timothy is to treat older men as fathers, younger men as brothers—implying that Timothy himself belongs to this category (cf. 4:12)—older women as mothers, and younger women as sisters.[264]

In the first instance, Paul adds that Timothy shouldn't rebuke an older man harshly (NASB, "sharply"; ἐπιπλήσσω)—which would be disrespectful (cf. πλήκτην in 3:3 and Titus 1:9)—but to appeal to him (παρακαλέω; cf. 1:3; 2:1; 6:2; 2 Tim 4:2; Titus 1:9; 2:6, 15) as though he were his father (§4.1.2.1).[255] Humility demands that older men in the church, even if not in leadership positions, be treated with respect in keeping with their age.[266] Later on, Paul calls on Timothy to rebuke sinning elders (presumably "older men"; vv. 19–20), and the apostle may be concerned that this be done properly and respectfully. In keeping with the household analogy, Paul instructs Timothy to treat younger men as brothers and older women as mothers.

In the final instance Paul elaborates that Timothy should treat older women as mothers and younger women as sisters, with absolute purity (ἁγνεία; elsewhere only in 4:12), which remains sound advice for younger ministers in particular (§4.1.2.2). In relating to younger women (νεωτέρας; see vv. 11, 14; cf. νέας in Titus 2:4),

---

[264] See the discussion of Barclay, "There Is Neither Old Nor Young?," at 4:12 above. Barclay notes that adults (ages thirty to sixty) in that day typically comprised no more than two generations, the "older" and the "younger." On "younger men," see Acts 5:6; Titus 2:6; 1 Pet 5:5 (νεώτεροι); Matt 19:20, 22; Mark 14:51; 16:5; Luke 7:14; Acts 2:17; 5:10; 23:18, 22; 1 John 2:13–14 (νεανίσκοι); Acts 7:58; 20:8; 23:17 (νεανίαν).

[265] I. L. Ramelli, "The Pastoral Epistles and Hellenistic Philosophy: 1 Timothy 5:1–2, Hierocles, and the 'Contraction of Circles,'" *CBQ* 73 (2011): 562–81, adduces parallels from the Greek Stoic writer Hierocles who uses the cognate nouns of ἐπιπλήσσω and παρακαλέω, urging respect rather than harsh treatment of one's elders (in particular, one's parents). The author notes the Stoic notion that around "one's mind, regarded as the center, there runs a series of ever wider concentric circles, beginning with that representing one's own body, then moving outward to circles representing one's parents, siblings, spouse, and children; on to more remote relatives; and then to members of the same deme and tribe, to fellow citizens, to those who belong to the same people or ethnos, [and eventually] . . . the entire human race" (p. 573). Hierocles, for his part, argued for a "contraction of the circles," that is, reducing the distance from each circle to the next, so as to create the closest-knit household possible.

[266] See A. J. Köstenberger, "Humility, II. New Testament," in *Encyclopedia of the Bible and Its Reception*, ed. C. Helmer et al., vol. 12 (Berlin/Boston: de Gruyter, 2016), 544–46.

leaders in the church should set the example, not getting entangled in any potentially compromising situations. Paul has already stipulated that overseers and deacons be held to a standard of marital faithfulness (3:2, 12). Yet younger women in the church—especially those improperly dressed (see 2:8–10)—may present strong sources of temptation. While temptation itself isn't sin—at times it may be impossible to avoid being tempted—it's vital to establish certain safeguards, such as proper accountability to others, in order to minimize such potential for stumbling. Particularly for leaders in the church, purity of heart (not limited to sexual purity) is absolutely essential (1:5; 4:12; v. 22). The devil is always on the prowl seeking to trap church leaders or to trip them up (3:6, 7).

Timothy himself may or may not have been married (though most likely, he was not, as the NT is silent with regard to any wife or family). In any case Timothy should relate to younger women as sisters. This doesn't mean he should stay away from young women altogether simply because they may be a source of temptation. To the contrary, he is charged to minister to them, which requires that he love rather than avoid them, but he must do so with absolute purity. Such purity in relationships with the opposite sex isn't a function of legalistic rules or dos and don'ts but a matter of the heart. Pure devotion to Christ—and devotion to one's wife in the case of married church leaders—is the best safeguard against improper relationships with the other sex.

Bridge

The instruction to treat older brothers and sisters in Christ with respect, even when rebuke may occasionally be called for, is of timeless significance, as is the exhortation to treat younger sisters in Christ with absolute purity. Similar but more extended instructions are given in Paul's letter to Titus (see 2:1–10). This speaks to a culture like ours where young men in leadership may at times be harsh, if not outright disrespectful, toward older people rather than valuing their wisdom and life experience, and where they may struggle with treating younger women in the church with all purity.

2. Ministering to Widows (5:3–16)

[3] Support widows who are genuinely in need. [4] But if any widow has children or grandchildren, let them learn to prac-

> tice godliness toward their own family first and to repay their
> parents, for this pleases God. 5 The widow who is truly in need
> and left all alone has put her hope in God and continues night
> and day in her petitions and prayers; 6 however, she who is
> self-indulgent is dead even while she lives. 7 Command this
> also, so that they will be above reproach. 8 But if anyone does
> not provide for his own family, especially for his own house-
> hold, he has denied the faith and is worse than an unbeliever.
> 9 No widow is to be enrolled on the list for support unless
> she is at least sixty years old, has been the wife of one hus-
> band, 10 and is well known for good works—that is, if she has
> brought up children, shown hospitality, washed the saints'
> feet, helped the afflicted, and devoted herself to every good
> work. 11 But refuse to enroll younger widows, for when they
> are drawn away from Christ by desire, they want to marry
> 12 and will therefore receive condemnation because they have
> renounced their original pledge. 13 At the same time, they also
> learn to be idle, going from house to house; they are not only
> idle, but are also gossips and busybodies, saying things they
> shouldn't say. 14 Therefore, I want younger women to marry,
> have children, manage their households, and give the adver-
> sary no opportunity to accuse us. 15 For some have already
> turned away to follow Satan. 16 If any believing woman has
> widows in her family, let her help them. Let the church not be
> burdened, so that it can help widows in genuine need.

Relation to Surrounding Context

Paul mentioned older and younger women in v. 2. He now proceeds to deal with a particular group among female church members, namely widows, counseling younger widows to remarry (v. 14) and instructing the church regarding criteria for financially supporting older widows (vv. 9–10) unless they have relatives to do so (vv. 4, 8, 16). He will move on to deal with (male) elders as another group that requires special instructions. In this way Paul structures this chapter chiastically, moving from older men (v. 1) and older women (v. 2) to dealing with older women (i.e., widows; vv. 3–16) and older men (i.e., elders; vv. 17–25).

Structure

As the following diagram shows, the structure of Paul's lengthy comments regarding widows oscillates between descriptions of a "real widow" and the principle "own family first":

General Command: Support Real Widows (v. 3)
Principle: Own Family First (v. 4)
Brief Initial Description of Real Widow (vv. 5–7)
Reiteration of Principle: "Own Family First" (v. 8)
Detailed Description of Real Widow (vv. 9–10)
At least sixty years old

- Faithful to her (now deceased) husband
- Reputation for good works
    - » Raised children
    - » Hospitality
    - » Served fellow believers
    - » Helped afflicted
    - » Devoted to every good work

No Younger Widows (vv. 11–15)
Final Reiteration of Principle "Own Family First" So Church Can Help Real Widows (v. 16)

5:3–6 Before returning to the subject of false teachers one last time (6:3–5), Paul now gives instructions on three important matters Timothy must address in God's household, each of which is introduced in terms of "honor" (τιμάω/τιμή, vv. 3, 17; 6:1): (1) caring for widows (vv. 3–16); (2) compensating elders and handling accusations against them (vv. 17–25); and (3) slaves submitting to their masters (6:1–2).[267]

First, Paul broaches the issue of caring for widows (§4.1.2.3): "Widowhood could be a severe test in the Greco-Roman world, since women were usually not the direct heirs of their husband's wills. Rather, the widow had her dowry as well as any stipulation which the testator made for her care to his heirs. . . . If the son or sons did not care for their mother (or often, their stepmother),

[267] See esp. Pao, "Let No One Despise Your Youth," with special reference to widows on pp. 753–54. For a helpful reconstruction of the scenario underlying Paul's instructions on widows in the present passage, see D. T. Thornton, "'Saying What They Should not Say': Reassessing the Gravity of the Problem of the Younger Widows (1 Tim 5:11–15)," *JETS* 59 (2016): 119–29. Thornton believes the problem was that the younger widows had been duped by the opponents and were promoting their false teaching and that the church, by supporting these widows, unwittingly contributed to the propagation of deviant doctrine.

the woman could be in a dire condition if her dowry was not substantial."[268] According to James, pure religion is this: "to look after orphans and widows in their distress" (1:27).

This contention receives ample support from OT teaching concerning widows (Exod 22:22–23; Deut 10:8; 14:29; 24:17–21; 26:12, 14; 27:19; etc.). Paul, for his part, counsels widows to remain unmarried like himself, unless they lack self-control, in which case marriage is preferable to succumbing to temptation (1 Cor 7:8–9). Caring for widows was an important part of the ministry of the early church. The Seven were appointed specifically to deal with this issue (Acts 6:1), and widows were a recognized group among the first Christians (Acts 9:39, 41).

It would be fair to say with L. T. Johnson that a particular construal of the scenario underlying 1 Tim 5:3–16 has provided many with "the essential key to the sociohistorical context of the Pastorals as a whole," reflecting an understanding of 1 Timothy as "a second-century patriarchal reaction to a protofeminist movement within early Christianity."[269] This revised understanding

---

[268] S. M. Baugh, "1 Timothy, 2 Timothy, Titus," 467; cf. Quinn and Wacker, *Letters to Timothy*, 412–49. On widows, see esp. J.-U. Krause, *Witwen und Waisen im Römischen Reich*, 4 vols., Heidelberger Althistorische Beiträge und Epigraphische Studien 16–19 (Stuttgart: F. Steiner, 1994–95), who observes that many widows in the ancient world were not elderly but women in their mid-thirties or forties with one or several (young) children on their hands and little chance to remarry because Roman women married young and Roman men married somewhat older, so the age differentiation led to a lot of widows. See also B. W. Winter, *Seek the Welfare of the City* (Carlisle/Grand Rapids: Paternoster/Eerdmans, 1994), 62–78; Winter, "*Providentia* for the Widows of 1 Timothy 5:3–16," *TynBul* 39 (1988): 83–99; and *NewDocs* 8:106–16. J. M. Bassler, "Limits and Differentiation: The Calculus of Widows in 1 Timothy 5.3–16," in *A Feminist Companion to the Deutero-Pauline Epistles*, FCNTECW, ed. A.-J. Levine with M. Blickenstaff (Cleveland: Pilgrim, 2003), 122–46, employs an "aggressive" feminist hermeneutic of suspicion, arguing unconvincingly that the author of 1 Timothy (not Paul) used this passage as a "calculus of suppression" (p. 146). See also M. T. LaFosse, "Age Matters: Age, Aging, and Intergenerational Relationships in Early Christian Communities, with a Focus on 1 Timothy 5" (Ph.D. diss., University of Toronto, 2011), who seeks to locate 1 Timothy 5 in the Roman cultural context but assumes the letter contains the fictive story of Paul and Timothy, postulated by the author of the heterographical (pseudepigraphical) letter of 1 Timothy in order to establish an ideal intergenerational relationship between Paul as an older man and Timothy as his adult child.

[269] Johnson, *Letters to Paul's Delegates*, 177–78. Representative of this understanding are J. M. Bassler, "The Widows' Tale: A Fresh Look at 1 Tim 5:3–16," *JBL* 103 (1984): 23–41; Bassler, "Limits and Differentiation," 122–46; E. S. Fiorenza,

sees at least a portion of the passage to be regulating an existing churchly "order of widows" who had taken a vow of future celibacy in order to devote themselves to certain duties in the church, in return for which they were supported by the church. In feminist interpretation, widows in such an order are often understood to have occupied a sort of church office parallel to the office of elder and deacon; they were "officials" in the church.[270]

Although the standard feminist interpretation of the passage relies on understanding it to describe a formal order of widows, this doesn't mean that all who see an order of widows in the passage subscribe to the standard feminist interpretation by default. By the same token, an order of widows in 1 Timothy 5 is used as support for pseudonymous authorship and a late date for the LTT, due to perceived similarity between such an order and similar groups in the post-apostolic church, but some who argue for an order of widows embrace Pauline authorship.[271] In sum, accepting the notion of an order of widows in 1 Timothy 5 is not incompatible with a conservative stance on the LTT.

Two lines of reasoning may be set forth as underlying the "order of widows" hypothesis. The first involves various positively presented features of the text that are suggestive of such an order.[272] (1) The command to "honor" true widows in 5:3, which

---

In Memory of Her: A Feminist Theological Reconstruction of Christian Origins (New York: Crossroad, 1983); L. M. Maloney, "The Pastoral Epistles," in *Searching the Scriptures, Volume 2: A Feminist Commentary*, ed. E. S. Fiorenza (New York: Crossroad, 1994), 361–80; B. Thurston, *The Widows: A Women's Ministry in the Early Church* (Minneapolis: Fortress, 1989); Thurston, "1 Timothy 5.3–16 and the Leadership of Women in the Early Church," in *Feminist Companion to the Deutero-Pauline Epistles*, 159–74.

[270] Thurston, "1 Timothy 5:3–16," 159.

[271] E.g., M. D. Moore, "The 'Widows' in 1 Tim. 5:3–16," in *Essays on Women in Earliest Christianity*, vol. 1, ed. C. D. Osburn (Joplin, MO: College Press, 1993; repr., Eugene, OR: Wipf & Stock, 2007), 321–66; Spicq, *Les épîtres pastorales*, 524–40.

[272] These are noted in Towner, *Letters to Timothy and Titus*, 333. Similarly, Thurston ("1 Timothy 5:3–16," 166–67) notes, "Key points in favor of an order include the context in 1 Timothy, the terms τίμα and καταλεγέσθω, and the suggestion of a vow or pledge taken upon admittance. That the widows appear in a roster of church officials including bishop, deacon, and elder suggests that they, too, are church officials. . . . While none of these elements alone provides conclusive proof of an order, taken together they are a classic case of the whole being more than the sum of the parts."

compared to the subsequent section's assertion that elders who rule well are worthy of "double honor," suggests the possibility of remuneration, or "payment corresponding to an office." (2) A limitation is set forth as to which widows may be "enrolled" in 5:9, and the term suggests to some a formal induction into office. (3) There's some similarity between some qualifications given for widows in 1 Timothy 5 and certain requirements set forth for overseers and deacons in 1 Timothy 3. (4) The first/previous πίστις that young widows might set aside in 5:12 is often considered to be a vow of celibacy required for entrance into an order of widows, given that its setting aside stems from a desire to marry (5:11).

A second line of reasoning finds certain points in 1 Tim 5:9–10 difficult to reconcile with the view that the entire passage addresses widows in need of benevolence.[273] Wagener notes, for instance, that the restrictive nature of the text (here she must especially be referring to 5:9–10) has led some to question whether Scripture would really exclude from support certain widows just because they didn't meet certain external or moral criteria.[274] Some suggest that some of the characteristics of 5:9–10, specifically showing hospitality and assisting those in distress (and perhaps "bringing up children" in the sense of caring for orphans), speak of a level of prosperity that is incompatible with needing the church's benevolence.[275] Others note that while the description of a "true widow" in 5:5 coheres with one who requires benevolence, the qualifications in 5:9–10 sound more like requirements for

---

[273] E.g., Bassler ("Limits and Differentiation," 135) avers that "the criteria put forward in [1 Tim 5:3–16] seem so contradictory that many find it difficult to maintain that vv. 3–8, 16 and vv. 9–15 refer to the same group."

[274] U. Wagener, *Die Ordnung des "Hauses Gottes": Der Ort von Frauen in der Ekklesiologie und Ethik der Pastoralbriefe*, WUNT 2.65 (Tübingen: Mohr-Siebeck, 1994), 115. Similarly, Moore, "The 'Widows' in 1 Tim. 5:3–16," 345–49; M. Tsuji, "Zwischen Ideal und Realität: Zu den Witwen in 1 Tim 5.3-16," *NTS* 47 (2001): 92–93. Mounce's simple answer to this objection is that while only certain widows were eligible for a formally agreed upon relationship of care (indicated by their "enrollment"), the church was certainly free to help other widows (say, those under sixty) as it chose to on an *ad hoc* basis. Mounce, *Pastoral Epistles*, 275–76.

[275] Tsuji, "Zwischen Ideal und Realität," 93.

church office similar to those given for the overseer and deacon in 1 Tim 3.11.[276]

For these reasons it's best not to place too much weight on the "order of widows" hypothesis in interpreting Paul's instructions in 1 Tim 5:3–16. While there are some surface similarities between widows and elders, this may pertain merely to the need to honor both, each in their own, appropriate way, and to deal with them as called for in the context of a given local congregation. In the present situation, the church may have cared for widows who had other sources of support, thus rendering it difficult to come alongside those widows who did not.[277] This may have been due to confusion as to who should support widows and/or the influence of the false teachers.[278]

In the ancient world widows were particularly vulnerable to those who preyed on them and sought to exploit their precarious state for financial gain. Jesus denounced the religious leaders in his day for "devour[ing] widows' houses" (Mark 12:40 par. Luke 20:47). He watched one poor widow cast her offering into the temple treasury and praised her devotion (Mark 12:41–43 par. Luke 21:1–4). Luke tells the story of Anna, a widow who prophesied regarding Jesus (2:37); preserves Jesus's reference to the widow in Zarephath in Elijah's day (4:25–26); records the raising of a widow's son (7:12); and includes the parable of the persistent widow (18:1–8). Jesus cared for widows, and so should his followers.

Paul's burden here isn't just to urge care for widows but to provide Timothy with specific guidelines for doing so. He first tells him to honor certain kinds of widows, whereby "honor" (τίμα) reflects the fifth commandment (cited in Eph 6:2, the only other Pauline instance of the term). Such "honor" entails not merely respect but has a material dimension as well: "The real issue for Paul . . . is the maintenance of culturally appropriate norms of reciprocity."[279] The widows Timothy is instructed to honor, then, are "widows who are genuinely in need" (v. 3, ὄντως χήρας; cf. vv. 5, 16), that is, those who meet the following qualifications.

---

[276] I'm indebted to C. Bumgardner for providing the above material on a possible "order of widows."

[277] Moore, "The 'Widows' in 1 Tim. 5:3–16," 1:337.

[278] Ibid.

[279] *NewDocs* 8:114.

First, they have no relatives to care for them, whether their own children (τέκνα; cf. 3:4, 12), grandchildren, or other descendants (ἔκγονα; cf. Gen 48:6 LXX). If they do, these relatives should support them. This is how they should learn (μανθάνω; positively, 2:11; 2 Tim 3:14; Titus 3:14; negatively, 1 Tim 5:13; 2 Tim 3:7) to put their religion into practice (lit., "to practice godliness," εὐσεβεῖν; translated "worship" in the term's only other NT occurrence, Acts 17:23). In so doing they will (literally) "return payments" (ἀμοιβὰς ἀποδιδόναι; the only NT occurrence of ἀμοιβή) to their parents and grandparents (προγόνοις; cf. 2 Tim 1:3; the word may mean "parents" or "ancestors").

Caring for one's family pleases (ἀπόδεκτος) God as a practical outworking of the fifth commandment to honor one's father and mother, as does living a peaceful and quiet life in all godliness and holiness (2:3, the term's only other NT occurrence). It's all too easy to relinquish the responsibility of caring for one's family members to the church. Yet church funds ought to be reserved for the neediest lacking other means of financial support.

Paul proceeds to provide a description of a "widow who is truly in need and left all alone"—without relatives to care for her (μεμονωμένη, a classical verb found only here in the NT)—and who has put her hope in God (ἤλπικεν, the perfect tense denotes a settled state as in 4:10; 6:17), continuing (προσμένω; lit. in 1:3) in petitions and prayers (δεήσεσιν . . . προσευχαῖς—the same phrase as in 2:1) "night and day." This mirrors Paul's self-description as praying night and day in 2 Tim 1:3 (cf. Eph 6:18; Phil 1:4) and recalls his exhortation in 1 Thess 5:17 (the reverse order "day and night" is found in Luke 18:7; Acts 9:24; Rev 4:8; etc.). For a NT example, see Anna the prophetess, who, "having lived with her husband seven years after her marriage, and was a widow for 84 years [or, perhaps more likely, was a widow until she was 84; so the NIV]. She did not leave the temple, serving God night and day, with fasting and prayers" (Luke 2:36–37).

Such a "widow who is truly in need" is not self-indulgent, living in pursuit of sensual pleasure (σπαταλάω; elsewhere in the NT only in Jas 5:5; cf. Ezek 16:49 LXX on Sodom), as some of the younger widows in Paul's day seem to have done (v. 13). Those widows were spiritually "dead" (τέθνηκεν, from θνήσκω, not elsewhere in the Pauline corpus) even while they were still alive physically (ζῶσα; cf. 2 Tim 4:1; contrast Rom 8:10; John 11:25).[280]

5:7–8 Timothy shouldn't keep these instructions to himself but pass them on to others in the congregation. In v. 8 Paul reiterates, in escalated form, the principle already enunciated in v. 4: whoever doesn't provide for (προνοέω; cf. Rom 12:17; 2 Cor 8:21) those in his own household, especially his immediate family (μάλιστα, "especially," also occurs in v. 17 and 4:10), has denied the faith (ἀρνέομαι; cf. 2 Tim 2:12–13; 3:5; Titus 1:16; 2:12)[281] and is worse than an unbeliever.[282] Even unbelievers, having God's requirements written on their hearts, take care of their own.[283] Claiming to be religious while failing to keep God's commandments is the epitome of hypocrisy. Paul's way of thinking here is similar to James's: a person's faith must show itself in concrete deeds, or it's not real faith at all (Jas 2:14–26; cf. Matt 7:21–23; 1 John 3:16–18).

---

[280] See I. L. Ramelli, "1 Tim 5:6 and the Notion and Terminology of Spiritual Death." *Aevum* 84 (2001): 237–50, who draws parallels between this passage and Stoic connections between spiritual death and moral corruption.

[281] On the verb ἀρνέομαι, see A. Fridrichsen, "Zu ἀρνεῖσθαι in N.T. insonderheit in den Pastoralbriefen," *ConBNT* 6 (1962): 94–96, who notes that the verb doesn't occur in Paul's other writings, but it is found seven times in the LTT (1 Tim 5:8; 2 Tim 2:12, 13; Titus 1:16; 2:12); and H. Riesenfeld, "The Meaning of the Verb ἀρνεῖσθαι," in *In honorem Antonii Fridrichsen sexagenarii edenda curavit Seminarium Neotestamenticum Upsaliense*, ConBNT 11 (Lund: C. W. K. Gleerup, 1947), 207–19.

[282] Translations variously render οἰκείων as "family members" (NRSV), "his own household" (NASB), or "those in their own household" (NLT). In its only other NT instances, the expression refers to the "household of faith," that is, fellow believers (Gal 6:10; Eph 2:19). For an argument that the present passage refers to fellow believers, see R. A. Campbell, "Καὶ μάλιστα οἰκείων: A New Look at 1 Timothy 5.8," *NTS* 41 (1995): 157–60. For discussions of the concept underlying the term προνοεῖ, "provide," see *TDNT* 4:1009–16; *NIDNTT* 1:693–95; Danker, *Benefactor*, 359–60; *NewDocs* 8:106–16, esp. 113–16; and Winter, "*Providentia* for the Widows of 1 Timothy 5:3–10," who argues that church members are urged to assume the legal responsibility imposed by custody of the dowry and that Christian women are called upon to accept responsibility for any widowed relatives.

[283] For a discussion of the relationship between aged parents and their adult offspring in the ancient Roman world, see K. Cokayne, *Experiencing Old Age in Ancient Rome* (London: Routledge, 2003), 153–72; T. G. Parkin, *Old Age in the Roman World: A Cultural and Social History* (Baltimore: Johns Hopkins University Press, 2003), 205–16. Parkin also helpfully discusses potential sources of welfare for the aged other than family (pp. 216–26).

5:9–10 In addition to these requirements, Paul establishes an age limit: to be eligible for church support (καταλέγω; only here in the NT), widows must be at least sixty years old, presumably because at that age remarriage was unlikely and/or because women under sixty were capable of working.[284] This would have kept the list reasonably short, especially since life expectancy was lower than it is today.[285] Younger widows should remarry (vv. 11–15; Roman legislation stipulated this for women under fifty).[286]

Not only must such widows live in prayerful dependence on God (v. 5); they must have been faithful to their deceased husbands (literally, a "one-man woman," ἑνὸς ἀνδρὸς γυνή, the female equivalent of μιᾶς γυναικὸς ἄνδρα, "faithful husband"; see on 3:2 above).[287] Also, they must be known (μαρτυρουμένη; cf. Heb 11:2, 4–5, 39) for their good deeds (v. 10; see on 2:10 above), five of which are singled

---

[284] Cf. L. K. Pietersen, "Women as Gossips and Busybodies: Another Look at I Timothy 5:13," *LTQ* 42 (2007): 23, who observes that sixty years of age was "the recognized age in antiquity when one was classified as 'old' and correspondingly less likely to remarry." See further K. Cokayne, *Experiencing Old Age in Ancient Rome*, 1; Parkin, *Old Age in the Roman World*, 36–56. Parkin notes, "In classical times, dying when one was in one's 60s or beyond was regarded—at least officially—as natural; to die younger was usually seen as a harsh and unusual fate" (p. 44).

[285] As Baugh ("Foreign World," 44–45) notes, women's life expectancy in antiquity was in the mid-twenties or thirties, so that a sixty-year-old widow would have outlived most of her children and other relatives. Parkin thoroughly examines extant data from the ancient Roman world and concludes that "we may assume that some 5–10 percent of the overall population of the Roman world at any one time would have been over the age of 60 years and that the vast majority of them would not have been affluent, to say the very least." He estimates more narrowly that 6–8 percent of the population being over sixty "is probable as a generalization over space and time." Parkin, *Old Age in the Roman World*, 50, 224. LaFosse argues this proportion would be consistent for early Christian communities as well ("Age Matters," 142–43).

[286] Winter, "*Providentia* for the Widows of 1 Timothy 5:3–10," 85, with further references.

[287] See Page, "Marital Expectations," 105–20. It's unlikely that Paul here stipulates that widows were literally to have been only *one* husband's wife, i.e., refrain from remarriage, because he in v. 14 directs younger widows to remarry. Cf. Köstenberger, "1–2 Timothy, Titus," 525: "Moreover, the idea of being married more than once is excluded because otherwise Paul first encourages younger widows to get remarried and would then later disqualify them on the grounds that they have (lit.) been wives of more than one husband" (with reference to P. Trummer, "Einehe nach den Pastoralbriefen," *Bib* 51 [1970]: 480).

out explicitly (by way of five conditional clauses increasing successively in length):

1. having brought up children (τεκνοτροφέω; see on 2:15);
2. having shown hospitality (ξενοδοχέω, only here in the NT, from ξενο- "stranger" and δοχή "banquet"; the more common NT word is φιλοξενία or φιλόξενος [Rom 12:13; Heb 13:2; 1 Pet 4:9; 1 Tim 3:2; Titus 1:8]), presumably opening her home to traveling believers, particularly teachers (3 John 5–8);
3. having washed the saints' feet (an idiom for humble service based on Jesus's literal washing of his disciples' feet: John 13; cf. Phil 2:1–11);
4. having helped (ἐπαρκέω, cf. v. 16) the afflicted (θλίβω, denoting various kinds of distress; e.g., 2 Cor 1:6; 4:8; 7:5–6);
5. having devoted herself (ἐπακολουθέω; cf. v. 24; 1 Pet 2:21) to every good work, a catch-all phrase frequently used in Paul's writings (2 Cor 9:8; Col 1:10; 2 Thess 2:17) including the LTT (2:10; 6:18; 2 Tim 2:21; 3:17; Titus 1:16; 3:1).

These requirements for widows, most of which pertain to the domestic sphere, are high, and in some respects even reminiscent of those for church leaders in chapter 3. No wonder some in Chrysostom's day cried out, "Heavens, what women there are among the Christians!"[288] By following these instructions, Timothy will make sure the church only aids widows who are worthy of financial assistance so that available funds are used only for those who lack other means of support.[289]

5:11–15 Paul's comments here give the reason for his instructions in vv. 9–10 that no widow under sixty be put on the list. Apparently, enrolled widows were expected to take a pledge (πίστις cf. 3:6) of singleness,[290] and Paul signifies that younger

---

[288] Chrysostom, *Letter to a Young Widow* 2, NPNF[1] 9:122

[289] Thornton, *Hostility in the House of God*, 151, notes that v. 10 contains only aorist verbs, indicating that the list of requirements "focuses on what widows have done in the *past*; the focus is not capacities for leadership or service in the *present*," which leads him to conclude that the passage doesn't present widows as holding an ecclesiastical office.

[290] The meaning "pledge" or "oath" for πίστις is well attested and more likely here than the usual meaning "faith." Note that the reference in the original is specifically to these women's "first πίστις" (τὴν πρώτην πίστιν), which may alternatively

widows should not be bound by such a pledge, which they may not be able to keep and thus incur judgment (κρίμα; cf. 3:6) when overcome by sensual desire (καταστρηνιάω, "overcome," is found only here in the NT; but see cognates in Rev 18:3, 7, 9).[291]

As Paul states elsewhere, it's better to marry than to burn (1 Cor 7:9). What's more, unmarried young widows may get into the habit[292] of being idle (ἀργαί; cf. Titus 1:12) and going from house to house (περιερχόμεναι; cf. Acts 19:13; Heb 11:37; Job 1:6–7 LXX), turning into gossips (φλύαροι; cf. 3 John 10; 4 Macc. 5:11) and busybodies (περίεργοι; note the possible wordplay ἀργαί/περίεργοι; cf. 2 Thess 3:11),[293] saying things they shouldn't (as the false teachers do; cf. Titus 1:11).

Paul's advice to younger widows (βούλομαι, expressing his apostolic will; cf. 2:8) is therefore to remarry (γαμεῖν), have children (τεκνογονεῖν), manage their households (οἰκοδεσποτεῖν)—elaborating on what is referred to as "childbearing" in 2:15 (where the cognate τεκνογονία is used)—and to give the enemy (τῷ ἀντικειμένῳ, lit. "the one who opposes"; cf. 1:10; Luke 13:17; 21:15; 1 Cor 16:9; Phil 1:28; 2 Thess 2:4) no opportunity for slander (ἀφορμὴν διδόναι; cf. 2 Cor 5:12; Paul's four pieces of advice are framed in phrases of increasing length; cf. vv. 9–10). Paul ominously hints

---

refer to their posture of faith in Christ. Perhaps the reference is to the possibility that these young widows may marry unbelievers (cf. 1 Cor 7:39), which, by choosing to follow her husband's pagan religious beliefs and practices, would amount to rejection of their own faith. Cf. Marshall, *Pastoral Epistles*, 580, 600–601; Mounce, *Pastoral Epistles*, 291–92; Towner, *Letters to Timothy and Titus*, 352

[291] On the apparent incongruity between the younger widows' desire to remarry (v. 11) and the false teachers forbidding people to remarry (4:3), see Thornton, *Hostility in the House of God*, 157, who says the younger widows are faced with a choice: (1) disregard their desire to remarry and follow the opponents' teaching (v. 15); (2) act on their desire to marry unbelievers and break with the false teachers while still bringing judgment on themselves (vv. 11–12); or (3) marry believers (Paul's advice, v. 14), break with the opponents, and take up their domestic role as part of their calling to good works (v. 14). See also Thornton, "'Saying What They Should Not Say': Reassessing the Gravity of the Problem of the Younger Widows (1 Tim 5:11–15)," *Journal of the Evangelical Theological Society* 59, no. 1 (2016): 119–29.

[292] Literally, "learn" (μανθάνω): the irony is palpable, as being lazy requires little (if any) education. Cf. Bjelland Kartzow, *Gossip and Gender*, 147.

[293] For helpful background on the term περίεργοι, see J. K. Brown, "Just a Busybody? A Look at the Greco-Roman Topos of Meddling for Defining ἀλλοτριεπίσκοπος in 1 Peter 4:15," *JBL* 125 (2006): 549–68.

that some have already turned away to follow Satan (Σατανᾶς, making explicit what is only intimated in 2:15; cf. 1:20), namely false teaching. Certainly the last thing the church would want to do is support indirectly the propagation of false teaching, as would be the case if they supported widows who spread the opponents' heresy.[294]

In summary, rather than failing to do what they should do (good works, prayer) and being what they should not be (idle, gossips, busybodies), young widows should devote themselves to their family, their domestic duties, and their divine calling.

5:16 Paul concludes his instructions regarding widows with an exhortation to believing women (daughters, daughters-in-law) to care for widows in their family in order to relieve the church (cf. vv. 4, 7–8).[295] In this way the church can help those widows who are "real widows," that is, those who meet the qualifications set forth by the apostle. Paul's discussion of this issue provides a helpful case study on how to deal with a practical matter in the church.

Bridge

The present passage provides a case study of the church's exemplary diligence in caring for those in their midst who truly need the church's help while at the same time seeking to be good stewards of the church's limited resources. The passage continues to affirm the regard for orphans and widows in OT times and by Jesus (see esp. Luke, e.g. 7:11–17; 18:1–8; 21:1–4) and the early church (Jas 1:27). As such, the passage provides the ethos, if not specific principles, for the church's benevolence ministry toward various needy groups in its midst today.

3. Dealing with Elders (5:17–25)

> [17]The elders who are good leaders are to be considered worthy of double honor, especially those who work hard at preaching and teaching. [18]For the Scripture says: **Do not muzzle an ox while it is treading out the grain**, and the worker is worthy of his wages.

---

[294] Cf. Thornton, *Hostility in the House of God*, 156.

[295] The word βαρέω ("weigh down") in the present context refers to imposing a financial burden on the church. Other NT references include Luke 9:32; 21:34; and 2 Cor 1:8.

> 19 Don't accept an accusation against an elder unless it is
> supported by two or three witnesses. 20 Publicly rebuke those
> who sin, so that the rest will be afraid. 21 I solemnly charge you
> before God and Christ Jesus and the elect angels to observe
> these things without prejudice, doing nothing out of favorit-
> ism. 22 Don't be too quick to appoint anyone as an elder, and
> don't share in the sins of others. Keep yourself pure. 23 Don't
> continue drinking only water, but use a little wine because
> of your stomach and your frequent illnesses. 24 Some people's
> sins are obvious, preceding them to judgment, but the sins of
> others surface later. 25 Likewise, good works are obvious, and
> those that are not obvious cannot remain hidden.

Relation to Surrounding Context

Paul has previously provided stipulations for candidates for overseer in 3:1–7. He now returns to the subject of elders, dealing with two specific issues that apparently arose with regard to existing elders: (1) financial remuneration; and (2) removal of sinning elders. This situation is different from that addressed in Titus, where Paul's apostolic delegate is charged with appointing first-time elders (Titus 1:5). The church in Ephesus is more established, and Timothy finds himself in the uncomfortable situation of having to deal with charges against elders who are currently serving, hence the need for Paul's instruction.

Structure

Paul first enunciates the principle that elders are worthy of honor, what is more, of "double honor," that is, both of respect and of financial remuneration (v. 17). In support, he cites two Scripture passages, one each from what we now designate as the Old Testament and the New Testament (the Gospel of Luke, the canon still being formed at that time; v. 18). In the remainder of the unit, Paul addresses the question of how to handle charges against existing elders (vv. 19–25) along the following lines: the customary two or three witnesses requirement (v. 19); public rebuke of sinning elders as a deterrent (v. 20); no partiality (v. 21); no premature appointment of elders (v. 22); taking care of illnesses (because of trouble with elders? v. 23); a final call to discernment (vv. 24–25).

5:17–18 Next Paul addresses various issues related to elders. He singles out three particular concerns: (1) elders' remuneration (vv. 17–18); (2) handling charges against elders (vv. 19–20); and

(3) premature appointment (vv. 21–25).[296] The elders (πρεσβύτεροι) mentioned here comprise the same group as the overseers in chapter 3 (cf. the parallelism between πρεσβύτερος and ἐπίσκοπος in Titus 1:5, 7).[297] This can be seen by the references to the work (κοπιάω; cf. 4:10; 2 Tim 2:6; "work hard" in CSB, NASB may be preferable to the NIV's "work") they are doing: preaching (λόγος; cf. 3:2) and teaching (διδασκαλία; both terms are also found in 4:6 and 12–13). "Direct the affairs . . . well" (NIV; προεστῶτες; NASB, "rule well"; the perf. ptc. denotes a present state) echoes 3:4 and 12 (cf. Rom 12:8; 1 Thess 5:12).[298]

Paul already stated that those who have served well attain to a high standing and great assurance in their faith (3:13, with specific reference to deacons). In addition, Paul now says elders should receive material recognition: they are worthy (ἀξιούσθωσαν, cf. v. 18) of "double honor," that is, both respectful submission (1 Cor 16:16; 1 Pet 5:5; Heb 13:17) and financial remuneration. The fact that the apostle must make a case for this may suggest that this wasn't (yet) universally recognized. Perhaps Paul viewed the inadequate remuneration of elders as the cause of other problems in the church, though this is only a possibility.[299]

In support, Paul cites "the Scripture" (γραφή; cf. Rom 10:11; §2.7.1), a rare occurrence in the LTT: "Do not muzzle an ox while it is treading out the grain" (Deut 25:4 LXX; also cited by Paul in

---

[296] See the study by W. Kowalski, "The Reward, Discipline, and Installation of Church Leaders: An Examination of 1 Timothy 5:17–22" (Ph.D. diss., University of Gloucestershire, 2005), who notes that in the Greco-Roman world leaders were often immune from accusations made by group members and any resulting discipline. He also observes that the idea that leaders were to receive financial support from those below them was foreign to many of these groups and was deemed not "honorable."

[297] See Merkle, *Elder and Overseer: One Office in the Early Church.*

[298] The CSB's "who are good leaders" may unduly diminish the ruling dimension of elders here.

[299] Virtually all translations render μάλιστα as "especially," implying that among the elders are some who direct the affairs of the church but don't also labor hard at preaching and teaching. It has been suggested that μάλιστα means "namely" (Skeat, "Especially the Parchments"), in which case the distinction between teaching and nonteaching elders would disappear. However, NT usage speaks decisively in favor of the meaning "especially" here and elsewhere in the LTT (cf. 4:10: see commentary and summary of critiques there; v. 8; 2 Tim 4:13; Titus 1:10). The pattern seems to be that a larger group is first named, from which subsequently a smaller group is singled out (cf. esp. Acts 25:26; Gal 6:10; Phil 4:22; Titus 1:10; 2 Pet 2:10).

1 Cor 9:9).[300] Strung together with this OT quotation is a second statement: "The worker is worthy of his wages" (Luke 10:7 par. Matt 10:10).[301]

Remarkably Jesus's words are juxtaposed with OT Scripture (though it's possible that only the first quotation is explicitly identified as such). The fact that the wording of Jesus's saying matches the version preserved in Luke's Gospel suggests that the latter may have been Paul's source (cf. 1 Cor 11:24–25; Luke 22:19–20).[302] Those who may not understand the OT saying (oxen were allowed an occasional bite of grain as they treaded out the corn) will recognize the principle enunciated by Jesus in straightforward language. A worker ought to be paid, including those who labor in the church (the close parallel 1 Thess 5:12 likewise features κοπιάω and προΐστημι).

While Paul himself typically chose to waive his right of remuneration (1 Cor 9:12, 15; 1 Thess 2:6–9), he insisted that Christian workers should be compensated financially (1 Corinthians 9). Paul's focus here appears to be on elders who are involved in regular preaching and teaching ministry (thus implying that not all elders were, see above), which would correspond to senior/lead and associate pastors in most churches today (though it may extend to other members of the pastoral staff as well).

---

[300] Only here in 1 Timothy; 2 Tim 2:19 cites Num 16:5 and 2 Tim 3:8 alludes to Exod 7:11, 22. There is no citation in Titus. See also the allusions to Deut 19:15 in v. 19 and to Isa 52:5 in 6:1 below. On the close relationship between Deut 19:15–20 and 1 Tim 5:19–21, see J. W. Fuller, "Of Elders and Triads in 1 Timothy 5.19–25," *NTS* 29 (1995): 258–63, who lists the following parallels: (1) the concern for fairness in the examination of a person, leading to the two or three witness requirement; (2) the resulting effect of the judgment in those who observe the trial, namely "fear"; (3) the warning against partiality in judgment; (4) the triads of persons ensuring due process, with 1 Timothy 5 substituting Christ for priests and angels for judges. See also D. A. Mappes, "The Discipline of a Sinning Elder," *BSac* 154 (1997): 333–43.

[301] See A. E. Harvey, "'The Workman Is Worthy of His Hire': Fortunes of a Proverb in the Early Church," *NovT* 24 (1982): 209–21, esp. 212. D. Instone-Brewer, "1 Corinthians 9:9–11: A Literal Interpretation of 'Do Not Muzzle the Ox,'" *NTS* 38 (1992): 554–65 argues that Paul interpreted "Do not muzzle an ox" literally, because in rabbinic exegesis the term "ox" was understood to refer to all kinds of workers, whether humans or animals.

[302] L. T. Swinson, *What Is Scripture? Paul's Use of* Graphe *in the Letters to Timothy* (Eugene, OR: Wipf & Stock, 2014), 1, 87, 93–113, 179 contends that Paul had Luke's Gospel in hand.

5:19–20 Having dealt with elders' remuneration, Paul now moves on to the second issue: accusations brought against elders. As Paul makes clear, such charges (κατηγορία; cf. Titus 1:6; John 18:29) are to be accepted (παραδέχομαι) only if corroborated by a minimum of two or three witnesses. This conforms to OT teaching (Deut 19:15) as well as the teachings of Jesus (Matt 18:16) and Paul elsewhere (2 Cor 13:1; both with reference to Deut 19:15).[303] Those who sin (ἁμαρτάνω), that is, elders in whose case the charges turn out to be accurate (the NASB's "continue to sin" may read too much into the Greek present tense here), are to be rebuked (ἐλέγχω; see 2 Tim 4:2; Titus 1:9, 13; 2:15; cf. Matt 18:15) publicly (lit., "before all"), that is, before the entire church (cf. Rom 12:17), as a warning to the rest (lit., "so that the rest may have fear" [φόβος]; cf. Deut 13:11; Acts 5:5, 11; Titus 3:11). "The rest" probably refers to the rest of the elders, though a public warning will also serve as a deterrent for the church as a whole. A public rebuke is in keeping with the public office held by these elders and by the fact that their sin has public as well as private consequences. Some sins may not be so obvious but in due course will be exposed (v. 24).

5:21 Paul then issues a solemn charge (διαμαρτύρομαι occurs with reference to Paul in Acts 18:5; 20:21, 23–24; 23:11; 28:23; cf. 1 Thess 4:6) "before God and Christ Jesus and the elect angels" (cf. 3:16; 1 Cor 4:9).[304] Timothy is to observe (φυλάσσω; cf. 6:20; 2 Tim 1:12, 14; 4:15; see also Rom 2:26; Gal 6:13) these instructions (lit., "these things") without partiality (πρόκριμα) or favoritism (πρόσκλισις; both words—close synonyms—occur only here in the NT, but the language is similar in 2 Tim 4:1).[305]

Paul's solemn appeal serves as a reminder that God is the witness and judge of people's actions. The divine judgment will take place through Christ following his return, in plain view of and as witnessed by God's elect, nonfallen angels (note the OT concept of the heavenly court; e.g., Ps 82:1). Once again (see on 4:14), one detects parallels between Paul's charge and Moses's solemn

---

[303] See H. van Vliet, *No Single Testimony: A Study on the Adaptation of the Law of Deut. 19:15 Par. into the New Testament* (Utrecht: Kreminck en Zoon, 1958).

[304] See J. W. Fuller, "Of Elders and Triads in 1 Timothy 5:19–25," *NTS* 29 (1983): 258–63.

[305] See the similar charges in 6:20 and 2 Tim 1:14 and the use of προσωπολημψία with a similar sense in Rom 2:11; Eph 6:9; Col 3:25; and Jas 2:1.

exhortation of the people of Israel in the wilderness (Deut 30:19; cf. 4:26; 8:19 LXX). It remains a challenge for pastors to refrain from partiality in the case of elders or candidates for elder, especially when their influence in the church is due to wealth or prestige. What matters is conformity to the requirements laid down for church leaders, particularly maturity of character, not status or money.

5:22 Moving on to his third and final concern related to elders, Paul urges Timothy not to be hasty (ταχέως; cf. 2 Tim 4:9) in appointing anyone as elder (lit., "laying on of hands").[306] As Paul mentioned earlier, appointing a new convert may render him vulnerable to Satan (3:6–7). Too many promising young leaders have fallen prey to the sins of arrogance, pride, and sexual immorality, forfeiting their high calling and bringing dishonor on the name of Christ. Finding mature, humble, godly men who were able to lead the church was doubtless a major challenge in the early days of the church and continues to be today.

Timothy, for his part, must not fall into the same trap. He ought not share in the sins of others (ἀλλοτρίαις; cf. Rom 14:4; 15:20; 2 Cor 10:15–16) and must keep himself pure (ἁγνός; cf. Titus 2:5; 2 Cor 7:11; 11:2; Phil 4:8; 1 Pet 1:22; 3:2; Jas 4:8; 1 John 3:3; see on 4:12 and 5:2 above). As Barrett comments, "Hastily to ordain an elder who later would bring reproach upon the Church and have to be publicly exposed (v. 20) would be an act of shocking irresponsibility, and it would involve Timothy in the sins of the unworthy ordinand."[307]

5:23–25 Paul's fatherly concern for his "son in the faith" (1:2) shines through when the apostle counsels his protégé to "use a little wine [along with water] because of your stomach and your frequent illnesses" (ἀσθενεία). This piece of conventional wisdom finds also expression in Jewish (b. Ber. 51a; b. B. Bat. 58b), Greek (Hippocrates, *Vet. med.* 13; Plutarch, *Advice about Keeping Well*), and

---

[306] Cf. D. A. Mappes, "The 'Laying on of Hands' of Elders," *BSac* 154 (1997): 473–79; Tipei, *Laying on of Hands in the New Testament*, 271–74. B. P. Irwin, "The Laying on of Hands in 1 Timothy 5:22: A New Proposal," *BBR* 18 (2008): 123–29 argues unconvincingly that the reference is to hastily accusing an elder of wrongdoing.

[307] Barrett, *Pastoral Epistles*, 81.

Latin writings (Pliny the Elder, *Nat.* 2.19).[308] Paul's words confirm the impression that Timothy may have been of a rather weak constitution (e.g., 2 Tim 1:6–7). Perhaps Paul's word of advice also indicates the apostle's concern that dealing with the false teachers was causing Timothy additional stress.

In an apparent afterthought to vv. 19–22, Paul proceeds to add that some people's sins are obvious while those of others surface later (ἐπακολουθέω; used in a positive sense in v. 10 for widows "following after" all kinds of good deeds). While in the former instance a candidate's character can be assessed more straightforwardly, in the latter case shortcomings would be exposed only subsequent to a premature appointment. A more deliberate course of action will allow time to bring a person's real character to light. This will also remove the need for discipline at a later time (vv. 19–20). Finally, Paul observes that just as some people's sins are obvious, so are good works; and even those that aren't obvious won't remain hidden for long. Sooner or later people's sins will be exposed, and so will their good works (cf. Dan 12:3; Matt 5:16; 13:43; Phil 2:15).

Bridge

Plurality of leadership is a vital NT principle pertaining to the church in that it alone provides for sufficient accountability among its leaders. The elders don't stand above the church; they're called out from among its members and remain accountable to it. If they sin, they must be held to account by the other elders and publicly reprimanded before the entire congregation. Too often today church leaders rule autocratically and are insufficiently accountable. In many cases this is a ticking time bomb that will explode in due course, leaving destruction in its wake. The wisdom principles enunciated by Paul in the present passage (such as not appointing untested men as church leaders) have stood the test of time and continue to be critically important (see also the principle for dealing with a divisive person in Titus 3:10–11; and cf. Matt 18:15–20).

---

[308] On 5:23, cf. Weidemann, "Engelsgleiche, Abstinente," esp. 48–65. For a discussion of the patristic exegesis of the verse, see B. Dehandschutter, "Μηκέτι ὑδροπότει: Some Notes on the Patristic Exegesis of 1 Timothy 5:23," *LS* 20 (1995): 265–70; Merkt, "Reading Paul and Drinking Wine," 71–74.

4. Instructions for Slaves (6:1–2a)

> [1] All who are under the yoke as slaves should regard their own masters as worthy of all respect, so that God's name and his teaching will not be blasphemed. [2] Let those who have believing masters not be disrespectful to them because they are brothers, but serve them even better, since those who benefit from their service are believers and dearly loved.

Relation to Surrounding Context

After widows (5:3–16) and elders (5:17–25), slaves are the third and final group singled out for specific comment by Paul. After this, Paul will return one final time to the subject of the false teachers.

Structure

In comparison with Paul's instructions regarding widows and elders, his comments regarding slaves are comparatively brief. In v. 1 he enunciates the principle of respect; v. 2 provides the rationale for obeying even believing masters.

6:1–2a These two verses complete the domestic code that commenced in 5:1. The brevity of Paul's remarks may indicate that he expected his audience to be familiar with his fuller treatment in Eph 6:5–9. Without clear transition (but note τιμή as in 5:3 and 17), Paul provides brief instructions regarding Christian slaves (§4.1.2.4).[309] These were necessitated by the fact that slaves made up a large number of the first-century population of Ephesus. Unlike Paul's other writings, 1 Timothy has no corresponding section on masters (cf. Eph 6:5–9; Col 3:22–4:1; but see Titus 2:9–10; 1 Pet 2:18–20).

"Under the yoke as slaves" is literally "slaves under yoke" (ὑπὸ ζυγὸν δοῦλοι; cf. Lev 26:13; Isa 9:4; Ezek 34:27; 1 Macc 8:18 LXX). The phrase "regard . . . as worthy of all respect" (τιμή; cf. Rom 13:7) is reminiscent of the earlier description of elders as "worthy of

---

[309] See further P. T. Towner, "Can Slaves Be Their Masters' Benefactors? 1 Timothy 6:1–2a in Literary, Cultural, and Theological Context," *Current Trends in Scripture Translation* 182/183 (1997): 43–50. On ancient slavery, see esp. G. E. M. de Ste. Croix, "Early Christian Attitudes to Property and Slavery," *Church and Politics*, ed. D. Baker (Oxford: Blackwell, 1975), 1–38; M. J. Harris, *Slave of Christ: A New Testament Metaphor for Total Devotion to Christ*, NSBT 8 (Leicester: InterVarsity, 2000); and C. Osiek, "Slavery in the Second Testament World," *BTB* 22 (1992): 174–79. See also S. S. Bartchy, "Slaves and Slavery in the Roman World," in *The World of the New Testament: Cultural, Social, and Historical Contexts*, ed. J. B. Green and L. M. McDonald (Grand Rapids: Baker, 2013), 169–78, with further references.

double honor" (5:17). Paul's exhortation is meaningful in a day when slaves were often disrespectful. To be sure, in Christ there's neither slave nor free (Gal 3:28), but this must not be used as an excuse for insubordination to earthly masters.

By urging slaves' submission, Paul sought to preserve the reputation of God's name (Isa 52:5; cf. Rom 2:24) and the effectiveness of Christian teaching, both of which would be hindered if slaves were unruly. God's honor and the preaching of the gospel are even more important than personal freedom. As any form of insubordination, lack of submission to one's master ultimately brought dishonor to the highest authority: God himself. Elsewhere, Paul observed that conversion transforms master-slave relationships into the family relationship of brothers (Phlm 16–17; v. 2).[310] Rather than crusade for the abolition of slavery, Paul therefore opted for a more indirect approach, confident that over time the power of the gospel would transform society from within (Rom 1:16; Gal 3:28; Phlm 16). That said, he does counsel slaves to pursue freedom if the opportunity presents itself (1 Cor 7:21). Spiritually speaking, the Christian gospel of salvation in Christ had brought about a reversal already (1 Cor 7:22).

Even those who have believing masters (the term δεσπότας, unlike the English "despot," need not connote tyranny; it elsewhere refers to God or Christ; Luke 2:29; Acts 4:24; 2 Pet 2:1; Jude 4; Rev 6:10) should not presume upon their Christian bond but rather than rebel or demand liberation show proper respect (lit., "not show contempt," καταφρονέω; cf. 4:12; Rom 2:4; 1 Cor 11:22). In fact, their service should be even more valuable because those who benefit (εὐεργεσία, cf. Acts 9:4) from it are believers and dear to them (ἀγαπητοί; cf. 2 Tim 1:2). In a stunning reversal Paul therefore casts slaves—rather than their masters—as benefactors,

---

[310] Horrell ("From ἀδελφοί to οἶκος θεοῦ") understands 1 Timothy to reflect a post-Pauline church scenario and contrasts Philemon's reception of Onesimus as "a beloved brother" as implying "a real change in the social relationship between slave and owner, and not merely a spiritual revaluation in the sight of God" (p. 302), with the exhortation of 1 Tim 6:2, where "slaves are warned *against* drawing from [the fact of their spiritual kinship with their masters] any ideas about the restructuring of the social relationship between slaves and masters" (p. 307). But note how Paul in the undisputed 1 Cor 7:20–24 encourages slaves not to be concerned about their social position while simultaneously calling them "brothers" (v. 24).

indicating that their service should be rendered from a position of strength, nobility, and honor.[311]

Building on the foundational teaching on church leadership and the life of faith in chapters 3 and 4, 1 Tim 5:1–6:2a covered further important congregational matters. These included dealing with different age groups in God's household, the church (5:1–2), caring for worthy widows (5:3–16), dealing with issues related to elders (5:17–25), and proper conduct for slaves (6:1–2a). In this way Timothy and other apostolic delegates like him, as well as elders/overseers in general, are cast in the role of being set over God's household as God's stewards or household managers. The instructions on various groups in the church—old and young, male and female, as well as widows, elders, and slaves—are thus vitally important in God-honoring stewardship if the apostolic mission is to succeed.

Bridge

Slavery was an ancient institution that shows signs of being transformed by Christianity as early as Paul's letter to Philemon (plus see already Paul's advice to slaves in 1 Cor 7:21, "But if you can become free, by all means take the opportunity"). In the present passage Paul is primarily concerned with believers honoring Christ in their present circumstances, even if they were slaves, which was even more important than for them to try to secure their liberation. Today, of course, slavery has largely been abolished, though the principle of believers honoring Christ by respecting those in authority over them continues to be vital "so that God's name and his teaching will not be blasphemed" (v. 2).

---

[311] A major interpretive issue in this passage relates to the question of whether οἱ τῆς εὐεργεσίας ἀντιλαμβανόμενοι refers to slaves (e.g., F. W. Danker, *Benefactor: Epigraphic Study of a Graeco-Roman and New Testament Semantic Field* [St. Louis: Clayton, 1982], 324; Towner, *Letters to Timothy and Titus*, 385–90) or their masters (e.g., Dibelius and Conzelmann, *Pastoral Epistles*, 82, Kidd, *Wealth and Beneficence*; Katherine Ann Shaner, "The Religious Practices of the Enslaved: A Case Study of Roman Ephesos" [Ph.D. dissertation, Harvard Divinity School, 2012], 159–61). The latter seems more likely.

V. Extended Final Exhortation (6:2b–19)

The first part of Paul's closing exhortation engages in a final indictment of the false teachers (6:2b–10) in which he contrasts the false teachers with Timothy, the "man of God," in terms of "godliness" (εὐσέβεια) and "gain" (πορισμός). Rather than being motivated by greed and using a form of godliness to exploit others, the true servant of God must couple godliness with contentment. Paul then draws on his considerable motivational skills to encourage Timothy. Calling him "man of God," the apostle evokes a long line of distinguished servants of God. Paul also refers to Timothy's "good confession" made in the presence of many witnesses (a possible reference to his ordination service), even linking it to the "good confession" made by Christ before Pilate (6:11–14). A reference to the hope of Christ's return is followed by a solemn doxology (6:15–16) and, almost as an afterthought, an exhortation to the rich (6:17–19).[312]

> [2b]Teach and encourage these things. [3]If anyone teaches false doctrine and does not agree with the sound teaching of our Lord Jesus Christ and with the teaching that promotes godliness, [4]he is conceited and understands nothing, but has an unhealthy interest in disputes and arguments over words. From these come envy, quarreling, slander, evil suspicions, [5]and constant disagreement among people whose minds are depraved and deprived of the truth, who imagine that godliness is a way to material gain. [6]But godliness with contentment is great gain. [7]For we brought nothing into the world, and we can take nothing out. [8]If we have food and clothing, we will be content with these. [9]But those who want to be rich fall into temptation, a trap, and many foolish and harmful desires, which plunge people into ruin and destruction. [10]For the love of money is a root of all kinds of evil, and by crav-

[312] The complex structure of 1 Tim 6:3–21 has occasioned lively scholarly discussion. Against those who emphasize incongruence, A. Schlatter, *Die Kirche der Griechen im Urteil des Paulus* (Stuttgart: Calwer, 1936), 159–75, argues that this final section in Paul's letter to Timothy is unified around the contrast between this-worldly concerns and the worship of God. J. Thurén, "Die Struktur der Schlußparänese 1.Tim. 6,3–21," *TZ* 26 (1970): 241–53, contends Paul here repeats two basic themes, the denunciation of Timothy's opponents and the encouragement of Timothy. See also V. Mihoc, "The Final Admonition to Timothy (1 Tim 6,3–21)," in *1 Timothy Reconsidered*, ed. K. P. Donfried, Colloquium Oecumenicum Paulinum 18 (Leuven: Peeters, 2008), 135–52.

ing it, some have wandered away from the faith and pierced themselves with many griefs.

[11] But you, man of God, flee from these things, and pursue righteousness, godliness, faith, love, endurance, and gentleness. [12] Fight the good fight of the faith. Take hold of eternal life to which you were called and about which you have made a good confession in the presence of many witnesses. [13] In the presence of God, who gives life to all, and of Christ Jesus, who gave a good confession before Pontius Pilate, I charge you [14] to keep this command without fault or failure until the appearing of our Lord Jesus Christ. [15] God will bring this about in his own time. He is the blessed and only Sovereign, the King of kings, and the Lord of lords, [16] who alone is immortal and who lives in unapproachable light, whom no one has seen or can see, to him be honor and eternal power. Amen.

[17] Instruct those who are rich in the present age not to be arrogant or to set their hope on the uncertainty of wealth, but on God, who richly provides us with all things to enjoy. [18] Instruct them to do what is good, to be rich in good works, to be generous and willing to share, [19] storing up treasure for themselves as a good foundation for the coming age, so that they may take hold of what is truly life.

Relation to Surrounding Context

The entire unit 6:2b–19 closely mirrors the opening section 1:3–20. The opening reference to "anyone [who] teaches false doctrine" by way of *inclusio* reiterates the rare word ἑτεροδιδασκαλέω from 1:3, signaling Paul's return to the primary occasion for the letter. He again identifies "godliness" as a distinguishing mark of the gospel and those who administer it (v. 3; cf. 3:16; 4:7–8; v. 6). Once again he elaborates on the characteristics of the false teachers (vv. 3–5). While earlier Paul focused on the false teachers' misuse of the Jewish law (1:3–7), he here strikes at their root motivation: a desire to get rich (vv. 9–10). The Christian antidote is godly contentment (vv. 6–8).

Structure

The extended closing instructions in the letter include a final indictment of the false teachers (vv. 2b–10); an encouragement to Timothy (vv. 11–14); a concluding doxology (vv. 15–16); and a final exhortation to the rich (vv. 17–19; cf. vv. 9–10). The doxology forms an *inclusio* with the opening doxology in 1:17, similarly concluding with an emphatic "Amen." In both cases eternal honor is ascribed to the King who is immortal and invisible, the only God, though the concluding doxology elaborates on some of these epithets in more detail.

1:17	6:15b–16
	He is the blessed and **only** Sovereign,
To the **King** of ages,	the **King** of kings,
	and the Lord of lords,
immortal,	who **alone** is **immortal**
	and who lives in unapproachable light,
invisible,	whom **no one has seen or can see**,
the **only God**,	
be **honor** and glory **forever and ever**.	to him be **honor** and **eternal** power.
Amen.	**Amen.**

6:2b The two imperatives, "Teach and encourage these things" (Ταῦτα δίδασκε καὶ παρακάλει; cf. esp. 4:11: Παράγγελλε ταῦτα καὶ δίδασκε), conclude Paul's instructions and transition into his extended final exhortation of Timothy. More narrowly, "these things" (Ταῦτα) probably refers to 5:22–6:2a (note the identical phrase in 5:21), though more broadly it may pertain to 5:1–6:2a,[313] if not ultimately the entire letter.[314] Paul customarily refers to "these things" before moving on to a new set of instructions (see 3:14; 4:6, 11, 15; 5:7, 21; 6:2, 11; Titus 2:15). In the present instance he may refer to the entirety of his instruction in the letter en route to concluding his missive to his apostolic delegate. Specifically Timothy is to teach and encourage adherence to the true gospel over against the opponents who propagate deviant doctrine (see v. 3 below).

6:3–5 As mentioned, vv. 3–5 refer all the way back to Paul's opening remarks in 1:3–4 (note the rare term ἑτεροδιδασκαλεῖ, "teach false doctrine," in both 1:3 and 6:3). Despite the statement's general nature ("If anyone"), the opponents are clearly in mind (see the reference to "people" in the plural in v. 5 below). Though the statement is couched in form of a first-class conditional clause (using indicatives and assuming the reality of the statement for

[313] Towner, *Letters to Timothy and Titus*, 393.

[314] Fee, *1 and 2 Timothy, Titus*, 140–41.

sake of argument) of which v. 3 is the protasis and vv. 4–5 the apodosis, the specific mention of Hymenaeus and Alexander in 1:20 shows that Paul's words are anything but hypothetical.[315] The term προσέρχομαι (only here in the LTT and in fact in all of Paul's writings) most likely denotes figurative (i.e., intellectual) movement (see the reference to "depraved minds" in v. 5 below), indicating that the false teachers' thoughts have wandered off from the true gospel to their own speculations (cf. 1:4).[316]

The phrases "sound teaching" and "teaching that promotes godliness" call to mind the similar phrase rendered "sound teaching" in 1:10.[317] "Sound" (ὑγιαίνω), which is part of the medical vocabulary found in the LTT,[318] relates to both the nature of the instruction and its effect in the lives of those who take it to heart. As in the case of the human body, for the body of apostolic teaching to be sound and healthy means to be free from any sickness or contamination, unlike the teaching of the opponents, which is unhealthy and causes those who listen to become spiritually sick (note the reference to the opponents' "unhealthy interest in disputes" in v. 4 below). "Of our Lord Jesus Christ" may mean "*concerning* our Lord Jesus Christ" (objective genitive) and/or designate teaching that has the Lord Jesus Christ as its *source*.[319]

"Teaching that promotes *godliness*" elaborates by focusing on the need for Timothy's teaching to be characterized and undergirded by εὐσέβεια (v. 3; §5.1.3).[320] In the NT εὐσέβεια is found only

---

[315] See Marshall, *Pastoral Epistles*, 638; Mounce, *Pastoral Epistles*, 336–37; Towner, *Letters to Timothy and Titus*, 393.

[316] See Thornton, *Hostility in the House of God*, 72, who refers to Plutarch, *Cat. Min*. 12.2; Epictetus, *Diatr*. 4.11.24; *Did*. 4.14. For discussions of προσέρχομαι, see Marshall, *Pastoral Epistles*, 638; and Towner, *Letters to Timothy and Titus*, 393. The CSB and ESV rendering "agree with" may be preferable to the NIV rendering "agree to."

[317] The expression "sound teaching" (διδασκαλία) also occurs in 1 Tim 1:10 and 2 Tim 4:3 (see also Titus 1:9; 2:1). "Sound message" (λόγος) occurs in 1 Tim 6:3 and 2 Tim 1:13.

[318] For a relevant study, see A. Malherbe, "Medical Imagery in the Pastoral Epistles," in *Paul and the Popular Philosophers* (Minneapolis: Fortress, 1989), 121–36 (though I cannot endorse all of his conclusions).

[319] Marshall, *Pastoral Epistles*, 639; see the discussion in Thornton, *Hostility in the House of God*, 73.

[320] See esp. 4:7–8 where εὐσέβεια is tied to a rejection of myths; and note the preponderance of the term εὐσέβεια in the present unit, which features four of the term's fifteen NT occurrences (vv. 3, 5, 6, 11).

in the LTT (10x), the book of Acts (1x), and 2 Peter (4x).[321] The term also occurs about sixty times in the LXX, most frequently in the apocryphal book 4 Maccabees (47x). While in Greek thought εὐσέβεια was a virtue tied to ritual acts, the term came to be used in a Hellenistic Jewish context to designate a disposition of reverence for God that is grounded theologically and expressed ethically.[322] In this way sound doctrine and righteous living are kept together, and any departure from sound doctrine necessarily results in lack of righteous living and vice versa.

As noted above, a church leader's teaching and personal life cannot be separated (4:7–8; cf. 4:15–16). In the following verses Paul elaborates on the contrast between true and false godliness. The false teachers surmise that godliness is a means to financial gain while in fact godliness must express itself in contentment and gratitude for God's provision (6:5–6). This is why Timothy, the man of God, should pursue godliness along with other Christian virtues. So closely is godliness tied to the essence of the Christian message that the expression can serve as a shorthand for the gospel itself (3:16). For this reason Timothy must combat false teaching with a pattern of instruction that conforms to Paul's own teaching and propagates sound doctrine in the context of a godly life.

As Paul makes clear, the opponents' propagation of deviant doctrine at the root betrays pride and ignorance (summed up well in the NEB's rendering "pompous ignoramus"). At the heart of the matter, therefore, is that the false teachers are conceited (τετύφωται, the perf. pass. indicating a settled condition).[323] In the two other NT instances of the term, Paul stipulates that overseers not be recent converts so that they not become conceited (τυφωθείς) and incur the same judgment as the devil (3:6) and presents conceit (τετυφωμένοι) as a mark of end-time apostasy (2 Tim 3:4).[324] This is highly instructive as Satan himself challenged God's authority and

[321] Acts 3:12; 1 Tim 2:2; 3:16; 4:7, 8; 6:3, 5, 6, 11; 2 Tim 3:5; Titus 1:1; 2 Pet 1:3, 6, 7; 3:11 (in the pl.).

[322] Marshall, *Pastoral Epistles*, 141; see the discussion in Thornton, *Hostility in the House of God*, 74–75.

[323] P. G. R. de Villiers, "The Vice of Conceit in 1 Timothy," *Acta Patristica et Byzantina* 7 (1996): 37–67.

[324] See the discussions in Marshall, *Pastoral Epistles*, 638–39; and Thornton, *Hostility in the House of God*, 75–76.

incurred divine judgment. It may also mean the opponents' conceit resulted from premature appointment to the office of elder, though this is mere conjecture. In any case they are presented as latter-day instruments of Satan who strive unsuccessfully to subvert God's plan.

The charge of ignorance ("understands nothing," v. 4) is a regular part of polemic directed against false teachers (cf. Jude 10). Throughout the letter Paul asserts that, in truth, the false teachers "don't understand what they are saying or what they are insisting on" (1:7). Most likely, this relates primarily to their misuse of the Mosaic law (cf. 1:8–11). Specifically, the apostle excoriates his opponents for having an unhealthy (NASB, "morbid") interest (νοσῶν, contrast "sound" in v. 3 above) in "disputes" (ζητήσεις; called "foolish" in both of its other instances in the LTT: 2 Tim 2:23; Titus 3:9) and "arguments over words" (lit., "word-fights," λογομαχίας, a NT hapax; but see the verb λογομαχέω in 2 Tim 2:14). Paul's primary concern is the devastating effect of such speculation on the practical outworking of people's faith. God's people must not be sidetracked by side issues but must focus on growing in Christian character as a natural outflow of having accepted the gospel. Church leaders must do the same, rebutting efforts to divert people's attention from holy living and promoting spiritual growth by wholesome teaching.

Failure to do so will result in five undesirable consequences (the last three of which are couched in the plural):[325] (1) envy (φθόνος; Titus 3:3; frequently found in NT vice lists: Rom 1:29; Gal 5:21; 1 Pet 2:1); (2) quarreling (ἔρις; Titus 3:9; cf. Rom 1:29; 13:13; Gal 5:20; the two terms are linked in Phil 1:15; strife was a particular problem in the Corinthian church: 1 Cor 1:11; 3:3; 2 Cor 12:20); (3) slander(s) (βλασφημίαι; NASB, "abusive language"; Matt 15:19; Mark 3:28; Jude 9; cf. 1 Tim 1:20); (4) evil suspicion or conjecture (ὑπόνοιαι πονηραί; only here in the NT; cf. verb ὑπονοέω in Acts 13:25; 25:18; 27:27; Sir 3:24); and (5) constant disagreement (pl. διαπαρατριβαί; only here in the NT).[326] "Envy" and "quarreling" are

---

[325] Vice lists were common in antiquity: see, e.g., Wis 14:25–26; *Did*. 3; Plutarch, *Mor*. 473B; Epictetus, *Diatr*. 3.22.61; cf. C. G. Kruse, "Virtues and Vices," *DPL*, 962–63.

[326] The piling up of prepositions (in the present case διά and παρά) may have the effect of compounding the root word's meaning, hence renderings such as "*constant* disagreement" (CSB) or "*constant* friction" (NASB, NIV).

closely related as cause and effect; "slander" refers to a person's speech, "evil suspicions" to their inner disposition, and "constant disagreement" to interpersonal relationships. Taken together, the deadly combination of these vices will have a cancerous effect (2 Tim 2:17), slowly but surely eating away whatever spiritual life remains in the congregation.

Paul closes with a threefold description of the false teachers as (1) "people whose minds are depraved" (the perf. ptc. διεφθαρμένων conveys the notion of a settled state; elsewhere in the NT the expression denotes decay or destruction; see Luke 12:33; 2 Cor 4:16; Rev 8:9; 11:18; cf. καταφθείρω in 2 Tim 3:8); (2) as those who have been "deprived of the truth" (ἀπεστερημένων, another perf. ptc., translated "defraud," "cheat," "deprive," or "failed [to pay]" in Mark 10:19; 1 Cor 6:7–8; 7:5; Jas 5:4); and (3) as those who imagine godliness as a means to material gain (πορισμός; repeated in v. 6; not elsewhere in the NT).[327] The passives "depraved" and "deprived" may be "diabolical" (implying Satan as the agent; cf. 2:14; 4:2). Earlier in the letter Paul stipulated that an elder not be "greedy" (3:3) and that a deacon not be "greedy for money" (3:8). The considerable number of references to wealth in this letter may suggest that this was a real issue in the Ephesian congregation.[328]

Cumulatively the three traits depict people whose thoughts and motives have been corrupted by the sinful ways of the world and who are driven by the desire to exploit others. As the repeated perfect participles indicate, this process of decay was the result of the opponents' previous rejection of the gospel.[329] On the whole, therefore, Paul paints a highly unflattering portrait of his opponents. Their doctrine is heterodox (v. 3), their attitude arrogant (v. 4a), and they thrive on controversy (v. 4b), with disastrous results (v. 4c). These negative effects are the result of spiritual blindness, which renders the false teachers devoid of truth (v. 5a). As a result, their religion becomes a means of selfish gain (v. 5b). By contrast

[327] See the discussion in Trebilco, *Early Christians in Ephesus*, 226, 404–22.

[328] See, e.g., 2:9; 3:3, 8; 5:16–18; 6:5–10, 17–19. Contra those (like R. J. Karris, "The Background and Significance of the Polemic of the Pastoral Epistles," *JBL* 92 [1973]: 552) who claim this represents merely the stock polemic of the day. Cf. D. T. Thornton, "'Saying What They Should Not Say,'" 119–29.

[329] Towner, *Letters to Timothy and Titus*, 397, notes that this rejection has both theological and ethical implications.

Paul never sought to profit personally from his preaching (Acts 20:33; 2 Cor 2:17; 1 Thess 2:5).

6:6–10 To drive these points home, the apostle strings together a chain of proverbial sayings:

> "But godliness with contentment is great gain." (v. 6)
>
> "For we brought nothing into the world, and we can take nothing out." (v. 7)
>
> "If we have food and clothing, we will be content with these." (v. 8)
>
> "For the love of money is a root of all kinds of evil." (Or, "of all evils"; v. 10)

Not all of these sayings are original with the apostle, however. As will be seen below, Paul frequently draws on commonly accepted truths attested in both biblical and extrabiblical literature to argue his case.[330]

In the first saying Paul asserts that true godliness (εὐσέβεια; see on 2:2) was accompanied by (μετά) contentment (αὐταρκεία; cf. 2 Cor 9:8: Phil 4:11; cf. Ps 34:10). Such contented godliness is truly profitable (note the wordplay involving "gain"; on πορισμός, see the previous verse).[331] Contentment, conceived as self-sufficiency, was considered a virtue in Greek (Cynic-Stoic) philosophy (e.g., Plato, *Resp.* 2.369B; Diogenes Laertius, *Lives of Eminent Philosophers* 10.130–131).[332] Paul, for his part, didn't advocate the Greek version

---

[330] The theme of wealth is largely absent from 2 Timothy and Titus. The NT writers most interested in this topic are Luke, Paul (in his letters to the Corinthians and Ephesians), James, and John (in Revelation but not the Gospel). See especially C. L. Blomberg, *Neither Poverty nor Riches: A Biblical Theology of Material Possessions*, NSBT 7 (Downers Grove: IVP Academic, 1999); and R. M. Kidd, *Wealth and Beneficence in the Pastoral Epistles: A "Bourgeois" Form of Early Christianity?*, SBLDS 122 (Atlanta: Scholars Press, 1990). See also D. E. Gowan, "Wealth and Poverty in the Old Testament," *Int* 41 (1987): 341–53; B. J. Malina, "Wealth and Poverty in the New Testament and Its World," *Int* 41 (1987): 354–67; and R. H. Weaver, "Wealth and Poverty in the Early Church," *Int* 41 (1987): 368–81.

[331] The adjective "great" (μέγας) modifying "gain" probably sets Paul's words into end-time perspective (the term is found eight times in the book of Revelation; see also 1 Tim 3:16). Cf. Quinn and Wacker, *Letters to Timothy*, 502.

[332] For a discussion of 1 Timothy 6 against the backdrop of popular pagan philosophers, see A. J. Malherbe, "Godliness, Self-Sufficiency, Greed, and the Enjoyment of Wealth. 1 Timothy 6:3–19: Part I," *NovT* 52 (2010): 376–405; Malherbe, "Godliness, Self-Sufficiency, Greed, and the Enjoyment of Wealth. 1 Timothy 6:3–19: Part II,"

of contentment but declared that true αὐταρκεία is satisfaction with Christ rather than self-reliance.[333] Such true contentment stands in contrast with greed and a desire for more, leading to the exploitation of others. At its essence, godliness is not a means of material gain; as a spiritual virtue it is gain in and of itself.[334] This message has strong countercultural implications in Western culture, which is increasingly materialistic. Even Christians are frequently drawn into a pattern of excessive debt, consumer spending, and defining status primarily based on material possessions.

The attitude Paul canvassed in the second and third sayings couldn't be more different: "For we brought nothing into the world, and we can take nothing out. If we have food [διατροφάς] and clothing [σκεπάσματα], we will be content with these" (or, "let us be content with that").[335] The future may be a Hebraism with the force of a command.[336] See the similar counsel by Jesus (Matt 6:24–34; Luke 12:16–32) and John the Baptist (Luke 3:14); see also

---

NovT 53 (2011): 73–96. For a comparison with Cynic ideas see N. Neumann, "Kein Gewinn = Gewinn: Die kynisch geprägte Struktur der Argumentation in 1 Tim 6:3–12," *NovT* 51 (2009): 127–47. For discussion of this passage in connection with a roughly contemporaneous ancient Greek novel about a wealthy Ephesian couple, see G. G. Hoag, *Wealth in Ancient Ephesus and the First Letter to Timothy: Fresh Insights from* Ephesiaca *by Xenophon of Ephesus*, BBRSup Series 11 (Winona Lake, IN: Eisenbrauns, 2015).

[333] F. E. Brenk, "Old Wineskins Recycled: *Autarkeia* in I Timothy 6.5–10," *Filología neotestamentaria* 3 (1990): 39–52, argues that Paul here "continued to speak the idiom of the Hellenistic world, but as elsewhere, employed it to depict a newer, higher, and more spiritual reality" (p. 50).

[334] Kidd, *Wealth and Beneficence in the Pastoral Epistles*, 97: "The gain εὐσέβεια brings is εὐσέβεια itself"; cf. Blomberg, *Neither Poverty nor Riches*, 210.

[335] Translations differ on the rendering of σκεπάσματα in v. 8. Some translate the term as "clothing" (e.g., ESV; cf. RSV, NIV), while others render it as "covering" (NASB) or "shelter" (NET). Both διατροφάς and σκεπάσματα are found only here in the NT. After an extended discussion and survey of the primary evidence, D. H. Wenkel concludes that the rendering "covering" or "shelter" lacks lexical support and strongly urges the translation "clothing" ("Lexicography to the Aid of a Problematic Pastoral Proverb: With What Should Christians Be Content in I Timothy 6.8?," *BT* 66 [2015]: 73–90). Thus, against the LXX backdrop of conceiving of life as a pilgrimage from nakedness to nakedness, Paul here "is urging all Christians to find contentment with a lifestyle compatible with pilgrimage and wandering," not "a lifestyle that is settled and sedentary."

[336] See, e.g., Marshall, *Pastoral Epistles*, 648; Quinn and Wacker, *Letters to Timothy*, 509; Towner, *Letters to Timothy and Titus*, 401n47.

the book of Hebrews (Heb 13:5); there are OT parallels as well (cf. Job 1:21; Eccl 5:14 LXX). While it's entirely appropriate to enjoy one's belongings, believers should cultivate an attitude of healthy detachment with regard to material possessions.

By contrast, Paul observes that the desire to get rich (πλουτεῖν; cf. v. 18; Rom 10:12; 1 Cor 4:8; 2 Cor 8:9) amounts to falling (ἐμπίπτω; cf. 3:6–7) into temptation (πειρασμός; only here in the LTT; cf. 1 Cor 10:13; Gal 4:14) and a trap (παγίς; cf. Luke 21:35; Rom 11:9; 1 Tim 3:7; 2 Tim 2:26). This tendency is bound to plunge (βυθίζω, elsewhere in the NT only in Luke 5:7 with reference to a sinking boat) people into many foolish (ἀνοήτους; Luke 24:25; Rom 1:14; Gal 3:1, 3; Titus 3:3) and harmful (βλαβεράς; only here in the NT; cf. Prov 10:26 LXX) desires. The false teachers may have relied on the support of others while not working themselves. This stands in sharp contrast to Paul's philosophy of ministry, work ethic, and pattern of teaching (Acts 18:3; 1 Corinthians 9; 1 Thess 1:5; 2:9; 4:11–12; 2 Thess 3:6–13). Similarly, the church today shouldn't support people who use the ministry as an excuse for not working.

The false teachers, for their part, will end up in utter ruin (ὄλεθρος; 1 Cor 5:5; 1 Thess 5:3; 2 Thess 1:9) and destruction (ἀπώλεια; Rom 9:22; Phil 1:28; 3:19; Heb 10:39; 2 Pet 2:1, 3; 3:7, 16; Rev 17:8, 11), two close Semitic-style synonyms. Similar to Jesus (Matt 6:24; Luke 16:13),[337] Paul traces such ruin back to a root evil (ῥίζα; cf. Heb 12:15): the love of money (φιλαργυρία).[338] Centuries before Paul, Hippocrates (4th/5th c. BC) already wrote that the love of money is the cause of all kinds of things (*Epid.* 17.43); another individual, Bion, called "love of money the mother-city of all evils" (Diogenes Laertius, *Lives of Eminent Philosophers* 6.50).

---

[337] See P. Dschulnigg, "Warnund vor Reichtum und Ermahnung der Reichen: 1 Tim 6,6-10.17.19 im Rahmen des Schlussteils 6,3-21," *BZ* 37 (1993): 60–77.

[338] The term φιλαργυρία ("love of money") doesn't occur elsewhere in the NT (though see φιλάργυροι, "lovers of money," in Luke 16:14 and 2 Tim 3:2 and ἀφιλάργυρος in 1 Tim 3:3; extrabiblical references include Philo, *Spec. Laws* 1.24; 1.281; 2.78; Epictetus, *Diatr.* 2.16.45; T. Jud. 18.2; 19.1). In the original Greek the word "root" (ῥίζα) is in first position for emphasis. There is no article; yet in keeping with Colwell's rule, according to which a definite predicate noun preceding the verb is usually anarthrous (cf., e.g., John 1:1), the term "root" can be definite ("the root") despite the absence of the article. However, this should not be pressed to suggest that money is the *sole* root of evil; rather, the statement includes an element of hyperbole (cf. Matt 6:24): money is the root of countless evils.

Paul ominously adds, "By craving (ὀρεγόμενοι; cf. 3:1; Heb 11:16) it (i.e., money) some (τινες, another oblique reference to the false teachers; cf. 1:6, 19; 4:1; 5:15; 6:21) have wandered away from the faith (ἀπεπλανήθησαν, cf. Mark 13:22; the passive may imply Satan as the agent of the false teachers' demise) and pierced themselves (περιέπειραν; only here in the NT; cf. Philo, *Flaccus* 1) with many griefs" (ὀδύναις; cf. Rom 9:2).[339] As Quinn and Wacker put it, "The riches . . ., so eagerly sought, leave those who have acquired them in desperate frustration and anguish, neither satisfying their greed nor healing their hearts."[340] Considering the ignominious outcome of the false teachers, believers in every age should consider the great harm caused by greed and make every effort to dig up this "root of all kinds of evil," cultivating godly contentment.

6:11–12 Following his concluding denunciation of the false teachers, Paul turns to his final charge (the same pattern as in 1:3–7 and chap. 4). In short Timothy is to be everything the false teachers aren't. Negatively Paul pleads with Timothy to flee from "these things" (i.e., the vices discussed in vv. 3–10, including unhealthy controversies and the love of money). Positively he should pursue the Christian virtues of righteousness, godliness, faith, love, endurance, and gentleness.[341]

The direct address "But you" was used by Jesus in relation to his disciples (or would-be disciples; Matt 6:6, 17; Luke 9:60). Paul frequently employs the phrase in his other letters (Rom 2:17; 11:17; 14:10) including the LTT (2 Tim 3:10, 14; 4:5; Titus 2:1; the phrase is also found in Jas 4:12). That the expression occurs toward the end of this letter and three times in the closing chapters of 2 Timothy underscores Paul's intensity and urgency in entreating Timothy.

The expression "man of God" (ἄνθρωπε θεοῦ; cf. 2 Tim 3:17) is found in the OT with reference to Moses (Deut 33:1; Josh 14:6; Ps 89:1), Samuel (1 Sam 9:6–10), David (2 Chr 8:14; Neh 12:24, 36),

---

[339] The term is used literally with the sense of "to pierce with a sword or stake" in Diodorus Siculus 16.80; 19.84; Josephus, *J.W.* 3.296.

[340] Quinn and Wacker, *Letters to Timothy*, 514.

[341] Towner (*1–2 Timothy & Titus*, 140–41) points out that the "flee-pursue" formula is rooted in the Greek OT and Second Temple Judaism where people are enjoined to "flee from sin" (Sir 21:2; Tobit 4:21) and to "pursue righteousness" (Deut 16:20; Prov 15:9; Isa 51:1; T. Reu. 5:5). Paul appropriates this language in several of his letters (Rom 9:30; 12:13; 1 Cor 6:18; 10:14; 14:1; 1 Thess 5:15).

Elijah (1 Kgs 17:18, 24; 2 Kgs 1:9–13; 4:9, 16, 22, 40), Elisha (2 Kgs 8:3; 13:19), and other servants of God. Paul's use of this lofty expression indicates the solemn responsibility resting on Timothy and the venerable trajectory of men of God preceding him.

Paul's directive for Timothy to "flee" (φεῦγε) from these vices and "pursue" (δίωκε) these virtues underscores the intensity with which his apostolic delegate is to fulfill his calling. Both "flee" and "pursue" are strong verbs, suggesting that Timothy must be deliberate in both directions—take flight from the vices of the false teachers and continue in hot pursuit of Christian virtues. The NT urges all people to flee from God's coming wrath (Matt 3:7; 23:33; 24:16), calling them to take seriously the destructive and eternal consequences of sin. In his first letter to the Corinthians, Paul urged them to flee sexual immorality and idolatry (1 Cor 6:18; 10:14) and to pursue love (14:1; cf. chap. 13). In his second and final letter to Timothy, Paul will plead with Timothy to "flee from youthful passions" and to "pursue righteousness, faith, love, and peace" (2 Tim 2:22).

"These things" (ταῦτα; v. 11) refers to the vices mentioned in the previous section (vv. 3–10), especially those related to false doctrine and greed. In comparison to 2 Tim 2:22, Paul here includes references to godliness, endurance, and gentleness while omitting reference to peace; righteousness, faith, and love are shared in common by both lists. These six virtues contrast with the five vices associated with the false teachers in vv. 4–5. Where the opponents exhibit envy, quarreling, slander, evil suspicions, and constant disagreements, Timothy must pursue righteousness (δικαιοσύνη; cf. 2 Tim 2:22; 3:16; 4:8), godliness (εὐσέβεια; 2:2; 3:16; 4:7–8; 6:3, 5–6; 2 Tim 3:5), faith (πίστις; cf. 1:4–5, 14, 19; 4:12), love (ἀγάπη; cf. 1:5, 14; 2:15; 4:12), endurance (ὑπομονή; 2 Tim 3:10; Titus 2:2), and gentleness (πραϋπαθία; only here in the NT; cf. 2 Tim 2:25).

To summarize, Timothy, and with him every man and woman of God, is to be fueled by a strong desire to put as great a distance as possible between himself and evil, avoiding ungodly associations of any kind, and doing everything in his power to exemplify righteousness, faith, love, and other Christian virtues. Followers of Christ are to love and do what is right (or, as Jesus put it, "hunger and thirst for righteousness"; Matt 5:6). They are to cultivate godly character, trust God in all things, love friends and foes alike, and display endurance and gentleness, particularly in dealing with opponents inside and outside the church.

As though these charges were not solemn enough, Paul intensifies his pleas still further, exhorting Timothy to "fight the good fight of the faith" and to "take hold of eternal life" to which he was called when making his "good confession" in the "presence of many witnesses." The imperatives "fight" and "take hold" are juxtaposed without a connecting "and" (asyndeton).[342] In "fighting the good fight" (ἀγωνίζου τὸν καλὸν ἀγῶνα), Timothy should follow the example of his teacher (1 Cor 9:25; Phil 1:30; Col 1:29; 2:1; 4:12; 1 Thess 2:2; 1 Tim 4:10; 2 Tim 4:7). Gospel ministry won't always be an easy calling; it involves struggle and hard work on behalf of others. Paul wants Timothy not to be soft or timid but realistic and tough-minded. Athletic metaphors and other illustrations depicting the struggle of Christian ministry are frequent in Paul (e.g., 1 Cor 9:24–27; 2 Tim 2:3–7).[343]

Timothy also is to "take hold of eternal life" to which he was called when making his "good confession" in the "presence of many witnesses." "Called" (ἐκλήθης; cf. 2 Tim 1:9) is a "divine passive" implying God as agent. "Eternal life" in Paul tends to invoke the future (Titus 1:2; 3:7), though the lines aren't always sharply drawn (cf. 1:16; 2 Tim 1:10). Immediately following this passage, Jesus Christ is said to have made the ultimate "good confession" before Pontius Pilate (v. 13). In Timothy's case the public acknowledgment in view is probably that made at his ordination service (1:18; 4:14; cf. 2 Tim 1:6). The reference to the "many witnesses" once again adds solemnity to Paul's charge, as does the connection Paul establishes between Timothy's "good confession" and that of Jesus. Now that Timothy has made this confession, he must not turn back (cf. Luke 9:57–62). Rather, he should constantly reaffirm his commitment by courageous witness that is not afraid to suffer for the truth.

Paul's exhortation for Timothy to "take hold" (ἐπιλαβοῦ) of eternal life is reminiscent of the apostle's own practice of pressing on to take hold of that which Christ Jesus took hold of for him (καταλαμβάνω; Phil 3:12–14; 1 Cor 9:24). Toward that end Timothy must

---

[342] S. E. Runge, *Discourse Grammar of the Greek New Testament* (Peabody, MA: Hendrickson, 2010), 20: "Asyndeton means that the writer did not specify a relation" (p. 20). It is used "where the relation between clauses is clear" (p. 21).

[343] Cf. Pfitzner, *Paul and the Agōn Motif*, 165–86.

lay aside all fears, scruples, and encumbrances and fight for the faith regardless of any opposition, suffering, or other negative consequences. Whether convenient or not, Timothy must preach the gospel (2 Tim 4:2). What's more, not only should Timothy embrace this goal; so should everyone, even the wealthy (v. 19). Unlike other places where he stresses the "already" side of the end times, Paul here focuses on the "not yet" part of the Christian life. Only the coming age will witness believers' entrance into eternal life, "what is truly life" (v. 19).

6:13–16 "In the presence of God" is yet another solemn phrase underscoring the seriousness of Paul's charge. Apart from introducing two trustworthy sayings (2:3; 5:4), the expression occurs elsewhere in Paul's letters to Timothy always with διαμαρτύρομαι (5:21; 2 Tim 2:14; 4:1); here Paul uses the roughly equivalent term παραγγέλλω (both translated "charge" in the CSB). In 5:21, Paul's charge is before God, Christ Jesus, and the elect angels; here it is before God, "who gives life to all" (ζῳογονοῦντος; cf. Luke 17:33; Acts 7:19), and Christ Jesus, "who gave a good confession before Pontius Pilate."

The view of God as the giver of life is firmly anchored in the Jewish concept of God the Creator. Jesus's testimony before Pontius Pilate, the Roman governor, is attested by all four Gospels (most of whom simply refer to "Pilate"; "Pontius" is found elsewhere only in Luke 3:1 and Acts 4:27) and forms part of early Christian witness and liturgy. Taken together, both descriptions add further weight to Paul's exhortation. "Good confession" provides the wider context for the reference to Timothy making the "good confession" in v. 12 (ὁμολογία, "confession," occurs elsewhere in the NT only in 2 Cor 9:13; Heb 3:1; 4:14; 10:23).

What, then, is Paul's charge? It is for Timothy to keep "this command" (the only instance of the singular ἐντολή in the LTT; cf. Acts 17:15), which probably invokes Paul's threefold exhortation in vv. 11–12 to "flee and pursue," "fight the good fight," and "take hold of eternal life" in summary fashion, though a more general reference is possible as well.[344] "Without fault or failure" combines the rough

[344] Note N. Eubank, "Almsgiving Is 'the Commandment': A Note on 1 Timothy 6.6–19," *NTS* 58 (2012): 144–50, who argues that "the commandment" was a common idiom in Rabbinic Judaism for almsgiving and has that meaning in 1 Tim 6:14, bringing 1 Tim 6:11–16 to better cohere with the surrounding paragraphs (6:6–10 and 6:17–19), both of which address wealth issues. Cf. similarly A. Giambrone, "'According to the Commandment' (*Did.* 1.5): Lexical Reflections on Almsgiving as

synonyms ἄσπιλος (Jas 1:27; 1 Pet 1:19; 2 Pet 3:14) and ἀνεπίλημπτος (3:2; 5:7; the more common NT term is ἄμωμος). In keeping with the requirements for overseers/elders, Timothy must be "blameless" (cf. 3:2). Paul closes with a reference to the Second Coming, the "appearing" (ἐπιφανεία; cf. 2 Thess 2:8; 2 Tim 4:1, 8; Titus 2:13; §6.6) of our Lord Jesus Christ (more common NT designations are παρουσία and ἀποκάλυψις, neither of which occurs in the LTT), assuring Timothy that God will bring it about in his own time (as in 2:6 and 4:1, the Greek is plural, καιροῖς ἰδίοις; cf. Titus 1:3). The reference is to God's sovereignty over all salvation history, including that still future.

In a great sevenfold closing doxology (cf. 1:17), Paul speaks of God (§3.1) as "the blessed and only Sovereign, the King of kings, and the Lord of lords, who alone is immortal and who lives in unapproachable light, whom no one has seen or can see." To this God, Paul says in concluding the doxology, "be honor and eternal power. Amen." It's possible that Paul adapts this from Hellenistic synagogue worship. "Sovereign" renders the rare term δυνάστης, found elsewhere in the NT only in Luke's writings where it refers to human rulers (Luke 1:52; Acts 8:27). Slightly more common is δεσπότης (Luke 2:29; Acts 4:24; 2 Pet 2:1; Jude 4; Rev 6:10; see esp. Jude 4, where Jesus Christ is called "our only Master and Lord"; see at 1 Tim 6:2a; much more frequent is κύριος, "Lord"). Paul calls that Sovereign both "blessed" (μακάριος) and the "only" Sovereign (μόνος), both common Jewish designations for God. "King of kings and Lord of lords" also has OT precedent (cf. esp. Deut 10:17: "God of gods and Lord of lords"; Ps 136:2–3), identifying God as the ultimate King and supreme Lord in characteristic Semitic style (similarly, Rev 19:16; cf. Rev 17:14).[345] The combination of the terms "Sovereign," "King," and "Lord" emphatically affirms God's sovereignty over human affairs (cf. Isa 40:12–31; Dan 4:35),

---

'The Commandment,'" *NTS* 60 (2014): 448–65. At least some of the rabbinic examples Eubank cites, however, are (as he notes) likely to be dated late enough that they would not inform Paul's use of ἐντολή here, and 1 Tim 6:11–16 sufficiently coheres with its context even without an explicit reference to wealth.

[345] Cf. G. K. Beale, "The Origin of the Title 'King of Kings and Lord of Lords' in Revelation 17.14," *NTS* 31 (1985): 618–20, who argues that Dan 4:37 (LXX), rather than 1 Enoch 9:4, is the source of the expression "king of kings and lord of lords" in Rev 17:14 (cf. Rev 19:11–21, esp. v. 16). See also T. B. Slater, "'King of Kings and Lord of Lords' Revisited," *NTS* 39 (1993): 159–60.

adding further weight and solemnity to Paul's charge. God's supreme authority dwarfs all competing claims by comparison.

In the second part of the doxology, Paul affirms that God alone is immortal (cf. 1 Cor 15:53–54) and lives in unapproachable light (cf. Ps 104:2: "He wraps himself in light as if it were a robe"). "Immortality" is a Greek concept corresponding to the notion of "eternal life" (see on v. 12 above). God alone is not subject to death (rather, death is subject to God). He is the giver of life (v. 13) and dwells in unapproachable (ἀπρόσιτος; only here in the NT) light, removed from human sight (cf. Exod 33:20; John 1:18), for he is too holy for sinful human beings to behold. This understanding of God as transcendent coheres with OT depictions of God (e.g., at Sinai). Paul fittingly closes the doxology with the words, "to him be honor [τιμή] and eternal power [κράτος; cf. 1 Pet 4:11; 5:11; Jude 25; Rev 1:6; 5:13]. Amen."

6:17–19 Almost as an afterthought (note the preceding benediction), the apostle adds a closing word of advice (on παράγγελλω, see v. 13 above) for "those who are rich in this present age" (cf. Titus 2:12; 2 Tim 4:10; §4.1.2.5).[346] This may refer to people who don't have to work for a living. Earlier in the chapter Paul spelled out the benefits of contentment in contrast to the opponents' desire to get rich, warning against the "love of money" (vv. 6–10). Now Paul counsels Timothy directly on how to deal with wealthy individuals in the Ephesian church, of which there may have been quite a few (cf. 2:9; 5:13). At the same time, the congregation also included slaves (vv. 1–2), needy widows (5:3–16), and people from a variety of socioeconomic backgrounds.

Paul's overriding concern is that such people not succumb to the sin of arrogance (ὑψηλοφρονεῖν; cf. Rom 11:20: ὑψηλὰ φρόνει) and place their ultimate confidence in material possessions. A person's self-worth and identity don't depend on external factors such as one's wealth or lack thereof. In fact, wealth is a highly precarious object of trust (ἀδηλότης, "uncertainty," occurs only here in the NT). As Paul wrote earlier: "We brought nothing into the world, and we can take nothing out" (v. 7). In the seven letters of Revelation, the risen Jesus excoriates the church of Laodicea for claiming to be rich while being in fact poor, spiritually speaking (Rev 3:17–18).

---

[346] For an analysis of 1 Tim 6:6–10 and 17–19, see Dschulnigg, "Warnung vor Reichtum und Ermahnung der Reichen."

Positively, well-to-do believers should put their hope in God, who richly (πλουσίως, a wordplay) provides us (ἡμῖν, the entire Christian community, cf. 2 Tim 1:7, 9, 14) with all things for our enjoyment (ἀπόλαυσις; with a negative connotation in Heb 11:25). Gratitude rather than conceit is the proper response to material blessing from the Lord. What's more, people who have been blessed with material possessions should recognize their special obligation to share their wealth with the needy. They are to "do what is good" (ἀγαθοεργεῖν; cf. Acts 14:17; the synonym ἀγαθοποιέω occurs in Luke's and Peter's writings and in 3 John 11) and to be "rich in good works" (another wordplay), generous (εὐμεταδότους), and willing to share (κοινωνικούς). For no one can ever outgive God (Titus 3:6).[347]

Rather than putting their confidence in the uncertainty of riches, the rich will thus store up treasure for themselves (ἀποθησαυρίζω, an intensification of θησαυρίζω; only here in the NT) that will serve as a good foundation (θεμέλιον καλόν; rare in ancient literature) for the age to come (contrasted with the present age in v. 17), so that they may take hold of "what is truly life" (cf. 5:3, 5, 16: "real widow"). This admonition mirrors Paul's earlier exhortation to Timothy to "take hold of eternal life to which you were called" (v. 12). Once again Paul's advice echoes that of Jesus, who told his followers to store up treasures in heaven rather than on earth (Matt 6:19–21; cf. Luke 6:35; 12:21, 33–34; 16:9). As Paul wrote to the well-off Corinthians, Jesus serves as the ultimate example: he was rich but became poor so that we might become rich through his poverty (2 Cor 8:9; cf. 4:8).

Paul, himself on occasion the beneficiary of wealthy patrons (e.g., Rom 16:1–2; Phlm 1–2, 5–7, 22) and no ascetic, doesn't disparage wealth as such. Yet he's concerned for the spiritual condition of the rich. Like Jesus he knows it's more difficult for those who have an abundance of material possessions to place their trust fully in God. He therefore counsels rich believers to turn such a potential spiritual liability into an advantage by sharing some of what they have with those who are in need. Similar to needy widows, the rich should place their hope exclusively in God (5:5; 6:17).

---

[347] See the study by M. E. Sheldon, "The Apostle Paul's Theology of Good Works, with Special Emphasis on 1 Timothy 6:17–19" (Ph.D. diss., Southeastern Baptist Theological Seminary, 2012).

In terms of biblical theology, the *inclusio* in 6:3 involving the use of the rare word ἑτεροδιδασκαλεῖν ("teach false doctrine"; cf. 1:3) brings the letter back to the original concern, that of subversion of the apostolic message and mission. Accordingly, the false teaching of the opponents is contrasted with the "healthy teaching" (ὑγιαίνω) of Paul and Timothy. Against the backdrop of the false teachers, the virtue of godliness is held up as paramount (the term εὐσέβεια occurs three times in 6:3, 5, and 6). As in 4:1–5, the activity of the false teachers, and the sphere of the apostolic mission, is set in an eschatological framework (§6) in at least three ways: (1) the reference to the "appearing of our Lord Jesus Christ" (6:13–14); (2) the reference to "the coming age" (6:19); and (3) the repeated reference to eternal life (6:12, 19). In this way the letter provides closure by ending as it began and by tying together the ecclesiological issues at stake in the apostolic mission within an overall end-time compass that serves the purpose of conveying a sense of urgency. While the threat of the false teachers is serious, the final outcome is not in doubt: God is on the throne; he is the judge; and Paul and Timothy are on the right side of history while the false teachers are not.

Bridge

On the whole the letter displays the apostle's deep concern for a local church and his apostolic delegate in the context of his mission to propagate the gospel of God's salvation in Christ. Like a mother hen Paul is jealously protective of the church and instructs Timothy to put the false teachers in their place, even to remove sinning elders if necessary, in order to preserve the church from falling into error. In this regard Paul's primary concern is with establishing and/or restoring proper leadership in the church, that is, a plurality of qualified, mature men who aspire to leadership in order to serve others rather than pursuing selfish gain, as is characteristic of the false teachers. The LTT make a unique contribution to the NT canon by highlighting the importance of the purity of the church as overseen by properly constituted and authorized leadership.

VI. Closing (6:20–21)

> [20] Timothy, guard what has been entrusted to you, avoiding irreverent and empty speech and contradictions from what is falsely called knowledge. [21] By professing it, some people have departed from the faith.
> Grace be with you all.

6:20–21 Paul concludes this letter with one last exhortation to Timothy, calling on him to oppose what is falsely called "knowledge" (see further below). The CSB doesn't translate the initial Greek word Ὦ: "O Timothy." In some of its seventeen NT instances, this appellation has the potential of indicating intensity and depth of emotion (e.g., Gal 3:1: "You foolish Galatians"; cf. Matt 15:28 par.; Luke 24:25). It may also function as a literary address (Acts 1:1; v. 11). In the present instance the expression underscores the solemnity of Paul's appeal to his foremost disciple; this is the second time in this letter Timothy is called by name (cf. 1:18).

Paul wants Timothy to "guard" (φυλάσσω; cf. 5:21) what has been entrusted to him (παραθήκη) for careful preservation—the apostolic teaching (contrast the heterodox views promoted by the opponents).[348] In his second letter Paul similarly urges Timothy to "guard the good deposit" entrusted to him with the help of the Holy Spirit (2 Tim 1:14). This faithfulness, in turn, is rooted in the faithfulness of God himself, who, Paul is convinced, is able to "guard" what "has been entrusted" to him until that final day (2 Tim 1:12).[349]

For Timothy, guarding what has been entrusted to him includes both faithful proclamation (4:12–14; 6:2b; etc.) and pure living (4:11–13; 5:22–23; 6:11–12). Unlike the false teachers, who have deviated from the faith (see on v. 21 below; cf. 1:5–6; 5:15),

---

[348] Of the twenty-one NT occurrences of διδασκαλία, fifteen are in the LTT. Also, in the NT it is only in the LTT that Paul is described as a διδάσκαλος (1 Tim 2:7; 2 Tim 1:11), and the adjective διδακτικός occurs in the NT only in 1 Tim 2:7 and 2 Tim 1:11. These observations point to the heightened significance of "teaching" in the LTT as a function of preserving sound doctrine.

[349] Note the shift from παράδοσις in Paul's earlier letters (1 Cor 11:2; 2 Thess 2:15; 2 Thess 3:6) to παραθήκη in the LTT. Towner, *Letters to Timothy and Titus*, 431, contends this shift is due to an increased stress on protection, while pseudonymity advocates cite the shift as evidence for post-Pauline authorship (e.g., Oberlinner, *Pastoralbriefe*, 1.309).

Timothy must continually avoid (ἐκτρεπόμενος, cf. 1:6; pres. ptc.) irreverent, empty speech and contradictions "from what is falsely called knowledge." For Paul this large-scale apostasy is a mark of the end times, when people "will turn away from hearing the truth and will turn aside to myths" (2 Tim 4:4). In 2 Timothy, Paul reiterates his warning against "godless chatter" (βεβήλους κενοφωνίας; 2 Tim 2:16–17). "Godless" (βέβηλος) is also used for the "ungodly" for whom the law is made (1:9) and for the "pointless myths" indulged in by Timothy's opponents (4:7).

"Contradictions" translates ἀντιθέσεις, a term not found elsewhere in the NT (but see Plutarch, *Mor.* 953B; Philo, *Drunkenness* 187).[350] Just as Jannes and Jambres, the Egyptian magicians, opposed Moses, so these false teachers oppose the truth (ἀνθίστημι; 2 Tim 3:8). Similarly Timothy must be on guard against Alexander, who "strongly opposed our message" (ἀνθίστημι; 2 Tim 4:15). The opponents erroneously (ψευδωνύμου; cf. Plutarch, *Mor.* 953B; Philo, *Moses* 2.171) designate their deviant teaching as "knowledge" (γνώσεως). Yet while the false teachers claim special inside knowledge of spiritual things, in reality such teaching masks massive ignorance of what God truly requires (1:7).

Rather than identifying Gnosticism (which only developed in the second century AD) as the likely background, it is more promising to turn to passages such as 2 Tim 2:18, according to which the opponents claimed that the resurrection had already taken place.[351] Perhaps the false teachers saw themselves as living already in the age to come and thus claimed special knowledge (cf., e.g., 2:15; 4:1, 3). Paul, however, sharply refutes such overrealized eschatology resulting in ignorant and harmful teachings, contending that only one body of teaching is entrusted to Timothy that corresponds to the "knowledge of the truth" and that all contrary teaching be rejected.[352]

---

[350] Cf. Schlarb, *Gesunde Lehre*, 62–66; Schlarb, "Miszelle zu 1 Tim 6:20," *ZNW* 77 (1986): 276–81, who notes that the author's contrasts involve use of terms built off the verb τίθημι, the prefixes ἀντί and ἀπό, and use of plurals.

[351] See esp. Towner, "Gnosis and Realized Eschatology," 104–5, who notes the close connection between 1 Tim 6:20–21 and 2 Tim 2:15–18.

[352] Cf. Paul's words in 1 Cor 13:12 affirming that knowledge in the present is only partial while full knowledge awaits the final state. Note that 1 Corinthians was written while Paul engaged in ministry in Ephesus (1 Cor 6:8), the same location where Timothy was located at the writing of 1 Timothy.

Interestingly, the letter concludes without any final greetings. Instead Paul closes rather abruptly with the words "grace be with you all" (CSB; there is no Greek equivalent to the English word "all" other than the plural of "you"). While not an uncommon parting greeting (cf. Col 4:18; 2 Tim 4:22), the expression was usually supplemented by more extensive qualifiers such as "with you *all*" (Titus 3:15; Heb 13:25), "the grace *of the* [or *'our'*] *Lord Jesus* [*Christ*]" (Rom 16:20; 1 Thess 5:28), or the like. The fact that "you" is in the plural indicates that the apostle intends to greet not only Timothy but the entire congregation to whom the letter was going to be read.[353]

[353] See J. Ellington, "Problem Pronouns in Private Letters," *BT* 50 (1999): 222–23, who notes that (1) the shift in pronouns from singular to plural is found only at the benediction; (2) the LTT all close with a similar plural address; (3) this greeting finds a precedent in Paul's earlier letters in the epistle to the Colossians. He concludes that these letters "were, at least at some point, meant for the Church as a whole" (p. 223). Cf. Knight, *Pastoral Epistles*, 277, who similarly contends that the use of plural pronouns "indicates that Paul expected this letter to be read to the believers, and it further indicates that all along he has had them, not just Timothy, in view." Other commentators, however, following Moulton, counter that similar to papyri letters the singular and plural may alternate with no apparent distinction in meaning.

EXPOSITION OF 2 TIMOTHY

Occasion and Purpose

Second Timothy marks the final chapter in Paul's story;[1] Bengel asserts, "This letter is Paul's testament and swan song."[2] A few years have likely passed since Paul wrote his first letter to Timothy. It's unknown whether Paul's visit (announced in 1 Tim 3:14–15 and assumed in 4:13) ever materialized. While Timothy is still on assignment in Ephesus, Paul is no longer in Macedonia (1 Tim 1:3) but once again in prison, most likely in Rome (2 Tim 1:8). Unlike his first imprisonment, when he stayed in his own rented house and received all who came to see him (cf. Acts 28:30), Paul is now suffering "to the point of being bound like a criminal" (2:9). As a result, he anticipates shortly "being poured out as a drink offering" (4:6), a reference to his imminent martyrdom (Eusebius, *Hist. eccl.* 2.22).

For these reasons Paul's second letter to Timothy is much more personal in nature than the first, which included specific

---

[1] See P. H. Towner, "The Portrait of Paul and the Theology of 2 Timothy: The Closing Chapter of the Pauline Story," *HorBT* 21 (1999): 151–69, who notes that Paul appears to have taken his missiological bearings from the OT prophets who proclaimed God's plan for the nations (cf. esp. Rom 15:1–13, 15–16, 21–24, Gal 1:15; 2 Cor 6:2) and that the climax of Paul's story (esp. 2 Timothy 4) harks back to Psalm 21 (LXX). Towner refers to T. L. Donaldson, *Paul and the Gentiles* (Minneapolis: Fortress, 1997), 249–60; M. Hengel, *Between Jesus and Paul* (London: SCM, 1983), 51–52; and R. Riesner, *Die Frühzeit des Apostels Paulus: Studien zur Chronologie, Missionsstrategie und Theologie*, WUNT 71 (Tübingen: Mohr-Siebeck, 1994), 207–13.

[2] J. A. Bengel, *Gnomon Novi Testamenti* (London: Nutt, Williams, and Norgate, 1855), 837.

instructions on how to deal with problems in the Ephesian church. Paul is in a reminiscent mood (1:3–6), and his second letter to Timothy assumes the character of a last testament in which Paul writes to his foremost disciple for the last time, appealing to him to "preach the word" of the Christian gospel (2 Tim 4:1–2) as he passes on the mantle to Timothy. While urging Timothy to come to him "soon . . . before winter" (4:9, 21), Paul may or may not actually have seen him one last time.

Timothy's role is all the more critical as many of Paul's associates have abandoned him when Paul writes his second and final letter to Timothy. Paul's ministry is rapidly drawing to a close; after his demise Paul's legacy and the continuation of the apostolic ministry will rest on Timothy's shoulders. In salvation history this book marks the transition from the apostolic to the post-apostolic period, during which believers are charged to build on the foundation of the apostles and to guard the "good deposit" made by them (2 Tim 1:12, 14). But the apostle touches on many topics of perennial significance in this letter that are not limited to the original circumstance to which they are addressed.[3]

The Opponents

Little overt attention is given to Timothy's and Paul's opponents in 2 Timothy. Nevertheless, there is reason to believe that the false teachers don't merely serve as a foil for Paul's exhortation of Timothy (though they do that) but in addition represent real opponents who misunderstand and mischaracterize the Christian teaching on the resurrection (see esp. 2 Tim 2:18). While the primary purpose of 2 Timothy is hortatory rather than aiming to repudiate the false teachers directly, the writer does confront teaching that reflects an overrealized eschatology.[4]

[3] E.g., the affirmation in 2 Tim 1:9–10; the "trustworthy saying" in 2:11–13; and the "inscription" in 2 Tim 2:19. For a discussion of the theology of 2 Timothy, see G. D. Fee, "Toward a Theology of 2 Timothy—from a Pauline Perspecive," in *Society of Biblical Literature 1997 Seminar Papers*, SBLSP 36 (Atlanta: Scholars Press, 1977), 732–49.

[4] See J. L. Sumney, "Studying Paul's Opponents: Advances and Challenges," in *Paul and His Opponents*, ed. S. E. Porter, Pauline Studies 2 (Leiden: Brill, 2005), 43; D. T. Thornton, *Hostility in the House of God: An Investigation of the Opponents in 1 and 2 Timothy*, BBRSup 15 (Winona Lake, IN: Eisenbrauns, 2016).

Structure

P. H. Towner outlines 2 Timothy as follows:

I. Opening Greeting (1:1–2)

II. Body of the Letter (1:3–4:8)

- A. Call to Personal Commitment (1:3–18)
- B. Call to Dedication and Faithfulness (2:1–13)
- C. The Challenge of Opposition (2:14–26)
- D. Prophecy, Commitment, and Call (3:1–4:8)

III. Final Instructions (4:9–18)

IV. Closing Greetings (4:19–22).[5]

An alternative outline is provided by C. Westfall:

I. Epistolary Opening and Thanksgiving (1:1–5)

II. Body of the Letter: Paul's moral exhortation to Timothy (1:6–4:8)

- A. Body Opening: Paul is Timothy's spiritual father and model (1:6–18)
- B. Body Middle (2:1–3:17)
  1. Timothy is entrusted with a gospel of suffering (2:1–13)
  2. Timothy's conduct in teaching and speech (2:14–21)
  3. Timothy's conduct in conflict with his opponents (2:22–26)
  4. Paul is Timothy's ultimate model (3:1–17)
- C. Body Closing: Paul's charge and Timothy's commission (4:1–8)

III. Epistolary Closing (4:9–22).[6]

---

[5] P. H. Towner, *The Letters to Timothy and Titus*, NICNT (Grand Rapids: Eerdmans, 2006), xi. Marshall's proposal (*Pastoral Epistles* [Edinburgh: T&T Clark, 1999], 38) is identical.

[6] C. L. Westfall, "A Moral Dilemma: The Epistolary Body of 2 Timothy," in *Paul and the Ancient Letter Form*, Pauline Studies 6, ed. S. E. Porter and S. A. Adams (Leiden/Boston: Brill, 2010), 251. D. T. Thornton, "Hostility in the House of God:

The commentary below proceeds on the basis of the following outline:[7]

I. Letter Opening (1:1–5)
   A. Greeting (1:1–2)
   B. Thanksgiving (1:3–5)

II. Body Opening: Personal Exhortation (1:6–18)
   A. Call to Suffering and Faithfulness (1:6–14)
   B. Faithless and Faithful Coworkers (1:15–18)

III. Body Middle: Ministry Metaphors and Additional Exhortations (2:1–4:8)
   A. Ministry Metaphors, Paul's Gospel, and a Trustworthy Saying (2:1–26)
      1. Three Ministry Metaphors: Soldier, Athlete, Farmer (2:1–7)
      2. Paul's Gospel and a Trustworthy Saying (2:8–13)
      3. Three Additional Ministry Roles: Workman, Instrument, Servant (2:14–26)
         a. Workman (2:14–19)
         b. Instrument (2:20–21)
         c. Servant (2:22–26)
   B. Additional Exhortations (3:1–4:8)
      1. Latter-Day Apostasy (3:1–9)
      2. Stay the Course (3:10–17)

IV. Body Closing: Preach the Word (4:1–8)

V. Letter Closing (4:9–22)
   A. Recent News (4:9–18)
   B. Final Greetings and Farewell (4:19–22)

An 'Interested' Investigation of the Opponents in 1 and 2 Timothy" (Ph.D. thesis, University of Otago, 2015), 25, outlines the body of 2 Timothy as follows:

Paul and Timothy: The Difficulties of Ministry (1:3–2:13)
Timothy and the Opponents (2:14–3:9)
Paul and Timothy: Fulfill Your Ministry (3:10–4:8)

[7] Cf. A. J. Köstenberger, "1–2 Timothy, Titus," in *Expositor's Bible Commentary*, vol. 12: *Ephesians–Philemon*, rev. ed. (Grand Rapids: Zondervan, 2005), 566. The outline used here mostly follows Westfall. In addition, it incorporates insights gained from Towner and other commentators.

Exposition of 2 Timothy

Paul's second letter to Timothy opens with the customary greeting and thanksgiving (1:1–7), followed by an exhortation for Timothy not to be ashamed of Paul, who is now in prison (1:8–14). After contrasting various coworkers (1:15–18), Paul instructs Timothy on the nature of Christian ministry by way of three metaphors: the soldier, the athlete, and the farmer. Each has an important lesson to teach regarding the proper disposition of the Lord's servant (2:1–7). After discussing his gospel and adducing a trustworthy saying (2:8–13), Paul employs three additional metaphors for Christian ministry: the worker, various household instruments, and the servant (2:14–26). Further instructions (on latter-day apostasy and staying the course; 3:1–17), as well as a solemn charge to preach the word (4:1–8), recent news (4:9–18), and final greetings (4:19–22) conclude this highly personal letter.

Genre

It's often suggested that 2 Timothy represents a farewell discourse or last will or testament. In fact, 2 Timothy is Paul's final letter to his foremost disciple containing various exhortations and instructions. In terms of formal literary characteristics, however, parallels between 2 Timothy and testamentary literature such as *Testaments of the Twelve Patriarchs* aren't particularly pronounced.[8] Instead, the setting depicts a shared context between Paul, the seasoned apostle, and Timothy, who is to continue his mentor's legacy. Paul asks Timothy to join him in ministry (1:8; 2:3), presents himself as a model in suffering (e.g., 1:11–14), and expresses his hope that he will see Timothy again (4:9, 21).

More likely, 2 Timothy presents a pattern of moral exhortation (paraenesis).[9] As Malherbe notes, "Paraenesis is the moral

[8] See, e.g., the study by C. A. Smith, "A Study of 2 Timothy 4:1–8: The Contribution of Epistolary Analysis and Rhetorical Criticism" (Ph.D. thesis, University of Bristol, 2005), on which see further the note at 4:1–8 below. See also Thornton, "Hostility in the House of God," 20–23.

[9] A. J. Malherbe, *Moral Exhortation: A Greco-Roman Sourcebook*, LEC 4 (Philadelphia: Westminster, 1986), 124, cited in Westfall, "Moral Dilemma," 223–25, who also refers to L. T. Johnson, *Letters to Paul's Delegates: 1 Timothy, 2 Timothy, Titus*, The New Testament in Context (Valley Forge, PA: Trinity Press International, 1996), 38–41.

exhortation in which someone is advised to pursue or abstain from something. . . . It contains useful rules for conduct in common situations and adopts styles that range from censure to consolation."[10] Moral exhortations contain a combination of some or all of the following elements:[11]

> Commands or admonitions (imperative, hortatory subjunctive, indirect commands with illocutionary force of commands)
>
> Traditional content that
>
> - is already known (cf., e.g., 1 Thess 2:9; 3:6)
> - is often signaled by a variation of the disclosure formula (e.g., 1 Thess 1:5; 2:2, 5, 11; 3:4; καθὼς οἴδατε)
> - is generally applicable (though applied to a specific person and/or circumstance)
> - has no need of further instruction (e.g., 2 Cor 9:1–2; 1 Thess 4:9; 5:1; οὐ χρείαν ἔχετε ὑμῖν)
>
> Commendations of what the recipient is already doing and encouragement to continue (1 Thess 4:1, 10; 5:11)
>
> Positive and/or negative examples to emulate or avoid (Acts 20:31–34; 1 Thess 1:6; 2:1–8; 2 Thess 3:7–9)
>
> Appeals to honor and/or shame

Remarkably, as Westfall notes, 2 Timothy possesses virtually every feature typical of first-century Greco-Roman moral exhortation.[12] Such advice, in turn, is often "associated with concerns of parental authority figures or mentors at the end of life."[13] This is where farewell discourses or final testaments and moral exhortation share common ground. In the present instance Paul issues a series of moral exhortations to Timothy ranging from commendations of Timothy's current conduct to exhortations to follow Paul's example and to avoid the negative examples of false teachers and appeals to join Paul in his shameful imprisonment that contributes to the greater honor of the gospel.

---

[10] Malherbe, *Moral Exhortation*, 124.

[11] See Westfall, "Moral Dilemma," 224–25, with primary reference to Malherbe, *Moral Exhortation*, 124.

[12] Westfall, "Moral Dilemma," 225.

[13] Ibid.

Commentary

I. Letter Opening (1:1–5)

The letter opening establishes common ground between Paul and Timothy in terms of a familial spiritual relationship of father and dearly loved son (v. 2). The intimacy is nurtured also by Paul's reference to Timothy's mother Eunice and grandmother Lois (v. 5), both by name. It is further accentuated by Paul's reminiscences of the history of his relationship with Timothy (see esp. the reference to "tears" in v. 4) and reinforced by various references to the intergenerational aspect of his and Timothy's common faith (including to Paul's "ancestors," v. 3). In this way the letter opening lays a strong foundation for references to Paul as Timothy's mentor and model in the faith (and in particular in suffering) later in the letter.[14]

A. Greeting (1:1–2)

[1] Paul, an apostle of Christ Jesus by God's will, for the sake of the promise of life in Christ Jesus:

[2] To Timothy, my dearly loved son.

Grace, mercy, and peace from God the Father and Christ Jesus our Lord.

1:1–2 The epistolary greeting resembles that of most contemporary Greco-Roman letters. Paul's second letter to Timothy opens almost exactly the same way as the first. Again Paul states his office ("apostle of Christ Jesus"), his divine appointment ("by God's will"), and his ministry focus ("for the sake of the promise of life in Christ Jesus").[15] On a minor scale, "will" replaces "command," and "for the sake of the promise of life in Christ Jesus"

---

[14] Westfall, "Moral Dilemma," 239.

[15] Note that the phrase "by the will of God" is found only in the LTT and several of Paul's other NT letters but rarely in other literature, whether the LXX, Philo, Josephus, or the apostolic fathers. R. W. Yarbrough, *1–2 Timothy, Titus*, PNTC (Grand Rapids: Eerdmans, forthcoming), commentary at 2 Tim 1:1. Yarbrough notes that the phrase conveys the following: (1) authority; (2) personal relationship with God; and (3) a strong tie to Jesus (ibid.).

takes the place of "God our Savior and of Christ Jesus our hope."[16] Rather than "my true son in the faith," Timothy is called "my dearly loved son."[17] The greeting in v. 2b is unchanged.

B. Thanksgiving (1:3–5)

> [3] I thank God, whom I serve with a clear conscience as my ancestors did, when I constantly remember you in my prayers night and day. [4] Remembering your tears, I long to see you so that I may be filled with joy. [5] I recall your sincere faith that first lived in your grandmother Lois and in your mother Eunice and now, I am convinced, is in you also.

Relation to Surrounding Context

Unlike 1 Timothy, 2 Timothy follows the more customary format of opening plus introductory thanksgiving. The more personal "my dearly loved son" in v. 2 is followed by a moving expression of affection in vv. 3–5, including references to Timothy's grandmother and mother, both of whom are mentioned by name. Paul's purpose at the outset is to encourage Timothy by reminding him of the strong roots in the faith he has through his maternal (though not paternal) line.

Structure

The entire thanksgiving, broken up in English for stylistic reasons, is one long sentence in the original Greek. It reads something like this: "I thank God . . . as I ceaselessly remember you in

---

[16] "Promise of life in Christ Jesus" anticipates the later reference to the prospect of imminent martyrdom (2 Tim 4:6). See also the reference in 1 Tim 4:8 to godliness holding "promise for the present life and also for the life to come."

[17] Thus the bond is perceived as even closer. Westfall ("Moral Dilemma," 232) notes that there's a marked contrast between the father-son relationship postulated in the letters to Timothy and Paul's other letters where Timothy is identified as a fellow bondservant (Phil 1:1), coworker (Rom 16:21; 1 Thess 3:2), or Paul's (spiritual) brother (2 Cor 1:1; 1 Thess 3:2; Phil 1:1). It's doubtful, however, whether this really means Timothy is there presented "as Paul's equal in the mission to the Gentiles," as Westfall claims (ibid.). More likely these terms present the Paul-Timothy relationship in terms of partnership and joint association in ministry, though not necessarily in terms of (unfettered) equality. For this reason it also seems advisable not to draw too sharp a contrast between Timothy's respective designations in the letters to Timothy and Paul's other letters (see also 1 Cor 4:17, where Paul presents himself as Timothy's and the Corinthians' spiritual father, as noted by Westfall).

my prayers night and day, longing to see you, remembering your tears, so that I may be filled with joy. I recall your sincere faith." While the cadence may appear a bit rambling in English, it shows that in the original Paul's thanksgiving is of one cloth, and his fond memory of Timothy fueled his constant current intercession.

1:3–5 As typical in ancient letters, the opening greeting is followed by a thanksgiving.[18] Paul doesn't specify Timothy's location, which presumably is still Ephesus. It's somewhat unusual for Paul to mention his ancestors (cf. Phil 3:4–5); he may do so to convey generational continuity in God's service (cf. v. 5; 3:15).[19] Paul's conscience is clear even though he is currently in prison (2 Tim 2:9); yet ultimately, not even his conscience determines his guilt or innocence, but God alone is his judge (1 Cor 4:4).[20]

In characteristic hyperbole Paul writes that he "constantly" (ἀδιάλειπτον) remembers Timothy (ἔχω τήν . . . μνείαν, another Latinism) in his prayers "night and day."[21] This shows Paul's faithfulness in prayer, even while in prison. It also indicates that this letter strikes a more personal note and is less devoted to pressing concerns. The use of four different expressions for remembering highlights Paul's reminiscent mood.

---

[18] The customary εὐχαριστέω is replaced by the less common χάριν ἔχω, a Latinism; cf. 1 Tim 1:12. Note that this is the only standard instance of thanksgiving, a regular feature in Paul's other letters, in the LTT (Westfall, "Moral Dilemma," 233n67; though see 1 Tim 1:12–17). The thanksgiving bears a certain resemblance to Rom 1:8–11. See J. D. Quinn and W. C. Wacker, *The First and Second Letters to Timothy*, ECC (Grand Rapids: Eerdmans, 2000), 577–78: "It is as if the thanksgiving prayer for the Roman church was here set in a new key as a thanksgiving prayer from Rome."

[19] Yarbrough points out that the opening thanksgiving highlights heritage in terms of (1) ancestry, (2) a shared history of life and ministry, and (3) family faith (*1–2 Timothy, Titus*, commentary at 2 Tim 1:3–5).

[20] Note that both 1 and 2 Timothy open with a reference to "conscience." See further the commentary at 1 Tim 1:5 above. Here the reference is to a "clear" conscience (lit., "clean" or "pure" conscience, καθαρός, cf. 1 Tim 3:9 with regard to deacons); in 1 Tim 1:5 and commonly in the NT, the reference is to a "good" conscience (καλός). There is little (if any) discernible difference in meaning.

[21] Or, as people today would say, "day and night." See 1 Tim 5:5; cf. Acts 20:31; 1 Thess 3:10. On the entire thanksgiving, see Rom 1:9; 9:2; 1 Thess 1:2; 2:13; 5:17; cf. Eph 1:16; Phil 1:3; Phlm 4. As Westfall ("Moral Dilemma," 233) notes, "The thanksgiving and prayer in 1:3–5 is [*sic*] dominated by the semantic chain of memory, and consists of a complex sentence, so that the unit is easily determined formally."

2 Timothy 1:3–5

Paul already called Timothy his "dearly loved son" (v. 2). He now recalls (μεμνημένος; elsewhere in Paul only in 1 Cor 11:2) Timothy's tears—presumably at the occasion of their last parting of ways (cf. Acts 20:31, 37–38)[22]—and expresses his longing to see him (ἐπιποθῶν; Rom 1:11; Phil 1:8; 1 Thess 3:6). Paul's reference here may be to his arrest by Roman soldiers and his separation from Timothy and any other coworkers. The apostle is now in prison, and virtually all of his associates have gone their own separate ways. Paul knows he's approaching the end of his life (2 Tim 4:6–8) and thus longs to see his trusted deputy (cf. Rom 1:11; 1 Thess 3:6; Phil 2:26).[23]

The reason for Paul's gratitude is Timothy's "sincere faith" (ἀνυπόκριτος; see 1 Tim 1:5; cf. Rom 12:9; 2 Cor 6:6), which bodes well for Paul's continued legacy. Just as Jesus built his church on Peter on the basis of his confession (Matt 16:18–19), Paul entrusts Timothy with the apostolic church on account of his sincere faith. The permanence of this faith is shown in that Timothy himself carries on the living faith of his grandmother Lois (the term μάμμη is an endearing term equivalent to "grandma")[24] and his mother Eunice (a Jewish believer; Acts 16:1; cf. 2 Tim 3:15).[25] Just as Paul serves (the only instance of λατρεύω in the LTT) God as his

---

[22] Alternatively, though perhaps less likely, Paul may be referring to some other grief or calamity in Timothy's life of which he was aware. So Yarbrough, who speaks of "a track record of mutual support" between Paul and Timothy (*1–2 Timothy, Titus*, commentary at 2 Tim 1:4).

[23] This is the only reference to joy (χαρά) in the LTT. By contrast Paul frequently refers to joy in his other letters (20x); see, e.g., Rom 15:13; 2 Cor 7:4; Phil 2:2. Cf. M. A. Elliott, *Faithful Feelings: Rethinking Emotion in the New Testament* (Grand Rapids: Kregel, 2006), 172–75.

[24] See C. Spicq, "'Loïs, ta grand'maman' (II Tim., I, 5)," *RB* 84 (1977): 362–64: "un mot affectueux d'enfant (cf. l'anglais *grannie*)" (pp. 362–63). "Lived" (ἐνοικέω) is used in the NT only by Paul. Elsewhere the word describes the indwelling Spirit (Rom 8:11; 2 Tim 1:14) or the word of Christ dwelling richly among believers (Col 3:16). Here Paul indicates that Timothy's grandmother's faith was alive and active rather than merely perfunctory. Note that the word ἐνοικέω is found in v. 5 at the closing of the thanksgiving in vv. 3–5 and again in v. 14 at the closing of the next section in vv. 6–14.

[25] The word "convinced" (πείθω) is found in the first person singular in the LTT also in 2 Tim 1:12; elsewhere in Paul's writings in Rom 8:38; 14:14; 15:14; Gal 1:10; 5:10; and Phil 2:24; and on Paul's lips also in Acts 26:26. Yarbrough notes that perhaps Timothy's grandmother and possibly even his mother may have passed away by that time (*1–2 Timothy, Titus*, commentary at 2 Tim 1:5).

ancestors did (v. 3; cf. Acts 23:1; 24:14), so does Timothy.[26] In his first letter Paul emphasized the importance of a clear conscience (1 Tim 1:5, 19; 3:9; cf. 4:2). He doesn't take Timothy's genuine faith for granted, aware that the outward appearance of faith may mask inner bankruptcy (cf. 3:5).

In terms of biblical theology, the letter opening marks this as a deeply personal communication at a crucial juncture of the apostolic mission. Paul the apostle (v. 1) writes to Timothy, his "dearly loved son" (v. 2), in order to pass on the baton of the mission as his life draws to a close. Correspondingly, he hints at an end-time context by speaking of the "promise of life" right at the beginning of the letter (v. 2) and grounds the message of the letter in both theology proper ("God the Father"; §3.1) and Christology ("Christ Jesus our Lord," v. 2; §3.2). The opening thanksgiving in vv. 3–5 establishes continuity and antiquity by referring to Paul's "ancestors" (v. 3) and Timothy's "sincere faith" in continuity with that of his grandmother and mother (v. 5). The tone is thus set for the remainder of the letter in a way that is both solemn and testamentary in character. Paul's words here underscore how the Christian faith is passed on through deep interpersonal relationships and ministry partnerships. Not only does the father-son relationship between Paul and Timothy attest to the importance of committed, long-term spiritual mentoring and ministry training, Paul also stresses the deep roots each of them has in the faith, which adds great power and conviction to their ministry.

Bridge

The passage bears telling testimony to the beauty and gospel significance of long-lasting mentoring relationships. In his old age, when close to death, Paul derives great joy from knowing that the one he mentored consistently over a long period is ready to carry on his legacy and continue his mission.

---

[26] "Serve" (λατρεύω) denotes the performance of religious duties. The term occurs three other times in Paul's NT letters (cf. Rom 1:9, 25; Phil 3:3). Cf. Westfall, "Moral Dilemma," 234, who notes that the passage "underscores a generational awareness for Timothy that is similar to Paul's with his ancestors." "Ancestor" (πρόγονος) occurs in the NT only in 1 Tim 5:4. The word is found frequently in 2, 3, and 4 Maccabees as well as in Josephus and Philo.

II. Body Opening: Personal Exhortation (1:6–18)

Following the opening greeting and thanksgiving, Paul opens the body of his letter with a call to suffering and faithfulness (1:8–14), which replaces the opening appeal in Paul's first letter to Timothy. The occasion for the letter is "that Paul is in chains and wants Timothy to treat him, his situation and his commission with honor rather than shame, and particularly to join him in his suffering and in his commission."[27] In this vein the introduction of the body of Paul's letter closes with a contrast between faithful and faithless coworkers (1:15–18).[28]

A. Call to Suffering and Faithfulness (1:6–14)

[6]Therefore, I remind you to rekindle the gift of God that is in
you through the laying on of my hands. [7]For God has not given
us a spirit of fear, but one of power, love, and sound judgment.
[8]So don't be ashamed of the testimony about our Lord, or of
me his prisoner. Instead, share in suffering for the gospel, relying on the power of God. [9]He has saved us and called us with
a holy calling, not according to our works, but according to his
own purpose and grace, which was given to us in Christ Jesus
before time began. [10]This has now been made evident through
the appearing of our Savior Christ Jesus, who has abolished
death and has brought life and immortality to light through
the gospel. [11]For this gospel I was appointed a herald, apostle,
and teacher, [12]and that is why I suffer these things. But I am
not ashamed, because I know whom I have believed and am
persuaded that he is able to guard what has been entrusted to
me until that day.

[13]Hold on to the pattern of sound teaching that you have
heard from me, in the faith and love that are in Christ Jesus.
[14]Guard the good deposit through the Holy Spirit who lives in
us.

Relation to Surrounding Context

The expression "therefore" links the present section with the preceding thanksgiving, as does the word "remind" (v. 6; see the threefold instance of "remember/recall" in vv. 3–5). Thus the

[27] Westfall, "Moral Dilemma," 238–39.

[28] As Westfall (ibid., 235) points out, "The body opening in 1:6–18 is structured around a series of imperatives/reminders, and three examples (two of which are antithetical), all of which are typical of moral exhortation."

apostle moves from his memories of the past to present exhortation: "rekindle" (v. 6), "don't be ashamed" (v. 8), "share in suffering" (v. 8). This is followed by a brief doxology centered on the saving work of Christ (vv. 9–10). The threefold description of Paul's calling in v. 11 in terms identical to 1 Tim 2:7 (herald, apostle, teacher) establishes an important link between the two letters. Paul consistently presents the gospel as a stewardship he is to guard until the end of his life and then pass on to others like Timothy, who must do the same.

Structure

Verses 6–8 commence Paul's exhortation to Timothy; Paul's mention of the gospel and of the saving power of God in v. 8 seamlessly transitions into a brief doxology in vv. 9–10 on the same topic. This is followed by Paul's self-reference and testimony of trust in God in vv. 11–12 and a second series of exhortations addressed to Timothy in vv. 13–14.

1:6–7 The body opening flows from the opening thanksgiving: on the basis of Paul's confidence in the faith living in Timothy, he issues a reminder and series of exhortations (δι' ἣν αἰτίαν, "therefore," means more literally "because of this").[29] The word "remind" in v. 6 (ἀναμιμνῄσκω) harks back to the instances of "remember" in vv. 3 (μνείαν) and 4 (μεμνημένος).[30] In the context of moral exhortation, this reminder accentuates the history of the mentoring relationship and highlights Paul's role as an example.[31] At the outset of his personal exhortation, Paul reminds Timothy of his installation to ministry (cf. 1 Tim 4:14; cf. 1:18). Possibly due to the lack of a strong father figure (Acts 16:1 says that Timothy's father was Gentile, while his mother was "a believing Jewish woman"; cf. v. 5), Timothy may at times have lacked boldness in dealing with his opponents (cf. 1 Tim 4:12).[32] The memory of his ordination service

---

[29] For other NT uses, see 2 Tim 1:12; Titus 1:13. See also Luke 8:47; Acts 22:24; and Heb 2:11. Westfall (ibid., 236) calls this a "moderately emphatic complex conjunction in terms of marking the transition."

[30] Other Pauline instances of the word ἀναμιμνῄσκω are found in 1 Cor 4:17 and 2 Cor 7:15.

[31] Westfall, "Moral Dilemma," 236.

[32] But see C. R. Hutson, "Was Timothy Timid? On the Rhetoric of Fearlessness and Cowardice," *BibRes* 42 (1997): 58–73, who demurs from the usual characterization of Timothy as timid and argues that the passage describes Timothy as he *should* be, not as he *is* (p. 68), and claims the reference to timidity is a mere rhetorical device in keeping with Greco-Roman literature.

ought to reinvigorate him, restore his confidence, and remind him of his solemn responsibility to persevere in his ministry.

Correspondingly, Paul encourages Timothy to "rekindle" (CSB) or "fan into flame" (NIV; ἀναζωπυρεῖν; only here in the NT) the gift of God.[33] This may or may not imply that Timothy's zeal had waned; after all, Timothy is about to replace none other than the apostle Paul. Just as anyone who has tended a fire knows that it needs occasional stirring, all of God's servants must periodically renew their passion for serving God. The "gift of God" (τὸ χάρισμα τοῦ θεοῦ) that is in Timothy through the laying on of Paul's hands may be the pastoral ministry assigned to Timothy at his ordination service (cf. 1 Tim 4:14).[34] Alternatively, the Holy Spirit may be in view, or a combination of the two (i.e., the Spirit as the source of Timothy's ministry assignment). In the face of timidity (v. 7) or persecution (v. 8), the divine gift will help Timothy overcome and persevere.

As Paul reminds youthful Timothy (4:12; cf. 1 Cor 16:10), "God has not given us[35] a spirit[36] of fearfulness" (πνεῦμα δειλίας; only here in the NT; cf. Lev 26:36 LXX; Ps 54:4; Rom 8:15). Similarly, Jesus encouraged his followers not to be afraid (Matt 8:26 par. Mark 4:40; John 14:27), and the apostle John observed that "perfect love drives out fear" (1 John 4:18). God has given us a spirit

---

[33] The term, not used elsewhere in the NT, is used figuratively in the sense of rekindling or reviving also in the LXX (Gen 45:27 LXX: Jacob's spirit reviving when seeing Joseph; 1 Macc 13:7: people's spirit reviving when Simon encouraged them); the apostolic fathers (*1 Clem*. 27.3: renewed faith in God; Ignatius, *Eph*. 1:1: new life through "God's blood"); and Josephus (*Ant*. 8:234; *J.W.* 1.444).

[34] See D. A. Carson, *Showing the Spirit: A Theological Exposition of 1 Corinthians 12–14* (Grand Rapids: Baker, 1987), 20. The term χάρισμα occurs in the NT almost exclusively in Paul (esp. in Romans and 1 Corinthians). Laying on of hands was in OT times used when dedicating a person to serving the Lord (e.g., Num 8:10; 27:18). The symbolism carried over into the NT church (e.g., Acts 8:17; 9:17; 13:2; 1 Tim 5:22).

[35] Note that Paul uses the first person plural rather than the second person singular: "God has not given us," presumably to make his exhortation sound less confrontational and direct.

[36] Most English translations refer to "spirit" in the lower case ("a spirit of timidity"). But see the NIV, which translates, "For the Spirit God gave us does not make us timid." However, the anarthrous πνεῦμα would seem to make the lowercase rendering more likely. In fact, it is hard to see how the Greek syntax allows for the NIV rendering: οὐ γὰρ ἔδωκεν ἡμῖν ὁ θεὸς πνεῦμα δειλίας.

of power (δυνάμεως; 45x in Paul; elsewhere in the LTT only in v. 8 and 3:5; cf. Mic 3:8), love (ἀγάπης; 75x in Paul; see v. 13; 2:22; 3:10), and sound judgment (σωφρονισμοῦ, only here in the NT; but cf. the use of cognates in 1 Tim 2:9, 15; 3:2; Titus 1:8; 2:2, 4–5, 12). Among other things, the triad of virtues shows that the power exercised by church leaders must be constrained by love (cf. Eph 4:15) and sound judgment.

1:8–12 Paul continues in his exhortation (οὖν, "so"; cf. 1 Tim 2:1, 8; 3:2; 5:14; 2 Tim 2:1, 21; not in Titus), calling on Timothy not to be ashamed to testify about "our Lord" (i.e., Christ) or of Paul his prisoner (cf. v. 16) in light of God's gracious provision (v. 7).[37] Just as he shouldn't avoid the shame of being identified with a crucified criminal (Jesus), he shouldn't shrink back from the social stigma attached to being associated with the imprisoned apostle (2:9; cf. 3:12).[38] Rather, Paul calls on Timothy to join him in his sufferings (συγκακοπάθησον; cf. 2:3, apparently a Pauline coinage), in contrast to many other former associates who deserted him (v. 15; 4:10, 14–16; but see vv. 16–18; 4:11–12, 19–21; Jesus had the same experience).[39] Paul himself isn't ashamed to suffer (v. 11). Timothy's commitment to Christ his Lord also requires him to identify openly with those, like Paul, who suffer for his sake (the same triad "Christ, Paul, and the gospel" is found in 2:8–10). At the end of the letter, the apostle will ask Timothy to visit him in prison (4:9, 21),

---

[37] "Testimony" (μαρτύριον) occurs elsewhere in the LTT in 1 Tim 2:6 and elsewhere in Paul in passages such as 1 Cor 1:6; 2 Cor 1:12; and 2 Thess 1:10. The term refers to the public attestation of the truthfulness of a given set of affirmations, in the present case the gospel about the Lord Jesus Christ. See G. A. Couser, "'The Testimony about the Lord,' 'Borne by the Lord,' or Both?," *TynBul* 55 (2004): 295–316, who suggests a possible plenary sense for the genitive τοῦ κυρίου (i.e., *both* "about" *and* "by" the Lord) but in the end opts for "a reference to the testimony the Lord bore in his word and life to the saving plan of God" (subjective genitive; p. 295). If so, Paul is saying here that Timothy shouldn't be ashamed of "the testimony borne by our Lord." Yarbrough notes that in the original Greek vv. 8–12 comprise a single sentence containing 105 words (*1–2 Timothy, Titus*, commentary at 2 Tim 1:8).

[38] See D. A. deSilva, "Honor and Shame," *DNTB*, 518–22. Similarly, see Rom 1:16.

[39] As Yarbrough notes, συγκακοπάθησον is the first formal imperative in 2 Timothy out of a total of some thirty-three imperatives found in the letter (*1–2 Timothy, Titus*, commentary at 2 Tim 1:8).

which is one concrete way he'll be able to identify with Paul by "the power of God" (cf. v. 7).

Verses 9–10 elaborate more fully on the work of God with great rhetorical elegance and eloquence:

> 9 He has saved us and called us with a holy calling, not according to our works, but according to His own purpose and grace, which was given to us in Christ Jesus before time began.
>
> 10 This has now been made evident through the appearing of our Savior Christ Jesus, who has abolished death and has brought life and immortality to light through the gospel.

God saved and called believers with a holy calling, not according to works but in keeping with his own purpose and grace. This is the message of Paul's gospel (εὐαγγελίον; vv. 8 and 10; 2:8; 1 Tim 1:11), which extols God's unconditional grace (χάρις; v. 9; 2:1; cf. 1 Tim 1:14). As Paul makes clear elsewhere, it is not by our own works but by grace that we are saved (Eph 2:8–9). Once saved by grace, we've been "called with a holy calling" (NASB; cf. Eph 4:1), "not according to our works"[40]—the holy God has set us apart for ministry.[41] For Paul, believers' salvation and their Christian vocation are closely intertwined. Yet as R. Yarbrough notes, Paul's emphasis is not on how humans should live but on "God's remarkable, effectual, and ennobling summons to deliverance, worship, and service."[42]

While God's grace is granted to us in Christ Jesus from eternity past (cf. Eph 1:4), it has "now" (a salvation-historical "now"; cf. Rom 11:30; Eph 3:5, 10) been revealed (φανερωθεῖσαν; cf. 1 Tim 3:16; Titus 1:3) through the "appearing" (ἐπιφανεία) of our "Savior" (σωτήρ; cf. 1 Tim 1:1; Titus 1:4; 2:13; 3:6) Christ Jesus in human history (v. 10).[43] The reference to God's gospel of grace and "the appearing of

---

[40] Good works play an important role in the theology of the LTT but as a result of salvation, not as a prerequisite (§5.2).

[41] Note the parallel with 1 Tim 1:12–16, where mercy and grace were bestowed on Paul by Christ Jesus in connection with both his conversion and his call to ministry.

[42] Yarbrough, *1–2 Timothy, Titus*, commentary at 2 Tim 1:9.

[43] This is the only instance in the LTT where ἐπιφανεία refers to Christ's first coming; all other references are to the Second Coming (1 Tim 6:14; 2 Tim 4:1, 8; Titus 2:13; §6.6).

our Savior Christ Jesus" triggers a brief doxology focused on the saving work of Christ (vv. 9b–10; §3).[44] Christ Jesus has destroyed (καταργέω) death (cf. 1 Cor 15:26; Heb 2:14) and brought life (ζωή, cf. 1:1) and immortality (ἀφθαρσία, a Hellenistic term used in the NT exclusively by Paul; cf. Rom 2:7; 1 Cor 15:42, 50, 53–54; Eph 6:24) to light (φωτίσαντος; cf. 1 Cor 4:5; Eph 3:9)[45] through the gospel (cf. 1 Cor 4:15; Eph 3:6; 2 Thess 2:14).

The mention of the gospel invariably triggers Paul's reference to his own calling as a herald (evangelist; κῆρυξ), apostle (ἀπόστολος), and teacher (διδάσκαλος).[46] Paul is setting the example, and Timothy is to follow in his steps (cf. 3:10–12).[47] In view of the proliferation of false teaching and of desertions by Paul's followers (possibly part of "these things," v. 12; cf. v. 15; 4:14–16), his exhortations take on even greater urgency. Believers needn't fear suffering or even martyrdom (cf. Heb 2:14–15; 1 Cor 15:54–58): God's gospel of salvation is worth all sacrifice, for it is true.[48] Paul knows whom he has believed (πεπίστευκα, the perfect tense conveys a settled conviction). He has full confidence (πέπεισμαι; cf. v. 5) that God is able (δυνατός; cf. Rom 4:21; 11:23) to guard what Paul has entrusted to him[49] (παραθήκη; cf. 1 Tim 6:20; v. 14: see below) "until

---

[44] On patronage, which entailed an exchange of favors and loyalties, privileges and dependencies, see D. A. deSilva, "Patronage," *DNTB*, 766–71.

[45] Καταργέω ("destroy" in the sense of "render ineffective" or "abolish") is here to be understood in terms of "God [putting] out of action . . . those destructive powers that threaten our spiritual well-being" (Silva, "καταργέω," *NIDNTTE* 2:641). Ζωὴν καὶ ἀφθαρσίαν (lit., "life and immortality") is best understood as a hendiadys (i.e., "immortal life"; so I. H. Marshall, *Pastoral Epistles*, ICC [Edinburgh: T&T Clark, 1999], 708). W. D. Mounce (*Pastoral Epistles*, WBC 46 [Dallas: Nelson, 2000], 485) equates the phrase with "eternal life."

[46] Cf. the identical threefold description in 1 Tim 2:7. The variant "of the Gentiles" is probably a scribal gloss; see 1 Tim 2:7. For background, see Acts 9:15.

[47] Cf. A. D. Clarke, "'Be Imitators of Me': Paul's Model of Leadership," *TynBul* 49 (1998): 354–57.

[48] Note the recurrence of "p" sounds in the original: πάσχω . . . ἐπαισχύνομαι . . . πεπίστευκα . . . πέπεισμαι.

[49] Cf. 2 Tim 4:17. παραθήκη literally reads "my deposit"; the object is left implicit. See note 51 below.

that day."[50] That "deposit" (παραθήκη) may be Paul's life; alternatively, it is the gospel God entrusted to Paul.[51]

1:13–14 Verses 13–14 each contain an important command: ἔχε ("Hold on to") and φύλαξον ("Guard"). First, Timothy should be careful to hold onto the pattern (ὑποτύπωσιν; with reference to Paul in 1 Tim 1:16; cf. Phil 3:17) of sound teaching (ὑγιαινόντων λόγων (cf. 1 Tim 1:10; 6:3; 2 Tim 4:3, lit. "of sound words"; §2.1) he received from Paul, who had in turn received the gospel message from others (1 Cor 15:3).[52] Faith and love in Christ Jesus are to be his trademark. This pattern can also be viewed as a "good deposit" (παραθήκη; see v. 12 above) made by Paul, who again is presented as a model for Timothy to emulate.

Second, Timothy must guard (φύλασσω; cf. 1 Tim 5:21; 6:20; 2 Tim 4:15) the deposit he received from his apostolic mentor from loss or damage with the help of the indwelling (ἐνοικοῦντος; God: 2 Cor 6:16; Christ: Col 3:16; Spirit: Rom 8:11; faith: 2 Tim 1:5) Holy Spirit (cf. Titus 3:15), just as God will guard the deposit of Paul's life until the final day (v. 12: παραθήκην μου φυλάξαι; v. 14: παραθήκην φύλαξον).[53] Human effort thus is imperative, albeit in reliance on divine enablement. The charge implies the necessity to defend the

---

[50] I.e., the final judgment and vindication triggered by Christ's return: see esp. 2 Tim 4:8. Cf. 1 Cor 3:13; 2 Cor 5:10; Phil 1:10.

[51] Cf. Paul's references to "my gospel" in 2 Tim 2:8; cf. Rom 2:16; 16:25. The first option (that which *Paul* has entrusted to *God*) is favored by the majority of English versions, such as the NASB, NIV, NKJV, and NLT (see also Marshall, *Pastoral Epistles*, 710–11). Others, such as L. T. Swinson (*What Is Scripture? Paul's Use of* Graphe *in the Letters to Timothy* [Eugene, OR: Wipf & Stock, 2014], 81–82, citing Towner, Mounce, et al.) contend the Greek favors reading this passage in terms of that which *God* has entrusted to *Paul*, namely the gospel message and his apostolic mission (cf. CSB: "what has been entrusted to me"; footnote: "Or *guard what I have entrusted to Him*, or *guard my deposit*").

[52] This implies an encouragement for Timothy to continue to do what he is already doing. So rightly Westfall, "Moral Dilemma," 238. "Pattern" suggests a fabric of interrelated doctrines, which cautions against a reductionistic understanding of the gospel. The concept is entirely Pauline: in Rom 6:17, the apostle speaks similarly of the "pattern of teaching" (τύπον διδαχῆς). Over the years Paul would have amassed a coherent body of instruction, and Timothy, who had followed his teaching closely, would have been thoroughly aware of it (2 Tim 3:10; cf. 2:2; 3:14).

[53] The fact that in v. 14 the "deposit" and "the Holy Spirit" are distinct may suggest that they are so also in v. 12 (see commentary at v. 12 above). Cf. A. J. Malherbe, "*Paulus Senex*," *ResQ* 36 (1994): 205, who speaks of Paul's desire "to transmit what is of value to the future."

apostolic gospel against heterodox threats. Paul's exhortation that began in v. 6 has now come full circle.

The opening exhortation is thoroughly God centered (§3.1). This is evident by the references to (1) the gift of God (v. 6); (2) the power of God (v. 8); and (3) the fact that God saved us and called us (v. 9). As common in the LTT, God's act of salvation is linked with Christ Jesus being our Savior (v. 10). Interestingly, the phrase "the appearing of our Savior Christ Jesus" here refers to the first rather than second coming of Christ. The fact that the gospel (mentioned twice in vv. 10, 11) is not by works but by grace sounds a thoroughly Pauline chord (cf., e.g., Eph 2:8–9). The reference to "that day" in v. 12 provides an eschatological framework (§6), and the reference to "the pattern of sound teaching" entrusted to Timothy in vv. 13–14 is tied to a (rare) reference to the "Holy Spirit who lives in us."[54]

Bridge

How do you find out who your friends are? Make a mistake. Better still, be imprisoned for the gospel! In the present case Timothy's allegiance to the gospel is shown by his loyalty to Paul, who wrote this letter from a damp Roman prison cell. In this Paul resembled his Lord who likewise was one, in keeping with Isaiah's prophecy, "like someone people turned away from" (Isa 53:3), one who was despised and not esteemed. As believers, we're called to "go to him [i.e., Jesus] outside the camp bearing his disgrace" (Heb 13:13). Rather than crave prestige and power in this world, we're to take up our cross and follow our crucified and risen Lord.

---

[54] In fact, this is the only reference to the "Holy Spirit" in the letters to Timothy (though 1 Tim 3:16 and 4:1 refer to "the Spirit"). The only other reference to the Holy Spirit in the LTT is found in Titus 3:5. See the brief survey in F. M. Young, *The Theology of the Pastoral Letters*, New Testament Theology (Cambridge: Cambridge University Press, 1994), 68–70. See also M. A. G. Haykin, "The Fading Vision? The Spirit and Freedom in the Pastoral Epistles," *EvQ* 57 (1985): 291–305; I. H. Marshall, "The Holy Spirit in the Pastoral Epistles and the Apostolic Fathers," in *The Holy Spirit and Christian Origins. Essays in Honor of James D. G. Dunn*, ed. G. N. Stanton, B. W. Longenecker, and S. C. Barton (Grand Rapids: Eerdmans, 2004), 257–69; J. D. Quinn, "The Holy Spirit in the Pastoral Epistles," in *Sin, Salvation, and the Spirit. Commemorating the Fiftieth Year of The Liturgical Press*, ed. D. Durken (Collegeville, MN: Liturgical Press, 1979), 345–68; and P. Trebilco, "The Significance and Relevance of the Spirit in the Pastoral Epistles," in *The Holy Spirit and Christian Origins: Essays in Honor of James D. G. Dunn*, ed. G. N. Stanton, B. W. Longenecker, and S. C. Barton (Grand Rapids: Eerdmans, 2004), 241–56.

B. Faithless and Faithful Coworkers (1:15–18)

> [15]You know that all those in the province of Asia have deserted me, including Phygelus and Hermogenes. [16]May the Lord grant mercy to the household of Onesiphorus, because he often refreshed me and was not ashamed of my chains. [17]On the contrary, when he was in Rome, he diligently searched for me and found me. [18]May the Lord grant that he obtain mercy from him on that day. You know very well how much he ministered at Ephesus.

Relation to Surrounding Context

"You know that" introduces a new subunit, building on the previous exhortation to Timothy not to be ashamed of the gospel or Paul his prisoner (v. 8). As he did in the first letter, Paul here cites a couple of negative examples, Phygelus and Hermogenes (v. 15), as well as a positive one, Onesiphorus, which he develops at greater length (vv. 16–18; cf. 1 Tim 1:18–20). Onesiphorus "was not ashamed" of Paul's chains; neither should Timothy be. In 2:1 Paul then resumes his instruction of Timothy from 1:14, marking 1:15–18 off as a sort of parenthesis.

Structure

Paul opens the present unit with a declaration of virtually universal desertion in the province of Asia where Ephesus was located (v. 15). This is followed by reference to a brief exception, not only Onesiphorus but his entire household (v. 16). Paul elaborates that not only was Onesiphorus not ashamed of Paul, but he actively sought him out when in Rome and visited him in prison (v. 17). This, in turn, triggers Paul's prayer that Onesiphorus may find mercy from God on judgment day (v. 18).

1:15–18 As Van Neste observes, "There is practically universal agreement that there is a break between 1:14 and 1:15."[55] The present unit begins and ends with a reference to Timothy's "knowing" (v. 15: Οἶδας τοῦτο ["You know that"]; v. 18: βέλτιον σὺ [emphatic] γινώσκεις: "You know very well"), an inclusion using a standard disclosure formula.[56] In keeping with the customary pattern for

---

[55] R. Van Neste, *Cohesion and Structure in the Pastoral Epistles*, JSNTSup 280 (New York: T&T Clark, 2004), 149.

[56] This is more conspicuous in the original Greek, where the first and the last word in the paragraph (1:15–18) are instances of "to know": Οἶδας . . . γινώσκεις. "You know that" is in keeping with Pauline terminiology (cf., e.g., Phil 1:6; 1 Thess 4:15).

moral exhortation, the emphasis isn't on telling Timothy something he doesn't already know but of reminding him of the importance of acting on what he does know and of encouraging him to continue to do what he's already been doing.[57] The unit features antithetical examples of desertion (Phygelus and Hermogenes, v. 15) and loyalty (vv. 16–18) and harks back to Paul's exhortation at the beginning of the body opening for Timothy not to be ashamed of the gospel or of Paul who is imprisoned on account of the gospel (v. 8, 11–12).

Verse 15 contains the first explicit reference to large-scale desertions (or the absence of coworkers) in this letter (cf. 4:10, 14). "All those in the province of Asia" (not the modern continent but the Roman province with Ephesus as its capital) have deserted (ἀπεστράφησαν; cf. 4:4; Titus 1:14) Paul. This may refer to the lack of support by believers from Asia Minor while Paul was on trial in Rome (cf. 4:16) or to large-scale defections at his arrest (in Troas? cf. 4:13). There may be an element of hyperbole in Paul's lament (note the exceptions of Timothy and Onesiphorus's entire family). "Deserted" doesn't necessarily imply that these former coworkers left the faith entirely (but cf. Titus 1:14); what is clear is that they no longer partner with Paul in ministry. No other information is available regarding Phygelus and Hermogenes. They may have taken the lead in the defection, or perhaps Paul's disappointment with them was particularly severe.

However, there's one bright spot (besides Timothy): Onesiphorus (the name means "profit-bearer" in Greek), who often "refreshed" (ἀνέψυξεν; cf. Acts 3:20; Luke 16:24) Paul—with his presence and in other ways—and wasn't ashamed (ἐπαισχύνθη; cf. Mark 8:38 par. Luke 9:26; Rom 1:16; 6:21; 2 Tim 1:8, 12; Heb 2:11; 11:16) of Paul's imprisonment (lit., "chains," ἅλυσιν; cf. Acts 21:33; 28:20; Eph 6:20), providing a role model for Timothy (see 1:8; cf. Matt 25:36, 39–40). He tracked down ("diligently searched," σπουδαίως; cf. Phil 2:28; Titus 3:13) Paul in Rome until he found him (εὗρεν, a wordplay with "find" mercy in v. 18) after having been helpful to him before (διηκόνησεν) in Ephesus (presumably prior to Paul's trip to Macedonia, cf. 1 Tim 1:3).[58] Onesiphorus's difficulty

---

[57] See the discussion under Genre above.

[58] See the brief study by W. D. Thomas, "New Testament Characters: XII. Onesiphorus," *ExpTim* 96 (1985): 116–17, who notes that Onesiphorus reported

in finding Paul, as well as the reference to the apostle's "chains," points to a second, more severe Roman imprisonment.

At the time of Paul's writing, Onesiphorus's family may have been in Ephesus while he had joined Paul in Rome (cf. 4:19). (The fact that the man had a family—as well that he was able to travel to track Paul down in Rome—suggests he was a freedman rather than a slave; slaves were usually unable to marry or have children of their own.) Prisoners in antiquity often depended on assistance from family and/or friends. Paul prays for mercy for both: for Onesiphorus's family to have all their needs met during his absence (cf. Phil 2:27; Titus 3:5) and for Onesiphorus to find favor in God's eyes "on that day" (see v. 12 above and 4:8 below).[59] In the double mention of κύριος ("the Lord . . . from him") in v. 18, the first reference is to Jesus Christ (cf. vv. 2, 8), while the second is to God (LXX).[60]

The section concludes with Paul's statement that Timothy knows "very well" (βέλτιον, a NT hapax, though a variant reading in Acts 10:28) how much Onesiphorus ministered (διακονέω; cf. 1 Tim 3:10, 13; Phlm 13) to Paul at Ephesus (perhaps during Paul's three-year ministry there: see Acts 19–20). The unit, with its reference to the virtually universal desertion Paul suffered in v. 15, in conjunction with the reference to "that day" in v. 18, continues to develop the picture of the dark storm clouds that threaten the progress of the apostolic mission.

Bridge

Onesiphorus's kind deed of visiting Paul in prison was in keeping with the words of the writer of Hebrews: "Remember those

---

optimistically on the condition of the churches and emphasized the positive possibilities in Paul's imprisonment.

[59] Some infer from Paul's well-wish that Onesiphorus had died, but Paul's separate prayers for Onesiphorus's household and for him may just as well be due to the distance separating them (so D. Guthrie, *The Pastoral Epistles*, TNTC, rev. ed. [Grand Rapids: Eerdmans, 1990], 148–49; J. R. W. Stott, *The Message of 2 Timothy*, The Bible Speaks Today [Downers Grove: InterVarsity, 1984], 45).

[60] See, e.g., Kelly: "More probably, however, *May the Lord* . . . refers to Christ, this being in harmony with the usage of the Pastorals . . ., and *from the Lord* to God, whom Paul elsewhere (e.g., Rom. ii. 6; iii. 6) represents as exercising judgment, and who in the Pastorals is regularly described as Saviour. This is supported by the LXX practice of using 'Lord' (Gk. *Kurios*) without the article of God" (*A Commentary on the Pastoral Epistles*, 170, emphasis original). Similarly, Mounce, *Pastoral Epistles*, 496.

in prison, as though you were in prison with them, and the mistreated" (Heb 13:3). Interestingly, Heb 13:23 mentions Timothy's release from an otherwise unknown imprisonment, which, if written after 2 Timothy, may indicate that Timothy did indeed identify with Paul and proved to be unashamed of the gospel. Contemporary ministries such as Prison Fellowship carry on this noble legacy and seek to minister to those in prison, even though their imprisonment, unlike Paul's, may in some cases be self-inflicted.

III. Body Middle: Ministry Metaphors and Additional Exhortations (2:1–4:8)

The body middle is introduced by the emphatic phrase "But you, my son" (Σὺ οὖν, τέκνον μου).[61] While chapter 1 contains only three imperatives (vv. 8, 13, 14), the remainder of the letter features an additional thirty imperatives.[62] The first part of chapter 2 is mostly devoid of references to false teaching, focusing instead on encouraging Timothy to persevere in his ministry. The exclamation point is a solemn "trustworthy saying." The second part of the chapter then returns to the issue of false teachers.

In his exhortation to Timothy his "son," Paul draws on three pictures illustrating the nature of Christian ministry: soldier, athlete, and farmer (2:1–7). Each of these conveys a key characteristic Paul wants Timothy to emulate. At the heart of the chapter is a carefully crafted mini-doxology (one of five "trustworthy sayings" in the LTT) focusing on Christ's saving work and its implications

---

[61] See 1 Tim 6:11; 2 Tim 3:10, 14; 4:5; Titus 2:1; cf. Rom 14:10. As Westfall ("Moral Dilemma," 235) observes, "This combination of emphatic features is a cluster of the most prominent discourse markers up to this point, which leads the reader to expect a transition to a new unit." As Westfall (ibid., 235–36n73) notes, the explicit second-person singular pronoun, the inferential particle, the nominative of direct address with the first-person possessive pronoun are all "extra words" that are unnecessary for the actual content of the letter. They serve as discourse markers signaling a new unit and also convey a high level of intimacy between Paul and Timothy that is consistent with personal letters between father and son or mentor and mentoree. See further the commentary below.

[62] Cf. Yarbrough, *1-2 Timothy, Titus*, commentary at II. Priorities for Timothy (2:1–3:9).

for God's workers (2:8–13).[63] The chapter closes with three additional ministry roles: workman, instrument, and servant (2:14–26).

Another disclosure formula transitions to a new subunit, still in the body middle: Τοῦτο δὲ γίνωσκε ("But know this," 3:1; cf. 1:15). This phrase introduces an ominous warning against difficult times in the last days. Jannes and Jambres, the Egyptian magicians or Jewish opponents (see at 3:6–9), are invoked as negative types of false teachers in Timothy's day. By contrast Timothy is urged to emulate the example of Paul, his mentor. The boundary at the other end of the body middle is the solemn phrase Διαμαρτύρομαι ἐνώπιον τοῦ θεοῦ, etc. in 4:1, which signals the body closing.

A. Ministry Metaphors, Paul's Gospel, and a Trustworthy Saying (2:1–26)

1. Three Ministry Metaphors: Soldier, Athlete, Farmer (2:1–7)

> 1 You, therefore, my son, be strong in the grace that is in
> Christ Jesus. 2 What you have heard from me in the presence
> of many witnesses, commit to faithful men who will be able
> to teach others also.
>
> 3 Share in suffering as a good soldier of Christ Jesus. 4 No
> one serving as a soldier gets entangled in the concerns of ci-
> vilian life; he seeks to please the commanding officer. 5 Also,
> if anyone competes as an athlete, he is not crowned unless he
> competes according to the rules. 6 The hardworking farmer
> ought to be the first to get a share of the crops. 7 Consider
> what I say, for the Lord will give you understanding in ev-
> erything.

Relation to Surrounding Context

The phrase "therefore" in v. 1 most likely relates to the large-scale defections mentioned in the previous unit (1:15). In the face of these desertions, Timothy is to be strong in Christ's grace and commit what he's learned from Paul to faithful men who'll be able to teach others also (v. 2). Suffering calls for the qualities of a

[63] For a defense of the cohesion of 2:1–13, see Van Neste, *Cohesion and Structure*, 160–66, who shows that this unit coheres around motifs such as end-time rewards and exhortations to endurance.

good soldier as well as those of an athlete and hardworking farmer (vv. 3–6). The three illustrations reinforce the pervasive theme of sharing in Paul's suffering for the sake of the gospel, which spans the entire letter.

Structure

The unit consists of three commands ("be strong," "commit," and "share," in vv. 1, 2, and 3 respectively), followed by three analogies (soldier, athlete, farmer, vv. 4–6), and a concluding exhortation in v. 7.

2:1–2 "You" (Σύ) continues Paul's personal address to Timothy (cf. 1:18) and marks a new unit (cf. 1 Tim 2:1; see also 2 Tim 3:10; regarding the phrase "but you," σὺ δέ, see on 1 Tim 6:11). The address follows on the heels of Paul's reference to those from the province of Asia who had turned away from him (1:15) and his commendation of Onesiphorus (1:16–18). "Therefore" (οὖν; cf. 1:8) grounds Paul's instructions that are about to follow in his earlier exhortation that Timothy "rekindle" or "fan into flame" the gift of God he had received (1:6), join him in suffering for the gospel (1:8), and "hold on to the pattern of sound teaching" he had heard from Paul (1:13–14). "My son" (τέκνον) reiterates earlier similar references (1 Tim 1:2, 18; 2 Tim 1:2; cf. Titus 1:4).

A series of three exhortations ensues, each continuing themes struck in the introduction: ἐνδυναμοῦ ("be strong," v. 1), παράθου ("commit," v. 2), and συγκακοπάθησον ("share in suffering," v. 3).[64] First, Timothy is to be strong—not fearful (1:7)—in the grace that is in Christ Jesus. This opening exhortation reveals Paul's concern as to the effect his own imprisonment may have on Timothy and seeks to strengthen his resolve to continue in ministry by way of strong moral encouragement.[65] Paul himself knew how to be strong in the Lord (ἐνδυναμοῦ; Phil 4:13; 1 Tim 1:12; 2 Tim 4:17; cf. Acts 9:22) and had previously issued a similar exhortation to Ephesian believers (Eph 6:10; cf. Eph 2:8–9). He had also urged Timothy to suffer with him for the gospel, "relying on the power of God," who "has saved us . . . according to his own purpose and grace" (1:8–9; χάρις).

[64] Cf. Westfall, "Moral Dilemma," 240. Cf. Marshall, *Pastoral Epistles*, 721: "The structure of this part of the letter is determined by a series of imperatives: vv. 1f, 3, 7, 8. These are followed by material that backs them up vv. [2b], 4–6, 9f, 11–13."

[65] Cf. Westfall, "Moral Dilemma," 240.

Timothy should continually rely on God's gracious enablement in performing his ministry (cf. 2 Cor 9:8; Titus 2:11–14).

Second, Timothy shouldn't only be strong in God's grace but also endeavor to entrust Paul's teaching to faithful men who will also be able to teach others (the original emphasis is on the fact that the teachings Timothy is to commit to others are those he previously heard from Paul; cf. 3:10–11; note the added ταῦτα, "these"). This exhortation expands the earlier set of commands in 1:13–14 where Paul told Timothy to hold onto Paul's pattern of sound teaching and to guard the good deposit.[66] The reference to the presence of "many witnesses"—which may include but is probably not limited to the individuals present at Timothy's ordination service—adds further solemnity to Paul's charge and points to the public nature of his instruction (cf. John 18:19–21). Timothy himself had made his "good confession in the presence of many witnesses" (1 Tim 6:12).

Timothy must not keep Paul's teaching to himself. He should commit it (παράθου; cf. 1 Tim 1:18) to faithful individuals (πιστοῖς ἀνθρώποις). While ἀνθρώποις is probably gender inclusive (see 3:2; 1 Tim 2:1, 4–5, etc.; cf. Col 1:2), it is nonetheless likely that the term here refers to men, presumably present or potential elders. These should be individuals who will be able (ἱκανοί; cf. 2 Cor 2:16; 3:5: "competent") to teach others as well (cf. 1 Tim 3:2; 2 Tim 2:24; contrast 1 Tim 2:12; Titus 2:3). Positively, faithfulness means conveying God's Word accurately; negatively, it means not misrepresenting Paul's teaching (2:15).

Essentially Paul, the seasoned apostle, seeks to impart to Timothy, his foremost disciple, the same mentoring mind-set (cf. 1 Tim 4:12) that had characterized his own apostolic ministry (see, e.g., 1 Cor 11:1). Just as Paul is concerned to transmit what is of value (i.e., the gospel) to the next generation, so Timothy should join him in this transmission process and actively participate in it. What Christian ministry requires isn't originality or innovation but faithfulness (πίστις; cf. 1 Tim 1:12; 3:11) and the ability to commit the teaching the minister has received to others who will be faithful in passing on the teaching to additional faithful individuals.[67] Paul lists four links in this chain: (1) Paul himself;

---

[66] See also 1:18 and the discussion at 1:13–14 above.

[67] See, e.g., C. A. Blaising, "Faithfulness: A Prescription for Theology," *JETS* 49 (2006): 5–16.

(2) Timothy; (3) faithful individuals; and (4) others. This chain of people who faithfully commit the Christian gospel to others—not the Roman Catholic notion of papal succession—encapsulates the biblical vision of spiritual reproduction.

2:3–4 In the two previous verses Timothy was exhorted, first, to be strong in God's grace and, second, to entrust Paul's teaching to faithful men who will also be able to teach others. The third exhortation in the body middle is this: "Share in suffering ("with me" is implied; so rightly the NASB, NIV; cf. 1:8; 2:9: κακοπαθῶ) as a good soldier of Christ Jesus." "Share in suffering" (συγκακοπάθησον) is another Pauline coinage harking back to 1:8, repeating and expanding his earlier admonition (cf. κακοπαθῶ in v. 9 and 4:5; cf. Jas 5:13). The significance of the expression "good soldier" (καλὸς στρατιώτης; cf. στρατεύομαι in 1 Cor 9:7; 2 Cor 10:3; 1 Tim 1:18; 2 Tim 2:4) is explicated in the following verse. In his letters to Timothy Paul speaks repeatedly of the "good" (καλός) fight of faith (4:7; 1 Tim 1:18; 6:12). He also exhorts Timothy to be a "good" (καλός) servant of Jesus Christ (1 Tim 4:6).

In the following verses Paul adduces three metaphors to illustrate the qualities needed for faithful gospel ministry: (1) the soldier; (2) the athlete; and (3) the farmer.[68] Not everyone serves in the military, competes as an athlete, or works as a farmer, but the analogies Paul draws serve as representative examples of the types of qualities believers, and Christian leaders in particular, ought to cultivate.

First, the soldier epitomizes the virtue of single-mindedness. Refusing to be sidetracked or entangled (ἐμπλέκεται; cf. 2 Pet 2:20) in "concerns of civilian life" (NASB, "the affairs of everyday life"), the soldier maintains his focus out of a desire to please his "commanding officer" (and possibly also a desire for recognition or a reward). For first-century Roman soldiers, this could mean refraining from marriage and serving as a soldier for twenty-five years or more (*NewDocs* 6:147–49).[69] Like regular warfare the battle for

[68] L. T. Johnson, *Letters to Paul's Delegates*, 62, calls these "stock examples in hellenistic moral discourse," citing Epictetus, *Diatr.* 3.15.2–7; 3.24.34–35; 4.8.35–40.

[69] Apparently Emperor Claudius reformed Roman military service at the census in AD 47–48, according to which a soldier obtained both his discharge and citizenship after twenty-five years of service. The prohibition from marrying during service for Roman soldiers wasn't eased until Septimus Severus (AD 197; *NewDocs* 6:148).

human souls demands single-minded focus. A halfhearted effort won't do (cf. Luke 9:62). The same principle was at stake when the early apostles were careful not to "neglect the ministry of the word of God in order to wait on tables" (NIV; Acts 6:2–4). While the need for single-minded service has special relevance for church leaders, it extends to all believers. The Lord Jesus Christ is our commanding officer, and the battle for human souls in pursuit of extending Christ's redemptive mission demands our utmost attention. How easy it is to be distracted by the things of this world! The plethora of ubiquitous distractions—even when coming in form of "harmless" diversions such as watching sports on TV or a variety of trivial pursuits—makes single-minded focus on serving Christ imperative.

2:5 Second, the athlete exemplifies the commitment to compete according to the rules (νομίμως; cf. 1 Tim 1:8).[70] If a competitor wants to receive the victor's crown (στεφανόω; cf. Heb 2:7, 9), he must submit to rigorous training, which requires self-discipline and a willingness to forego earthly pleasures. Competing according to the rules also means running the race to the finish. Paul uses a similar line of reasoning in 1 Cor 9:25. Elsewhere, he calls believers in churches he planted his "joy" and "crown" (1 Thess 2:19; Phil 4:1) and speaks of the "crown of righteousness" waiting for him in heaven, now that he has "finished the race" (4:7–8). Thus Paul's second point resembles the first. Similar to the soldier (note *καί*, "also," in v. 5), the athlete focuses single-mindedly on pursuing his goal. The servant of Christ must do no less.

2:6–7 Third, Paul invokes the imagery of the farmer (γεωργόν; cf. Jas 5:7).[71] In antiquity, "somewhere around 85 or 90 percent of the whole population was directly involved with growing or getting food as their primary occupation . . . [so that] Paul's analogy . . . would have been much more alive to his original readers than to many of us."[72] Paul commends the farmer's willingness to work hard (κοπιῶντα; 1 Tim 4:10; 5:17; cf. Acts 20:35; Rom 16:6, 12; 1 Cor

[70] The requirement to compete according to the rules is emphasized by the grammatical construction: see the analysis by S. Runge, *Discourse Grammar of the Greek New Testament* (Peabody, MA: Hendrickson, 2010), 88–89.

[71] Paul will discuss three additional ministry roles in 2:14–26 below.

[72] S. M. Baugh, "1 Timothy, 2 Timothy, Titus," in *1 & 2 Thessalonians, 1 & 2 Timothy, Titus*, by J. A. D. Weima and S. M. Baugh, *Zondervan Illustrated Bible Backgrounds Commentary*, ed. C. E. Arnold (Grand Rapids: Zondervan, 2001), 485.

4:12; 15:10; 16:16; Gal 4:11; Eph 4:28; Phil 2:16; Col 1:29; 1 Thess 5:12). The soldier may be decorated for his heroic service, and the athlete may receive the victor's crown. By contrast, the farmer's life is less glamorous; his reward is simply to receive a share of (μεταλαμβάνειν; cf. Heb 6:7) the crops (*NewDocs* 7:115).

As with the soldier and athlete, key to the farmer's success is undivided devotion to his task. His hard work will be rewarded with a share of the crops (καρπῶν; see esp. Jas 5:7, 18; cf. 1 Cor 9:7). Timothy, likewise, may look forward to the fruit of his labor (cf. Matt 9:36–38 par. Luke 10:2; John 4:34–38; 3 John 4). Even in this life Christian workers such as Timothy are entitled to be paid for their work (see on 1 Tim 5:17–18). The words "ought to be the first" (πρῶτον) may indicate that Timothy needed encouragement in this regard. While farms in Paul's day were often owned by absentee landlords, the apostle here upholds the principle that hardworking farmers should be the first to benefit from their own labors—a principle that is transferable to the spiritual realm as well.

Paul concludes this section with an appeal to Timothy to reflect (νοέω; cf. 1 Tim 1:7; Rom 1:20; Eph 3:4, 20) on the truth of his words, assuring him that God will give him understanding (σύνεσις; cf. 1 Cor 1:19; Eph 3:4; Col 1:9; 2:2) in everything.[73] In other words, Paul wants Timothy to take his instructions to heart. The present statement bears some resemblance to Paul's words in Phil 3:12–15 (cf. 4:8). The main point of Paul's threefold illustration is that Timothy must be willing to pay the price and endure hardship in the ministry according to the principle "no pain, no gain," remembering that "beyond warfare is victory, beyond athletic effort a prize, and beyond agricultural labour a crop."[74] Likewise, Timothy should be motivated by the prospect of a reward. Even Jesus endured the cross for "the joy that lay before him" (Heb 12:2).

This section, too, is better understood when placed within the larger biblical-theological purview of the letter. It is precisely because the end times are upon Timothy and the church that he

[73] See T. Nicklas, "'Denn der Herr wird dir in allem Einsicht geben!' (II Tim 2,7b): Übernahme und Transformation alttestamentlich-weisheitlichen Denkens in II Tim 2," in *Weisheit als Lebensgrundlage: Festschrift für Friedrich V. Reiterer zum 65. Geburtstag*, ed. R. Egger-Wenzel, K. Schopflin, and J. Diehl (Berlin: de Gruyter, 2013), 207–24.

[74] C. K. Barrett, *The Pastoral Epistles*, New Clarendon Bible (Oxford: Clarendon, 1963), 102.

must be strong in the grace of Christ Jesus (v. 1); that he must find faithful men to perpetuate the message (v. 2); and that qualities such as single-mindedness (v. 4), integrity (v. 5), and hard work (v. 6) are of supreme importance. This end-time orbit explains the urgency and intensity of Paul's instructions, an urgency and intensity that are often lacking in complacent Christianity today but that need to be recovered if the church wants to be a factor in the rapidly unraveling moral fabric of the surrounding culture and bear bold witness to the Lord Jesus Christ.

Bridge

In the present passage Paul seeks to impress on Timothy the importance of persevering in his ministry by way of three analogous occupations requiring similar traits: soldier, athlete, and farmer. These roles are all oriented toward a final reward reserved for those who cultivate the requisite characteristics of single-mindedness, a commitment to play by the rules, and a willingness to work hard. Like Timothy, all believers should seek to cultivate these traits in striving for their heavenly reward. Elsewhere, too, Paul uses athletic metaphors such as running or boxing (1 Cor 9:24–27) to underscore the importance of self-discipline in living the Christian life; so do other NT writers such as the author of the book of Hebrews (Heb 12:1–3).

2. Paul's Gospel and a Trustworthy Saying (2:8–13)

[8] Remember Jesus Christ, risen from the dead and descended from David, according to my gospel, [9] for which I suffer to
the point of being bound like a criminal. But the word of God
is not bound. [10] This is why I endure all things for the elect: so
that they also may obtain salvation, which is in Christ Jesus,
with eternal glory. [11] This saying is trustworthy:

For if we died with him,
we will also live with him;
12 if we endure, we will also reign with him;
if we deny him, he will also deny us;
13 if we are faithless, he remains faithful,
for he cannot deny himself.

Relation to Surrounding Context

The present unit continues Paul's call to Timothy to share in his suffering. The centerpiece of this unit is the sole "trustworthy saying" in this epistle in vv. 11–13. In an intriguing progression the saying reinforces both the notions of the need for human faithfulness and the reality of God's faithfulness even in the midst of human unfaithfulness. This puts the emphasis squarely on God.

Structure

Verses 8–10 connect Paul's present circumstances (i.e., his imprisonment) with the gospel, God's message, which isn't bound, even though Paul currently is (vv. 8–9). Paul's suffering isn't only for the gospel but also for the sake of the elect so they may obtain salvation (v. 10). Then vv. 11–13 feature a liturgical piece whose cadence makes for an interesting dynamic, especially the break of the pattern in the last instance, where a positive statement follows rather than the expected negative one.

2:8–10 Paul now moves from analogy to history, in a fourth command (see vv. 1, 2, and 3 above) calling on Timothy to "remember [μνημόνευε] Jesus Christ, risen from the dead and descended from David," according to Paul's gospel (cf. Rom 2:16; 16:25; 1 Cor 15:1–3, 11).[75] This continues the intergenerational emphasis in this letter, which reaches from David to Jesus to Paul to Timothy and to those he is called to mentor. Paul's exhortation to Timothy to "remember," later followed by the exhortation to "remind" the members of his congregation (v. 14), is part of the "remembrance" motif in this letter (1:3–6; 3:14–15; cf. Luke 17:32; Acts 20:31, 35; Heb 13:7). The remembrance theme, in turn, forms the backbone

[75] We know that the nature of the resurrection was a major bone of contention between Paul and the false teachers (2 Tim 2:18). This may be one reason Timothy in the present passage is told to remember "Jesus Christ, risen from the dead." This is mere speculation, but is it possible that Jesus as "descended from David" was a contentious issue as well? Rather than engaging in extensive conjecture about "myths and genealogies," is Paul's point here perhaps that the proper focus with regard to Jesus's ancestry is on his Davidic descent, indicating his messianic nature? Note the immediately following assertion, "This is 'according to my gospel,'" and see, e.g., Acts 13:34–37, where Jesus's resurrection and his Davidic descent are closely related in Paul's gospel preaching.

of Paul's moral exhortation of Timothy toward the end of Paul's life and ministry.[76]

The confession of Jesus as "risen from the dead and descended from David" stresses the historical reality of Christ's coming, particularly his Davidic descent (human sonship) and resurrection (divine sonship; cf. esp. Rom 1:3–4; see also Acts 13:23 and v. 11 below). Since Jesus's Davidic descent isn't a significant theme elsewhere in the LTT, it's possible that Paul here cites a liturgical fragment ("Risen from the dead, descended from David").[77] This is "according to my gospel," no matter how countercultural or counterintuitive: references to the gospel (εὐαγγέλιον) are rare in the LTT (1 Tim 1:11; 2 Tim 1:8, 10) but common in Romans, which underscores the affinity of the present verse with Paul's message there.

Paul continues to write with deep pathos and solemnity. He suffers for "it" (ἐν ᾧ, presumably the gospel [v. 8], or possibly for "him" [i.e., Jesus Christ], "bound (δεσμῶν, together with δέσμιος and ἅλυσις, here and in the Prison Epistles; cf. 1:8, 16; Eph 3:1; 4:1; Phil 1:7, 13–14, 17; Col 4:18; Phlm 1, 9–10, 13) like a [common] criminal" (κακοῦργος; cf. Luke 23:32–33, 39, referring to the two criminals crucified with Jesus). This is a dramatic way of putting things, as is the following affirmation that "the word of God [ὁ λόγος τοῦ θεοῦ; cf. 1 Tim 4:5; Titus 2:5] is not bound" (δέω; cf. Col 4:3; Rom 9:6; Acts 28:31). Clearly this kind of treatment represented a severe indignity for Paul who was not only a Roman citizen but innocent of any actual wrongdoing (for Paul's activities prior to his conversion, see 1 Tim 1:13).

The apostle here expresses his confidence in the sovereignty of God and in the effective power of his word in the face of mounting [Neronic] persecution (cf. Rom 1:16; Phil 1:12–18). While Paul's fate was closely tied to the progress of the gospel in early Christian history (Acts 9–28), he was convinced that the power of the gospel far transcended his own preaching of it. Ultimately, the fate of the gospel doesn't rest on any one human messenger, no matter how

---

[76] This is one of only six (out of thirty-one) times in the LTT and the only one (out of twelve) in 2 Timothy where the order is "Jesus Christ," not "Christ Jesus" (cf. 1 Tim 6:3, 14; Titus 1:1; 2:13; 3:6), with no apparent difference in meaning.

[77] See C. Burger, "Der Davidide in christlichen Bekenntnisformeln," in *Jesus als Davidssohn: Eine traditionsgeschichtliche Untersuchung* (Göttingen: Vandenhoeck & Ruprecht, 1970), 25–41.

important or influential; its victory is assured by its own inherent power (cf. Rom 1:16). In Acts and in Paul's letters, the gospel often takes on a virtual personal dimension as it marches forward and spreads irresistibly in the face of fierce opposition (Acts 6:7; 12:24; Rom 9:6; 1 Cor 14:36; 1 Thess 2:13; 2 Thess 3:1). Suffering abuse for the sake of the gospel creates a bond among believers across salvation history (Heb 11:32–12:3; 1 Pet 5:9).

The phrase "like a criminal" (κακοῦργος) may constitute a deliberate attempt to tie Paul's fate to Jesus's, similar to Paul's awareness that his suffering is "for the sake of the elect" (ἐκλεκτούς; Rom 8:33; Col 3:12; Titus 1:1; see also 1 Cor 4:9–13; Col 1:24).[78] Jesus's accusers before Pilate alleged similarly, "If this man weren't a criminal (κακὸν ποιῶν), we wouldn't have handed him over to you" (John 18:30). In the present passage Paul clearly enunciates his belief that God has chosen certain people for salvation and that Paul has the obligation to proclaim the gospel and suffer for it so that those who are chosen "also may obtain salvation, which is in Christ Jesus, with eternal glory" (cf. Acts 13:48; 18:10; Rom 8:28–30; Eph 1:4–5, 11; §3). The final phrase, "with eternal glory," serves to put believers' present suffering into eternal perspective.

2:11–13 Paul's words in vv. 3 and 9–10 trigger yet another "trustworthy saying" (cf. 1 Tim 1:15; 3:1; 4:8; see also 1 Tim 3:16; §2.6), in the present case a short liturgical piece, perhaps a hymn.[79] The present passage continues Paul's consistent emphasis that

---

[78] When Paul elsewhere uses the designation ἐκλεκτός, the term invariably refers to those who have already come to faith (e.g., Rom 8:33; 16:13; Col 3:12), not those who have yet to do so. If this is how ἐκλεκτός is to be understood here, then the reference is to believers in the church in Ephesus and other locations. At the very least, ἐκλεκτός *includes* those who have already come to faith. Compare also the similar language in Col 1:24–28 and 2 Cor 1:6 and the related passage in v. 19 below.

[79] The presence of the word "for" (γάρ) in v. 11b has suggested to some that vv. 11b–13 provide the reason for the "trustworthy saying" referred to in v. 11a rather than containing the saying itself. However, there's no compelling alternative. The phrase "Jesus Christ, risen from the dead and descended from David" in v. 8 is too far removed (and more of a liturgical piece than a saying), and vv. 9–10 are probably too personal to constitute a saying. It's therefore most likely that the γάρ in v. 11b is part of the "trustworthy saying" and that the saying is found in vv. 11b–13 (see G. W. Knight, *Commentary on the Pastoral Epistles*, NIGTC [Grand Rapids: Eerdmans, 1992], 400–402; Knight, *The Faithful Sayings in the Pastoral Letters*, Baker Biblical Monographs [Grand Rapids: Baker, 1979], 112–15, suggesting that γάρ has the weakened sense "namely" in the present context or is part of the cited hymn).

enduring hardship is a necessary part of the Christian life (note the switch from "my" and "I" in vv. 8–9 to "we" in vv. 11b–13; cf. 1 John 1:6–10). Paul reinforces this point in a variety of ways: with reference to God's grace and power (1:6–9, 12, 14; 2:1), by positive and negative examples (1:15–18), by secular analogies (2:3–6), by appeals to personal experience (2:8–10), and now by citing a "trustworthy saying." The saying/hymn reinforces Paul's message by focusing on the rewards for suffering and by affirming that God remains faithful even when his servants are not.

In light of the numerous Pauline parallels, it's likely that the saying/hymn is original to Paul (cf. 1 Corinthians 13; Rom 8:28–39).[80] The statement consists of four conditional clauses (εἰ + indicative verb), of which the first two deal with faithful service and the last two deal with disowning Christ, plus a main clause with a future (first three clauses) or present verb (final clause). The verb ἀρνέομαι occurs three times, indicating the hymn's primary subject. The final clause features an added reason for the assertion made in the saying: "For he cannot deny himself." The cadence makes for an interesting dynamic, especially the break of the pattern in the last instance, where a negative statement (conveying divine rejection) is expected but a positive one follows instead.[81]

[80] See, e.g., A. T. Hanson, *The Pastoral Epistles*, NCB (Grand Rapids: Eerdmans, 1982), 132, an avowed opponent of Pauline authorship who acknowledges that "the theology implied in the hymn is thoroughly Pauline." Alternatively, Paul used preformed tradition (M. M. Yarbrough, *Paul's Utilization of Preformed Traditions in 1 Timothy: An Evaluation of the Apostle's Literary, Rhetorical, and Theological Tactics*, LNTS 417 [London: T&T Clark, 2009], 42). If so, the trustworthy saying may have been excerpted from a longer piece in that it's not until κἀκεῖνος in v. 12b that there's a direct reference to the one with whom we die, live, and reign (vv. 11–12; cf. Quinn and Wacker, *Letters to Timothy*, 649–50). Jesus may have been mentioned in the original piece prior to the excerpt included in 2 Timothy 2. Then again, perhaps Paul is simply writing in a more poetic vein and using συν- compounds to refer to "Christ Jesus" in v. 10.

[81] Most likely the effect of the final line is to soften the categorical note of rejection in line 3 by making God's faithfulness, rather than human faithlessness, the overriding theme, which raises the possibility that, at least in some individual cases, human faithlessness may not have the last word, but divine faithfulness may prevail in the end. See the discussion in J. M. Bassler, "'He Remains Faithful' (2 Tim 2:13a)," in *Theology and Ethics in Paul and His Interpreters: Essays in Honor of Victor Paul Furnish*, ed. E. H. Lovering Jr. and J. L. Sumney (Nashville: Abingdon, 1996), 173–83.

11 For if we died with him, we will also live with him;	εἰ γὰρ συναπεθάνομεν, καὶ συζήσομεν·
12 if we endure, we will also reign with him;	εἰ ὑπομένομεν, καὶ συμβασιλεύσομεν·
if we deny him, he will also deny us;	εἰ ἀρνησόμεθα, κἀκεῖνος ἀρνήσεται ἡμᾶς·
13 if we are faithless, he remains faithful, for he cannot deny himself.	εἰ ἀπιστοῦμεν, ἐκεῖνος πιστὸς μένει, ἀρνήσασθαι γὰρ ἑαυτὸν οὐ δύναται.

The main subject of the four lines of the hymn isn't identified explicitly, though it can be reasonably inferred that it is Christ (see esp. v. 11: "For if we died with him"). Nevertheless, by way of *double entendre*, the reference to faithfulness in v. 13 may on a secondary level also extend to God.[82] As mentioned, the flow in logic is intriguing and defies simplistic characterization, moving from the promise of living and reigning with Christ ("die . . . live," "endure . . . reign"), to the severe consequences of denying Christ ("deny . . . deny"), to an affirmation of Christ's (and possibly God's) unshakable faithfulness even in the face of human faithlessness ("faithless . . . faithful"), which provides a climactic exclamation point, further accentuated by the element of surprise introduced by the unexpected turn in the final affirmation.

"For if we died with him, we will also live with him." The language and thought are thoroughly Pauline (see esp. Rom 6:8: "Now *if we died with Christ*, we believe that *we will also live with him*" [cf. v. 5; Gal 2:20; see also the verbal parallels with 2 Cor 7:3]). In view of these parallels, "died with him" likely refers to the believer's spiritual union with Christ rather than to martyrdom (though readiness to martyrdom may be implied on a secondary level). Similarly, "live with him" doesn't refer primarily to the believer's

[82] Bassler (ibid., 178) notes some confusion among commentators at this point. E.g., Knight (*Pastoral Epistles*) at one time or another affirms both that the "he" is God (p. 406) and Christ (p. 407). As Bassler observes, "The reference to faithfulness in the hymn is . . . a significant piece of the author's rhetorical strategy. It affirms the principle of divine faithfulness, which provides both the model for the faithfulness demanded of church leaders and the basis for the claims concerning the reliability of the church's message of salvation" (p. 180).

eternal state but to his present possession of spiritual life by virtue of his union with Christ.[83]

"If we endure, we will also reign with him." Once again the statement coheres with Paul's teaching elsewhere (see esp. Rom 5:17; note also the verbal similarity with 1 Cor 4:8 and the affinity with Jesus's teaching in Mark 13:13 // Matt 24:13; Matt 10:22 par.). As in the previous statement, the primary reference is to Christians' present reign with Christ (though a future dimension cannot be ruled out). The need for believers—including Timothy—to endure (ὑπομένω) is the frequent subject of Paul's instruction (v. 10; 3:10–11; 1 Tim 6:11; Rom 5:3–4; 15:4–5; 2 Cor 1:6; 6:4; 1 Thess 1:3; 2 Thess 1:4; 3:5; Col 1:11). Job and the prophets are examples of such endurance (Jas 5:10–11), which is a mark of Christian maturity (Titus 2:2; Jas 1:3–4, 12; 2 Pet 1:6).

"If we deny him, he will also deny us." This third conditional clause is most likely the primary reason Paul cites this "trustworthy saying."[84] His purpose is to strengthen Timothy's resolve to remain loyal to Paul and to the gospel in the crisis he faces and to remind him that apostates will suffer the negative consequences of their faithlessness.[85] The history of the church provides ample evidence that under pressure Christ's servants may succumb to temptation to avoid personal suffering and deny their Lord (see on 1:15 above and 4:10, 14–16 below). This is another example where Paul's words echo those of Jesus (Matt 10:33; Mark 8:38; Luke 12:9; cf. John 13:38; Acts 3:14; Rev 3:8).[86] Elsewhere in

[83] Contra G. Sellin, "'Die Auferstehung ist schon geschehen': Zur Spiritualisierung apokalyptischer Terminologie im Neuen Testament," *NovT* 25 (1983): 234, who speaks of a "Reapokalyptisierung" (reapocalypticization), possibly in conjunction with mounting persecution.

[84] As mentioned, the verb ἀρνέομαι occurs three times in the hymn, suggesting that the denial of Christ is the major concern underlying the author's use of the hymn in the context of the letter.

[85] The LTT contain numerous references to the false teachers denying Christ in this way: they've "departed" (ἀστοχέω) from a pure heart, good conscience, and sincere faith and thus have "turned aside" (ἐκτρέπω) to fruitless discussion (1 Tim 1:5–6); they've "departed" (ἀφίστημι) from the faith (1 Tim 4:1); they've "departed" (ἀστοχέω) from the truth (2 Tim 2:18); they have an appearance of godliness but deny (ἀρνέομαι) its power (2 Tim 3:5); and they profess to know God but deny (ἀρνέομαι) him by their works (Titus 1:18).

[86] See the discussion in H. Riesenfeld, "The Meaning of the Verb ἀρνεῖσθαι," in *In honorem Antonii Fridrichsen sexagenarii edenda curavit Seminarium*

the LTT Paul speaks of denying the faith (1 Tim 5:8), the power of godliness (2 Tim 3:5), and even God himself (Titus 1:6).

"If we are faithless, he remains faithful, for he cannot deny himself." If we deny him, Christ will deny us, but he cannot deny himself. The final clause with its reassuring message balances the frightening prospect of Christ's denying apostates in the previous line.[87] God's sovereignty and faithfulness remain unaffected by human faithlessness (ἀπιστέω).[88] While denying the Lord will incur severe consequences, God will always remain faithful and true to himself (1 Cor 10:13; 1 Thess 5:24), as Paul knew from personal experience. Prior to his conversion he acted in unbelief (ἀπιστία; 1 Tim 1:13–14), but now his greatest desire is to be faithful to his Lord (2 Tim 4:8), confident of God's preserving power and grace (1:12; 4:18).[89]

Once again Paul's affirmation coheres closely with his teaching elsewhere: "What then? If some were unfaithful [ἀπιστέω], will their unfaithfulness [ἀπιστία] nullify God's faithfulness [πίστις]? Absolutely not! Let God be true, even though everyone is a liar" (Rom 3:3–4). Paul draws comfort from the fact that God is sovereign and faithful at a time when he is confined to prison, deserted by all but his closest coworkers (1:15; 4:10, 14–16). As in v. 9, it's not human performance but divine faithfulness that serves as the ultimate ground of assurance. At the same time, the closing line may anticipate the reference to Hymenaeus and Philetus in v. 17, asserting that some people's faithlessness will not take away God's faithfulness to those he has chosen, especially church leaders. This holds out hope for those who were swayed by the preaching of Paul's opponents and fell into ungodliness, and even for the opponents themselves (cf. vv. 19, 24–26).[90]

Neotestamenticum Upsaliense, ConBNT 11 (Lund: Gleerup, 1947), 215–16.

[87] The shift in pattern suggests to some that the last line was added by the letter's author (see, e.g., Hanson, *Pastoral Epistles*, 133: "It is probably the author's own comment").

[88] Bassler ("'He Remains Faithful,'" 183) speaks of "the conflicting demands of divine justice . . . and divine faithfulness," which leads the author "to predict the downfall of his opponents, but also to hold out hope for their ultimate redemption."

[89] Another NT example is Peter's denial of Jesus (John 18:15–27; cf. 13:36–38) and his subsequent restoration (John 21:1–19).

[90] So Bassler ("'He Remains Faithful,'" 181): "It seems, then, that one important implication the author reads out of v. 13a is that the faithlessness of some will not jeopardize God's faithfulness to the elect, especially to faithful church leaders.

In terms of biblical theology, we see here clearly that Paul's focus is not on himself and his adverse personal circumstances (v. 8). Nor is it on his coworkers, who for the most part are failing him, or even on his mission itself as a movement he seeks to perpetrate at all cost. Rather, his focus on the risen Lord Jesus Christ (v. 9) and on God's message of salvation in him (v. 10). This underscores that the apostolic mission is thoroughly God centered, gospel centered, and unequivocally committed to preaching salvation as the gracious gift of God provided only in the Lord Jesus Christ (§3). The faithful saying in vv. 11–13 underscores our union with the crucified and risen Christ in our mission, except that our unfaithfulness in no way nullifies his faithfulness. This, of course, would have been of supreme comfort and encouragement for Paul and also Timothy as they faced the unfaithfulness of many of their coworkers (cf. 1:15–18).

Bridge

The overriding themes in this section are the power of God's word and the faithfulness of God. In Paul's dire circumstances the apostle recalls these unshakable realities and links his own destiny to them. In this the apostle is exemplary, for we, too, should lift our eyes away from our current adverse circumstances and look to our faithful God to sustain and deliver us. The covenant-keeping faithfulness and righteousness of God are also the themes of other Pauline letters, most notably the letter to the Romans, with which this section displays numerous parallels.

3. Three Additional Ministry Roles: Workman, Instrument, Servant (2:14–26)

a. Workman (2:14–19)

[14]Remind them of these things, and charge them before God not to fight about words. This is useless and leads to the ruin of those who listen. [15]Be diligent to present yourself to God as one approved, a worker who doesn't need to be ashamed, correctly teaching the word of truth. [16]Avoid

---

The apparent success of those who are faithless [and, one might add, the apparent failure of those, like Paul, who are faithful but presently find themselves in prison] does not imply that God's firm foundation of support for the faithful has crumbled."

> irreverent and empty speech, since those who engage in it will produce even more godlessness, [17] and their teaching will spread like gangrene. Hymenaeus and Philetus are among them. [18] They have departed from the truth, saying that the resurrection has already taken place, and are ruining the faith of some. [19] Nevertheless, God's solid foundation stands firm, bearing this inscription: **The Lord knows those who are his**, and let everyone who calls on the name of the Lord turn away from wickedness.

Relation to Surrounding Context

The present unit shifts the spotlight on the false teachers whose influence is said to be like gangrene. The two explicit references to Scripture (Num 16:5, 26) in v. 19 are noteworthy because scriptural quotations are not common in the LTT. Paul's dual point is that (1) despite growing defections, God is not deceived—he has known those who are his all along; and (2) the Ephesian believers must distance themselves from the false teachers.

Structure

The previous unit climaxed in a faithful saying; the present unit culminates in a dual reference to Scripture. Three commands to Timothy ("remind," "be diligent," "avoid," vv. 14–16) are followed by a dire prediction of the demise of the false teachers, two of whom are singled out by name (v. 17). Their false teaching is specified and their impact noted (v. 18). Again the unit ends on a note of confidence with an added element of exhortation (v. 19).

2:14 Until this point in the letter, Paul has primarily addressed Timothy personally (except for 1:15–18 and 2:2). Now the apostle instructs Timothy to instruct others. The opening three verses in the present section include three additional commands addressed to Timothy. He is to (1) "remind them of these things, and charge them before God not to fight about words" (ὑπομίμνῃσκε; v. 14); (2) "be diligent" to present himself approved to God, "a worker who doesn't need to be ashamed, correctly teaching the word of truth" (σπούδασον; v. 15); and (3) "avoid irreverent and empty speech," in contrast to the false teachers (περιΐστασο; v. 16).

First, having asked Timothy to remember (μνημονεύω) Jesus Christ (v. 8), Paul now urges him to "remind" (ὑπομιμνῄσκω; cf. Titus 3:1; 2 Pet 1:12; 3 John 10; Jude 5) the people in his church (esp. the "faithful men" in v. 2) of "these things" (see vv. 3–13 and following verses). The reminder is to be given in form of a charge.

The term underlying "charge" (διαμαρτύρομαι) occurs elsewhere in the LTT in two solemn charges before God and Christ (4:1) and the angels (1 Tim 5:21). Here the charge is made "before God" (cf. 1 Tim 5:4; the variant "Lord" is unlikely), that is, in his presence and with him as a witness, invoking courtroom language. Paul's charge relates to the danger of "quarreling about words" (λογομαχεῖν; cf. λογομαχία in the similar warning in 1 Tim 6:4–5; and see v. 23 below), an exercise in futility (cf. Ezek 15:4 LXX) whose only outcome bringing ruin (καταστροφή; cf. 2 Pet 2:6 [variant]) on those who listen (cf. v. 2 above and v. 16 below).[91] Such quarrels were spawned by the false teachers (1 Tim 1:4: ἐκζητήσεις). Similarly, believers today should avoid those who are self-absorbed, love to hear themselves talk, and are more interested in minor quibbles than in evangelizing the lost or building up the church.

2:15–16 Second, unlike the false teachers, Timothy must make every effort (σπουδάζω; cf. 4:9, 21; Titus 3:12; Gal 2:10; Eph 4:3; 1 Thess 2:17) to teach God's Word accurately. The Greek word underlying "Be diligent" (CSB = NASB; ESV and NIV: "Do your best"; NLT: "Work hard"; KJV: "Study") conveys the notion of intensity; Paul seeks to instill in Timothy a sense of urgency.[92] Teaching God's Word is no task to be performed in a cavalier manner. Rather, it is a matter of supreme importance that calls for energetic focus and dogged commitment. This is the case all the more because teachers are accountable to God, as those who should present themselves (παραστῆσαι—in a cultic sense in Rom 12:1, but here probably to God as a judge) to him on judgment day as tested and approved (δόκιμος; cf. Rom 14:18; 16:10; 1 Cor 11:19; 2 Cor 10:18; 13:7; the opposite ἀδόκιμος occurs in 3:8; Titus 1:16; cf. 1 Cor 9:27). The false teachers twist the Scriptures to fit their own theology; Timothy ought to model a proper use of God's Word.

Paul now employs the first of three additional images, that of a worker (ἐργάτης; cf. Matt 9:37–38 par.; 1 Tim 5:19 cf. Luke 10:7) who doesn't need to be ashamed (ἀνεπαίσχυντος, only here in the NT; cf. Josephus, *Ant.* 18.243) but correctly teaches the "word

---

[91] The term καταστροφή refers to God's bringing about physical destruction at the end-time judgment (Gen 19:29 LXX; 2 Chr 22:7 LXX; cf. *1 Clem.* 7.7); cf. 1 Tim 6:9.

[92] None of the major English translations fully captures the notion of intensity present in the Greek word σπουδάζω.

of truth," that is, Paul's apostolic gospel.[93] Paul previously told Timothy not to be ashamed of the gospel (e.g., 1:8). Here shame is not the result of fear of being identified with Christ (ultimately at God's judgment, 1 John 2:28) but of lack of proper training and skill in handling God's Word. Similarly, some today stand ready to identify with Christ and preach his Word but, due to inadequate training, fail to handle God's Word properly and thus will be put to shame. What such people need is not more courage or commitment but proper training in interpreting and communicating the scriptural message (cf. 3:16–17). Just as a worker takes pride in a job well done, the proper teaching of God's Word requires training and skill.

The word "correctly teaching" (ὀρθοτομέω) conveys the notion of "cutting straight" (rather than crooked), whether cutting a road in order to forge a straight path (cf. Prov 3:6 LXX; 11:5 LXX) or some other setting.[94] In an age when Roman roads were masterful examples of skilled engineering, this metaphor would have communicated well.[95] In any case, Paul's point is that a worker's task requires skill. Incompetence or shortcuts won't get the job done. In fact, an untrained worker will do more harm than good. Jesus observed that "everyone who is fully trained will be like his teacher" (Luke 6:40). Paul was educated under Gamaliel (Acts 22:3), and Jesus's disciples were recognized as having "been with Jesus" (Acts 4:13). God's Word must be interpreted and communicated in keeping with its intended purpose (cf. 2 Cor. 2:17; 4:2; contrast Acts 13:10).

Having been properly trained, not only must Timothy stay on the straight and narrow path himself; he must also make sure that those under his care are shown the paths of God's truth. There's no substitute for thorough training in the Scriptures, even in a day when modern technology has made learning the biblical languages

---

[93] On Paul's work ethic, see H. Mare, "The Pauline Work Ethic," in *New Dimensions in New Testament Study*, ed. R. N. Longenecker and M. C. Tenney (Grand Rapids: Zondervan, 1974), 357–69. I owe this reference to R. Yarbrough.

[94] Most church fathers interpret the term as plowing. Johnson, *Letters to Paul's Delegates*, 76, favors a surgical connotation due to the proximity of "gangrene" in v. 17.

[95] Quinn and Wacker, *Letters to Timothy*, 676, citing Moulton and Milligan, contend that the emphasis is on ὀρθο, with τομέω having largely faded out of consciousness. Other commentators, likewise, contend that the original sense of "cutting" may have faded from view (G. D. Fee, *1 and 2 Timothy, Titus*, NIBCNT 13 [Peabody, MA: Hendrickson, 1988], 255; Knight, *Pastoral Epistles*, 411–12).

easier and the Internet has opened new avenues of theological education. What's more, the primary subject of training for the Christian worker must be "the word of truth" (i.e., the word that is true; cf. Ps 119:43; Jas 1:8), not other subjects. Timothy's training had come largely as a result of being associated with Paul in ministry (3:10–11; cf. Acts 16:1–5). If training for the ministry is to be effective today, there must be similar mentoring or internship opportunities for young aspiring pastors and Christian workers. On the negative side, cults typically distort the teaching of Scripture with disastrous results for their converts and members.

As mentioned at v. 14 above, Paul issues three commands to Timothy, the first of which was to remind people in his church not to fight about words (v. 14) and the second being to be diligent to present himself to God as one approved in the way he handles God's word (v. 15). In v. 16, third, Timothy, and presumably those in his congregation, are once again warned to avoid (περιΐστημι; Titus 3:9; John 11:42; Acts 25:7, lit., "go around [so as to avoid something]") "irreverent and empty speech" (v. 16; cf. v. 14; 1 Tim 6:20; see also 1 Tim 1:6, 9; 4:7). For those who indulge in it will grow more and more ungodly (ἀσέβεια; cf. Titus 2:12; 3:9–11). Literally the latter phrase reads "progress more and more in ungodliness," involving a wordplay: those given to irreverent, empty speech—self-styled doctrinal "progressives," perhaps—will indeed "progress" (προκόπτω) but entirely in the wrong direction (cf. 3:9, 13; see also 1 Tim 4:15). Calvin's simile is apt: indulging in vacuous speech is like a "deep whirlpool, from which there is no escape and into which men plunge deeper and deeper."[96]

2:17–18 To illustrate his point, Paul uses yet another medical metaphor (cf. "pattern of sound teaching" in 1:13). He predicts that the false teachers' doctrine will spread (νομὴν ἕξει; cf. John 10:9: "find pasture") "like gangrene" (γάγγραινα, a medical term since Hippocrates [5th c. BC]). As cancer slowly but surely eats away at a person's body, the false teaching will sap the spiritual vitality of the church. Paul goes on to name two teachers who have "departed" (ἠστόχησαν; 1 Tim 1:6; 6:21) from the truth (cf. v. 15), Hymenaeus and Philetus. Despite Paul's not-so-subtle earlier demand that Hymenaeus be excommunicated (1 Tim 1:20),

---

[96] Calvin, *1 & 2 Timothy & Titus* (1556; repr., Wheaton: Crossway, 1998), 138.

Paul remains concerned about this individual; Philetus is not mentioned elsewhere.

Not only does Paul identify the false teachers by name, but he also specifies the nature of their teaching (cf. 1 Tim 4:3): the claim that the resurrection has already occurred. Apparently Paul faced a similar teaching in Corinth (1 Cor 15:12; cf. v. 29). The denial of a future resurrection may be an instance of overrealized eschatology (contrast 1 Thess 4:13–18). Irenaeus (2nd c. AD) reports that the Gnostic Menander claimed to have already experienced resurrection by virtue of being baptized (*Haer.* 1.23.5) and that other Gnostics held that resurrection takes place in the acquisition of truth (*Haer.* 2.48.2), since they were committed to the immaterial nature of the resurrection body.

The false teachers may also have distorted Paul's teaching regarding believers' present experience of being risen with Christ (e.g., Rom 6:1–14) as though this completely exhausts what sharing in Christ's resurrection entails. As Paul tells the Corinthians, however, the Christian hope of resurrection is more than a present spiritual experience (1 Cor 15:19). The driving force behind this false teaching may be the dualism inherent in Greek philosophy with its focus on the immortality of the soul and its disparagement of the human body (cf. 1 Tim 6:20–21). Even in our day people's notion of resurrection often bears greater resemblance to Greek philosophy than biblical teaching. In the original context Paul's opponents seem to have had a measure of success, having overturned (ἀνατρέπω; Titus 1:11; literally, John 2:15) the faith of some (cf. commentary at v. 13 above and v. 19 below). Asserting that believers experienced the full reality of Christ's resurrection already in the present, the opponents may have proceeded to maintain that it therefore didn't matter how they lived (cf. 1 Cor 4:8).

2:19 Nevertheless (μέντοι; only here in Paul), God's solid foundation stands firm, bearing this (twofold) inscription (lit., "bearing this seal," σφραγίς; cf. Rom 4:11; 1 Cor 9:2): (1) "The Lord knows those who are his" (Num 16:5 LXX)[97]—true about God (1 Sam 16:7), comforting for believers (Psalm 139), and a message of judgment to unbelievers (Matt 7:23)—and (2) "let everyone who calls on the

[97] The quotation is verbatim from Num 16:5 except that "God" is replaced with "the Lord."

name of the Lord [rather than "God," cf. Joel 3:5 LXX] turn away from wickedness" (Num 16:26–27 LXX; cf. Isa 26:13 LXX; §2.7.1). In 1 Tim 6:19 Paul calls generosity "a good foundation (θεμέλιον καλόν) for the coming age" (cf. 1 Cor 3:10–12; Eph 2:20). The adjective "solid" (στερεός) occurs elsewhere in the NT only in Heb 5:12, 14 and 1 Pet 5:9.

The terms "solid foundation," "stand firm," and "seal" all highlight the unshakable nature of the truths of Scripture that Paul invokes. By using the image of a "seal," Paul alludes to the fact that just as a seal warrants a letter's integrity, so "Christians' moral integrity manifests or seals the fact that Christ is present in them."[98] Specifically, these passages refer to God's knowledge and sovereign preservation of his own and believers' need to base their Christian confession on true repentance and a commensurate way of life. The "inscription" may be that on a building, a common sight in ancient life (cf. the house metaphor in vv. 20–21 below).

What are the two foundational truths Paul highlights? First, the apostle affirms that despite growing defections and the resulting disillusionment, God isn't deceived—he has known who are his own all along (Num 16:5; cf. John 6:70–71; 12:4–6; 13:10; 17:12). In the original instance this refers to the rebellion by Korah and his followers against Moses and Aaron and God's response of active support by destroying Korah and confirming Moses's leadership. In the present contexts this means that Hymenaeus, Philetus, and any other opponents don't belong to God's people (see on v. 13a above). Bound and approaching the end of his life, Paul draws comfort from his knowledge of the sovereign omniscience of God. Second, just as wilderness Israel needed to distance itself from rebellious Korah, the Ephesian believers must separate from the false teachers (Num 16:26). Truth and falsehood cannot permanently coexist.[99]

---

[98] C. Molina and E. van Eck, "Σφραγίς (*sfragis*) and Its Metaphorical Testimonial Presence in 2 Timothy 2:19," *Harvard Theological Studies* 67 (2011): 1–4 (quote from p. 2). As the authors note, "It was this aspect of Christian behavior, this voluntary isolation from moral corruption and idolatry, which attracted upon Christians humiliation and eventually persecution" (ibid., with reference to Ezekiel).

[99] Bassler, "'He Remains Faithful,'" 181–82, believes those who call on the name of the Lord may include those, both church leaders and ordinary Christians, who have embraced the message of the false teachers. This, she says, constitutes faithlessness but doesn't draw instant judgment. Instead, God remains faithful and doesn't

To sum up this section's overall biblical-theological contribution, the letter continues to be God focused (§3.1) and to unfold against an ominous eschatological backdrop (§6). In this vein there are references to God's approval in v. 15 and to God's solid foundation in v. 19, contrasted by the apostasy of the false teachers. In these increasingly dark days, God's servants must be firmly committed to sound apostolic teaching, not succumbing to social pressure or a tendency to please people. Instead they must stand firm against the prevailing winds of the culture and cling to "the word of truth" (v. 15). In the remainder of the chapter, this will be further developed as cultivating purity and as being set apart for God so as to be "useful . . . for every good work" (vv. 20–21) and as fleeing from youthful passions and pursuing Christian virtues "along with those who call on the Lord from a pure heart" (vv. 22).

Bridge

Paul's words to Timothy, "Be diligent to present yourself to God as one approved, a worker who doesn't need to be ashamed, correctly teaching the word of truth" (2:15), are set against the dark backdrop of the false teachers. Some claim early Christianity was diverse and there wasn't yet a clear notion of orthodoxy. While the word *orthodoxy* is a later coinage, however, the notion of "correct teaching" of the Word of God was certainly present when Paul wrote to Timothy. In fact, it is implicit in Paul's words to the Galatians: "I am amazed that you are so quickly turning away from him who called you by the grace of Christ and are *turning to a different gospel—not that there is another gospel*, but there are some who are troubling you and *want to distort the gospel* of Christ. But even if we or an angel from heaven should preach to you *a gospel contrary to what we have preached to you*, a curse be on him! As we have said before, I now say again: If anyone is preaching to you *a gospel contrary to what you received*, a curse be on him!" (Gal 1:6–9). It's hard to imagine a stronger denunciation of the notion of Christian diversity with regard to the gospel.[100]

---

abandon the genuinely elect even when they've been temporarily swayed by heresy. Rather, they're urged to turn from wickedness (see vv. 24–26; cf. Titus 1:13).

[100] See A. J. Köstenberger and M. J. Kruger, *The Heresy of Orthodoxy: How Contemporary Culture's Fascination with Diversity Has Reshaped Our Understanding of Early Christianity* (Wheaton: Crossway, 2010); A. J. Köstenberger,

b. Instrument (2:20–21)

> 20 Now in a large house there are not only gold and silver vessels, but also those of wood and clay; some for honorable use and some for dishonorable. 21 So if anyone purifies himself from anything dishonorable, he will be a special instrument, set apart, useful to the Master, prepared for every good work.

Relation to Surrounding Context

On the heels of describing Timothy's task as that of a worker, Paul follows up with a second illustration, that of being a special instrument useful to the Master. Below he will add a third, that of being a servant.

Structure

"Now" (δέ) in v. 20 is a development marker, indicating that Paul has moved on to another topic or illustration.[101] "So" (οὖν) in v. 21 indicates the result that follows. Paul will return to the notion of "every good work" in 3:17.[102]

2:20–21 To the workman metaphor (v. 15) Paul adds a second illustration: a useful household tool (cf. Rom 9:19–21; see also 1 Cor 12:12–29).[103] In the picture of a large house (presumably owned by a wealthy individual) with a variety of articles, the point is not so much that utensils made of gold and silver are intrinsically superior to those made of wood or clay (note the arrangement in decreasing order of value). All fulfill a useful function—expensive utensils as fine dinnerware for public meals, inexpensive ones as rough clay pots for storage, etc.—but some tools serve nobler purposes than others (such as those used for human waste or

---

D. L. Bock, and J. D. Chatraw, *Truth in a Culture of Doubt: Engaging Skeptical Challenges to the Bible* (Nashville: B&H Academic, 2014), 107–30.

101 On development markers in general, and δέ in particular, see S. E. Runge, *Discourse Grammar of the Greek New Testament* (Peabody, MA: Hendrickson, 2010), 28–36 and the charts on pp. 42 and 57.

102 On οὖν as a development marker conveying both continuity and development, see ibid., 43–48 and the chart on p. 57.

103 Some interpret this illustration almost like a parable, such as the parable of the wheat and the weeds (Matt 13:24–30), to the effect that in this age there'll still be some false teachers in Christendom. However, vv. 20–21 don't represent a parable but rather an illustration or analogy. The "large house" doesn't represent the church, and the presence of various types of utensils doesn't point to the presence of both true and false teachers. Paul's illustration merely establishes the principle that Timothy and others should strive to be instruments for noble use.

garbage, a possible allusion to opponents such as Hymenaeus and Philetus).[104] Timothy and all those desiring to be used by God (note the generic reference in v. 21; cf. v. 22: "along with those who call on the Lord from a pure heart") should aspire to be instruments for noble purposes.

In what follows, however, Paul moves beyond the original illustration in that clearly in the Ephesian situation "dishonorable [use]" requires conscious, thorough cleansing (the force of the intensifying ἐκ in ἐκκαθάρῃ; cf. 1 Cor 5:7; see also v. 22: καθαρᾶς καρδίας; Titus 2:14: καθαρίζω). The threefold result (listed in phrases of increasing length) is that such a person will be: (1) set apart (ἡγιασμένον; 1 Tim 4:5); (2) useful (εὔχρηστον; Mark in 4:11; Onesimus in Phlm 11) to the Master (in the original illustration, the master of the household; in a Christian context, Christ or God); and (3) prepared (ἡτοιμασμένον; see 3:17; Eph 2:10) for every good work. This should be the desire of every Christian: to be set apart exclusively for God's purposes (which requires a clean heart; see v. 22 below); to be useful for God's service; and to be ready for whatever good work God wants them to do.

Bridge

It's been said that a Christian should be faithful, available, and teachable. The image Paul employs in this passage, an instrument useful to the Master, requires that a person be wholly available to be used by the Master, which also entails prior purification. In this regard, one thinks of many who have been used by God in salvation history who were first set aside and prepared for the Master's use: Abraham, Joseph, Moses, Isaiah, Paul himself, and, above all, Jesus.

c. Servant (2:22–26)

[22] Flee from youthful passions, and pursue righteousness, faith, love, and peace, along with those who call on the Lord from a pure heart. [23] But reject foolish and ignorant disputes, because you know that they breed quarrels. [24] The Lord's servant must not quarrel, but must be gentle to everyone, able to teach, and patient, [25] instructing his opponents with gentle-

[104] On honor and shame, see the discussion on 1:8–12 above. See also 1 Tim 5:1–17, where honor is supposed to be extended to older church members as well as worthy widows and elders in charge of the congregation.

> ness. Perhaps God will grant them repentance leading them to the knowledge of the truth. [26]Then they may come to their senses and escape the trap of the devil, who has taken them captive to do his will.

Relation to Surrounding Context

This is now the third and final illustration designed to set Timothy's role and task into perspective. Not only are these comparable to a worker (v. 15) and a useful instrument (vv. 20–21), but they're also similar to a household servant.

Structure

The passage starts with the dual command to "flee" and "pursue" (v. 22). To this a negative command is added: "reject" (v. 23). Verses 24–26 then describe the proper demeanor of the Lord's servant, which may result in God's granting of repentance and deliverance from the devil.

2:22 A skilled worker (v. 15), a useful tool in the Master's hand (vv. 20–21)—Paul employs one more ministry metaphor: a household servant (vv. 24–25). The intensity of the apostle's pleading with Timothy continues unabated. Again Paul issues a series of three commands in vv. 22 and 23. First of all, Paul urges his protégé to "flee" (φεύγω) and "pursue" (διώκω; commands 1 and 2; see on 1 Tim 6:11; cf. 1 Cor 6:18; 10:14). Negatively, Timothy is urged to run from "youthful passions" (νεωτερικὰς ἐπιθυμίας), possibly in contrast with the earlier mentioned Hymenaeus and Philetus (v. 18; cf. the similar exhortation in 1 Tim 4:12). Positively, Paul calls on Timothy to pursue the traits of righteousness (moral uprightness, integrity), faith (trust in God), love (a charitable disposition toward others), and peace (harmony rather than contentiousness; see on 1 Tim 1:14).

The range of the "youthful passions" Timothy is urged to flee is likely broader than sexual lust (cf. NASB, "youthful lusts").[105]

---

[105] The expression "desire" or "passion" (ἐπιθυμία), often in the plural, is found frequently in Paul's letters, virtually always with a negative connotation and often in relation to believers' former way of life prior to their conversion when they lived lives controlled by their sinful nature (Rom 1:24; 6:12; 7:7, 8; 13:14; Gal 5:16, 24; Eph 2:3; 4:22; Col 3:5; 1 Thess 4:5; 1 Tim 6:9; 2 Tim 3:6; Titus 2:12; 3:3; but see Phil 1:23; 1 Thess 2:17). At times, but not invariably, the term has a sexual connotation (e.g., Rom 1:24). See Westfall, "Moral Dilemma," 245, who says that in the present

If the positive traits that are mentioned are any indication, the vices Timothy is urged to shun include unrighteousness (i.e., any form of immorality, including sexual sins, 3:6, and the desire to get rich, 1 Tim 6:9), unbelief (including improper self-reliance in conduct or teaching), an unloving disposition (contrast the self-centered nature of the false teachers), and restlessness (a frequent characteristic of young people). That said, not only young people must flee "youthful passions." In summary, Timothy should train himself in godliness (εὐσέβεια, 1 Tim 4:7–8). Yet the quest for holiness needn't be a lonely enterprise, as though believers should retreat to their closets and engage in quiet meditation. Instead, holiness should be pursued in community, "along with those who call on the Lord from a pure heart" (v. 22; cf. 1 Tim 1:5; a partial allusion to Joel 3:5 LXX; cf. v. 19 above).[106]

2:23–26 For the third time in this chapter (cf. vv. 14, 16), then, Paul urges Timothy to have nothing to do with pointless controversies (παραιτοῦ, v. 23; command 3). He is to shun "foolish and ignorant disputes" (NIV: "foolish and stupid arguments"; note the strong language; cf. 1 Tim 6:4; Titus 3:9).[107] For he knows they produce only quarrels (μάχας; v. 23: cf. Titus 3:9; 2 Cor 7:5; Jas 4:1; see also μάχεσθαι in v. 24). The "foolish debates, genealogies, quarrels, and disputes about the law" mentioned in Titus 3:9 are examples of this. As "the Lord's servant" (cf. 1 Tim 4:6), Timothy must not get entangled in fruitless disputes (cf. Isa 42:2) but rather should be gentle or kind (ἤπιον; cf. 1 Thess 2:7) to everyone (CSB, NIV; better NASB, "to all"), able to teach (διδακτικός; 1 Tim 3:2; cf. 2 Tim 2:2), and not resentful (ἀνεξίκακον, a NT hapax). He must speak the truth in love (Eph 4:15; cf. Matt 11:29). In all of this, Paul's concern for Timothy is that he knows how to properly deal with challenges, arguments, and disagreements of a doctrinal nature, ensuring that he stay on course and not get thrown off.[108]

---

passage Paul has in mind "the hot-headed tendency to argue and get involved in side issues and unprofitable hairsplitting."

[106] "Pure heart" may be the Semitic equivalent of "pure conscience," since Hebrew has no word for "conscience."

[107] "Foolish" translates μωρός (cf. 1 Cor 1:25, 27; 3:18; 4:10), while "ignorant" or "stupid" renders ἀπαίδευτος (lit., "uneducated"), a NT hapax that occurs in the LXX frequently in the book of Proverbs (e.g., 5:23; 8:5; 15:12, 14; 17:12; 24:8; 27:20) as well as in the apocryphal wisdom book Sirach.

[108] So rightly Westfall, "Moral Dilemma," 244–45.

Guided by this kind of inner disposition, the Lord's servant must instruct (παιδεύω; 1 Tim 1:20; Titus 2:12; cf. ἀπαιδεύτους in v. 23) his opponents with gentleness (ἐν πραΰτητι; cf. Titus 3:2; Gal 5:23; 6:1; 1 Cor 4:21; 2 Cor 10:1; Eph 4:2; Col 3:12; see *NewDocs* 4:169–70). He must not be guided by the desire to win an argument or to take revenge but by the hope that God might grant the false teachers repentance (cf. Acts 5:31; 11:18)[109] and the knowledge of the truth (cf. 3:7; 1 Tim 2:4; Titus 1:1; on truth, see vv. 15, 18), which most likely refers to the way of salvation in and through Jesus as conveyed by the apostolic gospel message. Perhaps they'll come to their senses (ἀνανήφω, another NT hapax), as if waking up and realizing they've been trapped, and escape the devil (διάβολος; cf. 1 Tim 3:6, 7, 11; see the comments at vv. 13 and 19 above). This is similar to Paul's teaching elsewhere (e.g., 2 Cor 4:4; 10:4–5).

The false teachers' problem isn't merely ignorance (v. 23); they've been trapped (παγίς; cf. 1 Tim 3:7; 6:9) by the devil "who has taken them captive [ἐζωγρημένοι; cf. Luke 5:10; 2 Chr 25:12 LXX] to do his will." The setting of traps, such as using nets to catch animals ranging from birds to deer, is a fitting metaphor for the bondage resulting from sin. Trapping people in a web of lies has been the devil's practice from the beginning (Gen 3:1–7). Those who persist in falsehood show that they're caught in spiritual bondage. As Paul wrote to the Ephesians, our struggle isn't against flesh and blood but against the devil and his forces (Eph 6:10–18). Christian ministry entails waging spiritual warfare (2 Cor 10:3–5; 11:2–3). Thus Timothy should adopt a ministering stance toward the false teachers; perhaps some of them can be set free from spiritual bondage. To that end he must "tread the narrow path between acquiescence in error, and too violent a rejection of it."[110]

Bridge

In Paul's first letter to Timothy, the apostle acknowledged, in effect, "There but for the grace of God go I." He was no better than the false teachers but had been shown mercy by the Lord (1 Tim 1:12–17). In the present passage Paul tells Timothy to instruct his

---

[109] See the treatment of 2 Tim 2:25 in M. J. Boda, *'Return to Me': A Biblical Theology of Repentance*, NSBT 35 (Downers Grove: InterVarsity, 2015), 173.

[110] Barrett, *Pastoral Epistles*, 108.

opponents with gentleness so that perhaps some might repent and be delivered from the devil's grasp. This highlights the importance of humility in dealing with one's opponents, which, in turn, must be balanced with the need to confront false teachers because of the deleterious effect they have on people in the church (cf., e.g., Galatians, Jude, and Jesus's dealings with the Pharisees).

B. Additional Exhortations (3:1–17)

After holding out hope, at least in principle, that Timothy's opponents may escape "the trap of the devil," Paul now puts the moral and religious decay of the times in broader perspective. As in his first letter to Timothy, about halfway through the letter Paul refers to the latter-day apostasy at work in the false teachers (3:1–9).[111] He also encourages Timothy to stay the course (3:10–17).

1. Latter-Day Apostasy (3:1–9)

> [1] But know this: Hard times will come in the last days. [2] For people will be lovers of self, lovers of money, boastful, proud, demeaning, disobedient to parents, ungrateful, unholy, [3] unloving, irreconcilable, slanderers, without self-control, brutal, without love for what is good, [4] traitors, reckless, conceited, lovers of pleasure rather than lovers of God, [5] holding to the form of godliness but denying its power. Avoid these people.
>
> [6] For among them are those who worm their way into households and deceive gullible women overwhelmed by sins and led astray by a variety of passions, [7] always learning and never able to come to a knowledge of the truth. [8] Just as Jannes and Jambres resisted Moses, so these also resist the truth. They are men who are corrupt in mind and worthless in regard to the faith. [9] But they will not make further progress, for their foolishness will be clear to all, as was the foolishness of Jannes and Jambres.

---

[111] See also Paul's use of Τὸ λοιπόν ("finally") halfway through his letter to the Philippians (Phil 3:1).

2 Timothy 3:1–5

Relation to Surrounding Context

Having just spoken of the "the trap of the devil," by which Satan ensnared some of Timothy's opponents (2:26; cf. 3:13; 1 Tim 3:6; 5:15; 6:9), Paul now turns to a general characterization of the "last days," which ominiously forecast the circumstances surrounding Jesus's second coming. The extended vice list makes for a scathing denunciation not only of the false teachers but of human society apart from God in general. The description of the false teachers in vv. 6–9 recalls Paul's concern for young widows in 1 Tim 5:11–15. Unlike Timothy these individuals won't make further progress (v. 9; cf. 1 Tim 4:15).

Structure

As in Paul's first letter to Timothy, halfway through the letter Paul sets his remarks within an eschatological framework. The introduction in v. 1 is followed by a vice list spanning vv. 2–5. Paul lists no fewer than nineteen negative characteristics in the form of a chiasm with διάβολοι ("slanderous") at the center. The warning at the end of v. 5 to avoid these people is then followed up by a description of the false teachers in vv. 6–9, who are ironically cast as "always learning and never able to come to a knowledge of the truth" (v. 7).

3:1–5 As in Paul's first letter to Timothy, the midway point is marked by a sharp turn, setting the current apostasy in the context of end-time prophecy (cf. 1 Tim 4:1–5; §6).[112] After adducing various positive and negative examples (1:8–18), using several ministry metaphors (2:3–7, 15, 20–21, 24), quoting a "trustworthy saying" (2:11–13), and invoking Scripture (2:19), Paul employs yet another weapon in his rhetorical arsenal.[113]

The introductory phrase, "But know this" (Τοῦτο δὲ γίνωσκε), sounds the alert (cf. 1:18; see also Gal 3:7). Paul reminds Timothy

---

[112] This is not to deny the fact that there are several "cohesive ties" between the preceding (2:14–26) and the present unit (3:1–17). See Westfall, "Moral Dilemma," 245, who cites the vice list in 3:2–4 and the behavior of Timothy's opponents in 2:25–27 [*sic*; presumably, 2:24–26].

[113] For a defense of 2 Tim 3:1–9 as a textual unit, see J. Tromp, "Jannes and Jambres (2 Timothy 3, 8–9)," in *Moses in Biblical and Extra-Biblical Traditions*, ed. A. Graupner and M. Wolter, BZAW 372 (Berlin: de Gruyter, 2007), 220, who writes, "So 2 Tim 3,1–9 is a distinct textual unit, neatly demarcated from both the preceding and the succeeding pericopes."

that "hard times" (καιροὶ χαλεποί; cf. Matt 8:28: "violent"; Isa 18:2 LXX: "aggressive") will come (ἐνιστήμι; cf. 2 Thess 2:2) in the "last days" (cf. Acts 2:17 citing Joel 3:1; Jas 5:3; see also the "apostolic prophecy" in Jude 17–18 // 2 Pet 3:3; and Heb 1:2). Rebellion will run rampant.

The defections of Paul's coworkers (1:15; 4:11) and the presence of false teachers in the Ephesian church (in keeping with Paul's own prediction, cf. Acts 20:29–31) are clear signs that the "last days" (i.e., the time preceding Christ's return) are at hand. As Paul has written to the Ephesians, believers should be wise in how they live and make the most of every opportunity "because the days are evil" (Eph 5:15–16).

Paul goes on to elaborate on the terrible conditions that will prevail in the days preceding the second coming, listing no fewer than nineteen negative characteristics which pertain not merely to the false teachers but to humanity at large (cf. the vice list in 1 Tim 1:9–11).[114] A chiasm is evident, with διάβολοι ("slanderous," possibly linked to the devil, διάβολος, cf. 2:26) at the center and as the emphatic exclamation point. People (ἄνθρωποι, used inclusively) will be:

- lovers of self (φίλαυτοι; only here in the NT);
- lovers of money (φιλάργυροι; only here in the NT; cf. Luke 16:14);
- boastful (ἀλαζόνες; cf. Rom 1:30; see also 1 John 2:16; Jas 4:16);
- proud (ὑπερήφανοι; cf. Luke 1:51; Rom 1:30; Jas 4:6; 1 Pet 5:5);
- demeaning (βλάσφημοι; cf. Acts 6:11; 1 Tim 1:13; 2 Peter 2:11);
- disobedient to parents (γονεῦσιν ἀπειθεῖς; cf. Rom 1:30; Titus 1:16; 3:3);
- ungrateful (ἀχάριστοι; cf. Luke 6:35);
- unholy (ἀνόσιοι; cf. 1 Tim 1:9);
- unloving (ἄστοργοι; cf. Rom 1:31; see also Rom 12:10);
- irreconcilable or unforgiving (ἄσπονδοι; only here in the NT);
- slanderous (διάβολοι; cf. 1 Tim 3:11; Titus 2:3);
- without self-control (ἀκρατεῖς; only here in the NT; cf. Prov 27:20 LXX);
- brutal (ἀνήμεροι; only here in the NT);

[114] See ibid., 221.

- without love for what is good (ἀφιλάγαθοι; only here in the NT);
- traitors (προδόται; cf. Luke 6:16: Judas; Acts 7:52);
- reckless (προπετεῖς; cf. Acts 19:36; see also Prov 10:14 LXX; 13:3);
- conceited (τετυφωμένοι; cf. 1 Tim 3:6; 6:4);
- lovers of pleasure (φιλήδονοι) rather than lovers of God (φιλόθεοι; both only here in the NT); and, in summary;
- holding to the form of godliness (μόρφωσιν εὐσεβείας; cf. Rom 2:20; 1 Tim 6:3) but denying its power (δύναμις; cf. 1:7, 8; regarding the whole phrase, see Titus 1:16).[115]

The list is striking in its rich and rare vocabulary: as many as seven words are found only here in the NT, and six words occur elsewhere only once. The list bears closest affinity to the vice list in Rom 1:29–32 (four shared words). In terms of literary form, five attributes pertain to people's misdirected love: lovers of self, lovers of money, not lovers of good, lovers of pleasure rather than lovers of God, with the first and the last two terms enveloping the entire list in form of a chiasm. Eight traits pinpoint the lack of a certain virtue (α privative): boastful, disobedient to parents, ungrateful, unholy, unloving, irreconcilable, without self-control, without love for what is good.

Some expressions relate to attitude, others to the manifestation of inner dispositions in speech or action; but all of them, in one way or another, depict a person's godless self-centeredness. The list as a whole isn't meant to serve as a comprehensive description of depraved humanity. Rather, the desired rhetorical effect is moral outrage. The list paints a picture of the evil condition and actions of people in the last days, which are also exhibited by the false teachers in the Ephesian church (cf. 1 Tim 1:9–11). Paul's advice for Timothy is to the point: "Avoid these people" (ἀποτρέπω; cf. 2:19, 21; cf. Titus 3:10–11). There's no basis for fellowship with false teachers in the same church.

[115] If "Satan disguises himself as an angel of light," it's not surprising "if his servants also disguise themselves as servants of righteousness" (2 Cor 11:14–15). This is what makes the false teachers so dangerous, and this is why their identity must be revealed and their true motives exposed (note the naming of specific false teachers in the LTT).

3:6–9 The connection to the previous verses (vv. 1–5) is more obvious in the original, where the false teachers are tied to end-time prophecy by the conjunction "for" (*γάρ*; translated in the CSB, ESV, and NASB but not in the NIV). The "people" (v. 2) whom Timothy should avoid (v. 5) are now described as those who, first, "worm their way" (ἐνδύνοντες; cf. Gal 2:4; Jude 4; 2 Pet 2:1) into homes (cf. Titus 1:11), and, second, deceive or overpower (αἰχμαλωτίζοντες; cf. Luke 21:24; Rom 7:23; 2 Cor 10:5) "gullible women" (γυναικάρια; probably in the diminutive or belittling sense of "frail" or "little women").

While the "typical large Greek home had a clear demarcation between the public areas of the house and the women's quarters (often on a second story)," a man might gain access as a "permanent guest under the patronage of the mistress of the house as a teacher or as a tutor for the children."[116] If the man's motives were deceptive, this obviously created a host of difficulties, most importantly that of turning the home away from the truth of the gospel by way of false teaching.[117]

As mentioned at 1 Tim 2:14–15, women are generally in a more vulnerable position than men and, if unprotected, can become an easy prey of Satan (cf. Gen 3:1–7). Concern for women's preservation from the evil one was one of the reasons Paul cited for assigning authoritative teaching and governing roles in the church to men (1 Tim 2:14; cf. v. 12; §3.5.7). A similar concern motivated his advice to younger widows to remarry (1 Tim 5:11–15; cf. v. 6). The latter passage, likewise, speaks of certain women living for pleasure (1 Tim 5:6), being overcome by sensual desires (v. 11), and needing to focus on their domestic duties (v. 14; cf. v. 13) in order not to fall prey to Satan (v. 15; cf. 1 Tim 2:14–15).

The women in the present passage are described by a series of participles: (1) loaded with or overwhelmed by (σεσωρευμένα, cf. Rom 12:20 citing Prov 25:22) sins (the perfect most likely expresses a present settled state of being); (2) led astray (ἀγόμενα; positively, Rom 8:14 and Gal 5:18; negatively, 1 Cor 12:2) by a variety of passions (ἐπιθυμία; see esp. Titus 3:3; cf. 1 Tim 6:9; 2 Tim 2:22; 4:3; Titus 2:12); and (3) always learning (μανθάνοντα; cf. 1 Tim 2:11) but never able (cf. v. 15) to come to a (full) knowledge of the truth (ἐπίγνωσιν;

[116] Baugh, "1 Timothy, 2 Timothy, Titus," 489–90.

[117] For a somewhat similar scenario, see 2 John 10–11.

v. 7; cf. 1 Tim 2:4; 2 Tim 2:25; Titus 1:1; similarly, Eph 4:14).[118] The overall picture is that these women lack dignity and self-restraint, are weak mentally and morally, are caught in bondage to their sinful desires, and are trapped in a cycle of futility, never attaining to true knowledge, which involves not merely passive listening but requires action as well (1 Tim 5:4, 13; 2 Tim 3:14; Titus 3:14; cf. Jas 1:22–25; Matt 7:24–27).[119]

Nevertheless, primary culpability rests not with the victims of the false teaching but with the false teachers. Drawing on extrabiblical information,[120] Paul likens these men to Jannes and Jambres, men who oppose (ἀνθίστανται; in 4:15 with reference to "Alexander the coppersmith"; cf. Gal 2:11) the truth (with Timothy being related to Paul the way Aaron was to Moses).[121]

---

[118] On Pauline communities as learning communities in a positive sense, see C. S. Smith, *Pauline Communities as "Scholastic Communities": A Study of the Vocabulary of 'Teaching' in 1 Corinthians, 1 and 2 Timothy and Titus*, WUNT 2/335 (Tübingen: Mohr-Siebeck, 2012).

[119] See the discussion in Johnson, *Letters to Paul's Delegates*, 85, who points out that the proclamation of a realized resurrection could in the case of these women have resulted in sexual promiscuity or sexual rigor (cf. 1 Cor 7:1); and G. P. C. Streete, "Bad Girls or Good Ascetics? The *Gynaikaria* of the Pastoral Epistles," in *Women in the Biblical World: A Survey of Old and New Testament Perspectives*, ed. E. A. McCabe (Lanham, MD: University Press of America, 2009), 155–64, who says these women are "not simply bad girls: they are bad ascetics and spiritual whores." She notes that "the Pastorals understand sexual gratification as included within and limited to heterosexual marriage, with the intent of reproducing orderly individual 'households' and thus building up the community or 'household of God.'"

[120] See especially CD 5:18–19 (2nd c. BC); Pliny, *Nat.* 30.1.11 (AD 77); and *Tg. Ps.-J.* to Exod 7:11–12 (on the date, see M. McNamara, *The New Testament and the Palestinian Targum to the Pentateuch*, AnBib 27 [Rome: PBI, 1966], 82–96, who argues that a previous version of the Targum was the source of the present reference; and the critique by L. Grabbe, "The Jannes/Jambres Tradition in Targum Pseudo-Jonathan and Its Date," *JBL* 98 [1979]: 393–401). See also the survey by S. Gero, "Parerga to 'The Book of Jannes and Jambres,'" *JSP* 9 (1991): 67–85. Jannes and Jambres are commonly identified as two of the Egyptian magicians/sorcerers who opposed Moses (cf. Exod 7:11, 22; 8:3, 8, 15; 9:11). However, Tromp, "Jannes and Jambres," 211–26, suggests in light of CD 5:17–19 that Jannes and Jambres may have been Jewish opponents of Moses from within Israel (see esp. 219). Cf. E. Schürer, *The History of the Jewish People in the Age of Jesus Christ*, vol. III.2, rev. and ed. G. Vermes, F. Millar, and M. Goodman (Edinburgh: T&T Clark, 1987), 781, who points out that "the names are almost certainly Semitic." Note also that Pliny identifies Jannes and Jambres as Jewish. As Tromp suggests, there may be two unrelated stories, one told in CD and 2 Timothy identifying Jannes and Jambres as Jewish opponents, and another in the *Apocryphon of Jannes and Jambres* and other later sources that link these individuals with Egyptian sorcerers.

[121] See BDAG, 464–65; H. Odeberg, "Ἰάννης, Ἰαμβρῆς," *TDNT* 3:192–93; A. Pietersma and T. R. Lutz, "Jannes and Jambres," in J. H. Charlesworth, ed., *The*

Jannes and Jambres may have been brothers (CD 5:18–19: "Jannes and his brother," with Jannes being the older of the two because he's mentioned first), which further accentuates the contrast with Moses and Aaron, who were brothers as well.[122] Similar to Jude, Paul employs typology, connecting OT figures to contemporaneous ones. The correspondence goes beyond the personages (pairs of brothers) and scenario (resisting the manifest power of God) to the outcome of the opposition to God's servants. Just as the attacks on Moses didn't succeed, the false teachers won't prevail against Timothy.[123]

God's vs. Satan's Servants	Relevant Passage(s)	Type of Characterization/ Additional Information
TYPES		
Moses and Aaron	Exodus 6–12	Positive; brothers
> Jannes and Jambres	2 Tim 3:8; cf. CD 5:18–19	Negative; brothers (?) raised up by Belial (Satan)
> Jonathan and Simon	Implied in CD?	Negative (from vantage point of DSS); brothers
ANTITYPES		
Paul and Timothy	1 Tim 1:2, 18; 2 Tim 3:10-11	Positive; spiritual father-son relationship
> Hymenaeus and Alexander	1 Tim 1:20	Negative; false teachers handed over to Satan

Old Testament Pseudepigrapha, vol. 2 (Garden City, NY: Doubleday, 1985), 427–36; E. Schürer, *The History of the Jewish People in the Age of Jesus Christ*, rev. and ed. G. Vermes, F. Millar, and M. Goodman (Edinburgh: T&T Clark, 1973), III.2.781–83; and Str-B 3:660–64.

[122] Tromp, "Jannes and Jambres," 217. Note that CD 5:19 says that "Belial, with his cunning, raised up Jannes and his brother," connecting the brothers explicitly with Satan. A. Pietersma, *The Apocryphon of Jannes and Jambres the Magicians*, RGRW 119 (Leiden: Brill, 1994), 19–22, posits a link between Jannes and James and the Maccabean leader Jonathan and his brother Simon (cf. 1 Maccabees).

[123] See Marshall, *Pastoral Epistles*, 778; Quinn and Wacker, *Letters to Timothy*, 727–33. See also Tromp, "Jannes and Jambres," 218, who sums up the message of the Damascus Document (CD) as follows: "Accordingly, many people calling themselves 'Israel' actually do not deserve that name, because they are trapped in Belial's nets and succumb to sin. Only those who follow the correct interpretation of the law will be saved, all others will perish."

> Phygelus and Hermogenes	2 Tim 1:15	Negative; deserted Paul in the province of Asia
> Hymenaeus and Philetus	2 Tim 2:17	Negative; false teachers: resurrection has taken place

The typology pitting God's servants against an axis of evil represented by Satan's servants (the false teachers) represents itself as follows:

Type	Antitype
Moses and Aaron resisted by Jannes and Jambres.	Paul and Timothy resisted by Hymenaeus, Alexander, Philetus.
Moses and Aaron won; opponents were judged.	Paul and Timothy will win; opponents will be judged.

It should be pointed out that understanding Jannes and Jambres as Jewish opponents who resisted Moses works considerably better as a typology in 2 Timothy, which is directed toward the church in Ephesus where in keeping with Paul's own prediction to the Ephesian elders, "men will rise up *even from your own number* [i.e., from within the church] and distort the truth to lure the disciples into following them" (Acts 20:30; emphasis added).

The false teachers resist or oppose the truth because of their depraved minds (κατεφθαρμένοι; cf. 1 Tim 6:5; see also Gen 6:12 LXX). Yet, ironically, it's not the truth that is rejected, but they themselves are cast away (ἀδόκιμοι; see esp. Titus 1:16; cf. Rom 1:28; 1 Cor 9:27; 2 Cor 13:5–7; Heb 6:8) with regard to the faith. What's more, in their rebellion they're not going to progress very far (προκόψουσιν; see on 2:16 above and on v. 13 below) because their foolishness (ἄνοια; cf. Luke 6:11; and OT wisdom literature: Ps 21:3; Prov 14:8; 22:15; Eccl 11:10; Job 33:23) will be clear (ἔκδηλος; only here in the NT) to all. This ought to reassure Timothy. At the same time he must be aware that there's the real danger of doing nothing. False tolerance that fails to take charge and confront the false teaching that threatens the spiritual well-being of the church would be deadly.

In vv. 1–9, then, the storm clouds grow even darker. Eschatology takes center stage and casts its shadow on ecclesiology, with the effect of throwing the need for the life of faith, the pursuit of virtue, and faithful gospel ministry into even sharper focus (§§4, 5, 6). Ecclesiology thus doesn't operate in a vacuum or consist merely of a static set of principles unrelated to God's activity in the present and future. Rather, the certainty of eventual divine judgment and of the second appearing of the Lord Jesus Christ requires that lines be drawn sharply even in the present so that the choice between the gospel of grace and salvation in Jesus Christ and the law-based, works-oriented alternative presented by the false teachers are presented in mutually exclusive terms. Similarly, today's church must preach the biblical, apostolic gospel of salvation by grace through faith in Jesus Christ with such clarity and conviction that any rival "gospel" is exposed as being in fact no gospel at all.

Bridge

The depiction of the last days in vv. 1–5 is part of Paul's eschatological outlook often categorized in terms of "already and not yet." While Jesus's return is still future, the dire state of affairs characteristic just prior to that event casts its ominous shadow foreward. For believers this spiritual darkness engulfing the world calls for godly separation, similar to God's call to Israel to be separate from the surrounding ungodly nations (cf. 2 Cor 6:17; Titus 3:10–11). This is in keeping with Jesus's prediction in the Olivet Discourse (Matthew 24 and parallels); with Paul's words elsewhere (2 Thess 2:1–12; cf. 1 Tim 4:1–15); and with the lengthy description of the last days in the book of Revelation.

2. Stay the Course (3:10–17)

[10]But you have followed my teaching, conduct, purpose,
faith, patience, love, and endurance, [11]along with the persecutions and sufferings that came to me in Antioch, Iconium,
and Lystra. What persecutions I endured—and yet the Lord
rescued me from them all. [12]In fact, all who want to live a
godly life in Christ Jesus will be persecuted. [13]Evil people and
impostors will become worse, deceiving and being deceived.
[14]But as for you, continue in what you have learned and firmly believed. You know those who taught you, [15]and you know
that from infancy you have known the sacred Scriptures,
which are able to give you wisdom for salvation through faith
in Christ Jesus. [16]All Scripture is inspired by God and is profitable for teaching, for rebuking, for correcting, for training

> in righteousness, [17] so that the man of God may be complete, equipped for every good work.

Relation to Surrounding Context

As Paul slowly but surely moves toward the end of his final letter, he recalls Timothy's loyal service in the past and calls him to continued faithfulness. This will issue in a solemn charge in the following unit (4:1–5). The end of Paul's life is near (4:6–8), and most have deserted the apostle (4:10–11). Timothy must cling to the sacred Scriptures and be willing to endure persecution.

Structure

Σὺ δέ ("But you") in v. 10 contrasts Timothy with the false teachers in the previous unit. The list of virtues in v. 10 contrasts with the vice list characteristic of the end times in vv. 2–5. Another contrast between Timothy and the false teachers in v. 14 is likewise expressed by σὺ δέ. The unit starts with Timothy's allegiance to Paul in the past (v. 10) and calls on him to continue in the Scriptures (vv. 14–17).

3:10–13 Having warned Timothy about difficult days ahead and about the devious ways of the false teachers (who serve as a foil for the following exhortation),[124] Paul urges his foremost disciple to be different (Σὺ δέ, "But you"; see 2:1; v. 14; 4:5; cf. 1 Tim 6:11; Titus 2:1).[125] For Timothy "has followed" (παρηκολουθέω; 1 Tim 4:6; Luke 1:3) closely all aspects of Paul's life and ministry (he lists nine; compare this "list of virtues" with the "vice list" in vv. 1–5 above). As in the parallel passage in Paul's first letter to Timothy, (1) the apostle's teaching takes pride of place (v. 10; cf. 1 Tim 4:6; "my"—rather than someone else's—teaching is stressed in the original and modifies the following nouns).[126]

---

[124] Westfall, "Moral Dilemma," 245.

[125] Westfall (ibid.) states that while "many have split 3:1–17 into two units (3:1–9, 10–17), there is not a comparable high level shift at 3:10." However, the phrase Σὺ δέ in 3:1 does seem to signal a shift in direction and topic, whether "high level" or not (cf. 2:1). Nevertheless, 3:1–17 does constitute the overarching unit.

[126] Teaching is a major theme in the LTT: see §2 in the Biblical-Theological Themes below. References to teaching in the LTT include 1 Tim 1:10; 4:1, 6, 13, 16; 5:17; 6:1, 3; 2 Tim 3:16; 4:3; cf. 1 Tim 3:2. Paul's teaching is contained in his thirteen NT letters (some of which were written in conjunction with Timothy: 2 Corinthians, Philippians, Colossians, 1 and 2 Thessalonians, Philemon); in addition, Timothy would have heard Paul preach and teach on numerous occasions.

Not only has Timothy been thoroughly exposed to Paul's teaching (cf. 2:2), he is also well acquainted with (2) Paul's conduct and way of life (ἀγωγή; cf. Esth 2:20; 10:3 LXX; 1 Clem. 47.6; 48.1). He knows about Paul's integrity and has seen the way in which he has conducted himself honorably in a variety of circumstances, many of them very trying. The passage makes clear that mentoring and disciple-making don't merely involve imparting a body of information but most vitally entail modeling of one's convictions in real life. The passage once again is typical of moral exhortation which commends people for doing what they've been doing and urges them to continue.[127]

Timothy is also aware of (3) Paul's purpose (πρόθεσις; elsewhere in Paul used only of God's purpose: 1:9; Rom 8:28; 9:11; Eph 1:11; 3:11). Similarly, Jesus claimed that he revealed to his followers everything he had learned from his Father (John 15:15; cf. 5:19–20). Paul lived and acted strategically (Rom 15:19–20, 28; 1 Cor 9:26–27), and Timothy, who had a significant part in no fewer than six of Paul's letters, knew exactly what Paul's driving motivation, strategic outlook, and overall plan were. Soon it would be time for Timothy to succeed Paul and to continue his legacy (cf. 4:5–7). He would no longer have Paul, but he would still have his legacy and the Scriptures.

Timothy also knew about Paul's (4) faith, (5) patience, and (6) love (triad 1; cf. Gal 5:22). Faith and love are frequently conjoined in the LTT (esp. 1:13; 2:22; 1 Tim 4:12; 6:11; cf. 1 Tim 2:15; Titus 2:2). Here "patience" (μακροθυμία) is placed between these two virtues (cf. 4:2; 2 Cor 6:6; Col 1:11). Paul didn't merely serve with a clear purpose in mind (while at the same time being fully submitted to God's overarching providence), he related to others with the Spirit-grown qualities of faith, patience, and love. This is why he was able to command intense love—even affection—and commitment from his followers (e.g., Acts 20:36–38; 21:12–14).

Finally, Timothy also knew about his mentor's (7) endurance (ὑπομονή; cf. 1 Tim 6:11; Titus 2:2), (8) persecutions (διωγμοῖς; Rom 8:35; 2 Cor 12:10; 2 Thess 1:4), and (9) sufferings (παθήμασιν; cf.

---

[127] Westfall, "Moral Dilemma," 246. More broadly on imitation and Paul's pattern of leadership, see Clarke, "Paul's Model of Leadership," 329–60, esp. 354–57. See also B. Fiore, *The Function of Personal Example in the Socratic and Pastoral Epistles*, AnBib 105 (Rome: Biblical Institute Press, 1986).

Rom 8:18; 2 Cor 1:5–7; Phil 3:10; Col 1:24; triad 2). We know from Paul's other letters that he viewed the present sufferings as not worthy of being compared with the glory to follow (Rom 8:18); that he regarded himself as "completing in my flesh what is lacking in Christ's afflictions" (Col 1:24); and that he knew himself united with Christ and other believers in his sufferings (2 Cor 1:5–7). In the present passage Paul refers to his sufferings in Antioch, Iconium, and Lystra at the beginning of his missionary career (Acts 13:13–14:23). This persecution included verbal abuse (13:45), expulsion from the region (13:50), swaying others against Paul (14:2), and even a conspiracy (14:5). In the end Paul was stoned and dragged outside the city, and people thought he was dead (14:19).

"Yet the Lord rescued me from them all" (ἐρρύσατο; cf. 2 Tim 4:17–18, here echoing Ps 33:5, 18, 20 LXX): in Antioch Paul shook the dust off his feet in protest and moved on (Acts 13:51); in Iconium he found out about the plot and fled to neighboring cities (14:6); in Lystra he got up and left for Derbe the next day; he later returned to the region with Barnabas, encouraging converts to remain true to the faith and reminding them that we must "go through many hardships to enter the kingdom of God" (14:20–22).

Paul exhibited great courage and faith during his many years of service. He was convinced of the power of God and of his saving gospel message and knew that nothing could stop its irresistible progress. Even though Timothy didn't join Paul until the beginning of his second missionary journey, he may have witnessed (or at least heard of) some of the persecutions Paul suffered on his first missionary journey in the region from which Timothy came. Timothy himself was from Derbe and well regarded in the region (Acts 16:2). When he chose to join Paul, he was well aware of the cost of preaching the gospel. Paul's reminder that all who want to live a godly life in Christ Jesus will be persecuted echoes Jesus's words to his followers (John 15:20; cf. Matt 10:22; Luke 21:12) and reiterates Paul's earlier warning (Acts 14:22).

Yet evil people and impostors (γόητες, "swindler, cheat," only here in the NT) will become worse (NIV: "go from bad to worse"; cf. 2:16; v. 9 above), deceiving others and being deceived themselves (πλανάω; cf. Titus 3:3; 2 Pet 2:15). The false teachers aren't only perpetrating improper teaching; they're also victimized by it (cf. vv. 8–9). While they may not suffer persecution (cf. v. 12), they'll nonetheless suffer harm because of their deception (cf. Rom 1:21–25).

3:14–17 "But as for you" (σὺ δέ) indicates the same contrast as in v. 10 above. While the false teachers continue to spiral downward, Timothy must continue (μένω; cf. 1 Tim 2:15) in the teachings he has learned (μανθάνω; cf. Eph 4:20; Phil 4:9) and firmly believed (πιστόω, only here in the NT).[128] For he has received them on good authority, from human sources—especially Paul (v. 10) and his mother and grandmother (1:5; in some MSS the plural is changed to the singular, presumably in order to accentuate Paul's role as Timothy's instructor)—and from the sacred Scriptures (ἱερὰ γράμματα; cf. γράμματα in John 5:47; 7:15; §2.7.2).[129] The most likely source of Timothy's education is the public reading of the Greek translation of the Scriptures (LXX) in a synagogue such as Lystra (cf. Acts 15:21).

Timothy has known them "from infancy" (ἀπὸ βρέφους, a stock phrase; cf. 1:5; Acts 16:1), and they're able to give him wisdom (σοφίζω; cf. 2 Pet 1:16; Pss 19:7; 105:22; 119:98) for salvation through faith in Christ Jesus (1 Tim 3:13; Gal 2:16; Col 1:4; cf. Rom 3:22; Gal 2:16; 3:22).[130] Most likely, "salvation" isn't here referring

[128] Cf. Marshall, *Pastoral Epistles*, 788: "to abandon the faith would mean abandoning that which Timothy has been taught from his earliest days." P. Dragutinović, "Die Schrift im Dienst der gesunden Lehre. Text-pragmatische Erwägungen zu 2 Tim 3,14–17," *Annali di Storia dell'Esegesi* 32 (2015): 309–24 provides a "text-pragmatic" analysis, contending that the author (whom he assumes to be pseudonymous) invoked the God-breathed nature of Scripture in the service of the institutionalization of Pauline tradition.

[129] The sacred writings Paul refers to in 3:15 are widely agreed to be equivalent to the OT. So, e.g., Marshall, *Pastoral Epistles*, 789; Quinn and Wacker, *Letters to Timothy*, 755–56. Cf. Philo, *Moses* 2.290, 292; *Embassy* 195; Josephus, *Ant*. 1.13; 10.210.

[130] Construed as an objective genitive, contra those who construe the meaning here in terms of the faithfulness of Jesus Christ (subjective genitive). Cf. D. J. Downs, "Faith(fulness) in Christ Jesus in 2 Timothy 3:15," *JBL* 131 (2012): 145; somewhat similarly, I. G. Wallis, *The Faith of Jesus Christ in Early Christian Tradition*, SNTSMS 84 (Cambridge: Cambridge University Press, 1995), 142. Johnson (*First and Second Letters to Timothy*, 420) asserts that Christ as the object of faith would be indicated by εἰς Χριστόν, not ἐν Χριστῷ (cf. Gal 2:16; Col 3:5). But see Col 1:4; Eph 1:15 as possible exceptions and note Harris's judgment that several times in the LXX "*en* after *pisteuō* denotes the object of faith" (*NIDNTT* 3:1212). Harris goes on to note, "In the 4 instances where *en* is to be construed with *pistis* (Eph. 1:15; Col. 1:4; 1 Tim. 3:13; 2 Tim. 3:15; but not Rom. 3:25 and probably not Gal. 3:26), the prep. phrase is as likely to mark out the sphere or realm in which faith was operative and evident

to *entrance* into salvation (conversion)[131] but to *future* salvation as a goal. Thus the function of Scripture is here not conceived as leading to conversion as aiding Timothy—and by implication, all believers—in attaining salvation as a future goal.[132] This coheres with the use of σωτηρία in 2:10, where Paul's endurance of all things contributes toward the elect obtaining the salvation that is in Christ, while here the sacred writings of Scripture are able to instruct Timothy toward the same goal.[133]

With regard to the false teachers, Paul's point here seems to be that the Scriptures (in which Timothy was reared from an early age and which he therefore knows well) are indeed of great value (see further below), but only if understood as pointing toward faith in Christ. Rather than using the Scriptures with an emphasis on law and the observance of its particular stipulations, a proper appreciation of the value of the Scriptures entails recognition of its true God-intended salvation-historical purpose. This coheres perfectly with the battles Paul fought earlier with the Judaizers and others who insisted on continued observance of the law by (Gentile) Christians.[134]

Without any conjunction (such as "for"), Paul elaborates on the supreme value of Scripture,[135] focusing primarily on two

---

as to specify the actual object of faith." Marshall (*Pastoral Epistles*, 790) notes that in the immediate context, Paul speaks of those who want to live in a godly way ἐν Χριστῷ Ἰησοῦ (v. 12).

[131] Knight, *Pastoral Epistles*, 444; cf. B. Mutschler, *Glaube in den Pastoralbriefen: Pistis als Mitte christlicher Existenz*, WUNT 256 (Tübingen: Mohr-Siebeck, 2010), 352–53.

[132] This is indicated by σε in 3:15; Timothy is specifically in view as being made wise for salvation. Of course, the OT was used evangelistically, as the gospel appeals in Acts clearly show (see Wieland, *Significance of Salvation*, 162–64, who reads the present passage in this light), but that is most likely not what is in view here.

[133] Downs, "Faith(fulness) in Christ Jesus in 2 Timothy 3:15," 143–60, seeks to enlist the passage in the πίστις Χριστοῦ debate, arguing unconvincingly that the phrase here refers primarily, though not exclusively, to the faithfulness of Christ.

[134] See, e.g., Galatians, esp. chaps. 3–4, and Romans, esp. chaps. 6–8, and the reference to Christ being the goal/end (τέλος) of the law in Rom 10:4.

[135] The rendering, "All Scripture is inspired by God and is profitable . . .," masks a difficult set of exegetical choices. The word πᾶς underlying "all" could also mean "every." However, since no specific passage is referred to, it's more likely that Paul here views Scripture in its totality ("all Scripture" used as a collective phrase). The second major question arises from the absence of the verb "is" in the original. Should the word be inserted after or before "inspired by God"? If the former,

aspects (with the emphasis being on the second element). First, Scripture, in fact, "all" Scripture (more likely than "every")—in the original context, the OT (but see 2 Pet 3:16; 1 Tim 5:18)[136]—is "inspired by God" (lit., "God breathed," θεόπνευστος).[137] The term, an apparent Pauline coinage, is found in subsequent Greek literature (Ps.-Phoc. 129; Sib. Or. 5:308; 5:407 [ca. AD 90–130]), but the concept of the creative, life-giving breath of God and the image of the word of God as breathed by God have deep OT roots (Genesis

---

Paul would be saying that "all inspired Scripture is also [an alternative meaning of καί] useful." However, this requires the highly improbable assumption that Paul believed there was also noninspired Scripture (Knight, *Pastoral Epistles*, 444–48; D. B. Wallace, *Greek Grammar Beyond the Basics* [Grand Rapids: Zondervan, 1996], 314).

[136] But note that in speaking of "all" Scripture (πᾶσα γραφή) in v. 16, Paul draws together the OT writings (ἱερὰ γράμματα, v. 15) and the nascent writings of the Christian faith containing the gospel of Christ which Paul preached (οἷς ἔμαθες καὶ ἐπιστώθης, v. 14; cf. 1 Tim 5:18). See on this point Swinson, *What Is Scripture?*, 115–59.

[137] See, e.g., B. B. Warfield, *Revelation and Inspiration* (New York: Oxford University Press, 1927), 80, who writes that Scripture "is the product of the creative breath of God, and, because of this its Divine origination, is of supreme value for all holy purposes." Many commentators point out the limitations of the English term "inspired," which means "breathed in" rather than "breathed out," which is the meaning of the Greek word θεόπνευστος (see, e.g., B. B. Warfield, *The Inspiration and Authority of the Bible* [Philadelphia: Presbyterian & Reformed, 1951), 153: "It is very desirable that we should free ourselves at the outset from influences arising from the current employment of the term 'inspiration.' This term is not a biblical term, and its etymological implications are not perfectly accordant with the biblical conception of the modes of the divine operation in giving the Scripture"; E. J. Young, "Scripture: God-breathed and Profitable," *Grace Journal* 7, no. 3 [1966]: 8: "The word 'inspiration' does not accurately represent Paul's thought"). For this reason A. T. B. McGowan, "The Divine Spiration of Scripture," *SBET* 21 (2003): 199–217; McGowan, *The Divine Spiration of Scripture: Challenging Evangelical Perspectives* (Nottingham: Apollos, 2007), suggests "divine spiration" as an alternative since "expiration" has unwelcome connotations in English (drawing one's *final* breath, i.e., death). J. Frame, in a review of McGowan's book (accessed 18 March 2016, http://www.frame-poythress.org/review-of-andrew-mcgowans-the-divine-spiration-of-scripture), responds that he has no objection to this vocabulary change, but neither does he have confidence that the church will adopt it. He recommends to "make the word conform in meaning to *theopneustos*, rather than to try to persuade the church to adopt another term." Frame also points out that, according to McGowan, God's "spiration" of Scripture includes errors, which is incompatible with the nature of God as being truthful. For this reason it's problematic to limit inspiration (or spiration) strictly to God's act of speaking because the latter has inexorable implications for the resulting product, i.e., the text of Scripture.

1–2; Ps 33:6; Isa 42:5), and the notion of inspiration is not foreign to the OT (Num 24:2; Hos 9:7). The present passage is one of the major biblical texts on the divine inspiration of Scripture, focusing on Scripture's origin in God himself. It is complemented by 2 Pet 1:19–21, which speaks to the process of inspiration.[138]

Second, because Scripture has God as its source, it is "profitable" (ὠφέλιμος; cf. 1 Tim 4:8; Titus 3:8) in a variety of ways (cf. Rom 15:4; 1 Cor 10:11). Employing chiasm, with the two positive features enveloping the two negative ones, Paul observes that Scripture is profitable for (A) teaching (διδασκαλία, a general term; see on v. 10 above and on 4:3 below); (B) rebuking (ἐλεγμόν, only here in the NT; cf. 1 Tim 5:20; 2 Tim 4:2; Titus 1:9, 13; 2:15); (B[1]) correcting (ἐπανόρθωσιν, only here in the NT); and (A[1]) training (παιδεία; Eph 6:4; Heb 12:5–11; cf. Prov 16:17) in righteousness.[139] As in raising children, growing in Christ involves both nurture and correction (cf. Eph 6:4).

The end result of such thorough training in the Scripture is that "the man of God" (see commentary at 1 Tim 6:11)—Timothy as well as other church leaders, and ultimately all believers[140]—will

---

[138] See the discussion of inspiration and inerrancy in A. J. Köstenberger, S. L. Kellum, and C. L. Quarles, *The Cradle, the Cross, and the Crown: An Introduction to the New Testament*, 2nd ed. (Nashville: B&H Academic, 2016), 38–52, esp. 47–49. See also D. A. Carson, "Three Books on the Bible: A Critical Review," *JETS* 26 (1983): 337–67; S. B. Ferguson, "How Does the Bible Look at Itself?," in *Inerrancy and Hermeneutics: A Tradition, A Challenge, A Debate*, ed. H. M. Conn (Grand Rapids: Baker, 1988), 47–66; L. I. Hodges, "Evangelical Definitions of Inspiration: Critiques and a Suggested Definition," *JETS* 37 (1994): 99–114; J. Murray, "The Inspiration of the Scripture," *WTJ* 2 (1940): 73–104 (a slightly revised version of his inaugural address at Westminster Theological Seminary); and W. E. Nix, "The Doctrine of Inspiration Since the Reformation," *JETS* 25 (1982): 443–54.

[139] The παιδεία-word group is represented in the LTT in 1 Tim 1:20, 2 Tim 2:25, Titus 2:12 (παιδεύω), 2 Tim 3:16 (παιδεία), and 2 Tim 2:23 (ἀπαίδευτος). For a monograph-length study of education (παιδεία) in the LTT, see F. Krumbiegel, *Erziehung in den Pastoralbriefen. Ein Konzept zur Konsolidierung der Gemeinden*, Arbeiten zur Bibel und ihrer Geschichte 44 (Leipzig: Evangelische Verlagsanstalt, 2013), who stresses the interface between education and dealing with the opponents in the LTT (pp. 39–53) and the embeddedness of education in the household metaphor (p. 105); see also the list of related terms in the semantic domain on pp. 77–78.

[140] Strictly speaking, Paul speaks here of "the man of God" (ὁ τοῦ θεοῦ ἄνθρωπος), but this is likely primarily a reference to Timothy (cf. 1 Tim 6:11); see Towner, *Letters to Timothy and Titus*, 592–93. If so, the NIV's "servant of God" is less than ideal, especially since there are other words for "servant" in the Greek (the NIV has "that you, a man of God," in a footnote). Note in this regard S. C. Martin, *Pauli*

be complete (ἄρτιος, only here in the NT), equipped (ἐξηρτισμένος; cf. Acts 21:5; the NIV collapses the two expressions into "thoroughly equipped") for every good work (see esp. 2:21; Titus 3:1). While salvation comes through faith in Christ (v. 15; cf. 1:9; Titus 3:5), all believers are called to good works, a major theme in Paul's correspondence with Timothy and Titus (1 Tim 2:10; 3:1; 5:10, 25; 6:18; 2 Tim 2:21; Titus 1:16; 2:7, 14; 3:1, 8, 14; §5.2).

Once again, these instructions cohere with Paul's teaching elsewhere (see, e.g., Eph 2:8–10). Christian training must first be grounded in Scripture (not merely general life experience or commonsense values). Second, it must be thorough—there are no shortcuts to true spiritual growth—including both instruction and correction, rather than focusing unilaterally on encouragement. Third, the purpose of such training isn't merely an individual's personal edification or intellectual stimulation; it's ministry to others.

In biblical-theological terms, the twofold emphatic introductory phrase, "But as for you" (vv. 10, 14), shows how Paul uses the dark eschatological backdrop epitomized by the false teachers as additional motivation for his exhortation to faithfulness. Rather than grounding this faithfulness merely in commitment or character, Paul roots it in the Holy Scriptures which are (1) able to give "wisdom for salvation through faith in Christ Jesus" (v. 15); (2) "inspired by God" and "profitable for teaching, for rebuking, for correcting, for training in righteousness" (v. 16); and (3) able to make the man of God complete and equip him "for every good work" (v. 17). In this way, the pursuit of virtue and the life of faith are shown to be deeply rooted in devotion to the Scriptures as the word of God, which form the foundation of the sound apostolic teaching concerning salvation being found solely in the Lord Jesus Christ.

Bridge

In this passage Paul notably affirms the divine origin of Scripture as "inspired by God" (lit., "God breathed"; v. 16). Elsewhere Peter indicates that in the case of scriptural prophecies

---

Testamentum: 2 Timothy and the Last Words of Moses, TGST 18 (Rome: Pontificia Università Gregoriana, 1999), 32–34, who argues that the "man of God" language in 3:17 is meant to echo the title of Moses and denote the authority of Timothy (and by extension, other teachers; cf. 2 Tim 2:2).

"men spoke from God as they were carried along by the Holy Spirit" (2 Pet 1:21). These affirmations are in keeping with Scripture's self-attestation in both Testaments (see, e.g., Psalms 19; 119; John 10:35). The trustworthiness of Scripture continues to be a bone of contention among critical scholars, but Scripture itself clearly affirms that it is trustworthy and profitable because it has its origin in none other than God himself.

IV. Body Closing: Preach the Word (4:1–8)

The body of the letter closes with an exceedingly solemn charge by the veteran apostle to Timothy to preach the Christian gospel.[141] Paul's plea is introduced by the lengthy phrase Διαμαρτύρομαι ἐνώπιον τοῦ θεοῦ καὶ Χριστοῦ Ἰησοῦ τοῦ μέλλοντος κρίνειν ζῶντας καὶ νεκρούς, καὶ τὴν ἐπιφάνειαν αὐτοῦ καὶ τὴν βασιλείαν αὐτοῦ ("I solemnly charge you before God and Christ Jesus, who is going to judge the living and the dead, and because of his appearing and his kingdom"). This charge forms the climax of the letter and sounds a note of great urgency.[142] This portion includes Paul's last recorded words, indicating his awareness that the end of his life and ministry was drawing near and revealing his profound concern that Timothy be faithful to his legacy.

> [1] I solemnly charge you before God and Christ Jesus, who is going to judge the living and the dead, and because of his appearing and his kingdom: [2] Preach the word; be ready in season and out of season; rebuke, correct, and encourage with great patience and teaching. [3] For the time will come when people will not tolerate sound doctrine, but according to their own desires, will multiply teachers for themselves because they have an itch to hear what they want to hear.
> [4] They will turn away from hearing the truth and will turn aside to myths. [5] But as for you, exercise self-control in every-

[141] See Smith, "Study of 2 Timothy 4:1–8," who argues that this final charge is totally dissimilar in form from farewell speeches, testaments, and Jewish deathbed speeches. Instead, the final charge at the end of the body of the letter serves as a summary of the role of a good Christian minister and of the paraenetic material in the preceding portions of the letter. Note also S. O. Stout, *Preach the Word: A Pauline Theology of Preaching Based on 2 Timothy 4:1–5* (Eugene, OR: Wipf & Stock, 2014).

[142] Marshall, *Pastoral Epistles*, 797. Similarly, Westfall, "Moral Dilemma," 247, remarks that the "density of the nine imperatives that follow in the context of the moral exhortation of the discourse create a discourse climax."

> thing, endure hardship, do the work of an evangelist, fulfill your ministry.
>
> [6]For I am already being poured out as a drink offering, and the time for my departure is close. [7]I have fought the good fight, I have finished the race, I have kept the faith. [8]There is reserved for me the crown of righteousness, which the Lord, the righteous Judge, will give me on that day, and not only to me, but to all those who have loved his appearing.

Relation to Surrounding Context

Paul's final charge to Timothy represents the emotional climax of the entire letter and indeed of Paul's correspondence with Timothy. Paul's triadic declaration that he himself has fought the good fight, finished the race, and kept the faith (v. 7), reminiscent of Jesus's cry on the cross, "It is finished" (John 19:30; cf. 17:4), continues the eschatological emphasis begun in 3:1 with a reference to Jesus's serving as end-time judge and dispenser of rewards at his second coming.

Structure

Verse 1 contains Paul's solemn final charge to Timothy. Verse 2 calls on Timothy to (1) preach the word, (2) be ready in season and out of season, (3) rebuke, (4) correct, and (5) encourage. In vv. 3–4 Paul returns to the subject of the end times; in v. 5 he reiterates the by-now-familiar contrast between Timothy and the false teachers by way of σὺ δέ ("But you") and calls on him to fulfill his ministry. The reason for Paul's charge of Timothy to faithfulness is given in vv. 6–8 (γάρ; compare also σύ in v. 5 with ἐγώ in v. 6).

4:1–2 As Paul's second and final letter to Timothy draws to a close, the apostle issues his closing appeal. "I solemnly charge you" (Διαμαρτύρομαι; note the absence of any conjunction) is a momentous introduction for the even more stirring phrase "before God and Christ Jesus, who is going to judge the living and the dead, and because of his appearing and his kingdom" (see 2:14; cf. 1 Tim 5:21; 6:13–14). Paul's appeal exceeds all previous charges in solemnity, intensity, and urgency. As Timothy discharges his duties as Paul's apostolic delegate and in keeping with Paul's own practice (2 Cor 5:9–11), the apostle wants Timothy to be ever conscious of the reality of God and the certainty of Christ's return (ἐπιφάνεια; cf. 1 Tim 6:14; v. 8; Titus 2:13). Christ is the end-time judge of all of humanity ("the living and the dead"; cf. Acts 10:42; Rom 14:9;

1 Thess 4:16–17; 1 Pet 4:5) and will establish his kingdom (βασιλεία; cf. v. 18 below; see also Acts 14:22; on Jesus as end-time judge, see Rom 14:9–12; 1 Cor 3:10–15; cf. John 5:27; Heb 9:27). "The living" are those alive at Christ's return, while "the dead" are those who died previously (1 Thess 4:15–17).

Paul's concluding appeal to Timothy ensues as follows (leading off a series of five imperatives):

1. "Preach the word" (κηρύσσω; cf. 1 Tim 3:16; cf. κῆρυξ in 1 Tim 2:7; 2 Tim 1:11; on "the word," see 1 Tim 4:12; 5:17). Timothy has been thoroughly grounded in the "sacred Scriptures" (3:14–17); it is the same message—God's Word (2:9), the "word of truth" (2:15)—that he is solemnly called upon to preach in his ministry (cf. Rom 10:8; 1 Cor 15:2). What's more, this preaching isn't limited to believers (v. 5). Timothy must impart sound teaching to his hearers rather than telling them what they want to hear. His primary motivation shouldn't be pleasing people; he should take his cue first and foremost from God's word. As J. Stott points out, "We have no liberty to invent our message, but only to communicate 'the word' which God has spoken and has now committed to the church as a sacred trust."[143] Is God's Word preached in our churches today? We must proclaim the Word rather than merely catering to people's "felt needs" or using the pulpit as a platform for building our own little kingdoms.
2. Paul adds that the preacher should be ready to preach the Word in season and out of season (εὐκαίρως ἀκαίρως, an oxymoron; Mark 6:21; 14:11; cf. v. 3). This is certainly borne out by Paul's own example: at times his preaching met a favorable response; at other times it didn't.[144] Paul's advice defied both Jewish and Greco-Roman wisdom. The OT preacher wrote that there is "a time to be silent and a time to speak" (Eccl 3:7). Similarly, according to Greco-Roman rhetoric, a speaker should carefully discern whether certain forms of address are opportune in a given context. As the philosopher Plato wrote, "Knowledge of the times for

[143] Stott, *Message of 2 Timothy*, 106.

[144] For examples, see the book of Acts. See also 1 Cor 16:9–10.

speaking and for keeping silence" is vital (*Phaedr.* 272A).[145] This background makes Paul's exhortation to Timothy to preach the Word even when inconvenient (some say the reference is merely to Timothy's *own personal* convenience, but this is unlikely) all the more remarkable. Judging by the book of Acts, Paul followed this maxim in his own preaching. In the end it's not up to the preacher to presume upon his audience's response. He must simply be faithful to his calling to proclaim God's Word.

3. Overall, the preacher must rebuke (ἔλεγξον; 1 Tim 5:20; Titus 1:9, 13; 2:15; cf. 2 Tim 3:16);
4. correct (ἐπιτίμησον; not elsewhere in Paul; cf. Jude 9);[146] and
5. encourage (παρακάλεσον; cf. 1 Tim 5:1; 6:2; on the triad, see 3:16) with great (ESV: "complete") patience (μακροθυμία; cf. 3:10) and teaching (διδαχή). The fact that the words rendered "rebuke, correct, and encourage" are all partially overlapping in meaning suggests that Paul is concerned here to convey the spectrum of functions a person such as Timothy will be called to exercise in the local congregation, ranging from encouragement and affirmation to mild correction or even strong rebuke. To know what is needed in a particular situation calls for considerable wisdom and discernment.

4:3–5 Timothy must be prepared to proclaim the message even when inconvenient because there'll be a time (καιρός; cf. 3:1–5; 1 Tim 4:1) when people won't tolerate (ἀνέξονται, i.e., listen willingly to; cf. Mark 9:19; 2 Cor 11:1, 4, 19–20; Heb 13:22) sound doctrine (ὑγιαίνω; cf. 1 Tim 1:10; 6:3; 2 Tim 1:13; Titus 1:9, 13; 2:1–2), a possible metonymy for those teaching it. In view of the thinly veiled reference to the false teachers (cf. esp. 1 Tim 4:1; 6:3), it appears that Paul believes this time has already arrived.

What's more, the opponents' message seems to have found a favorable reception among some in the Ephesian church. As Paul observes, people in the last days will multiply (ἐπισωρεύω;

---

[145] Cf. Abraham J. Malherbe, "'In Season and Out of Season': 2 Timothy 4:2," *JBL* 103 (1984): 235–43.

[146] Confusingly, the CSB translates commands 3 and 4 as "rebuke, correct," while the NIV and NLT render them as "correct, rebuke." Cf. NASB: "reprove, rebuke"; NKJV: "convince, rebuke."

cf. σωρεύω in 3:6) teachers for themselves to suit their own desires who tell them what their itching ears want to hear (κνήθω). These people merely want to have "'their ears tickled,' as if what they heard merely scratched their eardrums without penetrating further."[147] They don't want to grow spiritually but only to satisfy their curiosity (cf. Acts 17:20–21). Thus they turn aside from the truth (Hymenaeus and Philetus: 2:18; cf. 2:25; 3:7–8; "turn aside" need not imply that the false teachers once confessed the truth themselves) to myths (μῦθος; 1 Tim 1:4; 4:7; cf. Titus 1:14), that is, fabrications of their own that aren't rooted in actual fact (a contrast accentuated by the μέν . . . δέ construction).

In times like these, Timothy must be (four more imperatives in v. 5) markedly different (σὺ δέ; cf. 2:1; 3:10, 14; 4:5; 1 Tim 6:11):[148]

1. exercise self-control (νῆφω; cf. 1 Thess 5:6, 8; 1 Pet 1:13; 4:7; 5:8; NIV, "keep your head") in everything;
2. endure hardship (κακοπάθησον; cf. 1:8; 2:3, 9; Jas 5:13);
3. do the work (cf. 1 Tim 3:1) of an evangelist (εὐαγγελιστής; cf. Acts 21:8 [Philip]; Eph 4:11 [list of ministries]); that is, preach the gospel (see v. 1 above);[149] and
4. fulfill (πληροφόρησον) his ministry (διακονία; cf. 1 Tim 1:12; v. 11; Paul has come close to completing his: vv. 7, 17).[150] While the region surrounding Ephesus has already been evangelized (Acts 20:31), Timothy must continue to proclaim the gospel to those who haven't yet heard or responded to the message. Apparently, Timothy's calling

---

[147] Guthrie, *Pastoral Epistles*, 178.

[148] As Westfall ("Moral Dilemma," 248, with reference to Knight, *Pastoral Epistles*, 451), notes, of the nine imperatives, the first eight serve as a summary of the attitudes and aspects of Timothy's preaching ministry while the ninth and final imperative summarizes the thrust of Paul's entire moral exhortation.

[149] See D. A. Carson, "Editorial: Do the Work of an Evangelist," *Them* 39, no. 1 (2014): 1–4, who concludes that "doing the work of an evangelist" in the present context amounts to "an exhortation to engage . . . in gospel ministry, which includes what we today mean by evangelism but should not be restricted to it."

[150] Cf. Westfall, "Moral Dilemma," 249: "Paul has done precisely what he has charged Timothy to do: he has discharged *all* the duties of his ministry (cf. 4:5d)." In this way, 4:6–8 serves as the culmination of Paul's presentation of himself as the model that Timothy should emulate in his ministry (cf. Heb 12:1–3). This is also motivating for Timothy in that it holds up the promise of a reward, the "crown of righteousness," if he perseveres in his ministry to the end as Paul has done.

wasn't primarily that of pastor but that of an apostolic delegate who consolidated the fruit of Paul's preaching before moving on to other fields.[151]

4:6–8 The reason (*γάρ*) Paul wants Timothy to fulfill his ministry is he himself (note the emphatic ἐγώ) is already (cf. Phil 3:12: "not already") "being poured out as a drink offering" (σπένδομαι; elsewhere in the NT only in Phil 2:17, but there with "if"). "Drink offering" refers to Paul's imminent martyr's death, which he views as a sacrifice for others and an act of worship toward God.[152] The differences between Paul's two Roman imprisonments couldn't be more striking. While toward the end of his first imprisonment the apostle already made plans for the time following his release (Phlm 22), he now seems resigned to his fate: "The time for my departure is close" (ἀναλύσεως; cf. Phil 1:23: ἀναλῦσαι, fig. of death: cf. ἔξοδος in Luke 9:31).

Paul is comforted by the assurance that he has fulfilled his ministry and been faithful to the end (cf. John 17:4). What others may consider an ignominious outcome, the apostle views as glorious. Perseverance in the struggle and the faithful completion of his task will bring a heavenly reward. By way of another triad, Paul depicts his struggle as fighting a fight, finishing a race, and keeping the faith (in each case, the verb is in the perfect tense, indicating completion, and the object precedes the verb).[153]

---

[151] See W. W. Combs ("The Biblical Role of the Evangelist," *DBSJ* 7 [2002]: 44), who contends that "do the work of an evangelist" "is not actually identifying Timothy as an evangelist. Instead, the language more probably suggests that Timothy should *do the kind of work that is normally associated with an evangelist* even though he is functioning in more of a pastoral role and may not have been particularly gifted as an evangelist himself" (emphasis added). Combs continues, "An evangelist was primarily an *itinerant church planter*, but Timothy is now temporarily stationed in [*sic*] Ephesus area, in somewhat of a supervisory role. Still, even in that work, he must not neglect the task of proclaiming the gospel of salvation to unbelievers and forming them into churches" (ibid.; emphasis added).

[152] The term "drink offering" occurs nineteen times in the LXX, first with reference to Jacob pouring out a drink offering (Gen 35:14). In the Greco-Roman world, libations were commonly poured out to pagan deities. In the NT, particularly in Paul's writings, compare esp. the reference to believers offering their bodies as living sacrifices in Rom 12:1.

[153] But see C. Campbell, "Finished the Race? 2 Timothy 4:6–7 and Verbal Aspect," in *Appreciation*, vol. 3 of *Donald Robinson: Selected Works* (Camperdown, N.S.W.: Australian Church Record, 2008), 169–75, who suggests the translation "I am

2 Timothy 4:6–8

First, Paul has "fought the good fight" (ἀγῶνα ἠγώνισμαι; esp. 1 Tim 6:12; cf. 1 Tim 4:10; 6:12; 1 Thess 2:2; Phil 1:30; Col 1:29; 2:1; 4:12), an athletic (rather than a military) metaphor (perhaps running). Second, he has "finished the race" (δρόμος; cf. Acts 13:25; 20:24: Paul wants to "finish the race"; Phil 3:10–14).[154] Third, he has "kept the faith" (πίστις; thirty-three times in the LTT, usually with reference to continuation in or departure from apostolic teaching). In extrabiblical literature "keeping the faith" refers to loyalty to one's trust (Josephus, *Ant.* 15.134; *J.W.* 2.121; 6.345; Polybius, *Hist.* 6.56.13); here the reference may be to an athlete's pledge to compete according to the rules (cf. 2:5).

What applies to Paul also pertains to believers generally. The Christian ministry is like fighting a fight; it doesn't involve following the path of least resistance but entails overcoming many obstacles, including doctrinal opposition (cf. Acts 14:22). The ministry is also like running a long-distance race; it calls for endurance (cf. Heb 12:1–3). Paul knows this all too well. Many of his coworkers have abandoned him in this dark hour (1:15; vv. 10, 14–16). In this regard he is like Jesus who likewise was deserted by his closest followers at his arrest (Mark 14:50 par.). Finally, the ministry is about keeping the faith. This involves passing on the apostolic teaching or, as Jude puts it, "contend[ing] for the faith that was delivered to the saints once for all" (v. 3).

---

fighting the good fight, I am finishing the race, I am keeping the faith." However, apart from the merits of Campbell's construal of the perfect tense-form, his proposal seems difficult to square with the context and setting of the letter, which shows Paul as in prison aware that the end of his life is near and concerned with securing his legacy. Note also Paul's reference to the final judgment and his end-time reward in vv. 1 and 8.

[154] Note esp. the striking verbal similarity between Acts 20:24 (ὡς τελειῶσαι τὸν δρόμον μου) and 2 Tim 4:7 (τὸν δρόμον τετέλεκα). Riesner ("Paul's Trial and End according to Second Timothy, *1 Clement*, the Canon Muratori, and the Apocryphal Acts," in *The Last Years of Paul: Essays from the Tarragona Conference, June 2013*, ed. Armand Puig i Tàrrech, John M. G. Barclay, and Jörg Frey, WUNT 352 [Tübingen: Mohr-Siebeck, 2015], 400, referring to Boismard) claims that this suggests Luke wrote both statements (Riesner believes Luke served as redactor of the LTT). However, more likely Luke accurately recorded Paul's *ipsissima verba* in Acts 20:24, which would support the Pauline authorship of 2 Tim 4:7.

For Paul, the contest is all but over. What remains is receiving the prize (cf. 1 Cor 9:24–25; Phil 3:13–14).[155] Looking past his imminent martyrdom, Paul anticipates his heavenly reward (cf. Heb 12:2). What awaits him in the future (λοιπόν, in the sense of "finally"; cf. 2 Cor 13:11; 1 Thess 4:1) is the "crown of righteousness" (δικαιοσύνη; 1 Tim 6:11; 2 Tim 2:22; 3:16), that is, the crown (στέφανος; cf. Phil 4:1; 1 Thess 2:19) or reward consisting in righteousness (epexegetic gen.; cf. 1 Thess 2:19; 1 Pet 5:4; Jas 1:12; Rev 2:10). In that day Paul will at last attain the full righteousness that was his all along in Christ (see esp. Rom 6; 9:30–32; cf. Phil 3:9), in keeping with Paul's earlier statement, "by faith, we ourselves eagerly wait for the hope of righteousness" (Gal 5:5 ESV).

This crown or heavenly reward will be awarded by "the Lord" (i.e., Christ; cf. vv. 14, 18), "the righteous Judge," on "that day" to Paul and all those who have longed for his appearing (ἐπιφάνεια; see v. 1). On that future day believers' glorification will be complete (cf. Rom 8:17–30). Again this expectation is consistent with Paul's earlier teaching (e.g., 2 Thess 1:5–10; 1 Cor 3:10–15). Those who competed in Greek athletic races and won received a victor's crown composed of olive branches, while military victors were given special wreaths, and loyal subjects of Oriental sovereigns received awards for services rendered.[156] Those who are faithful to Christ till the end will receive the approval of Christ and attain full righteousness through the Lord Jesus Christ on judgment day. While righteousness is a divine gift granted on the basis of faith, believers must respond with a life of faithful, grateful service.

Similar to the first letter to Timothy, the present letter closes with a solemn appeal (vv. 1–8). Not only the activity of the false teachers but more importantly the expectation of the second coming of Christ and God's final judgment constitute the all-encompassing eschatological backdrop for Paul's final exhortation of Timothy. Because God, in Jesus Christ, will "judge the living and the dead" (v. 1), and "because of his appearing and his kingdom" (v. 2), Timothy must faithfully preach the Word of God, whether or not people are prepared to listen (v. 2). In this spirit he must

---

[155] For a study of the relationship between 2 Tim 4:6–8 and Philippians, see D. Cook, "2 Timothy IV.6–8 and the Epistle to the Philippians," *JTS* 33 (1982): 168–71.

[156] See Baugh, "1 Timothy, 2 Timothy, Titus," 492–93; Guthrie, *Pastoral Epistles*, 181.

also be prepared to endure hardship and strive to fulfill his ministry, just as his apostolic mentor is about to fulfill his (vv. 5–8). This raises the specter of faithfulness in ministry to the end. It also underscores the importance of mentoring and accountability in ministry. Timothy is fortunate enough to have Paul as an example in ministry to inspire him to continued faithfulness; we, too, must seek out godly role models to emulate if we want to be faithful to the end.

Bridge

"Fulfill your ministry" (v. 5). Jesus cried out at the cross, "It is finished" (John 19:30). Paul wrote, "I have finished the race" (v. 7). In Jesus's parable of the talents, the master tells his servant, "Well done, good and faithful servant! You were faithful over a few things; I will put you in charge of many things. Share your master's joy!" (Matt 25:21). In the words of Walter Henrichsen, "Many aspire, few attain."[157] It's easier to start well than to finish well. But the Christian race is a marathon, not a sprint (cf. Heb 12:1–3). It's through many trials that we must enter the kingdom of God (Acts 14:22). The ultimate reward is spending eternity in Christ's presence and hearing his "Well done, good and faithful servant" when giving an account of the way we lived our lives.

V. Letter Closing (4:9–22)

The letter concludes with some recent news from Paul who coordinated the mission of the early church even while in prison (4:9–18) and a farewell wish and greeting (4:19–22). In this letter closing Paul pursues at least three purposes: (1) to address practical concerns that arise from the complex nature of the Pauline mission, especially logistics with regard to the movement of individuals; (2) to tap into and enhance communication networks by naming people in the community, lending credibility to Paul and his cause; and (3) to reinforce some of the arguments made earlier in the letter.[158]

The letter closes with a few final greetings from specific individuals and issues a final plea for Timothy to try to come to Paul before winter. At the time of writing, only Luke is with Paul.

[157] See Walter A. Henrichsen, *Many Aspire Few Attain* (Colorado Springs: NavPress, 1975).

[158] See Johnson, *Letters to Paul's Delegates*, 99.

The apostle wants Timothy to bring Mark with him as well once Timothy is relieved by Tychicus who is to stay in Ephesus and take Timothy's place after delivering the letter to him. The letter concludes with a brief farewell and general greeting.

A. Recent News (4:9–18)

9 Make every effort to come to me soon, 10 because Demas
has deserted me, since he loved this present world, and has
gone to Thessalonica. Crescens has gone to Galatia, Titus to
Dalmatia. 11 Only Luke is with me. Bring Mark with you, for
he is useful to me in the ministry. 12 I have sent Tychicus to
Ephesus. 13 When you come, bring the cloak I left in Troas with
Carpus, as well as the scrolls, especially the parchments. 14 Alexander the coppersmith did great harm to me. The Lord will
repay him according to his works. 15 Watch out for him yourself because he strongly opposed our words.

16 At my first defense, no one stood by me, but everyone
deserted me. May it not be counted against them. 17 But the
Lord stood with me and strengthened me, so that I might
fully preach the word and all the Gentiles might hear it. So I
was rescued from the lion's mouth. 18 The Lord will rescue me
from every evil work and will bring me safely into his heavenly kingdom. To him be the glory forever and ever! Amen.

Relation to Surrounding Context

Together with the final greetings and farewell in vv. 19–22 below, this section concludes the letter with some recent news and a brief doxology (complete with a final "Amen"). Now that Paul has issued his final charge to Timothy, all that remains is to urge him to make haste in visiting Paul at his earliest convenience and to give some accompanying instructions. In the midst of considerable external persecution and internal opposition, Paul turns to his closest follower and ally for support.

Structure

This final section is made up of a laundry list of items Paul includes in order to orient Timothy as to his present circumstances and recent events (vv. 9–17). Despite great adversity, Paul ends this section with an expression of confidence in God (v. 18).

4:9–13 Following his final appeal to Timothy (vv. 1–8), Paul closes the letter by addressing some pressing matters (§1). The scenario cannot easily be accommodated within the scope of events narrated in the book of Acts but rather reflects conditions that took shape subsequent to Paul's first Roman imprisonment with which Acts closes. One way of reconstructing the data referred to in the following verses is as follows.

Paul spends the winter in Nicopolis (possibly having left Trophimus ill at Miletus; v. 20) and sends Zenas and Apollos to Crete in order to deliver his letter to Titus who is relieved by Artemas. Passing through Corinth, Paul leaves Erastus there (v. 20) and travels on to Troas (perhaps on his way to Ephesus), where he is arrested (perhaps opposed by Alexander; vv. 14–15), leaving behind his cloak and scrolls (v. 13), and taken to Rome to be tried. After his first defense (v. 16), sensing ultimate conviction but counting on legal delays, Paul tells Timothy to come before winter and to bring Mark with him (v. 11) as well as his cloak and scrolls (v. 13); he sends Tychicus to relieve Timothy in Ephesus after delivering to him the present letter (v. 12). The Pauline circle had broken up, with Demas going to Thessalonica, Crescens to Galatia, and Titus to Dalmatia (v. 10), leaving Luke as the only coworker still with Paul (v. 11).

First, the passage starts out, Timothy should do his best (Σπούδασον; cf. 2:15; v. 21; Titus 3:12) to come to Paul quickly (ταχέως; 1 Cor 4:19; Phil 2:19, 24). Paul and Timothy may have discussed this visit previously, and Paul may merely urge Timothy to delay no further (cf. 1:4). Later, Paul writes that he wants Timothy to come before winter (v. 21). Paul's urgency may be due to delays in the Roman legal system. It may also be triggered or exacerbated by the departure of several of his coworkers. There are several parallels between Paul's experience and that of Jesus (Mark 15:34 par.; cf. Ps 22:1).

Among those who abandoned Paul (ἐγκατέλιπεν; cf. v. 16; 2 Cor 4:9) is Demas (a familiar form of Demetrius; the fronted "me" in the original may indicate that Demas deserted Paul, though not necessarily the faith) who had gone to Thessalonica "since he loved this present world" (τὸν νῦν αἰῶνα, "the present age"; cf. 1 Tim 6:17; Titus 2:12).[159] Thessalonica may have been Demas's

[159] Marshall, *Pastoral Epistles*, 815, thinks Demas balked at martyrdom (cf. Pol. *Phil*. 9:2: "They [martyrs] did not 'love this present world' but him who died on our behalf, and was raised by God for our sakes") but may have continued as an

hometown. (In Phlm 24, Demas is mentioned with Aristarchus the Thessalonian; cf. Acts 20:4; 27:2.) In Col 4:14 Paul conveyed greetings from him (cf. Phlm 24; v. 11 below), but now he has left the Pauline circle for worldly comfort (cf. Mark 4:17–19 par.).

Two others have left as well (though they are not censured for their departure): Crescens (the name is Roman; only here in the NT) has gone to Galatia (central Asia Minor, modern Turkey; the variant "Galilee" lacks adequate MS support; "Gaul" may be a former name of Galatia: see Augustus's *Res Gestae*, Ancyra 29.1: "Spain, Galatia, Dalmatia"),[160] and Titus to Dalmatia (ranging from present-day Croatia to Albania; partially congruous with the Roman province Illyricum, Rom 15:19; see also 2 Cor 8:23; Gal 2:3). Titus's departure may be due to Paul's request to meet him in Nicopolis (Titus 3:12) and may indicate that his ministry in Crete (Titus 1:5, etc.) is now over.

Only Luke, the "dearly loved physician" of Col 4:14 (cf. Phlm 24), remains with Paul. Luke may have had a hand in the composition of this letter as Paul's amanuensis and/or may have provided medical or other assistance.[161] On his way Timothy is to pick up

---

active Christian, perhaps even as a missionary in Thessalonica. See also Calvin, *1 & 2 Timothy & Titus*, 164: "But we do not have to suppose that he denied Christ completely . . . but only that he cared more for his own convenience and safety than for Paul's life."

[160] See Towner, *Letters to Timothy and Titus*, 623n19, who favors the region Paul and Barnabas evangelized during their first missionary journey (Acts 13–14). Quinn and Wacker, *Letters to Timothy*, 802–4, prefer Gaul, conquered by Julius Caesar and located in today's France and Belgium.

[161] See, e.g., J.-D. Kaestli, "Luke-Acts and the Pastoral Epistles: The Thesis of a Common Authorship," in *Luke's Literary Achievement: Collected Essays*, ed. C. M. Tuckett, JSNTSup 116 (Sheffield: Sheffield Academic Press, 1995), 110–26. J. D. Quinn, "The Last Volume of Luke: The Relation of Luke-Acts to the Pastoral Epistles," in *Perspectives on Luke-Acts*, ed. C. H. Talbert, Perspectives in Religious Studies, Special Studies 5 (Macon, GA: Mercer University Press, 1978), 62–75, explores the possibility that the LTT serve as a sort of "epistolary appendix" for Luke-Acts. See also R. Riesner, "Once More: Luke-Acts and the Pastoral Epistles," in *History and Exegesis: New Testament Essays in Honor of Dr. E. Earle Ellis for His 80th Birthday*, ed. S.-W. Son (New York: T&T Clark, 2006), 239–58, who argues that Luke was involved in the compilation of the LTT and that the setting of 1 Timothy and Titus doesn't fit with the period after the conclusion of Acts. Westfall, "Moral Dilemma," 252, writes, "If some of the features or style of the letter seem more like Luke-Acts than the undisputed Pauline Epistles, it is highly likely that Luke, who was Paul's only companion at the time he wrote 2 Timothy, had some influence on the content, vocabulary and style." S. G. Wilson, *Luke and the Pastoral Epistles*

John Mark, the second evangelist and former missionary associate of Paul (Acts 12:25; 13:5), and bring him to Rome, "for he is useful to me in the ministry" (εὔχρηστος εἰς διακονίαν; 2:21; Phlm 11, cf. v. 5), which may entail not only ministry to others but also personal assistance to Paul (cf. Onesiphorus in 1:16–18). This amounts to a restoration of Mark to service (cf. Peter's restoration by Jesus in John 21:15–19), whom Paul refused to take on his second missionary journey after Mark had returned to Jerusalem at the beginning of the first journey (Acts 13:13). Later Mark teamed up with his uncle Barnabas (Acts 15:36–41). But now Paul, like Peter (1 Pet 5:13), considers Mark to be "useful . . . in the ministry" (cf. Col 4:10; Phlm 24).

Moreover, Paul anticipates sending Tychicus to Ephesus, presumably in order to deliver the present letter and perhaps also to relieve Timothy upon his arrival so that Timothy can depart for Rome to be with Paul. Tychicus was found in Paul's company several years earlier, shortly after the Ephesian riots (Acts 20:4), having helped to deliver the collection of the Gentile churches to the Jerusalem church. Later, he delivered Paul's letters to the Ephesians and Colossians and brought a report regarding the circumstances of Paul's first Roman imprisonment (Eph 6:21; Col 4:7). He is also mentioned in Paul's letter to Titus (3:12).

Paul asks Timothy to bring two things when he comes. First, Paul requests "the cloak" (φαιλόνην, a loanword from the Lat. *paenula*)—a seamless, thick woolen garment with a hole in the center for the head (like a poncho)—he left in Troas (emphasized in the original; Timothy must pass through Troas on the way from Ephesus to Rome) with Carpus (not mentioned elsewhere) or at Carpus's home (cf. 1 Cor 16:2 and several times in Luke-Acts). The warm coat would award Paul a measure of protection against the cold in his prison cell (especially with winter approaching; see v. 21).

Second, Paul asks for "the scrolls" (βιβλία; cf. Luke 4:17, 20; John 20:30; 21:25), "especially the parchments" (μεμβράνας, another Lat. loanword; "especially," μάλιστα, on which see note at 1 Tim 5:17 above, implies that there were also scrolls not made of

(London: S.P.C.K., 1979), claims Luke wrote the LTT after completing Acts, incorporating travel notes compiled while accompanying Paul on some of his missionary journeys.

parchment).[162] The scrolls may have contained portions of sacred Scripture, the parchments notebooks, perhaps "memoranda such as lists of Christians in various communities" or even "collections of Jesus's *logia*; scriptural *testimonia*; even the draft copies from which the final rolls of his epistles had been transcribed; perhaps the rough copies and drafts of preaching, teaching, and epistolary materials."[163]

4:14–18 "Alexander the coppersmith" (or metalworker; χαλκεύς; cf. Gen 4:22; 2 Chr 24:12) was a blacksmith who manufactured or repaired any copper, bronze, or iron implements. He may be the Alexander mentioned in 1 Tim 1:20, or the epithet "the coppersmith" may be designed to distinguish this Alexander from the one mentioned in Paul's first letter to Timothy. There Paul had urged Timothy to excommunicate the false teachers. Here Paul simply notes that Alexander has done him "great harm" (lit., "did many evil things to me," ἐνεδείξατο; cf. Gen 50:17). In fact, he had strongly (λίαν, fronted for emphasis, only here in Paul) opposed Paul's words (λόγοις). The term "opposed" (ἀντέστη) occurs elsewhere in the LTT only in 3:8, there with reference to Jannes and Jambres, who opposed Moses, so that Paul may seek to link Alexander implicitly to those ancient opponents of God's people. Paul wants Timothy to watch out (φυλάσσω; cf. 1:12, 14) for Alexander as well (καὶ σύ, "you also," is emphatic).

Alexander may have provided information leading to Paul's arrest (the possible legal connotation of ἐνεδείξατο), so that the apostle had to leave his cloak and scrolls in Troas (v. 13). This would be even more likely if Paul were recounting events here chronologically, which would place the "harm" caused by Alexander prior to Paul's "first defense" in Rome (v. 16). If Alexander is still in Troas, this would explain Paul's warning Timothy to be on guard

---

[162] See V. S. Poythress, "The Meaning of μάλιστα in 2 Timothy 4:13 and Related Verses," *JTS* 53 (2002): 523–32 (esp. 525), who concludes—contra T. C. Skeat, "'Especially the Parchments': A Note on 2 Timothy IV.13," *NTS* 30 (1979): 173–77, who argues for the meaning "that is" or namely"—that μάλιστα means "especially," not only in 2 Tim 4:13, but also in 1 Tim 4:10; 3:8, 17; and Titus 1:10. Among other concerns, Poythress notes the availability of the unambiguous expression τοῦτ' ἔστιν; the ambiguity of the evidence cited by Skeat; and the lexicographic principle of not unnecessarily multiplying meanings (see commentary at 1 Tim 4:10 above).

[163] Quinn and Wacker, *Letters to Timothy*, 812; Skeat, "Especially the Parchments," 177.

against him. In any case Paul knows his struggle is not against flesh and blood, resting content that the Lord (i.e., Christ; cf. vv. 8, 18) will repay this man for what he has done (2 Sam 3:39; Pss 28:4; 62:12; Prov 24:12; also cited in Rom 2:6; cf. 2 Sam 3:39; Ps 28:4). This coheres with Paul's earlier teaching not to take revenge but to leave room for God's wrath (Rom 12:17–21).

Continuing to paint a picture of virtual abandonment, Paul observes that at his first defense (ἀπολογία) no one stood by him (παρεγένετο; cf. 1 Cor 16:3) but everyone deserted him (ἐγκατέλιπον; see on v. 10 above; cf. 1:15). "First defense" probably relates to Paul's courtroom defense at the initial hearing of his trial in Rome, the *prima actio* or preliminary investigation of the proceedings.[164] If so, "stood by me" may refer to formal legal representation by a *patronus* or lawyer. This was not the first, and probably not the last, time Paul must defend himself against unjust charges (Acts 22:1; 25:16; 1 Cor 9:3), just as he viewed the "defense of the gospel" as the essence of his ministry (Phil 1:7, 16; cf. 1 Pet 3:15). Paul's attitude, like Jesus's, is one of forgiveness: "May it not be counted against them" (cf. Luke 23:34; see also Acts 7:60).

As in Jesus's case, human companions may prove unreliable (Mark 14:50 par.), but the Lord "stood with" Paul (fig. use of παρίστημι, corresponding to "stood by me" in the previous verse) and strengthened him (ἐνεδυνάμωσεν; 1 Tim 1:12; Phil 4:13; Acts 9:22; cf. John 16:32). The book of Acts records several similar instances (see esp. 22:17–21; 23:11; cf. 18:9–10). Yet even at this late stage of Paul's ministry, he retains a clear understanding of his purpose: that the gospel (κήρυγμα) might be fully proclaimed (πληροφορηθῇ) through him and that "all the Gentiles might hear it" (cf. 1 Tim

---

[164] See Quinn and Wacker, *Letters to Timothy*, 821–23. A minority demurs and believes "first defense" refers to an earlier trial that led to Paul's release. See Knight, *Pastoral Epistles*, 468–70; J. Murphy-O-Connor, *Paul: A Critical Life* (Oxford: Oxford University Press, 1996), 359–61; R. Riesner, "The Pastoral Epistles and Paul in Spain (2 Timothy 4:16–18)," in *Rastreando Los Origenes: Lengua y exegesis en el Nuevo Testamento*, ed. J. M. G. Perez (Madrid: Ediciones Encuentro/CEU Ediciones/Fundacion San Justino, 2011), 324–30 (see 329n52 for other advocates of this view); Riesner, "Paul's Trial and End," 397. But see the cogent critique by J. Herzer, "The Mission and the End of Paul between Strategy and Reality: A Response to Rainer Riesner," in *The Last Years of Paul: Essays from the Tarragona Conference, June 2013*, ed. A. Puig i Tàrrech, J. M. G. Barclay, and J. Frey, WUNT 352 (Tübingen: Mohr-Siebeck, 2015), 422.

2:7; Acts 9:15).[165] Whether figuratively (1 Pet 5:8; Ps 22:21) or literally (1 Sam 17:37; Heb 11:33; Dan 6:22), Paul was "rescued from the lion's mouth" (ἐρρύσθην; also in v. 18). Most likely the apostle was delivered from some extreme peril (cf. 2 Cor 6:4–10).[166]

Although Paul clearly laments the fact that no one in the Roman church stood by him at his first defense, he is convinced that the Lord (Christ, cf. vv. 8, 14; cf. Acts 23:11) won't fail him: he will rescue him (ῥύσεται; cf. 2 Tim 3:11; Rom 15:31; 2 Cor 1:10; 2 Thess 3:2) from every evil attack (cf. Matt 6:13)—whether by physical deliverance or spiritual preservation—and bring him safely (σώσει; cf. 1 Tim 2:15; 4:16) into his heavenly kingdom (βασιλεία; cf. v. 1). Earthly kings or emperors may persecute him, but the apostle knows that his eternal destiny is secure (cf. 1 Thess 4:13–18). As he waits for Timothy during a presumable delay in legal proceedings, Paul reaffirms that his entire life and ministry are devoted to the glory of Christ (cf. v. 18): "To him be the glory forever and ever! Amen" (a standard doxology: cf. 1 Tim 1:17; 6:15; Rom 9:5; Phil 4:20).[167]

A. Puig i Tàrrech draws attention to the fact that in this section Paul draws a sharp contrast between an earthly, just court and the divine tribunal, presided over by "the righteous judge" (4:8).[168] The former is marked by "evil work" (4:18) and the charge of Paul's being a "criminal" (2:9), which may suggest that the accusation of *seditio* (insurrection) before Festus (cf. Acts 25:26–27) may now have been ratified by the imperial court. If so, Paul, "a prisoner of Rome" (1:8, 17) and deserted by his associates in

---

[165] See the remarkable verbal similarity between 2 Tim 4:17 and Rom 15:19, both of which speak of Paul's "fully proclaiming" the gospel (2 Tim 4:17: πληροφορηθῇ; Rom 15:19: πεπληρωκέναι), in the former passage in conjunction with κήρυγμα, in the latter with εὐαγγέλιον.

[166] Riesner ("Paul's Trial and End," 407) believes the reference may hint at the Roman emperor (cf. Josephus, *Ant*. 18.228; cf. Eusebius, *Hist. eccl*. 2.22.4).

[167] According to tradition, Paul was beheaded at Aquae Salviae on the Ostian Way (*Via Ostiensis*). F. F. Bruce, *Paul, Apostle of the Heart Set Free* (Grand Rapids: Eerdmans, 1977), 450–51, says it was near the third milestone; V. Marotta, "St. Paul's Death: Roman Citizenship and *summa supplicia*," in *Last Years of Paul*, 260n76, reports that the *Apostolic Memoirs of Abdias* (8) indicate that a woman named Lucina buried Paul's body (after his martyrdom on July 3) near the second milestone on the Ostian Way. See also the introduction to Titus below.

[168] A. Puig i Tàrrech, "Paul's Missionary Activity during His Roman Trial: The Case of Paul's Journey to Hispania," in *Last Years of Paul*, 481.

the east (1:15; 4:10), would already have been unjustly sentenced. All this stands in contrast with the latter, divine tribunal, which Paul anticipates he'll face subsequent to his death at his arrival in the "heavenly kingdom" (4:18). Puig i Tàrrech contends that Paul uses four images to depict his imminent demise: (1) the sacrificial Roman cult; (2) the army; (3) stadium races; and (4) the maritime world (4:6–7).[169] Paul himself expects to receive the victor's crown (4:8) on "that day" (1:12; 4:8).

The "recent news" section in vv. 9–18 showcases Paul's determination fueling his ministry that he "might fully preach the word and all the Gentiles might hear it" (v. 17). Rather than merely providing incidental details the modern Bible reader may safely skip, this section underscores the real-life mission" context in which the LTT were written. The various theological assertions in these letters are firmly grounded in the apostolic mission rooted in the Scriptures and committed to proclaim God and Christ Jesus as Savior. In contrast to 1 Timothy and Titus, 2 Timothy doesn't devote detailed attention to the church as "God's household," presumably because in light of Paul's personal circumstances, his focus is predominantly on finishing his ministry and passing on the baton to Timothy as his trusted successor. In this regard the Moses-Paul typology provides an important salvation-historical grid (§7.1.3).

Bridge

The passage shows the closely knit first-century network of Christians in action. Sadly not all (or even most) stood with Paul, who spearheaded the church's mission to the Gentile world. Too often people in the church choose comfort and convenience over solidarity with their persecuted Christian brothers and sisters. Jesus called his followers to take up their cross and follow him (e.g., Matt 16:24). This calls for a realistic mind-set that expects persecution and supports others who are persecuted rather than withdrawing support out of fear or based on a false notion of Christian prosperity that attributes any suffering to personal sin and the withdrawal of God's favor.

[169] Ibid.

B. Final Greetings and Farewell (4:19–22)

19 Greet Prisca and Aquila, and the household of Onesiphorus. 20 Erastus has remained at Corinth; I left Trophimus sick
at Miletus. 21 Make every effort to come before winter. Eubulus greets you, as do Pudens, Linus, Claudia, and all the brothers and sisters.
22 The Lord be with your spirit. Grace be with you all.

4:19–22 Paul may be all but alone in Rome, but he's not friendless. He extends final greetings to two groups of people: Priscilla (*Prisca*, a short form) and Aquila, the well-known missionary couple (in the customary sequence, with Priscilla mentioned first, cf. Acts 18:18, 26; Rom 16:3; but see Acts 18:2; 1 Cor 16:19), and the household of Onesiphorus (cf. 1:16–18).[170] Apparently Priscilla and Aquila returned to Ephesus where they and Paul had previously joined forces (Acts 18:19–21).

Two more pieces of news are mentioned regarding Paul's coworkers. Erastus stayed in Corinth (Rom 16:23: "the city treasurer"; cf. Acts 19:22), while Trophimus "the Ephesian" (Acts 21:29), who had fallen ill (cf. Acts 20:4; see on v. 12 above), remained in Miletus, a seaport on the coast of Asia Minor roughly fifty miles south of Ephesus. A Latin inscription was found in Corinth in 1929 reading, "ERASTVS PRO AED[ILITATE] S[VA] P[ECUNIA] STRAVIT" ("Erastus in return for his aedileship laid [the pavement] at his own expense").[171]

---

[170] Late tradition supplies the names of the members of Onesiphorus's household as "Lectra, his wife, and Simaeas and Zeno, his sons" (*Acts of Paul and Thecla*, MSS 181 and 460 [11th and 13th c.]). See B. M. Metzger, "Names for the Nameless in the New Testament," in B. M. Metzger, *New Testament Studies: Philological, Versional, and Patristic*, NT Tools and Studies X (Leiden: Brill, 1980), 41.

[171] At least two major questions on Erastus continue to be debated. First, is the Erastus here the same person as in Rom 16:23 and Acts 19:22? This is almost certainly the case, for in each instance Erastus is connected with both Paul and Timothy, and arguably (whether explicitly or not) with Corinth (see H. J. Cadbury, "Erastus of Corinth," *JBL* 50 [1931]: 44–45), and appears to be relatively well known among the churches. As well, strengthening this argument, T. A. Brookins has recently demonstrated that the name "Erastus" was relatively uncommon in the time and geographical region in which Paul ministered ("The (In)frequency of the Name 'Erastus' in Antiquity: A Literary, Papyrological, and Epigraphical Catalog," *NTS* 59 [2013]: 496–513).

A second and more contentious question concerns the social status of Erastus, particularly whether he was a member of the elite class. It is disputed whether

For the second time (cf. v. 9) Paul urges Timothy to delay no further, possibly sensing that his martyrdom is imminent. For Timothy to be able to join Paul before winter, traveling from Ephesus to Rome mostly by ship, he would need to leave early enough to avoid seaports being closed due to inclement weather (the Mediterranean was impassable from November to March). In closing Paul sends greetings from several Roman Christians (with the exception of Eubulus, the names are Latin), including Eubulus, Pudens (a name used in upper-class families), Linus—according to early tradition bishop of Rome after the deaths of Paul and Peter (cf. Irenaeus, *Haer.* 3.3.3; Eusebius, *Hist. eccl.* 3.2.1; 3.4.8)—Claudia, "and all the brothers and sisters."

The final benediction resembles the one at the end of Galatians (6:18). Several manuscripts add "Jesus" or "Jesus Christ" to "Lord," but the shorter reading is to be preferred. "Your" (v. 22) is singular, referring to Timothy, who certainly could use encouragement (e.g., 1:5–8). "With you," on the other hand, is in the plural (cf. 1 Tim 6:21), indicating that the entire letter, while addressed to Timothy, is to be read in public (cf. Titus 3:15).[172]

Paul's final NT letter presents the apostle as still pulling the strings behind the early Christian mission, even from a dark, lonely prison cell. If not even prison walls and imminent execution can stop Paul, what can? Paul himself is convinced his death won't be the end; he'll receive a victor's crown when he stands before his righteous judge (2 Tim 4:8). What's more, the apostolic mission isn't ultimately about Paul, as important as he is to the progress of the gospel to the farthest regions of the then-known world; it's

---

"Erastus the aedile" in the Corinthian inscription should be identified with Paul's associate. An aedile was a high-ranking civic official, and the term οἰκονόμος used of Erastus (Rom 16:23) is not its direct Greek-language equivalent but could be used for a relatively low-ranking municipal functionary who might even be a civic slave (S. J. Friesen, "The Wrong Erastus: Ideology, Archaeology, and Exegesis," in *Corinth in Context: Comparative Studies on Religion and Society*, ed. S. J. Friesen, D. N. Schowalter, and J. C. Walters [Leiden: Brill, 2010], 245–48). The debate is rather involved, but the recent essay by J. Goodrich, "Erastus of Corinth (Rom 16:23): Responding to Recent Proposals on His Rank, Status, and Faith," *NTS* 57 (2011): 583–93 (now bolstered by Brookins, "(In)frequency") makes a plausible case for continuing to identify the Erastus of the NT with the Erastus of the Corinthian inscription.

[172] See the discussion in J. Ellington, "Problem Pronouns in Private Letters," *BT* 50 (1999): 222–23.

about the irresistible, unstoppable gospel of the Lord Jesus Christ. As Paul wrote, almost defiantly, while he was bound and imprisoned as a criminal, the Word of God could never be bound (2:9). Thus he remained undaunted: "This is why I endure all things for the elect: so that they also may obtain salvation, which is in Christ Jesus, with eternal glory" (2:10). Two millennia later, the apostle continues to set an example of faithfulness in ministry to the very end:

> This saying is trustworthy:
> For if we died with him,
> we will also live with him;
> if we endure, we will also reign with him;
> if we deny him, he will also deny us;
> if we are faithless, he remains faithful,
> for he cannot deny himself. (2:11–13)

EXPOSITION OF TITUS

Occasion

While not as close to Paul as Timothy, Titus was also a trusted coworker.[1] When Paul went to talk with the leaders of the Jerusalem church about the gospel he preached, he took Titus with him (Gal 2:1–3). Being Greek (i.e., a Gentile; Gal 2:3), Titus hadn't been compelled to be circumcised when converting to Christianity.[2] This served to illustrate the nature of Paul's gospel (Gal 2:3–5). While not mentioned in Acts,[3] Titus's name surfaces repeatedly in Paul's second letter to the Corinthians (2 Cor 2:12–13; 7:5–6; 8:6). His current

---

[1] Paul refers to him in 2 Cor 2:13 as his "brother" (ἀδελφός) and in 2 Cor 8:23 as his "partner" (κοινωνός) and "coworker" (συνεργός). A complete list of NT references to Titus is as follows: Gal 2:1, 3; 2 Cor 2:13; 7:6, 13, 14; 8:6, 13, 16; 12:18; and 2 Tim 4:10 (for text, see the introduction). See further C. K. Barrett, "Titus," in *Neotestamentica et Semitica: Studies in Honour of Matthew Black*, ed. E. E. Ellis and M. Wilcox (Edinburgh: T&T Clark, 1969), 1–14; J. Gillman, "Titus (person)," *ABD* 6:581–82; A. Mayer-Haas, "Titus im Zeugnis des Neuen Testaments: Eine Einführung," in *Ein Meisterschüler: Titus und sein Brief. Michael Theobald zum 60. Geburtstag*, ed. H.-U. Weidemann and W. Eisele, SBS 214 (Stuttgart: Katholisches Bibelwerk, 2008), 11–30; and the discussion below.

[2] Though note Barrett's comment that "the question whether or not he [Titus] was circumcised is warmly disputed, and by no means settled" ("Titus," 4–5). Relevant considerations include the text of Gal 2:4–5, the stress put on ἠναγκάσθη, and "the view taken of the general probabilities of the situation" (ibid., 4).

[3] Barrett (ibid., 2) notes that "it is surprising that Titus is not mentioned in Acts." He suggests the reason may be that "Titus was closely bound up with Paul's collection and with Corinth" and that Luke provides an abridged version of events (ibid.). After a discussion of dead ends in attempts to find references to Titus in Acts, Barrett concludes, "We leave Acts, therefore, having learnt nothing whatever about Titus" (p. 3).

assignment finds him on the island of Crete, where he's tasked with taking care of some unfinished business, appointing elders in every city (1:5). Upon receiving this letter, he's to meet Paul in Nicopolis (3:12; cf. 2 Tim 4:10). Cretan society was known for its immorality,[4] so Titus's task wasn't easy. Similar to Paul's first letter to Timothy, his missive to Titus is designed to encourage his apostolic delegate to complete the assignment given to him and to stand firm against his opponents.[5]

The letter to Titus was most likely written around the same time as the first letter to Timothy and for similar reasons.[6] The occasion is stated in 1:5 as follows: "The reason I left you in Crete was to set right what was left undone and, as I directed you, to appoint elders in every town."[7] This is followed by a set of qualifications for elders in 1:6–9. While initially given to provide guidance for Titus, this passage isn't limited to the original occasion but has abiding relevance for the church as it strives to ensure that its leaders meet biblical requirements. Beyond this immediate purpose, Paul provides a series of additional instructions for Titus to aid him in overseeing the life of the church in the cities of the island of Crete. In so doing the apostle articulates several crucial and perennial Christian doctrinal truths, including salvation

---

[4] See further the discussion below.

[5] There is little to commend the theory that Titus is one and the same person as Timothy, with "Titus" being the informal first name. See R. G. Fellows, "Was Titus Timothy?" *JSNT* 81 (2001): 33–58. For a critique, see Mayer-Haas, "Titus im Zeugnis des Neuen Testaments," 24–26.

[6] J. D. Quinn, *The Letter to Titus*, AB 35 (Garden City, NY: Doubleday, 1990), 7 thinks that Titus was the first letter among the LTT because its opening is much fuller and that Titus was designed to serve as the introduction for the collection of these three letters. Similarly, C. Schaefer, "Judentum und Gnosis? Die Gegnerpolemik im Titusbrief als Element literarischer Konstruktion," in *Ein Meisterschüler: Titus und sein Brief. Festschrift M. Theobald*, ed. H.-U. Weidemann and W. Eisele, SBS 214 (Stuttgart: Katholisches Bibelwerk, 2008), 76–79. C. L. Quarles, *Illustrated Life of Paul* (Nashville: B&H Academic, 2014), writes that "Paul probably wrote his first letter to Timothy at about the same time [as Titus]" (p. 259) and suggests that "Paul wrote his letter to Titus in the fall from Macedonia or Achaia as he was making plans to winter in Nicopolis (Titus 3:12)" (p. 258).

[7] See esp. G. M. Wieland, "Roman Crete and the Letter to Titus," *NTS* 55 (2009): 338–54.

apart from works, believers' regeneration and renewal by the Holy Spirit, and justification by grace (3:4–7).[8]

Chronology

The basic framework for establishing a chronology for the letter to Titus takes its point of departure from Paul's references to two Jerusalem visits subsequent to his conversion, after three and fourteen years, respectively, in the letter to the Galatians (1:18; 2:1; the reference to fourteen years may be exclusive or inclusive of the three years mentioned earlier). If Paul was converted in the year 34, and the reference in Gal 2:1 is inclusive, this would mean the second Jerusalem visit (most likely the famine visit of Acts 11:27–30) took place in approximately AD 46. Paul probably visited Corinth in the spring of AD 50 and stayed there for eighteen

---

[8] For a treatment of the authenticity of the letter to Titus, see D. A. Hagner, "Titus as a Pauline Letter," in *Society of Biblical Literature 1998 Seminar Papers, Part Two*, SBLSP 37 (Atlanta: Scholars Press, 1998), 546–58, who writes, "Why the situation assumed in Titus . . . could only exist in a period some considerable time *after* Paul remains unclear to me. It further remains unclear to me why Paul is regarded as so fixed in his ways that he cannot have written a different kind of letter when new circumstances required it of him" (p. 548). He approvingly cites Ellis, who laments that certain scholars "envision a Paul who is a rather narrow personality unable to combine charism and church order and passionately fixated for life on a very few theological issues. In the end this Paul is too small" (E. E. Ellis, "The Pastorals and Paul," *ExpTim* 104 [1992–93]: 46. In interaction with I. H. Marshall, who says that the Paul of Titus is "not the Paul that I know from the genuine letters," Hagner retorts that "it is nonetheless the 'real' Paul" if allowance is made for the later, different circumstances and an amanuensis such as Luke or Tychicus (p. 556, with reference to I. H. Marshall, "Prospects for the Pastoral Epistles," in *Doing Theology for the People of God: Studies in Honor of J. I. Packer*, ed. D. M. Lewis and A. E. McGrath [Downers Grove: InterVarsity, 1996], 139). Hagner concludes that "the possibility that Titus stems from Paul through an amanuensis can by no means be confidently ruled out. Indeed, it remains for many a persuasive possibility" (p. 558). See, however, "The Pastoral Epistles," in D. A. Hagner, *The New Testament: A Historical and Theological Introduction* (Grand Rapids: Baker, 2012), 614–42, where Hagner backs away from the Pauline authorship of the LTT including Titus and writes, "Although quite possibly by Paul (2 Timothy perhaps having the best claim), a slight probability favors a disciple or disciples of Paul, possibly making use of fragments stemming from Paul" (p. 615; see also p. 637: "probably the most we can say is that these letters were written by someone who was a close and trustworthy associate of Paul"; and most strongly, p. 622: "The Pastorals breathe a different atmosphere. . . . We have here the marks of an incipient early catholicism.").

months (roughly from March AD 50 to September AD 51), which means Paul would have been associated with Titus for about five years by that time.

Paul later spent three years in Ephesus (AD 51–54), followed by three months in Greece (early AD 55; cf. Acts 20:2–3), which most likely included a visit to Corinth, and then went to Jerusalem at Pentecost of the same year (Acts 20:16). The account in 2 Corinthians mentions that Paul was initially unable to find Titus at Troas and so departed to look for him in Macedonia, where they eventually connected (2 Cor 2:13). The story resumes in 2 Cor 7:5, recounting the good news that the Corinthians had responded well to Paul's letter Titus had delivered. Later, in 2 Cor 8:6, reference is made to the collection for the believers in Jerusalem. Finally, in 12:16–18 we read that Paul was accused of defrauding the Corinthians under the guise of taking up a collection for the poor. Paul's defense was that he had thus far taken no direct part in the collection but delegated it to trustworthy coworkers such as Titus.

Subsequently, Paul dispatched Titus to Crete, assigning to him the task of appointing qualified leaders in the churches in every city. The present letter, written most likely in the early to mid-60s AD, was probably penned sometime after the following events: Paul's arrest, which took place when he delivered the collection to the Jerusalem church; his lengthy and eventful transfer to Rome that included several interrogations by Roman government officials such as Felix, Festus, and Agrippa; his living under house arrest in Rome while awaiting trial; and his subsequent release and further ministry. By that time Paul had known and been associated with Titus in ministry for close to two decades, and Titus had proven himself as a coworker who could be entrusted with delicate and difficult tasks. In the present case Titus's challenge came not only from the magnitude of the task and the false teachers but was exacerbated by the general immorality of the Cretan culture.

We may surmise that later on, when Artemas took Titus's place on the island (Titus 3:12) and met up with Paul in Nicopolis, the apostle sent Titus to Dalmatia in Artemas's place (2 Tim 4:10). Alternatively Titus arrived in Nicopolis after Paul had already departed, and Paul sent Titus to Dalmatia at a later time after the apostle's arrival in Rome.[9] While in Rome, Paul was arrested again

[9] Quarles, *Illustrated Life of Paul*, 259.

and subjected to a more severe imprisonment. He wrote the second letter to Timothy in the mid-60s AD and subsequently, similar to the apostle Peter, suffered martyrdom under Emperor Nero (ruled AD 54–68) in Rome in approximately AD 65, 66, or 67. According to tradition (4th–5th c.?), Paul was beheaded at a place called "Aquae Salviae" (now known as *Tre Fontane* or "Three Fountains") near the third milestone on the Ostian Way (*Via Ostiensis*).[10]

Date	Event(s)	Scripture Passage
34	Paul's conversion	Acts 9
36	First Jerusalem visit	Gal 1:18
46	Second Jerusalem visit	Gal 2:1; cf. Acts 11:27–30
50–51	18 months in Corinth	Acts 18:11
51–54	3 years in Ephesus	Acts 20:31
55	Visit to Greece (incl. Corinth), Pentecost in Jerusalem	Acts 20:2–3, 16
55	Paul's arrest in Jerusalem	Acts 21–22
55–57	Transfer to Rome, interrogations by Felix, Festus, Agrippa	Acts 23–27
58–60/60–62	Arrival in Rome, house arrest, waiting for trial	Acts 28
62	Paul's release	—
63–65	Letter to Titus	Titus
65/66	Subsequent ministry by Titus and Paul, Paul's second arrest	2 Tim 4:10
65/66/67	Paul's martyrdom	—

[10] *Acts of Paul* 11.5; Eusebius, *Hist. eccl.*. 2.25.7; 3.31.4. A. Puig i Tàrrech, "Paul's Missionary Activity during His Roman Trial: The Case of Paul's Journey to Hispania," in *The Last Years of Paul: Essays from the Tarragona Conference, June 2013*, ed. A. Puig i Tàrrech, J. M. G. Barclay, and J. Frey, WUNT 352 (Tübingen: Mohr-Siebeck, 2015), 481n40, notes that "Dionysius of Corinth refers around 170 CE to Paul's martyrdom and about 200 CE Gaius, a Roman priest, already knows the trophy (*trophaeum*) of Paul on the Via Ostia, that is to say, his tomb, with the remains of his body. The trophy had been erected around 150 CE." See also the information provided by R. Penna, "The Death of Paul in the Year 58: A Hypothesis and Its Consequences for His Biography," in *Last Years of Paul*, 551n63.

Background

Paul's charge to Titus is "to set right what was left undone and, as I directed you, to appoint elders in every town" (κατὰ πόλιν; 1:5).[11] A literate audience would be familiar with the statement by the famous classical poet Homer, who spoke of "Crete of the hundred cities" (Homer, *Iliad* 2.649), no doubt by way of poetic hyperbole.[12] Along its extensive coastline, many of Crete's cities were connected by sea as well as roads on land.[13] During the Hellenistic period, some forty πόλεις are known.[14] About twenty πόλεις are attested in the Roman period, issuing coins of their own and being administered by their own magistrates.[15] The most prominent cities in the early Roman period were Gortyn (the administrative capital, known for its celebrated "Gortyn Code," a set of classical codified laws),[16] Knossos (a Roman colony most likely established by Augustus, famous for its Bronze Age palace), and the less-explored Eleutherna, Hierapytna, and Kydonia.[17] Gortyn, located in the south of the island, was not far

---

[11] The following summary of the Cretan literary and archaeological evidence is indebted to D. W. J. Gill, "A Saviour for the Cities of Crete: The Roman Background to the Epistle to Titus," in *The New Testament in Its First Century Setting: Essays on Context and Background in Honour of B. W. Winter on His 65th Birthday*, ed. P. J. Williams, A. D. Clarke, P. M. Head, and D. Instone-Brewer (Grand Rapids: Eerdmans, 2004), 220–30 (with additional bibliographic references). Note that the term πόλις occurs only infrequently in the NT epistles and in the letter to Titus apparently refers to "the urban, political units of the Roman province of Crete and Cyrenaica" (p. 220). For a contemporary account of Crete, see Strabo, *Geogr.* 10 (LCL, Jones).

[12] See P. Perlman, "One Hundred-Citied Crete and the 'Cretan *Politeia*,'" *CP* 87 (1992): 193–205.

[13] Wieland, "Roman Crete," 352.

[14] I. F. Sanders, *Roman Crete: An Archaeological Survey and Gazeteer of Late Hellenistic, Roman and Early Byzantine Crete* (Werminster: Aris & Phillips, 1982), 11.

[15] Ibid., 12.

[16] See A. S. Vasilakis, *The Great Inscription of the Law Code of Gortyn* (Heraklion: Mystis, n.d.); R. F. Willetts, ed., *The Law Code of Gortyn* (Berlin: de Gruyter, 1967); Vasilakis, "Cretan Laws and Society," in *Cambridge Ancient History* 3.3, 2nd ed., ed. J. Boardman and N. G. L. Hammond (Cambridge: Cambridge University Press, 1982), 237–48.

[17] For detailed discussion and additional references, see Gill, "Saviour for the Cities of Crete," 224–27. Knossos also was the home of Epimenides, whose prophecy

from the places Paul passed along the Cretan coast on his voyage to Rome.[18]

At one time Crete served as the center of the Minoan civilization (ca. 2700–1420 BC), which many regard as the earliest recorded civilization in the continent of Europe.[19] In the first century AD, the cult of Augustus and Roma appears to have been practiced in Gortyn, while the cult of the deified Claudius is attested for Knossos.[20] The cult of Asclepius, a god of healing, was confirmed in at least eighteen locations.[21] The Egyptian cult of Isis and Serapis is attested as well.[22] Under Tiberius (ruled AD 14–37), Crete was used for exiles from Rome (Tacitus, *Ann.* 4.21). In addition to the Roman administrators, a local leading official, the *Koinon*, organized quinquennial games and issued coins, seeking to maintain a distinct Greek identity.[23]

---

is cited in Titus 1:12. Cf. Diogenes Laertius (3rd c. AD), whose *Lives of Eminent Philosophers* devotes an entire chapter to Epimenides (chap. 10, par. 109).

[18] See Acts 27:7–8: "We sailed along the south side of Crete off Salmone. With still more difficulty we sailed along the coast and came to a place called Fair Havens [Καλοὶ λιμένες] near [i.e., 1.5 miles west of] the city [πόλις] of Lasea"; Acts 27:12: "Since the harbor was unsuitable to winter in, the majority decided to set sail from there, hoping somehow to reach Phoenix, a harbor on Crete facing the southwest and northwest, and to winter there." For a map, see J. Boardman, "Crete," in *Cambridge Ancient History* 3.3, 2nd ed., ed. J. Boardman and N. G. L. Hammond (Cambridge: Cambridge University Press, 1982), 224.

[19] For a report of a significant find documenting the supremacy and sophisticated nature of Cretan culture in the mid-second century BC, see Nicholas Wade, "Grave of 'Griffin Warrior' at Pylos Could Be a Gateway to Civilizations," *Science*, *New York Times*, October 26, 2015, accessed October 27, 2015, http://www.nytimes.com/2015/10/27/science/a-warriors-grave-at-pylos-greece-could-be-a-gateway-to-civilizations.html. The tomb of an ancient warrior was discovered in Pylos, an ancient city on the southwest coast of Greece near a palace that was part of the Mycenaean civilization, which at that time borrowed heavily from Minoan culture. The coffin has decayed, but remaining are the bones of a thirty- to thirty-five-year-old man lying on his back: "Placed to his left were weapons, including a long bronze sword with an ivory hilt clad in gold and a gold-hilted dagger. On his right side were four gold rings with fine Minoan carvings and some 50 Minoan seal stones carved with imagery of goddesses and bull jumpers."

[20] For details, see Gill, "Saviour for the Cities of Crete," 227.

[21] See ibid., n. 39.

[22] See further the discussion below.

[23] Sanders, *Roman Crete*, 8.

In light of the frequent use of the term "Savior" in the letter to Titus (1:3, 4; 2:10, 13; 3:4, 6; cf. 1 Tim 1:1; 2 Tim 1:10), it's noteworthy that an inscription was found at the sanctuary of Asclepius at Lebena near Gortyn, reading, "Diodorus dedicated to you, Savior (σωτήρ), two dreams in return for twofold eyes, light being restored" (2nd c. AD?).[24] Another similar Greek inscription, addressed to Zeus and attributed to a Corinthian named Plotius, was found at Knossos.[25] This evidence for the use of "Savior" with regard to Greek deities provides a crucial backdrop for Paul's references to God and Jesus as "Savior," designating them as the true provider and exclusive mediator of salvation, respectively (§3.3). There is also evidence for the presence of a Jewish community on Crete (Acts 2:11; note the references to "the circumcision party" and devotees to "Jewish myths" in Titus 1:10 and 14).[26] Thus the Alexandrian Jewish philosopher Philo writes in the early 40s AD that "not only are the mainlands full of Jewish colonies but also the most highly esteemed of the islands, Euboia, Cyprus, Crete" (*Alleg. Interp.* 282).[27]

In light of this background information, it's possible that Titus was based in or near Gortyn, the provincial capital,[28] and that his task as apostolic delegate was to establish a body of elders in the

---

[24] The inscription is reproduced in facsimile, Greek, and English translation in Gill, "Saviour for the Cities of Crete," 229.

[25] For details see ibid., 230.

[26] See esp. P. W. van der Horst, "The Jews of Ancient Crete," *JJS* 39 (1988): 183–200 (see additional bibliographic references on 83n3), who observes that from the Hellenistic period until the Middle Ages, the island enjoyed a unique period of peace (p. 183). He also notes that there are no remains of an ancient synagogue at Crete (ibid., n2) and suggests that some Jews may have fled to Crete during the time of the Maccabean revolt in the second century BC (1 Macc 15:22–23). See also commentary at 1:10 below.

[27] After a reference in Tacitus's *Histories* (V.2, 1–3), there is no literary evidence on Cretan Jews from the beginning of the second to the fifth century AD (van der Horst, "Jews of Ancient Crete," 189), perhaps because during this time "the Jews reached a high degree of integration into Cretan society" (van der Horst, 200). From Titus 1:10–14, van der Horst infers that "tensions ran high between Christians of Jewish and Gentile origins" in Crete (p. 188).

[28] C. Zimmermann, "Wiederentstehung und Erneuerung (Tit 3:5): Zu einem erhaltenswerten Aspekt der Soteriologie des Titusbriefs," *NovT* 51 (2009): 284, says that Titus was reportedly based in the city of Metropolis which was located near Gortyn. She also cites Eusebius's reference to a correspondence between the bishop Dionysius of Corinth (2nd c. AD) and Philip of Gortyn (*Hist. eccl.* IV 23.5, 7–8).

churches of every one of the twenty or so πόλεις on the island.[29] As Wieland notes, "Gortyn is traditionally held to be Crete's first ecclesiastical centre, and it would not be surprising if a Christian mission located itself in such a leading town, nor that both recruits and opposition to the Christian movement should come from the Jewish community already established there."[30] Crete is 3,219 square miles (8,336 m^2) in size, and because of the mountainous nature of the island, travel is not always easy, especially since "there is little evidence for a Roman road system."[31] Thus Titus was faced with a formidable challenge, both logistically and theologically (in light of the false teachers). It also shows how ambitious Paul and his associates were in targeting the entire island and all of its cities for evangelization.

The Opponents

At one point in his letter to Titus, Paul writes, "Let no one disregard you" (2:15). Earlier in the epistle, Paul specifies the nature of Titus's opposition as follows: "For there are many rebellious people, full of empty talk and deception, especially those from the circumcision party. It is necessary to silence them; they are ruining entire households by teaching what they shouldn't in order

[29] Cf. Wieland, "Roman Crete," 340, who notes that "of special interest is the city of Gortyn, which local tradition identifies as the site of the first Christian mission on Crete and the ministry of Titus" (with reference to excavations in Gortyn by the Cretan archaeologist A. Vasilakis; see, e.g., *Gortyn* [Iraklio: V. Kouvadis–V. Manouras, 2002]). The remains of a sixth-century AD Christian cathedral dedicated to Titus can still be seen in Gortyn today.

[30] Wieland, "Roman Crete," 352–53. Wieland notes that S. Spyridakis (*Ptolemaic Itanos and Hellenistic Crete*, University of California Publications in History 82 [Berkeley: University of California, 1970], 102n169) "locates the principal Jewish population in Gortyn, the administrative capital for the Roman proviunce of Crete and Cyrenia," contending that the Jews of Gortyn most likely hailed from the Egyptian city of Alexandria.

[31] Gill, "Saviour for the Cities of Crete," 221, who notes, however, that J. D. S. Pendlebury, *The Archaeology of Crete: An Introduction* (London: Methuen, 1939), 365, suggested the paved roads attributed to later times may be Roman in origin; see also O. Rackham and J. Moody, *The Making of the Cretan Landscape* (Warminster: Aris & Phillips, 1982), 155–56. Note also that a Roman official, Q. Paconius Agrippinus, is said to have repaired roads in the south of the island, in the region of Hieropytna, during Claudius's reign (Sanders, *Roman Crete*, 7).

to get money dishonestly" (1:10–11). Titus is to "rebuke them sharply, so that they may be sound in the faith and may not pay attention to Jewish myths and the commands of people who reject the truth" (1:13–14).

The NT contains multiple references to "those of the circumcision."[32] On one level, by synecdoche, this simply refers to those who practice circumcision and adhere to other religious customs such as food laws or Sabbath observance, that is, ethnic Jews. On another level it may denote Judaizers, that is, those who insist that Christians must still abide by Jewish customs such as these just mentioned, people whose teaching Paul fiercely opposed (Gal 2:11–14) and the Jerusalem Council decisively rejected (Acts 15). While certainty is elusive,[33] Titus's opponents may represent a local phenomenon rather than forming part of a larger pattern of opposition that has invaded the island of Crete from the mainland. The profile of the false teachers in the letter to Titus suggests that these opponents are Christian Jews who promulgate Torah observance based on an unduly narrow interpretation and application of the law that Paul rejects as improper for Gentile Christians. This includes purity regulations (1:15–16), though precisely which ones is unclear.[34]

---

[32] See, e.g., Acts 10:45; 11:2; Rom 4:12; Gal 2:12; and Col 4:11. In addition, the letter to the Galatians contains multiple references to circumcision and the Judaizers and their teaching.

[33] See R. J. Karris, "The Background and Significance of the Polemic of the Pastoral Epistles," *JBL* 92 (1973): 549–64.

[34] See J. L. Sumney, "Studying Paul's Opponents: Advances and Challenges," in *Paul and His Opponents*, ed. S. E. Porter, Pauline Studies 2 (Leiden: Brill, 2005), 44. C. Gerber, "Antijudaismus und Apologetik. Eine Lektüre des Titusbriefes vor dem Hintergrund der Apologie *Contra Apionem* des Flavius Josephus," in *Josephus und das Neue Testament: Wechselseitige Wahrnehmungen*, ed. C. Böttrich and J. Herzer with T. Reiprich (Tübingen: Mohr-Siebeck, 2007), 335–63, contends that Titus, in contrast to Josephus's *Against Apion*, contains anti-Jewish, even anti-Semitic, polemic that casts ominous dark clouds on Paul's legacy (p. 363), who in Galatians and Romans engaged his Jewish opponents. By contrast, Gerber argues, the author of Titus uses anti-Jewish polemic as well as Cretan stereotypes while leaving constructive apologetics behind. However, anti-Semitism is far too sweeping and inflammatory a charge in this case because the letter is addressed to Titus for the purpose of dealing with a set of local false teachers and, unlike in the case of Galatians and Romans, Titus is addressed to an individual rather than a church. In any case, if Paul wrote Titus, he was a Semite (e.g., Phil 3:5) and thus was unlikely to hold anti-Semitic beliefs. To the contrary, in Romans Paul expresses strong

Nevertheless, the message of Titus cannot be simply reduced to a polemic against a set of opponents. By quoting a Cretan prophet's critique of his own culture for its "impiety, injustice, and intemperance," by "insisting upon the opposite of these qualities among their leaders," and by "highlighting grace's education in sobriety, justice, and piety for Christians in general," the letter "challenges Cretan Christians to live out a kind of community that coheres with the social self-criticism of an important strand of Greek thought."[35]

As L. T. Johnson perceptively notes, the author believes that with Crete he has reached civilization's backcountry.[36] Consequently, "repulsed by a heritage of religious fabrication and its moral aftermath, the apostle understandably believes nascent Christian congregations here need instruction in the most basic elements of the human enterprise."[37] Paul's proposal is that Cretans can attain the ancient but elusive ideal of genuine humanity (being rightly related to God, others, and themselves) by pursuing lives that reflect "Christ's noble deed and redemptive beneficence," in appropriate social venues (2:1–10; 3:1–3) and by the impetus of the Holy Spirit (3:5–7).[38]

In contrast to Cretans' belief in humans who became gods and were rewarded for providing benefits to humanity, "Paul proclaims that the God-become-human has made available the ultimate human existence possible: a right relationship with deity, with other humans, and with oneself. What articulates the life of this God is a humanity enlivened with his attributes: his graciousness, his own love for humans, and the kindness of his bearing toward them."[39] In this way Titus speaks with a distinctive voice within the context of the writings of the NT, issuing "a clarion call to do theology for the outsider."[40] Christians are indeed a "new race" (*καινόν . . . γένος*).[41] As such, they neither reduplicate Israel's

---

affection for his Jewish compatriots and passionately longs for their conversion (9:1–5). Similar to Gerber is Schaefer, "Judentum und Gnosis?," 62–70.

[35] R. M. Kidd, "Titus as *Apologia*: Grace for Liars, Beasts, and Bellies," *HorBT* 21 (1999): 207.

[36] L. T. Johnson, *1 Timothy, 2 Timothy, Titus* (Atlanta: John Knox, 1987), 117.

[37] Kidd, "Titus as *Apologia*," 207.

[38] Ibid., 208.

[39] Ibid., citing also Matt 5:14–16; John 13:34–35; 17:21, 23.

[40] Ibid.

[41] See the reference in the second-century-AD *Epistle to Diognetus* I.

heritage nor simply accommodate themselves to the Greek host culture. Instead, the manifestation of God incarnate, and the salvation he came to bring, inexorably leads to "lives undergoing transformation and a community under construction."[42]

The approach used by Paul in evangelizing the people of Crete has important contemporary missiological implications (§1). First, Paul focused on urban centers (πόλεις; 1:5; see Background above); this made sense not only on an island such as Crete but is also consistent with Paul's missionary strategy attested in the book of Acts.[43] Second, Paul focused on establishing local church leadership in the form of a plurality of elders (1:5–9). Third, he built his missions strategy on a penetrating understanding of a given culture's moral condition (1:12–13). Fourth, he proclaimed the saving message of the gospel in the context of attaining genuine humanity in keeping with the highest (albeit elusive) ideals of a given culture (2:11–14) and against the backdrop of local pagan practices (3:4–8).[44] In all these respects, the approach in Titus bears an uncanny resemblance to Paul's strategy in Athens where he likewise framed his message in terms of the Athenians' religious and philosophical outlook and set the gospel in the context of humanity at large and its noblest ideals and insights (Acts 17).

Topic	Acts 17	Titus
Traces yet ignorance of true God	v. 23 (altar to unknown God; cf. v. 30)	1:16 (Cretans profess to know God)*
Universal reach of God	v. 24 (made world/everything in it)	2:4, 11 (kindness/grace of God our Savior)
Quote by local poet	v. 28 (Aratus)	1:12 (Epimenides)**
Future return/judgment	v. 31 (universal judgment by Son)	2:13 (waiting for Christ's return)
Resurrection/Redemption in Christ	vv. 31–32 (resurrection from the dead)	2:14 (gave himself to redeem us)

* See V. Wittkowsky, "'Pagane' Zitate im Neuen Testament," *NovT* 51 (2009): 121–23.

** Note that Wittkowsky (ibid., 111–15, 123) even attributes both sayings in Acts 17:28 and Titus 1:12 to Epimenides (see also his reference to Clement of Alexandria, *Strom.* 1.59.2–4; 1.91.1, 4–5).

[42] Kidd, "Titus as *Apologia*," 208–9.

[43] On Paul's missionary strategy, see esp. E. J. Schnabel, *Paul the Missionary: Realities, Strategies and Methods* (Downers Grove: InterVarsity, 2008).

[44] Such as the cult of Isis and Osiris; see the discussion at 3:4–8 below.

Genre and Literary Forms

The epistle to Titus represents a Hellenistic letter, an "ecclesial paraenesis,"[45] with a typical letter opening (1:1–4), body (1:5–3:11), and closing (3:12–15). It has an extended salutation but no thanksgiving.[46] The body opens with a statement denoting the immediate occasion (1:5), followed by a list of qualifications (1:6–9) and a denunciation of the false teachers (1:10–16), the latter of which may be occasioned by the reference to the need for elders to uphold sound teaching and to refute those who contradict it (1:9).[47]

Following a brief transition (2:1), Paul issues a series of instructions for different groups in the church in form of a household code (2:2–10). The rest of the body of the letter (2:11–3:11) alternates theological portions with imperatives:

2:11–14	Theology	2:15–3:3	Imperatives
3:4–8a	Theology	3:8b–11	Imperatives

Both 2:11 and 3:4 feature the word ἐπεφάνη, signaling the manifestation of God as Savior,[48] and each passage concludes with a ἵνα-clause specifying what God has done (2:14; 3:7). In this way Paul undergirds his imperatives with a weighty theological rationale.[49]

The letter closes with the customary travel plans, parting instructions, and a concluding imperative (3:12–14). No names are

---

[45] J. D. Quinn, "Timothy and Titus, Epistles to," *ABD* 6:565. See also A. J. Malherbe, "Paraenesis in the Epistle to Titus," in *Early Christian Paraenesis in Context*, ed. J. Starr and T. Engberg-Pederson, BZNW 125 (Berlin: de Gruyter, 2004), 297–317, who focuses particularly on 2:1–3:8.

[46] Arguments from silence are notoriously difficult, though some infer from the lack of a thanksgiving that the author of this letter was not pleased with the community addressed in this letter (see, e.g., B. Thurston, "The Theology of Titus," *HorBT* 21 [1999]: 174).

[47] See the possible *inclusio* framed by references to "sound teaching" in 1:9 and 2:1.

[48] Note that in his letter the author contextualizes the Christian message by using language denoting the manifestation of God in Christ as a divine epiphany bringing salvation to people. Such benefactors were described in antiquity as kind and generous. See F. W. Danker, *Benefactor: Epigraphic Study of a Graeco-Roman and New Testament Semantic Field* (St. Louis: Clayton, 1982).

[49] F. M. Young, *The Theology of the Pastoral Letters*, NT Theology (Cambridge: Cambridge University Press, 1994), 95.

given in the greetings (3:15a), and the unusually succinct closing lacks reference to Jesus Christ (3:15b).[50]

The letter evinces a considerable diversity of literary forms, both on the micro and macro levels, including polemical sayings and proverbs (1:12); virtue (1:8; 2:2, 3, 5, 7, 12; 3:2) and vice lists (1:6–7, 10; 2:12; 3:3); a household code (2:2–10); and creedal formulas (2:11–14; 3:4–7), possibly including a (baptismal) hymn (3:4–7).[51] As a matter of fact, some argue that the body of the entire letter is essentially a household code.[52]

Structure

As in the case of the letters to Timothy, the various proposals regarding the structure of Titus reveal a certain amount of consensus as well as differences in the details. Towner proposes the following outline:

I. Opening Greeting (1:1–4)

II. Body of Letter (1:5–3:11)
  - A. Instructions to Titus (1:5–16)
  - B. Instructions for the Church (2:1–3:11)

III. Personal Notes and Instructions (3:12–14)

IV. Final Greetings and Benediction (3:15).[53]

Towner's outline is similar to Mounce's, who breaks 1:5–16 down further into 1:5–9 and 1:10–16 (as does Van Neste) but keeps 3:12–15 together as a unit.[54] Marshall divides 2:1–3:11 further into 2:1–15 and 3:1–11 while Van Neste divides the same unit into

[50] Thurston, "Theology of Titus," 175.

[51] Ibid., 173–74.

[52] See R. Brown, *An Introduction to the New Testament* (New York: Doubleday, 1997), 643–44, for differences between the household codes in Titus and those in Ephesians and Colossians.

[53] P. H. Towner, *The Letters to Timothy and Titus*, NICNT (Grand Rapids: Eerdmans, 2006), xii.

[54] W. D. Mounce, *The Pastoral Epistles*, WBC 46 (Dallas: Nelson, 2000), cxxxvi.

2:1–3:8 and 3:9–11.[55] The structural proposal set forth below differs only slightly from these commentators:[56]

I. Opening (1:1–4)

II. Occasion for Writing (1:5–16)
  A. The Need to Appoint Qualified Elders (1:5–9)
  B. The Cretan Opposition (1:10–16)

III. Instructions Concerning Different Groups in the Church (2:1–15)
  A. Introduction (2:1)
  B. Household Code (2:2–10)
    1. Older Men (2:2)
    2. Older and Young Women (2:3–5)
    3. Young Men (2:6–8)
    4. Slaves (2:9–10)
  C. The Manifestation of the Grace of God in Christ and the Expectation of Christ's Return (2:11–14)
  D. Conclusion (2:15)

IV. Instructions on Doing What Is Good in the Context of the General Culture (3:1–11)

---

[55] I. H. Marshall, *The Pastoral Epistles*, ICC (Edinburgh: T&T Clark, 1999), 24; R. Van Neste, *Cohesion and Structure in the Pastoral Epistles*, JSNTSup 280 (New York: T&T Clark, 2004), 250, 262–63. See also the detailed "cohesion shift analysis" in Van Neste, "Structure and Cohesion in Titus: Problems and Method," *BT* 53 (2002): 118–33; cf. D. J. Clark, "Discourse Structure in Titus," *BT* 53 (2002): 101–17; and C. J. Classen, "A Rhetorical Reading of the Epistle to Titus," in *The Rhetorical Analysis of Scripture: Essays from the 1995 London Conference*, ed. S. E. Porter and T. H. Olbricht, JSNTSup 146 (Sheffield: Sheffield Academic Press, 1997), 427–44, esp. 444.

[56] A. J. Köstenberger, "1–2 Timothy, Titus," in *Expositor's Bible Commentary*, vol. 12: *Ephesians–Philemon*, rev. ed. (Grand Rapids: Zondervan, 2005), 603; cf. Marshall, *Pastoral Epistles*, 24. P. S. Jeon, *To Exhort and Reprove: Audience Response to the Chiastic Structures of Paul's Letter to Titus* (Eugene, OR: Pickwick, 2012), posits a chiastic structure for Titus, but similar to Gibson's proposal for 1 Timothy, his macro-chiasm seems contrived. Clark, "Discourse Structure in Titus," proposes three main sections in the letter, 1:5–13a, 13b–3:8a, and 3:8b–11, which comes at the cost of breaking the link with the description of the opponents in 1:10–12 (cf. Marshall, "Pastoral Epistles in Recent Study," in *Entrusted with the Gospel: Paul's Theology in the Pastoral Epistles*, ed. A. J. Köstenberger and T. L. Wilder [Nashville: B&H Academic, 2010], 283).

A. On Keeping the Peace (3:1–2)
B. The Manifestation of God's Kindness and Love in Christ and Regeneration by the Spirit (3:3–8a)
C. On Dealing with Divisive Persons (3:8b–11)

V. Conclusion (3:12–15)
A. Final Instructions (3:12–14)
B. Closing (3:15)

Similar to 1 Timothy, Paul moves straight to the point by reminding Titus of the reason Paul left him on Crete: "To set right what was left undone and . . . to appoint elders in every town" (1:5; cf. 1 Tim 1:3–4). Also similar to 1 Timothy, Titus receives various instructions on how to correct the enemies of the gospel while staying above the fray. Christians are to "adorn the teaching of God our Savior in everything" (2:10) and to devote themselves to "good work" (3:1). In keeping with the personal nature of the letter, Paul concludes with final instructions and a closing greeting (3:12–15).[57]

[57] On the theology of Titus, see esp. R. F. Collins, "The Theology of the Epistle to Titus," *ETL* 76 (2000): 56–72; and Thurston, "Theology of Titus." For contemporary studies, see G. K. A. Bonnah, "The Responsibilities of Titus on the Island of Crete: A Replica for the Leadership of the Church in the Contemporary West African Society," in *Ein Meisterschüler: Titus und sein Brief: Michael Theobald zum* 60. *Geburtstag*, ed. Hans-Ulrich Weidemann, Wilfried Eisele (Stuttgart: Verlag Katholisches Bibelwerk, 2008), 212–31; and G. M. Wieland, "Grace Manifest: Missional Church in the Letter to Titus," *Stimulus* 13 (2005): 8–11. On Roman Crete, see Jane E. Francis and Anna Kouremenos, eds., *Roman Crete: New Perspectives* (Oxford; Philadelphia: Oxbow, 2016).

Commentary

I. Opening (1:1–4)

> [1]Paul, a servant of God and an apostle of Jesus Christ, for the faith of God's elect and their knowledge of the truth that leads to godliness, [2]in the hope of eternal life that God, who cannot lie, promised before time began. [3]In his own time he has revealed his word in the preaching with which I was entrusted by the command of God our Savior:
>
> [4]To Titus, my true son in our common faith.
>
> Grace and peace from God the Father and Christ Jesus our Savior.

1:1 In spite of its relative brevity, Paul's letter to Titus has the third-longest opening greeting of any of his letters. The opening bears considerable resemblance to Paul's first letter to Timothy. While Timothy's and Titus's circumstances were not identical, they appear to have been similar enough to warrant substantial overlap in Paul's instructions. As in his letters to Timothy, Paul calls himself "an apostle of Jesus Christ" (though "Christ Jesus" is reversed). He adds two things: (1) a self-identification as "servant of God" (δοῦλος θεοῦ); and (2) an extended statement regarding the purpose of his apostolic office.

The expression "servant of the Lord" is used in the OT for Moses (Deut 34:5; Josh 1:1, 13, 15) and Joshua (Josh 24:29; Judg 2:8; see also Isaiah's Servant Songs). Elsewhere, Paul calls himself a "servant of Christ" (Rom 1:1; Gal 1:10; Phil 1:1; cf. Col 4:12; cf. 1 Pet 2:16; 2 Pet 1:1; Jude 1).[58] While Paul also regarded himself as a servant of other believers (2 Cor 4:5), he ultimately saw himself as a servant of God the Father (v. 3) and of Christ. The phrase "apostle of Jesus Christ" then connects Paul's role as apostle, commissioned by Jesus Christ (Acts 9:15; cf. 1 Tim 2:7; 2 Tim 1:11), to his service of God.[59]

Paul goes on to describe the purpose of his ministry as follows: his apostleship is for "the faith of God's elect and their knowledge

---

[58] "Servant of God" is also found in Jas 1:1.

[59] Note that the connective used is δέ rather than *καί*, which indicates development if not a mild adversative (i.e., a servant, yet an apostle).

of the truth that leads to godliness" (see 2 Tim 2:10; cf. Rom 1:5). "God's elect" (ἐκλεκτῶν) connects NT believers with God's "chosen people" Israel (Rom 8:33; Col 3:12; cf. 1:10, 14; 3:8–9; see also 2:14) and points to God's sovereign work of choosing certain individuals for salvation (cf. Acts 13:48). The sequence moves from faith (πίστις) to knowledge of the truth (ἐπίγνωσιν ἀληθείας; 1 Tim 2:4; 2 Tim 2:25; 3:7; cf. Heb 10:26). Conversion is the pathway to growing in knowledge.[60] Yet this knowledge must not be an end in itself but rather should lead to godliness (εὐσέβεια; only here in Titus; see on 1 Tim 2:2), that is, mature Christian character.[61]

1:2–3 The CSB rendering "in the hope" suggests that believers' faith and knowledge rest on (ἐπί) the hope of eternal life (so also the NASB and NIV).[62] The preposition ἐπί can have that force (e.g., Rom 4:18; 8:20; 1 Cor 9:10). Alternatively it may convey purpose (Gal 5:13; Eph 2:10; 1 Thess 4:7; 2 Tim 2:14), in which case Paul would add here a third goal of his apostolic ministry: not only faith and knowledge but also hope, using ἐπί rather than κατά for stylistic variation. Either rendering coheres well with other NT and Pauline teaching (Rom 4:18; 8:24–25; 1 Cor 9:10; 13:13; Gal 5:5; 1 Thess 1:3; 5:8; Heb 11:1; 1 Pet 1:21).

This hope is for "eternal life" (3:7; 1 Tim 1:16; 6:12; cf. 1 Tim 4:8; 2 Tim 1:1), a Pauline (Rom 2:7; 5:21; 6:22–23; Gal 6:8; cf. Acts 13:46, 48) and Johannine concept (e.g., John 3:16; 17:3; 1 John 5:13) firmly embedded in Jewish thought and Jesus's teaching (Matt 19:16, 29; 25:46; etc.). Not only is this life eternal, but in its indestructibility and joy it shares the qualities of the life of God himself. It is anchored in the promise of "God, who cannot lie" (lit., "the not-lying God," ἀψευδής; cf. Rom 3:4; Heb 6:18; 1 John 1:10; 5:10; cf. Num 23:19; 1 Sam 15:29; contrast 1 Tim 1:10 and esp. v. 12),

---

[60] Cf. the dictum, "faith seeking understanding" (*credo ut intellegam*), attributed to Augustine and others.

[61] Godliness is also an important theme in 2 Peter: see 1:3–11; 3:11.

[62] R. W. Yarbrough, "Schlatter on the Pastorals: Mission in the Academy," in *New Testament Theology in Light of the Church's Mission: Essays in Honor of I. Howard Marshall*, ed. J. C. Laansma, G. R. Osborne, and R. F. Van Neste (Eugene, OR: Wipf & Stock, 2011), 310 draws attention to the fact that A. Schlatter made the point in conjunction with this passage that Christian hope rests in historical fact, something that had been widely denied in German scholarship since Kant.

which he made "before time began" (lit., "before eternal times," πρὸ χρόνων αἰωνίων; cf. 2 Tim 1:9; Rom 16:25).

While issued in eternity past (the CSB's "before time began" is to be preferred over the NASB's "long ages ago"), the "word" (λόγος) of God's promise was revealed (ἐφανέρωσεν; elsewhere in the LTT only in 1 Tim 3:16; 2 Tim 1:10; cf. Rom 3:21; Col 1:26; 4:4) in history in God's "due time" (lit., "his own times," pl. καιροῖς ἰδίοις; cf. 1 Tim 2:6; 6:15; Eph 1:10; see also Acts 1:7; Rom 5:6 [sg.]; Gal 4:4 [sg.]).[63] This occurred through Paul's "preaching" of the gospel (κήρυγμα; cf. 2 Tim 4:17; Paul as a herald, κῆρυξ: 1 Tim 2:7; 2 Tim 1:11), which he considered a sacred stewardship (passive of πιστεύω; cf. 1 Tim 1:11; 1 Thess 2:4; note the emphatic ἐγώ).

Paul's gospel proclamation, which was grounded in a special commissioning by the risen Christ (Acts 9:15–16), took place by the command (ἐπιταγή, 2:15; see on 1 Tim 1:1) of "God our Savior" (see on 1 Tim 1:1). Paul consistently rooted his preaching in divine revelation rather than viewing it merely as a human message. The gospel originated with God, not Paul. By identifying God, and later Jesus, as Savior, Paul establishes a theocentric, Christocentric, and soteriological framework for the entire letter (the pattern recurs in 2:10, 13 and 3:4, 6), where Jesus is presented as both God in his own right (2:13) and the fulfillment of God's saving promises.[64]

1:4 As he does Timothy, Paul addresses Titus as his "true son" in the faith (see on 1 Tim 1:1). The expression "our common faith" may be designed to convey unity between Paul as a Jew and Titus as a Gentile. Regarding Titus's earlier association with Paul, see Occasion, Chronology, and Background in the introduction to the Exposition of Titus. His current assignment finds him on the island of Crete (see The Opponents in the introduction to the Exposition of Titus above and v. 5 below). The opening concludes with the greeting "Grace and peace [mercy is omitted; compare the

---

[63] The "time" references in the LTT and Paul's other NT letters cohere to such an extent that Ramsay could speak of "the Pauline philosophy of history as expressed in the Pastoral Epistles." W. R. Ramsay, *Historical Commentary on the Pastoral Epistles*, repr. ed., ed. M. Wilson (Grand Rapids: Kregel, 1996), 137–41. I owe this reference to R. Yarbrough.

[64] L. T. Johnson, *Letters to Paul's Delegates: 1 Timothy, 2 Timothy, Titus*, The New Testament in Context (Valley Forge, PA: Trinity Press International, 1996), 218–19; Quinn, *Titus*, 304–15.

openings of 1 and 2 Timothy] from God the Father and Christ Jesus our Savior" (cf. v. 3; both Father and Son are involved in salvation). The greeting anticipates Paul's exhortations in chap. 2 (see below).

By way of biblical-theological summary, the opening sets the frame for the letter by referring to Paul's apostleship (v. 1) and Titus his "true son" in the faith (v. 4). In a surprisingly full and theologically rich introduction, Paul:

1. identifies the purpose of his apostolic office as the building up of believers' faith and their knowledge of the truth leading to godliness (v. 1);
2. sets the salvation-historical canvas from God's promise "before time began" (v. 2) to the revelation of his message in Paul's proclamation "in his own time" (v. 3); and,
3. characteristically for the LTT, refers to "God our Savior" (v. 3; §3.3).

In the God-centered letter opening, God is identified as: (1) the one Paul serves (v. 1); (2) the one who elected believers (v. 1); (3) the one who promised before time began (v. 2); (4) the one who revealed the gospel in Paul's proclamation (v. 3); and as (5) "God our Savior" (v. 4; §3.1).

II. Occasion for Writing (1:5–16)

The occasion for the letter to Titus consists in the need to appoint qualified elders in every town (1:5–9), set in the context of Titus's Cretan opposition (1:10–16). The list of qualifications for church leaders in Titus 1:6–9 is roughly equivalent to the similar list in 1 Timothy 3:1–7, though there's no list of qualifications for deacons (cf. 1 Tim 3:8–12).

Although there are similarities in content, the structure of Titus differs from that of the first letter to Timothy in that qualifications for church leaders are stipulated at the outset of the letter rather than at a later point, as an expansion of the injunction to Titus to appoint elders in every city. The stern denunciation in 1:10–16 is equivalent to the section on the false teachers in 1 Tim 1:6–11. The less personal nature of Titus may be indicated by the absence of a unit corresponding to 1 Tim 1:12–17.

A. The Need to Appoint Qualified Elders (1:5–9)

> [5]The reason I left you in Crete was to set right what was left undone and, as I directed you, to appoint elders in every town. [6]An elder must be blameless: the husband of one wife, with faithful children who are not accused of wildness or rebellion. [7]As an overseer of God's household, he must be blameless: not arrogant, not hot-tempered, not an excessive drinker, not a bully, not greedy for money, [8]but hospitable, loving what is good, sensible, righteous, holy, self-controlled,
> [9]holding to the faithful message as taught, so that he will be able both to encourage with sound teaching and to refute those who contradict it.

Relation to Surrounding Context

Following the lengthy letter opening (vv. 1–4), the present unit states the immediate occasion for writing including qualifications for elders/overseers. This is similar to Paul's first letter to Timothy (cf. 1 Tim 1:3–4). In both cases Paul instructs his apostolic delegates to ensure that the church in their respective location is properly led and protected from false teachers.

Structure

While most English versions start a new sentence in v. 6, in the original Greek vv. 5–6 form a unit (but note the switch from "elders" in the plural to the generic τίς, "anyone"). Verse 7 begins with the phrase, "For it is necessary" (δεῖ γάρ), which introduces an elaboration on the requirement for an overseer to be blameless by listing six negative (v. 7) and six positive terms (v. 8) plus a final broad requirement related to sound teaching (v. 9).

1:5 As was customary for ancient letters, Paul recalls his most recent contact with the addressee. He had left (ἀπέλιπον; cf. 2 Tim 4:13, 20) Titus in Crete, a Mediterranean island Paul had previously passed on his sea voyage to Rome (Acts 27:7–13). As Paul makes clear in v. 12 below, the dishonesty, immorality, and laziness of the inhabitants of Crete were proverbial. Paul's leaving Titus in Crete may imply that Paul himself was there with him, however briefly (presumably at some point after the events recorded in Acts), planting churches in various cities on the island (see discussion of Pauline Chronology in the Introduction).[65]

---

[65] Quarles, *Illustrated Life of Paul*, 257 conjectures, "Perhaps it was on his return voyage from Spain that Paul stopped at Crete for some extensive work on the island

Specifically, Paul had directed (διεταξάμην, a fairly strong term; cf. 1 Cor 7:17; 9:14; 11:34; 16:1; note also the emphatic ἐγώ and the fronted position of σοι) Titus to "set right" ("straighten out," ἐπιδιορθώσῃ) some important unfinished business: appointing (καταστήσῃς; cf. Rom 5:19) elders in every town (Paul's pattern; see Acts 14:21–23).[66] Not only is ἐπιδιορθόω used only here in the NT, the term is also extremely uncommon in pre-Christian Greek writings. Intriguingly, the sole written instance is found in a second-century BC inscription from Hierapytna, a Cretan city, with reference to the activity of a regional local administrator.[67] Perhaps Titus's role mirrors that of this Cretan official.[68]

Compared with Timothy's assignment, Titus's task may have been a bit easier—Crete was no Ephesus, even though, as mentioned, it was known for its many cities ever since Homer—and

together with Titus (Titus 1:5)." Alternatively, Paul visited Crete at some point subsequent to his release from his first Roman imprisonment regardless of any mission to Spain. Quarles suggests Paul's work on the island must have been "extensive" and "time-consuming" (p. 284n18), though Paul's mission to Spain (envisaged in Rom 15:24, 28) is uncertain.

In fact, 2 Timothy is silent about such a trip (noted by J. Herzer, "The Mission and the End of Paul Between Strategy and Reality: A Response to Rainer Riesner," in *The Last Years of Paul*, 424). The Muratorian Canon (ca. AD 180) knows of the tradition, as do the apocryphal *Acts of Peter* (3rd c.?; cf. 1 Clem. 5.5–7 [ca. AD 96], which refers to Paul's "having reached the farthest limits of the West," a possible reference to Spain). Later, Epiphanius (4th c.) writes that "Paul went to Hispania" (*Pan*. 27). The first detailed examination of the question is J. J. Spier, *Historia Critica de Hispanico Pauli Apostolo Itinere ad Rom. XV, 24 & 28* (Wittenberg: E. G. Eichsfeld, 1742), cited in Puig i Tàrrech, "Paul's Missionary Activity," 469.

See also the discussion in Quarles (*Illustrated Life of Paul*, 255–57); the highly skeptical stances taken by J. M. G. Barclay, "The Last Years of Paul: What Are the Issues?," in *Last Years of Paul*, 12–13; and Herzer, "Mission and the End of Paul," 430–31; and the much more confident affirmative assessments by E. J. Schnabel, *Early Christian Mission*, 2 vols. (Downers Grove: InterVarsity, 2004), 1271–83; Riesner, "Paul's Trial and End," 391–409 (see the conclusion on p. 409); and Puig i Tàrrech, "Paul's Missionary Activity," 469–506, esp. 484–506 ("the Tarragona hypothesis"; but see the critique by C. Karakolis in the same volume).

[66] On the phrase κατὰ πόλιν, see Wieland, "Roman Crete," 352.

[67] *CIG* 2555.9 = *Inscriptiones Creticae* 3, 49–52, cited in Wieland, "Roman Crete," 351.

[68] See Wieland, "Roman Crete," 351, with reference to the use of local terms in the book of Acts discussed in C. J. Hemer, *The Book of Acts in the Setting of Hellenistic History*, WUNT 49 (Tübingen: Mohr-Siebeck, 1989), esp. chaps. 4–5 and the excursus, "Names and Titles in Acts" (pp. 221–43).

while Timothy found himself in a situation where elders had already been appointed (some of whom, at least, seem to have been in need of rebuke, 1 Tim 5:19–20), Titus is charged with the fresh appointment of elders (perhaps Paul and Titus planted the churches following Paul's first Roman imprisonment, with no time left to establish leadership at that time). Nevertheless, Titus, like Timothy, faces the challenge of false teachers, "especially those from the circumcision party" (NIV: "those of the circumcision group," v. 10).

1:6–9 As mentioned, the list of qualifications for church leaders is roughly congruous with the similar list in 1 Tim 3:1–7 (though there's no equivalent to 1 Tim 3:8–12; §4.3.2). "If" (εἴ) at the beginning of v. 6 (untranslated in the CSB and NIV) may indicate that Titus is to appoint elders only when qualified persons are available. The synonymous use of "elders" (πρεσβυτέρους, v. 5) and "overseer" (ἐπίσκοπον, v. 7) suggests that these two terms refer to the same office (cf. 1 Tim 3:2; Acts 20:28).

The requirements for elders/overseers—in the NT always a plurality of men (cf. Acts 20:17, 28; Phil 1:1; 1 Tim 5:17)—resemble those stipulated in 1 Timothy 3 fairly closely (among the minor differences is that there's no warning against appointing new converts in Titus, perhaps because the churches have been planted only recently; cf. 1 Tim 3:6; 5:22). In both passages emphasis is placed on a candidate's character and proven track record of conducting his marriage and family. Doctrinal orthodoxy is important as well.

In both instances, pride of place goes to an elder being (1) "blameless" (ἀνέγκλητος; vv. 6–7; 1 Tim 3:2: "above reproach"), that is, a man of integrity. Second in both lists is the requirement of (2) marital faithfulness (cf. 1 Tim 3:2). Similar to 1 Timothy 3, which stipulates that an overseer's children must obey him with full respect (v. 4), Paul here states that the elder must be a man who has (3) "faithful children who are not accused of wildness [ἀσωτίας; cf. Eph 5:18; 1 Pet 4:4; Prov 28:7 LXX] or rebellion" (lit., "unsubjected," ἀνυπότακτα; cf. Heb 2:8).[69]

---

[69] In 1 Tim 3:4–5, 15, Paul enunciates a more explicit connection between a man's ability to oversee his natural household and his ability to oversee the affairs of God's household, the church. In Titus, the candidate for overseer is called "God's

"Faithful" (πιστά) probably means "obedient and submissive to their father's orders" (cf. 1 Tim 3:11; 2 Tim 2:2, 13; note the possible inclusion with v. 9: "faithful message").[70] While πίστος can also mean "believing" (and does so most frequently in the LTT), this meaning is less likely here in view of the context and the parallel 1 Tim 3:4, not to mention the theological difficulties of squaring such a requirement with the doctrine of election and the question of how new churches could have had enough men with converted children.[71]

The fact that the other two NT references to "wildness" relate to orgies of drunkenness and the other two references to "rebellion" relate to outright mutiny (v. 10; 1 Tim 1:9) suggests that Paul isn't referring to occasional disobedience but deep-seated rebellion against parental authority. Anyone who aspires to serving as an elder in the church, which involves exercising authority over the congregation, must properly exercise authority at home, with his children responding in obedience and submission.

After this Paul reiterates the term "blameless" (see v. 6 above) and goes on to list further qualifications for "God's administrator" or "manager" (CSB: "overseer of God's household," θεοῦ οἰκονόμος; cf. 1 Cor 4:1–2; 1 Pet 4:10) in rapid succession (see 1 Tim 3:5, 15).

Including the initial expression, Paul lists six negative terms:

- blameless (ἀνέγκλητον; not to have blame; = 1 Tim 3:10; cf. 1 Tim 3:2)
- not arrogant or overbearing (μὴ αὐθάδη; cf. 1 Tim 3:2: "temperate"; 2 Pet 2:10; Gen 49:3, 7; Prov 21:24 LXX)

administrator" (1:7). On the "household" motif in the LTT, see §4.1 in the biblical-theological exposition below.

[70] N. C. Grubbs, "The Truth about Elders and Their Children: Believing or Behaving in Titus 1:6?," *Faith & Mission* 22/2 (2005): 3–15, who notes that πίστος means "faithful" in the vast majority of instances (ca. 92 percent) in the LXX, Philo, Josephus, the NT, and the Church Fathers (see Table 1 on p. 8) as well as in close proximity in Titus 1:9, also drawing attention to the close parallel 1 Tim 3:4 ("hav[ing] his children under control with all dignity").

[71] The reading "faithful" rather than "believing" which is argued in the above commentary is adopted by the CSB ("with faithful children"; footnote: "Or *believing*"), contra the NIV ("whose children believe"; footnote: "Or *children are trustworthy*"), NASB ("having children who believe"), ESV ("his children are believers"; footnote: "Or *are faithful*"), and NLT ("his children must be believers").

- not hot-tempered (μὴ ὀργίλον; cf. 1 Tim 3:3: "not quarrelsome"; Pss 17:49; 21:19; 22:24; 29:22; cf. 20:3 LXX)
- not an excessive drinker (μὴ πάροινον; = 1 Tim 3:3; cf. 1 Tim 3:8; Eph 5:18; Prov 20:1; 21:17; 23:20, 31; 31:4)
- not a bully or violent (μὴ πλήκτην; = 1 Tim 3:3)
- not greedy for money (μὴ αἰσχροκερδῆ; cf. v. 11; = 1 Tim 3:8; cf. 1 Tim 3:3; 1 Pet 5:2; see also 1 Sam 12:3–5).

This list of six negative characteristics is followed by a list of six positive traits:

- hospitable (φιλόξενον; = 1 Tim 3:2; cf. 1 Pet 4:9; Heb 13:2; 3 John 8)
- loving what is good (φιλάγαθον; no exact equivalent in 1 Timothy 3; cf. Wis 7:22; Philo, *Moses* 2:9)
- sensible or self-controlled (σώφρονα = 1 Tim 3:2; cf. Titus 2:2, 5)[72]
- righteous or upright (δίκαιον; cf. 1 Tim 3:2: "respectable"; cf. Titus 2:12; Phil 4:8; Col 4:1)
- holy (ὅσιον; no exact equivalent in 1 Timothy 3; but see 1 Tim 2:8; cf. Heb 7:26)[73]
- self-controlled or disciplined (ἐγκρατῆ; cf. 1 Tim 3:2; see "sensible" above).[74]

Paul concludes the list with an overall doctrinal requirement (cf. 1 Tim 3:2, 9): an overseer must hold to (ἀντέχω, cf. 1 Thess 5:14; Matt 6:24; Luke 16:13) "the faithful message as taught."[75] This will enable him to encourage others with sound teaching (see 1 Tim 1:10; 2 Tim 4:3; cf. 1 Tim 6:3; 2 Tim 1:13; §2.1) and to refute (ἐλέγχειν; cf. v. 13; 2:15; 1 Tim 5:20; 2 Tim 4:2) those who contradict it (ἀντιλέγοντας; cf. 2:9; Rom 10:21). "Refute" is further elaborated upon in v. 13 below. Since the NT was still in process of being written, "faithful message" (πιστοῦ λόγου) probably refers to (oral) apostolic teaching and preaching (cf. 1 Tim 5:17).

---

[72] See the excursus in Marshall, *Pastoral Epistles*, 182–91 ("The σώφρων word-group and related concepts").

[73] Regarding the two attributes, "righteous" and "holy," one hastens to observe that only God is perfectly righteous and holy, though church leaders should reflect these character qualities by virtue of their spiritual union with Christ.

[74] This final requirement climaxes the list as ἐγκράτεια does in Gal 5:23.

[75] Note the possible connection with the five "trustworthy sayings" included in the LTT (§2.6).

The organization into two (or three) general qualifications (blameless, faithful husband, faithful children) followed by an equal number of negative and positive characteristics provides a helpful checklist. Arrogance, a bad temper, and dishonesty disqualify a man from serving as an elder. The absence of such flaws isn't enough, however. Integrity, personal holiness, and love for all that's good are essential for anyone who aspires to the office of overseer. A church leader needs to exhibit personal maturity, stability of character, a proven track record, and doctrinal soundness.

In terms of biblical-theological contribution, vv. 5–9 identify the occasion for Paul's letter: appointing elders in every town (v. 5), in keeping with the apostle's customary missiological and ecclesiological practice. Such an "overseer" is identified more specifically as "an overseer of God's household" (v. 7). As an extension of Paul's apostolic ministry, and the ministry of his delegates, such overseers must hold "to the faithful message as taught" so as to "be able both to encourage with sound teaching and to refute those who contradict it" (v. 9). This highlights the importance of Scripture, the gospel, and faithful church leaders who are firmly grounded in the apostolic message (§2).

Bridge

The list of qualifications for church leaders in the present unit is roughly comparable to that in 1 Timothy 3, though here Paul lists those requirements at the beginning rather than later in the letter. Clearly for Paul appointing qualified leaders was at the top of his priority list when it came to church planting. In this regard Paul led by example, mentoring numerous men in what has come to be known as the "Pauline circle." Jesus, too, devoted most of his time on earth to leadership training and development (the Twelve). Today we neglect giving proper attention to leadership issues in the church at our peril and the church's detriment. Not only will the church, God's household, not be properly led and managed, but it will also be rendered vulnerable to the influence of false teaching, worldliness, and a variety of countervailing cultural and social trends.

B. The Cretan Opposition (1:10–16)

[10]For there are many rebellious people, full of empty talk
and deception, especially those from the circumcision party.
[11]It is necessary to silence them; they are ruining entire households by teaching what they shouldn't in order to get money
dishonestly. [12]One of their very own prophets said,"Cretans
are always liars, evil beasts, lazy gluttons." [13]This testimony is
true. For this reason, rebuke them sharply, so that they may
be sound in the faith [14]and may not pay attention to Jewish
myths and the commands of people who reject the truth.

[15]To the pure, everything is pure, but to those who are defiled and unbelieving nothing is pure; in fact, both their mind
and conscience are defiled. [16]They claim to know God, but
they deny him by their works. They are detestable, disobedient, and unfit for any good work.

Relation to Surrounding Context

Following the "as" (more literally, "for," γάρ) in v. 7, there is now a second "for" in v. 10. The first instance is positive, while the second reason is negative: the preponderance of rebellious people, "especially those from the circumcision party" (v. 10). Similar to the reference to those who would be teachers of the law in 1 Tim 1:7, this reference points to the Jewish background of the false teachers. In the present instance their presence adds urgency to Paul's instructions to Titus to appoint qualified leaders who will adhere to sound teaching so they "will be able both to encourage with sound teaching and to refute those who contradict it" (v. 9).

Structure

The declaration in vv. 10–11 regarding the corrupt nature of the false teachers is supported in v. 12 by a quote from "one of their very own prophets." The veracity of the quote is affirmed in v. 13, plus the apostle issues a command that Titus rebuke these individuals sharply. Paul proceeds to provide a sort of excursus on the consequences of adhering to false teaching (cf. 1 Tim 1:8–11; note the chiastic structure of v. 15a). Ironically, their concern for external ritual purity exposes their lack of internal purity and falsifies their Christian confession. Unlike Timothy, who was "equipped for every good work" (2 Tim 3:17), these people will be "unfit for any good work" (v. 16; note the identical original word order).

1:10 The final qualification for elders in v. 9 leads Paul to elaborate on the reason (γάρ) elders must hold fast to sound teaching: the need to refute the "many rebellious people, full of empty talk and deception."[76] Specifically, Paul identifies "especially those from the circumcision party" (lit. "those of the circumcision"), for whom Titus—a Gentile—would be an obvious target (cf. Gal 2:1–3).[77] Similar to Peter and Jude, Paul pinpoints the root of the false teaching as rebellion against authority (on ἀνυπότακτοι, see v. 6 above). Such people's talk is empty (ματαιολόγοι; cf. 3:9; 1 Tim 1:6; 2 Pet 2:18),[78] and their minds are deceptive (φρεναπάται; cf. Gal 6:3). This kind of futility is characteristic of humanity set against God (Acts 14:15; Rom 1:21; Eph 4:17; cf. 1 Pet 1:18). Among the "many" are "those of the circumcision" (cf. Acts 10:45; 11:2; Rom 4:12; Gal 2:12; Eph 2:11; Phil 3:3). These divisive persons are embroiled in "foolish debates, genealogies, quarrels, and disputes about the law" that are "unprofitable and worthless" (Titus 3:9).

1:11 It's necessary (δεῖ; cf. v. 7) to silence those false teachers because they're "teaching what they shouldn't" (δεῖ; cf. ἑτεροδιδασκαλεῖν in 1 Tim 1:3; 6:3). The wording mirrors that concerning certain younger widows in 1 Tim 5:13 who are saying things

---

[76] "Many" (πολλοί) carries a negative connotation and is used rhetorically: cf. 1 Cor 16:9; 2 Cor 11:18; Phil 3:18; 2 Pet 2:2; 1 John 2:18; 4:1; 2 John 7. While it's hard to determine just how numerous the opponents were, Paul's words make clear that these aren't just a few isolated individuals. An interesting contrast is provided by James, who writes that "not many" should be teachers (Jas 3:1).

[77] On "especially," μάλιστα, see note at 1 Tim 5:17. Regarding the false teachers, see the discussion under "The Opponents" in the introduction to Titus above. The presence of a Jewish community on Crete is supported by ample first-century evidence: Josephus, *Ant.* 17.327; *J.W.* 2.103: "the Jews of Crete"; *Vita* 76 (mentioning that his third wife was a Jewess from a notable Cretan family); Philo, *Embassy* 282; cf. Acts 2:11; 1 Macc 15:23. See the discussion in Wieland, "Roman Crete," 352–53. In favor of viewing this as a reference to a Christian group, "the circumcision party," is S. Sandmel, "Myths, Genealogies, and Jewish Myths and the Writing of Gospels," *HUCA* 27 (1956): 201–11. Sandmel proposes that the objection pertains to canonical Gospels such as Matthew and Luke, both of which include genealogies and "myths" (accounts of Jesus), which would make John's Gospel more amenable to the author of the Pastorals since it avoids such "myths and genealogies." However, this theory itself seems to be of the type of conjecture characteristic of myths and genealogies!

[78] For a discussion of the possible connection with Greco-Roman moral philosophical texts, see P. G. R. de Villiers, "'Empty Talk' in 1 Timothy in the Light of Its Graeco-Roman Context," *Acta Patristica et Byzantina* 14 (2003): 136–55.

they "shouldn't say" (5:13). Paul's recommended course of action here is not patient dialogue or peaceful arbitration for the sake of maintaining unity in the church; these opponents must be "silenced" (ἐπιστομίζειν), that is, their public teaching activity must be stopped, presumably in form of church discipline or public rebuke.[79] Such "zero tolerance" is required because these individuals are "ruining entire households" (ἀνατρέπω; see 2 Tim 2:18; cf. John 2:15), plunging their devotees into spiritual turmoil by overturning their previous convictions through persuasive argument.[80]

This doesn't necessarily mean the content of the false teaching addressed in the LTT is precisely the same—the teachers are doubtless different. In the present instance Paul specifically identifies "those of the circumcision." Yet the effect of false teaching remains one and the same: those who are led astray are unsettled and thrust into turmoil. The same phenomenon is observable today in the case of those unfortunate individuals who fall under the spell of a cult, to the chagrin of family members and friends. Paul warns that such false teachers don't have the well-being of their converts in mind. Rather than genuinely caring for others, these teachers are motivated by a desire to "get money dishonestly" (αἰσχρός, cf. 1 Cor 11:6; 14:35; Eph 5:12; see also v. 7; 1 Tim 3:8; and 1 Pet 5:2).

1:12–14 Titus's opponents seem to be native Cretans because Paul, in support of his command to silence those false teachers, cites as true prophecy—tongue firmly in cheek—the Cretan self-witness in the form of a Greek hexameter that "Cretans are always liars, evil beasts, lazy gluttons."[81] As Polybius writes, "So

---

[79] Regarding Paul's stern advice that Timothy "silence" his opponents, cf. Demosthenes, *Halon.* 7.33: "stop the mouths of us, his opponents"; Plutarch, *Mor.* 155A. The word ἐπιστομίζειν is used only here in the NT and is not found in the LXX. Note that this injunction anticipates the "Liar Paradox" in vv. 12–14 and the references to speech later in the letter (see P. Gray, "The Liar Paradox and the Letter to Titus," *CBQ* 69 [2007]: 310–13 and the discussion at vv. 12–14 below).

[80] Not only were households the center of ancient education; believers gathered in households for worship (Rom 16:5; 1 Cor 16:19; Col 4:15; 1 Tim 3:15; Phlm 2). See further the discussion at §4 below.

[81] Poets were viewed as "inspired" in Graeco-Roman culture and thus occasionally called "prophets." The saying is commonly attributed to the Cretan philosophical logician Epimenides (6th c. BC; see L. T. Johnson, *Letters to Paul's Delegates*,

much in fact do sordid love of gain and lust for wealth prevail among them, that the Cretans are the only people in the world in whose eyes no gain is disgraceful" (*Hist.* 6.46.3). Cicero wrote that Cretans regarded highway robbery as honorable (*De Republica* 3.9.15).[82] Paul's quotation taps into the common Greek convention

---

227; first in Clement of Alexandria, *Strom.* 1.59.2 [but see further below]; Jerome, *Comm. Tit.* 7). The first part of the saying is taken up later by another poet named Callimachus (3rd c. BC), who denounces Cretans as liars for claiming to have the grave of Zeus on their island (*Hymn.* 1.8–9; see Johnson, *Letters to Paul's Delegates*, 228; first in Theodore of Mopsuestia II, 243 and Theodoret III, 701). The expression "play the Cretan" or "speak like a Cretan" (κρητίζω) was a synonym for lying (LSJ 995: "*play the Cretan*, i.e. *lie*"); Plutarch, *Aem.* 34.6; *Lys.* 20.2; cf. S. M. Baugh, "1 Timothy," in *1 & 2 Thessalonians, 1 & 2 Timothy, Titus*, by J. A. D. Weima and S. M. Baugh, *Zondervan Illustrated Bible Backgrounds Commentary*, ed. C. E. Arnold (Grand Rapids: Zondervan, 2001), 502–3, who cites an episode recounted in Polybius, and many a writer labeled the Cretans a race of liars (cf. Lucian, *Philops.* 3; *Tim.* 6; cf. Kidd, "Titus as *Apologia*," 191–97). G. M. Lee ("Epimenides in the Epistle to Titus [I 12]," *NovT* 22 [1980]: 96), citing G. L. Huxley (*Greek Epic Poetry from Eumelos to Panyassis* [London: Faber & Faber, 1969], 81–82), suggests the author of Titus may have seen the citation personally as part of a collection of oracles on the island. Alternatively, the author took the saying from a florilegium (anthology of well-known sayings arranged alphabetically or topically), perhaps focused on moral issues (P. G. R. de Villiers, "A Pauline Letter and a Pagan Prophet," *Acta Patristica et Byzantina* 11 [2000]: 80–81, with reference to Quinn, *Titus*, 108), most likely the *Theogony* or *Chresmoi* of Epimenides (R. Renehan, "Classical Greek Quotations in the New Testament," in *The Heritage of the Early Church*, ed. D. Neiman and M. A. Schatkin, Orientalia Christiana Analecta 195 [Rome: Pontificium Institutum Studiorum Orientalium, 1973], 35; cf. J. R. Harris, "The Cretans Are Always Liars," *Exp* 7 [1906]: 305–17; Harris, "St. Paul and Epimenides," *Exp* 15 [1915]: 29–35). See also E. Koskenniemi, "The Famous Liar and the Apostolic Truth," *FilNeot* 24 (2011): 59–70, who points out that Clement of Alexandria only mentions Epimenides but not his work; the first to attribute the work to Epimenides is Jerome. Thus it is possible, as Koskenniemi contends, that the proverb is of unknown origin (stage 1); that the proverb later was used to construct a logical paradox (stage 2); and that Epimenides, the famous philosopher from Crete, was linked to the paradox only at a later time (stage 3). If so, the verse would not necessarily prove Paul's direct knowledge of the writings of Epimenides.

[82] See already a third-century BC source: "Cretans are thieves from way back, pirates; they never think along legal lines" (*Anthologia Graeca* 7.654 (NW II/2, 1024; cited by Yarbrough, *1-2 Timothy, Titus*, commentary at Titus 1:12). On ancient stereotyping, both positive and negative, see Tertullian, *An.* 20: "And here local influences, too, must be taken into account. It has been said that dull and brutish persons are born at Thebes; and the most accomplished in wisdom and speech at Athens, where in the district of Colythus children speak—such is the precocity of their tongue—before they are a month old. . . . The subject of national

of the "liar paradox" (or simply "the Liar," ὁ ψευδόμενος) as though one were to ask: "Everything that I say is a lie: Is this true?"[83] Gray unpacks this famous antinomy of the ancient world as follows:

> If Cretans are always liars, and if the speaker . . . is a Cretan, then he must be a liar. And if he is a liar, then his "testimony" cannot be true. On the other hand, if it is true that Cretans are always liars, then his testimony corresponds to the facts of the case and he is not lying. But this would mean that not all Cretans are lying all the time, which would mean that the beginning premise was false. So if he is lying, then he is telling the truth (when he says that Cretans are always liars); and if he is telling the truth, then he must be lying (since he himself disproves the stated rule that Cretans are always liars).[84]

---

peculiarities has grown by this time into proverbial notoriety. Comic poets deride the Phrygians for their cowardice; Sallust reproaches the Moors for their levity, and the Dalmatians for their cruelty; even the apostle brands the Cretans as 'liars.'" M. Vogel, "Die Kreterpolemik des Titusbriefes und die Ethnographie," *ZNW* 101 (2010): 263, wrongly states that all of Tertullian's ethnic examples are negative.

[83] See esp. Gray, "Liar Paradox," 302–14 and the bibliography cited on p. 303n4. A. Thiselton notes that, "If the speaker is a liar, the proposition 'I am now (or always) lying' constitutes a paradox of formal logic" ("The Local Role of the Liar Paradox in Titus 1:12, 13," *BibInt* 2 [1994]: 222; cf. S. Heyworth, "Deceitful Crete: *Aeneid* 3.84 and the *Hymns* of Callimachus," *The Classical Quarterly* 43 [1993]: 255–57). Rather than throwing "to the winds the courtesy, gentleness, and self-control" he urges throughout the letter, Paul "employs the liar paradox . . . to demonstrate the self-defeating ineffectiveness of making truth-claims which are given the lie by conduct which fails to match them" (Thiselton, "Liar Paradox," 214). The saying is obviously a generalization and shouldn't be taken to imply that, without exception, all statements uttered by Cretans are false. See already Ovid, *Am.* 3.10.19: *Nec fingunt omnia Cretes* ("Nor do Cretans lie about all things"; cited in Vogel, "Kreterpolemik des Titusbriefes," 254n12).

[84] Gray, "Liar Paradox," 303. See also the excellent detailed treatment "The Liar Paradox in Greco-Roman Antiquity" in ibid., 304–7. Gray demonstrates that "it seems improbable that anyone with a modicum of Hellenistic education would be unfamiliar with the Liar Paradox or that it would appear where it does in Titus by pure coincidence" (p. 307). He says the "Liar Paradox" was a way for an "author to poke fun at himself . . . and, in the same breath, to castigate the native population (as well as to cast aspersions on the opponents who are exploiting their vicious natural proclivities). Given that the implied reader of the correspondence is a close associate, the implied author could reasonably expect him to get the joke" (p. 309).

Rather confusing, isn't it? Paul exploits the shock value of this startling saying by linking it to the false teachers (cf. 3:3; Matthew 23). By contrast the overseer must be blameless so he can refute those empty talkers who contradict sound teaching, professing to know God but denying him by their actions (vv. 7, 9–10, 16). Living a life of obedience and honest work, believers must "slander no one," "avoid fighting," "be kind, always showing gentleness to all people" (3:1–2), and "avoid foolish debates," which are unprofitable (3:9–10).[85] Paul goes on to characterize Titus's opponents in three ways.

First, their "prophetic testimony" (μαρτυρία, cf. 1 Tim 3:7) indirectly proves they're liars (ψεῦσται; cf. 1 Tim 1:10); they distort the truth of Paul's gospel and later are identified as "men who reject the truth" (v. 14). This stands in stark contrast with Paul's desire for the Cretan believers to attain to a full "knowledge of the truth that leads to godliness" (v. 1). Paradoxically, the only thing that's "true" (ἀληθής, the only occurrence in the LTT) about those impostors is the incriminating testimony regarding them by one of their own!

Second, they're "evil beasts" (κακὰ θηρία); they act "by instinct" like "irrational animals" (Jude 10) and are insensitive to the things of God. As the false teachers condemned by Jude, they "follow mere natural instincts and do not have the Spirit" (Jude 19 NIV). Since Crete appears to have been known for its *lack* of wild beasts, it's "possible that the line is mildly ironic in alluding to the wild and barbaric *behaviour* of Crete."[86]

Third, they're "lazy gluttons" (γαστέρες ἀργαί, lit. "idle stomachs," cf. 1 Tim 5:13; Jas 2:20). They're self-indulgent and idle (ἀ-ἔργος, lit. "without deeds"), their primary concern being their own welfare. As Paul says elsewhere, "Their god is their stomach, and their glory is in their shame. Their mind is set on earthly things" (Phil 3:19 NIV). Titus's Cretan opponents are worldly through and through and devoid of the Spirit—the diametrical opposite of spiritually transformed, Spirit-led, mature men of God.

In view of this sweeping denunciation of Cretans' spiritual sensitivity, Titus must rebuke (ἐλέγχω; see v. 9; 2:15; cf. 1 Tim 5:20; 2 Tim 4:2) them sharply (ἀποτόμως; cf. 2 Cor 13:10). The intended

[85] See Gray, ibid., 310–13, for a discussion of the "liar paradox" in the context of proper and improper speech in the LTT.

[86] Marshall, *Pastoral Epistles*, 201–2 (emphasis added).

results are: (1) they will be sound in the faith (ὑγιαίνω; cf. v. 9; 2:1, 2; see also 1 Tim 1:10; 6:3; 2 Tim 1:13; 4:3; §2.3); and (2) pay no attention to "Jewish myths and the commands of people [i.e., the false teachers—a possible allusion to Isa 29:13 cited in Matt 15:9 par. Mark 7:7; cf. Col 2:22] who reject [lit., "turn away from," ἀποστρέφω; cf. 2 Tim 1:15; 4:4] the truth."

"Jewish myths" probably harks back to "those from the circumcision party" in v. 10 (see The Opponents in the above introduction to Titus). There may also be an affinity with the individuals denounced in 1 Timothy who "want to be teachers of the law" (1 Tim 1:7) and "pay attention to myths and endless genealogies" (1 Tim 1:4). Still closer at hand is the reference later in Titus to "foolish debates, genealogies, quarrels, and disputes about the law" (Titus 3:9; cf. 1 Tim 4:3). It appears, therefore, that the false teachers were preoccupied with certain minutiae of the OT law.

The function of the quote in 1:12 within the context of the argument of vv. 10–16 and the letter as a whole is "to show that doctrinal error is accompanied by moral corruption" and to impress upon the reader(s) the truth that, conversely, "true doctrine is accompanied by sound living."[87] Rather than representing a "racist slur, polemic invective, or philosophical dilemma," the quote serves "to exhort Titus and the Christians on Crete to see the basis, nature, and effect of joining sound teaching with good practice."[88] To this end the saying "is used not so much to denounce

[87] R. Faber, "'Evil Beasts, Lazy Gluttons': A Neglected Theme in the Epistle to Titus," *WTJ* 67 (2005): 145, 141.

[88] Ibid., 145. Contra W. Stegemann, "Anti-Semitic and Racist Prejudices in Titus 1:10–16," in *Ethnicity and the Bible*, ed. M. G. Brett, BIS 19 (Leiden: Brill, 1996), employing a "sociology of deviance," who detects "xenophobic prejudices" (p. 273), even "crass prejudices towards Jews and Cretans" (p. 278), in the context of a "negative labelling" and stigmatization of a heterodox Christian group in the present passage. According to social deviance theory, a society reconfirms its identity by excluding others who are different from the group (p. 281). Stegemann argues that the letter of Titus represents a post-Pauline phase in which humanity was no longer divided into Jews and Gentiles and Israel's salvation-historical privilege is no longer in view (pp. 276–77). He alleges that the letter is "heterophobic" (p. 284), "anti-semitic and racist" (p. 285; see further the elaboration on both counts on pp. 293–94).

the false teachers without argument as to encourage the Christian community by means of positive and negative *exempla*."[89]

1:15–16 The just-mentioned "Jewish myths" were apparently ascetic, an amalgam of Jewish food laws and a dualistic rejection of the material realm (cf. Col 2:21–22). This is confirmed by the nature of Paul's refutation in the present passage. The chiasm in Paul's saying presents itself as follows:

> All things are *pure* to the *pure*.
> But to those who are corrupted
> and do not believe,
> nothing is *pure*.

Whether Paul coined the saying (cf. esp. Rom 14:20), the contrast surrounds the distinction between what (or who) is pure (καθαρός) and what (or who) is corrupt (μιαίνω), which in turn is traced back to unbelief.[90] Already in the LXX, the term μιαίνω is used for ritual defilement (Lev 5:3; 11:24; 18:24; 1 Macc 1:63). Elsewhere in the LTT Paul speaks of a "pure heart" (1 Tim 1:5; 2 Tim 2:22; cf. Matt 5:8) or conscience (1 Tim 3:9; 2 Tim 1:3). James combines elements of both expressions when he speaks of "pure and undefiled religion" (1:27).

---

[89] Faber, "Evil Beasts, Lazy Gluttons," 145. Faber also notes that the linking of sound faith and practice is characteristic of Paul's undisputed writings, most notably Romans. He refers to Marshall (*Pastoral Epistles*, 100), who observes that "the same building of practice upon doctrine which lies at the heart of Pauline thinking" is found in the LTT (remarkable since Marshall doesn't hold to the Pauline authorship of Titus) and O. Merk, "Glaube und Tat in den Pastoralbriefen," *ZNW* 66 (1975): 91–102, who similarly points to the congruence between the relationship of faith and practice in Paul's undisputed writings and the letter to Titus.

[90] See also de Villiers, "Pauline Letter and a Pagan Prophet," who includes a section on "Epimenides as purifier" (pp. 83–85) and points out, "Already in his own times, it was reported, Epimenides was so well known that he was fetched from Crete to purify Athens from a plague during the 46th Olympiad (596–593 B.C.E.)" (p. 83). De Villiers also points to the prominence of the purification motif in Titus (1:9, 13, 15; 2:1, 8, 14; 3:5), noting that "the net effect of these references is that they create two antithetical configurations of ideas: on the one hand there are the commands and myths of the opponents who are impure, despite their attempts to become pure. On the other hand, God is delineated as the Purifier of sinners in order to bring them to do good deeds as true believers" (p. 84). According to de Villiers, the opponents' teaching most likely represents an amalgam of Jewish and pagan elements.

Even more instructive is Rom 14:20, the only other Pauline reference to what is "pure," where the apostle writes that "all food is clean [πάντα καθαρά], but it is wrong for a person to eat anything that causes someone else to stumble" (NIV; cf. Luke 11:41; John 15:3; cf. 13:10–11). The word μιαίνω is used in the sense of ritual defilement in John 18:28. Jude says his opponents "pollute their own bodies" (CSB: "defile their flesh"), a reference to their immoral lifestyle (Jude 8; cf. 4). As this sketch of NT references to what is "pure" or "corrupt" illustrates, Paul's primary concern is most likely with a Jewish focus on ritual purity coupled with a pagan lack of concern for righteous living. This deadly combination is sure to subvert the grace of God.

"To the pure, everything is pure": if a person's heart and conscience are pure, their actions will likely be pure as well.[91] "But to those who are defiled and unbelieving nothing is pure": if a person's heart is corrupted by sin and unbelief, their actions will predictably follow suit (cf. Hag 2:13–14). As far as "those who are defiled" are concerned, their corruption has affected both their minds (νοῦς; cf. 1 Tim 6:5; 2 Tim 3:8) and their consciences (συνείδησις; cf. 1 Cor 1:10; 8:7). In 1 Tim 6:5 Paul speaks similarly of "people whose *minds* are depraved and deprived of the truth," and in 2 Tim 3:8 he denounces false teachers as "men who are *corrupt in mind* and worthless in regard to the faith."

While the false teachers "claim" or "profess" (ὁμολογέω; cf. 1 Tim 6:12) to know God (emphasized in the original)—which makes them all the more dangerous and deceptive—they deny him by their actions ("works," ἔργοις). Their lifestyle betrays their pious posturing. This was probably the result of a dualistic dichotomy between spirituality and morality (cf. 1 John 1:6, 8, 10), perhaps coupled with a kind of Jewish ritualism that claimed superior insight into the Mosaic law. Paul's verdict is categorical: such people are, first of all, "detestable" (βδελυκτοί; cf. Rom 2:22; Prov 17:15 LXX). The irony is apparent: by avoiding what they consider ritually detestable, the false teachers become detestable themselves. As Jesus said, "What people value highly is detestable in God's sight" (Luke 16:15 NIV).

---

[91] See the summary of A. Schlatter's discussion of this verse in Yarbrough, "Schlatter on the Pastorals," 311–12, with reference to Schlatter's commentary *Die Kirche der Griechen im Urteil des Paulus* (Stuttgart: Calwer, 1936), 186–89.

Second, the false teachers are "disobedient" (ἀπειθεῖς), like anyone who is outside of Christ (Titus 3:3). In fact, disobedience is at the core of a sinful, unregenerate nature that refuses to submit to authority (cf. Rom 1:30; 2 Tim 3:2). In the case of the false teachers, a certain irony rears its head once again: with all their attention to minutiae of the Mosaic law, they are still found to be "disobedient" because they mistakenly reject true Christianity (which centers on salvation by grace through faith) in favor of their own brand of religion.

Third and finally, their rebellion renders the false teachers and their adherents "unfit" or "disqualified" and unable to do anything of value (lit., "every good work," πᾶν ἔργον ἀγαθόν; contrast the identical phrase in 2 Tim 3:17), despite their claims to the contrary (ἀδόκιμοι; cf. 2 Tim 3:8; contrast 2 Tim 2:21; 3:17; see also 2 Cor 9:8). This doesn't mean an unsaved person can't do anything good, but that any good work starts properly with salvation in Christ, *followed* by good works (Eph 2:8–10). This is clear from the principle evoked by Paul in v. 15 and Paul's teaching elsewhere, such as 2 Cor 13:5–7, where being "disqualified" (ἀδόκιμοι) is tantamount to being outside of Christ. Even as an apostle, Paul made sure he continued in faithful service so as not to be disqualified (1 Cor 9:27).

On the whole, then, vv. 10–16 elaborate on vv. 5–9 by explaining why it's so important for Titus to appoint elders in every town. If the apostolic mission is to succeed, it's paramount that people knowledgeable in the Scriptures and thoroughly conversant with the true gospel are able to defend the faith against those who misrepresent it. In light of such grave challenges, elders must stand for the truth and exhibit godliness, particularly in as immoral an environment as ancient Crete. Likewise, church leaders today should be thoroughly equipped to explain the biblical gospel and defend it against misrepresentations. They should also live out the gospel in their own lives by example, which will be a powerful witness to its truthfulness in a spiritually dark and morally corrupt cultural environment.

Bridge

Paul and Timothy were engaged in a fierce battle for the heart and soul of the church on the island of Crete. Powerful spiritual forces sought to impede their progress in establishing a set of churches in that location, and resolute action was required both in terms of identifying suitable leadership and resisting those whose unregenerate mind-set and ungodly actions disqualified them from service. The history of God's people is in many ways a history of its leaders, whether godly or ungodly. On the positive side are Abraham, Moses, and David; on the negative side, many kings in the north and south of Israel during the days of the divided kingdom. The quest for godly leadership centers in Jesus the "Good Shepherd" who came to take the place of Israel's faithless shepherds and called his followers to be faithful undershepherds of God's flock, leaders who deeply and sacrificially care for the sheep rather than exploiting them for selfish gain.

III. Instructions Concerning Different Groups in the Church (2:1–15)

After a transitional verse (v. 1), Paul, in form of a household code, turns to specific instructions on what Titus should teach to specific groups in the church (vv. 2–10; cf. 1 Tim 5:1–2): older men (v. 2), older and young women (vv. 3–5), young men (vv. 6–8), and slaves (vv. 9–10). He follows these instructions by adducing two major incentives for faithful service: (1) the grace of God, which appeared in Christ (v. 11; cf. 3:4) and which also instructs (v. 12); and (2) the return of Christ (vv. 11–14). Paul concludes this section with the injunction to Titus: "Let no one disregard you" (v. 15).[92]

The instructions in vv. 2–10 bear some resemblance to the "house tables" in Col 3:18–4:1 and Eph 5:21–6:9. In the present case, however, the customary pattern of delineating responsibilities for interrelated pairs is replaced by a discussion of different age groups from older to younger, following a chiastic pattern:[93]

older men (v. 2)
    older women (v. 3)
    young women (vv. 4–5)
young men (vv. 6–8)

---

[92] For a helpful sketch of the structure of Titus 2 followed by an analysis of the chapter (despite his assumption of post-Pauline authorship), see A. Weiser, "Titus 2 als Gemeindeparänese," in *Neues Testament und Ethik. Für Rudolf Schnackenburg*, ed. H. Merklein (Freiburg: Herder, 1989), 400–401.

[93] See ibid., 409 (cf. 411).

Also, there's no instruction to masters or married men as such. Paul's instructions are congruent with Greco-Roman treatments of household management.[94]

Relation to Surrounding Context

After addressing the question of leadership (whether proper or improper) in chapter 1, Paul now turns to God's household at large and addresses the question of how to deal with different groups in the church.

Structure

The chapter begins with the customary "But you" (Σὺ δέ; cf., e.g., 2 Tim 3:10). The introductory word of instruction in v. 1 is followed by a household code in vv. 2–10 providing instructions on how to treat the various members of God's household, whether older men (v. 2), older and younger women (vv. 3–5), young men (vv. 6–8), or slaves (vv. 9–10). Note that, as mentioned above, vv. 2–8 form a chiasm. Then, in vv. 11–14 Paul elaborates (γάρ) on the phrase "God our Savior" in v. 10, specifying two major incentives for faithful service: the saving grace of God and the second coming of Christ. The unit closes with a brief conclusion mirroring the introduction (v. 15; note the repetition of λαλέω).

A. Introduction (2:1)

> [1] But you are to proclaim things consistent with sound teaching.

2:1 In the phrase "But you" (Σὺ δέ; cf. 1 Tim 6:11; 2 Tim 3:10, 14; 4:5), "you" is emphatic, and "but" establishes a contrast between the false teachers (referenced in 1:10–16) and Titus. Used in Titus only here and in v. 15 (and elsewhere in the LTT only in 1 Tim 5:13), λαλέω ("proclaim") serves to frame Paul's instructions in the entire chapter (see the similar use of διδάσκω in 1 Tim 6:2; cf. Eph 6:20; Col 4:4).[95] The expression continues the contrast between Paul's char-

[94] Johnson, *Letters to Paul's Delegates*, 232–33.

[95] Yarbrough notes that while chapter 1 only contained one formal imperative (1:13: "rebuke them sharply"), chapters 2–3 feature an additional thirteen imperatives (*1–2 Timothy, Titus*, introduction to Titus 2:1–10). Apart from three personal requests to Titus (3:12, 13, 15), the remaining ten imperatives canvass well Titus's pastoral duties: "proclaim" (2:1; the NIV's "teach" may be too restrictive), "encourage" (2:6), "proclaim," "encourage," "rebuke," "let no one disregard" (2:15),

acterization of Titus and the false teachers, who are "full of empty talk" and must be silenced because they're "teaching what they shouldn't" (1:10–11). Titus, however, must say what is "consistent with" (πρέπει; cf. 1 Tim 2:10; 1 Cor 11:13; Eph 5:3) sound teaching that promotes the spiritual health of its recipients.[96] The connection between true and false teaching is corroborated by church history, where heresy has frequently served as the impetus for the cultivation of sound, orthodox doctrine.

B. Household Code (2:2–10)

1. Older Men (2:2)

> Older men are to be self-controlled, worthy of respect, sensible, and sound in faith, love, and endurance.

2:2 Paul starts his specific instructions regarding dealing with people of different ages and genders with a brief set of remarks on old(er) men (§4.1.2.1).[97] The word for "older men" (πρεσβύτης) is rare in the NT, occurring only twice apart from the present passage (in Phlm 9 Paul, in prison in Rome and likely around sixty years of age, calls himself "an old man"; see also Luke 1:18 referring to Zechariah, father of John the Baptist).

Titus is to teach older men in the church to be (1) self-controlled or temperate (νηφαλίους), also required of elders and deacons (1 Tim 3:2, 11); (2) worthy of respect or respectable (σεμνούς), also required of both male and female deacons (1 Tim 3:8, 11); and (3) sensible or self-controlled (σώφρονας), also required of elders (1 Tim 3:2; Titus 1:8) and younger men (v. 6), older and younger women (vv. 4–5; cf. 1 Tim 2:9, 15), and all believers (v. 12); self-control is the most frequently mentioned characteristic in this chapter (vv. 2, 4, 5, 6, 12).

Finally, older men are (4) to be sound (see v. 1) in (a) faith, (b) love (see at 1 Tim 1:5), and (c) endurance (ὑπομονή; cf. 1 Tim 6:11;

"remind" (3:1), "avoid" (3:9), "reject" (3:10), "let our people also learn" (3:14). In addition, other tense forms may have imperatival force.

[96] In all of its occurrences in the LTT, "sound teaching" (ὑγιαινούσῃ διδασκαλίᾳ) contrasts with false teaching (cf. 1 Tim 1:10; 2 Tim 4:3; Titus 1:9).

[97] Given average life expectancy in the ancient world, this likely pertained to men of about fifty years of age or older. Cf. Marshall, *Pastoral Epistles*, 239.

2 Tim 3:10). Trust in God, love toward others, and hope-inspired perseverance (in keeping with the familiar Pauline triad "faith, love, and hope," with ὑπομονή replacing ἔλπις) are indications of serious, healthy Christian commitment and spiritual seasoning.

All the above-mentioned traits are marks of spiritual and personal maturity that should characterize an older person in the faith. Blessed is the church that has among its members such older men who can serve as models of dignity, respectability, and wisdom.

2. Older and Young Women (2:3–5)

> [3] In the same way, older women are to be reverent in behavior, not slanderers, not slaves to excessive drinking. They are to teach what is good, [4] so that they may encourage the young women to love their husbands and to love their children, [5] to be self-controlled, pure, workers at home, kind, and in submission to their husbands, so that God's word will not be slandered.

2:3 In the same way (ὡσαύτως; cf. 1 Tim 2:9; 3:8, 11; v. 6 below), Titus should challenge older women (πρεσβύτις) to exemplify the following four characteristics, the first and the last positive, the second and third couched in terms of avoiding negative traits (a chiasm; §4.1.2.2):

1. reverent (ἱεροπρεπεῖς) in behavior (*κατάστημα*, only here in the NT; not found in the LXX);
2. not slanderers (μὴ διαβόλους; cf. 2 Tim 3:3; also required of female deacons: 1 Tim 3:11);
3. not slaves to excessive drinking (μὴ οἴνῳ πολλῷ δεδουλωμένας, a stronger term than in the parallel in 1 Timothy; lit. "bound" or "enslaved," passive of δουλόω; cf. 2 Pet 2:19; Rom 6:18, 22; 1 Cor 7:15; Gal 4:3), required also of elders and deacons (1 Tim 3:3, 8);
4. teach what is good (lit., "teachers of the good." *καλοδιδασκάλους*; apparently a Pauline coinage).

Older women who avoid slander and excessive drinking are sure to stand out in their immoral Cretan context. The restricted movement often resulting from advanced age makes older people (then as today) particularly susceptible to fill their days with pastimes such as gossiping or drinking. This calls for godliness and self-control.

2:4–5 "So that" introduces a purpose clause (ἵνα). Older women are to cultivate virtues, not as ends in themselves but for the purpose of encouraging (σωφρονίζω, only here in the NT) young (CSB, NASB; better than "younger," NIV) women (νέας; cf. 1 Tim 5:2).[98] Interestingly, Titus isn't told to teach young women directly. It's worth noting that growth in godly character shouldn't be pursued in isolation from service to others in the context of healthy relationships in the church. Otherwise, such spirituality can easily foster pride and a judgmental attitude toward others who are perceived as less spiritual.

In ancient Crete, where men's halls served as the center of male community life, the lives of women revolved around the household.[99] While there's nothing uniquely Cretan about older women instructing young women in their proper domestic role, it's unusual that the role of the older women is cast in almost priestly terms (ἱεροπρεπεῖς, v. 3).[100] There's evidence for young women performing votive offerings in the temple of Athena in Gortyn during a period of service that may have been part of their education. It's possible that Paul frames the role of Christian women within the local Cretan context, suggesting that fulfilling their domestic and familial calling is their proper service offered to God.

In fact, it's impossible to train others in qualities a person doesn't possess herself. There's a dire need in the church today

---

[98] See the excursus in Marshall, *Pastoral Epistles*, 182–91 ("The σώφρων Word-Group and Related Concepts"), esp. the discussion of the occurrences in Titus 2 on p. 184. Marshall notes that ten of sixteen occurrences in the NT are found in the LTT, which makes this word group "both characteristic and distinctive in the PE" (p. 182). On p. 247, Marshall notes the role of personal example in inculcating Christian values.

English translations struggle as to how to render the rare verb σωφρονίζω in v. 4. Based on related terms such as σώφρων (vv. 2, 5; cf. 1:8), the sense seems to be to instill self-control and sensibility in young women (the suffix -ίζω may convey a causative notion). The NIV's, ESV's, and NLT's "train" evokes unwarranted associations with other kinds of training (e.g., of pets). The CSB's, NASB's, and NRSV's "encourage" is better. Perhaps best is the CEB's "mentor."

[99] The insights in this paragraph are indebted to Wieland, "Roman Crete," 344, who also refers to Barclay, "'There Is Neither Old Nor Young?'"; and M. Prent, *Cretan Sanctuaries and Cults: Continuity and Change from Late Minoan IIIC to the Archaic Period*, RGRW 154 (Leiden: Brill, 2005), 636.

[100] See Quinn, *Titus*, 134, who speaks of "terminology practically unexampled [*sic*] in this correspondence or in biblical Greek" in Titus 2:3–4a.

for older women who are godly and obey the biblical directive to train young women in the faith. Many young women long for more mature women to take them under their wings and to teach them how to live the Christian life, especially since many lack godly role models in their own families. Notably, such mentoring (σωφρονίζω; see on v. 2 above)—involving private rather than public instruction—should focus on the domestic sphere.

On the whole, requirements for Christian wives don't differ significantly from the customary ideal of the day.[101] Paul groups instructions for young women in three pairs, starting and ending with their relationship to their husbands.

First, they're to be certain kinds of wives and mothers:

- love their husbands (lit., "husband-lovers," φιλάνδρους)[102] and
- love their children (lit., "children-lovers," φιλοτέκνους).

Second, they're to cultivate Christian character:

- self-controlled (σώφρονας; see at v. 2 above) and
- pure (ἁγνάς; cf. 1 Tim 5:22; 2 Cor 11:2; Phil 4:8; 1 Pet 3:2; 1 John 3:3).[103]

Third, they're to be engaged in activities with the right kind of attitude:

- homemakers (lit., "busy at home," οἰκουργούς; cf. 1 Tim 5:14: οἰκοδεσποτεῖν)[104] and

---

[101] H. Baltensweiler, *Die Ehe im Neuen Testament: Exegetische Untersuchungen über Ehe, Ehelosigkeit und Ehescheidung* (Zurich: Zwingli, 1967), 242 (see the discussion on pp. 241–42).

[102] S. M. Baugh, "A Foreign World: Ephesus in the First Century," in *Women in the Church*, 3rd ed., 47n51, cites a grave inscription from Prusias-on-Hypius (Bithynia), where "Aur(elia) Chrestiniane Rufina, known as Himeris, was the modest and husband-honoring wife [ἡ σώφρων καὶ φίλανδρος γυνή] of the silversmith Aur(elius) Socratianos Pasikrates, she lived a decorous [κοσμίως] life for 31 years" (*IvPrusias* 89). *Die Inschriften von Priene*, ed. C. J. Fredrich and F. Hiller von Gaertringen (Berlin: Reimer, 1906). Baugh notes that the editor of these inscriptions calls the phrase "a typical characterization of a wife" and supplies further examples. On marriage in the ancient world, see K. M. Campbell, ed., *Marriage and Family in the Biblical World* (Downers Grove: InterVarsity, 2003).

[103] Cf. Baltensweiler, *Ehe im Neuen Testament*, 242.

[104] The essence of the phrase is that wives are managing their household well. The textual variant οἰκουρούς, "keepers at home," is secondary (see S. N. Helton, "Titus 2:5: Must Women Stay at Home?," in *Essays on Women in Earliest Christianity*, vol 1,

- kind (lit., "good," ἀγαθάς; cf. 1 Thess 5:15; Eph 4:28).

Finally, they're to be:

- subject in submission to their husbands (ὑποτασσομένας τοῖς ἰδίοις ἀνδράσιν; cf. Eph 5:24; Col 3:18; 1 Pet 3:1, 5).

The desired result of wifely submission and diligent household management is that no one will slander (βλασφημέω) God's Word (cf. Rom 9:6; 1 Thess 2:13).[105] The same kind of reasoning is found in vv. 8 and 10 (cf. 1 Tim 6:1). While verbal proclamation is essential, believers' lives play a vital role in the church's witness.

Several general and practical observations flowing from Paul's instructions regarding women in vv. 3–5 may be noted.

1. The present passage complements other NT instructions for wives. While their duty to love isn't mentioned in the parallels in Ephesians, Colossians, and 1 Peter, Paul here urges women to love their husbands and children.
2. While marriages should be strong, young women need other significant relationships. They should be mentored by older women who possess the life experience, skill, and wisdom that come from years of practicing Christian virtues.
3. Love of husbands is listed before love of children. The two go together and are at the heart of a woman's calling. Both qualities were admired in wives in Jewish and Greco-Roman culture.
4. Wives are called both to love and to submit to their husbands. Their submission is not to be grudging or perfunctory but loving. Of course, we know from passages elsewhere that husbands, in turn, are called to love their wives (e.g., Eph 5:25).

---

ed. C. D. Osburn [Eugene, OR: Wipf & Stock, 1993]," 369–72). "Self-controlled" and "workers at home" are juxtaposed in Cassius Dio, *Hist.* 36.3 (second century BC): "For is there anything better than a wife who is *chaste, domestic*, a good housekeeper, a rearer of children . . . ?" Helton ("Titus 2:5," 367–76) contends that the burden of this passage is not to urge women to stay at home but rather "to supervise their households with discretion and industry" (p. 376).

[105] The thesis of A. Padgett, "The Pauline Rationale for Submission: Biblical Feminism and the ἵνα Clauses of Titus 2:1–10," *EvQ* 59 (1987): 39–52, that Paul, by calling on wives to submit to their husbands, merely accommodated himself to surrounding cultural norms, unduly presupposes that Paul held an egalitarian view of gender roles.

5. Women need self-control in dealing with their husband and children. As wives, they should exhibit sexual fidelity; as mothers, they should maintain a loving disposition toward their children rather than grow irritable, viewing them as blessings from God rather than a burden.
6. Women's hearts should be pure and their attitude toward others in the home kind rather than adversarial, antagonistic, or hostile. Such strength of character, virtue, and dignity can be a wonderful female and motherly trait.
7. To a day when devotion to married life and childrearing is often disparaged (in contrast to antiquity where this was a highly lauded virtue), Paul speaks of the blessing God has in store for women who focus on their God-given calling focused on family and the home.

3. Young Men (2:6–8)

> [6] In the same way, encourage the young men to be self-controlled [7] in everything. Make yourself an example of good works with integrity and dignity in your teaching. [8] Your message is to be sound beyond reproach, so that any opponent will be ashamed, because he doesn't have anything bad to say about us.

2:6 "In the same way" once again marks the transition to a different group in the church (cf. v. 3 above). Paul's instructions concerning this group—perhaps more direct than his previous remarks (note the use of the imperative)—are to the point: Titus should encourage (παρακάλεω; cf. 1:9; v. 15) young men (νεωτέρους, the male equivalent to νέας, "young women," in v. 4 above; cf. 1 Tim 5:1; Acts 5:6) to be self-controlled (σωφρονεῖν; see at v. 2 above) in everything (§4.1.2.1).[106]

In short, Titus is to call young men (presumably ca. twenty to thirty years of age; *TDNT* 4:897)—who might tend to lack restraint—to a level-headed, disciplined life. This self-mastery involves "control of temper and tongue, of ambition and . . . bodily appetites."[107]

---

[106] "In everything" probably modifies "self-control" rather than the following phrase (CSB; contra NIV).

[107] J. R. W. Stott, *Guard the Truth: The Message of 1 Timothy & Titus*, The Bible Speaks Today (Downers Grove: InterVarsity, 1996), 189.

The critical importance of self-control is underscored by the fact that "self-control in everything" makes up the entirety of Paul's instruction to young men in this passage (2 Tim 1:7; cf. 1 Tim 4:7–8, 12; 2 Tim 2:22).

2:7–8 Like Paul (Phil 3:17; cf. 1 Cor 4:16; 11:1; 2 Thess 3:7, 9) and Timothy (1 Tim 4:12), Titus should lead by example (τύπος; cf. 1 Pet 5:3) in good works (cf. 2 Tim 2:21; 3:17). This stands in sharp contrast with the false teachers who deny God (whom they claim to worship) by their works and are disqualified from any good work (1:16). With church leaders setting the example, the entire congregation should follow suit and become a people "eager to do good works" (v. 14).

On the basis of an exemplary life, Titus should exhibit the following virtues in his teaching: (1) integrity (ἀφθορία, "incorruption"; cf. Esth 2:3 LXX); (2) dignity (σεμνότης; cf. v. 2; 1 Tim 2:2; 3:4, 8, 11); and (3) soundness in delivering the Christian message (see vv. 1 and 2 above) in a way that is "beyond reproach" (ἀκατάγνωστος), exhibiting blamelessness with regard to his teaching and preaching. Similarly, Greek oratory required of public speakers *ethos* (character), *pathos* (passion), and *logos* (rhetorical skill; Aristotle, *On Rhetoric*).

As a result, Titus's opponent (cf. 1:9–16; cf. Mark 15:39) will be ashamed (ἐντρέπω) because he doesn't have anything bad (φαῦλος; cf. Rom 9:11; 2 Cor 5:10; Jas 3:16) to say about him or his associates. Charges against Christians are frequently attested in first and second-century AD literature (see, e.g., Tacitus, *Ann.* 15.44; Pliny, *Ep.* 10.96).[108] Earlier the apostle had written along similar lines that the Thessalonians must not associate with anyone who doesn't obey the instructions contained in his letter, "so that he may be ashamed" (2 Thess 3:14).

4. Slaves (2:9–10)

[9] Slaves are to submit to their masters in everything, and to be well-pleasing, not talking back [10] or stealing, but demonstrating utter faithfulness, so that they may adorn the teaching of God our Savior in everything.

[108] Dickson, *Mission-Commitment in Ancient Judaism and in the Pauline Communities*, 278–82, speaks of this as an "ethical apologetic."

2:9–10 Paul now moves from issuing instructions to various age groups in the church to dealing with slaves (cf. 1 Tim 6:1–2; Eph 6:5–8; Col 3:22–25; §4.1.2.4). Rather than seeking to overturn the entire socioeconomic system in his day (though see 1 Cor 7:21–22; Phlm 15–21), Paul tells Titus to teach slaves:[109]

1. to submit (ὑποτάσσω; see at v. 5) to their masters in everything (see the similar phrase "self-controlled in everything" in vv. 6–7 above);
2. to be well pleasing to them (εὐαρέστος, a term used in the NT regularly for believers pleasing their Lord; cf. Rom 12:1–2; 14:18; 2 Cor 5:9; Eph 5:10; Phil 4:18; Col 3:20; Heb 12:28; 13:21);
3. not to talk back to them (ἀντιλέγω; cf. 1:9; Rom 10:21); and
4. not to steal from them (νοσφίζω; cf. Acts 5:2–3; cf. Josh 7:1 LXX), but
5. to demonstrate utter faithfulness (lit., "showing all good faithfulness").

"God our Savior" is a familiar phrase in the LTT (cf. 1:3; 3:4; 1 Tim 1:1; 2:3; 4:10; §3.3). As in vv. 5 and 8, Paul places proper Christian conduct within the larger framework of believers' witness to the surrounding world: "so that they may adorn the teaching [διδασκαλία; cf. 1:9; 2:1, 7] of God our Savior in everything" (cf. 1 Tim 6:1; on κοσμέω, "make attractive," cf. 1 Pet 3:5). Remarkably, this includes even Christian slaves.

To sum up, the teaching of vv. 1–10 spells out in some detail the roles and responsibilities Titus is to promote with regard to the various members of God's household, whether older men (v. 2), older and young women (vv. 3–5), or young men (v. 6). Titus himself is to set the example (vv. 7–8).[110] The set of guidelines for proper conduct in God's household is completed by instructions for slaves (vv. 9–10).

---

[109] See A. du Toit, "Sensitivity towards the Reaction of Outsiders as Ethical Motivation in Early Christian Paraenesis," in *Sensitivity towards Outsiders*, ed. J. Kok, T. Nicklas, D. T. Roth, and C. M. Hays, WUNT 2/364 (Tübingen: Mohr-Siebeck, 2014), 350–51.

[110] Note the literary *inclusio* marked by terms translated as "sound" in vv. 1 (ὑγιαινούσῃ) and 8 (ὑγιῆ).

The common denominator in Paul's instructions is believers' witness to the gospel in their unbelieving environment:

- "so that God's word will not be slandered" (v. 5);
- "so that the opponent will be ashamed, because he doesn't have anything bad to say about us" (v. 8); and
- "so that they may adorn the teaching of God our Savior in everything" (v. 10).

While this series of references to the surrounding culture doesn't indicate that the instructions regarding proper conduct in God's household are merely culturally relative, it does show that the first Christians were sensitive to the reception of the Christian message in the larger world around them. These references also demonstrate that believers were determined not to put any unnecessary stumbling blocks into people's paths that kept them from responding to the gospel.

C. The Manifestation of the Grace of God in Christ and the Expectation of Christ's Return (2:11–14)

> [11] For the grace of God has appeared, bringing salvation for all people, [12] instructing us to deny godlessness and worldly lusts and to live in a sensible, righteous, and godly way in the present age, [13] while we wait for the blessed hope, the appearing of the glory of our great God and Savior, Jesus Christ. [14] He gave himself for us to redeem us from all lawlessness and to cleanse for himself a people for his own possession, eager to do good works.

2:11–12 Paul now elaborates (γάρ) on the phrase "God our Savior" in v. 10, specifying two major incentives for faithful service: (1) the saving grace of God (vv. 11–12); and (2) the second coming of Christ (v. 13; see further 3:3–8 below). Apart from 3:7, the term "grace" (χάρις) is as uncommon in the LTT (cf. 1 Tim 1:14; 2 Tim 1:9; and 2:1) as it is common in Paul's other writings (e.g., Rom 6:15; 1 Cor 1:4; 3:10; 2 Cor 6:1). While this is intriguing, it need not imply different authorship.[111] This is the only instance of σωτήριος, "saving," in the NT.

Paul here affirms that God's saving grace in Christ has appeared to all (kinds of) people at Jesus's first coming. "Appeared" (ἐπιφαίνω; see esp. 3:4; see also Luke 1:79; cf. Isa 9:2) is emphasized in the original. "All (kinds of) people" includes slaves and "us" in vv. 8, 12, 14 (cf. 1 Tim 4:10). Rather than giving believers license to unbridled liberty, God's saving grace in Christ instructs them (παιδεύω; cf. 1 Tim 1:10; 2 Tim 2:25) in at least two ways, the first negative and the second positive:

1. to say "no" (ἀρνέομαι; unlike the false teachers who deny God by their actions, 1:16; cf. 2 Tim 3:5; see also 2:12–13) to ungodliness (ἀσέβεια; see 2 Tim 2:16; cf. Rom 1:18; 11:26) and to worldly passions (ἐπιθυμία; cf. 3:3; 1 Tim 6:9; 2 Tim 2:22; 3:6; 4:3); and
2. to live in a (a) sensible (σωφρόνως, only here in the NT; see cognates in 1:18; 2:2, 4, 5, 6 above), (b) righteous (δικαίως; see esp. 1 Thess 2:10), and (c) godly way (εὐσεβῶς; cf. 2 Tim 3:12; see also 1:1) in the present age (ἐν τῷ νῦν αἰῶνι, lit., "in the now-age," the same phrase as in 1 Tim 6:17).

The pattern of negative instruction followed by positive exhortation is frequent in Paul's writings (e.g., Rom 6:5–14; Gal 5:16–26; Col 3:8–14). The triad "sensible, righteous, and godly" contextualizes Christian teaching in a Greek environment where these kinds of virtues were highly esteemed.

Development of virtue as the purpose and goal of education (παιδεία) was a common notion in Greek thought.[112] The difference here is that, in Christian teaching, it is not human self-effort but divine grace that enables—even requires—virtuous and godly living.[113]

---

[111] It's difficult to determine what accounts for the paucity of references to grace in the LTT. Perhaps one of the reasons is that the focus is more on establishing churches by appointing or restoring proper leadership and less on setting forth the essentials of the gospel message itself as in some of the earlier letters.

[112] See references in Johnson, *Letters to Paul's Delegates*, 241.

[113] On grace as instructor (παιδαγωγός) in Gal 3:24–25 and Titus 2:11–12, see W. Eisele, "Vom 'Zuchtmeister Gesetz' zur 'erziehenden Gnade' (Gal 3,24f.; Tit 2,11f.): Religiöse Erziehung in der Paulustradition," *BZ* 56 (2012): 65–84.

While not advocating asceticism (cf. 1 Tim 4:3–5, 7–8; see also Col 2:16–23), Paul's call to self-denial (properly understood) and a commitment to a godly, disciplined life is in keeping with Jesus's teaching that his followers must deny themselves, take up their cross, and follow him (e.g., Mark 8:34 par.).

2:13–14 Paul concludes his series of exhortations with a doxology, aiming to motivate believers by setting their present efforts into eternal perspective. He does this by evoking their active expectation (προσδέχομαι, "wait")[114] of the "blessed hope" (ἐλπίς; cf. Col 1:5; Gal 5:5; see also 1:2; 3:7), "the appearing of the glory" (i.e., glorious appearance, ἐπιφάνεια; cf. ἐπιφαίνω in v. 11) of "our great God and Savior, Jesus Christ" (cf. 1 Thess 4:13–18; §3.3).[115] Since "blessed hope" and "glorious appearance" are governed by the same article, they refer to the same event. While Jesus was lowly at his first coming, the second coming will be glorious.

The final phrase—correctly rendered in translations such as CSB and NIV as referring to one person, Jesus Christ—represents a remarkably high Christological confession.[116] While Greeks were freely affixing the epithets "savior" and "god" to human benefactors and rulers, Romans were a bit slower to deify emperors (though this became more common over time). Jews such as Paul, in view of their strong monotheism, would never have done so

---

[114] In English, "wait" may suggest a passive disposition, as in waiting for a ride. In NT terms, however, the term frequently denotes an active expectation, desire, or longing that causes people to live their lives in accordance with future realities (see, e.g., Luke 23:51; Acts 24:15; Jude 21; cf. 2 Pet 3:12).

[115] B. W. Winter, *Divine Honours for the Caesars: The First Christians' Responses* (Grand Rapids: Eerdmans, 2015), 72, cites Roman parallels for the phrase "great God," such as an AD 37 inscription referring to Gaius [i.e. Caligula] as ruling with the "great gods" (τηλικούτων θεῶν; *Inscriptiones Graecae ad Res Romanas Pertinentes* 4, 145, line 9) and a second-century AD Delphic inscription referring to Hadrian as a "great god" (θεός τηλικοῦτος; *Fouilles de Delphes* 3.4.3).

[116] R. M. Bowman Jr., "Jesus Christ, God Manifest: Titus 2:13 Revisited," *JETS* 51 (2008): 733–52 (including a critique of the work of G. Fee); M. J. Harris, "Titus 2:13 and the Deity of Christ," in *Pauline Studies*, ed. D. A. Hagner and M. J. Harris (Grand Rapids: Eerdmans, 1980), 262–77; Harris, *Jesus as God: The New Testament Use of* Theos *in Reference to Jesus* (Grand Rapids: Baker, 1992), 173–85, 301–13; Knight, *Pastoral Epistles*, 321–26; Marshall, *Pastoral Epistles*, 277–82; Mounce, *Pastoral Epistles*, 426–31; and Wallace, *Greek Grammar Beyond the Basics*, 276.

apart from divine revelation.[117] This makes the reference to Jesus as "our great God and Savior" in the present passage all the more remarkable.

The same Savior whose return we await as our "blessed hope" "gave himself for us" at his first coming (echoing Mark 10:45 par. Matt 20:28; cf. 1 Tim 2:6; Gal 1:4; 2:20; Eph 5:2, 25). By using the related terms "appeared" and "appearing" (ἐπιφαίνω, ἐπιφάνεια) for Jesus's first and second coming, Paul stresses that the reality of Jesus's gracious incarnation (v. 11) is ground for our hope in his glorious return (v. 13). In Jesus's first coming his purpose was twofold:

1. to redeem us (λυτρόω; adapting Ps 130:8 and Ezek 37:23 LXX; cf. 1 Pet 1:18; Luke 24:21; see v. 12; see also ἀπολύτρωσις in Rom 3:24; 8:23; 1 Cor 1:30) from all lawlessness (ἀνομία; cf. Rom 4:7; 6:19 [2x]; 2 Cor 6:14; 2 Thess 2:3, 7); and
2. to purify or cleanse for himself (καθαρίζω; cf. 2 Cor 7:1; Eph 5:26) a people for his own possession (λαὸν περιούσιον; Exod 19:5; cf. Deut 4:20; 7:6; 14:2; 26:18; 1 Pet 2:9; see also the reference to "God's elect" in Titus 1:1), eager (ζηλωτής; Deut 26:18; cf. 1 Pet 3:13; Gal 4:18; Eph 2:10) to do good works (§5.2).[118]

In the context of slavery, the language of redemption, whether literal (vv. 9–10) or spiritual ("from all lawlessness," v. 14), was no dead metaphor. Only Jesus could break the chains of sin and its dire effects by his substitutionary sacrifice. By using OT terminology, Paul sets the NT church within the framework of salvation history reaching from OT Israel to the NT community of God consisting of both believing Jews and Gentiles.[119]

---

[117] Baugh, "1 Timothy, 2 Timothy, Titus," 506.

[118] "Eager" conveys enthusiasm (1 Cor 14:12), not fanaticism (Gal 1:14; cf. 3:1–2 below). Cf. B. L. Lappenga, "'Zealots for Good Works': The Polemical Repercussions of the Word ζηλωτής in Titus 2:14," *CBQ* 75 (2013): 704–18 stresses the polemical force of the term ζηλωτής and points to Paul's three uses of the word ζηλόω in Gal 4:17–18 and Paul's similar endorsement of "zeal" in Rom 10:2; 1 Cor 12:31; 14:1, 12, 39; 2 Cor 7:7, 11; 11:2; and Gal 4:18. Note that Lappenga has incorporated his work on ζηλωτής in Titus 2:14 into his *Paul's Language of* Ζῆλος*: Monosemy and the Rhetoric of Identity and Practice*, BIS 137 (Leiden: Brill, 2016), 205–8.

[119] Contra Stegemann, "Anti-Semitic and Racist Prejudices," 276–77, who claims the post-Pauline author no longer thinks in those terms.

The series of theological affirmations in vv. 11–14, coming on the heels of the instructions regarding proper conduct in God's household in vv. 1–8, is unusually rich theologically and makes a significant biblical-theological contribution to the theology of the LTT and the NT. Central in this affirmation, in keeping with the prominence of the theme in the LTT, is the salvation word group ("salvation," v. 11; "our great God and Savior, Jesus Christ," v. 13).[120]

Redemption in Christ is set within the context of living in a "sensible, righteous, and godly way in the present age" (v. 12) while believers "wait for the blessed hope, the appearing" of Jesus Christ (v. 13). Salvation and redemption in Christ result in believers' cleansing for Christ as a people for his own possession who are "eager to do good works" (v. 14). Salvation thus results in ethics and mission, set in an eschatological context (§6).

D. Conclusion (2:15)

> 15 Proclaim these things; encourage and rebuke with all authority. Let no one disregard you.

2:15 Paul's directives on how to instruct various groups in the church draw to a close.[121] The term λαλέω ("proclaim"; NIV: "teach") concludes the unit that began with the same expression in v. 1 (a literary *inclusio*).

"Encourage" (παρακαλέω; 1:9; v. 6) and "rebuke" (ἐλέγχω; 1:9, 13) refer to the positive and negative dimensions of Titus's teaching (both terms are juxtaposed in 1:9; see commentary there). He is

---

[120] As mentioned, the expression "our great God and Savior, Jesus Christ" in v. 13, is truly remarkable and constitutes one of the highest Christological affirmations and attributions of deity in the entire NT.

[121] For an analysis of v. 15, see E. R. Wendland, "'Let No One Disregard You!' (Titus 2.15): Church Discipline and the Construction of Discourse in a Personal, 'Pastoral' Epistle," in *Discourse Analysis and the New Testament: Approaches and Results*, ed. S. E. Porter and J. T. Reed, JSNTSup 170 (Sheffield: Sheffield Academic Press, 1999), 334–51, who contends that 2:15 is the fulcrum or midpoint of the entire letter, maintaining that "the pivotal nature of 2.15 within the epistle as a whole is signaled by the various structural and thematic links that it has with other key points in the discourse" (p. 339; see the formal, semantic, and functional overview of Titus in Fig. 1 on p. 345).

to encourage and rebuke "with all authority" (ἐπιταγή; used in 1:3 and 1 Tim 1:1 with reference to the command of God).

Paul closes this section by reassuring Titus, "Let no one disregard you" (περιφρονέω; cf. 1 Tim 4:12).[122] This encouragement likely aims to encourage Titus and to support him at the public reading of this letter, since not all seem to have respected his authority.

Bridge

The heart of this unit is the doctrinal section in vv. 11–14 where Paul cites two major incentives for faithful service: the saving grace of God and the second coming of Christ. Remarkably, in the same passage Jesus is called both "God" and "Savior." Paul also notes that Jesus gave himself for believers not only to redeem them from all lawlessness but also to cleanse for himself "a people for his own possession, eager to do good works" (echoing the OT designation of Israel in Exod 19:5 and several passages in Deuteronomy). This merits careful reflection. Believers shouldn't only revel in their salvation but also allow Christ to cleanse them so they're useful in his service. And they should be motivated both by gratitude for God's grace and by the certain prospect of Christ's return, entailing both judgment and reward.

IV. Instructions on Doing What Is Good in the Context of the General Culture (3:1–11)

The closing general instructions focus on believers' need to be "ready for every good work" (v. 1). They include remarks on keeping the peace (vv. 1–2), comments on salvation in Christ and renewal by the Spirit (vv. 3–8a), and a final warning (vv. 8b–11). At the outset Paul describes non-Christians in terms of seven characteristics, emphasizing that it is only by God's grace that he, Titus, and other believers are different.

The first two verses complete the directives in 2:1–10 by providing instructions on how Christians should relate to outsiders, particularly governing authorities. After a transitional verse (3:3), this is followed by an important compressed soteriological affirmation in 3:4–7, which further develops aspects of the similar

[122] See the above-mentioned analysis of this verse in the context of the entire letter in Wendland, "Let No One Disregard You!" (introduction to chap. 2).

affirmation in 2:11–14 (note the presence of the term "appeared," ἐπεφάνη, in both 2:11 and v. 4), and a few closing remarks.

A. On Keeping the Peace (3:1–2)

> [1] Remind them to submit to rulers and authorities, to obey, to be ready for every good work, [2] to slander no one, to avoid fighting, and to be kind, always showing gentleness to all people.

Relation to Surrounding Context

Following Paul's directives that wives and slaves submit (2:5, 9), he now speaks of the need for all believers to submit to rulers and authorities. He also continues to reiterate the need to be ready for every good work, which is a major emphasis pervading the entire letter (cf. 1:16; 2:7, 14; 3:1, 8).

Structure

This short unit features seven commands: the first three in v. 1 in form of infinitives, with "to submit" as the head command; the remaining four in v. 2, whereby commands 4 and 5 are likewise in the infinitive, 6 is a simple adjective, and the final command an extended participial construction. In the original Greek, v. 2 moves from "no one" to "all people."

3:1 "Remind" (Ὑπομίμνησκε; cf. 2 Tim 2:14; 2 Pet 1:12) implies that people already know they're supposed to submit to the governing authorities (in the present case, the civil authorities of Crete, who in turn were under the larger jurisdiction of Rome). The presence of similar commands in other Pauline (and NT) letters suggests this was standard Christian teaching (cf. Rom 13:1, 5; 1 Pet 3:12; see also 1 Tim 2:1–2). "Submit to" (ὑποτάσσω) has been used earlier in this letter with regard to wives' submission to their husbands (2:5) and slaves' submission to their masters (2:9).

The present reference continues the familiar triadic instruction to wives in relation to husbands, slaves in relation to masters, and citizens in relation to the governing authorities (1 Pet 2:13, 18; 3:1, 5). The ideal is a submitted life that brings glory and honor to God by respecting the order the Creator instituted (see also the references to submission to church leaders in 1 Cor 16:16; Heb 13:17; and 1 Pet 5:5; and of children to parents in Eph 6:1 and Col 3:20).

The combination "rulers-authorities" (ἀρχαῖς, ἐξουσίαις; note that there is no "and" in the original), a likely hendiadys by way of asyndeton, is also attested in Jesus's teaching (Luke 12:11); the closest Pauline parallel is Rom 13:1 (ἐξουσίαις). In other places Paul uses these terms to refer to heavenly forces (e.g., Eph 1:21; 3:10; 6:12); here the reference is to earthly rulers (cf. Luke 12:11; 20:20; see *TDNT* 1:482–84).

"To obey" underscores believers' need to submit to governing authorities (πειθαρχεῖν; cf. Acts 5:29, 32; 27:21; cf. πειθώ, in Heb 13:17–18), while "to be ready" (ἑτοίμους; 2 Cor 9:5; 10:6, 16) "for every good work" (cf. 2 Cor 9:8) constitutes a general reference to their need to engage in good deeds in order to create goodwill and a conducive environment for spreading the gospel (1 Tim 2:10; 5:10; 6:18; 2 Tim 2:21; 3:17; Titus 2:7, 14). The concern for good works (though not for the sake of procuring salvation: v. 5) frames and pervades the entire chapter (see vv. 1, 8, 14; §5.2).

3:2 By way of *inclusio*, the verse begins with "no one" (μηδένα) and ends with "everyone" (πάντας ἀνθρώπους), indicating the all-encompassing nature of Paul's commands. Part of creating such goodwill in the surrounding world is slandering no one (βλασφημεῖν); it's enough that Christians and their gospel are the object of slander (see 2:5; 1 Tim 1:20; 6:1; cf. Rom 2:24; 3:8). Also, believers should avoid fighting (lit., "not-fighting," ἀμάχους), be kind (ἐπιεικεῖς; both in 1 Tim 3:3; cf. Phil 4:5; Jas 3:17; 1 Pet 2:18), and show "all" gentleness (πραΰτητα) toward all, a virtue found supremely in Jesus Christ (Matt 11:29; 21:5; 2 Cor 10:1; Phil 2:55–11). In this way believers will ensure that the only offense caused is that of the gospel and that careless speech, contentiousness, or arrogance not stand in the way.

The instruction for believers to "submit to rulers and authorities," "to be ready for every good work," and always to show "gentleness to all people" in vv. 1–2 continues to develop the mission theme in this portion of the letter. It follows on the heels of repeated references to believers' witness "so that God's word will not be slandered" (2:5), "so that the opponent will be ashamed, because he doesn't have anything bad to say about us" (2:8), "so that they may adorn the teaching of God our Savior in everything" (2:10), and subsequent instructions "to deny godlessness and worldly lusts and to live in a sensible, righteous, and godly way in the present age" (2:12) and to live as cleansed "people for his own possession, eager to do good works" (2:14). In this regard Paul's instructions bear a remarkable similarity to Peter's instructions in 1 Peter.

Bridge

Paul's teaching here reflects standard NT teaching. Believers are to submit to the governing authorities (except, of course, under extreme circumstances) and devote themselves to good works. In this way they will commend the gospel and put no unnecessary obstacle in its way.

B. The Manifestation of God's Kindness and Love in Christ and Regeneration by the Spirit (3:3–8a)

3 For we too were once foolish, disobedient, deceived, enslaved by various passions and pleasures, living in malice and
envy, hateful, detesting one another.
4 But when the kindness of God our Savior and his love for
mankind appeared, 5 he saved us—not by works of righteousness that we had done, but according to his mercy—through
the washing of regeneration and renewal by the Holy Spirit. 6 He poured out his Spirit on us abundantly through Jesus
Christ our Savior 7 so that, having been justified by his grace,
we may become heirs with the hope of eternal life. 8 This saying is trustworthy.

Relation to Surrounding Context

The following verses provide the reason for Paul's directives in vv. 1–2, essentially God's saving kindness and mercy toward believers who once were disobedient just as the rest of humanity.

Structure

The present unit explains why believers are to be kind toward all and devote themselves to good works. Verse 3 provides a vice list specifying seven past characteristics of believers prior to conversion; vv. 4–7 set forth what in v. 8 is identified as another "trustworthy saying" about "the kindness of God our Savior and His love for mankind."

3:3 The following verses give the reason (γάρ; untranslated in the NIV) for Paul's instructions in vv. 1–2. The vice list in v. 3 (cf. 1 Cor 6:9–11) paints a dim picture of believers' preconversion way of life. This serves to remind them that they're different from their pagan neighbors solely because of God's grace. Paul describes the state of non-Christians—"we too were" implies that they still are—by way of seven characteristics (a 2–3–2 pattern):

1. foolish (ἀνόητοι; cf. 1 Tim 6:9; Rom 1:14; Gal 3:1, 3; Luke 24:25), i.e. lacking spiritual understanding;
2. disobedient (ἀπειθεῖς; cf. 1:16; 2 Tim 3:2; Rom 1:30), i.e., rebellious against God;
3. deceived (πλανώμενοι; cf. 2 Tim 3:13; 1 Pet 2:25 citing Isa 53:6) and
4. enslaved (δουλεύοντες; cf. John 8:33) by various passions and pleasures (cf. 2:12);
5. living (διάγοντες; cf. 1 Tim 2:2) in malice (κακίᾳ; Rom 1:29) and envy (φθόνῳ; Rom 1:29; Gal 5:21);
6. hateful (NIV: "being hated"; στυγητοί; see θεοστυγής in Rom 1:30: "God-haters"); and
7. detesting one another (μισοῦντες ἀλλήλους; common in Matthew, Luke, John, and 1 John).

"Deceived" may imply Satan as the agent or refer to self-deception (cf. 1 Tim 1:20; 2 Tim 3:13); "enslaved by various passions and pleasures" constitutes the peak of the vice list. The desired cumulative rhetorical effect is most likely that of a powerful reminder of believers' dismal preconversion state for the purpose of moving them to compassion toward those who are still outside of Christ. The list also reflects the sentiment of an appropriate, sincere revulsion of a Christian looking back on his life prior to becoming a believer (cf. Phil 3:7–9).

The review of believers' lives before God's saving initiative in Christ echoes similar passages in Paul's other letters (e.g., Eph 2:1–10). Both God and Christ are called "our Savior" (cf. v. 11), though ultimately all saving work is attributed to God the Father, with Christ serving as his agent in both salvation and the giving of the Spirit, and with the Spirit serving as his agent in regeneration.[123] Following a series of down-to-earth instructions, Paul focuses on God before closing the letter with one final warning against the false teachers and some final remarks.

[123] Cf. J. D. Quinn, "The Holy Spirit in the Pastoral Epistles," in *Sin, Salvation, and the Spirit*, ed. D. Durken (Collegeville, MN: Liturgical Press, 1979), 345–53.

3:4–8a These verses flesh out the contrast set up in v. 3 (ποτέ . . . ὅτε δέ: "once . . . But when . . .").[124] While humanity languished in depravity, God took the initiative in salvation (§3). As v. 8 indicates, the doctrinal summary in vv. 4–7 (note the contrast with the vice list in v. 3) constitutes another "trustworthy saying" (cf. 1 Tim 1:15; 3:1; 4:8; 2 Tim 2:11–13). The saying, a concise summary of Pauline soteriology and trinitarian in nature, focuses on God's salvation of believers through Christ and his regenerating work through the Holy Spirit.

Paul initially refers to the appearing (ἐπεφάνη, cf. 2:11) of the kindness (χρηστότης; cf. Eph 2:7; Rom 2:4; 11:22 [3x]) and love for humanity (φιλανθρωπία) of God our Savior (see at 1 Tim 1:1) at the first coming of Christ (cf. 2 Tim 1:9–10). The term for "love" occurs elsewhere in the NT only in Acts 28:2 (cf. Acts 27:3); the singular verb form may suggest that Paul viewed God's kindness and love in unity (though note the definite article with both words). The term χρηστότης may be intended as a wordplay with "Christ" (Χριστός).

Paul's terminology casts God as the supreme benefactor of humanity akin to Greco-Roman rulers:[125] "The thought here is that of a sovereign Lord who makes an act of unprompted and undeserved favour to his subjects, and does so in a personal appearance."[126] As Jesus taught, God is kind (χρηστός) even to the ungrateful and wicked (Luke 6:35; cf. Pss 24:17; 30:19; 67:10; 103:28 LXX). While accomplished historically at the time of Jesus's first coming, the saving benefits of his work are applied to believers at the point of conversion.

Paul states emphatically that God saved us, "not because of righteous things that we had done, but according to his mercy" (ἔλεος; cf. Eph 2:4; see also 1 Tim 1:13, 16).[127] This salvation was accomplished "through the washing of regeneration and renewal by the Holy Spirit," whom God poured out on us abundantly

---

[124] See A. Malherbe, "'Christ Jesus Came into the World to Save Sinners': Soteriology in the Pastoral Epistles," in *Salvation in the New Testament*, NovTSup 121, ed. J. G. van der Watt (Leiden: Brill, 2005), 351.

[125] See Johnson, *Letters to Paul's Delegates*, 244.

[126] C. K. Barrett, *The Pastoral Epistles*, New Clarendon Bible (Oxford: Clarendon, 1963), 141.

[127] Note that in the original Greek, the entire phrase "not by works of righteous that we had done, but according to his mercy" precedes the verb "saved" for emphasis.

through Jesus Christ our Savior (note the trinitarian thrust). The desired result of God's gracious regeneration and justification is that believers might become heirs (κληρονόμοι; cf. Rom 4:13–14; 8:17; Gal 3:29; 4:1, 7) with the hope of eternal life (cf. 1:2).

"Rebirth" (παλιγγενεσία; CSB, NASB, "regeneration") and "renewal" (ἀνακαίνωσις) are both tied to the metaphor of "washing" by the Holy Spirit (λουτρόν, see Eph 5:26; cf. 1 Cor 6:11; Heb 10:22). Παλιγγενεσία ("rebirth") is found elsewhere in the NT only in Matt 19:28 (cf. John 3:3, 5; Rom 6:4; 1 Pet 1:3, 23); ἀνακαίνωσις ("renewal") is a likely Pauline coinage first used in Rom 12:2 (cf. 2 Cor 4:16; Col 3:10).[128] The expressions are roughly synonymous, though the emphasis may be slightly different, with "rebirth" referring to spiritual regeneration and "renewal" to inner transformation.

The primary OT passage referring to inner cleansing and renewal is Ezek 36:25–27. NT teaching on the new birth is found in various writers (John 3:3–8; 1 John 3:9; 4:7; 5:1, 4, 18; Jas 1:18; 1 Pet 1:3, 23; cf. 2:2). The notion of rebirth or regeneration is also present in Hellenistic literature (e.g., Plutarch, *Is. Os.* 35).[129] The gener-

---

[128] See also the reference to a "new creation" (καινὴ κτίσις) in 2 Cor 5:17 and Gal 6:15. Cf. C. Zimmermann, "Wiederentstehung und Erneuerung," 272–95 (with additional bibliographic references on 273n1); and R. W. Wall, "Salvation's Bath by the Spirit: A Study of Titus 3:5b–6 in Its Canonical Setting," in *The Spirit and Christ in the New Testament and Christian Theology: Essays in Honor of Max Turner*, ed. I. H. Marshall, V. Rabens, and C. Bennema (Grand Rapids: Eerdmans, 2012), 198–212.

[129] See C. Zimmermann, "Wiederentstehung und Erneuerung," 283–89. Zimmermann also points out (pp. 284–85) that excavations on Crete indicate that the Isis and Serapis cult was practiced on the island, particularly in coastal cities such as Gortyn, Itanos, Hierapytna, Phaistos, Poikilasion, Phoinike, and Lasaia (see K. Sporn, *Heiligtümer und Kulte Kretas in klassischer und hellenistischer Zeit*, Studien zu antiken Heiligtümern 3 [Heidelberg: Archäologie und Geschichte, 2002], 339). The presence of the Isis and Serapis cult on the island can be traced to the influence of Ptolemaic Egypt. The Iseum in Gortyn (which dates to the second century BC and was renovated in the first and second centuries AD) is still visible. It features a crypt with a lavatory that presumably served to ritually recall the flooding of the Nile and may have represented the dead and life-giving god Osiris (R. Salditt-Trappmann, *Tempel der ägyptischen Götter in Griechenland und an der Westküste Kleinasiens*, Études préliminaires aux religions orientales dans l'Empire romain 15 [Leiden: Brill, 1970], 54–56). It's also possible that rites existed in which initiates reenacted the death and resurrection of Osiris (B. W. R. Pearson, "Baptism and Initiation in the Cult of Isis and Sarapis," in *Baptism, the New Testament and the Church: Historical and Contemporary Studies in Honour of R. E. O. White*, JSNTSup 171, ed. S. E. Porter and A. R. Cross [Sheffield: Sheffield Academic Press, 1999], 56).

ous "pouring out" (ἐκχέω) of the Spirit evokes the language used by the OT prophets (Zech 12:10; Joel 3:1–2 LXX; cf. Acts 2:17–18, 33; Rom 5:5). The term "abundantly" (πλουσίως) is found in the LTT also in 1 Tim 6:17–18 (cf. Col 3:16; 2 Pet 1:11). The addition of the phrase "through Jesus Christ our Savior" in v. 6 completes the passage's trinitarian scope, following references to God [the Father] in vv. 4–5 and the Spirit in v. 5.

Verse 7 conveys the result of God's saving work: "so that, having been justified by his grace, we may become heirs with the hope of eternal life." The concepts of justification by grace, believers' inheritance, and their living in hope of eternal life are all Pauline concepts (justification by grace: Rom 3:24, 26, 28; 5:1, 9; 8:30, 33; Gal 2:16–17; 3:24; 5:4; believers' inheritance: Rom 8:17; Gal 3:29; Eph 1:14, 18; Col 3:24; hope of eternal life: 1:2; Rom 5:2, 5; 8:20, 24; 12:12; 1 Cor 13:13; Col 1:5).[130] Justification allows believers to enter into their inheritance, which is still future and thus the object of hope.

The biblical-theological contribution of vv. 4–7 is considerable. This is one of only two references to the Holy Spirit in the LTT (the other is found in 2 Tim 1:14; and cf. 1 Tim 3:16; 4:1), and of these two, the present passage is more extensive. The trinitarian thrust of the passage is also highly remarkable. Both God and Jesus Christ are identified as "our Savior" (vv. 4, 6), and the Holy Spirit is identified as the agent of "the washing of regeneration and renewal" (v. 5). Justification by grace (v. 7) rather than salvation by works (v. 5) is mentioned as well (v. 7).

The message of vv. 4–5 has been poetically paraphrased by Walter Lock as follows:[131]

For the potential relevance of this background material for the interpretation of παλιγγενεσία in Titus 3:5 see the discussion in Zimmermann ("Wiederentstehung und Erneuerung," 289–92).

[130] "Hope" is a pervasive theme in the LTT: 1 Tim 1:1; 3:14; 4:19; 5:5; 6:17; 2 Tim 2:25; Titus 1:2; 2:13.

[131] Walter Lock, *A Critical and Exegetical Commentary on the Pastoral Epistles*, ICC (Edinburgh: T&T Clark, 1924), 151. In personal email correspondence dated November 25, 2015, Gordon Franz states his belief that many of the "trustworthy sayings" were early hymns or spiritual songs that Paul either composed or adopted from the church "hymnal." Cf., e.g., D. Guthrie, *The Pastoral Epistles*, TNTC, rev. ed. (Grand Rapids: Eerdmans, 1990), 216, commenting on v. 5: "The apostle next seems to quote from a Christian hymn."

But when in gracious love for man
Our Savior God unveiled His plan,
'Twas not for merit of our own
But on His pitying care alone

He saved us, by a heavenly birth
Cleansing away the stains of earth
And on our heads in rich largess
Pouring His Spirit's holiness.

Bridge

Following 2:11–14, Paul's comments in vv. 4–7 mark the second doctrinal highlight in this letter. In eloquent terms the apostle speaks of God's saving action with particular focus on the work of the Holy Spirit. Paul explicitly notes "the washing of regeneration and renewal by the Holy Spirit" (v. 5) and notes, in an implicitly trinitarian formulation, that God "poured out this Spirit on us abundantly through Jesus Christ our Savior" (v. 6). He also speaks of justification by God's grace and believers becoming heirs in hope of eternal life (v. 7). Against the dark backdrop of believers' preconversion existence, this puts in stark relief God's saving grace resulting in regeneration and renewal, enabling believers' good works (cf. Eph 2:8–9). It also shows that the only thing separating believers from unbelievers is the saving grace of God.

C. On Dealing with Divisive Persons (3:8b–11)

> I want you to insist on these things, so that those who have believed God might be careful to devote themselves to good works. These are good and profitable for everyone. [9] But avoid foolish debates, genealogies, quarrels, and disputes about the law, because they are unprofitable and worthless. [10] Reject a divisive person after a first and second warning. [11] For you know that such a person has gone astray and is sinning; he is self-condemned.

Relation to Surrounding Context

"These things" in v. 8a refers back to vv. 1–7, while "these" later on in the verse refers to good works. The passage continues the emphasis struck on the importance of engaging in good works in the previous unit. The specific guidance on how to deal with a divisive person is a new piece of instruction. The present unit concludes the letter apart from final personal instructions and greetings.

Structure

This final set of instructions starts with "I want" (βούλομαι) plus the specified purpose of devotion to good works (v. 8b). The development marker δέ in v. 9 indicates movement to the converse, devotion to unprofitable and worthless debates about the law. Both "foolish debates" (v. 9) and "divisive person" (v. 10) are fronted in the Greek for emphasis, with the final v. 11 providing a concluding rationale.

3:8b In one of his customary summary comments (cf. 2:15), Paul urges (βούλομαι, a strong command; cf. 2:8; 5:14) Titus to insist on (διαβεβαιοῦσθαι; cf. 1 Tim 1:7) "these things" (i.e., the content of vv. 1–7; cf. 2:15) so that believers (those who have put their trust in God) may be careful (φροντίζω; only here in the NT; cf. LXX: Ps 39:18; Job 23:15) to devote themselves to good works (see vv. 1 and 5 above and v. 14 below; §5.2). Reflection on the kindness, love, and mercy of God in salvation and on his generous justifying and regenerating work should inspire works of service.[132] A true appreciation of the gifts of God will engender willing, even eager, ministry on behalf of others. Paul's comment that "these [things] (i.e., doing good) are good and profitable (ὠφέλιμος; cf. 1 Tim 4:8; 2 Tim 3:16) for everyone" contrasts with his remark below (v. 9) that foolish debates are unprofitable (ἀνωφελής; cf. Heb 7:18) and worthless (μάταιος; cf. Acts 14:15; 1 Cor 3:20; 15:17; Jas 1:26; 2 Pet 2:18; see also 1:10; 1 Tim 1:6).

3:9–11 Mirroring his opening warning (1:10–16), and similar to his remarks in 2 Tim 2:23–26, Paul warns Titus one last time to avoid "foolish debates" (ζητήσεις; cf. 1 Tim 6:4; 2 Tim 2:23),

---

[132] Zimmermann, "Wiederentstehung und Erneuerung," 293–94, points out that the characteristics attributed to God in Titus 3:4 mirror attributes of the Roman emperor, such as χρηστότης, φιλανθρωπία, ἐπιφάνεια, and σωτήρ (cf. Philo, *Embassy* 73; F. Jung, *Σωτήρ: Studien zur Rezeption eines hellenistischen Ehrentitels im Neuen Testament*, NTAbh N.F. 39 [Münster: Aschendorff, 2002]; M. Karrer, "Jesus, der Retter (Σωτήρ): Zur Aufnahme eines hellenistischen Prädikats im Neuen Testament," *ZNW* 93 [2002]: 153–76; K. Läger, *Die Christologie der Pastoralbriefe*, Hamburger Theologische Studien 12 [Münster: Lit, 1996], 111; E. Plümacher, "φιλανθρωπία," *EDNT* 3:424–25; see also the references in Zimmermann, "Wiederentstehung und Erneuerung," 294nn74–75).

genealogies (γενεαλογίας; cf. 1 Tim 1:4), quarrels (ἔρεις; in the NT only in Paul: 1 Tim 6:4; Rom 1:29; 13:13; 1 Cor 1:11; 3:3; 2 Cor 12:20; Gal 5:20; Phil 1:15), and disputes (μάχας; cf. 2 Tim 2:23–24; 2 Cor 7:5; Jas 4:1–2) about the law, because they're unprofitable and worthless (cf. 1:10–16; see "The Opponents" in the introduction to Titus above).

The proper procedure for dealing with a divisive person (αἱρετικός; only here in the NT; cf. 1 Cor 11:19; Gal 5:20; 2 Pet 2:1) is as follows: Titus should issue a warning (νουθεσία; cf. 1 Cor 10:11; Eph 6:4) to such a person, and then, if needed, a second warning; after that, he should have nothing to do with that individual (παραιτέομαι; 1 Tim 4:7; 5:11; 2 Tim 2:23). This procedure resembles that of Jesus (Matt 18:15–17; cf. 1 Tim 1:19–20; 2 Tim 2:25–26).[133]

For such a person "has gone astray" or "is warped" (ἐκστρέφω; only here in the NT, the perfect tense pointing to a settled condition) and persists in sin (ἁμαρτάνω; cf. 1 Tim 5:20). He is self-condemned (αὐτοκατάκριτος; not elsewhere in the NT; cf. Luke 19:22; Gal 2:11), continuing in sin despite repeated warnings to stop his divisive behavior. Paul's letter to the Romans concludes with a similar warning (16:17–18).

Bridge

The letter proper concludes with a stern note on how to deal with divisive individuals. This underscores Paul's concern for unity as well as doctrinal purity in the church. Jesus, in his farewell prayer, similarly prayed for his followers' unity (John 17). Unity is important but should not be construed as enforced uniformity. It is spiritual unity brought about by what believers share in common in Christ and guarded by the Holy Spirit (Eph 4:1–7). At the same time, there's diversity in the body of Christ in terms of spiritual gifts and contributions by individual believers to the common good. This is a delicate balance to strike that calls for wisdom and maturity.

---

[133] See T. G. Kitchens, "Parameters of Corrective Church Discipline," *BSac* 148 (1991): 208–10.

V. Conclusion (3:12–15)

A. Final Instructions (3:12–14)

> [12] When I send Artemas or Tychicus to you, make every effort to come to me in Nicopolis, because I have decided to spend the winter there. [13] Diligently help Zenas the lawyer and Apollos on their journey, so that they will lack nothing. [14] Let our people learn to devote themselves to good works for pressing needs, so that they will not be unfruitful.

3:12–14 Paul concludes by making some final arrangements. First, Titus should meet him at Nicopolis ("Victory City"), a Roman colony on the western coast of Greece that served as provincial capital, having been founded by Augustus in 31–29 BC in order to celebrate his triumph over Mark Anthony at Actium. This is where the apostle has decided to spend the winter (παραχειμάζω; 1 Cor 16:6; Acts 27:12; 28:11; cf. 2 Tim 4:21). Nicopolis, the preeminent location for trade with Rome in western and northern Greece, was known for its mild climate.[134] The city's two harbors provided access to the cities at the coast of the Adriatic Sea.[135] Nicopolis was more than 300 miles from Crete, a five-to-ten-day journey by ship.[136]

Titus should leave as soon as Artemas, an otherwise unknown figure (late tradition makes him one of the seventy or seventy-two [see Luke 10:1] and the first bishop of Lystra) or Tychicus, Paul's better-known associate from the province of Asia who earlier carried letters to Ephesus and Colossae (Acts 20:4; Eph 6:21; Col 4:7; 2 Tim 4:12), has replaced him at Crete. Since Tychicus was sent to Ephesus (2 Tim 4:12), it was probably Artemas who was dispatched to Crete. Following this, Titus left for Dalmatia, up the coast from Nicopolis (2 Tim 4:10). The purpose for this planned meeting with Titus is unstated but presumably involved further coaching on how to deal with the situation at Crete.

Second, Titus should help Zenas the lawyer, presumably a Roman jurist (νομικός; otherwise unknown), and Apollos, the eloquent Alexandrian (mentioned in Acts 18:24 and 1 Cor 1:12; etc.)

---

[134] Quarles, *Illustrated Life of Paul*, 259.

[135] Ibid., with reference to C. E. Fant and M. G. Reddish, *A Guide to Biblical Sites in Greece and Turkey* (Oxford: Oxford University Press, 2003), 88.

[136] Schnabel, *Early Christian Mission*, 2.1287, 1234.

on their way (προπέμπω; cf. Acts 15:3; 20:38; 21:5), so that they have everything they need (cf. Rom 15:24; 1 Cor 16:6; 2 Cor 1:16; 3 John 6). In all probability these men delivered the present letter.[137] Note that the Jewish community at Crete may have hailed from Alexandria, Egypt, which would explain the connection with Apollos.[138] Apparently, "it was common for lawyers to visit Crete in Roman times."[139]

Third, Paul reminds Titus one last time of the importance of doing what is good (cf. verbal parallels with v. 8; "our people" may serve to distinguish believers from the followers of the false teachers) to provide for pressing needs (cf. 2 Cor 8:6 for an earlier example) and so as not to lead unproductive lives (cf. 2 Thess 3:12–13; Rom 1:13; 15:28).[140]

The closing portions of the letter contain repeated references to believers' "good works" (2:14; 3:8, 14; §5.2), underscoring the importance of the mission and witness theme that pervades the entire letter. The specific instructions in 3:12–13 also contribute to the theme of the apostolic mission as it is extended through Paul's apostolic delegates and believers in their congregations (§1).

B. Closing (3:15)

> [15] All those who are with me send you greetings. Greet those who love us in the faith. Grace be with all of you.

3:15 As customary for ancient letters, the letter closes with greetings from Paul and those with him to those "who love us in the faith" (possibly hinting at the disloyalty of some) and a

---

[137] Ibid., 2.1286.

[138] See Wieland, "Roman Crete," 353: "If the sort of Hellenistic Judaism that flourished in Alexandria furnished part of the environment envisaged by the author, who better to help than Apollos (3.13), the learned Alexandrian Jew encountered in Acts 18.24–28; 1 Cor 3.4–6, and so on?"

[139] See Wieland (ibid.), who writes, "The famous stone panels on which were inscribed the Law Code of Gortyn dated from c. 450 BCE but had been restored under Roman rule and were prominently displayed to facilitate study." Thus "Crete became 'a centre of pilgrimage for legal inspiration'" (ibid., citing Willetts, "Cretan Laws and Society," 237).

[140] "Let (them) learn" (μανθανέτωσαν) in v. 14 is the final imperative in the book, a challenge to committed discipleship resulting in good works.

final grace wish (cf. 1 Tim 6:21; 2 Tim 4:22) to Titus (the pronoun "you" in the first part of the verse is singular) and the believers in Crete (the second pronoun at the end of the verse, "all of you," is plural).[141]

With this parting greeting and grace wish, the letter to Titus has come to an end. In it Paul has instructed his apostolic delegate to "set right what was left undone and, as I directed you, to appoint elders in every town" (1:5). In addition Paul provided instructions on how to order the affairs in God's household, including qualifications for church leaders, and on caring for the various members of the congregations.

Mission accomplished? Paul certainly discharged his apostolic duties to follow up on the mission work in Crete. As far as Titus is concerned, it is difficult to determine what took place in the years following his receipt of Paul's letter. Yet the letter is not merely written to Titus but also to us. Will we be faithful to God's call and join him on his mission? In every age, there are those who follow his call and complete their mission. May you and I be among those who do.

[141] See J. Ellington, "Problem Pronouns in Private Letters," *Bible Translator* 50/2 (1999): 224. See also Quinn, *Titus*, 269, who calls Titus "a personal letter with a public function."

BIBLICAL AND THEOLOGICAL THEMES

"The author of the Pastorals had no theology of his own. He is a purveyor of other men's theology," writes A. T. Hanson.[1] Others view the theology of the LTT as a collection of preformed traditions, "a fairly arbitrary, inconsistent, unthought-out amalgam with little coherence."[2] It's true that a good deal of the most significant theological formulations in the LTT are found in liturgical material (Introduction, III.D, "Use of Preformed Traditions"), whether in the "trustworthy sayings" (§2.6) or other confessions or hymns.[3] At the same time, it's curious that scholars often deny the coherence of the theological outlook found in the LTT, on the assumption of their pseudonymity, while simultaneously setting these writings off from the undisputed Pauline NT letters. Rather than engaging in an attempt to argue for the coherence and distinctiveness of the LTT's theology at the outset, we'll let the following discussion speak for itself. Contrary to Hanson's assertion, I believe I'll show beyond any reasonable doubt that the author of the LTT did, in fact, have a theology of his own.[4]

---

[1] A. T. Hanson, *Studies in the Pastoral Epistles* (London: S.P.C.K., 1968), 110.

[2] The quote is from F. M. Young, *The Theology of the Pastoral Letters*, NT Theology (Cambridge: Cambridge University Press, 1994), 47. Young herself does not subscribe to this view; this is rather her summary of the general estimation of scholars on the theology of the LTT.

[3] E.g., 1 Tim 2:5–6; 3:16; 6:13–17; 2 Tim 1:9–10; 2:11–13; Titus 3:4–7.

[4] For works on the theology of the LTT considered together, see, in addition to treatments in commentaries, the following: J. W. Aageson, *Paul, the Pastoral Epistles, and the Early Church*, Library of Pauline Studies (Peabody, MA: Hendrickson, 2008), 57–69; Aageson, *Windows on Early Christianity: Uncommon Stories, Striking Images, Critical Perspectives* (Eugene, OR: Cascade, 2016), 114–20; M. L. Bailey, "A Theology of Paul's Pastoral Epistles," in *A Biblical Theology of the*

The remainder of this commentary, then, is devoted to discussing significant biblical-theological themes in the LTT. The primary focus will be on the theological convictions held by the author (whom I believe to be the apostle Paul) expressed by his distinctive vocabulary and thematic emphases in these letters. In the organization of the following themes and subthemes, every effort has been made to present the material in as organic and authentic a manner as possible, in recognition that the various major and minor themes interrelate closely. To be sure, while, as discussed in the Introduction, each letter should be read and understood on its own terms, the LTT are best viewed as a cluster in that they exhibit shared characteristics. In addition, since the LTT are part of the Pauline corpus, this material can subsequently be integrated into the larger Pauline theology as it emerges from his other ten letters included in the NT canon (§7.2).[5] An exploration of major and

---

New Testament, ed. R. B. Zuck (Chicago: Moody, 1994), 333–67; D. A. Hagner, *The New Testament: A Historical and Theological Introduction* (Grand Rapids: Baker, 2012), 626–34; I. H. Marshall, *New Testament Theology* (Downers Grove: InterVarsity, 2004), 407–19; F. J. Matera, *New Testament Theology: Exploring Diversity and Unity* (Louisville: Westminster John Knox, 2007), 240–58; U. Schnelle, *Theology of the New Testament*, trans. M. E. Boring (Grand Rapids: Baker, 2007), 578–601; G. Strecker, *Theology of the New Testament* (Berlin: DeGruyter, 2000), 576–94; P. H. Towner, *The Goal of Our Instruction: The Structure of Theology and Ethics in the Pastoral Epistles*, JSNTSup 34 (Sheffield: Sheffield Academic, 1989), 47–142; "The Pastoral Epistles," in *New Dictionary of Biblical Theology*, ed. T. D. Alexander and B. S. Rosner (Leicester: Inter-Varsity, 2000), 332–36; Young, *Theology*.

The theology of each of the three individual LTT is treated in Aageson, *Paul, the Pastoral Epistles, and the Early Church*, 18–56; I. H. Marshall's work in *Dictionary for Theological Interpretation of the Bible*, ed. K. J. Vanhoozer (Grand Rapids: Baker, 2005), 803–4, 806, 809; Marshall, *New Testament Theology*, 397–406; F. S. Thielman, *Theology of the New Testament* (Grand Rapids: Zondervan, 2005), 408–37.

For a treatment of the theology of 1 Timothy, see also L. T. Johnson, "*Oikonomia Theou*: The Theological Voice of 1 Timothy from the Perspective of Pauline Authorship," in L. T. Johnson, *Contested Issues in Christian Origins and the New Testament: Collected Essays*, NovTSup 146 (Leiden: Brill, 2013), 383–403. For 2 Timothy, see also G. D. Fee, "Toward a Theology of 2 Timothy—from a Pauline Perspective," in *Society of Biblical Literature 1997 Seminar Papers*, SBLSP 36 (Atlanta; Scholars Press, 1977), 732–49; P. T. Towner, "The Portrait of Paul and the Theology of 2 Timothy: The Closing Chapter of the Pauline Story," *HorBT* 21 (1999): 151–70. For Titus, see also R. F. Collins, "The Theology of the Epistle to Titus." *ETL* 76 (2000): 56–72; B. Thurston, "The Theology of Titus," *HorBT* 21 (1999): 171–84.

[5] Note the comments on the relative (or total) neglect of the LTT in NT theology in I. H. Marshall, "Faith and Works in the Pastoral Epistles," *SNTSU-A* 9 (1984):

minor themes in the LTT will also provide valuable insights into practical matters such as missions, discipleship, and leadership training in the local church (§§1, 4).[6]

At the outset of this biblical-theological exposition, it'll be helpful to provide a brief account of how the various major and minor themes were chosen that are discussed below. In essence, this distillation occurred in the context of a dynamic interplay between two factors: (1) a repeated inductive reading of the LTT employing a biblical-theological methodology; (2) a perusal of the relevant secondary literature on the biblical theology of the so-called "Pastoral Epistles." While the repeated reading of the LTT was primary and ultimately determinative in the formation of the following categories, reading the secondary literature provided a helpful framework for evaluating the chosen categories and at times occasioned a rethinking of these, whether by adding a subcategory, resequencing the treatment, or adding further insights and nuances.

In terms of the order in which various themes in the LTT will be treated in this biblical-theological exposition, it seems appropriate to start with a discussion of Paul's apostolic *mission* and his conception of his apostleship and apostolic authority, righteous suffering, the role of apostolic delegates, and his larger mission theology and strategy (§1). A second, closely related theme is that of *teaching*. Under this rubric I will cover topics such as healthy teaching, "the faith," the trustworthy sayings, and Paul's use of and teaching on Scripture (§2). The next cluster of topics to be addressed is *God, Christ, and salvation*. This includes in particular the distinctive designation of both God and Christ as "our Savior" and a detailed examination of the various corollaries of salvation in the LTT (§3). Next I will turn to the subject of the church as *God's household*, including a discussion of order and authority and responsibilities by the household's various members. Also treated

---

203–4: "It is no exaggeration to say that the contribution of the Pastorals to the study of NT theology is undervalued and even ignored." This situation is improving, even as there has been somewhat of a resurgence of scholarly commentaries which affirm Pauline authorship of the LTT, but much work remains to be done.

[6] As mentioned in the introduction, Titus and Timothy aren't, strictly speaking, local pastors but apostolic delegates. Also, the various themes in these letters are to some degree specific to the circumstances in Ephesus and Crete (for relevant information see the Introduction to this volume).

will be the tasks of ministry, church officers, and goals of ministry (§4). The ensuing section on the *Christian life* focuses primarily on the pursuit of Christian virtues and good works, as well as on good citizenship (§5). Last but not least will be a treatment of *the last days*. Under this heading the following topics will be covered: Satan, demons, and angels; the false teachers; virtues and vices; the need for perseverance; the resurrection of believers; and the appearing of Christ in final judgment and salvation (§6). The concluding portion of the biblical-theological exposition will round out our treatment with an attempt to ascertain the LTT's *contribution to the canon*. Toward this end we'll discuss the LTT and the OT; the LTT and Paul's other letters; the LTT and Acts; and the LTT and the non-Pauline NT letters (§7).

Yet the following presentation is more than a sequenced treatment of major topics in the LTT. It proceeds in the understanding that a truly adequate portrayal of the biblical theology exhibited by a given set of writings needs to do more than merely list and discuss a series of theological themes and subthemes. While this is certainly an important part of such a task, it is at least equally important to probe the interrelation between the various major themes, as well as the interrelation between these major themes and the various subthemes. This is based on the conviction that ultimately the biblical theology of a given set of writings is an interwoven fabric of interrelated major and minor themes, a matrix not unlike a spiderweb that is characterized by careful integration, cohesion, and interpenetration. Thus the following treatment will not merely present major and minor themes but regularly and consistently discuss the interrelation between these themes. The following types of questions will be asked: What is the relationship between the LTT's ecclesiology and eschatology? How are these grounded in the mission of Paul and of his apostolic delegates? What is the relationship between soteriology and ecclesiology, and between soteriology, ecclesiology, and mission?

As we present our biblical-theological exposition of the LTT, then, we are mindful of the complexity of thought represented in these letters. The seamless garment of this body of literature defies simplistic analysis, whether in its own right or in relation to the remaining Pauline letter corpus. For this reason, as well, we plead in particular with those who hold that the LTT are pseudonymous to keep an open mind about the following presentation.

There is surely a need for a certain amount of latitude in analyzing the theology of these letters that provides space for Paul to express himself in a way that best serves the needs of his apostolic mission at the particular salvation-historical juncture represented by these letters. It is this mission, then, that forms the appropriate starting point for our investigation.

§1 Mission

One of the most important questions concerning the LTT is the way these writings are grounded in the mission of the early church in general and in the mission of Paul in particular and thus convey his apostolic authority.[7] It's highly probable that these letters were written after the other ten Pauline letters included in the NT canon. It's also evident that these letters are concerned with issues related to Paul's legacy and the organization of the church at the onset of the subapostolic period. In this regard it's of some importance whether these instructions are grounded directly and personally in the mission of the apostle. If so, Paul himself prior to his martyrdom conveyed his ideas, vision, and instructions regarding the ordering of the church to his apostolic delegates who in turn were to pass these on to others. Thus the vital contents of these letters would become part and parcel of the apostolic foundation of the church, which would remain authoritative and normative throughout subsequent history.

This question, in turn, impacts canonicity, because it may be argued that whether these letters are authentically Pauline, they were included in the canon and are thus normative. Conversely, others may question whether the inclusion of these letters in the canon is legitimate if the letters weren't written by Paul, since the evidence overwhelmingly suggests that the church accepted these letters into the canon believing they were written by the apostle. For this reason it could be argued that if the church was mistaken

[7] Cf., e.g., the approach adopted by A. Schlatter, who, in contrast to pseudonymity advocates who explain the LTT "from a hypothetical scenario decades after Paul's death," provides a reconstruction that "grows out of the life of Paul and Paul's convictions about Christ, the God who sent him, and the gospel message that by the Spirit makes him known savingly to sinners, foremost Paul himself" (Yarbrough's summary: "Schlatter and the Pastorals," 309).

in this, these letters should be removed from the canon and be assigned to the category of subapostolic writings.[8] Some might adduce the parallel of Hebrews, but the important difference here is that Hebrews is formally anonymous, and the text asserts no claim of authorship, while the LTT each contain an attribution to the apostle Paul.

For this reason it's appropriate to start a discussion of the major and minor themes in the LTT with a treatment of the early church's mission and the related questions of apostolicity and authority. Specifically, the coverage of major themes in the LTT will commence with a discussion of these letters in relation to the Pauline mission. This will be followed by a treatment of the closely related matters of the Pauline conception of apostleship, righteous suffering, the role of apostolic delegates, and Paul's larger missionary strategy. After this, attention will turn to a second, related theme, tradition and Scripture, covering such topics as the faith, sound teaching, the trustworthy sayings, and Paul's use of and teaching regarding Scripture.

§1.1 The Pauline Mission

The NT documents are properly viewed as "the documents of a mission," recording the inauguration of the mission work of Jesus and its extension through his followers.[9] Whether one holds to the Pauline authorship of the LTT, it's clear that these letters portray an extension of Paul's mission to the Gentiles as he interacts with his delegates in Ephesus and Crete. After an

---

[8] See, e.g., W. Schenk, "Die Briefe an Timotheus I und II und an Titus (Pastoralbriefe) in der neueren Forschung (1945–1985)," in *ANRW* 2.25.4 (1987), 3428n93, who calls for a "de-canonization" of the LTT. DeSilva, *Introduction to the New Testament*, 736, who himself favors pseudonymity, seeks to ward off such a conclusion by arguing that "the church determined these *texts* to have been inspired" regardless of Pauline authorship. Similarly, P. J. Achtemeier, J. B. Green, and M. M. Thompson, *Introducing the New Testament: Its Literature and Theology* (Grand Rapids: Eerdmans, 2001), 461, assert that the LTT "have proved of value regardless of their author."

[9] Marshall, *New Testament Theology*, 34–35 (even though Marshall places those letters at a later point of composition subsequent to the earthly departure of Paul). J. Dickson, *Mission-Commitment in Ancient Judaism and in the Pauline Communities: The Shape, Extent, and Background of Early Christian Mission*, WUNT 2/159 (Tübingen: Mohr Siebeck, 2003), examines Paul's letters in light of Second Temple literature, concluding that Paul's outlook on mission was influenced significantly by his Jewish heritage.

initial visit to Ephesus, Paul established a mission work there (Acts 18:19–21). In 1 Timothy, Paul has left Timothy with this established church in order to put an end to false teaching that is detrimental to Paul's larger mission (1 Tim 1:3–4), teaching contrary to the sound doctrine that "conforms to the gospel concerning the glory of the blessed God, which was entrusted to me" (1 Tim 1:11). In Crete, Titus is to complete what appears to be an initial setting up of churches throughout the island by appointing qualified local church leaders (Titus 1:5).[10]

On a Pauline reading of these letters, in particular, it's clear that the LTT are "mission documents" by which Paul guides and encourages his delegates in their ministries with regard to an established (Ephesus) and a more recent work (Crete).[11] The centrality of mission is captured well by Ho, who speaks of the "missionary outlook" of these letters, conveying an "overarching framework of thought that has missions at its center."[12] Indeed, the LTT, particularly 1 Timothy and Titus, portray the apostle as engaged in the mission to which God called him, relying on colaborers to handle matters in particular locales as his delegates as he

---

[10] Apart from the letter to Titus, we possess no direct indication of a Pauline mission to Crete, though Paul's ship stopped there briefly on the way to Rome (Acts 27:8). If Paul had followed his usual pattern of planting churches by preaching in the local synagogue (Acts 13:5, 14; 14:1; 17:1–2, 10; 18:4, 19), he would have found such Jewish beachheads in Crete (cf. Acts 2:11; Philo, *Alleg. Interp.* 282; Josephus, *Ant.* 17.327; *J.W.* 2.103; P. W. van der Horst, "The Jews of Ancient Crete," *JJS* 39 [1988]: 183–200). Wieland argues on the basis of parallels between the letter and the distinctive culture of Crete that Titus is "understood most satisfactorily as a product of early Christian mission and an intriguing example of creative missionary engagement with a specific environment." G. M. Wieland, "Roman Crete and the Letter to Titus," *NTS* 55 (2009): 354.

[11] Barram notes that "inasmuch as Paul's letters aim to nurture the faith of established Christian communities, they are themselves *mission in action*—tools used by Paul to fulfill the terms of his apostolic commission. Everything in Paul's letters—autobiographical details and travel itineraries, theological assertions and benedictions, even the epistolary and rhetorical framing of the letters—serves a missional function for the apostle." M. Barram, *Mission and Moral Reflection in Paul*, StBibLit 75 (New York: P. Lang, 2006), 136.

[12] C. E. Ho, "Mission in the Pastoral Epistles," in A. J. Köstenberger and T. L. Wilder, eds., *Entrusted with the Gospel: Paul's Theology in the Pastoral Epistles* (Nashville: B&H Academic, 2010), 242. Ho's work in this essay is grounded in his dissertation, "Do the Work of an Evangelist: The Missionary Outlook of the Pastoral Epistles" (Ph.D. thesis, University of Aberdeen, 2000).

is engaged in travel or occupied elsewhere.[13] Specifically, in conjunction with the larger idea of his mission, we find Paul speaking of his appointment as a preacher, apostle, and teacher of the Gentiles (1 Tim 2:7; cf. 2 Tim 1:11).

In 2 Timothy Paul seeks to prepare Timothy for assuming the mantle of Paul's mission. With regard to his larger mission, Paul closes 2 Timothy with the intriguing statement that at his first defense "the Lord stood with me and strengthened me, so that I might fully preach (πληροφορηθῇ) the word and all the Gentiles (πάντα τὰ ἔθνη) might hear it" (2 Tim 4:17). The connection between πάντα τὰ ἔθνη and the "fullness" or "completeness" of Paul's proclamation of the apostolic message indicates that more is in view than Paul's being able to complete his presentation without interruption on this occasion.[14] Paul's words in 2 Tim 4:6–7 indicate that he believes he has reached the end of his life and ministry, which supports an understanding of "fully proclaim" (πληροφορηθῇ) that has the Gentile world in view. In any case, Paul has his larger mission in mind as he closes his final canonical letter.[15]

As Towner observes, Paul doesn't expect only his apostolic delegates to participate in his Gentile mission but individual congregations as well: "The theme of witness that underlies much of the ethical teaching reveals one important way in which the Christian communities are to participate in the mission to the Gentiles."[16]

---

[13] Note also the future plans Paul has for his own travels (1 Tim 3:14–15) and those of his associates (Titus 3:12–13). For details see the Introduction to this volume.

[14] C. Spicq, *Les épîtres pastorales*, 4th ed., EBib 39 (Paris: Gabalda, 1969), 820. There is merit in Mounce's reading of the verse's final καί as epexegetical, so that the complete proclamation of the message is specified to *involve* all the nations hearing it. It may be that the reference is forward looking: the Lord carried Paul through his trial so that his apostolic ministry to all the Gentiles might continue. Or it may simply be that Paul viewed the occasion of his first defense (ἀπολογία) as the point at which he had in some sense fully completed his mission to the Gentiles, whether in reaching the political capital of the empire or in reference to his variegated Roman audience as representative of the entire Gentile world. W. D. Mounce, *The Pastoral Epistles*, WBC 46 (Nashville: Nelson, 2000), 596.

[15] Towner argues that what Paul says in his figurative statement of 2 Tim 4:7 "on the historical (and missiological) plane translates into 'I have fully accomplished my mission to the Gentiles.'" P. H. Towner, "1–2 Timothy and Titus," in *Commentary on the New Testament Use of the Old Testament*, ed. G. K. Beale and D. A. Carson (Grand Rapids: Baker, 2007), 911.

[16] P. H. Towner, "The Pastoral Epistles," *NDBT*, 333. See on this point more thoroughly Towner, *Goal of Our Instruction*, 169–99.

To use the language of Titus 2:10, this is how believers whose character and conduct reflect their Christianity "adorn the teaching of God our Savior."[17] Another way Paul calls on his churches to participate in his mission is through prayer. In 1 Tim 2:1–6 the apostle urges that prayers be uttered, first, for all people (ὑπὲρ πάντων ἀνθρώπων), and, second, for kings and those in authority. While these latter prayers may also have the salvation of the rulers themselves in view, "Christians who pray for the authorities of state and city implore God 'to let them create the necessary free space in which the expansion of the gospel is possible.'"[18]

From a larger biblical-theological perspective, Paul's language in 2 Tim 4:17 (ἵνα δι' ἐμοῦ τὸ κήρυγμα πληροφορηθῇ καὶ ἀκούσωσιν πάντα τὰ ἔθνη, "so that through me the message might be fully proclaimed and all the Gentiles might hear it"; ESV, NIV) stands in pronounced continuity with the reference to "all the nations" (πάντα τὰ ἔθνη) in the Abrahamic promises (Gen 18:18; 22:18; 26:4 LXX; cf. Gal 3:8) culminating in the Great Commission (Matt 28:19) and other teachings and instructions of Jesus (e.g., Mark 13:10; Luke 24:45–47).[19] The use of πάντα τὰ ἔθνη here and elsewhere in Paul's writings thus reflects his larger understanding of his mission as bringing to culmination something that had begun long ago (cf., e.g., Rom 1:1–6; 16:26). Just as the Great Commission was given to the apostles representing the new messianic community's (the church's) leadership (Matt 28:18–20), spearheading the early church's mission is a critical element of Paul's mission, extended to his apostolic delegates and successors. This sort of understanding is also reflected in the opening of the letter to Titus, where Paul speaks of his mission as follows:

---

[17] Ho rightly argues that "the ethical posture of the Pastorals is not defensive and merely inward-looking as some commentators have suggested but is also outward-looking and missionary in orientation" ("Mission in the Pastoral Epistles," 242; note his treatment of the "good witness" motif on pp. 245–46).

[18] E. J. Schnabel, *Early Christian Mission*, vol. 2: *Paul & the Early Church* (Downers Grove: InterVarsity, 2004), 1470, citing P. Lampe and U. Luz, "Nachpaulinisches Christentum und pagane Gesellschaft," in J. Becker, et al., *Die Anfänge des Christentums: Alte Welt und neue Hoffnung* (Stuttgart: Kohlhammer, 1987), 213. See also I. H. Marshall, "Biblical Patterns for Public Theology," *EuroJTh* 14 (2005): 79–83.

[19] See A. J. Köstenberger and P. T. O'Brien, *Salvation to the Ends of the Earth: A Biblical Theology of Mission*, NSBT 11 (Downers Grove: InterVarsity, 2001), 101–6.

> Paul, a servant of God and an apostle of Jesus Christ, for the faith of God's elect and their knowledge of the truth that leads to godliness, in the hope of eternal life that *God*, who cannot lie, *promised before time began. In his own time he has revealed his word in the preaching with which I was entrusted* by the command of God our Savior. (Titus 1:1–3; emphasis added)

In speaking of that with which he has been entrusted, Paul highlights his stewardship of the hope of eternal life, a gift God was intent to give before the world began.[20] "In his own time," this truth was revealed through the gospel, which, in turn, occupied a central place in the apostle's preaching. In this way Paul grounds his ministry firmly in God's overarching plan: something new in this plan has been revealed, which has prompted Paul's mission to "all the nations" while at the same time grounding this mission in something ancient.[21] Thus Paul's mission unfolds as part of a trajectory that reaches back at least as far as God's commission to Abraham, which already envisioned a universal blessing through his seed (the Messiah) to all the nations of the earth (Gen 12:1–3; cf. Gal 3:16).

Along similar lines, one is struck by the intriguing connection between 1 Tim 2:8 and Mal 1:11.[22] When Paul commands, "I want the men in every place (ἐν παντὶ τόπῳ) to pray" (1 Tim 2:8), he is almost certainly appropriating the phrase ἐν παντὶ τόπῳ from Mal 1:11 (LXX): "For from the rising of the sun to its setting my name is glorified among the nations, and in every place (ἐν παντὶ τόπῳ) incense is brought to my name, and a pure offering, for my name

---

[20] The stewardship motif, in conjunction with the metaphor of "God's household," is a central plank in the LTT's ecclesiology (§4).

[21] Towner observes, "It is hardly to be disputed that the Paul of the earlier letters regarded his apostolate as a decisive element within the story of redemption. Although previously he imagined that plot complications would find their resolution in another way, the death and resurrection of the Messiah extended the story in an unexpected way. In short, *he discovered that his mission to the Gentiles was to be instrumental in the fulfillment of God's plan to extend the covenant to the whole world*." Towner, "Portrait of Paul and the Theology of 2 Timothy," 152 (emphasis added).

[22] C. K. Barrett briefly mentions the connection in *The Pastoral Epistles* (Oxford: Clarendon, 1963), 54; see also E. Ferguson, "Τόπος in 1 Timothy 2:8," *ResQ* 33 (1991): 65–73; and Towner, "1–2 Timothy and Titus," 893.

is great among the nations, says the Lord Almighty."[23] As Towner notes, the prayers uttered in the churches Paul planted become a sign of "the fulfillment of God's promise to offer salvation to 'the nations,'" and it's noteworthy that Paul's exhortation to prayer follows on the heels of his self-identification as "a herald, an apostle, . . . and a teacher of the Gentiles" (1 Tim 2:7).[24]

One final point relates to the specific mission-related information referenced in the LTT. In 1 Timothy this includes the charge to confront the false teachers in Ephesus (1 Tim 1:3–4), particularly Hymenaeus and Alexander (1 Tim 1:18–20). Interestingly, there are no concluding mission-related instructions in 1 Timothy. In this regard 1 Timothy contrasts with 2 Timothy, which, in addition to mentioning Hymenaeus and Philetus (2 Tim 2:17), concludes with a long list of specific personal references. As many as seventeen individuals (not counting Timothy) are mentioned by name (underlined below):

> Make every effort to come to me soon, because <u>Demas</u> has deserted me, since he loved this present world, and has gone to Thessalonica. <u>Crescens</u> has gone to Galatia, <u>Titus</u> to Dalmatia. Only <u>Luke</u> is with me. Bring <u>Mark</u> with you, for he is useful to me in the ministry. I have sent <u>Tychicus</u> to Ephesus. When you come, bring the cloak I left in Troas with <u>Carpus</u>, as well as the scrolls, especially the parchments. <u>Alexander</u> the coppersmith did great harm to me. . . .
>
> At my first defense, no one stood by me, but everyone deserted me. May it not be counted against them. But the Lord stood with me and strengthened me, so that I might fully preach the word and all the Gentiles hear it. So I was rescued from the lion's mouth. The Lord will rescue me from every evil work and will bring me safely into his heavenly kingdom. To him be the glory forever and ever! Amen.
>
> Greet <u>Prisca</u> and <u>Aquila</u>, and the household of <u>Onesiphorus</u>. <u>Erastus</u> has remained at Corinth; I left <u>Trophimus</u>

[23] Translation from A. Pietersma and B. G. Wright, *A New English Translation of the Septuagint* (Oxford: Oxford University Press, 2007), 820.

[24] Towner, "1–2 Timothy and Titus," 893.

> sick at Miletus. Make every effort to come before winter. Eubulus greets you, as do Pudens, Linus, Claudia, and all the brothers and sisters. (2 Tim 4:9–14a, 16–21)

Similarly, Titus is instructed to appoint elders in Crete (Titus 1:5), and the letter closes with several mission-related instructions (though not nearly as extensive as those concluding 2 Timothy), including four individuals being mentioned by name:

> When I send Artemas or Tychicus to you, make every effort to come to me in Nicopolis, because I have decided to spend the winter there. Diligently help Zenas the lawyer and Apollos on their journey, so that they will lack nothing. (Titus 3:12–13)

It may seem obvious but nonetheless bears repeating: these mission-specific references (most of them to coworkers in the apostolic mission) strongly underscore the primacy of the mission motif in general and the foundational significance of the Pauline mission for the theology of the LTT as a whole. While contemporary readers of the LTT often tend to skip these sections and consider them irrelevant for application due to their time-bound nature, it shouldn't be overlooked that these mission references provide powerful support for the centrality of the mission theme in these documents (opponents are identified in the chart below).

Individuals Mentioned by Name in the Letters to Timothy and Titus

1 Timothy	2 Timothy	Titus
Hymenaeus (1:20; false teacher)	Hymenaeus (2:17; cf. 1 Tim 1:20)	Artemas (3:12)
Alexander (1:20; false teacher)	Philetus (2:17; false teacher)	Tychicus (3:12)
	Demas (4:10; deserter)	Zenas (3:13)
	Crescens (4:10)	Apollos (3:13)
	Titus (4:10)	
	Luke (4:11)	
	Mark (4:11)	
	Tychicus (4:12)	

Individuals Mentioned by Name in the Letters to Timothy and Titus (continued)

1 Timothy	2 Timothy	Titus
	Carpus (4:13)	
	Alexander (4:14; did great harm)	
	Prisca (4:19)	
	Aquila (4:19)	
	Onesiphorus (4:19)	
	Erastus (4:20)	
	Trophimus (4:20)	
	Eubulus (4:21)	
	Pudens (4:21)	
	Linus (4:21)	
	Claudia (4:21)	

In what follows, we'll discuss the important contribution made by the LTT to our understanding of Paul's mission in a number of areas: his apostolic authority; the significance of his apostolic suffering for his mission; his use of apostolic delegates; and the conception of his larger missionary strategy. Moreover, in these letters Paul is well along in his mission and thus concerned to pass on the baton prior to his earthly departure. In this vein he highlights what he refers to as the "deposit" of his teaching—apostolic tradition—and demonstrates his concern that the sound teaching of the faith be preserved in dealing with false teachers. Aspects of this deposit are reflected in the "trustworthy sayings" scattered throughout these letters. Another dimension is Paul's use of and teaching on Scripture.

§1.2 Apostolic Authority and Suffering

Paul's apostolic identity is explicitly affirmed at the outset of each of the LTT[25] and is evident throughout.[26] Although the letters are addressed to Paul's delegates—who doubtless need little

[25] 1 Tim 1:1; 2:7; 2 Tim 1:1, 11; Titus 1:1.

[26] The word ἀπόστολος appears only four times in the LTT (1 Tim 1:1; 2:7; 2 Tim 1:1, 11), but words and concepts reflecting apostolic authority are common (see discussion below).

reminder of Paul's status as an apostle—they are apparently not meant to be received solely and privately by Timothy and Titus but also to be overheard by their respective congregations.[27] Paul's apostolic authority finds forceful expression in the authoritative language used,[28] whether in the form of direct commands or third-person imperatives addressed to the congregations.[29] Paul considers himself able to speak authoritatively not only to the congregations at large but also to their local leadership[30] and to Timothy and Titus in particular, who as apostolic delegates are portrayed as outranking local church leaders.[31]

Of particular note regarding Paul's apostolic authority is his statement in 1 Tim 1:20 that he has "delivered to Satan" two false teachers, Hymenaeus and Alexander (note that Hymenaeus, along with Philetus, is mentioned also in 2 Tim 2:17–18 as being among those who falsely taught that the resurrection had already taken place). It's likely that some of the opponents at Ephesus (possibly including these two individuals) were either current or previous elders, and Paul's action of formally excluding them from the congregation emphatically underscores his stance of apostolic authority.[32] In the same vein Paul later lays down guidelines

[27] This is suggested by the closing plurals in 1 Tim 6:21; 2 Tim 4:22; and Titus 3:15, as well as the third-person imperatives in the letters. See various approaches to an audience beyond the LTT's named recipients in J. Ellington, "Problem Pronouns in Private Letters," *BT* 50 (1999): 222–23; M. Harding, *Tradition and Rhetoric in the Pastoral Epistles* (New York: P. Lang, 1998), 85; L. T. Johnson, *The First and Second Letters to Timothy*, AB 35A (Garden City, NY: Doubleday, 2001), with his *mandata principis* hypothesis; L. Kidson, "1 Timothy: An Administrative Letter," *Early Christianity* 5 (2014): 97–116; F. Young, "The Pastoral Epistles and the Ethics of Reading," *JSNT* 45 (1992): 105–20. Recognizing the congregation as audience goes a long way to answering contentions such as that of Collins, who argues that the use of the term "apostle" "seems out of place in letters addressed to such companions and beloved co-workers [*sic*] as Timothy and Titus." R. F. Collins, "The Image of Paul in the Pastorals," *LTP* 31 (1975): 148.

[28] E.g., βούλομαι (1 Tim 2:8), διαμαρτύρομαι (2 Tim 4:1), οὐκ ἐπιτρέπω (1 Tim 2:12), παραγγέλλω (1 Tim 6:13), παραγγελία (1 Tim 1:5, 18), and παρακαλέω (1 Tim 1:3; 2:1).

[29] E.g., 1 Tim 2:11; 3:10, 12; 4:12; 5:4, 9, 16, 17; 6:1, 2; Titus 2:15; 3:14. Such imperatives are conspicuously absent from 2 Timothy, and nearly so from Titus.

[30] E.g., 1 Tim 5:17.

[31] E.g., 1 Tim 1:3–5, 18; 4:11, 12; 5:7, 21; 6:2, 13, 17; 2 Tim 2:14; 4:1–2; Titus 1:3; 2:15.

[32] As Marshall observes, the congregational involvement in "handing over to Satan" the sexually immoral man of 1 Corinthians 5 is not necessarily at odds with what appears to be a more unilateral action on Paul's part in the present passage. In 1 Corinthians 5, Paul's apostolic "presence" and pronouncement of judgment

for Timothy his apostolic delegate in handling the discipline or removal of errant elders (1 Tim 5:19–20).

More than once Paul speaks of his apostolic office, which may be part of his strategy to legitimate the authority of his teaching and directives (and thus that of his delegates) over against the false teachers.[33] For example, after Paul opens 1 Timothy by addressing the issue of false teaching at Ephesus (1:3–11), he uses his own contrasting example to highlight the nature of his gospel as one of mercy, grace, and transformation rather than genealogies, myths, and law (1:12–17). In this connection Paul goes on to refer to the juncture at which Jesus appointed him to his service, that is, Paul's ministry as an apostle (1:12).[34] In this context Paul draws particular attention to the gracious nature of his apostolic calling.[35] Later in the letter (and similarly in 2 Timothy) Paul reiterates certain aspects of his gospel and observes that it was for the proclamation of this gospel that he was called to be a preacher, apostle, and teacher of the Gentiles (1 Tim 2:7; 2 Tim 1:11).

In 2 Timothy a particular emphasis emerges on the apostle's suffering that runs through the entire letter.[36] As Paul the prisoner (1:8, 16; 2:9) opens the letter, the topic of his suffering at once

---

on the man are noted (vv. 3–4), and here Paul's nonmention of any congregational involvement doesn't preclude it. I. H. Marshall, *Pastoral Epistles*, ICC (Edinburgh: T&T Clark, 1999), 414.

[33] On the so-called "Pauline polemic," see the discussion in the Introduction to this volume.

[34] This is suggested to be the case by Paul's immediately preceding statement that he was entrusted with the gospel (cf. 2 Tim 1:12; Titus 1:3). He relates his apostleship at various points to the promulgation of the gospel (cf. 1 Tim 2:7; 2 Tim 1:10–11; Titus 1:1—the gospel is that *to which* he was appointed a preacher and *apostle* and teacher). Note in Acts 20:24 (in his address to the Ephesians elders) Paul's closer specification of his διακονία as διαμαρτύρασθαι τὸ εὐαγγέλιον τῆς χάριτος τοῦ θεοῦ. Note also the connection in Rom 11:13 between his assertion εἰμι ἐγὼ ἐθνῶν ἀπόστολος and his reference to διακονίαν μου.

[35] In connection with 1:12–17, Mounce wonders if the emphatic form and placement of δι' ἐμοῦ in 2 Tim 4:17 may not highlight "Paul's wonder that God would use one such as he [*sic*]" (*Pastoral Epistles*, 596).

[36] The vocabulary of suffering in the LTT as a whole is largely confined to 2 Timothy and includes κακοπαθέω (2x: 2 Tim 2:9; 4:5), συγκακοπαθέω (2x: 2 Tim 1:8; 2:3), πάθημα (1x: 2 Tim 3:11), and πάσχω (1x: 2 Tim 1:12), as well as the use of διώκω in 2 Tim 3:12. On the topic of Paul's suffering more generally, see D. E. Frederickson, "Paul, Hardships, and Suffering," in *Paul in the Greco-Roman World: A Handbook*, vol. 1, ed. J. P. Sampley (New York: Bloomsbury T&T Clark, 2016).

comes to the fore (1:8–12). In v. 8 the veteran apostle challenges Timothy not to shrink from the proclamation of the gospel or from associating with Paul as the Lord's prisoner. Instead, Timothy must join with Paul in suffering for the gospel. After stepping back for a big-picture look at the gospel in vv. 9–10 and highlighting his own appointment as a preacher, apostle, and teacher of that gospel, Paul acknowledges that it's because of this appointment that he's currently suffering. In what follows, he engages the language of his challenge to Timothy as he points to himself as a model for his foremost disciple. Just as Timothy must not be ashamed (ἐπαισχύνομαι) of Paul and his gospel proclamation but must join him in suffering (συγκακοπαθέω) for the gospel (εὐαγγέλιον; 1:8), so Paul is suffering (πάσχω) for the gospel (εὐαγγέλιον) and is not ashamed (ἐπαισχύνομαι; 1:10–12). Given this correspondence in language, the grounds for Paul's lack of shame are implied to be Timothy's as well: Paul knows the God in whom he trusts, and he's convinced that God will guard his deposit.[37]

This progression—from Paul to Timothy to faithful men to others—is significant in its connection with the suffering that accompanies the apostolic ministry as well. In fact, 2 Timothy reflects a passing of the torch from Paul to Timothy, and 1:8–12 suggests that Timothy may have been fearful (lacking one of the Greek cardinal virtues, i.e., courage) with regard to the suffering his own ministry would continue to entail. After an aside regarding those who have deserted him (1:15) and one who has remained loyal to him (1:16–18), Paul returns to encouraging Timothy, continuing to tie suffering to the ministry of the gospel as he calls his foremost disciple to be strong in Jesus's grace (2:1). Paul also urges Timothy to perpetuate Paul's gospel ministry in the lives of other trustworthy men and to share in his suffering (συγκακοπαθέω). In particular, Timothy is called to share in suffering as a good soldier of Christ Jesus, which may imply continuity with Jesus's suffering as well.

At the same time, it's of note that in spite of the connection between Paul's and Jesus's suffering (cf. 2 Cor 1:5–7; 4:8–14; Col 1:23–26), and in spite of 2 Timothy's oblique references to Jesus's suffering (1:8; 2:8–10), the suffering of Jesus is nowhere directly

---

[37] On the interpretation of this phrase see the commentary above.

mentioned in the letter. Instead, Jesus is overtly portrayed—doubtless for Timothy's encouragement—on the other side of the grave, having abolished death and brought life and immortality to light through the gospel (1:10), having risen from the dead (2:8), and serving as the righteous judge of the living and the dead (4:1, 8). To be sure, Paul's suffering for the gospel is tied to the death of Christ in 2:11,[38] but only as part of what is probably a preformed tradition, and as a passing protasis ("If we died with him") on the way to a hopeful apodosis ("we will also live with him"). In 2:9 Paul reiterates that it's the gospel for which he, bound as a criminal, is suffering. Because God's gospel message isn't bound, however, Paul is willing to endure all things for the sake of God's elect (2:10). Paul's suffering thus leads to a desirable end, similar to how dying with Christ leads to being alive with him (2:11).

After reminding Timothy to avoid the false teachers who are described at some length in 3:1–9, Paul points out that in contrast to these individuals, Timothy has known and followed Paul's example.[39] One aspect of Paul's model that Timothy should continue to emulate is that of accepting persecution (διωγμός) and suffering (πάθημα). Timothy is familiar with the persecutions and sufferings Paul underwent on his first missionary journey in Pisidian Antioch, Iconium, and Lystra (3:11; cf. Acts 13:49–52; 14:4–6, 19–22), which came to a head when Jews from the first two cities caught up with him at Lystra, stoned him, and left him for dead outside the city. Even this last instance of persecution, however, is included in Paul's affirmation that "the Lord rescued me from them *all*" (2 Tim 3:11). What's more, with 2 Tim 3:11 echoing Ps 34:17, 19, as Towner notes, Paul "makes explicit his interest in a theology of suffering built on the OT theme of the righteous sufferer" and goes on in v. 12 to

---

[38] Note that Paul speaks of the *death* of Christ, with no mention of suffering *per se*, although Christ's death in 2:10 does parallel Paul's suffering hardship (κακοπαθέω) in 2:8, and his enduring (ὑπομένω) all things in 2:9.

[39] On the nuance of παρηκολούθησας ("followed") here, see Spicq, *Les épîtres pastorales*, 781. To be sure, Timothy has further to go in imitating Paul—hence Paul's exhortations throughout the letter—but the term here doesn't *merely* mean that Timothy carefully observed Paul, as shown by the contrast with those characterized in the previous verses.

present an affirmation "which is essentially a contextualized form of Ps. 33:20a LXX."[40]

Remarkably, then, Paul ties together the virtue of godliness (εὐσέβεια), so characteristic of the letters to Timothy, with suffering for the gospel: "In fact, *all who want to live a godly life* in Christ Jesus will be persecuted" (2 Tim 3:12). A striking contrast is thus established with the preceding vv. 1–9 and the following v. 13. On the one side are those who display only an outward veneer of godliness (ἔχοντες μόρφωσιν εὐσεβείας, 3:5), in particular the false teachers whom Timothy must confront. On the other side are Paul (model of right teaching, moral living, and proper affections), Timothy, and all those who desire to live in a godly way.[41] Although the lines aren't explicitly drawn, it would seem that Timothy and other faithful believers shouldn't merely expect persecution in a generic sense but particularly from those described in the contrasting category (i.e., the false teachers). In the same vein Paul uses Jannes and Jambres as analogues for the opponents and notes that the former stood against Moses with whom Paul appears to align himself in 2 Timothy (§2.7).[42] Similarly, when Paul highlights the specific persecutions he has suffered in 3:11, he doesn't speak of his present imprisonment but of his hounding by the Jews who rejected his teaching.

As 2 Timothy draws to a close, Paul challenges Timothy one final time to "endure hardship" (4:5). His own suffering is reflected shortly thereafter in his reference to Psalm 22 (21 LXX) in the latter half of chapter 4.[43] Having made the point that all who desire to live a godly life will suffer persecution, the apostle now draws on this psalm depicting the righteous sufferer to assist him in

---

[40] Towner, "1–2 Timothy and Titus," 908.

[41] As Knight rightly notes, this "is not a designation of a subgroup of Christians who desire a more godly life but rather a description of real Christians in distinction from those who follow false teaching" (G. W. Knight, *The Pastoral Epistles*, NIGTC [Grand Rapids: Eerdmans, 1992], 441).

[42] Although he approaches his work from a stance of pseudonymity, Martin's work connecting Paul with Moses in 2 Timothy is largely compatible with a reading of 2 Timothy from the stance of authenticity: S. C. Martin, *Pauli Testamentum: 2 Timothy and the Last Words of Moses*, TGST 18 (Rome: Pontificia Università Gregoriana, 1999). See further discussion below.

[43] Towner has made a conclusive case for Paul's use of this psalm and his identification with David as righteous sufferer ("1–2 Timothy and Titus," 909–13).

weaving together a number of themes related to suffering. As Towner points out, Paul is here concerned "to interpret his final episode of suffering for the gospel in terms of the tradition of Jesus's passion."[44] Space prohibits a full discussion of the complex web of interconnections between the psalmist, Jesus, and Paul as righteous sufferers, but the following points may be noted.

First, Paul's suffering was heightened by his sense of abandonment (2 Tim 4:16; cf. 1:15), similar to the psalmist (Ps 22:1) and Jesus (Mark 15:34 par.). Second, in his suffering Paul was helped by the presence of the Lord (2 Tim 4:17), a presence likewise craved by the psalmist (Ps 22:19). Third, Paul was rescued (ῥύομαι) from previous persecutions (2 Tim 3:11; 4:17) and was confident that he would be similarly rescued (ῥύομαι) from every evil deed (2 Tim 4:18), just as the psalmist (Ps 22:8) and Jesus (Matt 27:43) eventually experienced the reality of the rescue (ῥύομαι) that was only mockingly mentioned in connection with their suffering.

Finally, a particularly striking connection can be detected between 2 Timothy 4 and Psalm 22 (LXX Psalm 21) in conjunction with Paul's mission to the Gentiles: the psalmist asserts as one result of God's rescuing him "from the lion's mouth" (Ps 22:21) that "all the ends of the earth will remember and turn to the Lord. All the families of the nations (πᾶσαι αἱ πατριαὶ τῶν ἐθνῶν) will bow down before you" (Ps 22:27); Paul notes that God strengthened him to fully proclaim the gospel message, with "all the Gentiles" (πάντα τὰ ἔθνη) hearing it, and *in conjunction with this* Paul was rescued "from the lion's mouth" (2 Tim 4:17).

These connections place the suffering of Paul and his apostolic delegates, as well as other faithful believers, against the backdrop of an entire biblical trajectory of righteous suffering that encompasses David, the prototypical righteous sufferer (especially at the hands of Saul), and the latter-day son of David, Jesus Christ, the suffering Servant who endured a violent cross-death to atone for the sins of humanity (e.g., 1 Pet 2:21–25; cf. Isa 52:13–53:12). In this way Paul's apostolic mission, reaching to the ends of the earth and including the Gentile nations, is shown to involve (vicarious) suffering that finds validating biblical-theological precedent

[44] Ibid., 912.

in previous servants of the Lord such as David and, climactically, Jesus himself (cf. Col 1:24; see discussion above).

§1.3 The Role of Apostolic Delegates

The apostolic mission, which is rooted in the Great Commission and carried forward in Paul's mission to the Gentiles, significantly involves the use of apostolic delegates who carry out the apostle's orders.[45] Notably, while nomenclature used for Timothy and Titus in the LTT is diverse,[46] neither is said to be an apostle.[47] There is a sense in which they might be considered such in a

---

[45] Cf. Young, *Theology*, 67, who views the apostolic mission as taking place between two epiphanies or imperial visits of Christ, at which time authority is vested in the apostle and his delegates, who in turn are over God's household, the church.

[46] In 1 and 2 Timothy, Timothy is spoken of as Paul's true or beloved child (τέκνον) in the faith (1 Tim 1:2, 18; 2 Tim 1:2; 2:1), as a good servant (διάκονος) of Christ Jesus (1 Tim 4:6), as a man of God (ἄνθρωπος θεοῦ, 1 Tim 6:11; ὁ τοῦ θεοῦ ἄνθρωπος, 2 Tim 3:17), as a good soldier (στρατιώτης) of Jesus Christ (2 Tim 2:3), as a workman (ἐργάτης, 2 Tim 2:15), and as the Lord's servant (δοῦλος, 2 Tim 2:24; "servant of the Lord" in 2 Tim 2:24 is probably meant to refer to church leaders in addition to Timothy but likely includes Timothy as well). Elsewhere in the NT, Timothy is said to be a disciple (μαθητής, Acts 16:1), Christ's servant (δοῦλος, Phil 1:1), and God's coworker (συνεργός, 1 Thess 3:2), as well as Paul's helper (διακονούντος, Acts 19:22), coworker (συνεργός, Rom 16:21), child (τέκνον) in the Lord (1 Cor 4:17), and brother (ἀδελφός, 2 Cor 1:1; Col 1:1; 1 Thess 3:2). Titus, not nearly as prominent in the NT, is spoken of as Paul's brother (ἀδελφός, 2 Cor 2:13), partner (κοινωνός, 2 Cor 8:23), coworker (συνεργός, 2 Cor 8:23), and as his true child (τέκνον) in their common faith (Titus 1:4).

[47] So R. F. Collins, "Where Have All My Siblings Gone? A Reflection on the Use of Kinship Language in the Pastoral Epistles," in *Celebrating Paul. Festschrift in Honor of Jerome Murphy-O'Connor, O.P., and Joseph A. Fitzmyer, S.J.*, ed. P. Spitaler, CBQMS 48 (Washington, DC: Catholic Biblical Association of America, 2011), 333–34, who notes the lack of sibling language in the LTT in general (with the exception of 1 Tim 4:6; 6:2; 2 Tim 4:21). Neither are they given the titles of the church leaders with whom Paul is concerned (ἐπισκοπή, πρεσβύτερος), an observation made by B. Fiore, *The Pastoral Epistles*, SP 17 (Collegeville, MN: Liturgical Press, 2007), 179; see also J. P. Meier, "*Presbyteros* in the Pastoral Epistles," *CBQ* 35 (1973): 342; M. M. Mitchell, "New Testament Envoys in the Context of Greco-Roman Diplomatic and Epistolary Conventions: The Example of Timothy and Titus," *JBL* 111 (1992): 652. While Timothy is listed with Paul and Silas as a sender of 1 Thessalonians and had accompanied them on their initial mission foray into Thessalonica, Paul's statement in 1 Thess 2:7 ("we could have been a burden as Christ's apostles") should be understood as limited to Paul and Silas. For discussion, see G. D. Fee, *The First and Second Letters to the Thessalonians*, NICNT (Grand Rapids: Eerdmans, 2009), 64.

nontechnical sense—*Paul's ἀπόστολοι*, sent by Paul with his apostolic authority backing them as they act as his representatives.[48] Titus and Timothy are repeatedly instructed to authoritatively communicate Paul's instruction; on Paul's behalf they are to command (παραγγέλλω),[49] teach (διδάσκω),[50] urge (παρακαλέω),[51] remind (ὑπομιμνῄσκω),[52] and insist on (διαβεβαιόομαι)[53] the things Paul has set forth.[54] However, they were apparently lacking in the necessary qualifications of an apostle as such; unlike Paul, they had probably not "seen Jesus" (cf. 1 Cor 9:1).

Whether the term ἀπόστολος can be properly applied to Timothy and Titus, the fact remains that the canonical documents don't do so. E. E. Ellis observes that among Paul's numerous associates, some seem to have played a more collaborative and somewhat independent role (e.g., Apollos, Priscilla and Aquila, Barnabas, Silas), while others "appear as Paul's subordinates, serving him or being subject to his instructions."[55] Given the tenor of the LTT, we may place Timothy and Titus, as Ellis does, in the latter category, and it has been common to style such coworkers as "apostolic delegates."[56] Such a position might be simply defined as "a subor-

[48] In connection with "apostolic delegates," consider the significance of the laying on of hands by Paul in 2 Tim 1:6, cf. 1 Tim 4:14. Cf. J. F. Tipei, *The Laying on of Hands in the New Testament: Its Significance, Techniques, and Effects* (Lanham, MD: University Press of America, 2009), 268: "In the manner of a Jewish Rabbi who ordains his own student to become a teacher of the Law, so Paul ordains Timothy as his delegate in order to preserve the established apostolic teaching. Like his Rabbinic counterpart, Timothy is not installed into a given office with precisely defined administrative duties. As an apostolic delegate, he is an intermediary link between the apostolic authority and the mon-episcopacy of the second century."

[49] 1 Tim 1:3; 4:11; 5:7; 6:17.

[50] 1 Tim 4:11; 6:2.

[51] 1 Tim 5:1; 6:2; 2 Tim 4:2.

[52] 2 Tim 2:14; Titus 3:1.

[53] Titus 3:8.

[54] Probably because the LTT are written primarily to Timothy and Titus themselves, Paul doesn't use vocabulary that would be equivalent to "apostolic delegate," such as *συνεργός* or *διακονούντος*. What the LTT teach about the role of apostolic delegates must be inferred more indirectly.

[55] E. E. Ellis, "Paul and His Coworkers," *DPL* 183.

[56] Funk uses the equivalent term *apostolic emissary*. R. W. Funk, "The Apostolic *Parousia*: Form and Significance," in *Christian History and Interpretation: Studies Presented to John Knox*, ed. W. R. Farmer, C. F. D. Moule, and R. R. Niebuhr (Cambridge: Cambridge University Press, 1967), 249.

dinate of an apostle who acts with his authority in his absence." Elsewhere in the NT, we read of Paul's coworkers functioning as apostolic delegates in this sense,[57] and the LTT contribute to our understanding of Paul's missionary practice and strategy by detailing some of the specifics of such a role. We find that both Timothy and Titus, as Paul's delegates, have been left in a certain locale to represent Paul and to further his mission—Timothy in Ephesus (1 Tim 1:3) and Titus in Crete (Titus 1:5).[58]

With regard to Timothy, his marching orders in 1 Timothy (προσμεῖναι ἐν Ἐφέσῳ . . . ἵνα) pertain to correcting those who teach false doctrine in the church (1:3–4). Throughout the letter Paul issues instructions on this and other matters, not only to Timothy directly but also to the congregation. As Paul's delegate, Timothy is responsible to convey Paul's instructions to the congregation and to hold people accountable to follow these instructions. This is regularly made explicit as Paul pauses to instruct Timothy to "command and teach these things" or the like.[59] As to the specific church-related responsibilities given to Timothy, he is to (1) stop the false teachers from teaching false doctrine (1:3–4); (2) authoritatively communicate what Paul is commanding and teaching in the letter (4:6, 11; 5:7; 6:2, 17); (3) provide a godly example for the congregation (4:12, 15–16); (4) devote himself to the public reading of Scripture and to the exhortation and teaching that follow from such reading (4:13); (5) exhort various members of the congregation in the context of the church family, giving consideration to their age and gender, possibly in relation to guiding them away from false teaching they may have embraced to proper belief and behavior (5:1–2);[60] (6) honor true widows by regulating the

---

[57] Timothy is portrayed as Paul's delegate to various churches other than that at Ephesus; see Acts 18:5; 19:22; 1 Thess 3:2; Phil 2:19 (potentially); 1 Cor 4:17; 16:10–11. Similarly, Titus: 2 Cor 7:6–15; 8:6, 16–23; 2 Tim 4:10.

[58] It should probably be assumed that Timothy was still in Ephesus when Paul wrote 2 Timothy. This is hinted at in 2 Tim 1:18 and suggested by the textual location of Paul's note that he is sending Tychicus to Ephesus (2 Tim 4:12), situated as it is between Paul's request to Timothy to bring Mark with him when he comes to Paul (2 Tim 4:11) and Paul's request that Timothy bring Paul's cloak, books, and parchments when he comes (2 Tim 4:13). The references to Timothy's coming to Paul surrounding 4:12 suggest that Tychicus is coming to Ephesus to replace Timothy, at least for a time.

[59] 1 Tim 4:11; 5:7; 6:2.

[60] It's likely that these verses aren't wholly generic, merely giving general instruction to Timothy as to the way in which he should relate to various groups in

church's support program (5:3–16); (7) handle accusations against elders by accepting only substantiated charges and rebuking persistently sinning elders in the presence of the congregation (5:19–21); and (8) avoid haste in appointing men to the office of elder (5:22).

In 2 Timothy, Paul seems less concerned with church matters and more intent on encouraging Timothy to remain loyal to Paul and his gospel in spite of suffering. That said, church matters are by no means out of view: as Paul's delegate, Timothy is to (1) entrust Paul's teaching to other faithful men for its perpetuation (2:2); (2) remind the congregation of Paul's teaching (2:14); (3) charge the congregation not to engage in the fruitless debates that apparently characterized the false teachers (2:14, 16); (4) kindly and adeptly correct his opponents, with gentleness and without quarreling (2:24–25); (5) engage in "the faithful presentation of the Christian message to the church with the accompanying discipline that is needed for people who are tempted not to listen or to heed it"[61] (4:2); and (6) do the work of an evangelist, that is, proclaim the gospel (4:5).

The letter to Titus, similar to 1 Timothy, provides a straightforward statement of Paul's purpose for his delegate (1:5). In general terms, Titus is to complete aspects of Paul's mission to Crete that have remained unfinished; more specifically, he is to appoint elders in the cities of Crete where Christian congregations have been established. In addition, he is, (1) along with the elders he appoints, to silence the false teachers present in the churches (1:9–14); (2) to teach what is consistent with healthy doctrine, urging proper conduct to various age groups within the church (2:1–6); (3) to model good works and blameless teaching (2:7–8); (4) to authoritatively declare and remind the Cretan believers of Paul's teaching and to exhort and rebuke his hearers as necessary

---

the congregation. That this is the case is suggested by the immediately preceding admonition of 4:16: Timothy is to keep a close watch on his own life and doctrine and should follow Paul's teaching carefully because in doing so he will help preserve both himself and those who listen to him. The first verses of chapter 5, then, detail how Timothy is to relate to various groups of those who listen to him. What's more, when Timothy is told not to rebuke (ἐπιπλήσσω) an older man but to appeal (παρακαλέω) to him, this seems to imply the possibility that something may warrant rebuke.

[61] Marshall, *Pastoral Epistles*, 799. This includes preaching the word, and doing so in an urgent way, reproving, rebuking, and exhorting the hearers.

(2:15–3:1; 3:8); (5) to avoid participating in worthless disputes with the false teachers (3:9); and (6) after warning factious people twice, to reject (παραιτέομαι) them, which probably involves their formal exclusion from the congregation.[62]

This survey of responsibilities given to Timothy and Titus provides insight into the role of an apostolic delegate.

1. The role entails a considerable measure of *authority*. This is evident in the strong language of command Paul uses when speaking of their interaction with their respective congregations, their significant role in appointing elders and excluding false teachers from the congregation, their role of teaching apostolic doctrine, and Paul's insistence that their congregations are not to reject or despise them (1 Tim 4:12; Titus 2:15).

2. Their authority is not *intrinsic* but *delegated*. Time and again Paul insists that they teach and urge their congregations to heed his instructions and commands.[63] Similarly Paul insists that they bring the Scriptures to bear upon their congregations: the God-breathed Scriptures equip the man of God (2 Tim 3:16–17), and it is to the public reading and exhortation and teaching of this Scripture that Timothy must devote himself (1 Tim 4:13).

3. The *preservation and perpetuation of the apostolic teaching* is paramount in their work: they must be sure to teach what is consistent with sound doctrine, fight against false teaching, and entrust Paul's teaching to faithful men.

4. The role of Timothy and Titus as apostolic delegates was *temporary*: Timothy is envisioned as leaving Ephesus to come to Paul (2 Tim 4:9, 11–13, 21), and a similar situation obtains with Titus (Titus 3:12; cf. 2 Tim 4:10). Similarly, Paul indicates that Timothy's ministry of bringing Scripture to bear on the Ephesian congregation is to be done "until I come" (ἕως ἔρχομαι, 1 Tim 4:13), which implies that Paul will take the reins back at that time.[64]

---

[62] As with appointing elders to office, this imperative to Titus does not necessitate unilateral action on his part.

[63] As Mitchell shows ("New Testament Envoys," 649–51), this was commensurate with the standard role of an envoy in Greco-Roman culture, although Paul's own conception of his delegates may well have been shaped more significantly by the role of the Jewish *shaliach* or his own role as an apostle of Christ.

[64] See Meier, "*Presbyteros* in the Pastoral Epistles," 342; B. L. Merkle, "Ecclesiology in the Pastoral Epistles," in *Entrusted with the Gospel*, 196–97.

5. Paul's apostolic delegates were *competent*. As Mounce notes, "The often-painted picture of Timothy as a weak, timid person is not supported by the evidence. He was Paul's 'first lieutenant,' someone Paul felt comfortable sending into difficult situations, as he did repeatedly throughout Acts."[65] This assessment is underscored by Phil 2:19–22, where Paul speaks of Timothy's "proven worth" (τήν ... δοκιμὴν αὐτοῦ).

Why did Paul send delegates to churches, as opposed to going himself? Doubtless, at least part of the reason lies in the multiplicity of needs Paul encountered in the many churches under his care. Many congregations required special attention beyond what their nascent leadership could provide, but Paul could physically be in only one place at a time. Through his delegates, however, his apostolic "presence" could extend to numerous churches.[66]

---

[65] Mounce, *Pastoral Epistles*, lviii. Note in this connection C. R. Hutson, "Was Timothy Timid? On the Rhetoric of Fearlessness (1 Corinthians 16:10–11) and Cowardice (2 Timothy 1:7)," *BR* 42 (1997): 58–73, who concludes that "the testimony of both Acts and Paul regarding Timothy is entirely positive. There is no indication in these writings that the historical Timothy was anything but a strong, dependable, and self-sacrificing evangelist" (p. 65). He reads "spirit of cowardice" in 2 Tim 1:7 as "a rhetorical device . . . to appeal to Timothy's sense of shame in order to goad him on to what is noble" (p. 73).

[66] Mitchell challenges the assumption that Paul always considered his personal presence to be preferable in all ways to his presence in form of a letter or envoy ("New Testament Envoys," 641–62). She argues instead that "in certain instances, Paul sent envoys or letters (or both) to represent him because he thought that they might be more effective than a personal visit in dealing with a particular situation that was facing a church" (p. 642). Her case studies focus not on the LTT (which she considers to be deutero-Pauline) but on Timothy's envoyship to and from the Thessalonians (1 Thessalonians 3; cf. Acts 17–18), and on Titus's similar role in 2 Cor 7:5–16. She concludes, "Hardly mere substitutes for the universally preferable Pauline presence, these envoys were consciously sent by Paul to play a complex and crucial intermediary role that he could not play, even if present himself" (p. 662). However, it is not clear that Timothy and Titus fulfilled the same role in Ephesus and Crete, since they weren't *sent* (strictly speaking) by an absent Paul but were *left* in their respective locations by Paul as he departed to minister elsewhere (1 Tim 1:3; Titus 1:5). What's more, in Timothy's case one gets the impression that upon Paul's return at least some of Timothy's responsibilities would revert to Paul (1 Tim 4:13).

§1.4 Paul's Larger Mission Theology and Strategy and the LTT

Before concluding our discussion of the mission motif in the LTT, it'll be instructive to cast our net a bit wider in order to view the LTT's mission motif within a larger framework, namely Paul's overall mission strategy. N. T. Wright seeks to probe the underlying dynamic of Paul's mission in his later years.[67] He locates Paul's motivation in "Jewish apocalyptic," understood not as pertaining narrowly to the end of the world but as broad "strategy for both narrating and living the counter-imperial story in which Israel's God, the creator, dethrones the present world rulers and exalts a messianic figure in their place."[68] In Christ a "new moment" had come, which constituted "the long-awaited fulfillment of ancient prophecies and promises," ensuing, in keeping with prophecies such as those found in Daniel 2 and 7, "after a historical sequence characterized by a succession of world empires" in the "fullness of time" (Gal 4:4).[69] As an "apocalyptic thinker," Paul espoused an eschatology "rethought around Jesus as Israel's Messiah and around the fresh gift of the divine spirit," which "necessarily involved an important though oblique confrontation with the last great world empire, that of Rome."[70]

Wright contends that, "If we want to understand what Paul thought he was called to do in the last years of his life, we need to place his vision of creation renewed in fulfillment of the Abrahamic promises and under the sovereignty of Israel's Messiah at its heart."[71] This, in turn, involves understanding Paul's statement regarding a future mission in Spain in Rom 15:24, 28 in the buildup to this passage in the book of Romans. In Rom 4:13 Paul affirms that God's promise to Abraham and his offspring pertained to their inheritance of *the world*, not merely some geographical territory in the Middle East. Thus, in keeping with the universal rule promised the future Davidic king, and Psalm 8's vision of glory (i.e., sovereignty) being given over all of creation, Paul in Romans 8 shows the retold

[67] N. T. Wright, "Paul's Western Missionary Project: Jerusalem, Rome, Spain in Historical and Theological Perspectives," in *Last Years of Paul*, 49–66.

[68] Ibid., 53.

[69] Ibid., 54.

[70] Ibid.

[71] Ibid., 57.

exodus story coming to a climax: "The people who leave the state of slavery by coming through the waters of baptism (Romans 6; compare 1 Corinthians 10.1–2), who then arrive at Mount Sinai to face the challenge of Torah (Romans 7), are now led by the divine presence through the challenging wilderness (Romans 8.12–17) to the 'inheritance' which is the Messiah's and which he will share with his people (8.18–30)."[72]

This, in turn, fleshes out Paul's gospel, which he understood to be not merely about Jewish restoration but about "the redemption and renewal of creation itself, and of humans within that."[73] Thus the gospel isn't merely about justification by faith, vital as that is, but also about the announcement of the universal lordship of the Lord Jesus Christ, the long-awaited Messiah who had come, died atoningly, and risen triumphantly. All of this climaxes in Rom 15:7–13, in particular the catena of OT passages cited in vv. 9–12, all of which prophesy the Messiah's rule over, and outreach to, the Gentiles.[74] Romans 15:7–13, in turn, lays the foundation for Paul's missionary strategy enunciated in Rom 15:14–32.[75] What is instrumental to this strategy, then, is Paul's self-designation, unique to the LTT, of being a herald (κήρυξ; 1 Tim 2:7; 2 Tim 1:11) whose role was to make an initial announcement (cf. the use of the ἐυαγγέλιον

---

[72] Ibid., citing Wright, "New Exodus, New Inheritance: The Narrative Structure of Romans 3–8," in *Romans and the People of God: Essays in Honor of Gordon D. Fee on the Occasion of His 65th Birthday*, ed. S. K. Soderlund and N. T. Wright (Grand Rapids: Eerdmans, 1999), 26–35; and S. C. Keesmat, *Paul and His Story: (Re) Interpreting the Exodus Tradition* (Sheffield: Sheffield Academic Press, 1999).

[73] Wright, "Paul's Western Missionary Project," 57.

[74] See also the citation of the beginning of Isaiah's fourth Servant Song (Isa 52:15) in Rom 15:21, noted by R. Riesner, "Paul's Trial and End according to Second Timothy, *1 Clement*, the Canon Muratori, and the Apocryphal Acts," in *Last Years of Paul*, 391 (see also Riesner's other publication noted in ibid., n. 4). But see the critique by J. Herzer, "The Mission and the End of Paul between Strategy and Reality: A Response to Rainer Riesner," in *Last Years of Paul*, 411–31, esp. 413–17.

[75] Wright points out that the Jewish expectation of a worldwide messianic kingdom can be found in Second Temple literature, especially related to Deuteronomy (Wright, "Paul's Western Missionary Project," 58). He also notes that while Paul contextualizes his gospel in a Greco-Roman environment, he proclaims a thoroughly Jewish message (citing an unpublished paper delivered at an SNTS meeting by W. Horbury, "Jewish Imperial Thought and [the] Pauline Gospel" [Leuven, 2012]).

word group in Isa 40:9; 52:7).[76] In this vein Paul conceived of his mission in terms of announcing "Jesus as Messiah and Lord *across the key parts of Caesar's empire*."[77] Thus, having made initial proclamation in Asia, Macedonia, Achaea, and Illyricum, Paul intended to proceed to make initial proclamation of Jesus's lordship at the end of Caesar's earth, Spain.[78]

In this way Paul focused his missionary strategy on Roman provinces and major urban centers. What place, then, do the LTT have within the orbit of Paul's mission? The letters were written at a time when Paul himself had made sufficient proclamation of Christ's universal lordship in most of the Greco-Roman world, including Ephesus. While he himself endeavored to push forward, he didn't therefore abandon the churches he had previously planted. Rather, he assigned their care to trusted deputies such as Timothy and Titus who were charged with dealing with various issues in the local congregations under their care, whether sinning elders (Timothy) or the need to appoint proper leadership (Titus). In this way Paul was able to continue to spearhead the early Christian mission while consolidating the work he had previously done so his efforts would prove not to be in vain (1 Cor 15:58; 1 Thess 3:5; Phil 2:16). As mentioned above, the LTT show Paul engaged in his apostolic mission in his last years until the end (see 2 Tim 4:9–22; see esp. v. 10, indicating that Titus had now moved on to Dalmatia). Whether Paul ever went to Spain, he laid the foundation for the worldwide proclamation of the good news of salvation in the Lord Jesus Christ on which subsequent generations were able to build (cf., e.g., 2 Tim 2:2).[79]

---

[76] Wright, "Paul's Western Missionary Project," 60. Cf. the use of *κήρυγμα* in Rom 16:25; 1 Cor 1:21; 2:4; 15:14; and the numerous instances of *κηρύσσω* in Paul's letters (e.g., Rom 10:8, 14, 15; 1 Cor 1:23; 9:27; 15:11, 12; etc.).

[77] Ibid., 61 (emphasis original).

[78] Ibid., 62, in critical interaction with K. Magda, *Paul's Territoriality and Mission Strategy*, WUNT 2/266 (Tübingen: Mohr-Siebeck, 2009), chap. 4. On the question of whether there were Jews in Spain in Paul's day, see Wright, "Paul's Western Missionary Project," 64–65, esp. n. 50, and the scholarly literature cited there.

[79] Wright ("Paul's Western Missionary Project," 66) makes the intriguing comment that whether Paul ever reached Spain, in God's sovereign providence his desire to go to Spain via the church in Rome led the apostle to write the book of Romans, which has proven to be a major contribution regardless of whether Paul's plans to missionize Spain ever materialized.

§1.5 Conclusion

The theology of the LTT is firmly embedded in the Pauline mission. This is indicated not only by the presence of Paul's delegates but also by the congruence of the mission strategy in these letters with the other Pauline correspondents and Paul's *modus operandi* in the book of Acts. His commitment to appoint qualified leaders in every church and in every city, his commitment to purge the church of sin and to remove sinning elders, his global vision, his apostolic authority and self-understanding as a herald of the gospel, and his preparedness to suffer for the cause of Christ tie the LTT inextricably to the mission of Paul as depicted in the book of Acts and Paul's other ten NT letters.

Within this mission it's evident that these letters are to be located toward the end of Paul's missionary career at a time when the apostle passed on his legacy to his trusted associates. In characteristic fashion Paul is shown to prepare his delegates for the challenges they will face and to formulate a theology that is not a mere carbon copy or extrapolation of that found in his other letters (as a later follower of Paul might have done) but a contextualized theology that, as will be seen further below, effectively engages the world in which Paul and his associates lived and ministered. In this way Paul, as a missionary and a theologian, serves as a powerful example for those who are called to lead and participate in the church's mission today.

The LTT thus make important contributions to the understanding of Paul's mission in a number of areas: (1) Paul's apostolic authority; (2) the significance of his apostolic suffering for his mission; (3) his use and training of apostolic delegates; and (4) the connection between the LTT and Paul's broader mission strategy and theology as evident particularly in the book of Romans culminating in chapter 15. In these ways these missives to Paul's apostolic delegates bear telling testimony to Paul's understanding, performance, and continuation of his mission.

§2 Teaching

In a sense the LTT in their entirety contain *paraenesis*, that is, ethical instruction and exhortation.[80] This body of teaching is to be understood in the context of first-century Greco-Roman education[81] and the depiction of the church as God's ho usehold (§4.1). Within the household, moral conduct is imperative, as are properly aligned relationships and adherence to tradition. This pertains to God's household, the church, just as it did to the natural household in the first-century Greco-Roman world: "The predominant concern is about correct relationships, duties and obligations in a community which regards itself as a teaching environment with a pattern of virtuous behavior and a set of authoritative writings."[82] Thus the household was the primary place where ancient education took place.[83] This, in turn, explains why Paul was perturbed when certain false teachers invaded households (e.g., 2 Tim 3:6) and sought to infiltrate them with their teaching that was contrary to apostolic doctrine.

Throughout the LTT, reference is made to some in the church who were perpetrating teachings contrary to Paul's gospel. This heretical threat relates directly to Paul's mission (§1), because "countering heresy and [doing] missions are not mutually exclusive endeavors. . . . Warning and protecting believing communities against the insidious teachings of heretics have been a part of the apostle Paul's mandate as 'Apostle to the Gentiles.'"[84] In response Paul's delegates were to preserve and perpetuate what Paul taught (§3.5.5), and Paul uses a number of terms to describe this apostolic

---

[80] See Young, *Theology*, 78, who cites terminology such as παραγγέλλω, παραγγελία, παρακαλέω, παράκλησις, μανθάνω, παιδεία, and παιδεύω. See also C. S. Smith, *Pauline Communities as "Scholastic Communities": A Study of the Vocabulary of 'Teaching' in 1 Corinthians, 1 and 2 Timothy and Titus*, WUNT 2/335 (Tübingen: Mohr-Siebeck, 2012), who after thorough examination concludes that E. A. Judge's characterization of believing communities as "scholastic" (or, better, "learning communities") is appropriate in the cases of Corinth, Ephesus, and Crete.

[81] As Young (*Theology*, 79) notes, "The education of mind and body through *paideia* was the classical Greek ideal" (citing relevant literature in ibid., n. 2).

[82] Ibid., 83.

[83] Cf. Young (ibid., 82), who states, "Indeed, it was in the household that much education and training must have taken place. The head of the household was responsible for the appropriate nurture of family and servants."

[84] Ho, "Mission in the Pastoral Epistles," 248.

teaching,[85] usually in contexts where it is contrasted with false teaching. If false teaching is rightly understood as the main problem faced across the three letters, it would make sense to say that "the fundamental interest of the Pastorals would appear to be 'healthy' or 'sound teaching.'"[86] Vocabulary covering the content of Paul's apostolic mission is diverse and includes references to "healthy teaching," "the truth," "the faith," "the word of God," and "the deposit."[87]

§2.1 Healthy Teaching

The phrase "healthy teaching" is part of the LTT's distinctive vocabulary.[88] The phrase hints at the existence of teaching that is not healthy. In fact, the connection between the gospel and deviant instruction comes into focus at once in the LTT. When identifying false teaching as the primary problem Timothy must address in Ephesus, Paul makes immediate reference to proper teaching.[89] He speaks of the false teachers' misuse of the law, noting that the law wasn't laid down for the righteous but for sinners, and, after referencing various types of sinners, states that the law was laid down

---

[85] Key terms in the LTT include διδασκαλία (1 Tim 1:10; 4:6, 13, 16; 5:17; 6:1, 3; 2 Tim 3:10, 16; 4:3; Titus 1:9; 2:1, 7, 10) and ὑγιαίνω (1 Tim 1:10; 6:3; 2 Tim 1:13; 4:3; Titus 1:9, 13; 2:1, 2); other related terms are discussed below. R. Van Neste (*Cohesion and Structure in the Pastoral Epistles*, JSNTSup 280 [London: T&T Clark, 2004]) demonstrates the cohesion of the LTT through tracing "semantic chains," defined as "a set of words in a discourse which are related to each other semantically because they refer to the same person/concept or to the same general class of people/concepts" (p. 16). L. T. Swinson (*What Is Scripture? Paul's Use of* Graphe *in the Letters to Timothy* [Eugene, OR: Wipf & Stock, 2014]), building on Van Neste's work, proposes that at the time of writing the letters to Timothy, Paul viewed both his own letters and Luke's Gospel as Scripture and included the apostolic writings alongside the OT in his reference to "all Scripture" (πᾶσα γραφή) in 2 Tim 3:16.

[86] Young, *Theology*, 74.

[87] See in this conjunction also the remembrance theme in the LTT, on which see commentary on 2 Tim 2:8–10. For a survey of many of the following motifs see Hagner, *New Testament*, 626–30, who discusses "Protecting Orthodoxy and Orthopraxy," "The Deposit," "The Faith," "The Truth," "The Teaching or Doctrine," "Healthy Doctrine," and the trustworthy sayings.

[88] See the discussion in Hagner, *New Testament*, 629.

[89] See 1 Tim 1:3. Van Neste argues that the charge (παραγγελία) in 1:5 (and 1:18) is part of the semantic chain related to teaching in 1 Timothy (*Cohesion and Structure*, 109). The present treatment, however, is more concerned with proper teaching considered holistically as a body of teaching, and Paul's charge seems to be fairly narrow in scope.

for "whatever else is *contrary to healthy teaching* (ἕτερον τῇ ὑγιαινούσῃ διδασκαλίᾳ;[90] 1 Tim 1:10). Paul then proceeds to refer to the standard of the gospel (κατὰ τὸ εὐαγγέλιον) in v. 11. Whether Paul is setting forth the gospel as the epitome of "healthy teaching" or as the corollary to the correct use of the law (vv. 9–10), Paul's message stands in contrast to the false teaching being propagated at Ephesus (cf. 2 Tim 2:8).[91] This contrast between true and false teaching is sustained throughout the LTT. Paul refers to "healthy teaching" (and the equivalent "healthy words") repeatedly in his correspondence with Timothy and Titus.[92] In addition, the references to false teaching in 1 Tim 1:3 and 6:3 constitute important bookends enveloping the entire letter.

§2.2 The Truth

Proper teaching is described not only in terms of health but also in terms of truth (ἀλήθεια).[93] Thus not only is apostolic doctrine life giving and sustaining; it also corresponds to the actual revelation of God. In 1 Tim 2:4 Paul affirms that God wants all people to be saved and to come to the knowledge of the truth. The church is the pillar and foundation of the truth (1 Tim 3:15). Adherents to Paul's teaching believe and know the truth (1 Tim 4:3), while the false teachers are deprived of it (1 Tim 6:5).

---

[90] Marshall (*Pastoral Epistles*, 381) considers ὑγιαίνουσα διδασκαλία "a technical term in the PE for the approved apostolic doctrine" and contrasts the singular διδασκαλία with the demonic "teachings" mentioned in 1 Tim 4:1.

[91] The relationship between ὑγιαίνουσα διδασκαλία and τὸ εὐαγγέλιον is difficult to determine. Aageson remarks that "presumably, Paul's instruction is influenced and affected by the gospel. Or, at least, it is thought to be consistent with the gospel" (J. W. Aageson, *Paul, the Pastoral Epistles, and the Early Church* [Peabody, MA: Hendrickson, 2008], 96). Marshall (*Pastoral Epistles*, 168) suggests that "teaching" may have the believing congregation in view while "gospel" may be aimed toward outsiders.

[92] Timothy: 1 Tim 6:3; 2 Tim 1:13; 4:3; Titus: Titus 1:9; 2:1–2. Malherbe notes that these expressions "represent a major theme of the letters, viz., that orthodox teaching alone issues in a moral life." A. J. Malherbe, "Medical Imagery in the Pastoral Epistles," in *Light from the Gentiles: Hellenistic Philosophy and Early Christianity*, ed. C. R. Holladay, et al., NovTSup 150 (Leiden: Brill, 2014), 1:117.

[93] Marshall, *Pastoral Epistles*, 168. See also Hagner, *New Testament*, 628–29; and J. D. Quinn, *The Letter to Titus*, AB 35 (Garden City, NY: Doubleday, 1990), 276–82 ("Truth and *epignōsis alētheias* in the PE").

Paul's delegate must rightly handle the word of truth (2 Tim 2:15), for the false teachers have departed from it (2 Tim 2:18), though gentle correction by God's servant may possibly lead them to the knowledge of the truth (2 Tim 2:25). The opponents are always learning but never able to come to the knowledge of the truth (2 Tim 3:7). In fact, they resist the truth (2 Tim 3:8). Those who are swayed by the false teachers likewise won't endure sound teaching but turn away from hearing the truth (2 Tim 4:3–4).

In his letter to Titus, Paul states his desire to advance the knowledge of the truth (1:1) while the false teachers reject it (1:14). In our day, too, there's a clear line of demarcation between true, apostolic doctrine and deviant, heretical teaching. This critical distinction applies particularly to the person and work of Jesus Christ and the message of the gospel.[94] Today's church and its leaders, too, must hold firm to the notion that the gospel of Jesus Christ, and it alone, is true.

§2.3 The Faith

Proper teaching is also spoken of as "the faith" (πίστις).[95] In the following instances, at least, πίστις indicates a body of doctrine to be believed. Timothy was trained in the words of the faith (1 Tim 4:6) and is to fight the good fight for the faith (1 Tim 6:12). Facing the end of his earthly life, Paul declares that he has kept the faith (2 Tim 4:7). Deacons are to hold to the mystery of the faith (1 Tim 3:9); the Cretan Christians must be sharply rebuked so that they may be sound in the faith (Titus 1:13); older men in the congregation are to be sound in the faith as well (Titus 2:2). False teachers have shipwrecked the faith (1 Tim 1:19) and are disqualified concerning it (2 Tim 3:8). Some will follow them and thus depart and swerve from the faith (1 Tim 4:1; 6:21); similarly, craving money causes some to wander from the faith (1 Tim 6:10). Finally, those who don't provide for their relatives have denied the faith (1 Tim 5:8).

---

[94] A. J. Köstenberger, "Orthodoxy," in *The Encyclopedia of Christian Civilization*, 4 vols., ed. G. T. Kurian (Oxford: Blackwell, 2011), 1735–43.

[95] Marshall (*Pastoral Epistles*, 214) refers to this use of πίστις as "the content of what is believed, 'the Christian faith,' i.e., a fixed body of doctrine comparable to 'the truth.'" Mounce (*Pastoral Epistles*, cxxx–cxxxi) speaks of the "objective sense" of πίστις: "a body of truth, 'the faith.'" See also Marshall, "Faith and Works," 213–14; and Hagner, *New Testament*, 628.

What these references make clear is that when the LTT were written, there existed a body of apostolic teaching that represented the standard for sound Christian doctrine.[96] While there were certainly those who challenged this norm—the false teachers being a prime example—this departure from accepted apostolic teaching drew sharp rebuke from Paul and his delegates and in some cases even resulted in excommunication (e.g., 1 Tim 1:20; Titus 3:10–11). The existence of this firm body of apostolic doctrine at the time of writing of the LTT doesn't prove their lateness or pseudonymity, however. As early as in Acts 2:42, reference is made to the fact that the early Christians "devoted themselves to the apostles' teaching."

In Galatians, his first NT letter, the apostle Paul excoriates the Galatian believers for "turning to a different gospel" (Gal 1:6), quickly adding, "not that there is another gospel" (v. 7). Paul goes on to say that "even if we or an angel from heaven should preach to you a gospel contrary to what we have preached to you, a curse be on him" (v. 8). Later Paul affirms that "that the gospel preached by me is not of human origin. For I did not receive it from a human source and I was not taught it, but it came by a revelation of Jesus Christ" (vv. 11–12).

Clearly then the core message of salvation—the gospel—existed virtually from the inception of the church, which is why Paul could write to the Corinthians, "For I passed on to you as most important what I also received: that Christ died for our sins according to the Scriptures, that he was buried, that he was raised on the third day according to the Scriptures" (1 Cor 15:3–4). Thus the references to "the faith" in the LTT take their place in a long string of NT passages that attest to the fact that the Christian faith was centered around a clearly delineated body of teaching concerning the person and work of Jesus Christ and the salvation available in and only through him (e.g., John 14:6; Acts 4:12; 1 John 5:11–12).

This body of apostolic teaching regarding Jesus, in turn, was seen to be firmly grounded in God's promises to his people Israel

---

[96] For a book-length treatment of this issue, see A. J. Köstenberger and M. J. Kruger, *The Heresy of Orthodoxy: How Culture's Fascination with Diversity Has Reshaped Our Understanding of Early Christianity* (Wheaton: Crossway, 2010). See also Köstenberger, "Orthodoxy"; and A. J. Köstenberger, D. L. Bock, and J. D. Chatraw, *Truth in a Culture of Doubt: Engaging Skeptical Challenges to the Bible* (Nashville: B&H Academic, 2014), 107–30.

in OT times. This is nowhere clearer than in the opening words of Romans, where Paul speaks of "the gospel of God—which he promised beforehand through his prophets in the Holy Scriptures—concerning his Son, Jesus Christ our Lord" (Rom 1:1–3). For this reason it's no wonder that much dispute surrounded the proper interpretation of the OT Scriptures (cf., e.g., 1 Tim 1:8–11) and that the accurate understanding of the Scriptures took on supreme importance, as will be discussed in greater detail below (§2.7).

§2.4 The Word of God

In the LTT, "the word" or "message" (λόγος) can at times be equivalent to "the gospel."[97] We've already noted references to "healthy words" (1 Tim 6:3; 2 Tim 1:13) and the "word of truth" (2 Tim 2:15). In addition, "word of God" in 1 Tim 4:5 may pertain to the gospel message,[98] as it does in 2 Tim 2:9. Timothy is to preach the word (2 Tim 4:2); God's promise was shown forth in his word (Titus 1:3); overseers are to be devoted to the trustworthy word which is in accordance with sound teaching (Titus 1:9); and young women are to live godly lives so that the Word of God will not be maligned (Titus 2:5).

Various other expressions also refer to the body of proper teaching in the LTT. In connection with the "words of the faith" in 1 Tim 4:6, Timothy is also trained in the "good teaching" (καλῆς διδασκαλία). In 1 Tim 6:1, in the context of his ministry, he is to give attention to both himself and his teaching. That the body of apostolic teaching has moral implications is reflected in the reference to the "teaching that promotes godliness" with which the false teachers aren't properly aligned (1 Tim 6:3). Paul tells Titus that slaves are to live in such a way that they adorn the teaching about God (Titus 2:10).

Arguably, the references to Scripture in 1 Tim 5:18 and 2 Tim 3:16 encompass, at least by implication, the emergent NT writings and thus include the apostolic teaching (§2.7). Moreover, in 1 Tim 4:13 Timothy is to give attention to the public reading

---

[97] Mounce, *Pastoral Epistles*, 250.

[98] The referent of λόγου θεοῦ here is difficult to determine. Mounce may be on the right track when he sees a reference to God's evaluation of his creative work (including all foods) as good, an evaluation reasserted in the gospel (*Pastoral Epistles*, 241; cf. p. 250).

of Scripture—probably including the extant apostolic writings—along with the exhortation that grows out of that reading and teaching (most likely the body of apostolic doctrine in the light of which Scripture was to be read). The "promise of life" (2 Tim 1:1) may be equivalent to the gospel. Paul instructs Timothy to commit to faithful men "what you have heard from me," which seems to encompass the whole of Paul's apostolic teaching (2 Tim 2:2). As Paul considers the completion of his apostolic mission, he refers to "the proclamation" (κήρυγμα) the Lord gave him strength to fulfill (2 Tim 4:17).

§2.5 The Deposit

One additional term deserves brief comment, the "deposit" (παραθήκη) to which Paul refers in the letters to Timothy. In 1 Tim 6:20 Paul ends the letter with a serious charge to Timothy, enjoining him to "guard the deposit." In 2 Tim 1:14, similarly, Timothy is urged to "guard the good deposit."[99] The term παραθήκη is not used elsewhere in the NT, and Towner registers the important observation that this "language reflects a development in the notion of 'tradition' from the letters of the earlier Paul."[100] He elaborates,

> In the earlier Pauline literature, the technical language of tradition includes παράδοσις (1 Cor. 11:2; Gal. 1:14; 2 Thess. 2:15; 3:6), παραδίδωμι (1 Cor. 11:2), and παραλαμβάνω (Col. 2:6), terms which play no part in the PE. Associated verbs (κατέχω, 1 Cor. 11:2; κρατεῖν, 2 Thess. 2:15; ἑστηκέναι, 1 Cor. 15:1) suggest that for Paul the interest was in accepting and maintaining the growing body of apostolic tradition. But the verbs associated with παραθήκη (παρατίθημι, 2 Tim. 2:2; 1 Tim. 1:18; φυλάσσω, 1 Tim. 6:20; 2 Tim. 1:12; τηρέω, 2 Tim. 4:7) suggest a changed interest in protecting the deposit and transmitting it safely to future generations.[101]

---

[99] As noted above, the term is also used in 2 Tim 1:12; but there seems to have a slightly different nuance, perhaps referring to Paul's life devoted to gospel ministry, which he was confident God would preserve through the perpetuation of his ministry in Timothy. See also 1 Tim 1:11 (entrusted with the gospel) and Titus 1:3 (entrusted with the κήρυγμα, "preaching"). See the discussion in Hagner, *New Testament*, 627–28.

[100] Towner, "Pastoral Epistles," 333.

[101] Towner, "Pauline Theology or Pauline Tradition," 306–7.

Towner rightly associates this development with the impending departure of Paul as well as with the present danger of false teachers in the church.

With considerable variety in terminology, then, Paul expresses his concern throughout the LTT that his teaching—which, in the ultimate analysis, was not original with him—be maintained over against the false teaching present at Ephesus and Crete (e.g., 1 Tim 1:3; 6:3, 20) and be entrusted to and embraced by the leaders of the churches (e.g., 2 Tim 2:2; Titus 1:9). In this way Paul serves as a crucial link between the apostolic teaching about Jesus in the first few decades of the NT church and the subapostolic church that would build on Paul's legacy subsequent to his martyrdom, and the LTT make a significant contribution to NT theology in this regard.

§2.6 Trustworthy Sayings

One of the features that strikingly binds the LTT together as a cluster is the phrase πιστὸς ὁ λόγος ("The saying [is] trustworthy") which is used five times in the three letters and nowhere else in Paul's other writings or anywhere else in the NT.[102] This phrase likely refers to preformed material (whether unmodified or including Pauline material) immediately preceding or following the phrase.[103]

---

[102] Yarbrough avers that the "formulaic expression (πιστὸς ὁ λόγος) . . . draws attention to the literary expression unlike any other formula in the NT." M. M. Yarbrough, *Paul's Utilization of Preformed Traditions in 1 Timothy: An Evaluation of the Apostle's Literary, Rhetorical, and Theological Tactics*, LNTS 417 (London: T&T Clark, 2009), 67.

[103] The demonstration that πιστὸς ὁ λόγος refers to previously existing material rather than serving merely to highlight Paul's own teaching is one of the goals of G. W. Knight III, *The Faithful Sayings in the Pastoral Letters*, Baker Biblical Monographs (Grand Rapids: Baker, 1979). Yarbrough, *Paul's Utilization of Preformed Traditions*, employs a more sophisticated method. Marshall (*New Testament Theology*, 407) suggests that πιστὸς ὁ λόγος isn't so much a marker for preformed material as "primarily a statement of the trustworthiness of the material in question," though he acknowledges that "at least some of these sayings may rest on tradition" (cf. Marshall, *Pastoral Epistles*, 326–29 ["The trustworthy sayings"]). Ellis thinks that, "given their Pauline themes and vocabulary, most 'faithful Word' sayings were probably Paul's compositions" ("Pastoral Letters," *DPL* 664; cf. Ellis, "Traditions in the Pastoral Epistles," in *Early Jewish and Christian Exegesis*, ed. C. A. Evans and W. F. Stinespring [Atlanta: Scholars Press, 1987], 237–53). Towner opines similarly that "there is good reason to think Paul fashioned these set pieces himself—that is, they are more than oft-recited hymns or confessions" ("1–2 Timothy and Titus," 891). Swinson, building on his examination of semantic streams in the letters to Timothy, argues that ὁ λόγος in πιστὸς ὁ λόγος refers not

While debate continues as to what comprises each "faithful saying,"[104] a solid case can be made for the following:[105]

1 Timothy

1. 1 Tim 1:15	Christ Jesus came into the world to save sinners.
2. 1 Tim 3:1	If anyone aspires to be an overseer, he desires a noble work.
3. 1 Tim 4:8	The training of the body has limited benefit, but godliness is beneficial in every way since it holds promise for the present life and also for the life to come.

2 Timothy

4. 2 Tim 2:11–13	For if we died with him, we will also live with him; if we endure, we will also reign with him; if we deny him, he will also deny us; if we are faithless, he remains faithful, for he cannot deny himself.

Titus

5. Titus 3:4–7	When the kindness of God our Savior and his love for mankind appeared, he saved us—not by works of righteousness that we had done, but according to his mercy—through the washing of regeneration and renewal by the Holy Spirit. He poured out his Spirit on us abundantly through Jesus Christ our Savior, so that, having been justified by his grace, we may become heirs with the hope of eternal life.

This interesting literary feature of a "trustworthy saying," together with other linguistic, literary, and theological elements,

---

to a bounded saying but to "a report of a basic gospel truth" (p. 26). In his view πιστὸς ὁ λόγος "serves as an affirmation and confirmation of the firm reliability of the apostolic gospel message" (pp. 31–32) with which it is associated in each of its uses in the LTT. L. T. Swinson, "Πιστὸς ὁ λόγος: An Alternative Analysis" (paper presented at the annual meeting of the Society of Biblical Literature, New Orleans, LA, November 22, 2009).

[104] Campbell deploys form-critical methodology to argue that the writer of the letters tended to "add parentheses and additional comments to his basic formula, comments which incidentally have the effect of obscuring the limits of the saying itself" (R. A. Campbell, "Identifying the Faithful Sayings in the Pastoral Epistles," *JSNT* 54 [1994]: 77). This way of looking at the sayings allows him consistently to identify the "saying" as what follows the introductory phrase. He sees the author of the letters as having interrupted preexisting swaths of paraenetic material with material such as the trustworthy sayings.

[105] Knight makes this case in *Faithful Sayings*. See also the identical list in Hagner, *New Testament*, 630.

provides a degree of coherence for this body of literature. Beyond this, there is considerable variety among these five "trustworthy sayings." The first (1 Tim 1:15) is reminiscent of Jesus's statement in Luke 19:10 and accompanied by the phrase "deserving of full acceptance" (as in 1 Tim 4:9), which is also attested in Hellenistic literature.[106]

In the second "trustworthy saying" (1 Tim 3:1), Paul underscores the propriety of aspiring to the office of overseer and the nobility of the task, similar to Jesus's solemn affirmation, "Truly I tell you" (ἀμήν, ἀμήν; see John 1:51).

The third saying in 1 Tim 4:8 is subject to considerable controversy. Some claim that the saying is found in v. 10 rather than v. 8.[107] On balance, however, v. 8 is to be preferred for the following reasons: (1) v. 8 has the form of a proverbial saying; (2) γυμνασία ("training"; once in the NT) and σωματική ("of the body"; twice in the NT) are rare words, which makes adaptation as a "trustworthy saying" more likely; (3) v. 8 (but not v. 10) speaks of an action for which v. 9 seems to call; and (4) v. 8a can be better explained as part of a saying.

The fourth saying (2 Tim 2:11–13) focuses on the rewards of suffering while affirming that God remains faithful even if his servants are not. In light of the numerous Pauline parallels (see especially Rom 8:28–39), the saying was most likely coined by Paul himself. The statement consists of four conditional clauses, the first two dealing with faithful service, the last two with denying Christ. The last clause features an added reason: "for he cannot deny himself." The cadence makes for an interesting dynamic, especially the breaking of the pattern in the last element where an expected negative statement is replaced by a positive one.

The fifth saying (Titus 3:4–7) constitutes a summary of Paul's soteriology in highly condensed form and with trinitarian import, centering on God's salvation of believers through Christ and his regenerating work through the Holy Spirit.

The range of "trustworthy sayings" in the LTT includes therefore (1) a possible adaptation of a saying of Christ (1 Tim 1:15); (2) a

---

[106] See Philo, *Flight* 129; *Rewards* 13.

[107] Interestingly, v. 8 is favored as the "trustworthy saying" by a vast majority of commentators but not translations.

solemn apostolic affirmation about church leaders (1 Tim 3:1); (3) an apostolic pronouncement about the value of godliness (1 Tim 4:8); (4) a hymn-like, artistically crafted affirmation of God's faithfulness in the face of human faithlessness (2 Tim 2:11–13); and (5) a summary of Paul's soteriology in trinitarian terms (Titus 3:4–7). Also, two of the five sayings have the formula after the referent (1 Tim 4:8; Titus 3:4–7).[108]

Important to recall is the likelihood that Timothy and Titus were not meant to be the sole audience of the letters of which they were the primary recipients. As noted above, it appears to be assumed that others will be listening in: the leaders and congregations of the churches in view, possibly including (or as an eventual audience) the false teachers and their adherents.

The trustworthy sayings in particular, then, may each serve one or more of a number of functions: (1) bolstering Paul's authority (as do his references to his apostleship);[109] (2) building rapport with his audience; (3) reminding the congregation and its leaders of accepted Christian doctrine;[110] and (4) tacitly challenging the false teachers and their followers to return to the fold.

§2.7 Scripture

Few treatments of the theology of the LTT view Scripture as a major theme.[111] However, this cluster of letters makes an indis-

[108] Yarbrough, in his study of preformed traditions in 1 Timothy, highlights several likely reasons for the inclusion of preformed material: (1) strengthening the literary cohesion of the letter; (2) providing "rhetorical leverage" with his audience; and (3) leveling theological salvos against the false teachers (*Paul's Utilization of Preformed Traditions*, 142–95).

[109] Yarbrough notes that this occurs in that preformed traditions "represent an authority beyond the apostle himself" and "stand as the agreement of the church at large" (ibid., 170).

[110] Although he does not specifically engage the context of false teaching here, Wall rightly notes, "Sharply put, these sayings articulate the core theological agreements of a Pauline grammar of faith and set normative guideposts for the formation of a healthy congregation." R. W. Wall, *1 & 2 Timothy and Titus*, THNTC (Grand Rapids: Eerdmans, 2012), 73.

[111] An exception is Towner (*Letters to Timothy and Titus*, 58–59), who treats "the authority and use of Scripture" among the six examples of "shared elements of theology" he finds in the three letters.

pensable contribution to the theology of Scripture in the NT.[112] Below it will therefore be beneficial to consider both Paul's use of Scripture and his teaching regarding Scripture in the LTT (§7.1).

§2.7.1 Paul's Use of Scripture[113]

Formal OT citations in the LTT are rare, with Paul's usage tending to be more allusive.[114] At the same time it's not as though the OT is absent. While Paul cites the OT only a few times, the OT substructure underlying these letters suggests deep familiarity with the Hebrew Scriptures.[115] As to the manner in which

[112] The last full-orbed treatment of Scripture in the LTT from the perspective of Pauline authorship was produced by B. P. Wolfe, "The Place and Use of Scripture in the Pastoral Epistles" (Ph.D. diss., University of Aberdeen, 1990). For a treatment from the perspective of pseudonymous authorship, see G. Häfner, *"Nützlich zur Belehrung" (2 Tim 3,16). Die Rolle der Schrift in den Pastoralbriefen im Rahmen der Paulusrezeption*, Herders biblische Studien 25 (Freiburg: Herder, 2000).

[113] More detailed treatments can be found in the exegetical portion of this commentary; here we take a more synthetic approach.

[114] Because of this relative paucity of citations, and the presumed pseudonymity of the LTT, treatments of the OT in these letters have not been common, though the situation is improving. See esp. Towner ("1–2 Timothy and Titus"), who provides an excellent thorough treatment of the major quotations and allusions to the OT in these books; and A. J. Köstenberger, "The Use of Scripture in the Pastoral and General Epistles and the Book of Revelation," in *Hearing the Old Testament in the New Testament*, ed. S. E. Porter (Grand Rapids: Eerdmans, 2006), 230–54. See also Elengabeka, *L'exploitation des Ecritures*; Häfner, *"Nützlich zur Belehrung"*; A. T. Hanson, "The Use of the Old Testament in the Pastoral Epistles," *IBS* 3 (1981): 203–19; H. Hübner, *Vetus Testamentum in Novo*, vol. 2: *Corpus Paulinum* (Göttingen: Vandenhoeck & Ruprecht, 1997), 583–657; B. Kowalski, "Zur Funktion und Bedeutung der alttestamentlichen Zitate und Anspielungen in den Pastoralbriefen," *SNTSU–A* 19 (1994): 45–68; H. K. Moulton, "Scripture Quotations in the Pastoral Epistles," *ExpTim* 49 (1937–38): 94; C. M. Nielsen, "Scripture in the Pastoral Epistles," *PRSt* 7 (1980): 4–23; B. P. Wolfe, "Scripture in the Pastoral Epistles: Premarcion Marcionism?," *PRSt* 16 (1989): 5–16; Wolfe, "Place and Use of Scripture in the Pastoral Epistles"; Wolfe, "The Sagacious Use of Scripture," in *Entrusted with the Gospel*, 199–218. In addition, C. Spicq is a rarity among commentators in providing a discrete section treating the LTT and the OT (*Saint Paul: les Épîtres pastorales* [Paris: J. Gabalda, 1947], 215–23). P. T. Towner treats "the authority and use of Scripture" as a discrete section in his article on the LTT in *NDBT*, 334–35.

[115] Kowalski, "Zur Funktion und Bedeutung," 67. She finds fifty-eight OT allusions in the letters (p. 49n15). Malherbe notes that "the influence of the OT on the language of the letters is evident throughout." A. Malherbe, "How to Treat Old Women and Old Men: The Use of Philosophical Traditions and Scripture in 1 Timothy 5," in *Light from the Gentiles*, 1:480n8.

Paul uses Scripture in the LTT, Wolfe observes, "There is in the PE no deeply engaging theological argumentation involving the Scriptures, as one finds, for example, in Romans or Hebrews. One gets the impression that all this has already been worked out."[116] He maintains, "The Scriptures provide guidelines for leadership and public worship and ethical exhortation. The opponents are insubordinate and unethical. Accordingly, the uses of Scripture are for practical purposes."[117] However, as will be seen below, on closer scrutiny the OT substructure underlying the LTT is considerably more robust than meets the eye. It includes references to the Torah (esp. Genesis), the historical books (patterning the Paul-Timothy relationship after the Moses-Joshua relationship), and the Psalms (esp. to David as the righteous sufferer; §7.1).

OT Usage in the Letters to Timothy and Titus

1 Timothy	OT Passage(s)*	Type of Usage	Basic Content
2:5	Num 24:7, 17; Deut 6:4; Isa 19:20	Allusion/Echo?	The coming ruler and savior
2:8	Mal 1:11	Allusion	Worship in every place
2:13–15	Gen 2:7–8, 15; 3:13, 16	Allusion	Order of creation, fall scenario
4:3–5	Genesis 1, esp. v. 31	Allusion	Goodness of creation
5:18	**Deut 25:4 (cf. 1 Cor 9:9)**	**Quotation**	**Don't muzzle an ox**
5:19	Deut 19:15	Allusion	Need for two or three witnesses
6:1	Isa 52:5	Echo	Name of God not blasphemed
2 Timothy	**OT Passage(s)***	**Type of Usage**	**Basic Content**
2:19	**Num 16:5; Isa 26:13; cf. Num 16:26–27**	**Quotations**	**Confess Lord's name, Korah's rebellion**

[116] Wolfe, "Sagacious Use of Scripture," 218.
[117] Ibid.

OT Usage in the Letters to Timothy and Titus (continued)

3:8	Exod 7:11, 22; 9:11?	Allusion	Jannes and Jambres
3:11	Ps 34:17, 19	Echo	Rescue from persecution
4:14	Ps 62:12; Prov 24:12: 27:4	Allusion/Echo	God repays accord- ing to works
4:16–18	Psalm 22, esp. vv. 8, 21, 27	Allusion/Echo	Rescue from lion; all the nations
Titus	**OT Passage(s)***	**Type of Usage**	**Basic Content**
2:14	Ps 130:8; cf. Ezek 37:23; cf. 36:25–33	Allusion	Cleansing terminology
*Citations are in bold. In addition, see the listing of Paul-Moses typology below.			

The *formal citations* of Scripture in the LTT include the brief quotation of Deut 25:4 in 1 Tim 5:18 in support of Paul's argument concerning the remuneration of elders. The argument moves from the lesser to the greater: if oxen may benefit from their labor, how much more workers for the gospel?[118] The pastiche in 2 Tim 2:19 most likely refers to Num 16:5; Isa 26:13; and, on a more conceptual plane, Num 16:26–27.[119] The Isaianic passage is applied to the faithful who acknowledge Jesus in contrast to the false teachers who have "departed from the truth," while the reference to

[118] See Köstenberger, "Use of Scripture in the Pastoral and General Epistles," 233–34; Towner, "1–2 Timothy and Titus," 900. Beale considers this usage an example of his categories "to indicate an analogical or illustrative use of the OT" and "to indicate an abiding authority carried over from the OT" (G. K. Beale, *Handbook on the New Testament Use of the Old Testament: Exegesis and Interpretation* [Grand Rapids: Baker, 2012], 73). D. Instone-Brewer argues that this usage isn't necessarily allegorical, contending that for Jewish exegetes the term "ox" in the Torah included any type of laborer, human or animal ("1 Corinthians 9:9–11: A Literal Interpretation of 'Do Not Muzzle the Ox,'" *NTS* 38 [1992]: 554–65). J. L. Verbruggen, "Of Muzzles and Oxen: Deuteronomy 25:4 and 1 Corinthians 9:9," *JETS* 49 (2006): 699–711 explains the reference in the context of "a law dealing with the economic responsibility of someone using someone else's property," telling a man not to muzzle an ox he rented from his neighbor (p. 711).

[119] See Köstenberger, "Use of Scripture in the Pastoral and General Epistles," 235, including n. 14.

Korah's rebellion in Numbers serves as an indirect challenge to those who might entertain following, or are already following, the false teachers.[120]

Without formally citing Scripture, Paul *echoes* or *alludes* to the OT in several other places in the LTT.[121]

- A possible allusion to the coming ruler and savior mentioned in Num 24:7, 17 and Isa 19:20 is found in 1 Tim 2:5.[122]
- The connection between 1 Tim 2:8 and Mal 1:11 has already been noted in the discussion of the Pauline mission above.
- The Genesis accounts of the creation of Adam and Eve and of the scenario at the fall are referenced in 1 Tim 2:13–15.[123]
- The discussion of God's good creation by the word of God in 1 Tim 4:3–5 invokes the first chapter of the Genesis creation narrative.
- The reference to the two-or-three-witness requirement in 1 Tim 5:19 harks back to Deut 19:15.[124]

---

[120] Wolfe ("Sagacious Use of Scripture," 203) suggests that in his references to the account of Korah, Paul isn't engaging the OT directly but "an established tradition that asserts the incompatibility of God's people and evil, often incorporating OT characters [Cain, Balaam, Korah] as negative examples."

[121] For discussions of several of these references (along with the citation of Deut 25:4 in 1 Tim 5:18), see J. W. Aageson, "Genesis in the Deutero-Pauline Epistles," in *Genesis in the New Testament*, ed. M. J. J. Menken and S. Moyise, LTNS 466 (London: Bloomsbury T&T Clark, 2012), 117–29; G. Häfner, "Deuteronomy in the Pastoral Epistles," in *Deuteronomy in the New Testament*, ed. M. J. J. Menken and S. Moyise, LNTS 358 (New York: T&T Clark, 2007), 136–51.

[122] See Towner, "1–2 Timothy and Titus," 892–93.

[123] For a detailed discussion of the use of Genesis 2–3 in 1 Tim 2:13–15, see Köstenberger, "Use of Scripture in the Pastoral and General Epistles," 231–33. For further relevant literature, see the extensive bibliography in A. J. Köstenberger and T. R. Schreiner, eds., *Women in the Church: An Analysis and Application of 1 Timothy 2:9–15*, 3rd ed. (Wheaton: Crossway, 2016), 363–406.

[124] J. W. Fuller, "Of Elders and Triads in 1 Timothy 5:19–25," *NTS* 29 (1983): 258–63. Note also the important monograph by H. van Vliet, *No Single Testimony: A Study of the Adaptation of the Law of Deut. 19:15 Par. into the New Testament* (Utrecht: Kerminck en Zoon, 1958). See also G. Couser, "Divergent, Insurgent or Allegiant? 1 Timothy 5:1–2 and the Nature of God's Household" (paper presented at the annual meeting of the Evangelical Theological Society, Atlanta, GA, November 19, 2015), 11–12, who argues that the instructions to care for widows (1 Tim 5:3–16) and the instructions with regard to elders (1 Tim 5:17–25) are based on a firm OT substructure: the OT call to care for widows as an implication of the fifth commandment (Exod 20:12; cf., e.g., Lev 19:2, 9, 14) and the OT teaching regarding the fair examination of those who are alleged of sinning (e.g., Deut 10:15; 19:15–21). On

- Paul's words in 1 Tim 6:1 on God's name not being blasphemed may echo OT passages such as Isa 52:5.
- The reference to Jannes and Jambres in 2 Tim 3:8 may link the false teachers to the episode of Pharaoh's magicians opposing Moses in Exodus 7–9, though this is disputed.[125]
- Paul's words in 2 Tim 4:14 may echo OT passages about God's repaying people according to their works, such as Ps 62:12; Prov 24:12; 27:4.
- The connection between 2 Tim 4:16–18 and Psalm 22 has already been noted above.
- The letter to Titus has little in the way of overt connections with the OT, except that 2:14 seems to invoke Ps 130:8 in its language of redemption from all lawlessness and to echo OT texts such as Ezekiel 36–37 in its "cleansing" terminology.

What's more, in an interesting discussion of possible connections between the OT and the LTT, Martin argues at some length that there is likely a large-scale link between the presentation of Paul in 2 Timothy and Moses in relation to Joshua.[126]

- Regarding the incident with Korah in Numbers 16, Alexander and Hymenaeus parallel the false teachers, while Paul and Timothy parallel Moses and Aaron (2 Tim 2:19).
- The Egyptian magicians in Exodus 7 and 9, named Jannes and Jambres in later tradition and referenced in 2 Tim 3:8–9, prefigure the false teachers.
- "Laying on of hands" in 2 Tim 1:6 is connected with Moses's laying on of hands on Joshua in Num 27:18–23; Deut 34:9.
- The title "servant of the Lord" in 2 Tim 2:24 is connected with Moses "the servant of the LORD" in Deut 34:5 (cf. 2 Kgs 18:12).

---

the former, see M. Sommer, "Witwen in 1 Tim 5: Eine subkulturelle Annäherung aus der Perspektive der Schriften Israels und ihrer Auswirkungen auf das frühe Christentum," *ASE* 32 (2015): 287–307. On the latter, see W. Fuller, "Of Elders and Triads in 1 Timothy 5.19–25," *NTS* 29 (1983): 258–63.

[125] For extrabiblical parallels see CD 5:19; Pliny, *Nat*. 30.2.11; Tg. Ps.-J. to Exod 7:11–12. See the discussion of this passage in the commentary portion of this volume.

[126] Martin (*Pauli Testamentum*, 19–43) argues from the perspective of pseudonymous authorship, but his observations are pertinent for a Pauline reading of 2 Timothy as well.

- The title "man of God" in 2 Tim 3:17 is connected with Moses "the man of God" in Deut 33:1.
- Paul's exhortation to Timothy to "be strong" (2 Tim 2:1) parallels the similar exhortation by Moses to Israel and Joshua in Deut 31:6–7.[127]

Beyond this, the letters contain other OT echoes and general references to Scripture.[128]

§2.7.2 Paul's Teaching on Scripture

This survey will commence with an examination of three pertinent texts in Paul's first letter to Timothy: 1:8–11; 4:13; and 5:18.[129] After this we'll discuss the central text for examining Paul's perspective on Scripture in the LTT: 2 Tim 3:14–17.

1. In *1 Tim 1:8–11* Paul addresses the proper function of the law. This passage contributes to the theme of Scripture in that the law is the foundational portion of the Hebrew Scriptures. The false teachers emphasized the Mosaic law in their teaching,[130] but Paul insists that these self-styled "teachers of the law" (νομοδιδάσκαλοι) lack proper understanding as to its true nature and purpose.[131] The law, Paul maintains, is good[132]—if a person uses it appropriately

---

[127] Ibid.

[128] See the excellent discussion in Towner, "1–2 Timothy and Titus."

[129] The key term highlighting Paul's doctrine of Scripture in the LTT is *γραφή* (2x: 1 Tim 5:18; 2 Tim 3:16). The term *νόμος*, also significant in this regard, is used only in 1 Tim 1:8–9.

[130] At times, of course, *νόμος* can have reference to the OT as a whole (e.g., Rom 3:19, preceded by a catena of citations from Psalms and Proverbs) or "law" as principle. Here, though, the reference of *νόμος* to the Mosaic law seems assured by (among other reasons) the commonly recognized connection between the Decalogue and the various categories of the "unlawful" in 1:9–10. That *νόμος* should encompass the entire Torah and not be limited to, say, the Decalogue alone or the moral law, is suggested by "genealogies" (1:4) being within the purview of the *νομοδιδάσκαλοι* (Mounce, *Pastoral Epistles*, 27, 32). It should be noted that "genealogies" shouldn't be limited to genealogies, properly speaking (e.g., Genesis 5), but involves broader historical content as well, as argued by F. J. A. Hort, *Judaistic Christianity: A Course of Lectures* (New York: Macmillan, 1894), 135–38.

[131] See Johnson, *First and Second Letters to Timothy*, 167: "The would-be teachers know neither the language nor the substance of the Law."

[132] It may be that Paul is here insisting that the law is *καλός* because the false teachers portrayed him as antinomian or as seeing the Mosaic law as entirely without value.

(1:8).[133] What, then, is the appropriate use of the law? While some have inferred from the following verses that the law's proper use pertains to revelation of sin, restraint of sin, or condemnation of the unrighteous,[134] S. Westerholm rightly notes that the answer to this question isn't overtly stated in this passage.[135] Paul isn't so much concerned to indicate the precise purpose of the law as to insist that the false teachers are *misapplying* the law to *believers*: "The law is not meant for a righteous person" (v. 9).[136] Instead it has its proper application to those who live counter to its morals and to "whatever else is contrary to the healthy teaching" as set forth in Paul's gospel (1:10–11).

What, then, is the contribution 1 Tim 1:8–11 makes to the doctrine of Scripture in the LTT? It would be hasty to conclude from this passage that Paul here teaches that the OT Scriptures no longer have any place in the Christian life, for the apostle elsewhere in the LTT cites passages from the Torah and applies them to the believing community. However, this passage demonstrates that in at least some ways the Mosaic law, which forms the backbone of

---

[133] Paul uses νομίμως here in a wordplay with the preceding νόμος and with ἄνομος in 1:9. In the term's only other NT occurrence, 2 Tim 2:5, it clearly means "according to the rules [i.e., of the athletic contest]"; its use here is somewhat more generic: "properly," "appropriately," "in line with its intended purpose." Marshall is right: "νομίμως can mean 'in accordance with the law'; but here where 'the law' is the object of χρῆται, 'appropriately' makes better sense" (*Pastoral Epistles*, 376). See the discussion in B. S. Rosner, *Paul and the Law: Keeping the Commandments of God*, NSBT 31 (Downers Grove: InterVarsity, 2013), 74–75.

[134] Revealing sin: Towner, *Letters to Timothy and Titus*, 125; restraint of sin: J. Calvin, *1 & 2 Timothy & Titus*, Crossway Classic Commentaries (Wheaton: Crossway, 1998 [1556]), 24; T. R. Schreiner, *The Law and Its Fulfillment: A Pauline Theology of Law* (Grand Rapids: Baker, 1993), 86–87; condemnation of the unrighteous: Rosner, *Paul and the Law*, 75.

[135] S. Westerholm, "The Law and the 'Just Man' (1 Tim 1, 3–11)," *ST* 36 (1982): 83.

[136] The nuance of δίκαιος is hotly debated. The major division of opinion is between those who see justification specifically in view—positional righteousness—and those who favor an emphasis on moral virtue—ethical righteousness. For the former, see J. D. Quinn and W. C. Wacker, *The First and Second Letters to Timothy*, ECC (Grand Rapids: Eerdmans, 2000), 94; for the latter, see Knight, *Pastoral Epistles*, 82–83; Westerholm, "Law and the 'Just Man,'" 84–85. It is best, however, to see both aspects of the Christian's righteousness in play: the law "does not apply to the Christian who is made righteous through faith and who lives righteously" (Mounce, *Pastoral Epistles*, 35; note the excellent discussion on pp. 33–36).

the OT Scriptures, is not the primary frame of reference for NT believers (cf., e.g., Rom 10:4).

A further contribution may be suggested by looking at the description of the Ephesian opponents' false teaching. While the teaching involved the Mosaic law (1:7), it is also consistently tied to "myths" (1:4).[137] The precise relationship between νόμος and μῦθος is difficult to determine, but given Paul's description of myths in Titus 1:14 as "Jewish,"[138] a case can be made for the opponents' use of speculative Second Temple literature—specifically, expansions of the Pentateuch—to inform their teaching of the law. For Paul and his contemporaries, μῦθος was equivalent to "tale" or "fable"; the term conveyed an account that was deceitful in character, illusory, unreal, and untrustworthy.[139] Various kinds of connections have been made between Second Temple Jewish literature and the false teaching described as "myths and genealogies."[140] If Paul's

---

[137] 1 Tim 1:4; 4:7; 2 Tim 4:4; cf. Titus 1:14. Mounce observes that in 1 Tim 1:4, "'Endless myths and genealogies' are almost epexegetical to 'another teaching' [1:3] . . . one of the few hints in the PE regarding the content of the Ephesian heresy" (*Pastoral Epistles*, 20). While one shouldn't assume that the false teaching is the same in Ephesus and Crete, sufficient common ground exists to suggest they are related. For a list of commonalities, see Mounce, *Pastoral Epistles*, 15; more generally, J. L. Sumney, "Studying Paul's Opponents: Advances and Challenges," in *Paul and His Opponents*, ed. S. E. Porter, Pauline Studies 2 (Leiden: Brill, 2005), 48–50.

Some treat descriptions of the false teaching—such as the term μῦθοι—as merely polemical (see esp. M. Dibelius and H. Conzelmann, *The Pastoral Epistles*, trans. P. Buttolph and A. Yarbro, Hermeneia [Philadelphia: Fortress, 1972]). R. J. Karris, "The Background and Significance of the Polemic of the Pastoral Epistles," *JBL* 92 (1973): 549–64 argues that the letters appropriate polemical language used by philosophers (e.g., Philo, Aristotle, Dio Chrysostom) against sophists. However, much research in this area is hampered by the assumption that the opponents are merely fictional and/or that the polemic is merely stereotypical and rhetorical in nature.

[138] In defense of understanding the reference to "Jewish myths" in Titus to inform the nature of the "myths" in Timothy, note the previously mentioned likelihood that the false teachings in Crete and Ephesus were similar; in particular, note that the "genealogies" associated with the "myths" of 1 Tim 4:14 find a parallel in Titus 3:9.

[139] Spicq, *Les épîtres pastorales*, 93–94. Strabo contrasts the mythical (μυθώδης) with the historical (ἱστορικός; *Geogr.* 11.5.3; see the list of similar contrasts in Greek writers on pp. 94–96), and Philo regularly contrasts myths with truth (see the numerous excerpts in Spicq, "μῦθος," *TLNT* 2:533).

[140] Specific pseudepigraphical works most often adduced are Jubilees, Pseudo-Philo (Liber Antiquitatum Biblicarum), and the Genesis Apocryphon (1QapGen). For Jubilees, see K. Berger, "Jesus als Pharisäer und frühe Christen als Pharisäer," *NovT* 30 (1988): 260; É. Cothenet, "La lecture liturgique des Épitres pastorales," *Esprit*

opponents were indeed drawing on Second Temple material that was not part of the accepted Hebrews Scriptures, this would indicate a further reason for Paul's emphasis on the Scriptures in the letters to Timothy.

2. The next passage, *1 Tim 4:13*, is part of Paul's discussion of the Ephesian opponents and their variant teaching (4:1–5) and a resultant series of instructions aimed at encouraging Timothy to convey healthy teaching in both word and life (4:6–16).[141] Earlier in the letter Paul noted that the false teachers are "devoted" (προσέχω) to myths and genealogies (1:4). In the present context he warns Timothy to stay away from such myths (4:7), instructing him instead to "devote" (προσέχω) himself to three related practices that would aid in countering the influence of the false teachers in the congregation: the public reading of Scripture (τῇ ἀναγνώσει), exhortation (τῇ παρακλήσει), and teaching (τῇ διδασκαλίᾳ; 4:13). All three activities were apparently standard practice in the early church[142] and were meant to take place during the public worship service of the assembly.[143]

---

et Vie 114 (2004): 18; Fee, *1 and 2 Timothy, Titus*, 41; Hort, *Judaistic Christianity*, 136–37; W. Lock, *A Critical and Exegetical Commentary on the Pastoral Epistles*, ICC (Edinburgh: T&T Clark, 1924), 8; B. J. Oropeza, "1, 2 Timothy and Titus: The Influence of False Teachers in the Pastoral Letters," in *Jews, Gentiles, and the Opponents of Paul: The Pauline Letters*, Apostasy in the NT Communities 2 (Eugene, OR: Cascade, 2012), 294; G. Kittel, "Die γενεαλογίαι der Pastoralbriefe," *ZNW* 20 (1921): 51; Marshall, *Pastoral Epistles*, 336; Mounce, *Pastoral Epistles*, lxx, 20; Spicq, *Les épîtres pastorales*, 102–3. For Pseudo-Philo, see Fee, *1 and 2 Timothy, Titus*, 41; Lock, *Pastoral Epistles*, 8–9; Marshall, *Pastoral Epistles*, 336; Mounce, *Pastoral Epistles*, lxx, 20; Oropeza, "1, 2 Timothy and Titus," 294. For the Genesis Apocryphon, see Marshall, *Pastoral Epistles*, 336; Oropeza, "1, 2, Timothy and Titus," 294; Spicq, *Les épîtres pastorales*, 103.

[141] Van Neste divides 4:6–16 into two textual units (vv. 6–10 and 11–16) but notes that the two units are "closely linked . . . so the shifts between units are not great" (*Cohesion and Structure*, 51).

[142] Spicq notes that the repeated article before these nouns indicates that these functions are defined and well known (*Les épîtres pastorales*, 514). Marshall (*Pastoral Epistles*, 562) and Mounce (*Pastoral Epistles*, 260) concur, as do Quinn and Wacker (*Letters to Timothy*, 390), who also highlight the crisp asyndeton. Towner observes, "These [three ministry commands] were certainly not innovations in the worship service, but rather activities that needed to be continued (or possibly resumed) in view of the disruption caused by the false teaching" (*Letters to Timothy and Titus*, 316).

[143] Theoretically, each of these elements could occur in private settings. At least two points, however, suggest that public reading is in view, and the parallel exhortation and teaching would follow suit: (1) the parallel with synagogue practices (cf.

What precisely is Timothy to read publicly? While the object of Timothy's communication is not made explicit, it's widely agreed that the OT Scriptures are at least partly in view.[144] In addition, Paul doubtless meant for Timothy to set forth Paul's own (and perhaps other) apostolic writings.[145] Support for this contention is found in repeated indications elsewhere that Paul expects his missives to his churches be read in the assembly.[146] It would, of course, be expected that a letter to, say, the church of the Thessalonians would be read aloud in that church's assembly. Note, however, that Paul also instructed churches to read each other's letters (e.g., Col 4:16). The truth of Paul's gospel as communicated in his letters would stand against the improper use of the law set forth by the false teachers and would demonstrate the proper way to use the OT Scriptures.

The three functions given in this passage to counter the false teachers seem to be intentionally sequenced, each one presupposing the previous one.[147] "Reading" (ἀνάγνωσις) would find Timothy setting forth the authoritative text, perhaps over against alternative texts which the false teachers used alongside the Mosaic law.[148] After the text had been read aloud, "exhortation" (παράκλη-

---

the use of ἡ ἀνάγνωσις in 2 Cor 3:14 and esp. Acts 13:15; cf. Luke 4:16–20; see P. H. Towner, "The Function of the Public Reading of Scripture in 1 Timothy 4:13 and in the Biblical Tradition," *Southern Baptist Journal of Theology* 7 [2003]: 44–48); (2) the context of the passage (see E. Elengabeka, "Une médiation pastorale entre le livre et la communauté: L'anagnôsis en 1 Tm 4,13," *RevScRel* 79 [2005]: 122).

[144] The point is generally assumed rather than argued. See, e.g., Knight's observation that what was read would have been "those writings that were regarded as authoritative," which would have included the OT (*Pastoral Epistles*, 207); Swinson points to Paul's use of Torah in the letters to Timothy (*What Is Scripture?*, 73).

[145] So, e.g., Knight, *Pastoral Epistles*, 207; Marshall, *Pastoral Epistles*, 563; G. J. Stiekes, "Liturgy in the Pastoral Epistles," *Artistic Theologian* 2 (2013): 46–47. Swinson takes a step further and argues that the primary referent of ἡ ἀνάγνωσις is "some written form of the apostolic gospel message"—and more specifically, Luke's Gospel—and that the OT is also involved (*What Is Scripture?*, 101–2).

[146] E.g., 2 Cor 7:8; Col 4:16; 1 Thess 5:27; 2 Thess 3:4. J. P. Heil argues that Paul's letters ought to be viewed as "epistolary rituals of worship . . . performed publicly in a liturgical assembly," being "aimed to enable and facilitate the worship of the assembly" (*The Letters of Paul as Rituals of Worship* [Eugene, OR: Wipf & Stock, 2011], 1).

[147] Quinn and Wacker, *Letters to Timothy*, 390.

[148] While this reading served as a ground for the subsequent exposition, Towner rightly points out its function of identity formation as well; modern hermeneutics

σις) would follow as Timothy laid the moral weight of the text upon his hearers in exhorting them toward proper living;[149] this function would be equivalent to a sermon.[150] What, then, would distinguish this exhortation from the "teaching" (διδασκαλία) that immediately followed? Given the typical use of διδασκαλία in the LTT as a technical term to denote "apostolic or Christian teaching as a whole,"[151] it may be that its use here doesn't so much contrast sermonic exhortation with classroom-like instruction but points to a demonstration to the faithful of how various texts contribute toward a coherent theology.[152]

As far as its contribution to the doctrine of Scripture in the LTT is concerned, 1 Tim 4:13 highlights the role Scripture plays in combating false teaching. It should be noted, however, that Scripture wasn't merely read to the congregation, as important and foundational a practice as that was. It also formed the basis for the ethics and theology of the faithful as it was expounded in preaching and teaching, not in accordance with the myths and genealogies of the false teachers but in connection with Paul's gospel.[153] What's more, 1 Tim 4:13 suggests that reading, exhortation, and teaching were standard practices in the worship services of the early church.

3. The following passage, *1 Tim 5:18*, juxtaposes an OT citation with a saying of Jesus found in Luke's Gospel, which poses a series of intriguing questions. In continuing his instructions on proper conduct in God's household in 1 Timothy 5, Paul first turns to a discussion of widows in the church (5:3–16) and subsequently to

---

discussions agree that "reading/hearing certain significant texts influences the formation, shaping, defining, and redefining of individual and corporate identity" (*Letters to Timothy and Titus*, 318).

[149] In translating παράκλησις, "exhortation" is better than "comfort." Knight suggests that either nuance might be in view depending on which text is read (*Pastoral Epistles*, 208), but Paul doubtless means to emphasize exhortation in the Ephesian situation given the opponents' teaching. Johnson points out that since the related verb παρακαλέω is consistently used in 1 Timothy with the sense of "exhort" (not "comfort"; 1:3; 2:1; 5:1; 6:2, with διδάσκω), a similar nuance is likely in view here (*First and Second Letters to Timothy*, 252).

[150] Spicq, *Les épîtres pastorales*, 515; Towner, "Function," 48. Note the striking parallel in Acts 13:15 with Paul's resultant λόγος παρακλήσεως in vv. 16–41.

[151] H.-F. Weiss, "διδασκαλία," *EDNT* 1:317. Cf. Spicq, *Les épîtres pastorales*, 516.

[152] Spicq, *Les épîtres pastorales*, 516.

[153] Quinn and Wacker describe the "teaching" as "the explanation and application of the OT according to Pauline hermeneutics" (*Letters to Timothy*, 390).

various issues regarding elders (5:17–25). In discussing the remuneration of elders, he grounds his instruction in a quotation from Deut 25:4 and a dominical saying found in Luke 10:7. The connection between ἡ γραφή, and 1 Tim 5:18c contributes to the question of whether apostolic writings were considered to be Scripture in the first-century church.

REFERENCES TO SCRIPTURE IN 1 TIMOTHY 5:18

λέγει γὰρ ἡ γραφή, Βοῦν ἀλοῶντα οὐ φιμώσεις, καί,	οὐ φιμώσεις βοῦν ἀλοῶντα (Deut 25:4 LXX)
Ἄξιος ὁ ἐργάτης τοῦ μισθοῦ αὐτοῦ.	ἄξιος γὰρ ὁ ἐργάτης τοῦ μισθοῦ αὐτοῦ (Luke 10:7)

Several major approaches to the juxtaposition of ἡ γραφή and Jesus's saying have been set forth.[154] (1) "Scripture" does not apply to the second part of the verse.[155] (2) By the time Luke's Gospel was written, it had attained the status of Scripture, and the pseudonymous writer uses a term that would have been anachronistic in Paul's day.[156] (3) The writers of 1 Timothy and of Luke's Gospel both appropriated the saying of 1 Tim 5:18c from a common source, which is categorized as Scripture.[157] (4) Paul appropriated a saying

[154] The proposal by Quinn and Wacker doesn't fit neatly into any of the following categories. They propose that Luke appropriated Jesus's words from an early collection of *logia*, adapted it for his Gospel, then reused the saying when he (Luke) composed and redacted the present portion of the LTT (*Letters to Timothy*, 462–63). As an interesting possibility, they also allow that the writer of Luke's Gospel may have appropriated the *logion* from 1 Timothy.

[155] Writing from the perspective of authentic authorship, Fee provides two grounds for this position: (1) Luke's Gospel had probably not been written at this point; (2) while the teaching of Jesus was seen as authoritative, "the term *Scripture* means *only* the OT for Christians until the end of the second century" (*1 and 2 Timothy, Titus*, 134, emphasis original). See also Johnson, *Letters*, 286, who claims Paul was "careless in his syntax"; Mounce, *Pastoral Epistles*, 311; and Towner, *Letters to Timothy and Titus*, 364–67, who asserts that ἡ γραφή "normally meant the OT . . . the [equally] authoritative Jesus-saying is added as further proof." Dibelius and Conzelmann (*Pastoral Epistles*, 79) and Quinn and Wacker (*Letters to Timothy*, 462) also note this as an option.

[156] See Dibelius and Conzelmann, *Pastoral Epistles*, 78–79, who set this forth as a possibility.

[157] Quinn and Wacker mention this view (*Letters to Timothy*, 462). J. Roloff discounts that 1 Tim 5:18c draws from Luke's Gospel and suggests a collection of Jesus

of Jesus recorded in Luke's Gospel, which the writer considered to be Scripture.[158]

What, then, does 1 Tim 5:18 contribute to the understanding of Scripture in the LTT? With the working assumption that "Scripture" encompasses both citations in the verse, it appears that at least by this point in his ministry, Paul's understanding of Scripture had grown from encompassing only the OT to include other writings. In addition, although Luke's Gospel no doubt had Paul's enthusiastic backing—if not input—it's noteworthy that it was not written by an apostle. This being the case, 1 Tim 5:18 indicates that direct apostolic authorship was not a requirement for a postresurrection writing to be considered Scripture. A further implication of Paul's use of Scripture with reference to Luke's Gospel is that a piece of writing could apparently be considered Scripture within a relatively short time of composition.

4. The final passage, *2 Tim 3:14–17*, is contained in Paul's last written communication to his trusted and beloved protégé as the veteran apostle has reached the end of his life and ministry. In this letter Paul calls Timothy to faithful gospel ministry despite his share of suffering that surely awaits him. Shot through the book are references to opponents of Paul's gospel. This theme is particularly prominent at the onset of chapter 3, where Paul characterizes the opponents in some detail (3:1–9). In the concluding portion of the chapter, Paul sets up a contrast between the enemies of the gospel and Timothy (3:10–17).[159] Timothy has faithfully followed Paul's teaching and example (3:10–12), and while the

sayings that was used in congregational worship as a possible source (*Der erste Brief an Timotheus*, EKKNT 15 [Zurich: Benziger, 1988], 41). Both R. F. Collins (*1 and 2 Timothy and Titus*, NTL [Louisville: Westminster John Knox, 2002], 146) and A. E. Harvey ("'The Workman Is Worthy of His Hire': Fortunes of a Proverb in the Early Church," *NovT* 24 [1982]: 212) propose the author of 1 Timothy appropriated a common proverb and mistakenly identified it as Scripture.

[158] Knight, *Pastoral Epistles*, 234; A. Schlatter, *Die Kirche der Griechen im Urteil des Paulus: Eine Auslegung seiner Briefe an Timotheus und Titus*, 2nd ed. (Stuttgart: Calwer, 1958), 150–51. Swinson, *What Is Scripture?*, 91–111, argues that ἡ γραφή, in the letters to Timothy is not "limited strictly to the Law, Prophets, and Writings" but "includes at least some of the apostolic writings that now appear in the NT."

[159] As Van Neste notes, the return to direct address in Timothy in 3:10 ("But you") marks the opening of a new unit; while 3:10–17 is closely connected to the following unit (4:1–8), the topic shifts from Timothy's stance to what he is supposed to do (*Cohesion and Structure*, 178–79).

opponents will continue in a downward spiral of deception (3:13), Paul calls Timothy to continued faithfulness, in conjunction with the Scriptures (3:14–17).

Timothy's call to continued faithfulness to what he has been taught is grounded in two facts. First, Paul indicates that Timothy knows his teachers,[160] likely a reference to their character over against that of the opponents (cf. 3:13). Second, Timothy knows that from his earliest days he has known "the sacred writings" (τὰ ἱερὰ γράμματα),[161] which are able to give him wisdom concerning salvation through faith in Christ. To ground his assertion about the sacred writings, Paul provides a theological rationale for the usefulness of Scripture in Timothy's situation: "All Scripture is inspired" (πᾶσα γραφὴ θεόπνευστος). That is to say that all of Scripture, by virtue of being God breathed, is beneficial for the things Timothy is called to do, particularly with regard to the opponents in Ephesus:[162] positively, to teach proper doctrine and train in righteousness;[163] negatively, to refute error and correct false teaching.[164] As a result of using Scripture to these ends,[165] "the man of God"—Timothy (1 Tim 6:11) and potentially any church leaders brought back from the error of their ways (cf. 2 Tim 2:24–26)—will be adequately equipped for the good works that constitute the concrete outworking of the gospel.

Paul's brief statement as to the origin of Scripture—πᾶσα γραφὴ θεόπνευστος—has generated considerable debate.[166] The best

[160] In the context of 2 Timothy, "those who taught you" (3:14) the Scriptures would have included Lois and Eunice (1:5, esp. given the subsequent reference to Timothy's upbringing) and Paul himself (3:10–11).

[161] The phrase ἱερὰ γράμματα was a technical term for the Hebrew Scriptures; see the primary source examples adduced in BDAG 205d, which also notes that the phrase can have this reference whether articular or anarthrous. This being the case, a decision on the textual variant involving the article is not strictly necessary.

[162] Mounce notes the chiastic structure of the four prepositional phrases (positive-negative-negative-positive) as well as the apparent divide between the doctrine-oriented pair that opens the list and the behavior-oriented pair that closes it (*Pastoral Epistles*, 570).

[163] See, e.g., 1 Tim 4:11; 4:13; 6:2; 2 Tim 2:2.

[164] See, e.g., 1 Tim 1:3; 5:20; 2 Tim 2:14; 4:2.

[165] The conjunction ἵνα is best taken as indicating purpose ("in order that"). See the discussion in Marshall, *Pastoral Epistles*, 796.

[166] While the contribution of this passage to Paul's view of Scripture in the LTT is clearly important, the significance of this issue may have been overstated at times. Even if πᾶσα γραφὴ θεόπνευστος were to mean "every inspired Scripture," it would

reading of this phrase is arguably "all Scripture is God breathed." Space precludes detailed discussion of all of the lexical, grammatical, and syntactical issues involved in this interpretation,[167] but a few points may be briefly noted. (1) Whether πᾶσα is understood as "all [Scripture]" or "every/each [passage of Scripture]" isn't finally determinative of the sense of the verse, though each option has implications.[168] (2) It's preferable to understand θεόπνευστος as predicative, not attributive.[169] (3) While the precise nuance of θεόπνευστος continues to be debated, it seems clear that at a minimum Paul is indicating that πᾶσα γραφή has its source in God.[170]

What does 2 Tim 3:14–17 contribute to the understanding of Scripture in the LTT? Paul's expanded view of Scripture inferred from 1 Tim 5:18 finds even more explicit expression here: "Scripture" includes both OT (2 Tim 3:15) and apostolic writings (2 Tim 3:14). What's more, the OT—presumably in connection with

---

be rather jarring to the context to suggest that Paul also has in mind some part of canonical Scripture that is *not* θεόπνευστος (Mounce, *Pastoral Epistles*, 567).

[167] See esp. H. W. House. "Biblical Inspiration in 2 Timothy 3:16," *BSac* 137 (1980): 54–63; J. W. Johnston, *The Use of* Πᾶς *in the New Testament*, Studies in Biblical Greek 11 (New York: Peter Lang, 2004), 178–83, who argues for the translation "every [passage of] scripture is inspired"; Knight, *Pastoral Epistles*, 444–50; Marshall, *Pastoral Epistles*, 790–96; Mounce, *Pastoral Epistles*, 565–71; Swinson, *What Is Scripture?*, 146–54; D. B. Wallace, *Greek Grammar Beyond the Basics: An Exegetical Syntax of the New Testament* (Grand Rapids: Zondervan, 1996), 313–14.

[168] It seems that at times interpreters have been eager to argue for "all" so as to undermine the interpretation of the passage as saying that "every inspired Scripture—as opposed to those which are not—is profitable." However, as Mounce points out, Paul could be thinking of the Scripture as "the sum total of its parts" (*Pastoral Epistles*, 566); see also Wallace, *Greek Grammar*, 314n57 ("an attributive θεόπνευστος . . . could be descriptive [of all scripture] rather than restrictive").

[169] That is, "All Scripture is inspired " and not "All inspired Scripture . . ." Points of support include: (1) the καί joining θεόπνευστος and ὠφέλιμος is best taken as coordinate ("and"), not ascensive ("also"), conjoining the two adjectives; it is preferable to construe both as predicative since it would be awkward to construe both as attributive ("Every God-breathed and profitable Scripture [is] for teaching, etc."); (2) according to Wallace, "In πᾶς + noun + adjective constructions in equative clauses the πᾶς, being by nature as definite as the article, implies the article, thus making the adjective(s) following the noun outside the implied article-noun group and, therefore, predicate" (*Greek Grammar*, 314).

[170] Swinson, *What Is Scripture?*, 134–59, as part of a detailed study, surveys ἡ γραφή in Philo, Josephus, the LXX, the NT, and the apostolic fathers (p. 161) and concludes that the term requires a written referent. In light of 1 Tim 5:18, Swinson conjectures that this may have been a version of Luke's Gospel (p. 179).

the apostolic gospel—is able to bring wisdom concerning salvation through faith in Christ. In addition, Paul emphasizes the essential nature of Scripture in properly equipping Timothy to handle the challenges before him by highlighting a theological point about Scripture's origin: it is God breathed, that is, has its ultimate source in God. Given this quality of Scripture, believers may have confidence in its sufficiency for refuting the false teaching and for leading them to right thinking and conduct.

§2.8 Conclusion

Built on the foundation of the mission theme (§1), the teaching motif, with its associated subthemes, makes a distinctive contribution to NT and biblical theology. One thinks here of a long trajectory which includes the giving of the law; priests/Levites teaching it to the people (Deut 33:10); the importance of intergenerational passing on of the message about Israel's God and his deliverance (Deut 6:4–9; Josh 4:6–7; Ps 78:5–8); the continual significance of teaching and learning in the OT; the references to earlier Scripture in later OT writings; and the prominence of the OT in Jesus's teaching and non-Pauline NT writings.[171]

The LTT's concern for sound doctrine in keeping with OT teaching and apostolic tradition regarding Jesus Christ is expressed by diverse vocabulary that includes references to healthy teaching, the truth, the faith, the Word of God, and the deposit. In addition, Paul uses Scripture in strategic and significant ways and provides instruction regarding the nature of Scripture. The LTT thus contribute both to our understanding of the content of Paul's missional teaching and of the development of his concept of Scripture as a function of the perpetuation of his apostolic ministry and legacy (cf. Rom 15:4; 1 Cor 10:6).

---

[171] E.g., Luke 24:25–27, 45–47; John 5:46; 10:35; 2 Pet 1:16–21. Among the vast literature on the subject, see G. K. Beale and D. A. Carson, eds., *Commentary on the New Testament Use of the Old Testament* (Grand Rapids: Baker, 2007); D. A. Carson and H. G. M. Williamson, eds., *It Is Written: Scripture Citing Scripture. Essays in Honour of Barnabas Lindars, SSF* (Cambridge: Cambridge University Press, 1988); A. J. Köstenberger with D. W. Jones, *God, Marriage, and Family: Rebuilding the Biblical Foundation*, 2nd ed. (Wheaton: Crossway, 2010), 92–96.

§3 God, Christ, the Holy Spirit, and Salvation

The themes of God, Christ, the Holy Spirit, and salvation are so closely intertwined as to be often virtually inseparable, which is why they will be treated jointly under the present heading.[172] This is nowhere clearer than in the distinctive terminology found in the LTT regarding God and Christ "our Savior," which will be discussed shortly below (§3.3). At the same time, as will become evident in the following discussion, there are places where God or Christ is mentioned in contexts other than salvation so that it would be inappropriate to subsume God or Christ entirely under the rubric of salvation. Nevertheless, it seems justified to treat the theme of salvation at some length, revealing the various facets of the LTT's teaching on this topic so as to do justice to the significance of this theme in these letters.

In fact, the salvation theme is so prominent in the LTT that the question arises whether the LTT display a Christology apart from their soteriology. Demonstrably, the LTT's teaching on Christ focuses primarily on his role as Savior so that by and large salvation is the overarching theme while Christology is subservient to it. This, of course, doesn't mean that Christ is dispensable; to the contrary, he provides salvation. What it means, however, is that the LTT's teaching on Christ focuses not so much on his person, nature, or other characteristics in their own right but on God's provision of salvation in and through him. As N. T. Wright notes, "'Christology' is not about an abstract proposition concerning the 'divinity' of Jesus, but the dynamic announcement that in Jesus, Israel's Messiah, Israel's God has become king of the world, with immediate effect and urgent consequences."[173] Arguably, the key "effect" is salvation, and the key "consequence" is mission.

---

[172] Cf., e.g., the observation by Belleville, "Christology," 226: "The title Χριστός Ἰησοῦς and soteriology are intimately connected in the Pastorals." Hetzler notes the pairing of God and Christ in a number of shared activities in 1 Timothy, including the calling of Paul (1:1, 11, 12–17); granting the gift of salvation to humankind (1:1, 15; 2:3-6; 4:10); bestowing grace, mercy, and peace (1:2, 14, 16); being the object of the Christian's hope (1:1; 4:10; 5:5; 6:17). C. O. Hetzler, "Our Savior and King: Theology Proper in 1 Timothy" (Ph.D. diss., The Southern Baptist Theological Seminary, 2008), 135.

[173] Wright, "Paul's Western Missionary Project," 60.

This biblical-theological exposition of major themes in the LTT, therefore, is based on the conviction that by and large salvation is the predominant theme while theology proper and Christology are for the most part subsumed under that larger salvific motif.[174] In this way, the message of salvation in Christ is integrally connected with the core content of the apostolic mission (§1), the apostolic message concerning God's salvation in Christ (§2), and the LTT's theological, Christological, and pneumatological teaching. This understanding flows from a comparison between the LTT and the other Pauline letters, not to mention the rest of the NT writings, as well as from the observation that the "salvation" word group, including the description of both God and Christ as Savior, is strikingly prominent, especially in Titus. We'll discuss possible contextual or other reasons why salvation is particularly conspicuous in the LTT further below.

§3.1 God

Theology proper has been a largely neglected theme in the literature on the LTT.[175] However, while at times in the background, God sustains a significant presence throughout the letters.[176]

---

[174] Towner, e.g., observes that "the author's presentation of God has a distinct soteriological orientation" (*Goal of Our Instruction*), 51.

[175] G. A. Couser, "God and Christian Existence in 1 and 2 Timothy and Titus" (Ph.D. thesis, University of Aberdeen, 1992), 2.

[176] There are forty-eight references to God (θεός) in the LTT; the term occurs twenty-two times in 1 Timothy, thirteen times in 2 Timothy, and thirteen times in Titus. Typically, statements made about "God" (θεός) in the LTT refer specifically to God the Father; this is evident in that Jesus is often contextually present as well (but note the important exception in Titus 2:13). In addition, Paul specifically refers to God as Father as well (1 Tim 1:2; 2 Tim 1:2; Titus 1:4). Relevant works on theology proper in the LTT include Bailey, "Theology of Paul's Pastoral Epistles," 340–43; G. A. Couser, "God and Christian Existence in 1 and 2 Timothy and Titus"; Couser, "God and Christian Existence in the Pastoral Epistles: Toward *Theo*logical Method and Meaning." *NovT* 42 (2000): 262–83; Couser, "The Sovereign Savior of 1 and 2 Timothy and Titus," in *Entrusted with the Gospel*, 105–36; J. A. Fitzmyer, "The Savior God," in *The Forgotten God: Perspectives in Biblical Theology. Essays in Honor of Paul J. Achtemeier on the Occasion of His Seventy-fifth Birthday*, ed. A. A. Das and F. J. Matera (Louisville: Westminster John Knox, 2002), 181–96; Hetzler, "Our Savior and King: Theology Proper in 1 Timothy"; Schnelle, *Theology of the New Testament*, 579–82; Spicq, *Les épîtres pastorales*, 243–45; J. L. Sumney, "'God Our Savior': The Fundamental Operational Theological Assertion of 1 Timothy," *HorBT* 21 (1999): 105–23; Sumney, "'God Our Savior': The Theology of 1 Timothy," *LTQ* 33 (1998): 151–61; Towner, *Goal of Our Instruction*, 49–51.

Indeed, theology proper provides important grounding at a foundational level for all that Paul teaches and enjoins.[177]

In the letter opening to 1 Timothy, God is identified as Savior and Father (1:1, 2). Paul also speaks of "God's plan, which operates by faith" (1:4) and of "the gospel concerning the glory of the blessed God" with which he was entrusted (1:11). His thanksgiving climaxes in the doxology: "Now to the King eternal, immortal, invisible, the only God, be honor and glory forever and ever. Amen" (1:17). Chapter 2 again opens with a reference to "God our Savior" (2:3) and the affirmation that there is "one God and one mediator between God and humanity, the man Christ Jesus" (2:5). In the instructions regarding church leaders, reference is made to "God's church" in conjunction with a man's household (3:5), followed by Paul's purpose statement: he has written this letter to instruct Timothy on how people ought to act in "God's household," "the church of the living God" (3:15). In chapter 4, over against the false teachers, Paul affirms that everything God created is good, "and nothing is to be rejected if it is received with thanksgiving, since it is sanctified by the word of God and by prayer" (4:3–5). Later Paul says he and other believers have put their hope in "the living God," who is the Savior of "all people" (4:10; cf. 3:15). When providing instructions regarding widows, Paul writes that it pleases God when children take care of their parents (5:4). Widows worthy of church support have put their hope in God (5:5). Paul's instructions regarding dealing with (sinning) elders contain a solemn charge "before God and Christ Jesus and the elect angels" (5:21). Later he urges slaves to obey their masters so that God's name and teaching not be blasphemed (6:1). Toward the end of the letter, Paul charges Timothy, the "man of God," in the presence of God, to keep his instructions until Christ's return, which God will bring about in his own time (6:11, 13). Finally, the rich are exhorted to put their hope in God rather than on uncertain riches (6:17). Throughout the letter, the phrase "before God" (ἐνώπιον τοῦ θεοῦ in 2:3; 5:4, 21; 6:13) highlights God's cognizance of and involvement

[177] Sumney finds that "the fundamental and *operative* theological conviction of 1 Timothy is the conception of God as Savior, with the inseparable notion that faith in this God entails piety" ("'God Our Savior': The Theology of 1 Timothy," 33); similarly, Hetzler argues that Paul describes God in 1 Timothy "as both Savior and King, in major part, to ground and focus his entire message to Timothy" ("Our Savior and King," 2).

in the works of Timothy and the Ephesian church.[178] This emphasis on God's presence, the designation of God as "Savior" in a letter which majors on soteriology, and the doxologies which at some level frame the letter, all point to the significant role theology proper plays in 1 Timothy.[179]

In the letter opening to 2 Timothy, Paul acknowledges that he is an apostle by God's will (1:1) and, as in the first letter, refers to God the Father (1:2; cf. 1 Tim 1:2). His thanksgiving is framed by references to God as the recipient of the thanksgiving (1:3) and the giver of power, love, and sound judgment (1:7). In the following verse Paul urges Timothy to join him in suffering for the gospel and to rely on the power of God (1:8). While Paul suffers, God's Word is not bound (2:9). He calls on Timothy to exhort people not to fight about words (2:14) and to present himself approved to God, correctly teaching his word (2:15). For God's solid foundation stands firm: he knows those who are his (2:19). As Timothy instructs his opponents gently, perhaps God will grant them repentance (2:25). All Scripture is inspired by God, so that the man of God may be complete and equipped for every good work (3:17). The final chapter opens with a solemn charge before God and Jesus Christ in view of the upcoming judgment and Christ's return (4:1).

The letter opening to Titus is particularly saturated with references to God, featuring two references to God in v. 1 and one each in vv. 2, 3, and 4. Paul identifies himself as a servant of God whose purpose is to build up the faith of God's elect (1:1). God, "who cannot lie," promised eternal life before time began (v. 2). In vv. 3 and 4 God is identified as Savior and Father (cf. 1 Tim 1:2; 2 Tim 1:2). In the list of qualifications for church leaders, overseers are those who are given charge of God's household (1:7; cf. 1 Tim 1:4). The false teachers claim to know God but deny him by their works (1:16). Older women must instruct young women so that God's message may not be slandered (2:5; cf. 1 Tim 6:1). Slaves, too, must adorn the teaching of God our Savior in everything (2:10). In the theologically rich passage that follows, Paul writes that the

---

178 Hetzler, "Our Savior and King," 68.

179 In addition, Sumney ("'God Our Savior': The Theology of 1 Timothy," 37) contends that the argumentation of 1 Timothy is consistently grounded in "God and God's character/activity as life-giving creator."

grace of God appeared at Jesus's first coming (2:11).[180] In the following chapter Paul writes similarly of the appearing of the kindness of "God our Savior" (3:4) and urges that "those who have believed God might be careful to devote themselves to good works" (3:8).

Our survey of references to God in the LTT has yielded a rich biblical-theological harvest. As the above passages document, from beginning to end, God is characterized in many ways which reflect both OT and NT antecedents: as the Father,[181] Savior,[182] Creator,[183] the living God,[184] the one who inspired Scripture, and the one in whom believers are to set their hope. Likewise, the doxologies of 1 Tim 1:17 and 6:15–16 contribute significantly to a biblical-theological view of God: God is the "King eternal" (1:17) and the "blessed and only Sovereign" (6:15) and "King of kings and Lord of lords" (6:15); he is "immortal" (1:17; 6:16); is "invisible" (1:17) and cannot be seen by humans (6:16);[185] dwells in "unapproachable light" (6:16); and is the only God (1:17).[186] These doxologies highlight God's transcendence, but the immanence of God is on display as well throughout the letters by way of his portrayal as Savior and as the one whose "ongoing presence and provision likely stands

---

[180] The passage continues to state that believers "wait for the blessed hope, the appearing of the glory of our great God and Savior, Jesus Christ" (2:13). This astonishing affirmation is the first and only reference to Jesus as God (θεός) in the LTT.

[181] Though he doesn't deal directly with the LTT, note A. M. Mengestu, *God as Father in Paul: Kinship Language and Identity Formation in Early Christianity* (Eugene, OR: Wipf & Stock, 2013), who examines God as Father in the OT, ancient Jewish writings, and Paul.

[182] See §3.3 "God and Christ as Savior."

[183] See Aageson, "Genesis in the Deutero-Pauline Epistles," 123–24; and esp. Couser, "Sovereign Savior," 120–22.

[184] See Goodwin, "Pauline Background of the Living God as Interpretive Context for 1 Timothy 4:10."

[185] Note A. S. Malone, "The Invisibility of God: A Survey of a Misunderstood Phenomenon," *EvQ* 79 (2007): 311–29, who argues that the idea of God's "invisibility" in 1:17, expanded to the idea that no one has seen him or can see him in 6:16, doesn't indicate that the Father is intrinsically unable to be seen. Instead, Malone argues, the emphasis is on God's transcendence: he is typically "unseen" (perhaps a better translation than "invisible") because he is other than and apart from humankind. He notes that the adjective ἀόρατος simply refers to something that is "unavailable to human sight" without commenting on why it is—sometimes it may indeed be because something is literally "unseeable" (such as the human soul), but this idea is not intrinsic to the word.

[186] See Fitzmyer, "Savior God," 182–85.

behind Paul's repeated reference to believers as those who 'hope in God'" (1 Tim 4:10; 5:5; 6:17).[187]

Every major theme highlighted in this biblical-theological exposition finds its grounding in God. Paul's apostleship is by God's will and God's command (§1). The message Paul is proclaiming is God's word, God's message, God's gospel (§2). God—not any human ruler—is Savior (§3.3). The church is God's household, the church of the living God (§4.1). Believers are to perform good works on the basis of the grace they've received from God, by faith (§5.2). They are to wait eagerly in hope for the second appearing of God's grace in form of Christ's return (§6.6). As we'll explore further below, God the Father is portrayed as conjoined with the Lord Jesus Christ as Savior of humankind in God's plan which is to be administered by Paul and the leaders of the church.

§3.2 Christ

Whether in conjunction with salvation or otherwise, Christology is one of the most pronounced themes in the LTT and one of its most discussed points of biblical theology.[188] The

---

[187] Couser, "Sovereign Savior," 116.

[188] Among studies on the LTT's Christology, see esp. A. Y. Lau, *Manifest in Flesh: The Epiphany Christology of the Pastoral Epistles* (Tübingen: Mohr-Siebeck, 1996), and more briefly, I. H. Marshall, "The Christology of the Pastoral Epistles." *SNTSU-A* 13 (1988): 157–77; and P. H. Towner, "Christology in the Letters to Timothy and Titus," in *Contours of Christology in the New Testament*, ed. R. N. Longenecker (Grand Rapids: Eerdmans, 2005), 219–44. For historical overviews of the conversation on the letters' Christology, see Marshall, "The Christology of the PE," 158–62; H. Stettler, *Die Christologie der Pastoralbriefe*, WUNT 2/105 (Tübingen: Mohr-Siebeck, 1998), 3–22; and Lau, *Manifest in Flesh*, 1–11. For other studies on the LTT's Christology, see D. L. Akin, "The Mystery of Godliness Is Great: Christology in the Pastoral Epistles," in *Entrusted with the Gospel*, 137–52; Bailey, "Theology of Paul's Pastoral Epistles," 343–47; J. M. Bassler, "A Plethora of Epiphanies: Christology in the Pastoral Letters," *Princeton Seminary Bulletin* 17 (1996): 310–25; Bassler, "Epiphany Christology in the Pastoral Letters: Another Look," in *Pauline Conversations in Context: Essays in Honor of Calvin J. Roetzel*, ed. J. C. Anderson, P. Sellew, and C. Setzer, JSNTSup 221 (Sheffield: Sheffield Academic Press, 2002), 194–214; L. L. Belleville, "Christology, Greco-Roman Religious Piety, and the Pseudonymity of the Pastoral Letters," in *Paul and Pseudepigraphy*, ed. S. E. Porter and G. P. Fewster, Pauline Studies 8 (Leiden: Brill, 2013), 221–44; Belleville, "Christology, the Pastoral Epistles, and Commentaries," in *On the Writing of New Testament Commentaries. Festschrift for Grant R. Osborne on the Occasion of His 70th Birthday*, ed. S. E. Porter and E. J. Schnabel, Texts and Editions for NT Study 8 (Leiden: Brill, 2012), 317–36; Brox, *Pastoralbriefe*, 161–66; G. D. Fee, *Pauline*

Christological data present themselves as follows. "Christ Jesus" occurs twenty-five times in the LTT,[189] while "Jesus Christ" is used a mere six times.[190] "Lord" (κύριος) occurs twenty-two times, almost always with reference to Jesus,[191] while "Savior" (σωτήρ) is applied to Christ four times out of the ten times it appears in the LTT.[192] Significant Christological teaching is also conveyed by way of probable preformed materials, such as a faithful saying (1 Tim 1:15: Jesus came to save sinners), a creedal statement (1 Tim 2:5–6: Jesus the mediator between God and humanity in providing salvation), and a hymnic confession (1 Tim 3:16: the mystery of godliness concerning Christ's death, resurrection, etc.).[193]

Christology: An Exegetical-Theological Study (Peabody, MA: Hendrickson, 2007), 418–78; V. Hasler, "Epiphanie und Christologie in den Pastoralbriefen," *TZ* 33 (1977): 193–209; K. Läger, *Die Christologie der Pastoralbriefe*, Hamburger theologische Studien 12 (Münster: Lit, 1996); Marshall, *New Testament Theology*, 408–11; Marshall, *Pastoral Epistles*, 287–96 ("Christology and the concept of 'epiphany'"); F. J. Matera, *New Testament Christology* (Louisville: Westminster John Knox, 1999), 158–72; Schnelle, *New Testament Theology*, 582–85; H. Simonsen, "Christologische Traditionselemente in den Pastoralbriefen," in *Die Paulinische Literatur und Theologie*, ed. S. Pederson, Teologiske Studier 7 (Göttingen: Vandenhoeck & Ruprecht, 1980), 51–62; T. Söding, "Das Erscheinen des Retters: Zur Christologie der Pastoralbriefe," in *Christologie in der Paulus-Schule: Zur Rezeptionsgeschichte des paulinischen Evangeliums*, ed. K. Scholtissek, SBS 181 (Stuttgart: Katholisches Bibelwerk, 2000), 149–92; Spicq, *Les épîtres pastorales*, 245–54; G. Strecker, *Theology of the New Testament* (Berlin: de Gruyter, 2000), 58–82; P. H. Towner, "Christology in the Letters to Timothy and Titus," in *Contours of Christology in the New Testament*, ed. R. N. Longenecker (Grand Rapids: Eerdmans, 2005), 219–44; Towner, *Goal of Our Instruction*, 51–56; Towner, *Letters to Timothy and Titus*, 59–68 ("In Search of a Christological Center: Savior and Epiphany"), 416–18 ("The Epiphany Concept"); C. M. Tuckett, *Christology and the New Testament: Jesus and His Earliest Followers* (Louisville: Westminster John Knox, 2001), 84–88; W. Windisch, "Zur Christologie der Pastoralbriefe," *ZNW* 34 (1935): 213–38; Young, *Theology*, 59–68.

[189] 1 Tim 1:1 (2x), 2, 12, 14, 15, 16; 2:5; 3:13; 4:6; 5:21; 6:13; 2 Tim 1:1 (2x), 2, 9, 10, 13; 2:1, 3, 10; 3:12, 15; 4:1; Titus 1:4.

[190] 1 Tim 6:3, 14; 2 Tim 2:8; Titus 1:1; 2:13; 3:6. Though it is unclear whether there is any significant difference between the two, and if so, what it would be (but see Belleville, "Christology, the Pastoral Epistles, and Commentaries," 322). Note that "Jesus Christ" is more common in Titus while "Christ Jesus" is the prevalent expression in the letters to Timothy.

[191] 1 Tim 1:2, 12, 14; 6:3, 14, 15; 2 Tim 1:2, 8, 16, 18 (2x); 2:7, 19 (2x), 22, 24; 3:11; 4:8, 14, 17, 18, 22 (note the curious absence of κύριος in the letter to Titus).

[192] 2 Tim 1:10; Titus 1:4; 2:13; 3:6; note the frequency in Titus.

[193] See Belleville, "Christology, the Pastoral Epistles, and Commentaries," 323–35; Lau, *Manifest in Flesh*, 64–178; Marshall, "Christology of the Pastoral

In the letter opening to 1 Timothy, Paul ties his apostleship to Christ Jesus (1:1) and connects Christ Jesus with God the Father (1:2). Paul's thanksgiving in vv. 12–17 includes four references to Christ Jesus: he appointed Paul to ministry (v. 12, cf. v. 1); the faith and love in Christ Jesus are connected with God's grace (v. 14); the "faithful saying" in v. 15 speaks of Christ Jesus coming into the world to save sinners; and v. 16 refers to the demonstration of his patience by extending mercy to Paul who had persecuted him. Chapter 2 attests to Christ Jesus as the one mediator between God and humanity who gave his life as a ransom for all (v. 5). Toward the end of chapter 3, Paul writes that deacons who serve well acquire a good standing in the faith in Christ Jesus (v. 13). In 4:6 Paul speaks to Timothy about being a good servant of Christ Jesus. In 5:11 Paul expresses his concern for young widows who are drawn away from Christ by their desires. In the midst of his instructions to Timothy on how to deal with errant elders is a charge "before God and Christ Jesus and the elect angels" (5:21). In 6:3 Paul references opposition to "the sound teaching of our Lord Jesus Christ." Toward the end of the letter, 6:13 includes another solemn charge in the presence of God and Christ Jesus, and the following verse speaks of the future appearing of the Lord Jesus Christ (v. 14).

Similar to the first letter, 2 Timothy opens with multiple references to Christ Jesus: in conjunction with Paul's apostleship, in relation to the promise of life in him (v. 1), and in connection with God the Father (v. 2). It is hard to imagine God the Father and the Lord Jesus Christ being more intricately intertwined than they are in vv. 1 and 2 of the letter opening to 2 Timothy: they are joint sources from which the blessings of life, grace, mercy, and peace flow. Paul's testimony in vv. 9 and 10 speaks of the grace given to believers in Christ Jesus before time began and of life brought through the first coming of "our Savior Christ Jesus." The reference to "faith and love . . . in Christ Jesus" in v. 13 echoes the similar reference in 1 Tim 1:14. In chapter 2 Paul urges Timothy to be strong in the grace that is in Christ Jesus (v. 1), to share in suffering as a good soldier of Christ Jesus (v. 3), and to focus his attention on Christ Jesus as "risen from the dead and descended from David"

Epistles," 164–65.

(v. 8). Paul himself endures all things for those chosen for salvation in Christ Jesus (v. 10). In chapter 3, Paul makes references to living a godly life in Christ Jesus (v. 12) and to salvation through faith in him (v. 15). Similar to the first letter, 2 Timothy concludes with a solemn charge before God and Christ Jesus (4:1; cf. 1 Tim 6:13).

References to Christ are much sparser in the letter to Titus. In v. 1 Paul links his apostleship to Christ Jesus, and in v. 4 he calls Christ Jesus "our Savior." In both passages Christ Jesus is closely tied to God the Father. The Christological high point in the letter, if not the LTT altogether, is the reference to the "appearing of the glory of our great God and Savior, Jesus Christ" in 2:13. This is the only place in the LTT where Jesus is identified as θεός, "God."[194] The final Christological reference in Titus is in fact a trinitarian reference: God poured out his Spirit on believers through "Jesus Christ our Savior" (3:6). While Christological references in Titus, therefore, are not as frequent as in the letters to Timothy, the letter contributes some striking and significant Christological contributions to the LTT and to the NT canon as a whole.

Similar to our discussion of references to God in the LTT above (§3.1), a close reading of the LTT shows significant breadth in its Christological scope.[195] Apart from references to Christ as Savior (further discussed under the next heading), Jesus Christ—or, more commonly, Christ Jesus—is referenced as the one who appointed Paul to be an apostle; he is identified not only as the source of salvation but also as the source of faith and love, as well as life, and the instrument of God's grace. Importantly, he is the one mediator between God and humanity who gave himself as a

[194] See esp. M. J. Harris, "Titus 2:13 and the Deity of Christ," in *Pauline Studies: Essays Presented to Professor F. F. Bruce on His Seventieth Birthday*, ed. D. A. Hagner and M. J. Harris (Grand Rapids: Eerdmans, 1980), 262–77. See also Knight, *Pastoral Epistles*, 322–26; Marshall, *Pastoral Epistles*, 276–82.

[195] Towner examines the Christology of the LTT letter by letter, finding that "1 Timothy reflects a decided emphasis on the humanity of Christ. Titus explores in greater depth the co-equal [*sic*] status of God and Christ. 2 Timothy brings the promises of resurrection and vindication, as well as the eschatological functions of Christ, to bear on the harsh realities of suffering and death that confronted Timothy and challenged his faithful endurance." "Christology in the Letters to Timothy and Titus," 243.

ransom for all; and he, along with God and the elect angels, is the frequent grounds on which Paul makes his urgent, solemn appeals to Timothy. He is confessed as risen from the dead and descended from David. He is "our great God and Savior"![196] And he is also the one through whom God poured out his Spirit on believers. This inventory shows that the scope of the LTT's Christology is rather impressive and varied. It is also clearly in keeping with the teaching of Paul's other letters and of the NT as a whole.[197]

An important aspect of the Christology of the LTT is Paul's use of the term ἐπιφάνεια ("appearance"),[198] once to refer to Christ's first coming (2 Tim 1:10) and four times to his second coming (1 Tim 6:14; 2 Tim 4:1, 8; Titus 2:13). In fact, in Titus 2:11–13 the grace of God has appeared (ἐπιφαίνω) through Christ in the past, and believers now look for the future appearing (ἐπιφάνεια) of Christ.[199] Paul uses the term in this sense only once elsewhere

---

[196] For other ways in which the deity of Christ is indicated in the LTT, see D. N. Howell, "God-Christ Interchange in Paul: Impressive Testimony to the Deity of Jesus," *JETS* 36 (1993): 467–79; Marshall, "Christology of the Pastoral Epistles," 174–75.

[197] Fee carefully works through the various Christological passages in the LTT and concludes that "nothing in these letters appears to be either more or less Christologically aware than what appears in the earlier [Pauline] corpus"; indeed, the LTT possess "a Christology so like the earlier letters, and often so subtle and unrehearsed, that one could use these findings to argue rather strongly for Pauline authorship" (*Pauline Christology*, 472–73).

[198] Relevant literature on this point includes R. F. Collins, "From παρουσία to ἐπιφανεία: The Transformation of a Pauline Motif," in *Unity and Diversity in the Gospels and Paul: Essays in Honor of Frank J. Matera*, ed. C. W. Skinner and K. R. Iverson, ECL 7 (Atlanta: Society of Biblical Literature, 2012), 273–99; Hasler, "Epiphanie und Christologie"; Lau, *Manifest in Flesh*, esp. 179–259; D. Lührmann, "Epiphaneia: Zur Bedeutungsgeschichte eines griechischen Wortes," in *Tradition und Glaube: Das frühe Christentum in seiner Umwelt: Festgabe für Karl Georg Kuhn zum 65. Geburtstag*, ed. G. Jeremias et al. (Göttingen: Vandenhoeck & Ruprecht, 1971); Marshall, *Pastoral Epistles*, 287–96; L. Oberlinner, "Die 'Epiphaneia' des Heilswillens Gottes in Christus Jesus: Zur Grundstruktur der Christologie der Pastoralbriefe." *ZNW* 71 (1981): 310–25; E. Pax, ΕΠΙΦΑΝΕΙΑ*: Ein religionsgeschichtlicher Beitrag zur Biblischen Theologie*, Münchener theologische Studien 1/10 (Munich: Karl Zink, 1955); A. J. Vermeulen, "Epiphaneia," *Graecitas et latinitas christianorum, Supplementa fasciculus I*, ed. C. Mohrmann, et al. (Nijmegen: Dekker and Van de Vegt, 1964), 9–44.

[199] The use of the term in all three of the LTT provides another commonality among the letters. Note also the use of ἐπιφαίνω in a related sense in Titus 2:11 and 3:4; and φανερόω in 1 Tim 3:16, 2 Tim 1:10, and Titus 1:3. M. Silva notes that "the

(2 Thess 2:8), which renders its repeated use in the LTT remarkable.[200] As to its use in the Greco-Roman world, Silva notes that "by the Roman period this noun had almost become a technical term for the manifestation of divine power, esp. the appearance of an otherwise hidden deity to a worshiper in need."[201] Similarly, Collins observes that ἐπιφάνεια was typically used to speak of "helpful divine interventions."[202] The term would thus have resonated with Gentiles in Ephesus.[203] However, its use in the context of the LTT is better understood to be grounded in the OT and Hellenistic Judaism. In this latter context it is used especially "in reference to the angel(s)-of-the-Lord tradition or to God's sending of supernatural agent(s) to assist His people in military context."[204]

Important to understand is that in using ἐπιφάνεια to describe both the first and second comings of Christ, the emphasis is not on the "appearance" of Christ *per se* but on the *purpose* of that appearance: to intervene for those in need.[205] Thus, as noted earlier, the Christology of the LTT largely serves its soteriology.[206] As well, it should be noted that some have denied that the LTT have anything

---

ἐπιφαίνω word group, when used with theological import, is found almost exclusively in the context of the revelation of Yahweh in the OT and of Jesus Christ in the NT" ("φαίνω, κτλ.," *NIDNTTE* 4:590–91).

[200] The use of ἐπιφανεία is also noteworthy in that Paul typically uses παρουσία in speaking of the return of Christ.

[201] M. Silva, "φαίνω, κτλ.," *NIDNTTE* 4:585–86. See examples from Greco-Roman sources in Lau, *Manifest in Flesh*, 182–89; Pax, ΕΠΙΦΑΝΕΙΑ, 24–84.

[202] Collins, "From παρουσία to ἐπιφανεία," 296.

[203] Apparently, as with various Greco-Roman deities, Artemis of the Ephesians was understood to "manifest" herself to her worshipers, and the ἐπιφανεία language of the LTT may stand over against this. See Trebilco, *Early Christians in Ephesus*, 356–57.

[204] Lau, *Manifest in Flesh*, 223, who comes to this conclusion after examining the use of ἐπιφανεία in 4 Maccabees and elsewhere.

[205] This point is brought out in Bassler, "Plethora of Epiphanies," 314–15. She helpfully points to the work of Lührmann, who demonstrates that the use of ἐπιφανεία typically emphasized the aspect of revelation less than that of "helpful intervention" ("*helfendes Eingreifen*"; Lührmann, "Epiphaneia," 190). Though she views the LTT as pseudonymous, Bassler's essay is helpful because it understands the LTT to encompass a coherent theology; a subsequent essay, "Epiphany Christology in the Pastoral Letters," in which she does not assume common authorship of the three LTT, is less helpful.

[206] This, in turn, provides an explanation for the atypical use of ἐπιφανεία in the LTT, which has been marshalled by some as evidence for pseudonymous authorship.

to say about the preexistence of Christ.[207] As observed earlier, however, the assertion that Christ Jesus "came into the world" in 1 Tim 1:15 is difficult to explain if some notion of preexistence were not present. Moreover, Christ's preexistence is implied in 1 Tim 3:16, which refers to Christ's being manifested in the flesh, and 2 Tim 1:9–10, where Paul speaks of God's bestowing his grace on us in Christ Jesus from eternity past.

§3.3 God and Christ as Savior

The frequent designation of both God and Christ as Savior (σωτήρ) is one of the most poignant soteriological features of the LTT.[208] As Talbert states,

> In the PE God is Savior (1 Tim 1:1; 2:3; 4:10; 2 Tim 1:8–9; Titus 1:2–4; 2:10; 3:4). Jesus is the human agent who carries out God's plan and, as such, can also be called Savior (2 Tim 1:10; Titus 1:4; 2:13; 3:6). Jesus's saving work is described mainly in terms of two epiphanies: past incarnation (1 Tim 1:10; Titus 1:4; 3:6) and future coming (Titus 2:13).[209]

In this way the mission and salvation motifs lay a theological foundation for the LTT on which Paul builds the themes of God's household (ecclesiology; §4), the Christian life (including the pursuit of

[207] Notably, see J. D. G. Dunn, *Christology in the Making: A New Testament Inquiry into the Origins of the Doctrine of the Incarnation*, 2nd ed. (Grand Rapids: Eerdmans, 1989), 237–39.

[208] See, e.g., F. F. Bruce, "'Our God and Saviour': A Recurring Biblical Pattern," in *The Saviour God*, ed. S. G. Brandon (Manchester: Manchester University Press, 1963), 55–63; R. F. Collins, *I & II Timothy and Titus*, 308–18; Fitzmyer, "Savior God," 181–96; Sumney, "God Our Savior: The Fundamental"; Sumney, "'God Our Savior': The Theology of 1 Timothy."

[209] Talbert, "Between Two Epiphanies," 59. However, in light of the striking ascriptions of deity to Jesus in the LTT, I take strong exception to Talbert's calling Jesus a mere "human agent." Also, while God in 2 Tim 1:8–9 is said to have saved us, he is not specifically called σωτήρ.

various virtues; §5),[210] and the last days (eschatology; §6), all of which will be discussed below.[211]

How is one to account for the frequency and preeminence of the concept of salvation and the distinctive characterization of God and Christ as "Savior" as epitomized by the "Savior/salvation" word group in the LTT?[212] First, in terms of *contextualization*, Paul likely sought to present Jesus as Savior in contrast to other gods or the emperor.[213] In the first century "Savior" was a title regularly attributed to rulers, including Roman emperors such as Nero (AD 54–68).[214] In contrast Paul maintains that the Christian God, and he alone, is "our Savior," rejecting competing claims by contemporaneous savior figures. With regard to references to the term in Paul's letters to Timothy (1 Tim 1:1; 2 Tim 1:10), evidence is strong that in Ephesus the title "Savior" (σωτήρ) was used as "a title or description of gods, emperors, provincial proconsuls, and local patrons."[215]

---

210 On the connection between the LTT's soteriology and the life of faith/ethics, see ibid., 59–60: "The time between the two epiphanies is provided for training (παιδεύουσα—Titus 2:11–12) that will produce progress (ἡ προκοπή—1 Tim 4:15) in virtuous living (1 Tim 4:7, 15; 2 Tim 3:16; Titus 2:12) and lead to inheritance of the blessed hope (Titus 2:13).... The ethics of the PE are grounded in their understanding of salvation."

211 Note also the connection between the distinctive salvation language (σωτήρ) and ἐπιφάνεια language (referring to God's or Christ's "appearing") in the LTT, which is noted by F. Jung, ΣΩΤΗΡ*: Studien zur Rezeption eines hellenistischen Ehrentitels im Neuen Testament*, NTAbh N.F. 39 (Münster: Aschendorff, 2002), 330–31.

212 The frequency of the σῴζω word group in the LTT is commonly and rightly adduced as evidence for the thematic centrality of salvation in the letters. See esp. I. H. Marshall, "Salvation in the Pastoral Epistles," in *Geschichte—Tradition—Reflexion: Festschrift für Martin Hengel zum 70. Geburtstag*, vol. 3: *Frühes Christentum*, ed. H. Lichtenberger (Tübingen: Mohr-Siebeck, 1996), 450–52. Cf. J. D. Quinn, *The Letter to Titus*, AB 35 (New York: Doubleday, 1990), 304–15 ("The PE on Salvation"); Towner, *Goal of Our Instruction*, 75–77.

213 See esp. Jung, ΣΩΤΗΡ, 321–32.

214 See H. O. Maier, *Picturing Paul in Empire: Imperial Image, Text and Persuasion in Colossians, Ephesians and the Pastoral Epistles* (London: Bloomsbury T&T Clark, 2013), 157–63; B. W. Winter, *Divine Honours for the Caesars: The First Christians' Responses* (Grand Rapids: Eerdmans, 2015), 36, 40–44, 71–73. Cf. Young, *Theology*, 64–65, who notes that not only "Savior" language but also terms such as εὐαγγέλιον and παρουσία are paralleled in Greco-Roman literature. In fact, Young contends that in the LTT the Christ-cult is consciously contrasted with the Caesar-cult (ibid.).

215 S. M. Baugh, "'Savior of All People': 1 Tim 4:10 in Context," *WTJ* 54 (1992): 335. Baugh notes that inscriptional evidence specifically names the patron goddess

With regard to the remarkably frequent use of the term "Savior" in the letter to Titus (1:3, 4; 2:10, 13; 3:4, 6), we mentioned in the introduction to Titus that an inscription was found at the sanctuary of Asclepius at Lebena near Gortyn, reading, "Diodorus dedicated to you, Savior (σωτήρ), two dreams in return for twofold eyes, light being restored" (2nd c. AD?).[216] Another similar Greek inscription, addressed to Zeus and attributed to a Corinthian named Plotius, was found at Knossos.[217] This and other similar evidence for the use of "Savior" with regard to Greek deities provides a crucial backdrop for Paul's references to God and Jesus as Savior, designating them as the true provider and exclusive mediator of salvation, respectively.

Second, the *false teaching* Paul opposed in the LTT was in all probability soteriological in nature and most likely exclusivist or elitist in orientation.[218] Rather than salvation being attained by adhering to various myths and genealogies (1 Tim 1:4), or in worshiping a pagan ruler or deity, Paul contended in conjunction with his Gentile mission that salvation was for all people (1 Tim 2:4) and came through Christ the Savior, and him alone (1 Tim 1:15; 2:3–4; 4:10; Titus 2:10–11; cf. Titus 3:2, 4). What is more, though eternal salvation is most often in view when Paul uses the "Savior/salvation" word group, several passages also speak of believers' safe preservation in this life (especially from Satan and his demons using the false teachers as their instruments) and their safe passage into the next (1 Tim 2:15; cf. v. 14; 4:16; 2 Tim 4:18).[219]

---

of Ephesus, Artemis, as "Artemis Soteria," and also records a plea for "salvation" to Artemis (335n18); see also S. Glahn, "The Identity of Artemis in First-Century Ephesus," *BSac* 172 (2015): 316–34, for the backstory that ties Artemis of the Ephesians tightly to the notion of salvation; and R. Oster, "The Ephesian Artemis as an Opponent of Early Christianity," in *JAC* 19 (1976): 40. On the use of σωτήρ in the ancient world, see further B. Witherington III, *Letters and Homilies for Hellenized Christians*, vol. 1: *A Socio-Rhetorical Commentary on Titus, 1–2 Timothy and 1–3 John* (Downers Grove: InterVarsity, 2006), 103–5; M. Silva, "σῴζω, κτλ.," 420–21.

[216] The inscription is reproduced in facsimile, Greek, and English translation in D. W. J. Gill, "A Saviour for the Cities of Crete: The Roman Background to the Epistle to Titus," in *The New Testament in Its First Century Setting: Essays on Context and Background in Honour of B. W. Winter on His 65th Birthday*, ed. P. J. Williams, A. D. Clarke, P. M. Head, and D. Instone-Brewer (Grand Rapids: Eerdmans, 2004), 229.

[217] For details see ibid., 230.

[218] See Marshall, *Pastoral Epistles*, 429; Towner, *Letters to Timothy and Titus*, 180.

[219] See further the discussion below.

Third, though the Ephesian situation may have prompted the repeated designation of God as Savior, Paul already had this language at hand in the LXX, where θεός and σωτήρ are regularly combined and provide "a natural and an ample biblical precedent."[220] The *Scriptures* with which Paul was familiar consistently refer to God as "the God who saves," "the God (or rock) of my salvation," etc. (1 Sam 10:19; Pss 23:5 [24:5]; 24:5 [25:5]; 26:1, 9 [27:1, 9]; 61:7 [62:7]; 78:9 [79:9]; 94:1 [95:1]; Hab 3:18; Isa 12:2), and this designation in the LTT serves the biblical-theological underscoring of "the continuation of God's redemptive act."[221] What's more, since both in the LTT and elsewhere in the NT Jesus is designated as "Savior"—an epithet even more striking in the LTT where God and Christ are both called "Savior"—we're reminded that God's work as Savior in the OT has in the NT taken on a new dimension in the work of Christ.

§3.4 The Holy Spirit

Although the Holy Spirit doesn't play a prominent role in the LTT,[222] he does make a contribution to their theological message, in particular their soteriology.[223] In Titus 3:4–7, Paul states the

[220] Couser, "God and Christian Existence in 1 and 2 Timothy and Titus," 20. Cf. Fitzmyer: "The use of 'Savior' for God in the pre-Christian Jewish world is well attested, and it acquires a specific Jewish nuance of the Creator God as giver of life and providing for his people" ("Savior God," 186). Interestingly, apart from the LTT, σωτήρ is used of God in the NT only in Luke 1:47 (note the strong OT connections in the Magnificat) and in Jude 25, while the title is associated with Jesus twelve times.

[221] Pao, "Let No One Despise Your Youth," 751.

[222] Though to speak of the "absence" of Pauline theological themes such as the Holy Spirit from the LTT is hyperbolic. E. J. Schnabel, "Paul, Timothy, and Titus: The Assumption of a Pseudonymous Author and of Pseudonymous Recipients in the Light of Literary, Theological, and Historical Evidence," in *Do Historical Matters Matter to Faith?*, ed. J. K. Hoffmeier and D. R. Magary (Wheaton: Crossway, 2012), 392.

[223] Hence the treatment of the Holy Spirit under the present rubric. On the Spirit in the LTT, see esp. Bailey, "Theology of Paul's Pastoral Epistles," 347–49; M. Clark, "The Pastoral Epistles," in *A Biblical Theology of the Holy Spirit*, ed. T. J. Burke and K. Warrington (Eugene, OR: Wipf & Stock, 2014), 213–25; M. A. G. Haykin, "The Fading Vision? The Spirit and Freedom in the Pastoral Epistles," *EvQ* 57 (1985): 291–305; I. H. Marshall, "The Holy Spirit in the Pastoral Epistles and the Apostolic Fathers," in *The Holy Spirit and Christian Origins: Essays in Honor of James D. G. Dunn* (Grand Rapids: Eerdmans, 2004), 257–69; J. D. Quinn, "The Holy Spirit in the Pastoral Epistles," in *Sin, Salvation, and the Spirit*, ed. D. Durken (Collegeville, MN:

means by which salvation is applied: a washing that brings about regeneration and renewal, which is effected by the Holy Spirit whom God poured out on believers abundantly through Jesus Christ their Savior. G. Fee describes this as "the absolutely crucial event that effects both the washing away of the sins in which we all once walked [Titus 3:3] and the regeneration necessary for the good works now urged upon God's new people [Titus 3:1–2, 8]."[224]

The reference to the Holy Spirit in Titus 3 is part of the "trustworthy saying" in vv. 4–7, the only one of the five such sayings in the LTT that contains a reference to the Spirit. The saying, a concise summary of Pauline soteriology and trinitarian in nature, focuses on God's salvation of believers through Christ and his regenerating work through the Holy Spirit. Paul states that God saved us, "not by works of righteousness that we had done, but according to his mercy" (v. 5). This salvation was accomplished "through the washing of regeneration and renewal by the Holy Spirit," whom God poured out on us abundantly through Jesus Christ our Savior (v. 6). "Regeneration" and "renewal" are both tied to the metaphor of "washing" by the Holy Spirit (Ezek 36:25–27). The generous "pouring out" (ἐκχέω) of the Spirit evokes OT prophetic language (Zech 12:10; Joel 3:1–2 LXX).[225]

One additional cluster of references to the Holy Spirit in the LTT pertains to Timothy's preservation of Paul's apostolic teaching (§2). In 1 Tim 6:20 Paul exhorts Timothy to guard (cf. 5:21) what has been entrusted to him (παραθήκη) for careful preservation—the apostolic teaching. In his second letter Paul similarly urges Timothy to guard the "good deposit" entrusted to him with the

---

Liturgical Press, 1979), 35–68; Spicq, *Les épîtres pastorales*, 254–56; Schnelle, *New Testament Theology*, 585–86; Towner, *Goal of Our Instruction*, 56–58; P. Trebilco, "The Significance and Relevance of the Spirit in the Pastoral Epistles," in *The Holy Spirit and Christian Origins: Essays in Honor of James D. G. Dunn*, ed. G. N. Stanton, B. W. Longenecker, and S. C. Barton (Grand Rapids: Eerdmans, 2004), 241–56. Cf. J. Brug, "A Rebirth-Washing and a Renewal-Holy Spirit," *Wisconsin Lutheran Quarterly* 92 (1995): 124–28; R. W. Wall, "Salvation's Bath by the Spirit: A Study of Titus 3:5b–6 in Its Canonical Setting," in *The Spirit and Christ in the New Testament and Christian Theology: Essays in Honor of Max Turner*, ed. I. H. Marshall, V. Rabens, and C. Bennema (Grand Rapids: Eerdmans, 2012), 198–212.

[224] G. D. Fee, *God's Empowering Presence: The Holy Spirit in the Letters of Paul* (Peabody, MA: Hendrickson, 1994), 779.

[225] For additional detailed exegetical information, see commentary at Titus 3:4–7.

help of the Holy Spirit (2 Tim 1:14; cf. 1 Tim 5:21; 6:20; 2 Tim 4:15). Timothy must guard the deposit he received from his apostolic mentor with the help of the indwelling (ἐνοικοῦντος) Holy Spirit, just as God will guard the deposit of Paul's life until the final day (2 Tim 1:12, 14). This underscores the importance of not only sustained and committed effort on the part of Timothy but also of the need for the indwelling Holy Spirit's enablement.

The Holy Spirit is also mentioned repeatedly in the LTT in conjunction with Timothy's appointment to ministry (§4). In 1 Tim 4:14 reference is made to his ordination service when the council of elders laid hands on him (cf. 1:18). Paul urges Timothy not to neglect his gift but to exercise it diligently. In context, "gift" may refer to Timothy's empowerment for ministry given by the Holy Spirit. The "gift of God" (τὸ χάρισμα τοῦ θεοῦ), mentioned in 2 Tim 1:6,[226] that is in Timothy through the laying on of Paul's hands may be the pastoral ministry assigned to Timothy at his ordination service. Alternatively, the Holy Spirit may be in view or a combination of the two (i.e., the Spirit as the source of Timothy's ministry assignment). In the face of timidity (v. 7), or persecution (v. 8), the divine gift will help Timothy overcome and persevere.

The LTT are often understood as having been written pseudonymously at a stage in the early church where the regular, powerful, and visible work of the Spirit has faded and where charismatic ministry has been replaced by institutionalization,[227] particularly in the realm of leadership in the church. Yet in these

---

[226] Haykin, "Fading Vision?," 298, suggests that "2 Tim 1:6 and its wider context contain the richest pneumatological vein in the Pastoral Epistles." He notes the conceptual similarity between this verse and 1 Thess 5:19, where "the Thessalonian believers are admonished not to quench the fiery power and light of the Spirit either by refusing to allow the exercise of the gifts of the Spirit or by ignoring them" (p. 299).

[227] Note, e.g., Dunn, *Jesus and the Spirit: A Study of the Religious and Charismatic Experience of Jesus and the First Christians as Reflected in the New Testament* (1975; repr., Grand Rapids: Eerdmans, 1997). He discusses the LTT in §57.3 (pp. 347–50) and finds a number of contrasts between what he considers to be authentic Pauline pneumatology and that of the LTT. "The vision of charismatic community has faded . . . *Spirit and charisma have become in effect subordinate to office, to ritual, to tradition*" (349, emphasis original). Trebilco, "Significance and Relevance," strikes a sort of mediating position; he sees the LTT as post-Pauline but argues that the pseudonymous author does not neglect the work of the Spirit but "relates the Spirit to crucial issues he faces, makes connections between the Spirit and other facets

letters we actually see "a high regard for the manifestation of prophecy" (1 Tim 1:18; 4:14), the activity of the Spirit in gifting Timothy for (noninstitutionalized!) ministry in the context of the church (1 Tim 4:14; 2 Tim 1:6), and a body of believers upon whom the Spirit has been poured out richly (Titus 3:6).[228] Since the Spirit is connected with salvation's rebirth and transformation (Titus 3:5), it is clear that the Spirit's initial and ongoing activity in each believer is presumed.[229] What's more, the instruction to Timothy to guard "through the Spirit who lives in us" the teaching of Christ passed down through Paul (2 Tim 1:13–14) also presumably applies to the faithful men who follow in Timothy's steps (2 Tim 2:2). The Spirit thus continues to be active in the church in the LTT.[230]

While the Holy Spirit is not referred to often in the LTT—though the half dozen or so above-mentioned references are hardly insignificant, clustering around soteriology, ecclesiology, and the teaching ministry of Paul's apostolic delegates—he is certainly not absent from these letters. The work of the Spirit is bound up with other important themes in the LTT,[231] and the pneumatology of

---

of his theology, and understands the Spirit's activity to involve new and different areas" (241).

228 Marshall, "Holy Spirit in the Pastoral Epistles and the Apostolic Fathers," 258 notes the connection between the language of the "pouring out" of the Spirit in Titus 3:5–6 and the description of Pentecost (Acts 2:17–18, 33; cf. 10:45); cf. Quinn, "Holy Spirit in the Pastoral Epistles," 351–52. Marshall also points out that from the earliest stages of the church there was "a system of leadership and oversight alongside the tasks of ministry (1 Thessalonians; 1 Corinthians), and there is overlap in that some leadership is more by appointment (e.g., apostleship and local eldership), whereas other leadership is more charismatic" (p. 268).

229 As to the believer's ongoing transformation, Trebilco ("Significance and Relevance," 252) connects the key soteriological role the Spirit plays in Titus 3:5 with the life of good deeds and Christian ethics enjoined in the context (vv. 1–8).

230 We might also mention Paul's reference to the Scripture being "God-breathed" (θεόπνευστος, 2 Tim 3:16). Marshall ("Holy Spirit in the Pastoral Epistles and the Apostolic Fathers," 258n3) points out that this is "a term which might arouse echoes of πνεῦμα for readers"; cf. also Quinn, "Holy Spirit in the Pastoral Epistles," 361–64. As noted above, it is likely that under the rubric of "Scripture" Paul included his own and other apostolic writings which were still being produced, thus pointing to the continuing work of the Spirit via the inspiration of Scripture in the church.

231 Trebilco, "Significance and Relevance," 251–54, explores the connection of the pneumatology of the LTT with the letters' teaching on salvation, the Christian life, and Christ.

the letters is consistent with that of Paul elsewhere.[232] Especially through the remarkable "trustworthy saying" in the letter to Titus, the LTT make a significant contribution to NT pneumatology in conjunction with the Holy Spirit's role in salvation and in particular his work of rebirth, regeneration, and renewal, which is mentioned only infrequently elsewhere in the NT.[233]

§3.5 Salvation

In conjunction with the mission theme and the twin motifs of tradition and Scripture in the LTT, the theme of salvation arguably serves as the fulcrum or center of gravity in these letters.[234] As P. Towner observes, "At the center of the theology of the Pastoral Epistles is the theme of salvation."[235] How does Paul present and develop the theme of salvation in the LTT? The following components of the LTT's teaching on salvation will be considered below: God and Christ as Savior, the need for salvation, the provision of salvation, the recipients of salvation, the nature of salvation, the reception of salvation, and the results of salvation.

C. Talbert lists a series of soteriological questions raised by the LTT that are addressed in the relevant literature:[236]

---

[232] See esp. Fee, *God's Empowering Presence*. Trebilco demurs but notes certain shared features of pneumatology of the LTT and that of Paul's letters elsewhere: "the importance of the Spirit at conversion, the concept of the indwelling Spirit, the Spirit and living the Christian life, the Spirit and power, the Spirit and love, the Spirit and eschatology, and the connection between Christ and the Spirit" ("Meaning and Significance," 254).

[233] See, e.g., John 1:13; 3:3, 5, 7; 1 Pet 1:23; cf. 2 Pet 1:4; 1 John 2:29; 3:9; 5:1, 4.

[234] For a basic survey, see Young, *Theology*, 50–55 (God as Savior), 56–59 (salvation), though note that she holds to pseudonymous authorship of the LTT. See also her discussion of Christology on pp. 59–68 (both κύριος and liturgical tradition).

[235] P. H. Towner, "The Pastoral Epistles," *NDBT*, 332; Towner, *Goal of Our Instruction*, chap. 5. U. Schnelle similarly speaks of the "central location of soteriology in the comprehensive theological conception of the Pastoral Epistles" and the letters' "basic soteriological orientation" (*Theology of the New Testament*, trans. M. E. Boring [Grand Rapids: Baker, 2009], 586). For a helpful study see G. M. Wieland, "The Function of Salvation in the Letters to Timothy and Titus," in *Entrusted with the Gospel*, 153–72, which is grounded in Wieland, *The Significance of Salvation: A Study of Salvation Language in the Pastoral Epistles* (Milton Keynes, UK: Paternoster, 2006).

[236] The list is adapted from C. H. Talbert, "Between Two Epiphanies: Clarifying One Aspect of Soteriology in the Pastoral Epistles," in *Getting "Saved": The Whole*

- whether salvation is effective for all by virtue of Christ's first coming or only becomes effective through faith;[237]
- whether the LTT espouse limited atonement;[238]
- whether the LTT endeavor to counteract an overemphasis on Jesus's death;[239]
- whether the LTT subsume Christology under soteriology, thus limiting Christ to two appearances;[240]
- whether the LTT's soteriology is part of contextualization in the surrounding Hellenistic nature;[241]
- whether the LTT's soteriology stands in continuity with Paul's earlier letters;[242] and
- whether the soteriology espoused in the three LTT differs from letter to letter.[243]

Talbert himself concludes that there is in fact "continuity with the understanding of soteriology in the undisputed Pauline letters."[244] The LTT see grace as operating in the believer's life from the beginning (regeneration, e.g., Titus 3:4–7) to its progress and fulfillment for the Lord's servants on mission (2 Tim 4:17–18): "The emphasis, therefore, is on divine enablement of Paul, Titus, and Timothy in the period between the first and second epiphanies of the Lord."[245] Without addressing the above list of questions one by one, the discussion below will survey salvation language in the LTT in its various dimensions before moving on to a discussion of

---

Story of Salvation in the New Testament, ed. C. H. Talbert and J. A. Whitlark (Grand Rapids: Eerdmans, 2011), 58–59.

[237] A. Klöpper, "Zur Soteriologie der Pastoralbriefe," *ZWT* 47 (1904): 57–88.

[238] I. H. Marshall, "Universal Grace and Atonement in the Pastoral Epistles," in *The Grace of God, the Will of Man*, ed. C. Pinnock (Grand Rapids: Zondervan, 1989), 51–69.

[239] D. Gerber, "1 Tim 1:15b: L'indice d'une sotéeriologie pensée prioritairement en lieu avec la venue de Jésus?," *RHPR* 80, no. 4 (2000): 463–77.

[240] L. R. Donelson, *Pseudepigraphy and Ethical Argument in the Pastoral Epistles*, HUT 22 (Tübingen: Mohr-Siebeck, 1986), 133–54.

[241] J. D. Quinn, "Jesus as Savior and Only Mediator," in *Fede e cultura alla luce della Bibbia: Atti della sessione plenaria 1979 della Pontificia Commissione Biblica* (Torino: Editrice Elle Di Ci, 1981), 249–60.

[242] I. H. Marshall, "Salvation, Grace and Works in the Later Writings in the Pauline Corpus," *NTS* 42 (1996): 339–58. See Talbert's own conclusion: "Between Two Epiphanies," 71 cited below.

[243] Wieland, *Significance of Salvation.*

[244] Talbert, "Between Two Epiphanies," 71.

[245] Ibid.

the LTT's teaching on the church as God's household, the Christian life, and the last days.

§3.5.1 *The Need for Salvation*

The notion of "saving" or "rescuing" implies a danger or dangers from which salvation is needed. From what do people need to be saved? A key passage in the LTT in this regard is 1 Tim 1:12–17, where Paul notes that Jesus came into the world to save sinners (v. 15), thus highlighting sin as that from which people require saving. In bearing testimony to his own conversion and call to service, Paul speaks of his past, describing himself as a blasphemer, persecutor, and man of insolent violence (v. 13).[246] Although he sinned ignorantly "in unbelief" (v. 13), he still calls himself the "the worst of [sinners]" (v. 15) in need of grace and mercy. Paul is more direct in Titus 2:14 regarding that from which people must be saved, asserting that Jesus gave himself for us to redeem us from "all lawlessness" (ἀνομία).[247]

§3.5.2 *The Provision of Salvation*

As mentioned, both God and Jesus are portrayed as Savior (σωτήρ) in the LTT,[248] and both are active in making salvation available to sinners. The fact that Paul uses the same title for both God

---

[246] Although θεομάχος ("fighter against God"; cf. Acts 5:39) isn't used in this passage, the term has been applied to Paul's description of his former life by M. Wolter, "Paulus, der bekehrte Gottesfeind. Zum Verständnis von 1. Tim. 1:13," *NovT* 31 (1989): 48–66; and R. van Houwelingen, "A Godfighter Becomes a Fighter for God," in *Coping with Violence in the New Testament*, Studies in Theology and Religion 16, ed. P. G. R. de Villiers and J. W. van Henten (Leiden: Brill, 2012), 83–100.

[247] This corresponds to 1 Tim 1:8–11, where the lawless (ἄνομος) are one example of sinners for whom the law was given (v. 9) and who are characterized as contrary to the sound teaching of the good news of salvation (vv. 10–11).

[248] Interestingly, in 1 Timothy, Paul speaks of God, but not Christ, as σωτήρ (1:1; 2:3; 4:10); in 2 Timothy, he speaks of Christ, but not God, as σωτήρ (1:10); and in Titus, he applies σωτήρ to both God (1:3; 2:10; 3:4) and Christ (1:4; 2:13; 3:6). Against the background of Israel's deliverance from Egypt, the title σωτήρ is repeatedly used for God in the LXX (Deut 32:15; 1 Sam 10:19; Pss 23:5 [24:5 MT]; 24:5 [25:5 MT]; 26:1 [27:1 MT]; 29:6 [27:9 MT]; 61:3 [62:2 MT]; 61:7 [62:6 MT]; 64:6 [65:5 MT]; 78:9 [79:9 MT]; 94:1 [95:1 MT]; Mic 7:7; Hab 3:18; Isa 12:2; 17:10; 45:15, 21), but apart from the LTT, the term occurs only rarely in the NT (Luke 1:47, where Mary may be using the language of Hab 3:18 LXX; and Jude 25). Apart from the LTT, σωτήρ is associated with Jesus twelve times (Luke 1:47; John 4:42; Acts 5:31; 13:23; Eph 5:23; Phil 3:20; 2 Pet 1:1, 11; 2:20; 3:2, 18; 1 John 4:14). Interestingly, σωτήρ is used five times in 2 Peter but doesn't occur in 1 Peter.

the Father and Jesus Christ is remarkable and points to the high regard in which he held the latter. In the LTT the Father's role is portrayed as somewhat more "behind the scenes" as the "ultimate source or originator of the plan of salvation,"[249] whereas Jesus's role is actively "front and center" as "the means that God used to execute his plan of salvation."[250]

God desires "everyone" to be saved (1 Tim 2:4), and God is designated Savior of "all people" (1 Tim 4:10). At the same time Paul speaks of "God's elect" (ἐκλεκτῶν θεοῦ),[251] pointing toward God's choice of some to salvation (§3.1.3). Looking to eternity past, Paul paints God's salvific role in broad strokes, noting that he "saved us and called us with a holy calling, not according to our works, but according to his own purpose and grace, which was given to us in Christ Jesus before time began" (2 Tim 1:9). Paul speaks of the possibility of God granting repentance (μετάνοια) to the Ephesian opponents, resulting in knowledge of the truth.[252] As another "behind the scenes" role, Paul notes that God is the ultimate source of the Scriptures (they are "God breathed," θεόπνευστος), which have the capacity of giving people "wisdom for salvation" (2 Tim 3:15–16). In addition, Paul, at the close of his testimony (1 Tim 1:12–16), may allude to God's initiative in salvation as he directs a doxology to "the King eternal, immortal, invisible, the only God" (1 Tim 1:17).[253]

Jesus is closely associated with salvation throughout the LTT.[254] Paul refers several times to Jesus's "appearing" (ἐπιφάνεια),

---

[249] Towner, *Goal of Our Instruction*, 77. He notes in this regard Paul's reference to God's will (θέλω, 1 Tim 2:4) and purpose (πρόθεσις, 2 Tim 1:9).

[250] Ibid.

[251] Titus 1:1; cf. 2 Tim. 2:10. When Paul elsewhere uses the designation ἐκλεκτός, the term refers to those who have already come to faith (Rom 8:33; 16:13; Col 3:12), not those who have yet to do so. If this is how ἐκλεκτός is to be understood here, then Paul is referring to believers when he speaks of the elect as those for whose faith and knowledge of the truth he is an apostle (Titus 1:1) and those for whom he endures all things (2 Tim 2:10).

[252] Note the similar language in Acts 11:18, where God is observed to have "granted" (δίδωμι) the Gentiles repentance (μετάνοια) resulting in life.

[253] Towner, *Goal of Our Instruction*, 81.

[254] Notably, the LTT never use the term "Son" (υἱός) as a title for Jesus. Statements made about the "Lord" (κύριος) typically, though not always, refer to Jesus, often in contrast to God (the Father), without denying his deity. Paul also speaks of "Jesus Christ," "Christ Jesus," and "Christ Jesus our Lord."

both past and future, in conjunction with (past and future) salvation.[255] He describes this appearing as a coming into the world to save sinners (1 Tim 1:15): Jesus entered the stage of human history on a divine rescue mission. Christ's appearing was a striking manifestation of God's salvific grace (2 Tim 1:9; cf. Titus 2:11). Paul hints at Jesus's death when he speaks of believers having died together with Christ (2 Tim 2:11) and highlights Jesus's giving himself as a ransom for all (1 Tim 2:5) and for believers (Titus 2:14).[256] With striking language, Paul proclaims that when Jesus appeared, he abolished death and brought life and immortality to light through the good news of salvation (2 Tim 1:10).

Paul also asserts that "salvation . . . is in Christ Jesus," a salvation that, while secured in the past, will be consummated in the future, necessitating faithfulness and perseverance on the part of gospel messengers such as Paul (2 Tim 2:10). Paul's statement that salvation is "in Christ Jesus" (ἐν Χριστῷ Ἰησοῦ) could be understood to indicate merely that Christ is the *source* of salvation,[257] but the trustworthy saying that follows (vv. 11b–13) suggests a fuller meaning: salvation is not merely *provided* by Christ, but is *effected individually* through vital union with Christ.[258] While the believer isn't here directly said to be "in Christ," "salvation in Christ Jesus" is connected with having died with him (v. 11), the same connection Paul makes when speaking of union with Christ in Romans 6.

---

[255] Past: 2 Tim 1:10; Titus 3:4; cf. Titus 2:11. Future: 1 Tim 6:14; 2 Tim 4:1, 8; Titus 2:13.

[256] The phrase "giving oneself" need not invariably refer to death, but the early church would have assumed that Jesus's death is in view in 1 Tim 2:6. The saying in Mark 10:45 // Matt 20:28 (from which 1 Tim 2:6a is almost certainly drawn) is more explicit: Jesus gave *his life* as a ransom for many. See also N. Perrin, "The Use of (Para)didonai in Connection with the Passion of Jesus in the New Testament," in *A Modern Pilgrimage in New Testament Christology* (Philadelphia: Fortress, 1974), 94–103, who discusses (παρα)δίδωμι (as in 1 Tim 2:6) as a technical term for the passion of Christ.

[257] E.g., J. A. Allen, "The 'In Christ' Formula in the Pastoral Epistles," *NTS* 10 (1963): 115–21 sees "no compelling reason to regard the formula in the Pastorals as doing more than indicate Christ as the source of faith, love, godly living, etc." (p. 117); viewing the LTT as pseudonymous, he avers that "the writer of the Pastorals seems to have taken a Pauline phrase which probably expresses Paul's characteristic 'in Christ' mysticism and to have used it in a sense by no means mystical" (p. 120).

[258] Cf. D. J. Downs, "Faith(fulness) in Christ Jesus in 2 Timothy 3:15," *JBL* 131 (2012): 155; Kelly, *Pastoral Epistles*, 178.

Paul's regard for Jesus's role in salvation is perhaps seen most clearly in his testimony of conversion and call to ministry in 1 Tim 1:12–17. There the reader immediately senses the deep gratitude Paul has for what Jesus has done for him in and through his coming to faith in Christ: Jesus empowered him for service (v. 12), showered him with abundant grace and mercy (vv. 13–14), brought him to experience the faith and love that are found in Jesus (v. 14), and displayed the full extent of his patience in Paul as an example for others (v. 16).

Several times Paul strikingly juxtaposes God and Jesus in connection with salvation.[259] Just after highlighting God's desire that all people be saved, he speaks of Jesus as the mediator between God and humankind who gave himself a ransom for all (1 Tim 2:3–6). In 2 Tim 1:9–10 Paul speaks of God who "has saved us" (v. 9) and in the same context refers to "the appearing of our Savior Christ Jesus" (v. 10). The OT Scriptures, which were breathed out by God, are able to make one wise for salvation through the faith that is in Christ Jesus (2 Tim 3:15–16). In the introduction of his letter to Titus, Paul refers both to God (1:3) and Christ Jesus as "our Savior" (1:4), putting them on par with regard to their role as Savior of humankind (though without confusing their distinctive roles).

Also, in a remarkable trinitarian passage, Paul asserts,

> But when the kindness of God our Savior and his love for mankind appeared, he saved us—not by works of righteousness that we had done, but according to his mercy, through the washing of regeneration and renewal by the Holy Spirit. He poured out this Spirit on us abundantly through Jesus Christ our Savior, so that, having been justified by his grace, we may become heirs with the hope of eternal life. (Titus 3:4–7)

[259] Cullmann notes, "We have already mentioned that Jesus is called *Soter* primarily in those writings which bestow this title of honour also upon God. This is above all true of the Pastoral Letters, in which God repeatedly appears as Saviour." He goes on to speak of "the transfer to Jesus of an Old Testament divine attribute. Jesus is the *Soter* because he will save his people from their sins." O. Cullmann, *The Christology of the New Testament*, rev. ed., trans. S. C. Guthrie and C. A. M. Hall, NTL (Philadelphia: Westminster, 1963), 241–42.

Again, Paul assigns to both God the Father and Jesus Christ the role of Savior of humanity, for he understands the entire triune Godhead as integrally involved in providing and applying salvation.[260] Both God the Father (2 Tim 1:9; Titus 2:11; 3:7) and Jesus Christ (1 Tim 1:14) give grace in order to effect salvation. This grace, in turn, is the means by which we are justified (Titus 3:7).[261]

§3.5.3 *The Recipients of Salvation*

Who is understood to be the recipient of salvation, whether actual or potential, in the LTT? Paul sets forth a number of specific people and groups of people who are, either directly or by implication, the recipients of salvation. Paul speaks of *his own* conversion and call to ministry in 1 Tim 1:13–17 and in the process indicates that Jesus came to save *sinners*, even the greatest of them (v. 15). At the end of that passage, it is said to be *those who believe in him* who receive eternal life (v. 16; cf. 1 Tim 4:10).

Gentiles aren't excluded from salvation but are potential recipients of it, as shown by Paul's appointment as "teacher of the Gentiles" (1 Tim 2:7) and especially his statement that the Lord strengthened him so that through him the message might be fully proclaimed and all the Gentiles might hear (2 Tim 4:17).

Timothy is told that by following Paul's guidance, keeping a close eye on himself and on his teaching, he would save both *himself* and *those who hear him*. Paul endures all things so that *the elect* might receive salvation (2 Tim 2:10), and in the following context it seems that *those who died together with Christ* and *those who endure* are also in view as receiving salvation, spoken of in terms of living and reigning with Christ (vv. 11–12).

Since those who are "saved" in 1 Tim 2:4 are also those who "come to the knowledge of the truth," it would seem logical to understand those *opponents to whom God grants repentance* leading to a knowledge of the truth as also being potential recipients of salvation. In 2 Tim 3:14–16, it is implied that, like Timothy, *the person who is taught by the Scriptures from the perspective of the faith that*

[260] As Spicq notes, "La théologie trinitaire des Pastorales est soteriologique" (*Les épîtres pastorales*, 258).

[261] Note the discussion of justification in the LTT in M. A. Seifrid, *Christ Our Righteousness: Paul's Theology of Justification*, NSBT 9 (Downers Grove: InterVarsity, 2001), 90–91.

is in Christ Jesus will have the resources he needs to continue in what he has learned and to produce the good works for which he has been equipped; this sort of life is one that has final salvation as its end. Titus 3 indicates that *those who are justified by Jesus's grace* (v. 7)—described also as *those who have believed in God* (v. 8)—are recipients of salvation.

The LTT contain statements about recipients of salvation that appear to be in tension with one other. On the one hand, there are statements which seem to indicate a certain degree of universality. Thus Paul urges that prayers be offered for "everyone" (πάντων ἀνθρώπων);[262] that God desires "everyone" (πάντας ἀνθρώπους) to be saved and to come to the knowledge of the truth (1 Tim 2:4); that Christ Jesus died as a ransom for all (πᾶς; 1 Tim 2:6); that the living God is the Savior of "all people" (πάντων ἀνθρώπων; 1 Tim 4:10); and that the grace of God has appeared, bringing salvation for "all people" (πᾶσιν ἀνθρώποις; Titus 2:11).

On the other hand, Paul uses language that puts certain constraints on that universality.[263] In 1 Tim 4:10, not only does Paul designate the living God as the Savior of all people, but he goes on to clarify that God is "especially (μάλιστα) of those who believe."[264] In 2 Tim 2:10 and Titus 1:1 he speaks of the "elect."[265] Since 2 Tim 1:9 indicates that God's saving grace was given to us "before time began" (πρὸ χρόνων αἰωνίων), it would seem that this divine election occurred in eternity past.

It's not possible here to completely resolve the tension between passages affirming God's desire that all people be saved and passages portraying the recipients of salvation as a

---

[262] Presumably, given the following context, the prayers are for the conversion of those being prayed for.

[263] In addition to the following references, see 2 Tim 2:19b ("The Lord knows [γινώσκω] those who are his").

[264] T. C. Skeat proposed that in some cases the term μάλιστα might mean "that is" or "namely," as opposed to its standard meaning, "particularly" or "especially" ("'Especially the Parchments': A Note on 2 Tim 4:13," *JTS* 30 [1979]: 173–77). Adopting this understanding in 1 Tim 4:10 would remove any hint of universalism: God is the Savior of all people, *that is*, of those who believe. However, while adopted by some, Skeat's proposal is unlikely (see discussion in commentary at 1 Tim 4:10 above).

[265] As noted above, "elect" (ἐκλεκτός) is probably best understood in terms of those who are already converted (cf. Rom 8:33; 16:13; Col 3:12) but still alludes to the "electing" God exercised at some point.

more select group. However, contextual indicators suggest that "all people" should be typically understood in the LTT as "all *kinds of* people," which goes some way to alleviate the apparent tension between the two types of passages mentioned above.[266] For instance, in 1 Tim 2:3–4, where Paul writes that "God our Savior wants everyone to be saved," he may simply be emphasizing the extension of salvation beyond the limits set by the false teachers in Ephesus to include others (e.g., the Gentiles). Several contextual indicators suggest this to be the case.

First, Paul's mission to the Gentiles is alluded to in the previous context. He has introduced himself as Christ Jesus's apostle (1:1), and "for Paul, apostleship and the gospel for the Gentiles belonged indissolubly together."[267] Not long before the injunction of v. 1, he has noted Christ Jesus "appointing [him] to the ministry" (1:12), a reference to his commission to the Gentiles. Second, the deployment of the *Shema* in v. 5 is similar to its use in Gal 3:15–20 and Rom 3:28–30 where the inclusion of Gentiles is in view.[268] Third, the progression of vv. 6–7 culminates in Paul's Gentile mission: Jesus gave himself as a ransom "for all"; this truth is arguably the "testimony" Paul has in mind; and in this regard he was appointed "a teacher of the Gentiles."

§3.5.4 The Nature of Salvation

What is salvation like? This is a broad question, but we may offer some brief observations from the LTT in connection with its threefold portrayal of salvation as past, present, and future.[269]

Salvation is *past* in terms of Christ's provision and one's conversion to Christ and entrance into the life of faith. Paul presents Christ's death as having obtained salvation (Titus 2:14; 3:6), and in this regard speaks to Titus of salvation as having already occurred: "When the kindness of God our Savior and his love for mankind appeared, he saved us" (Titus 3:4–5a). Paul also describes salvation in past terms to Timothy when he speaks of God as the one

[266] See Towner, *Goal of Our Instruction*, 83–84.

[267] Marshall, *Pastoral Epistles*, 434.

[268] See C. Bruno, "One God, One People, One Mediator: The Use of the One God Formula in the Disputed Pauline Epistles" (paper presented at the annual meeting of the Evangelical Theological Society, Atlanta, GA, November 2015), 9–15.

[269] Mounce, *Pastoral Epistles*, cxxxii; M. Silva, "σῴζω, κτλ.," 432.

who "saved us and called us with a holy calling" (2 Tim 1:9) and of believers as having died together with Christ (2 Tim 2:11).

Salvation can also be understood as *present* in terms of its practical outworking in believers' lives and their existence in Christ.[270] Thus, for instance, Paul's conversion exemplifies the trustworthy saying that "Christ Jesus came into the world to save sinners," and as a result, the faith and love that are in Christ Jesus now characterize him, and Christ's perfect patience is on display in and through him (1 Tim 1:14–16). In fact, "the appeal to Paul's conversion experience as 'the prototype' establishes the continuing reality of salvation" for those who have yet to believe in Christ.[271]

Finally, rather often salvation is portrayed in the LTT as *future* (§6.6).[272] In this regard Paul asserts, "This is why I endure all things for the elect: so that they also may obtain salvation, which is in Christ Jesus, with eternal glory" (2 Tim 2:10). In addition, believers are described as "heirs with the hope of eternal life" (Titus 3:7) and told that if they died together with Christ, *they'll live together* with him, and if they endure, *they'll reign together* with him (1 Tim 3:16). While believers experience life in Christ in the here and now, the fact that it is *eternal* life (1 Tim 1:16; 6:12; Titus 3:7) entails the future experience of salvation, as does the future appearing of Christ (Titus 2:13).[273]

§3.5.5 The Reception of Salvation

The means by which salvation was provided, namely the plan of God and the work of Christ, has already been discussed. But how is salvation experienced? Because Paul is using the LTT to encourage Timothy and Titus in their ministry as his delegates, we naturally find him emphasizing the gospel ministry throughout these

---

[270] Indeed, Towner ("Christology in the Letters to Timothy and Titus," 222) finds that "all of the theological elements of these letters serve the broader theme of 'salvation in the present age.'"

[271] Towner, *Goal of Our Instruction*, 80.

[272] If, as Towner suggests, the false teaching in view in the LTT involved an over-realized eschatology, Paul's emphasis on the future aspect of salvation is even more understandable. P. H. Towner, "Gnosis and Realized Eschatology in Ephesus (of the Pastoral Epistles) and the Corinthian Enthusiasm," *JSNT* 31 (1987): 95–124.

[273] "Throughout the Pastorals eternal life is never divisible from the reality of salvation in the present age, which itself originates in the Christ-event." Towner, *Goal of Our Instruction*, 81.

letters. And it is *the teaching and preaching of the gospel* that communicates this good news to people for their salvation (§2). Regarding the gospel message (as encapsulated in 1 Tim 2:5–6), Paul emphasizes that he was made a preacher, apostle, and teacher of the Gentiles (1 Tim 2:7; 2 Tim 1:8–11).

Though numerous aspects of the Christ-hymn in 1 Tim 3:16 are debated, it seems clear that it centers on Christ and the salvation he wrought, and there, in two of the lines, Christ is proclaimed among the nations and believed on in the world. Paul speaks of "labor and strive" in 1 Tim 4:10, and while he doesn't make explicit that these are connected with his mission to the Gentiles, the conclusion is inescapable,[274] and the reason Paul engages in this missionary labor is that his hope is set on the living God[275] who is the Savior of all.

In his exhortation to Timothy in 2 Tim 2:8–10, Paul connects his preaching of the gospel not only with his suffering (vv. 8–9a; §1.2) but also with the free course of God's word which has its work among the elect "that they also may obtain salvation, which is in Christ Jesus." Perhaps it is in Titus 1:1–3 that Paul most directly sets forth preaching as the appointed means to convey the good news of salvation. There he speaks of having been made an apostle for the sake of the faith of God's elect and their knowledge of the truth and exults in the eternal life God promised in eternity past,

[274] "Toil" (κοπιάω) is used elsewhere in connection with his ministry (1 Cor 15:10; Gal 4:11; Phil 2:16; and esp. Col 1:28–29; cf. Rom 16:12; 1 Thess 5:12; 1 Tim 5:17; 2 Tim 2:6) and is joined with "labor" (ἀγωνίζομαι) in Col 1:28–29. See Spicq, "κοπιάω, κόπος," *TLNT* 2:327–29; M. J. Goodwin, "The Pauline Background of the Living God as Interpretive Context for 1 Timothy 4:10," *JSNT* 61 (1996): 71–72; J. N. D. Kelly, *A Commentary on the Pastoral Epistles*, BNTC (London: A. & C. Black, 1963), 101.

[275] After examining the designation "the living God" in the OT and in Hellenistic Judaism (where it is typically used in prayer, missionary appeal, and idol polemic), M. Goodwin (*Paul, Apostle of the Living God: Kerygma and Conversion in 2 Corinthians* [Harrisburg, PA: Trinity Press International, 2001]) surveys various uses of the epithet in Paul's writings (1 Thess 1:9–10; 2 Cor 3:3; 6:16; Rom 9:25–26) and writings he views as standing in the Pauline tradition (Acts 14:15; 1 Tim 3:10; 4:10; *Acts of Paul*). He argues that "the living God has a kerygmatic significance associated with the theme of Gentile conversion" (p. 1) and that Paul's use of the designation "living God" has its roots in its connection with Gentile conversion to Judaism. Cf. Goodwin, "Conversion to the Living God in Diaspora Judaism and Paul's Letters" (Ph.D. diss., Yale University, 1992), 54–60.

drawing a direct connection to the preaching with which Paul has been entrusted.

Once gospel truth is heard by means of preaching, it must be believed; the means by which salvation is appropriated is *faith*. The apostle implies this in 1 Tim 1:12–17 where he speaks of himself persisting in unbelief (ἀπιστία) before his conversion and then subsequent to his conversion presents himself as a model for those who have yet to believe (πιστεύω). Paul makes this point even more explicit when he refers to God in 1 Tim 4:10 as the Savior of all people, but especially of believers (πιστός), and when he speaks personally of this relationship of faith in assuring Timothy that he "knows whom he has believed" (πιστεύω; 2 Tim 1:12).

In the Christ-hymn of 1 Tim 3:16, Jesus is said to have been "believed on [πιστεύω] in the world" after being "preached among the nations." The soteriologically rich passage Titus 3:3–7 presents salvation from God's perspective: his goodness and loving-kindness appeared; he saved us; he poured the Holy Spirit out on us for renewal and regeneration; he justified us by his grace; and made us heirs in expectation of eternal life. It's not until v. 8 that Paul touches on the human part in all of this when he speaks of those whom God saved as "those who have believed [πιστεύω] God." With this emphasis on faith, it's no surprise that works are denied any role in salvation. While the LTT present good works as an important outflow of the Christian life,[276] Paul presses the point that God didn't save us according to our works (2 Tim 1:9; Titus 3:5).[277]

A means by which people are instructed for salvation is indicated in 2 Tim 3:15: *the Scriptures*, which are able to make Timothy (and, by implication, anyone) wise for salvation. This is clarified as the Scriptures are described as to their divine origin and usefulness for teaching, reproof, correction, and instruction in righteousness (2 Tim 3:16; §2.7.2).[278]

---

[276] Cf. 1 Tim 2:10; 5:10, 25; 6:18; Titus 2:7, 14; 3:8, 14.

[277] On the role of the Holy Spirit in salvation, see §3.4 above.

[278] Though the Scriptures certainly communicate the gospel message of salvation that leads to conversion, conversion is likely not in view in the concept of being made "wise for salvation" in 2 Tim 3:15, and this for two reasons: (1) Timothy is specifically in view as the one to be made wise for salvation, and he was already converted; (2) Paul likely parallels the use of Scripture to make Timothy wise for salvation (in its present or future sense) in v. 15, and the usefulness of Scripture to

§3.5.6 The Results of Salvation

Once people enter into salvation, what results may they expect? Perhaps the broadest and most significant is that of *eternal life*, life that begins in the present when the Holy Spirit gives them new life (Titus 3:5) and that extends indefinitely into the future (1 Tim 1:16; 6:12; Titus 1:1–3; 3:7). Belief in Christ ultimately results in eternal life (1 Tim 1:16), and those who become heirs of eternal life (Titus 3:7) have confident hope of eternal life (Titus 1:2). At the same time, Timothy is challenged to "take hold" of the eternal life to which he was called (1 Tim 6:12; §6).

Another dimension of salvation in the LTT is coming to a *knowledge of the truth*. In 1 Tim 2:4, Paul connects God's desire that all people be saved with their coming to the knowledge of the truth. In 2 Tim 2:25 Paul states that repentance leads to the knowledge of the truth. In Titus 1:1 Paul describes the purpose of his apostolic office as building up "the faith of God's elect and their knowledge of the truth." The opposite dynamic—failure to apprehend the truth—can be seen in the case of the false teachers (1 Tim 6:5; 2 Tim 3:7; 4:4).

Throughout the LTT Paul stresses that salvation and the accompanying knowledge of the truth are to result in *godliness* (§5.1.3; Titus 1:1). He enjoins prayer for those in authority so that believers can live godly and holy lives (1 Tim 2:2); urges Timothy to train himself and to pursue godliness (1 Tim 4:7–8; 6:11); and affirms that godliness with contentment is great gain (1 Tim 6:6). Negatively, there are those who consider "godliness" a means to financial gain (1 Tim 6:5) and who hold to a form of godliness while denying its power (2 Tim 3:5).

Paul's expectation as to the future aspect of salvation, both for himself and for all believers, is that of *eternal glory*. "This is why I endure all things for the elect," he writes, "so that they also may obtain salvation, which is in Christ Jesus, with eternal glory" (2 Tim 2:10). Later he writes, "The Lord will rescue me from every evil work and will bring me safely into his heavenly kingdom. To him be the glory" (2 Tim 4:18). Similarly, he speaks of waiting for the "blessed hope, the appearing of the glory of our great God and Savior, Jesus Christ" (Titus 2:13).

---

make the "man of God"—which surely primarily has Timothy in view—complete and equipped for every good work.

Other corollaries of salvation mentioned in the LTT are found in the Christ-hymn in 2 Tim 2:11–13, which speaks of believers' expectation that they will live with Christ and reign with him: "For if we died with him, we will also live with him; if we endure, we will also reign with him." Further entailments of salvation, such as performing good works, living a life of faith and love, and being liberated from sin will be discussed under §5 below.

§3.5.7 The Preservation of Believers

The preservation of believers is an often overlooked theme because σῴζω is rigidly understood to refer without exception in the LTT (and elsewhere in Paul) to eternal salvation. Yet the LTT exhibit a demonstrable and consistent concern for believers' preservation from Satan or demonic forces.[279] In 1 Tim 1:20 Paul writes that he has delivered two false teachers to Satan in order for them not to blaspheme. He mentions that Eve was deceived at the fall and provides instructions for women on how to escape a similar fate (1 Tim 2:14–15; cf. 5:14–15 with reference to young widows). He warns against appointing new converts to positions of church leadership, lest they become conceited and fall into the condemnation incurred by the devil (1 Tim 3:6). This also requires that candidates for ecclesiastical office be above reproach and enjoy a good reputation with those outside the church (1 Tim 3:7).

Paul also denounces those who teach others to refrain from marriage or to abstain from certain foods because of a false dichotomy between material and spiritual things described as "teachings of demons" (1 Tim 4:1–3). Another area from which believers need to be preserved spiritually is the desire to get rich (1 Tim 6:9–10; see 2 Tim 2:26). Paul warns Timothy to guard himself against "irreverent and empty speech and contradictions from what is falsely called knowledge" (1 Tim 6:20). This apparently relates to a kind of teaching which espouses a dualism between matter and spirit, disparaging all things created (see 1 Tim 2:14–15; 4:1–3).

Paul explains that the false teachers have been ensnared by the devil and held captive to do his will (2 Tim 2:26). In contrast to these opponents, Timothy is repeatedly exhorted to guard what had been entrusted to him (1 Tim 6:12; 2 Tim 1:12, 14; 4:7, 15, 18)

[279] See Köstenberger, "Ascertaining Women's God-Ordained Roles," 107–44, esp. 130–33. Cf. Schlarb, *Gesunde Lehre*.

so that he may elude the grasp of the false teachers and pursue Christian virtue (1 Tim 6:11; 2 Tim 2:22). As Paul's apostolic delegate, he is to be conscientious with regard to himself and his teaching and to persevere in these things, for by doing so he will "preserve" both himself and his hearers (1 Tim 4:16). By contrast, the false teachers have "wandered away from the faith," having "strayed" or "turned aside," so that their faith has suffered "shipwreck" (see 1 Tim 1:6, 19; 5:13, 15; 6:9, 10, 21).

§3.6 Conclusion

The LTT frequently, and characteristically, refer to God the Father and the Lord Jesus Christ as Savior and to the salvation God provides in Christ.[280] Paul considers salvation to be a joint operation of the triune Godhead—Father, Son, and Spirit—in which each has distinct yet complementary roles: the Father initiates salvation, the Son secures it, and the Spirit applies it.

In 1 Timothy Paul identifies himself at the outset as "an apostle of Christ Jesus by the command of God our Savior and of Christ Jesus our hope" (1 Tim 1:1). By speaking of "Christ Jesus our hope," the apostle invokes the future prospect of end-time salvation. Later on, he speaks of "God our Savior who wants everyone to be saved and to come to the knowledge of the truth" (1 Tim 2:3–4); and refers to God as "the Savior of all people, especially of those who believe" (1 Tim 4:10). In addition, in one of the trustworthy sayings, he asserts that "Christ Jesus came into the world to save sinners" (1 Tim 1:15).

In 2 Timothy Paul speaks of God who "has saved us" (2 Tim 1:9) and in the same context refers to "the appearing of our Savior Christ Jesus" (2 Tim 1:10). He also asserts that "salvation . . . is in Christ Jesus," a salvation that, while secured in the past, will be consummated in the future, necessitating faithfulness and perseverance in the faith (2 Tim 2:10). The source of knowledge regarding this salvation through faith in Christ Jesus are the Hebrew Scriptures, that is, the OT, which spoke prophetically of him (2 Tim 3:15). Several passages in Paul's letters to Timothy also speak of believers' safe preservation in this life and their safe passage into the next (1 Tim 2:15; 4:16; 2 Tim 4:18).

---

[280] See, e.g., Mounce, *Pastoral Epistles*, cxxxii–cxxxv.

In the introduction of his letter to Titus, Paul refers to both God and Jesus Christ as "our Savior" (1:3–4), putting them on par with regard to their role as Savior of humankind. This teaching is further developed in the body of the letter, where Paul speaks of "the teaching of God our Savior," according to which "the grace of God has appeared, with salvation for all people," teaching them to live righteous and godly lives in the present while waiting for the return of "our great God and Savior, Jesus Christ" (2:10–13). The theme reaches its climax when Paul toward the end of the letter writes that "when the kindness of God our Savior and His love for mankind appeared, he saved us. . . . he poured out his Spirit on us abundantly through Jesus Christ our Savior" (3:4–7).

As we've seen, the LTT's rich teaching on God, Christ, and the Holy Spirit in conjunction with the salvation they jointly provide occupies a central plank in the theology of the LTT as a whole. It is also clear that the salvation theme flows organically from Paul's apostolic mission (§1) and his teaching (§2)—and that of his delegates—on the salvation provided by God and Christ "our Savior" (§3). The salvation theme, in turn, leads inexorably to the formation of God's household, the church, which will be discussed under the next heading.

§4 The Church

As N. T. Wright observes, "Ecclesiology," for Paul, "was not a pragmatic addendum to a gospel of individual faith and salvation."[281] Rather, "Paul seems to have supposed that it was his task to plant cells of people loyal to Jesus as *kyrios* right across Caesar's empire."[282] For this reason it is proper to ground our discussion of the church and its ministry in Paul's mission theology and strategy (§1) and his concomitant teaching (§2), particularly regarding salvation in and through God, and Christ, "our Savior" (§3). At the same time, our discussion of the church and its ministry will lay the proper foundation for exploring the ethical dimension of the LTT below (§5), which, in turn, is embedded in the LTT's distinctive eschatology (§6).

---

[281] Wright, "Paul's Western Missionary Project," 62.

[282] Ibid.

To highlight the significant connection between the LTT's eschatology and their theology of the church and Christian life, we may consider Dibelius's influential "bourgeois Christianity" (*bürgerliches Christentum*) proposal, mentioned above in the Introduction.[283] In this proposal the LTT reflect a time after Paul's death when the church has realized that Christ's return might be delayed for some time and has thus reoriented itself, shifting from intense eschatological anticipation to the establishment of "peaceful coexistence with the various orders of the world."[284] The letters, it is suggested, represent an attempt to bring the church to be more in line with the norms of the surrounding culture, an accommodation that stands over against the earlier teaching of Paul (e.g., Phil 3:20). As a result of this shift in eschatology, Dibelius finds, egalitarianism has now been exchanged for hierarchy, charismatic ministers for formally qualified church officers, and an expectation of conflict in the world for the pursuit of a secure life in the world: "A static, secular type of ethic thus came to replace the gospel-inspired eschatological impulse to live in a redemptive way in this temporal world."[285]

In this view the charismatic outlook of, say, 1 Corinthians 12–14, where Paul regulates the use of various spiritual gifts in the church, is replaced by an institutionalized model that stipulates formal qualifications for officeholders such as elders or deacons. This model, it is maintained, resembles the power of the *paterfamilias* in the first-century Greco-Roman patriarchal household. In such a model, it is argued, the church is viewed as God's household, and defined, "not primarily upon one's spiritual or organizational resources of giftedness" but "according to the patriarchal standards of Greco-Roman society."[286]

---

[283] See C. The Social Setting of the Letters to Timothy and Titus above, under II. Historical Context in the introduction. Dibelius's proposal in *Die Pastoralbriefe* (1955) reached the English-speaking world through M. Dibelius and H. Conzelmann, *The Pastoral Epistles*, Hermeneia, trans. P. Buttolph and A. Yarbro (Philadelphia: Fortress, 1972), 39–41. See also Pao, "Let No One Despise Your Youth," 743, to whom some of the discussion in this section is indebted, and Towner, *The Goal of Our Instruction*, 9–16.

[284] Towner, *Goal of Our Instruction*, 9–10.

[285] Ibid., 10.

[286] E. S. Fiorenza, *In Memory of Her: A Feminist Theological Reconstruction of Christian Origins* (New York: Crossroad, 1983), 289, 291.

However, the problem with a view such as Dibelius's is that it unduly minimizes the eschatological outlook in the LTT, which has important ramifications for ecclesiology as well. Specifically, the LTT's view of the end times as being already inaugurated (though not yet completely realized, 2 Tim 2:17–18) in the age of the church[287] necessitates that the lists of qualifications for elders and deacons[288] are set within this larger end-time framework.[289] Thus it is unduly dichotomous to pit the concern for proper church organization in these letters against their eschatology. To the contrary, the latter provides an important, even indispensable, framework for the former (§6).

While Paul uses the household as the central metaphor for the church in the LTT and indicates that God's household, as in the larger culture, is to be marked by male leadership, he doesn't merely accommodate himself to the surrounding culture and abandon believers' eschatological hope. In fact, because of satanic and demonic activity seeking to subvert God's work in the church (a sign of the end times), appointing properly qualified church leaders takes on special urgency and end-time significance. In this way the church, God's household, is "the church of the living God, the pillar and foundation of the truth" (1 Tim 3:15) in the world. One of the ways Satan is seeking to subvert God's household, and God's created order, is by blurring gender lines, in terms of both identity and role.[290]

---

[287] See esp. 1 Tim 4:1–5; 2 Tim 3:1–5.

[288] 1 Tim 3:1–13; Titus 1:5–9.

[289] See G. K. Beale, *A New Testament Biblical Theology: The Unfolding of the Old Testament in the New* (Grand Rapids: Baker, 2011), 819–23; Beale, "The Origin of the Office of Elder and Its Relationship to the Inaugurated Eschatological Tribulation" (paper presented at the annual meeting of the Evangelical Theological Society, Atlanta, GA, November 2015). Beale argues that the office of elder is rooted in the predicted rise of false teaching in the last days and that elders are part of God's provision to help the church endure until the end.

[290] Note that in keeping with the Genesis creation account, the LTT assume a binary created order, humanity as male and female, throughout (see, e.g., 1 Tim 2:8–15, esp. vv. 13–14). This indicates that transgenderism, as gender identity confusion, diffusion, or rebellion, is a result of the fall. Without endorsing everything written in these works, see, e.g., M. A. Yarhouse, *Understanding Gender Dysphoria: Navigating Transgender Issues in a Changing Culture* (Downers Grove: InterVarsity, 2015); and S. A. Andreades, *enGendered: God's Gift of Gender Difference in Relationship* (Wooster, OH: Weaver, 2015).

In the following discussion we'll first briefly examine the Greco-Roman background of the household imagery and probe its relationship to Paul's purpose in writing. After this, two interrelated aspects of the imagery will be examined: order and authority, and responsibilities in God's household on the part of different groups: older and younger men, older and younger women, widows, slaves, and the wealthy.[291] Following a discussion of another metaphor Paul uses to describe the church in the LTT, that of a pillar and foundation of the truth, we'll discuss how ministry is envisaged in these letters. This includes tasks of ministry—such as preaching and teaching the Word, caring for the members of God's household, and prayer—as well as qualifications for elders/overseers and deacons, and the goals of ministry.[292]

§4.1 The Church as the Household of God

Whereas the LTT feature Paul's instructions to his apostolic delegates assigned to care for congregations in his place, explicit terminology related to the church appears only intermittently.[293] This should not be surprising, however, as the church is presupposed throughout these letters.[294] Paul uses the common NT term for the church, ἐκκλησία, only three times in the LTT, all in 1 Timothy (3:5, 15; 5:16). More common is the depiction of the

---

[291] See Towner, *Letters to Timothy and Titus*, 273.

[292] Literature on the ecclesiology of the LTT (in addition to that on elders and deacons, for which see below) includes Bailey, "Theology of Paul's Pastoral Epistles," 354–65; C. R. Hutson, "Ecclesiology in the Pastoral Epistles," in *The New Testament Church: The Challenge of Developing Ecclesiologies*, ed. J. Harrison and J. D. Dvorak, McMaster Divinity College Biblical Studies 1 (Eugene, OR: Pickwick, 2012), 164–88; Marshall, *New Testament Theology*, 414–17; Marshall, *Pastoral Epistles*, 512–21 ("The Church in the Pastoral Epistles"); B. L. Merkle, "Ecclesiology in the Pastoral Epistles," in *Entrusted with the Gospel*, 173–98; Schnelle, *Theology of the New Testament*, 592–99; and G. Strecker, *Theology of the New Testament* (Berlin: de Gruyter, 2000), 586–94. Note that the contribution of the LTT as Pauline is included in D. J. Downs, "Pauline Ecclesiology," *PRSt* 41 (2014): 243–55.

[293] See also Young's interesting discussion of Paul as teacher (e.g., 1 Tim 2:7) and of Timothy and Titus as "philosopher-chaplains" in keeping with contemporary educational mores in first-century Greco-Roman culture (*Theology*, 89–90).

[294] See Merkle, "Ecclesiology in the Pastoral Epistles," 173. However, following an appropriate critique of extremes in the relevant literature, Merkle may overreact when he approvingly cites Mounce (*Pastoral Epistles*, 221): "The metaphor of the house is relatively minor in the PE. . . . The metaphor is not a dominating force in the thought of the author." See further the discussion below.

church as "God's household," whether explicitly (οἶκος θεοῦ; 1 Tim 3:15; cf. 3:4, 5) or implicitly (see, e.g., 1 Tim 5:1–2; Titus 2:1–10).

The concept of God's people as a family isn't unique to Paul but finds its roots in the OT where God's people Israel are physically descended from Jacob (later renamed Israel). As early as Gen 46:27, the nascent nation is referred to as "Jacob's household," a phrase which, along with "the house of Israel," occurs approximately 170 times in the OT.[295] The familial nature of the people of God is carried into the NT where, in the teachings of Jesus and Paul, the spiritual relationship among believers is highlighted over against their ethnic characteristics (see, e.g., Matt 12:46–50; Rom 8:14–16).

While the phrase οἶκος θεοῦ can be rendered as either "house of God" (e.g., Matt 12:4) or "household of God" (e.g., Eph 2:19), the latter is commonly in view in the LTT.[296] Based on the premise that believers are members of one and the same spiritual family, Paul depicts them as members of a joint household, a concept with a rich background in the Jewish and particularly the Greco-Roman world.[297] While the concept of God's household thus builds on the reality of the church as the family of God, the LTT use this household metaphor to convey how Paul's apostolic delegates should carry out their roles and how believers should conduct themselves in the church.[298]

---

[295] The phrase normally refers to the people of Israel as a whole (e.g., Exod 19:3; Lev 17:10), though on a few occasions it refers specifically to the northern kingdom of Israel (e.g., 1 Kgs 12:21; 20:31).

[296] F. A. Tomlinson, "The Purpose and Stewardship Theme within the Pastoral Epistles," in *Entrusted with the Gospel*, 69–70, 75–82 demonstrates that the controlling metaphor in the LTT is household stewardship, pointing to the use of stewardship language at important junctures in the letters: e.g. οἰκονομίαν θεοῦ (1 Tim 1:4), παραγγελία (1 Tim 1:5, 18), ἐκκλησία θεοῦ (1 Tim 3:15), παραθήκη (1 Tim 6:20; 2 Tim 1:12, 14), παρατίθημι (2 Tim 2:2), ἐπιστεύθην (Titus 1:3), θεοῦ οἰκονόμον (Titus 1:7). In addition, there's a focus not only on the household of God but on the literal household as well (1 Tim 3:4–5, 12; 5:4, 8, 13–14).

[297] The designation of the church as the "household of God" occurs first in Eph 2:19. It's not surprising that Paul draws on this imagery again when writing to Timothy in Ephesus.

[298] This is not a unique theme in the LTT but is more developed there than in Paul's other letters (see 1 Cor 4:1–2; 9:17; Col 1:25; Gal 6:10; Eph 2:19; 3:14–15). D. G. McCartney, "House, Spiritual House," *DLNT* 509–11; Towner, *Letters to Timothy and Titus*, 57, 273; Towner, "Pauline Theology or Pauline Tradition in the Pastoral Epistles: The Question of Methodology," *TynBul* 46 (1995): 308.

Contrary to Dibelius's proposal, the LTT's ecclesiology with their prominent household metaphor ought to be viewed against the backdrop of the threat of the false teachers (1 Tim 1:3–4) who diminish the gospel for the sake of the law (1 Tim 1:8–11) and divert the church from its purpose—whether internally (family members loving and caring for one another) or externally (bearing witness to God and Christ our Savior). Paul advocates the "reappropriation (or reclamation) of the social spaces in the secular household toward the fulfillment of God's purposes in and through his family. As such, they are coopted and reinvested with new norms which both overlap and diverge from their secular counterparts."[299]

The household metaphor used for the church in the LTT, as mentioned, would have resonated significantly with Paul's audience.[300]

---

[299] Couser, "Divergent, Insurgent or Allegiant?," 11–12; cf. Couser, "'Prayer and the Public Square: 1 Tim. 2:1–7 and Christian Political Engagement," in *New Testament Theology in Light of the Church's Mission*, ed. J. Laansma, G. Osborne, and R. Van Neste (Eugene, OR: Cascade, 2011), 291–93. Couser appropriately questions whether the conventional nomenclature of "fictive kinship" is a proper way of describing the teaching of the LTT with regard to believers' relationships with one another in the household of God (contra, e.g., Towner, *Letters to Timothy and Titus*, 330).

[300] For relevant literature, see J. K. Goodrich, "Overseers as Stewards and the Qualifications for Leadership in the Pastoral Epistles," *ZNW* 104 (2013), 77–97; M. B. Yarnell, "*Oikos Theou:* A Theologically Neglected but Important Ecclesiological Metaphor," *Midwestern Journal of Theology* 2 (2003): 53–65; K. Zamfir, "Is the ἐκκλησία a Household (of God)? Reassessing the Notion of οἶκος θεοῦ in 1 Tim 3.15," *NTS* 60 (2014): 511–28, esp. 526–28. See also J. M. Holmes, "Disciplining Performance and 'Placing' the Church: Widows, Elders and Slaves in the Household of God (1 Tim 5,1–6,2)," in *1 Timothy Reconsidered*, ed. K. P. Donfried, Colloquium Oecumenicum Paulinum 18 (Leuven: Peeters, 2008), 109–34; Holmes, "From ἀδελφοί to οἶκος θεοῦ: Social Transformation in Pauline Christianity," *JBL* 120 (2001): 293–311; A. J. Malherbe, "Overseers as Household Managers in the Pastoral Epistles," in *Text, Image, and Christians in the Graeco-Roman World: A Festschrift in Honor of David Lee Balch*, ed. A. C. Niang and C. Osiek. Princeton Theological Monograph 176 (Eugene, OR: Pickwick, 2012), 72–88; and L. Portefaix, "'Good Citizenship' in the Household of God: Women's Position in the Pastorals Reconsidered in the Light of Roman Rule," in *A Feminist Companion to the Deutero-Pauline Epistles*, Feminist Companion to the NT and Early Christian Writings, ed. A.-J. Levine with M. Blickenstaff (Cleveland: Pilgrim, 2003), 147–58. More broadly, D. L. Balch, "Paul, Families, and Households," in *Paul in the Greco-Roman World: A Handbook*, vol. 1; R. W. Gehring, *House Church and Mission: The Importance of Household Structures in Early Christianity* (Peabody, MA: Hendrickson, 2004); K. Lehmeier, *Oikos und Oikonomia: Antike Konzepte der Haushaltsführung und der Bau der Gemeinde bei Paulus*, Marburger theologische Studien 92 (Marburg: N. G. Elwert, 2006); and

In the Greco-Roman world the household was the foundational unit of society. Rather than viewed as a matter of expediency or social construction, it was held to be divinely instituted and a foundational part of the natural order,[301] consisting not only of the nuclear family but also of slaves and the extended family. The male head of the household, the *paterfamilias*, served as the final authority responsible for overseeing the affairs of the entire household, all of whom were expected to follow his guidance in every respect.[302] For example, they were to worship his gods, though in addition they might also have been devoted to other gods privately. At times this authority was delegated to a steward (οἰκονόμος) whose role was to manage some aspect of the household. Because the household was viewed as the integral societal unit, its proper ordering was considered to be essential to the health of society. Consequently, a large volume of philosophical works was dedicated to the right ordering of the household and the proper conduct of its members.[303]

The household imagery, while appropriating language and conceptualities from Greco-Roman culture, nonetheless finds its theological foundation in the OT and Jesus, as briefly discussed above. Therefore, rather than reflecting a capitulation to the standards of the culture in order to survive, household imagery is an apt metaphor for describing the unique relationships believers have with one another, which reflects biblical theology and would

---

C. Osiek and D. L. Balch, *Families in the New Testament World: Households and House Churches* (Louisville: Westminster John Knox, 1997).

[301] Johnson, *1 Timothy, 2 Timothy, Titus*, 149. Young's summary is apt: "The theology of the Pastorals unquestionably assumes that God is the apex of a hierarchically ordered society in which obedience is a prime value. The church is God's household, and he is King of the Universe. By God's grace and favour, Christians are members of his household" (*Theology*, 94; see her discussion of obedience on pp. 91–94).

[302] On the power and responsibilities of the *paterfamilias*, see L. M. White, "Paul and *Pater Familias*," in *Paul in the Greco-Roman World: A Handbook*, vol. 2, ed. J. P. Sampley (New York: Bloomsbury T&T Clark, 2016).

[303] M. Harding, *What Are They Saying About the Pastoral Epistles?* (Mahwah, NJ: Paulist, 2001), 47–48; K. Jobes, *1 Peter*, BECNT (Grand Rapids: Baker Academic, 2005), 181–83; C. S. Keener, "Family and Household," *DNTB* 353–68; H. Kuhli, "οἰκονόμος," *EDNT* 2:499; D. G. McCartney, "Household, Family," *DLNT*, 511–13; P. H. Towner, "Households and Household Codes," *DPL* 417–19; Osiek and Balch, *Families in the New Testament World*, 82–83; D. C. Verner, *The Household of God: The Social World of the Pastoral Epistles*, SBLDS 71 (Chico, CA: Scholars Press, 1983), 28–29.

have resonated with people living in a culture where the household was considered to be the foundational unit of society.[304]

Not only is the household metaphor the predominant way in which Paul conceives of the church in the LTT, this designation occupies a central place in his purpose for writing. The reference to the church as God's household in 1 Tim 3:15, for instance, is part of Paul's purpose statement, suggesting that "1 Timothy is not merely *ad hoc* instruction but rather has application to the 'household' more broadly."[305] While the immediate occasion is given in 1 Tim 1:3–4 (dealing with false teachers), the instructions that follow aren't so narrowly construed as to be limited to the original context. Thus the entire letter, not merely small portions of it, is predicated on the conception of the church as God's household.

Consequently, Paul's concern for rightly ordering the household of God is connected to his mission to the Gentiles (§1) as he promotes "God's plan" (οἰκονομίαν θεοῦ, 1 Tim 1:4), that is, his redemptive arrangement (§3).[306] His desire is to see that believers carry out their responsibilities as members of God's household, living appropriately (§5) in light of the coming return of Christ (§6). As Towner observes,

> As Paul applies [the idea of God's οἰκονομία] to Christian existence, the term is expansive, encompassing the whole social, political, and religious world of life in much the same way as the Emperor would take to himself the role of the father or householder and regard the Empire and its inhabitants as his household. Understood this way, the whole of life is subject to the divine will (or is meant to be). The implications for a Christian understanding of the church in the world and mission are enormous.[307]

---

[304] See Tomlinson, "Purpose and Stewardship Theme," 68; Merkle, "Ecclesiology in the Pastoral Epistles," 176.

[305] Tomlinson, "Purpose and Stewardship Theme," 53, with reference to A. J. Köstenberger, L. S. Kellum, and C. L. Quarles, *The Cradle, the Cross, and the Crown: An Introduction to the New Testament* (Nashville: B&H Academic, 2009), 646.

[306] Tomlinson, "Purpose and Stewardship Theme," 68–69; Towner, *Letters to Timothy and Titus*, 238; see comments on 1 Tim 1:4.

[307] Towner, *Letters to Timothy and Titus*, 69; Towner, *Goal of Our Instruction*, 172.

§4.1.1 Order and Authority in the Household of God

The household imagery becomes particularly salient in the discussion of *order* in the church. Paul's first directive in 1 Timothy is to deal with the opponents, whose teaching promotes empty speculation. This is set in contrast with the apostolic pattern of instruction, which promotes "God's plan" (οἰκονομίαν θεοῦ; 1 Tim 1:4). Paul's use of the word "plan" (οἰκονομίαν) calls to mind the stewardship of a household. This term relates specifically to God's way of ordering his redemptive plan while preparing the way for Paul's explicit discussion of God's household.[308] As mentioned, this is one of Paul's central purposes in writing the LTT.[309] God has a distinct way of ordering the world at large and his church in particular,[310] and the teaching Timothy is to correct produces a way of life that is opposed to this order.[311] Timothy and Titus, as Paul's apostolic delegates, are charged with helping to bring order to the church so that the members of God's household conduct themselves properly (e.g., 1 Tim 1:5; 3:14–15; 2 Tim 2:4–15; Titus 1:13–14; §§4.1.2).

The reference to Timothy's being given instruction also uses stewardship language (παρατίθεμαί), seeking to ensure that the household is run properly (1 Tim 1:18).[312] This same idea is present in Paul's statement to Titus that the elder is "God's administrator" (θεοῦ οἰκονόμον; Titus 1:7). First Timothy also contains an interesting variation on the common household codes in the NT (1 Tim 2:1–6:2). In this extended section Paul addresses the proper ordering of God's household, discussing the church at large (2:1–7), men and women (2:8–15), elders/overseers (3:1–7), deacons (3:8–13), Timothy himself as the servant of Christ Jesus (chap. 4), different age groups (5:1–2), widows (5:3–16), elders (5:17–25), and slaves (6:1–2), with occasional general instructions interspersed. These exhortations have been influenced by the language of traditional Greco-Roman household codes, a form Paul likely chose because of

---

[308] See Towner, *Letters to Timothy and Titus*, 112–14.

[309] See Johnson, *1 Timothy, 2 Timothy, Titus*, 149.

[310] In 1 Tim 1:4, the οἰκονομία of God is further designated as being in reference to the faith, οἰκονομίαν θεοῦ τὴν ἐν πίστει. Tomlinson ("Purpose and Stewardship Theme," 79) proposes that the final phrase is a wordplay, suggesting that the stewardship is carried out "in trust" and also that it is in reference to "the faith."

[311] See Towner, *Letters to Timothy and Titus*, 113.

[312] Tomlinson, "Purpose and Stewardship Theme," 78–79.

his overriding conception of the church as God's household.[313] The emphasis on teaching throughout the letters, therefore, doesn't merely reflect a concern with proper doctrine for its own sake but with being a faithful steward in the household of God, rightly ordering the people of God to carry out the mission of God.[314]

The idea of order, in turn, dovetails with the notion of *authority*. This is seen most clearly in Paul's designation of elders as God's administrators (θεοῦ οἰκονόμον; Titus 1:7) and the injunction that an elder/overseer who is unable to manage his own household can't be expected to be able to oversee the church (1 Tim 3:4–5). In addition, the concept of authority may be present where household imagery is absent, such as in the authority Paul has granted to Timothy and Titus as his apostolic delegates (§1.3) and in the instructions to appoint elders/overseers who will lead the churches (§4.3.2.1). The language does not, however, suggest that there should be a rigid structure of authority imposed upon the church where it actually functions as a household, as we will see.[315]

The implicit assumption is that the ultimate *authority*, and thus the source of *order*, is God; elders are simply *stewards*. Titus and Timothy, while functioning in unique roles as apostolic delegates, are nonetheless not heads of households. Even Paul is not the *paterfamilias*; that role belongs to God alone: the church is *his* household (1 Tim 3:15). Those with authority in the household serve with delegated responsibility and are accountable to God, one another, and the members of the household. This set of assumptions should cause us to take Paul's instructions that much more seriously. God's household is not ours to order as we see fit. Inasmuch as God has given us instructions, it is incumbent upon us to follow them. This is not to suggest that the LTT answer every question we may have regarding church order, structure, and

---

313 Towner, *Goal of Our Instruction*, 170–71.

314 Towner, "Pauline Theology or Pauline Tradition in the Pastoral Epistles," 310–11.

315 Mounce, *Pastoral Epistles*, 221; Tomlinson, "Purpose and Stewardship," 68; Towner, *Letters to Timothy and Titus*, 238; contra Verner, *Household of God*, 1, 147, 160, 182. Arguing that the church is ordered as an actual house pushes the metaphor to the point of breaking it. It wouldn't be possible, for example, for Timothy to have authority as Paul's apostolic delegate on the one hand and to treat older men like fathers (1 Tim 5:1) on the other. It would be a father, as the *paterfamilias*, who would have held authority in a "household-church."

authority, but it does serve as a reminder that the church is not ultimately ours to structure or lead as we desire.

§4.1.2 Responsibilities in the Household of God

While household imagery doesn't demand that each person in the local body fill a particular role corresponding to a role in the household, it nonetheless helps convey the idea that there is proper behavior in the church, just as there is in the home. The LTT also demonstrate a certain degree of fluidity in moving from a discussion of the church as household to issuing commands to people in their natural households. As Verner rightly notes, Paul "never addresses the subject of the household life of church members as a topic in its own right. Rather, whenever he introduces the topic of household life, he does so in the course of discussing one aspect or another of life in the household of God."[316] The LTT thus contain both instructions directly pertaining to life in the household of God—such as how Timothy and Titus are to relate to members of the household—as well as instructions on how members of God's household should conduct themselves in their own households. As Towner observes, "Just as there are rules of accepted behavior, relationships to observe, and responsibilities to fulfill within the household, so there are analogous patterns to be observed in God's church."[317]

The following sections will discuss the roles and responsibilities of various members in God's household as described in the LTT: older and younger men, older and younger women, widows, slaves, and wealthy individuals who would have lived in the extended household. In these sections Paul instructs Timothy on how to relate to these various members, providing specific instructions they are to receive. There is a certain affinity with the so-called *Haustafeln* ("house tables") found in other parts of the NT, including several of Paul's own letters (e.g., Eph 5:21–6:9; Col 3:18–25; cf. 1 Pet 2:13–3:9), even though the form of instruction is slightly different.[318] What's more, Paul's instructions to the members of God's household consistently contain a missionary

[316] Verner, *Household of God*, 128.

[317] Towner, *Letters to Timothy and Titus*, 273–74.

[318] See ibid., 31–32, 192–93. See also Marshall, *Pastoral Epistles*, 231–36 ("Household codes and station codes").

dimension that relates to their function as witnesses to the gospel in the surrounding world, as will be discussed further below.

§4.1.2.1 Older and Younger Men

While serving as Paul's apostolic delegate and exercising authority over the local church, Timothy is nonetheless still a young man (at least by then-current societal standards).[319] But despite his age, he is called upon to serve as an example to the rest of the body. In 1 Tim 4:12 Paul instructs Timothy, "Don't let anyone despise your youth, but set an example for the believers in speech, in conduct, in love, in faith, in purity." He further tells him to exercise his spiritual gifts so that his progress may be evident to all: "Practice these things; be committed to them, so that your progress may be evident to all" (v. 15). As mentioned, here again is evidence that the household serves as a metaphor and doesn't indicate that the church should be strictly ordered as an actual household.[320]

In 1 Tim 5:1 Paul writes, "Do not rebuke an older man, but exhort him as a father, younger men as brothers," implying that Timothy himself belongs to the latter category and stressing the importance of familial relationships. Particular care and concern are to be directed toward older men, and humility demands that they be treated with respect in keeping with their age.[321] This is true even when they don't serve in leadership positions. Later on, Paul tells Timothy to rebuke sinning elders (presumably "older men"; vv. 19–20), and he may be concerned that this be done properly and respectfully.

---

[319] On the notion that the LTT are "man-to-man" communications in keeping with ancient ideals of masculinity, see J. A. Glancy, *Protocols of Masculinity in the Pastoral Epistles*, in *New Testament Masculinities*, ed. J. Capel Anderson and S. D. Moore, SBL Semeia Studies 45 (Atlanta: Scholars Press, 2003), 235–64; M. Rose D'Angelo, "'Knowing How to Preside over His Own Household': Imperial Masculinity and Christian Asceticism in the Pastorals, *Hermas*, and Luke-Acts," in ibid., 265–95; and H.-U. Weidemann, "Selbstbeherrschte Hausherren: Beobachtungen zur rhetorischen Funktion des Maskulinitätsideals in den Pastoralbriefen," in *Lukas–Paulus–Pastoralbriefe: Festschrift für Adolf Weiser zum 80. Geburtstag*, ed. R. Hoppe and M. Reichardt (Stuttgart: Katholisches Bibelwerk, 2014), 271–302.

[320] See L. T. Johnson, *Letters to Paul's Delegates: 1 Timothy, 2 Timothy, Titus* (Valley Forge, PA: Trinity Press International, 1996), 176.

[321] See A. J. Köstenberger, "Humility," in *Encyclopedia of the Bible and Its Reception* 12 (Berlin/Boston: de Gruyter, 2015).

In Titus 2:2 Paul again brings forward the importance of personal example in instructing his other apostolic delegate. He writes, Older men are to be self-controlled, worthy of respect, sensible, and sound in faith, love, and endurance." Later on in the same passage, he continues,

> In the same way, encourage the young men to be self-controlled in everything. Make yourself an example of good works with integrity and dignity in your teaching. Your message is to be sound beyond reproach, so that any opponent will be ashamed, because he doesn't have anything bad to say about us. (2:6–8)

The apostolic delegates, as well as older men in the church, should therefore set the example for the younger men in word and action, in character and godliness.

§4.1.2.2 Older and Younger Women

Paul provides a set of instructions regarding women in 1 Tim 2:9–15:

> Also, the women are to dress themselves in modest clothing, with decency and good sense, not with elaborate hairstyles, gold, pearls, or expensive apparel, but with good works, as is proper for women who profess to worship God. A woman is to learn quietly with full submission. I do not allow a woman to teach or to have authority over a man. . . . But she will be saved through childbearing, if they continue in faith, love, and holiness, with good sense.

We'll cover the instructions on female deacons (or deacons' wives) in 1 Tim 3:11 as part of dealing with the roles of men and women in the church below (§4.3.2).

In 1 Tim 5:2 Paul instructs Timothy to treat "older women as mothers, and the younger women as sisters with all purity." Timothy himself may or may not have been married (most likely he was not, as the NT is silent with regard to any wife or family). In any case he should relate to younger women as sisters. Here again familial language is used. The language of "sister," however, isn't simply one of spiritual kinship (Matt 12:50) but points to a particular form of care and concern: sexual purity. The passage on widows in 1 Tim 5:3–16 will be discussed separately below (§4.1.2.3). For now we note that younger widows are encouraged to remarry, to have children, and to manage their household, while worthy widows should be supported by family members or, if needed, the church.

In 2 Tim 1:5 Paul acknowledges the vital role Timothy's grandmother Lois, as well as his mother Eunice, had in raising Timothy in the Scriptures. Paul's reference to these women highlights the importance of godly women, especially when (as may have been the case in Timothy's situation) the father is not a believer. Similarly, in Titus 2:3–5 Paul writes,

> In the same way, older women are to be reverent in behavior, not slanderers, not slaves to excessive drinking. They are to teach what is good, so that they may encourage the young women to love their husbands and children, to be self-controlled, pure, workers at home, and in submission to their husbands, so that God's word will not be slandered.

Here Paul demonstrates that concern for God's household also entails concern for the familial household (see 1 Tim 3:5, 12; Titus 1:6).

While neither Titus nor Timothy (and by extension, elders) are absolved from shepherding and providing instruction for all the members of the local church, male and female alike, Paul indicates that the older women have a particular responsibility toward young women. This mentoring mandate is doubtless predicated on the model of the household where mothers take their daughters under their wing and teach them important life skills in connection with their God-given role in the household.[322]

§4.1.2.3 Widows

The instructions Paul gives Timothy on caring for worthy widows in 1 Tim 5:3–16 are the most extensive anywhere in the NT. Earlier we quoted S. M. Baugh:

> Widowhood could be a severe test in the Greco-Roman world, since women were usually not the direct heirs of their husband's wills. Rather, the widow had her dowry

[322] See Verner, *Household of God*, 31.

> as well as any stipulation which the testator made for her care to his heirs. . . . If the son or sons did not care for their mother (or often, their stepmother), the woman could be in a dire condition if her dowry was not substantial.[323]

Many widows in the ancient world were not elderly by modern standards but women in their mid-thirties or forties with one or several (young) children on their hands and little chance to remarry because Roman women married young and Roman men married somewhat older, so the age differentiation led to a large number of widows.[324]

In the present situation the church may have cared for widows who had other sources of support, thus rendering it difficult to help those widows who lacked such resources.[325] This may have been due to confusion as to who should support widows and/or the influence of the opponents. (In the ancient world widows were particularly vulnerable to those who preyed on them and sought to exploit their precarious state for financial gain.) Paul's burden in 1 Tim 5:3–16, then, isn't so much to urge care for widows but to provide Timothy with specific guidelines for doing so. He first tells him to honor certain kinds of widows in keeping with the fifth commandment. Such "honor" entails not merely respect but has a material dimension as well. The widows Timothy is instructed to honor, then, are those who are "truly in need" / "in genuine need" (vv. 5, 16)—that is, those who meet a series of qualifications:

- they have no relatives to care for them, whether children, grandchildren, or other descendants; otherwise, these relatives must support them so that church funds can be used for the neediest with no other means of financial support (v. 4; cf. v. 8);

---

[323] S. M. Baugh, "1 Timothy," in *1 & 2 Thessalonians, 1 & 2 Timothy, Titus*, by J. A. D. Weima and S. M. Baugh, *Zondervan Illustrated Bible Backgrounds Commentary*, ed. C. E. Arnold (Grand Rapids: Zondervan, 2002), 467; cf. Quinn and Wacker, *Letters to Timothy*, 412–49.

[324] J.-U. Krause, *Witwen und Waisen im Römischen Reich*, 4 vols., Heidelberger Althistorische Beiträge und Epigraphische Studien 16–19 (Stuttgart: F. Steiner, 1994–95).

[325] M. D. Moore, "The 'Widows' in 1 Tim. 5:3–16," in *Essays on Women in Earliest Christianity*, vol. 1, ed. C. D. Osburn (Eugene, OR: Wipf & Stock, 1993), 337.

- they must put their hope in God, continuing in petitions and prayers (v. 5);
- they must not be self-indulgent, pursuing sensual pleasure, as some of the younger widows in Paul's day seem to have done (v. 6; cf. v. 13);
- they must be at least sixty years old (v. 9), presumably because at that age remarriage was unlikely and/or because women under sixty were capable of working; this would have kept the list reasonably short, especially since life expectancy was lower than it is today; younger widows should remarry, have children, manage their households, and give the enemy no opportunity for slander (vv. 11–15; Roman legislation stipulated this for women under fifty);
- they must have been faithful to their husband while married (v. 9); and
- they must have a reputation for good works, including bringing up children, showing hospitality (presumably opening their homes to traveling believers, particularly teachers), washed the saints' feet (an idiom for humble service), helping the afflicted, and devoting themselves to every good work (v. 10).

By following these instructions, Timothy will ensure that the church helps only those widows who are truly worthy of financial assistance so that available funds are used for those who lack other means of support. Here again there is an overlap between the actual household and the household of God. It is incumbent on believers to care for those in their own natural household precisely so that the household of God can best serve the needs of its members.

Paul's concern for widows, in turn, is part of a larger biblical-theological pattern of God's people caring for the widows among them.[326] God himself is the "champion of widows" (Ps 68:5; cf. Deut 10:18; Ps 146:9; Prov 15:25). The law stipulates that the

---

[326] See S. G. Dempster, "Widow," in *Baker's Evangelical Dictionary of Biblical Theology*, ed. W. A. Elwell (Grand Rapids: Baker, 1996), 816–19; A. J. Köstenberger with D. W. Jones, *God, Marriage, and Family: Rebuilding the Biblical Foundation*, 2nd ed. (Wheaton: Crossway, 2010), 192–93. See also Couser, "Divergent, Insurgent or Allegiant?," 11–12, who argues that the instructions to care for widows (1 Tim 5:3–16) and the instructions with regard to elders (1 Tim 5:17–25) are based on the OT's call to care for widows as an implication of the fifth commandment (Exod

Israelites are not to take advantage of widows (Exod 22:22; Deut 27:19) but instead should provide for their needs (Deut 24:19–20; 26:12–13). Indeed, proper care of widows is an implication of the fifth commandment.[327] The prophets warned against the mistreatment of widows (Isa 1:17; Jer 7:6; 22:3; Zech 7:10). Jesus likewise cared for widows (Luke 7:11–17) and condemned the Pharisees' exploitation of them (Mark 12:40). The earliest church ensured that the widows among them were provided for (Acts 6:1–6) and saw their care as part of "pure and undefiled religion" (Jas 1:27). In this vein Paul's instructions in 1 Tim 5:3–16 provide a significant set of principles for the care of widows in the church.

§4.1.2.4 Slaves

With slaves there's sharp discontinuity between the idea of the church as the household of God and the natural household. Paul doesn't provide instructions for slaves to function as slaves in the church but gives guidance on how they're to function in their natural households. In 1 Tim 6:1–2 Paul continues the domestic code as follows:

> All who are under the yoke as slaves should regard their own masters as worthy of all respect, so that God's name and his teaching will not be blasphemed. Let those who have believing masters not be disrespectful to them because they are brothers, but should serve them even better, since those who benefit from their service are believers and dearly loved.[328]

Titus 2:9–10 contains similar instructions: "Slaves are to submit to their masters in everything, and to be well-pleasing, not talking back or stealing, but demonstrating utter faithfulness, so that they may adorn the teaching of God our Savior in everything.

20:12; cf., e.g., Lev 19:2, 9, 14) and on the OT's teaching regarding the fair examination of those alleged of sinning (e.g., Deut 10:15; 19:15–21; see further §2.7.1 above).

[327] Couser, "Divergent, Insurgent or Allegiant?," 8; P. D. Miller, *The Ten Commandments* (Louisville: Westminster John Knox, 2009), 219–20; Knight, *Pastoral Epistles*, 215–16; T. C. Oden, *First and Second Timothy and Titus*, Interpretation (Atlanta: John Knox, 1989), 155.

[328] On ancient slavery, see the bibliographic information provided in the commentary at 1 Tim 6:1–2a.

The Bible has much to say on the topic of slavery.[329] It's instructive that the first biblical reference to slavery comes in the context of a curse (Gen 9:25–27). In the OT, slavery is neither instituted nor abolished but regulated.[330] Meadors suggests that "the legal codes for that regulation (Exod 21; Lev 25; Deut 15) and the numerous texts that reflect Israel's development in this domain indicate an increasing humanization of slavery in contrast to the rest of the ancient Near East."[331] That is, slaves were seen in the OT as human beings, not merely property, a fitting stance for a nation whose forebears had been slaves in Egypt (Exod 1:8–14; cf. Deut 15:12–15). Slaves were to be treated humanely, had a number of possibilities for manumission (Exod 21:2–4, 7–11, 26–27; Lev 25:40–43, 48–55; Deut 21:14), and could benefit from a surprisingly generous asylum law (Deut 23:15–16).

In the NT, Paul indicates that slaves are to take advantage of legitimate opportunities for gaining their freedom but otherwise to accept their slavery on a human level, recognizing that they are simultaneously "the Lord's freedman" (1 Cor 7:20–24). Elsewhere Paul instructs slaves to provide good, respectful, and sincere service to their masters, recognizing that this good service would be repaid by the Lord (Eph 6:5–8; Col 3:22–24). Peter indicates that this sort of service ought to be given even to masters who are crooked (1 Pet 2:18–20). In his letter to Philemon, Paul addresses him as a slaveholder (v. 16), a ministry partner (v. 17), and a Christian brother (v. 20). He highlights the Christian brotherhood of Philemon's slave Onesimus and appeals for Onesimus's freedom, laying the groundwork for Christian efforts toward the abolition of slavery.

---

[329] Note G. T. Meadors, "Slave, Slavery," in *Evangelical Dictionary of Biblical Theology*, 740–41. Within the American antebellum context, both the proslavery and antislavery positions marshaled biblical teaching in support of their position; see, e.g., M. A. Noll, *The Civil War as a Theological Crisis* (Chapel Hill, NC: The University of North Carolina Press, 2006), esp. chap. 3.

[330] C. J. H. Wright, *Old Testament Ethics for the People of God* (Downers Grove: IVP Academic, 2004), 329–30, suggests that slavery, along with polygamy and divorce, was an example of "some customs and practices common in the ancient world [that] were tolerated within Israel, without explicit divine command or sanction, but with a developing theological critique that regarded them as falling short of God's highest standards."

[331] Meadors, "Slave, Slavery," 740. Cf. also Wright, *Old Testament Ethics*, 333–37.

Of course, in most parts of the world today, there is no slavery so that the instructions to slaves in 1 Timothy and elsewhere no longer have direct application. Nevertheless, on a principial level, submission to authority in the economic realm is still required by and pleases God. What this set of instructions demonstrates is the importance of members of God's household living rightly in their own households as a part of carrying out God's mission. Here again we see the close connection between the natural household and God's household, the church. Yet while Paul instructs Timothy to treat older men as fathers, older women as mothers, younger men as brothers, and younger women as sisters (1 Tim 5:1–2), there's no group he is to treat "as slaves." Slaves don't function as slaves in God's household. Rather, they would have been included in the previous groups: fathers, mothers, brothers, and sisters. This is further evidence for the church not to be slavishly modeled after the socioeconomic world of Greco-Roman culture.

§4.1.2.5 The Wealthy

In 1 Timothy Paul has choice words for "those who are rich in this present age" (6:17–19; cf. Titus 2:12; 2 Tim 4:10).[332] Over against the opponents' desire to use ministry as an avenue for gaining wealth, Paul stresses the benefits of contentment, warning against the "love of money" (vv. 6–10). In addition, he instructs Timothy on how to deal with the contingent of wealthy individuals in the Ephesian church (cf. 2:9; 5:13).[333] Paul's concern is that such people not succumb to the sin of arrogance and unduly place their confidence in material possessions. A person's self-worth and identity don't depend on external factors such as these. In fact, wealth is a highly precarious object of trust (v. 7).

Wealthy believers should put their hope in God, who richly provides believers with all things for their enjoyment. Gratitude rather than conceit is the proper response to material blessing from the Lord. What's more, people who have been blessed with

[332] For relevant research, see II. Historical Context, C. The Social Setting of the Letters to Timothy and Titus in the Introduction to this volume. See the treatment of the LTT in C. L. Blomberg, *Neither Poverty nor Riches: A Biblical Theology of Possessions*, NSBT 7 (Downers Grove: InterVarsity, 2000), 206–11.

[333] At the same time, as mentioned above, the congregation also included slaves (vv. 1–2), needy widows (5:3–16), and people from a variety of socioeconomic backgrounds.

the things of this world should recognize their special obligation to share what they have with the needy. They are to "do what is good" and to be "rich in good works," "generous," and "willing to share" (1 Tim 6:18). Rather than putting their confidence in uncertain riches, those well off will thus store up for themselves a supply that will serve as a good foundation for the age to come, so that they may take hold of "what is truly life" (1 Tim 6:19).

On occasion Paul himself was the beneficiary of wealthy patrons, whether male or female (e.g., Rom 16:1–2; Phlm 1–2, 5–7, 22). He was certainly no ascetic. Yet while he doesn't disparage wealth as such, he is deeply concerned for the spiritual condition of those of means. Like Jesus, he knows that it's more difficult for those who have an abundance of material possessions to place their trust fully in God. He therefore counsels rich believers to turn such a potential spiritual liability into an advantage by sharing some of what they have with those who are in need. Similar to needy widows, the wealthy should place their hope exclusively in God (1 Tim 5:5; 6:17).

§4.2 The Church as Pillar and Foundation of the Truth

Certain metaphors for the church, such as the "body of Christ," which are prominent in some of Paul's other letters (e.g., Rom 12:3–8; 1 Corinthians 12–14; Ephesians 4–5), are absent from the LTT. The only other ecclesiastical metaphor besides that of God's household is that the church is "the pillar and foundation of the truth" (1 Tim 3:15). "Pillar and foundation" would have been an evocative building metaphor in booming first-century Ephesus.[334] Similar language occurs in 2 Tim 2:19: "Nevertheless, God's solid foundation stands firm, having this inscription: The Lord knows those who are his, and let everyone who calls on the name of the Lord turn away from wickedness."[335] Some wonder how to reconcile "household of God" with "pillar and foundation of the truth,"

[334] On "pillar" (στῦλος) see Gal 2:9; "foundation" (ἑδραίωμα) occurs only here in the NT; "truth" (ἀληθεία) sets true believers apart from the false teachers (1 Tim 2:4; 4:3; 6:5; etc.). Note that Paul also uses a somewhat different building metaphor for the church in Eph 2:19–22, on which see J. van Nes, "Under Construction: The Building of God's Temple according to Ephesians 2,19–22," in *Paul's Graeco-Roman Context*, ed. C. Breytenbach, BETL 277 (Leuven: Peeters, 2015), 631–44.

[335] See Towner, *Letters to Timothy and Titus*, 530.

as the metaphor shifts from household to building.[336] But mixed metaphors aren't uncommon in Scripture,[337] and Paul's point is clear enough: the church, as God's household, serves as a bastion for the truth, standing against false teaching and testifying to the watching world.

Although the imagery of the church as a foundation occurs only in the letters to Timothy, the notion of standing for the truth recurs frequently throughout the LTT. On the one hand, Paul repeatedly stresses the need for Timothy and Titus to teach true doctrine and rebuke false teachers.[338] "Truth" language occurs fifteen times in the LTT.[339] It is most often connected with right knowledge of God and can be applied positively to knowing or teaching the truth (e.g., 1 Tim 2:4; 2 Tim 2:15) or negatively to false teachers who are devoid of the truth (e.g., 1 Tim 6:5; Titus 1:14). On the other hand, the church also bears witness to the watching world. This theme is particularly common in the LTT's household portions. Thus the church should pray for those in authority with a view toward proclaiming the gospel (1 Tim 2:1–7); slaves are to honor their masters "so that God's name and his teaching will not be blasphemed" (1 Tim 6:1) and "so that they may adorn the teaching of God our Savior in everything" (Titus 2:10); Paul gives his own life as an example of enduring all things in order that the elect may be saved (2 Tim 2:8–10) and exhorts Titus to let his life be an example and his teaching be sound "so that any opponent will be ashamed, because he doesn't have anything bad to say about us" (Titus 2:8); and older women are to teach the young women to live rightly "so that God's word will not be slandered" (Titus 2:5).

Through these two metaphors, "household" and "pillar and foundation of the truth," Paul powerfully communicates the role of the local church in ways that would have resonated deeply with the believers in Ephesus and Crete. They were to regard themselves as family, with unique responsibilities toward one another, similar to the members of a household. And they were to stand for the truth against false teachers who sought to undermine right doctrine and godly behavior and were to bear witness to a lost

---

[336] Johnson, *Letters to Paul's Delegates*, 157–58.

[337] See, e.g., Pss 18:1–2; 23; 2 Cor 5:2; 1 Pet 2:4–5.

[338] 1 Tim 1:3–11; 4:1–16; 6:2–16, 20–21; 2 Tim 2:14–3:9; 4:1–5; Titus 1:5–16.

[339] 1 Tim 2:4, 7 (2x); 3:15; 4:3; 6:5; 2 Tim 2:15, 18, 25; 3:7–8; 4:4; Titus 1:1, 13–14.

world, so that God's goodness and graciousness would be made manifest.

§4.3 The Church and Its Ministry

Given Paul's purpose in writing the LTT, particularly seeing the mission to the Gentiles continued through the establishment and organization of healthy churches in Ephesus and Crete (§1), it's not surprising that the ministry of the local church and its various aspects are continually and consistently discussed in these letters.[340] In addressing ministry from a biblical-theological perspective, we must take care to understand the roles of Timothy and Titus in these congregations and determine in what ways the instructions given to them can be applied to church leaders today.

As mentioned, Timothy and Titus weren't pastors as such but rather Paul's apostolic delegates (Introduction; §1.3). While elders today don't serve as apostolic delegates, their ministry nonetheless displays certain similarities. The most significant difference is that Timothy and Titus were tasked with accomplishing specific objectives in Paul's absence. These largely centered on dealing with false teaching (e.g., 1 Tim 1:3–4; 2 Tim 2:14, 16; Titus 1:9–14), passing on Paul's apostolic message (e.g. 1 Tim 4:6; 2 Tim 2:14; Titus 2:15–3:1), and, in the case of Titus, finishing what Paul had left incomplete, that is, appointing elders (Titus 1:5).

While therefore elders today don't function as apostolic delegates, they nonetheless find themselves appointed as overseers in the post-apostolic church who are tasked with serving as stewards of God's household (1 Tim 3:5; Titus 1:7). Paul himself, as well as Timothy and Titus, serves as an example of how this task is to be carried out (1 Tim 4:12; 2 Tim 1:13; Titus 2:7), and his instructions to Timothy and Titus continue to be relevant today. This section will discuss the various tasks of ministry, qualifications for church officers, and goals of ministry enunciated by Paul in the LTT.

§4.3.1 The Tasks of Ministry

As Paul provides instructions to Timothy and Titus, he discusses three general aspects of ministry: (1) the ministry of the

[340] See A. D. Clarke, *A Pauline Theology of Church Leadership*, LNTS 362 (London: T&T Clark, 2008), who rightly includes the LTT in his consideration of Paul's theology of leadership in the church. Cf. J. Barentsen, *Emerging Leadership in the Pauline Mission: A Social Identity Perspective on Local Leadership Development in Corinth and Ephesus*, Princeton Monograph Series 168 (Eugene, OR: Wipf & Stock, 2011).

word; (2) the ministry of caring for God's household; and (3) the ministry of prayer.

§4.3.1.1 The Ministry of the Word

From a biblical-theological standpoint, God has consistently been concerned with the ministry of the word, the verbal propagation of his revelation through proclamation and teaching.[341] In addition, when needed (and it often was!) prophets sent by God spoke words of divine rebuke and judgment. Jesus himself came teaching and preaching and at times delivered messages of rebuke and judgment as well. In like manner, those whom he sent out—his apostles—also preached and taught the gospel, correcting false representations of God's message where necessary.

Along this trajectory, we find that language related to teaching, instructing, rebuking, testimony, doctrine, etc. forms an integral part of the LTT (§2). The purpose statements of 1 and 2 Timothy both focus on some aspect of teaching. In 1 Timothy Paul writes, "As I urged you when I went to Macedonia, remain in Ephesus so that you may instruct certain people not to teach false *doctrine*" (1 Tim 1:3). In 2 Timothy he urges, "Hold on to the pattern of sound *teaching* that you have heard from me, in the faith and love that are in Christ Jesus. Guard the good deposit through the Holy Spirit who lives in us" (2 Tim 1:13–14); and "I solemnly charge you before God and Christ Jesus, who is going to judge the living and the dead, and because of his appearing and his kingdom: Preach the *word*; be ready in season and out of season; rebuke, correct, and encourage with great patience and teaching" (2 Tim 4:1–2). In Titus the purpose is more generally given as appointing elders (Titus 1:5); these elders, once appointed, must hold "to the faithful message as taught, so that he will be able both to encourage with sound *teaching* and to refute those who contradict it" (Titus 1:9).

The message that Timothy and Titus were charged with teaching was the written word, both the Hebrew Scriptures and apostolic teaching committed to writing, and possibly even authoritative non-apostolic writings, such as the Gospel of Luke (1 Tim 4:13; 5:18, §2.7) and the apostolic teaching directly from

[341] See J. C. Meyer, *Preaching: A Biblical Theology* (Wheaton: Crossway, 2015); H. O. Old, *The Reading and Preaching of the Scriptures in the Worship of the Christian Church*, vol. 1: *The Biblical Period* (Grand Rapids: Eerdmans, 1998).

Paul (1 Tim 1:3–4; 2 Tim 1:3). Both the Hebrew Scriptures and the apostolic teaching, whether directly from an apostle or an apostolic associate, and whether written or unwritten, were equally authoritative, and while there was a distinction when the LTT were written, Paul's recorded apostolic teachings are now a part of the text of Scripture, both in the LTT and in his other letters. As a result, while no elder today serves as apostolic delegate in an original, narrow sense, every pastor bears the responsibility for teaching the authoritative Word of God, both OT and NT, in its entirety.

Outside the purpose statements, the LTT are permeated by a focus on teaching and preaching the Word.[342] A good teacher—exemplified by Paul—must preach and teach the gospel of Jesus Christ (1 Tim 2:5–7; 6:2; 2 Tim 1:8; 2:8–9) and healthy doctrine (2 Tim 1:13; Titus 1:9; 2:1), specifically the apostolic message (2 Tim 2:2; Titus 1:9). Timothy is encouraged to engage in reading, exhortation, and teaching in Paul's absence (1 Tim 4:13; 2 Tim 4:2). Both are to appoint overseers who are capable, faithful teachers (1 Tim 3:2; 2 Tim 2:24; Titus 1:9), some of whom will labor hard at preaching and teaching (1 Tim 5:17). Timothy is told that in his instruction of what is true, he is himself "nourished by the words of the faith and the good teaching that you have followed" (1 Tim 4:7). What's more, he must watch his teaching, as it is essential for his own spiritual health and that of his hearers (1 Tim 4:16). Timothy is also charged with doing the work of an evangelist (2 Tim 4:5), engaging in the work of gospel ministry.[343] Finally, Timothy and Titus are both tasked with encouraging those under their care (1 Tim 5:1; 6:2; 2 Tim 4:2; Titus 1:9; 2:6, 15).

In addition, they—and the elders they appoint—are tasked with rebuking false teachers (1 Tim 1:3; 2 Tim 4:1–4; Titus 1:9–13) and sinning elders (1 Tim 5:20). While the false teachers confronting Timothy and Titus weren't necessarily the same, nor will their errors necessarily be identical to those confronting us today, what

---

[342] Words related to preaching (the κηρύσσω and εὐαγγελίζω word groups), teaching (the διδάσκω word group), and the word (λόγος) occur fifty times in the LTT. This count does not include other important words such as παρακαλέω, ἐλέγχω, etc. For the specific nuances of the various terms, see the commentary. Cf. Smith, *Pauline Communities as "Scholastic Communities."*

[343] D. A. Carson, "Editorial: Do the Work of an Evangelist," *Them* 39, no. 1 (2014): 1–4.

they share in common is the fact that they distort God's message in one way or another. Thus Paul says the opponents are teaching "false doctrine" (1 Tim 1:3; 6:3–5), desiring to be "teachers of the law" while failing to understand the law (1 Tim 1:7). In fact, their teaching is a part of the end-time apostasy, and they promulgate "the teachings of demons" (1 Tim 4:1). Yet despite the presence of false teachers and the mounting threat of persecution, God's word cannot be bound (2 Tim 2:9). Nevertheless, this ministry of the word, as is clear from the many injunctions given, requires diligent labor on the part of those who teach (1 Tim 5:17; 2 Tim 2:3–6, 15). The importance of right teaching stems from at least three places.

1. The apostolic message is the word of God (1 Tim 4:5; 2 Tim 2:9; 3:16; Titus 2:5)[344] and characterized by knowledge of the truth (1 Tim 2:4; 2 Tim 2:15, 25; 3:7; 4:4; Titus 1:1), while the false teachers promote demonic teachings (1 Tim 4:1) and are deprived of truth (1 Tim 6:5, 20–21). Proper instruction isn't so much a matter of being right but of accurately representing God. The gospel message Paul proclaims, as he makes clear in both the LTT and his earlier letters, isn't his own but was revealed to him by God and confirmed by the other apostles (Gal 1:11–2:2; Eph 3:3; 1 Tim 1:11; Titus 1:3).[345] To fail to preach this message isn't merely to place oneself outside Paul's camp, as it were, but outside God's camp.

2. The apostolic message, because it is God's word, results in godliness (1 Tim 1:5; 4:6–7, 16; 6:3; 2 Tim 3:16–17; Titus 1:1, 15; 3:8), while the false teachers' message results in ungodliness (1 Tim 6:4–5, 9–10; 2 Tim 2:17; 3:5; Titus 1:15–16).[346] Orthodoxy (correct belief) is never sufficient apart from orthopraxy (correct actions) and orthopathy (correct affections) but always has as one of its goals the transformation of lives into the increasing likeness of Jesus Christ.

3. The apostolic message is also centered on God's mission and is thus concerned with the salvation of unbelievers from out of the world. This occurs through the proclamation of the saving message (1 Tim 1:15; 2:1–7; 4:7–10; 2 Tim 1:8–11; 2:8–10; 3:15; 4:5, 17) and is attested by the transformed lives produced by it (1 Tim 6:1; Titus 2:5, 8, 10). To engage in a ministry of the word that reflects

---

[344] See also the reference to "the words of the faith" (1 Tim 4:6).

[345] See Peter's similar discussions in 1 Pet 1:12; 2 Pet 1:16–2:3.

[346] Or at best, they're "fruitless," failing to promote godliness, 1 Tim 4:7.

the concerns of the LTT and Scripture as a whole is to be concerned with the salvation of the lost and the preservation of believers. Rather than being insular and defensive, it is a ministry that aims at advancing God's mission.

§4.3.1.2 The Ministry of Caring for God's Household

The depiction of the church as God's household constitutes one of the most distinctive biblical-theological contributions of the LTT. While not unique to these letters, it is developed here in a unique manner, providing another helpful metaphor for what it means for overseers to care for God's people. Those who care for the church are "administrators" (Titus 1:7, *οἰκονόμος*), stewards who have been tasked by the true Lord and father of the household with caring for his family.[347] A. Malherbe's summary of the "job description" of the overseer of God's household is apt and may serve as the point of reference for further discussion below:

> The terms describing the preaching and pastoral care of the orthodox distinguish them from their opponents: they are to preach (2 Tim. 4:2) and speak what befits sound doctrine (Tit. 2:1; cf. 15) and are to charge (1 Tim. 1:3; 4:11; 5:7; 6:17), instruct (1 Tim. 4:6, 11, 16; Tit. 3:14; cf. 1 Tim. 3:3; Tit. 1:9), correct (Tit. 1:5), and remind (2 Tim. 2:14) others. They should be careful in chastising those within the community (1 Tim. 5:1; 6:2; 2 Tim. 4:2; Tit. 1:9; 2:6) and honor (1 Tim. 5:3, 17) them. Only seldom are they commanded to engage in censure (2 Tim. 4:20) [*sic*] and severe rebuke, harsh treatments reserved primarily for those who persist in sin (1 Tim. 5:20; cf. 2 Tim. 4:2; Tit. 2:15) and for the heretics (Tit. 1:9, 13) who must be silenced (Tit. 1:11). The evangelists are to present themselves as examples in their speech and conduct, in love, faith, and purity (1 Tim. 4:12), which requires that they constantly give attention to their own progress in the Christian virtues (e.g., 1 Tim. 4:12-16; 5:22; 6:11-14; 2 Tim. 2:1-8, 22; 3:10, 14; 4:5, 15).[348]

[347] Goodrich, "Overseers as Stewards," 85–87, 96–97.

[348] A. Malherbe, "Medical Imagery in the Pastoral Epistles," in *Paul and the Popular Philosophers* (Minneapolis: Fortress, 1989), 125.

In keeping with the discussion above, therefore, we can survey the ministries with which Timothy, Titus, and elders in the churches are charged in the LTT as follows.

1. Caring for God's household involves proper *instruction* in the Word of God as mentioned above. As Goodrich notes, stewards "lead and direct trusted delegates (διάκονοι, 1 Tim 3:8–13) and the rest of the *familia* by promoting genuine faith and sound doctrine."[349] This isn't just the responsibility of Paul's delegates and the elders. Deacons, too, are required to hold to "the mystery of the faith" (1 Tim 3:8). Although it is not their responsibility to teach, they likewise must stand firm against false teachers.

2. Overseeing God's household requires *caring* for needy family members, particularly widows.[350] The overlap between the responsibilities of the natural household and God's household are striking here: believers must care for widows in their own household so the church can care for those who truly are widows in God's household (1 Tim 5:3–4, 8, 16).

3. Though only mentioned briefly, caring for God's household also involves *hospitality*.[351] Both overseers and widows are enjoined to be hospitable (1 Tim 3:2; 5:10; Titus 1:8), a concept pertaining not primarily to entertaining friends but to caring for strangers, especially traveling believers.[352]

4. Caring for God's household involves setting an *example*. In his earlier letters Paul calls on believers to imitate him (1 Cor 4:16;

---

[349] Goodrich, "Overseers as Stewards," 97.

[350] A. Malherbe ("Paul: Hellenistic Philosopher or Christian Pastor?," in *Paul and the Popular Philosophers*, 67–78) suggests that Paul was familiar with Greco-Roman moral philosophers of his day, adopting and adapting aspects of their "philosophic pastoral methods" for use with his own congregations (p. 68; see also Malherbe, *Paul and the Thessalonians: The Philosophic Tradition of Pastoral Care* [Minneapolis: Fortress, 1987]). Though he views the LTT as pseudonymous, he situates them similarly, placing their common medical imagery in this philosophical context ("Medical Imagery in the Pastoral Epistles," 121–36). See the summary in Harding, *What Are They Saying about the Pastoral Epistles?*, 73–74.

[351] On hospitality, see S. C. Barton, "Hospitality," *DLNT* 501–7; J. T. Fitzgerald, "Hospitality," *DNTB* 522–25; and esp. A. Arterbury, *Entertaining Angels: Early Christian Hospitality in Its Mediterranean Setting* (Sheffield: Sheffield Phoenix, 2005).

[352] So T. R. Hobbs, "Hospitality in the First Testament and the 'Teleological Fallacy,'" *JSOT* 95 (2001): 21; W. A. Vogels, "Hospitality in Biblical Perspective," *Liturgical Ministry* 11 (2002): 171.

11:1; Phil 3:17; 2 Thess 3:7, 9).[353] In the LTT, too, he presents his life as an example, specifically of how God saves the undeserving (1 Tim 1:15–16). He also provides a pattern of sound teaching for Timothy to follow and pass on to others (2 Tim 1:13; 2:2). Both Timothy and Titus are exhorted to present themselves as examples to their congregations. To Timothy he says,

> Don't let anyone despise your youth, but set an example for the believers in speech, in conduct, in love, in faith, and in purity. . . . Practice these things; be committed to them, so that your progress may be evident to all. Pay close attention to your life and your teaching; persevere in these things, for in doing this you will save both yourself and your hearers. (1 Tim 4:12, 15–16)

Similarly, to Titus he writes, "Make yourself an example of good works with integrity and dignity in your teaching" (Titus 2:7).

5. Finally, caring for God's household also involves *hard work*. In fact, diligence is one of the virtues of the Christian life (§5), and ministering in God's household not only involves working hard but also, as mentioned, setting an example for others to follow. The work of an elder is a "noble work" (1 Tim 3:1), and elders who work hard at preaching and teaching are worthy of their wages (1 Tim 5:17–18). In fact, rightly handling God's word is presented as being the task of a "worker" (2 Tim 2:15). In 2 Tim 2:3–7 Paul uses a series of metaphors to stress the hard work and suffering involved in ministry: Timothy is to engage in ministry as a soldier who suffers and pleases his commanding officer; as an athlete who competes according to the rules; and as a hardworking farmer. Each of these metaphors also points to the rewards in store for the faithful Christian. The same connection between the minister's hard work and the final judgment is in view when Paul tells

---

[353] The topic of Paul's example has been treated extensively. For an overview of the research and bibliography since the seminal treatment of W. Michaelis ("μιμέομαι, κτλ.," *TDNT* 4:667), see B. Dodd, *Paul's Paradigmatic 'I': Personal Example as Literary Strategy*, JSNTSup 177 (Sheffield: Sheffield Academic Press, 1999), 18–29; B. Fiore, *The Function of Personal Example in the Socratic and Pastoral Epistles*, AnBib 105 (Rome: Biblical Institute Press, 1986), esp. 198–208; and Fiore, "Paul, Exemplification, and Imitation," in *Paul and the Greco-Roman World: A Handbook*, vol. 1.

Timothy to "fight the good fight of faith . . . until the appearing of our Lord Jesus Christ" (1 Tim 6:11–14; cf. 2 Tim 4:6–8). In addition, Timothy is equipped by Scripture for every good work (2 Tim 3:17)[354] and is to do the work of an evangelist (2 Tim 4:5). In all this Paul makes abundantly clear that ministry is not the path of least resistance. As all of the Christian life, if not more so, it involves labor and toil, yet the reward will be great.

§4.3.1.3 The Ministry of Prayer

As Paul makes a transition from urging Timothy to address false teachers to caring for the household of God, his first instruction is that the people of God should pray (1 Tim 2:1–2). The immediate context indicates that Paul isn't simply interested in believers' getting by peacefully in the world but rather that he is focused on God's people accomplishing God's mission in the world around them (v. 3). The inclusion of "thanksgiving" in Paul's command highlights the confidence we are to have in God as the Creator and Lord who is accomplishing his purposes.

It would be easy to overlook the importance of this command, given the centrality of teaching in the letter. However, while Timothy and Titus, as well as the elders, are to be diligent in teaching, prayer should occupy a prominent place in the ministry of the church if she is to have an effective witness in the world (cf. 2 Tim 2:22: "Call on the Lord from a pure heart").[355] Paul also testifies to the importance of prayer in his own life in his greeting to Timothy (2 Tim 1:3)[356] as well as in his instructions concerning widows, where one mark of a godly widow worthy of church support is faithful prayer (1 Tim 5:5; cf. Luke 2:36–37; 1 Thess 5:17).

§4.3.2 Church Officers

The LTT provide a rich deposit of information regarding two church offices, those of elder/overseer and deacon, highlighting

---

[354] See comments on 2 Tim 3:17 for Paul's use of "man of God."

[355] Young finds prayer in the context of the LTT to be "the principal activity of the household of God" (*Theology*, 34). Solevåg comments on this verse: "Earnest prayer is one of the signifying traits of the true believer." A. R. Solevåg, "Prayer in Acts and the Pastoral Epistles: Intersections of Gender and Class," in *Early Christian Prayer and Identity Formation*, ed. R. Hvalvik and K. O. Sandnes, WUNT 1/336 (Tübingen: Mohr Siebeck, 2014), 148 (though we cannot endorse all of her conclusions).

[356] Prayer formed a regular part of Paul's ministry, as attested by his letters (1 Cor 1:4; Eph 1:15–19; Phil 1:3–11; Col 1:3, 9–14; 1 Thess 1:2–4; 2 Thess 1:3; Phlm 4–6).

qualifications for those who serve in these offices. In what follows we'll briefly comment on qualifications for elders/overseers and those for deacons. For details see the commentary; here we'll briefly discuss a few broad theological considerations related to ministry.

§4.3.2.1 Elders/Overseers

One of the major contributions of the LTT is its discussion of church leaders.[357] The threat of the false teachers provides the backdrop for Paul's stipulations in this area. Since church leaders are charged with doctrinal oversight of local congregations, it's absolutely essential that they be chosen carefully in keeping with clearly delineated standards for character and integrity. For this reason it is fitting that a considerable portion of Paul's correspondence with Timothy and Titus is given to instructions on qualifications for church leaders.

Paul's discussions concerning appointing elders/overseers are connected with his use of household imagery (§4.1). As discussed above, the metaphor illustrates how church leaders are to function in and care for members of the household. While shepherding imagery associated with church leadership is more common in Scripture,[358] the household metaphor has something unique and distinctive to offer to our understanding of the task

---

[357] For helpful treatments on the subject, see Köstenberger, "Church Government"; Köstenberger, "1 Timothy," 521–30; W. Kowalski, "The Reward, Discipline, and Installation of Church Leaders: An Examination of 1 Timothy 5:17--22" (Ph.D. thesis, University of Gloucestershire, 2005); D. A. Mappes, "Moral Virtues Associated with Eldership," *BSac* 160 (2003): 202–18; the excursus in Marshall, *Pastoral Epistles*, 170–81 ("Overseers and Their Relation to Elders"); B. L. Merkle, *The Elder and Overseer: One Office in the Early Church*, StBibLit 57 (New York: P. Lang, 2003); Merkle, *40 Questions about Elders and Deacons* (Grand Rapids: Kregel, 2008); Merkle, "Are the Qualifications for Elders or Overseers Negotiable?," *BSac* 171 (2014): 172–88; P. A. Newton and M. Schmucker, *Elders in the Life of the Church: Rediscovering the Biblical Model for Church Leadership* (Grand Rapids: Kregel, 2013); Trebilco, *Early Christians in Ephesus*, 448–587. For presentations of different views, see C. O. Brand and R. S. Norman, eds., *Perspectives on Church Government: Five Views of Church Polity* (Nashville: B&H, 2004); and S. B. Cowan, gen. ed., *Who Runs the Church? 4 Views on Church Government* (Grand Rapids: Zondervan, 2004).

[358] E.g., Psalm 23; Ezekiel 34; John 10; Heb 13:20; 1 Pet 5:1–4. See T. S. Laniak, *Shepherds after My Own Heart: Pastoral Traditions and Leadership in the Bible*, NSBT 20 (Downers Grove: IVP Academic, 2006); D. Tidball, *Skilful Shepherds: Explorations in Pastoral Theology* (Leicester, UK: InterVarsity, 1996).

of church leaders.[359] The group of people that elders are charged with overseeing is not monolithic but highly diverse. Any given congregation will differ from any other with regard to age, gender, ethnicity, and socioeconomic status. Christ has truly made us one body consisting of many members, and none of these differences pose any barrier to church membership (Rom 10:12; 1 Cor 12:13; Gal 3:28).

Nevertheless, a competent overseer will understand that different people have different needs that require wisdom and maturity to meet. The overseer, serving as a steward in the household of God, must care for everyone entrusted to him.[360] Paul impresses this responsibility on both of his delegates. To Timothy he insists that the elder must be able to manage (προΐστημι) his own household well, or else he won't be able to care for the church (1 Tim 3:4–5).[361] He later reiterates this point when he tells Timothy that elders who are good leaders (προΐστημι) are worthy of a double honor (1 Tim 5:17). To Titus he writes that an elder is "an overseer of God's household" (οἰκονόμος; Titus 1:7). What's more, this kind of responsibility is evident in Paul's instructions on how elders are to care for various groups in the church (1 Tim 5:1–6:2; Titus 2:1–10).

According to Paul's instructions, then, church leaders, variously called "overseers" or "elders," are to meet the following qualifications (1 Tim 3:1–7).[362] They are to be above reproach;

[359] See J. N. D. Kelly, *A Commentary on the Pastoral Epistles*, BNTC (London: A. & C. Black, 1963), 78.

[360] Goodrich, "Overseers as Stewards and the Qualifications for Leadership in the Pastoral Epistles," 81–82, 87–96, argues that the qualities given by Paul to Timothy and Titus are precisely the kinds of skills and character qualities that were necessary for good stewards in the Greco-Roman culture. B. A. Paschke, "The *cura morum* of the Roman Censors as Historical Background for the Bishop and Deacon Lists of the Pastoral Epistles," *ZNW* 98 (2007): 105–19 explores the *cura morum* ("care of manners") practiced by Roman censors investigating the private life of candidates for the Roman senate.

[361] Just as the requirements of being a faithful husband (1 Tim 3:2; Titus 1:6) and having obedient children (1 Tim 3:4; Titus 1:6) assume but don't necessitate the elder being married and having children, so Paul's requirement here assumes but doesn't demand that an overseer (and deacon, see 1 Tim 3:12) is in charge of a household. The character quality of being a faithful and competent manager is what's important. See Marshall, *Pastoral Epistles*, 479; Mounce, *Pastoral Epistles*, 170–71, 177–78; Towner, *Letters to Timothy and Titus*, 254–55; Verner, *Household of God*, 132–33.

[362] See the comparative chart in Köstenberger, "1–2 Timothy, Titus," 523–24.

faithful husbands;[363] self-controlled; sensible; respectable; hospitable; able to teach; not an excessive drinker; not violent but gentle; not quarrelsome; and not greedy. They are to manage their own household well, with their children in proper submission; are not to be new converts; and are to have a good reputation with those outside the church.[364] I've elaborated on these qualifications in some detail in the commentary above.

The instructions on remuneration for elders (1 Tim 5:17–18)—apart from suggesting that at least some were not wealthy householders—is consistent with what Paul teaches elsewhere (1 Cor 9:4–14) and in 1 Tim 5:18 is explicitly tied to biblical precedent both in the OT (Deut 25:4; cf. 1 Cor 9:9) and in Jesus's teaching (Luke 10:7; cf. Matt 10:10). Elders who "are good leaders" should be *considered worthy* of both respect and remuneration—not that they're obligated to accept pay for their work: Paul's insistence that he not be paid for his ministry while planting a church (cf. 1 Cor 9:12, 15, 18; 2 Thess 3:7–9) demonstrates that the gracious refusal of remuneration is a live option for ministers of the gospel.

Uniquely, 1 Tim 5:19–20 provides guidance for handling accusations against church elders, detailed in the commentary above.[365] This guidance reflects a biblical-theological pattern in

---

[363] This implies that overseers/elders are to be male: cf. 1 Tim 2:11–15, esp. v. 12. Paul stipulates in 1 Tim 2:12 that he doesn't allow women to teach or exercise authority over men in the church. This prohibition would seem to preclude women from serving in roles of ultimate church leadership responsibility, such as senior pastor or elder (see commentary above and the discussion and additional resources cited there). The injunction reflects God's overarching design of male headship in both the natural household and the household of God, a headship that is not unique to the conditions in Ephesus and Crete reflected in the LTT but is part of a larger biblical-theological pattern grounded in the first chapters of Genesis; see the extended treatment of this pattern in A. J. Köstenberger and M. E. Köstenberger, *God's Design for Man and Woman: A Biblical-Theological Survey* (Wheaton: Crossway, 2014). On the LTT, see "Paul's Legacy (Letters to Timothy and Titus)," chap. 6 in ibid., 193–236. On the "faithful husband" requirement, see Köstenberger with Jones, *God, Marriage, and Family*, 259–64 (see esp. the chart listing the different views on p. 263).

[364] A similar list is found in Titus 1:6–9. A separate list of qualifications is provided for deacons and women (whether women deacons or deacons' wives; 1 Tim 3:8–13; see Acts 6:1–6; Rom 16:1–2). For a discussion of these qualifications, see Köstenberger, "1–2 Timothy, Titus," 522–30, 606–8.

[365] In 1 Tim 5:19–20 Timothy is presumably in view as the one who is to "accept an accusation against an elder" (or not) and who is to "publicly rebuke [a sinning

at least three respects. First, God has always held the leaders of his people responsible to model godliness for those they lead[366] and has brought correction when leaders have failed to do so.[367] For instance, Moses was penalized for his lapse in obedience in that he was not allowed to enter the promised land (Num 20:7–12; 27:12–14; Deut 1:37; 32:48–52), and when leaders in Israel sinned, they were confronted and rebuked by God's prophets (e.g., David; 2 Samuel 11–12).[368] Second, the need for "two or three witnesses" reflects a repeated biblical guideline grounded in Deut 19:15–21.[369] Third, the public nature of the rebuke intended as a deterrent echoes other biblical examples of God's correction enacted with an eye toward warning those who hadn't yet sinned in a similar way but might be tempted to. One might think of the OT example of the public challenge of Moses by Korah and company being met by the equally public response of God's judgment, so that the people

---

elder] in the presence of all." This would have been appropriate for him as an apostolic delegate, but the passage is still instructive for today's churches, with the congregation (perhaps through other church leaders) functioning in Timothy's place. Note the congregational role in calling out an unrepentant professing believer in Matt 18:17, and the congregational obligation to expel the unrepentant man involved in sexual immorality in 1 Cor 5:5, 13.

[366] David, the pinnacle of OT Israelite kingship, though not perfect, was a man after God's own heart (1 Sam 13:14). In 1 Pet 5:3 elders are enjoined to be "examples to the flock."

[367] Kowalski ("Reward, Discipline, and Installation of Church Leaders," 131–97) examines the discipline of leaders in Paul, the rest of the NT, the apostolic fathers, the OT and other Jewish literature, Greco-Roman civil life, and voluntary associations of the day. He finds the guidance of 1 Tim 5:19–21 to be "much closer to the intent and practice of the Jewish Scriptures and what is known of rabbinic practice than to any other contemporary cognate group" (195). Notably, he finds distinct differences between the discipline of leaders in 1 Tim 5:19–21 and similar practices in Paul's Greco-Roman context, where witnesses were not always necessary, eloquence was often prized over truth, and "accusations against one's social superiors were not permitted except in those situations which were defined as threatening the society (treason and adultery)" (p. 195).

[368] Cf. Isaiah's announcement of Yahweh's judgment on exploitive elders and princes (Isa 3:11–15) and Ezekiel's vision of Yahweh's pronouncement of judgment on Israel's idolatrous elders (Ezekiel 8).

[369] See H. van Vliet, *No Single Testimony: A Study on the Adaptation of the Law of Deut. 19:15 Par. into the New Testament* (Utrecht: Kreminck en Zoon, 1958).

would clearly recognize the fate of those who stood against God's appointed leaders (Numbers 16).[370]

§4.3.2.2 Deacons

The second office regulated in the LTT is that of deacon.[371] The fact that Paul provides qualifications for deacons in 1 Timothy but not in Titus may be accounted for by the fact that the church in Ephesus is more developed than that in Crete. While not as evident as in the case of elders, the household motif isn't completely absent. The deacons likely function in a similar way to the Seven who were appointed in the early church to serve, assisting the apostles in caring for members of the church, particularly widows (Acts 6:1–6).[372]

Qualifications for deacons include the following: worthy of respect; not hypocritical; not drinking a lot of wine; not greedy for money; holding to the mystery of the faith with a clear conscience; faithful husbands; managing their children and their own households competently (1 Tim 3:8–10, 12). To this is added the requirement that these deacons first be tested (v. 10) and that serving well as deacons brings a good standing and great eternal rewards

---

[370] Kowalski ("Reward, Discipline, and Installation of Church Leaders," 165) notes that "the Pentateuch is replete with examples of public punishment meant as a deterrent." The public nature of God's judgment on Ananias and Sapphira (Acts 5) is not explicitly said to have been for the purpose of deterring sin but certainly had the effect of bringing great fear on those who learned of it (vv. 5, 11).

[371] For discussion of deacons in the LTT, see A. Hentschel, *Diakonia im Neuen Testament: Studien zur Semantik unter besonderer Berücksichtigung der Rolle von Frauen*, WUNT 2/226 (Tübingen: Mohr-Siebeck, 2007), 383–406 ("Διακονέω, κτλ. in den Deuteropaulinen"); G. W. Knight, "Two Offices (Elders/Bishops and Deacons) and Two Orders of Elders (Preaching/Teaching Elders and Ruling Elders): A New Testament Study," *Presbyterion* 11 (1985): 1–12; Marshall, *Pastoral Epistles*, 486–88 ("Deacons and Their Relation to Overseers"); T. Söding, "1 Timotheus 3: Der Episkopos und die Diakone in der Kirche," in *1 Timothy Reconsidered*, ed. K. P. Donfried, Colloquium Oecumenicum Paulinum 18 (Leuven: Peeters, 2008), 63–86; T. Thatcher, "The Deacon in the Pauline Church," in *Christ's Victorious Church: Essays on Biblical Ecclesiology and Eschatology in Honor of Tom Friskney*, ed. J. A. Weatherly (Eugene, OR: Wipf & Stock, 2001), 53–67; P. Trebilco, *Early Christians in Ephesus*, 458–60.

[372] Goodrich, "Overseers as Stewards," 97; J. D. Quinn, "Ministry in the New Testament," in *Lutherans and Catholics in Dialogue IV: Eucharist and Ministry* (New York: National Committee of the Lutheran World Federation; Washington, DC: United States Catholic Conference, 1970), 97–98; Towner, *Letters to Timothy and Titus*, 261–62.

(v. 13). An interesting question arises with regard to the presence of qualifications for women (γυναῖκας) in 1 Tim 3:11, referring either to women married to deacons (deacons' wives) or to women who are themselves serving as deacons (deaconesses). Both interpretations are possible and advocated in major commentators and translations.[373] Some fear that appointing women as deacons would compromise the NT (and Pauline) principle of reserving leadership roles in the church and ordination to the ministry for men.[374] However, this fear is unnecessary if it is kept in mind that "deacon" (διάκονος) means "servant" and that, unlike the role of elder or overseer (1 Tim 3:2; Titus 1:9), the role of deacon doesn't entail the exercise of teaching or governing authority over the church. In all likelihood these women are called to engage in various forms of practical service in the congregation. In any case they are to be "worthy of respect, not slanderers, self-controlled, faithful in everything" (1 Tim 3:11).

§4.3.3 The Goals of Ministry

Much has already been said about the goals of various ministries in the preceding sections. Here we are left to draw some general conclusions. The LTT present two general purposes of the various ministries they specify.

1. Paul is intimately concerned in the LTT, as elsewhere, with the growth in *godliness* of God's people (§5.1.3). Both the positive instruction of God's people and the correction of false teachers are directed toward this end. Yet the LTT don't present godliness as a mere personal quality, a measure of spiritual sanctity determined simply by avoiding sin. Instead, godliness has visible outward manifestations. In 1 Timothy, Paul writes that the goal of apostolic instruction is love (1 Tim 1:5). This is true not only for Paul himself but also for his delegates and the elders they appoint.

[373] See the discussion and literature cited in Köstenberger, "1–2 Timothy, Titus," 529–30. In addition, note J. Hübner, *A Case for Female Deacons* (Eugene, OR: Wipf & Stock, 2014); J. McKinley, "Towards a Fuller Expression of Complementarianism in the Church" (paper presented at the annual meeting of the Evangelical Theological Society, San Diego, CA, November 21, 2014). Among translations the CSB has "wives" (footnote: "Or *The women*"); the NASB "women" (footnote: "I.e. either deacons' wives or deaconesses"); and the NIV "the women" (footnote: "Possibly deacons' wives or women who are deacons").

[374] See esp. 1 Tim 2:12 and the "faithful husband" requirement for elders/overseers in 1 Tim 3:2 and Titus 1:6.

This stands in contrast to the fruitlessness and godlessness of the teaching set forward by the opponents (1 Tim 1:3–11; 6:3–5; 2 Tim 3:1–5, 16–17; Titus 1:1, 15–16). The primacy of love is consistent with the OT commandments (e.g., Lev 19:18; Exod 20:1–17; Deut 6:4–9; Mic 6:8) as summarized by Jesus (Matt 22:34–40) and Paul in his earlier letters (e.g., Rom 12:9–21; 1 Cor 13). Similarly in Titus, Paul writes that God's grace has appeared in order that believers might "live in a sensible, righteous and godly way in the present age," for God has redeemed them to be a people "eager to do good deeds" (Titus 2:11–14).

2. This transformed life is also directed toward *mission* (§1). The church prays for believers to be able to live peaceful and godly lives in the world so the gospel can be proclaimed and believed (1 Tim 2:1–7). The transformed lives of believers guard against the danger of God's name and teaching being defamed among unbelievers (Titus 2:1–10). Timothy is to rebuke his opponents in the hope that they be saved (2 Tim 2:24–26). As the gospel is defended against false teachers and faithfully proclaimed, it results in God's people growing in godliness and in God's glory being displayed before the unbelieving world.

§4.4 Conclusion

While explicitly mentioned only a handful of times, the church is at the heart of the biblical theology of the LTT. The letters were written to Paul's apostolic delegates to encourage them in conducting their ministries in the local congregations to which Paul had sent them, providing leadership, instruction in sound doctrine, and correction of false teaching. The dominant image in these letters is that of a household, which complements the language of "flock" and "body" used elsewhere in Scripture to describe God's people. This household image and its implications are an important contribution of these letters, providing us not only with instructions on ordering the local church but also furnishing an image of the church that informs our understanding of the roles of elder/overseer, deacon, and the other members of God's household.

Building on the theology of the OT, as well as on Jesus's and Paul's earlier teaching, the description of the church as God's household highlights the importance of order, authority, responsibility, and distinctions in role. The LTT do not, however, provide merely abstract instructions on ecclesiology. Rather, they're vitally concerned with how ministry is to be carried out in the context of the household. In this respect the dominant ministry is that of teaching, both in its formative and corrective aspects. The letters also highlight the importance of prayer, as well as the broad focus of caring for God's household, a task that pertains to teaching but also involves meeting the needs of the members, showing hospitality, and setting an example, all of which involve diligent work.

In all of this, Paul is focused on his mission of reaching the lost. The proper ordering of God's household helps fulfill this goal. The preservation of sound doctrine and the establishment of proper order and authority in local churches are twin components of reaching the lost: false teachers can be corrected; the gospel can be rightly proclaimed; and a lost world can see God's glory through the lives of his people. The LTT thus serve as an important reminder that church order and mission are intimately and integrally related.[375] We do a disservice to our goal of being involved in God's mission if we fail to take seriously the diligent stewardship of God's household. Conversely, we gain much by conceiving of the task of church leaders in terms of stewardship over God's household, caring for its diverse members and meeting their needs.

§5 The Christian Life

The LTT are eminently practical letters. Paul provides instructions for his apostolic delegates to help them address false teaching and to shepherd the churches under their care.[376] Much of what Paul writes to Timothy and Titus is aimed at helping believers know how to conduct their lives.[377] Thus Paul tells Timothy that he has written so that "if I should be delayed . . . you will know how people ought to conduct themselves in God's

[375] See Towner, "Pauline Theology or Pauline Tradition in the Pastoral Epistles," 310–11.

[376] The LTT contain a higher frequency of imperatives than any other NT book except James.

[377] In the discussion of the LTT in his *New Testament Theology*, Marshall discusses "the life of believers" on pp. 411–14. Note also J. W. Thompson, *Moral Formation according to Paul: The Context and Coherence of Pauline Ethics* (Grand Rapids: Baker, 2011), who discusses the LTT under his treatment of "Ethics and the Disputed Letters of Paul," pp. 200–206.

household" (1 Tim 3:15). He later urges him to "set an example for the believers in speech, in conduct, in love, in faith, and in purity" (1 Tim 4:12). The life of faith is connected to both salvation (§3) and eschatology (§6). It is, as Talbert has labeled it, a life "between two epiphanies."[378] Jesus Christ came and brought salvation (2 Tim 1:10; Titus 2:11), and he will return to bring judgment and final salvation (1 Tim 6:14; 2 Tim 4:1, 8; Titus 2:13). In addition, as Barram has demonstrated, Paul's mission (§1) explains "why" he strives to morally guide his churches: it "provides the crucial link between his theology and his ethics."[379]

The time between these appearances in which Christians now live their lives "is provided for training (παιδεύουσα; Titus 2:11–12) that will produce progress (ἡ προκοπή; 1 Tim 4:15) in virtuous living (1 Tim 4:7, 15; 2 Tim 3:16; Titus 2:12) and lead to inheritance of the blessed hope (Titus 2:13)."[380] Throughout the letters Paul gives instructions that address proper conduct in the church (e.g. 1 Tim 2:1–3:13; Titus 1:5–9; cf. §4) and in believers' lives in general (e.g., 1 Tim 6:1–2, 17–19; Titus 2:1–3:11; see below). Guthrie attests to the importance of virtues and ethics in the LTT when he writes that Paul "did not consider these virtues as in any sense optional extras. They are part and parcel of normal Christian standards. They stand out vividly against the background of evils to be avoided, which in themselves reflect clearly the moral environment in the midst of which the patterns of Christian behaviour were forged."[381]

In examining this theme, it'll be particularly instructive to note the role of both positive and negative examples throughout the letters. Paul reminds Timothy of his own way of life (2 Tim 1:13) and stresses that both Timothy and Titus are to be examples to those under their care (1 Tim 4:12; Titus 2:6–8). The false teachers, too, serve an important role in this respect. Paul does not simply refer to them so that Timothy, Titus, and the people in their congregations can be on guard against them. They also serve as negative examples—as a foil for Paul's instruction of his

[378] Talbert, "Between Two Epiphanies."

[379] Barram, *Mission and Moral Reflection in Paul*, 139–40. See also R. G. Grams, "Gospel and Mission in Paul's Ethics" (Ph.D. diss., Duke University, 1989).

[380] Talbert, "Between Two Epiphanies," 59–60.

[381] D. Guthrie, *New Testament Theology* (Downers Grove: InterVarsity, 1981), 922.

apostolic delegates—whose teaching and lifestyle exhibit what the Christian life ought not to look like.[382] This is seen perhaps most clearly in Paul's words to Timothy with regard to ascetic false teachers. Following a brief discussion of their error, Paul writes, "If you point these things out to the brothers and sisters, you will be a good servant of Christ Jesus, nourished by the words of the faith and the good teaching that you have followed. But have nothing to do with pointless and silly myths. Rather, train yourself in godliness" (1 Tim 4:6–7). As a result, the Christian life in the LTT can be examined through the positive instructions Paul gives and also through the negative portrayals of the false teachers.

The ethical instruction of the LTT can largely, though not exclusively, be considered under the rubric of virtues (§6.3).[383] Virtue lists, and their negative counterparts, vice lists, occur regularly in the NT, including in Paul's earlier letters and the LTT.[384] As J. D. Charles observes, during the Socratic era philosophical reflection on ἀρετή ("virtue") moved from the theoretical dimension toward its practical outworking.[385] Ethical lists had an epideictic function, that is, they were designed to bestow praise or shame on individuals in one's audience. By standardizing a type of attitude or behavior, ethical lists thus became common fixtures in paraenetic (hortatory) discourse. Plato, in his *Republic*, identified four cardinal virtues: courage, wisdom, prudence, and justice. Similarly, there were four cardinal vices: folly, licentiousness, injustice, and cowardice.[386] The Stoics continued to develop ethical catalogs, in particular as part of the rhetorical arsenal of moral philosophers.

---

[382] See Talbert, "Between Two Epiphanies," 66–68.

[383] Owing to space constraints, not every quality listed in Paul's virtue lists will be addressed here but only those that are particularly important in the LTT. For a discussion of the remainder of these virtues, see the commentary.

[384] C. G. Kruse, "Virtues and Vices," *DPL* 692–93; virtue lists: Gal 5:22–23; Phil 4:8–9; Col 3:12; vice lists: Rom 1:29–31; 13:13; 1 Cor 5:9–11; 6:9–10; 2 Cor 12:20; Gal 5:19–21; Eph 5:3–5; Col 3:5, 8.

[385] J. D. Charles, "Vice and Virtue Lists," 1252–57, to whom some of the following discussion is indebted. In addition to the bibliography mentioned in the following footnotes, see also the resources listed at III.D. in the Introduction.

[386] Ibid.; D. J. Downs, "Vices and Virtues, Lists of," in *Dictionary of Scripture and Ethics*, ed. J. B. Green (Grand Rapids: Baker, 2011), 808–9; J. T. Fitzgerald, "Virtue/Vice Lists," *ABD* 6:857.

Most scholars today believe that "NT ethical catalogs in form and function derive from Hellenistic usage."[387]

The LTT contain the densest usage of ethical lists in the NT, which may suggest that "the foundations of morality are being called into question."[388] Notably, Titus 2:12 features adverbial forms of three of the four above-mentioned Platonic cardinal virtues (wisdom, prudence, and justice), together with the verb παιδεύω ("to train").[389] This concentration of virtue terminology designates the ethical end of salvation, in keeping with the moral goal upheld by Greek philosophy.[390] N. J. McEleney identifies five basic elements in the LTT: (1) reference to the law; (2) background of pagan idolatry; (3) moral dualism (virtue versus vice); (4) transfer of Hellenistic conceptions of virtue and vice to the Christian context; and (5) end-time punishment.[391] It's sometimes argued that the focus on virtues and the tenor of the LTT's ethical instruction served to help integrate the church with society in order to preserve its stability while isolation would have threatened the church's existence.[392] However, this misses the close connection in the LTT not only between ethics and mission (§1) but also between ethics and eschatology (§6.3).

In general terms NT virtue lists display both similarities and differences in comparison with pagan ethical lists. With regard to similarities, the qualifications for elders listed in 1 Timothy 3 resemble those for military generals and other public officials. Likewise, the ethical lists in Phil 4:8; Titus 1:7–8; and 3:1–2

---

[387] Charles, "Virtues and Vices," 1254, who cites an array of Greco-Roman ethical literature including Philo (ca. 20 BC–AD 50), Seneca (ca. 4 BC–AD 65), Epictetus (ca. AD 50–130), Musonius Rufus (ca. AD 65–80), Dio Chrysostom (ca. AD 40–120), and Plutarch (AD 50–120). See also J. D. Charles, *Virtue Amidst Vice: The Catalog of Virtues in 2 Peter 1*, JSNTSup 150 (Sheffield: Sheffield Academic Press, 1997).

[388] Charles, "Vice and Virtue Lists," 1255, who notes the affinity with 2 Peter (on virtue and vice lists in the non-Pauline corpus, see D. G. Reid, "Virtues and Vices," *DNTLD* 1190–94). See also J. T. Fitzgerald, "Virtue/Vice Lists," *ABD* 6:857–59; C. G. Kruse, "Virtues and Vices," *DPL* 962–63.

[389] S. C. Mott, "Greek Ethics and Christian Conversion: The Philonic Background of Titus 2:10–14 and 3:3–7," *NovT* 20 (1978): 22–48.

[390] See also the reference to "training in righteousness" in 2 Tim 3:16.

[391] N. J. McEleney, "The Vice Lists of the Pastoral Epistles," *CBQ* 36 (1974): 203–19.

[392] Schnelle, *Theology of the New Testament*, 592, as part of a section on the ethics of the LTT (pp. 589–92); see similarly Dibelius and Conzelmann, *Pastoral Epistles*, 39–41.

are similar to their pagan counterparts.[393] Conversely, NT virtue lists such as those in Gal 5:22–23 and 1 Tim 6:1 are distinctively Christian. Two further points regarding Paul's stress of virtues vis-à-vis the surrounding culture should be made. First, Paul's treatment of ethics and virtues only aligns with the culture at certain points. To be sure, he desires for there to be peace with the surrounding culture if possible, but this is ultimately for the goal of *mission*, not simply stability or survival (1 Tim 2:1–7; 4:6–10; 5:14; 6:1; Titus 2:1–14).[394] At other times the ethics and virtues presented are countercultural.[395] Paul's injunctions to women to avoid costly and immodest attire, for example, stand in contrast to prevailing cultural norms (1 Tim 2:9–10),[396] and his admonition to slaves casts them in the role of benefactors to their masters (1 Tim 6:1–2).[397] The LTT, and 2 Timothy in particular, also contain repeated exhortations to endure suffering inflicted by the culture for the sake of the gospel in order that people might be saved: Paul suffers for the gospel "to the point of being bound like a criminal. But the word of God is not bound. This is why I endure all things for the elect: so that they also may obtain salvation, which is in Christ Jesus, with

---

[393] B. S. Easton, "New Testament Ethical Lists," *JBL* 51 (1932): 11; see several examples (in Greek with English translation) in Dibelius and Conzelmann, *Pastoral Epistles*, 158–60.

[394] Contra the *bürgerliches Christentum* proposal of Dibelius and Conzelmann, *Pastoral Epistles*, 158–60.

[395] Towner, *Letters to Timothy and Titus*, 387 observes: "Paul has been known to co-opt the language and concepts so dominant in his culture in the effort to redefine, challenge and rather intentionally subvert the 'givens' of his day on the basis of the transforming truth of the gospel he preached." He later adds, "Tension is unavoidably created as God's values clash with the world's. Paradoxically, the household codes sought to control the effects of this tension while also sustaining it; they kept Christians engaged in the culture and urged against any radical dismantling of the social structure. Yet the instruction also encourages critical assessment of traditional assumptions and values that shape the institutions, by placing human household relationships under the Lordship of Christ and redefining things such as honor and benefaction with agape and service" (p. 389).

[396] See S. M. Baugh, "A Foreign World: Ephesus in the First Century," in *Women in the Church*, 3rd ed., 57–58; B. W. Winter, *Roman Wives, Roman Widows: The Appearance of New Women and the Pauline Communities* (Grand Rapids: Eerdmans, 2003), 97–109; and D. T. Thornton, *Hostility in the House of God: An Investigation of the Opponents in 1 and 2 Timothy*, BBRSup 15 (Winona Lake, IN: Eisenbrauns, 2016), 105–6.

[397] See Towner, *Letters to Timothy and Titus*, 385–88.

eternal glory" (2 Tim 2:9–10; §5.2.1). A final distinctive element of the LTT vice lists is that they at times occur in polemical or eschatological contexts (e.g., 1 Tim 1:9–10; 6:3–5; 2 Tim 3:2–5; §6.3).

Second, while the *form* of Paul's lists, both here and elsewhere in his letters (e.g., Gal 5:19–23; Eph 4:25–32; Col 3:12–14), is almost certainly styled after that of Greek ethical lists, the *content* is not uniquely Hellenistic.[398] The underlying basis for all of Paul's instructions is twofold: the Scriptures (1 Tim 4:13; 2 Tim 3:15–17; §2.7)[399] and apostolic teaching (1 Tim 4:6; 2 Tim 2:2; Titus 1:3; §2.1).[400] This connection with Scripture and tradition is important, especially since we enter into Paul's conversation with Timothy and Titus (and the churches at Ephesus and Crete) midstream, as it were. Paul had spent significant time with each of these men teaching and instructing them, and as the LTT make clear, the basis for that instruction was not Hellenistic ethics but God's Word.[401] While Paul has no hesitation in using forms derived from his culture, therefore, even content that overlapped and resonated with the culture, his primary frame of reference consists of OT ethics and apostolic teaching.[402] In considering the Christian

[398] However, the virtue lists contain fewer parallels in Hellenistic Judaism; C. G. Kruse, "Virtues and Vices," *DPL* 963. See G. E. Ladd, *A Theology of the New Testament*, rev. ed., ed. D. A. Hagner (Grand Rapids: Eerdmans, 1993), 557.

[399] This likely includes the Gospel of Luke that is already being considered Scripture. See commentary on 1 Tim 5:18; 2 Tim 3:14–17.

[400] See Towner, *Goal of Our Instruction*, 167, who says that "Christian existence is the interplay between correct (apostolic) doctrine, as the basis of faith in Christ, and outward, corresponding behavior."

[401] Thompson highlights the "integral relationship between Paul's theological and moral reflection" (*Mission and Moral Reflection in Paul*, 137), a point also highlighted in V. P. Furnish, *Theology and Ethics in Paul* (1968; repr., NTL; Louisville: Westminster John Knox, 2009); and Towner, *Goal of Our Instruction*.

[402] We shouldn't neglect relevant background information, as this may be important for properly interpreting Paul's teaching. Nevertheless, we also need to take seriously what Paul himself identifies as his source(s) of instruction and authority and what he constantly sets forward, and commands to be set forward, namely Scripture and the apostolic teaching. As to why Paul uses Hellenistic moral vocabulary in the LTT, Fee's comment on εὐσέβεια may point us in the right direction: "For many it is difficult to imagine Paul's using such a word, which belongs to Hellenism and Hellenistic Judaism (see esp. Ecclesiasticus and 4 Maccabees), to describe either the Christian faith or Christian behavior. But the answer to this, as with many such terms in the PE . . . , lies with the false teachers. Most likely this is *their* word, being used by Paul to counteract them (cf. the use of *wisdom* in 1 Cor. 1–3)." Fee, *1–2 Timothy, Titus*, 63; similarly, D. G. Peterson, *Possessed by God: A*

life, then, we will examine love, faith and faithfulness, godliness, self-control, good works, and good citizenship.

Virtue Lists in the LTT	Vice Lists in the LTT
1 Tim 4:12	1 Tim 1:9–10
1 Tim 6:11	1 Tim 6:3–5
2 Tim 2:22	2 Tim 3:2–5
2 Tim 3:10	Titus 3:3

§5.1 Christian Virtues

Paul urges his apostolic delegates, and by implication all believers, to pursue a number of Christian virtues. Among these are love, faith and faithfulness, godliness, and self-control. In addition, he calls believers to good works and good citizenship, all in the context of bearing Christian witness in the surrounding culture. In what follows we will first discuss the primary virtues enjoined by Paul and then turn to a discussion of good works and good citizenship.

§5.1.1 Love

As Paul opens his first letter to Timothy, urging him to correct false teachers, he notes the contrast between the result of the opponents' instruction and the goal of apostolic teaching. The false teachers promote nothing but empty speculation while "the goal of our instruction is love that comes from a pure heart, a good conscience, and a sincere faith" (1 Tim 1:4–5).[403] Love is not only assigned a place of central importance in this opening passage but continues to occupy a prominent position throughout the LTT.[404] In the first place, Paul affirms that love ultimately flows from God:

New Testament Theology of Sanctification and Holiness, NSBT 1 (Downers Grove: InterVarsity, 2001), 89.

[403] On the use of "love" vocabulary in the LTT, see R. Fuchs, "Ist 'die Agape das Ziel der Unterweisung' (1. Tim 1,5)? Zum unterschiedlichen Gebrauch des ἀγαπ- und des φιλ- Wortstammes in den Schreiben an Timotheus und Titus," *JETh* 18 (2004): 93–125.

[404] See T. B. Madsen II, "The Ethics of the Pastoral Epistles," in *Entrusted with the Gospel*, 228–29. Paul's instructions use both the ἀγαπάω word group and the φιλέω word group, the latter being used exclusively in compound words. See commentary on 1 Tim 1:6 for a discussion of the usage of these two word groups. Note that C. Spicq, one of the more important commentators on the LTT, has also produced *Agapè dans le Nouveau Testament: analyse des textes*, 3 vols. (Paris: Gabalda, 1958–1959), translated as *Agape in the New Testament*, 3 vols., trans. M. A. McNamara and

"And the grace of our Lord overflowed, along with the faith and love that are in Christ Jesus" (1 Tim 1:14). The same idea recurs in his second letter to Timothy, where he encourages him to "rekindle the gift of God" he had received: "For God has not given us a spirit of fear, but one of power, love, and sound judgment" (2 Tim 1:6–7).

Love, having its source in God, is also to be pursued as part of the Christian life. In the LTT, it most frequently occurs in virtue lists. Paul's own love is evident in the introductions to each of his letters, identifying Timothy as his "true son in the faith" (1 Tim 1:1) and "dearly loved son" (2 Tim 1:2) and Titus as his "true son" (Titus 1:4). In his directions regarding proper conduct in the church, Paul exhorts women to pursue love, along with faith, holiness, and good judgment (σωφροσύνη; §5.1.4)[405] as they devote themselves to their domestic and familial roles (1 Tim 2:15).[406] Shortly afterward, he lists two qualifications for overseers related to love: they're to be hospitable, that is, to love strangers (1 Tim 3:2, φιλόξενον) but must not love money (1 Tim 3:3, ἀφιλάργυρον), a vice later identified as "a root of all kinds of evil" that causes people to stray from the faith (1 Tim 6:10). Paul also urges Timothy to set an example for believers in love, listing it as a virtue alongside speech, conduct, faith, and purity (1 Tim 4:12). Slaves who have believing masters are to serve them all the more since their masters are "dearly loved" (ἀγαπητοί; 1 Tim 6:2). Later Paul tells Timothy to flee from the vices associated with the false teachers and to pursue love, along with righteousness, godliness, faith, endurance, and gentleness (1 Tim 6:11).

Paul also highlights the importance of pursuing love against the backdrop of the failure of the false teachers. In direct contrast to the apostolic instruction, which has as its goal "love that comes from a pure heart, a good conscience, and a sincere faith" (1 Tim 1:5), the opponents "have departed from these and turned aside to fruitless discussion" (1 Tim 1:6), eschewing God's order and love.[407] They're further identified as men who view godliness as a means to material gain and as those who love money (φιλαργυρία) and in

M. H. Richter (1963–66; repr., Eugene, OR: Wipf & Stock, 2006), with instances of ἀγάπη in the LTT being discussed in vol. 2.

[405] The high occurrence of the σωφρονέω word group is a unique feature of the LTT.

[406] See the commentary for a discussion of this challenging verse.

[407] See Towner, *Letters to Timothy and Titus*, 119–20.

pursuing riches have "wandered away from the faith and pierced themselves with many griefs" (1 Tim 6:10). Timothy, for his part, is not to be like them (1 Tim 6:11–12).

Similar admonitions are found in 2 Timothy. Paul speaks of adhering to the sound teaching "in the faith and love that are in Christ Jesus" (2 Tim 1:13). In an exhortation that is similar to that found in 1 Tim 6:11, he tells Timothy to "flee from youthful passions" and to pursue love along with righteousness, faith, and peace (2 Tim 2:22). Paul presents his own life as an example to Timothy, with love being one of the qualities that Timothy has emulated, along with his teaching, conduct, purpose, faith, patience, endurance, and sufferings (2 Tim 3:10). At the end of the letter, Paul says he looks forward to a future reward, "the crown of righteousness," which is reserved for "all those who have loved his appearing" (2 Tim 4:8). He then closely contrasts this with the example of Demas, who deserted Paul "since he loved this present world" (2 Tim 4:10).

Demas isn't the only negative example of love in 2 Timothy. Paul says that in the last days people will display various kinds of unloving behavior. Among other ungodly characteristics they will be "lovers of self" (φίλαυτοι), "lovers of money" (φιλάργυροι), "unloving" (ἄστοργοι), "without love for what is good" (ἀφιλάγαθοι), and "lovers of pleasure" (φιλήδονοι) rather than being "lovers of God" (φιλόθεοι; 2 Tim 3:1–4).[408] It's not only that the ungodly don't exhibit love but that the love they do exhibit is seriously misdirected. They love what they ought not to love! Finally, although "love" terminology is not used, Phygelus and Hermogenes, who had deserted Paul, and the household of Onesiphorus, who had searched diligently for Paul in Rome and refreshed him, are contrasting examples of those who did or didn't demonstrate love (2 Tim 1:15–17).

Paul's instructions concerning love in Titus fall along similar lines. As in 1 Timothy, elders are to be appointed who are hospitable (i.e., those who love strangers, φιλόξενον) and who love what is good (φιλάγαθον; Titus 1:8). Titus is to teach older men to be "sound in faith, love, and endurance," along with being self-controlled, respectable, and sensible (Titus 2:2). Similarly, older women are to teach the younger women to be lovers of their husbands (φιλάνδρους) and children (φιλοτέκνους; Titus 2:4). Paul also

[408] Almost one-third of the negative characteristics in these verses involve love.

describes God's love for humankind (φιλανθρωπία) as the basis for our salvation (Titus 3:4). While this is not directly set forth as a virtue, God's kindness and love are set in contrast with the behavior of unbelievers of whom we were once a part: "foolish, disobedient, deceived, enslaved by various passions and pleasures, living in malice and envy, hateful, detesting one another" (Titus 3:3). God's love thus implicitly forms an expectation for how we are to live. As Towner states, "Yet the main point in describing the epiphany as a display of these specific virtues—as a demonstration of God's character—is to explain that God has communicated the qualities needed to live the life prescribed in 3:1–2."[409]

We may sum up the essence of the LTT's teaching on love as follows.

1. Love is seen as the primary Christian virtue. The LTT not only explicitly affirm the centrality of love in the Christian life (1 Tim 1:5) but implicitly demonstrate this through the prevalence of love terminology in virtue lists and other ethical admonitions. Timothy and Titus are to pursue love themselves and should help the believers in Ephesus and Crete to do so as well.

2. Love isn't only urged positively but illustrated negatively. Both the false teachers and the unbelieving world are characterized, not so much as unloving, but as loving the wrong things. Rejecting God and hating others is but one type of failure to love. Negative examples help illustrate what a lack of love looks like: to love pleasure or money or oneself or to be caught up in fruitless discussions—all of these are marks of a failure to love as God desires.

3. There's a close connection between love and faith in the LTT.[410] The two are regularly paired, sometimes by themselves (1 Tim 1:5; 2 Tim 1:13) but more commonly with other virtues.[411] Along with love, faith is the central virtue in the LTT. The LTT,

---

[409] Towner, *Letters to Timothy and Titus*, 778–79.

[410] Towner rightly views the sense of "faith and love" in 2 Tim 1:13 as equivalent to their sense in "Gal 5:6 ('... faith working itself out through love') as a summary of Christian existence.... Together the two terms encompass the vertical relationship of trust in God and the horizontal outworking of this in service to others" (*Letters to Timothy and Titus*, 142).

[411] E.g., 1 Tim 1:14; 2:15; 2 Tim 2:22; Titus 2:2. This is but one more area in which Paul's theology in the LTT is thoroughly consistent with his theology in his other letters (1 Cor 13:13; Gal 5:6, 22–23; Eph 1:15; 6:23; Col 1:4; 1 Thess 1:3; 3:6; 5:8; 2 Thess 1:3; Phlm 5). See Marshall, *Pastoral Epistles*, 215.

and Scripture as a whole, remove any pretention that it is possible to have sound faith but lack love. Thus failure to love isn't simply an ethical shortcoming; it's a deficiency that is profoundly theological.

§5.1.2 Faith and Faithfulness

Faith is one of the key concepts in the LTT.[412] The "faith" word group occurs sixty-one times in the LTT, an extremely high number given the brevity of the letters.[413] In the LTT the majority of references are to "faith" (πίστις), which tends to pertain to "the faith," that is, the authoritative body of Christian teaching and belief.[414] Of thirty-two occurrences,[415] about half refer to the content of faith,[416] while the other half refer to the believer's trust in God.[417] When compared with Paul's earlier letters, the LTT demonstrate a greater focus on the former but not to the exclusion of the latter.[418] In fact, there is a close connection between individual

[412] Marshall, "Faith and Works in the Pastoral Epistles," *SNTSU-A* 9 (1984): 216; Marshall, *Pastoral Epistles*, 214, as part of an excursus on the πίστις word group (pp. 135–44). See also R. F. Collins, *I & II Timothy and Titus*, 93–95; W. Eisele, "Der gemeinsame Glaube der Auserwählten Gottes: Zum Glaubensbegriff der Pastoralbriefe nach Tit 1,1–4," in *Ein Meisterschüler: Titus und sein Brief. Michael Theobald zum 60. Geburtstag*, ed. H.-U. Weidemann and W. Eisele, SBS 214 (Stuttgart: Katholisches Bibelwerk, 2008), 81–114; G. Kretschmar, "Der paulinische Glaube in den Pastoralbriefen," in *Glaube im Neuen Testament: Studien zu Ehren von Hermann Binder anläßlich seines 70. Geburtstags*, ed. F. Hahn and H. Klein (Neukirchener-Vluyn: Neukirchener, 1982), 115–40; B. Mutschler, *Glaube in den Pastoralbriefen: Pistis als Mitte christlicher Existenz*, WUNT 256 (Tübingen: Mohr-Siebeck, 2010); Quinn, *Titus*, 271–75 ("*Pistis* Terminology in the PE").

[413] The number of occurrences of the various words is as follows: πίστις (33); πιστός (17); πιστεύω (6); ἄπιστος (2); ἀπιστέω (1); ἀπιστία (1); πιστόω (1). First Timothy and Titus have the two highest concentrations of the πιστ- word group in the NT, with 2 Timothy only three spots behind, following 2 Thessalonians and Galatians.

[414] Schnelle, *Theology of the New Testament*, 588.

[415] There are actually thirty-three uses of πίστις, but the reference in 1 Tim 5:12 refers not to Christian faith but to a "pledge."

[416] 1 Tim 1:2, 19; 3:9, 13; 4:1, 6; 5:8; 6:10, 12, 21; 2 Tim 3:8; 4:7; Titus 1:4, 13; 2:2; 3:15.

[417] 1 Tim 1:4, 5, 14, 19 (there are two occurrences in this verse, in all likelihood being used in two different ways); 2:7, 15; 4:12; 6:11; 2 Tim 1:5, 13; 2:18, 22; 3:10, 15; Titus 1:1. The other occurrence, Titus 2:10, refers to trustworthiness. The active focus of faith is also present in the uses of πιστεύω, πίστις, and the instances where α-prefixed negatives are used (ἄπιστος, ἀπιστέω, ἀπιστία). See the discussion in Towner, *Letters to Timothy and Titus*, 99n31.

[418] The more frequent reference of πίστις to the content of faith is often adduced as evidence of a later, pseudonymous authorship of the LTT (see, e.g., Dunn, *Neither*

faith and "the faith" in the LTT, which simply brings into sharper focus what is already present in Paul's earlier letters (Gal 1:6–10; 3:1–14; Col 2:1–23), namely that the personal dimension of trusting *in* God is closely tied to right belief *about* God. This section will focus on the active aspect of trusting in God. The role of faith and faithfulness in the LTT can be helpfully discussed in two ways: (1) faith as a virtue; and (2) faith and salvation.

§5.1.2.1 Faith as a Virtue

The centrality of faith for the Christian life is highlighted at the beginning of Paul's first letter to Timothy where Paul urges his foremost disciple to correct the opponents whose teachings "promote empty speculations rather than God's plan, which operates by faith" (1 Tim 1:4). God has ordered his redemptive purposes so that faith is the driving dynamic by which his plan is accomplished.[419] This is true both for salvation (see below) and the Christian life as a whole. The importance of faith in the Christian life is further attested in v. 5, where Paul lists "sincere faith" as one of the qualities that lead to love, which is "the goal of [his] instruction." The importance of faith for living the Christian life is highlighted further at the end of the opening section, where Paul encourages Timothy to carry on the fight, which requires having "faith and a good conscience" (v. 19).[420] Three times in this opening section, Paul affirms that the Christian life is to be lived by faith. This stands in contrast to false teachers such as Hymenaeus and Philetus who through their teaching were "ruining the faith of some" (2 Tim 2:18).

Paul also highlights the role of faith in the Christian life through his own testimony. Though he was a blasphemer and persecutor of the church who acted in unbelief (ἀπιστίᾳ), "the grace of our Lord overflowed, along with the faith and love that are in Christ Jesus" (1 Tim 1:14). As discussed above (§5.1.1), there's a strong connection between faith and love in the LTT as they address "the vertical relationship of trust in God and the horizontal outworking

Jew nor Greek, 679–80), but this is easily explained by the recipients of the letters being Paul's coworkers with whom he uses more specialized terminology.

[419] See Marshall, *Pastoral Epistles*, 368.

[420] See Knight, *Pastoral Epistles*, 109.

of this in service to others."[421] Paul also encourages women in the pursuit of faith, love, holiness, and good judgment as they carry out their responsibilities as wives and mothers (1 Tim 2:15). He also urges Timothy to pursue love, which both sets an example for other believers (1 Tim 4:12) and distinguishes him from the false teachers (1 Tim 6:11).

First Timothy also stresses the importance of faithfulness in the believer's life. Paul's own testimony, as mentioned, is that God showed him mercy as one who acted in unbelief (ἀπιστίᾳ; 1 Tim 1:13); the gospel was entrusted (ἐπιστεύθην) to him (v. 11), and God considered him to be faithful (πιστόν; v. 12). The point isn't that God determined that Paul was trustworthy and therefore saved him and called him to ministry but that God's calling made the unbelieving Paul faithful. As Towner helpfully articulates, the focus is on "the potency of divine calling to achieve certain results in human lives."[422] The importance of faithfulness in the Christian life surfaces four more times, all in relation to how Timothy is to ensure order in the household of God. Three of these pertain to those with responsibility in the church: elders and deacons are to be faithful husbands (3:2, 12),[423] and "the widow who is truly in need" (5:16) too, must have been faithful in marriage (1 Tim 5:9). Female deacons (or deacon's wives)[424] should be women who are "faithful in everything" (1 Tim 3:11), In these passages, then, there's an overlap between faith in God and faithfulness toward others. Faithfulness is a mark of those who possess and pursue faith in God.

In his second letter to Timothy, Paul continues to sound the theme of pursuing faith. He once again sets this forward as a goal for Timothy (2 Tim 1:13; 2:22), noting also that faith, along with other virtues, characterized his own life as well (2 Tim 3:10). Paul also encourages Timothy on the basis of his "sincere faith" (2 Tim 1:5), a statement that speaks well of Timothy's ability to carry on Paul's ministry and contrasts him with the false teachers who have

---

[421] Towner, *Letters to Timothy and Titus*, 142; see Marshall, *Pastoral Epistles*, 390; Mounce, *Pastoral Epistles*, 51.

[422] Towner, *Letters to Timothy and Titus*, 138.

[423] See commentary at 1 Tim 3:2.

[424] See commentary at 1 Tim 3:11.

"the form of godliness but [deny] its power" (2 Tim 3:5).[425] The importance of faithfulness surfaces twice in 2 Timothy. Timothy is to pass on the apostolic teaching to "faithful men" who will continue to teach it faithfully (2 Tim 2:2). Thus just as Paul (1 Tim 1:11) and Timothy (1 Tim 6:20; 2 Tim 1:14) were entrusted with the gospel, so now the message must be passed on to others. Faithfulness, then, must be understood not simply as intellectual competency but as spiritual fidelity. These are men who have trusted in God, having accepted the apostolic message, whose lives are marked by faith.[426]

The pursuit of faith as a virtue is less prevalent in Titus. Nevertheless, in his opening greeting Paul notes that his ministry has as one of its purposes to build up "the faith of God's elect" (Titus 1:1). The importance of faithfulness is expressed when Paul tells Titus what he told Timothy: that God has entrusted him (ἐπιστεύθην) with his message (Titus 1:3)[427] and that elders are to be faithful in their marriages (Titus 1:6). In addition to focusing on the pursuit of faith and the demonstration of faithfulness, the LTT also, in typical Pauline fashion, stress that faith is central for salvation.

§5.1.2.2 Faith and Salvation

As in all of Paul's letters, salvation is presented in the LTT as being appropriated by faith. The letters don't contain an explicit defense of this doctrine, which isn't surprising considering their recipients. Rather, in addition to some short sections commenting on being saved by faith, the concept is presupposed and occurs throughout the letters as a foundational reality that propels believers on in the life of faith. Paul's assertion that God's plan operates by faith (1 Tim 1:4) not only implicitly affirms that salvation is built upon faith[428] but sets this salvation in contrast to the false teachers whose instruction promotes speculation rather than love (vv. 3, 5).

---

[425] The contrast between Timothy and Paul and these teachers is made explicit in 2 Tim 3:10.

[426] The lexical connection between being "faithful" (πίστος) and being "entrusted" (πιστεύω) only occurs in 1 Tim 1:11. First Timothy 6:20 and 2 Tim 1:14 use παραθήκη, a word which is nonetheless in the same semantic range. See L&N, "παραθήκη, -ης," 1:463.

[427] The message itself is declared to be faithful (πιστοῦ) shortly after this (Titus 1:9).

[428] Knight, *Pastoral Epistles*, 76, states that "what is referred to is the outworking, administration, or stewardship of God's plan of salvation through the gospel and its communication."

Paul presents his own life as a testimony to this reality. While he had previously acted in unbelief (ἀπιστίᾳ), God's grace overflowed into his life and he became "an example to those who would believe in him for eternal life" (1 Tim 1:16). God's plan operates by faith, and Paul has been appointed a herald, apostle, and teacher to the Gentiles "in faith and truth" (1 Tim 2:7).[429] The "mystery of godliness" in 1 Tim 3:16 includes the assertion that Christ was "believed on in the world." In his second letter Paul tells Timothy similarly that the Scriptures give wisdom that leads to salvation "through faith in Christ Jesus" (2 Tim 3:15).

In addition, in both 2 Timothy and Titus there are explicit assertions that salvation is by faith, not works: "He has saved us and called us with a holy calling, not according to our works, but according to his own purpose and grace, which was given to us in Christ Jesus before time began" (2 Tim 1:9); "But when the kindness of God our Savior and his love for mankind appeared, he saved us—not by works of righteousness that we had done, but according to his mercy, through the washing of regeneration and renewal by the Holy Spirit" (Titus 3:4–5).

While faith is not explicitly mentioned in either of these verses, its presence in the LTT in the immediate contexts of both passages (cf. 2 Tim 1:12; Titus 3:8) and the fact that God is the giver of this salvation strongly suggest that faith is the human means of receiving the salvation God is bestowing. Marshall maintains, "The total disqualification of works is a clear indicator that the only possible response to grace is faith."[430] In fact, God's grace is so great and his sovereignty so all encompassing that even in the face of human faithlessness (ἀπιστέω) God remains faithful to his gracious promises (2 Tim 2:13).[431]

Finally, the first letter to Timothy features another, slightly more implicit way of presenting faith's role in salvation. Six times in the letter, Paul refers to Christians as those who believe (1 Tim

[429] T. Lea and H. P. Griffin Jr., *1, 2 Timothy, Titus*, NAC 34 (Nashville: B&H, 1992), 92, affirm that "faith" here refers to "the subjective response to the gospel." See also Knight, *Pastoral Epistles*, 127.

[430] Marshall, *Pastoral Epistles*, 216.

[431] J. M. Bassler, "'He Remains Faithful' (2 Tim 2:13a)," in *Theology and Ethics in Paul and His Interpreters: Essays in Honor of Victor Paul Furnish*, ed. E. H. Lovering Jr. and J. L. Sumney (Nashville: Abingdon, 1996), 183.

4:3, 10, 12; 5:16; 6:2 [2x]). In each case the term πιστός ("faithful") is applied to believers. The use of πιστός to designate believers occurs relatively infrequently outside the first letter to Timothy (cf. Acts 10:45; 16:1; 2 Cor 6:15; 1 Pet 1:21).[432] Christians are not foundationally those who love or are pious or possess any other distinguishing characteristic; they are first and foremost those who *believe*.

The LTT also connect faith and good works. Paul affirms that the outworking of faith, along with a pure heart and good conscience, is love, which is the goal of his instruction. The Christian life of love, which implies love for both God and others, and therefore involves good works, is impossible apart from faith (§5.1.1). In 1 Tim 1:19 Paul exhorts Timothy to engage in battle and to carry out his ministry in the face of difficulties, including dealing with false teachers. The means by which he is to do so are faith and a good conscience.[433] The lack of such qualities led false teachers such as Hymenaeus and Alexander to shipwreck the faith and to be handed over to Satan (1 Tim 1:19–20). Thus not only does faith lead to good works, but the lack of faith leads to spiritual bankruptcy. This portrayal of the importance of faith for good works by its converse is also seen in Titus 1:15, where the unbelieving (ἀπίστοις) are said not only to deny God by their works but also to be disqualified from every good work.

What should be evident from this discussion is that the LTT envision the entirety of the Christian life, from salvation onward, as operating by faith. While some have argued for the absence of justification by faith from the LTT,[434] Marshall concludes that "this verdict flies in the face of the evidence," citing 2 Tim 1:9, 12 and Titus 3:4–8.[435] It's true that the LTT stress the role of good works (§5.2), but this is not materially different from Paul's other letters (e.g., Eph 2:10; Phil 2:12–13). And while Paul in the LTT discusses grace less than in some of his other letters,[436] grace is nonetheless

[432] Πιστεύω is also used as a substantival participle to refer to a believer in 1 Cor 14:22 (2x) and 1 Thess 2:10.

[433] See Towner, *Letters to Timothy and Titus*, 157–58.

[434] See B. S. Easton, *The Pastoral Epistles* (New York: Scribner, 1947), 203–4.

[435] Marshall, *Pastoral Epistles*, 216.

[436] Χάρις occurs only thirteen times in the LTT: five times in 2 Timothy and four times each in 1 Timothy and Titus.

present and serves as the basis for salvation (1 Tim 1:14; 2 Tim 1:9; Titus 2:11; 3:7).

The emphasis on faith, not only in salvation but also in the Christian life, is further evidence that faith is the primary focal point of the Christian life. Paul makes this point explicit in the opening of his first letter to Timothy: God's entire redemptive plan (οἰκονομία) operates by faith (1 Tim 1:4). As Madsen observes, "The life that pleases God begins with his own redemptive acts and follows as a response to them. We do what we are, and our lives are an outworking of several definitive and irreversible changes secured by the cross and effected individually by the Spirit."[437] The Christian life and pursuit of virtues is therefore thoroughly God centered: it is initiated by him (1 Tim 1:14; Titus 3:4–7), focused on him (1 Tim 1:4, 17; 2 Tim 4:18), empowered by him (1 Tim 1:12; 2 Tim 3:16–17; 4:17–18; Titus 3:15), and lived in anticipation of him (1 Tim 6:14; 2 Tim 4:1; Titus 2:13).[438]

§5.1.3 Godliness

The concept of "godliness" or "piety" (εὐσέβεια) was prevalent in Greco-Roman virtue lists and inscriptions, referring generally to reverence and more specifically to behavior that was pleasing to the gods, including in carrying out cultic responsibilities.[439] The term is rare in the NT, occurring outside the LTT only

[437] Madsen, "Ethics of the Pastoral Epistles," 224.

[438] See Talbert, "Between Two Epiphanies," 68–71.

[439] Marshall, *Pastoral Epistles*, 138, as part of an excursus on εὐσέβεια (pp. 135–44). See also Dibelius and Conzelmann, *Pastoral Epistles*, 39; M. Engelmann, *Unzertrenntliche Drillinge? Motivsemantische Untersuchungen zum literarischen Verhältnis der Pastoralbriefe*, BZNW 192 (Berlin: de Gruyter, 2012), 345–63; W. Foerster, "Εὐσέβεια in den Pastoralbriefen," *NTS* 5 (1959): 213–18; M. Silva, "σέβομαι," *NIDNTTE* 4:272–73. See also discussions in R. F. Collins, *I & II Timothy and Titus*, 122–26; S. Mathews, "'Great Is the Mystery of Godliness': A Historical and Biblical Study of ΕΥΣΕΒΕΙΑ" (Ph.D. diss., Trinity International University, 1998); Quinn, *Titus*, 282–91 ("*Eusebeia* and Its Cognates in the PE"); D. G. Peterson, "Godliness in the Pastoral Epistles," in Peterson, *Possessed by God*, 89–91; A. Standhartinger, "*Eusebeia* in den Pastoralbriefen: Ein Beitrag zum Einfluss römischen Denkens auf das enstehende Christentum," *NovT* 48 (2006): 51–82; Towner, *Letters to Timothy and Titus*, 171–75 ("Godliness and Respectability"); J. J. Wainwright, "*Eusebeia*: Syncretism or Conservative Contextualization?," *EvQ* 65 (1993): 211–24; and M. Wieger, "*Eusebeia* dans la Septante et dans les épîtres pastorales," in *Die Septuaginta—Entstehung, Sprache, Geschichte*, ed. S. Kreuzer, M. Meiser, and M. Sigismund (Tübingen: Mohr-Siebeck, 2012), 311–34.

in 2 Peter and Acts.[440] The LTT, however, contain a significant concentration of words in the εὐσεβ- word group.[441] The high number of uses in the LTT and the paucity of occurrences in the rest of the NT highlight the distinctive emphasis on the virtue of piety in the LTT.[442] The prevalence of the term in Greco-Roman culture and the scarcity of the term in the NT, except in connection with that culture, have been adduced in support of the argument that the term should be understood in light of its Hellenistic background and that it reflects an accommodation to secular cultural morality.[443] However, this ignores both the usage in the OT, including the apocrypha, as well as the fact that while the LTT seek to contextualize the Christian faith in the Hellenistic culture, they are at the same time grounded in OT and apostolic teaching.[444]

---

[440] Acts 3:12; 10:2, 7; 17:23; 2 Pet 1:3, 6, 7; 2:9; 3:11.

[441] The words occur a total of thirteen times in the LTT, predominantly in 1 Timothy. Godliness, εὐσέβεια, is used most frequently (10x), followed by εὐσεβῶς (2x) and εὐσεβέω (1x). In addition, ἀσέβια occurs twice and ἀσεβής and θεοσέβεια both occur once.

[442] The word group is used rarely in the OT, though the word occurs somewhat regularly in the apocrypha, especially 4 Maccabees. Of the ninety-six uses in the LXX, only ten occur in the canonical OT (four in Proverbs and six in Isaiah). Sixty of the remaining eighty-six occurrences occur in 4 Maccabees. Not surprisingly, 4 Maccabees is a work that seeks to demonstrate that Judaism can thrive in the Hellenistic world (see J. W. Van Henten, "Maccabees, Fourth Book of," ed. J. J. Collins and D. C. Harlow, *The Eerdmans Dictionary of Early Judaism* [Grand Rapids: Eerdmans, 2010], 910).

[443] See the discussion in Marshall, *Pastoral Epistles*, 135–44, who argues against this understanding. Cf. also Wainwright, "*Eusebeia*." In a recent dissertation Hoklotubbe engages the use of "godliness" (εὐσέβεια) in the LTT. He finds that in Greco-Roman writings, claims to *pietas* (the Latin equivalent of εὐσέβεια), because of "the virtue's broad cultural currency and prestige" (p. iii), often served to legitimate claims to power, honor, knowledge of the divine, etc.; they "advanced socio-political aims and reinforced cultural values and ideological assumptions" (p. 258). Similarly, he finds that in the LTT a pseudonymous author rhetorically engages εὐσέβεια to legitimate various (interrelated) points of his agenda, including his presentation of a reworked Pauline tradition, the reinforcement of traditional gender values, and a portrayal of the Christian community that would counter Roman suspicions of it. T. C. Hoklotubbe, "The Rhetoric of PIETAS: The Pastoral Epistles and Claims to Piety in the Roman Empire" (Th.D. diss., Harvard Divinity School, 2015).

[444] Sumney notes, "That this piety is conceived largely in terms of contemporary social values is not surprising; it is the same with all New Testament authors. And like those other writers, these values are not merely accepted. There is also dialogue (with implicit critique) and dissent." "God Our Savior: The Theology of 1 Timothy," 38.

Marshall notes that when the LXX uses εὐσέβεια and there is a Hebrew equivalent in the MT, it translates the phrase יראת יהוה, "the fear of the Lord."[445] Interestingly, where the term is prominent in the NT, the use of the φόβος word group, which is often used in the LXX to translate "fear," is less prominent. While "godliness" occurs five times in 2 Peter, the term is absent from 1 Peter,[446] yet references to fearing God are prominent in 1 Peter[447] while being absent from 2 Peter. Similarly, the φόβος word group is used twenty-one times in Acts but almost never in the same contexts as "godliness" terminology.[448] The LTT demonstrate the same pattern. While "godliness" terms abound, "fear" occurs only once, in 1 Tim 5:20, which refers specifically to fearing judgment that stems from sin.[449] The "godliness" word group, then, constituted a useful set of words to convey a similar idea to "fear of the Lord" in a Gentile context.[450] "Godliness," therefore, refers to a particular way of living that reflects knowing God and being in a close, reverent relationship with him.[451] As Marshall helpfully summarizes, "The word-group functions to describe the life (noun) or manner of life (adverb) which is true Christianity. . . . 'Godliness' has a theological basis in the Christ-event (1 Tim 3.16; 2 Tim 3.12; cf. Tit 2:12), and it is integrally related to the knowledge of God (or of the gospel, the truth, etc.; Tit 1.1; 1 Tim 6.3, 5, 6, 11)."[452]

Unlike many of the other qualities found in virtue lists, godliness normally appears outside these lists. Only in 1 Tim 6:11 and Titus 2:12 does εὐσέβεια occur paired with other virtues. Rather, Paul normally speaks of this virtue in more specific situations.[453]

---

[445] Marshall, *Pastoral Epistles*, 140.

[446] Although the related term ἀσεβής occurs once in 1 Pet 4:18.

[447] 1 Pet 1:17; 2:17, 18; 3:2; also, the use of ὁμοίως in 1 Pet 3:1, 7 flows from the "fear" that is enjoined in 1 Pet 2:18 (see Jobes, *1 Peter*, 189–90; 202–3).

[448] The exception is Acts 10:2, where Luke says Cornelius was "a devout man and feared God" (εὐσεβὴς καὶ φοβούμενος τὸν θεόν). It may be that the two terms are both used here because Cornelius is specifically being identified as a "God-fearer"; see D. Bock, *Acts*, BECNT (Grand Rapids: Baker, 2007), 385–86; E. J. Schnabel, *Acts*, ZECNT (Grand Rapids: Zondervan, 2008), 485–86.

[449] Towner, *Letters to Timothy and Titus*, 371–72; Mounce, *Pastoral Epistles*, 314.

[450] See Marshall, *Pastoral Epistles*, 140–41; Mounce, *Pastoral Epistles*, 83; Towner, *Letters to Timothy and Titus*, 173.

[451] Towner, *Letters to Timothy and Titus*, 174.

[452] Marshall, *Pastoral Epistles*, 143.

[453] Towner suggests that there is a danger in thinking of godliness as simply one virtue to be pursued. Rather, "The whole of the data strongly confirms its function

In 1 Timothy, Paul describes one of the goals of praying for those in authority as being able to live godly lives (1 Tim 2:2), connecting godliness with the goal of living on mission in pagan society.[454] Paul directly ties godliness to the life, death, resurrection, ascension, and preaching of Christ (1 Tim 3:16), grounding the term theologically rather than merely culturally.[455] Godliness is to be demonstrated also in families with widows where children and grandchildren must "learn to practice godliness toward their own family first and to repay their parents, for this pleases God" (1 Tim 5:4).

Throughout the LTT Paul uses the false teachers as foils for true shepherds and by extension for how Christians should live.[456] This is not simply a rhetorical move but an essential application of what it means to pursue godliness. Because godliness is connected with a right knowledge of God, it follows that sound doctrine will lead to godliness and false doctrine will fail to have this effect. In 1 Timothy, the false teachers, who are intent on making use of the law, misconstrue how the law actually functions. It is not meant for the righteous but for those who live in opposition to the gospel, including the "ungodly" (ἀσεβέσι; 1 Tim 1:9–11). Paul later draws a contrast between true godliness and the false teachers who forbid marriage and certain foods (4:1–5). But asceticism is not a mark of godliness; while such practices involve harsh treatment of the body, they don't build spiritual maturity and Christlikeness. While physical training has some value, spiritual exercise is needed to develop godliness, which has value both in this life and for all

---

of describing, in one term, authentic Christian existence as the interplay of the knowledge of God (variously expressed) and its observable outworking in behavior that is appropriate to that knowledge" (*Letters to Timothy and Titus*, 174).

[454] Cf. Tertullian, *Apol.* 32 (PL 1, 508–9): "There is also another and a greater necessity for our offering prayer in behalf of the emperors, nay, for the complete stability of the empire, and for Roman interests in general." See also Tertullian, *Apology* 39 (PL 1, 532): "We pray, too, for the emperors, for their ministers and for all in authority, for the welfare of the world, for the prevalence of peace, for the delay of the final consummation." Cited in G. Wainwright, "Praying for Kings: The Place of Human Rulers in the Divine Plan of Salvation," *ExAud* 2 (1986): 121.

[455] Marshall, *Pastoral Epistles*, 143.

[456] See L. T. Johnson, "II Timothy and the Polemic against False Teachers: A Reexamination," *JRelS* 6–7 (1978): 1–26, who argues that the false teachers serve as a foil for how Timothy and Titus should shepherd and serve as examples for the flock.

eternity (4:7–8). Accordingly, godliness is to be strenuously pursued (4:10; §5.2.2). Later Paul writes that the opponents fail to promote godliness and are conceited, devoid of understanding, and ill intentioned. In addition, their teaching not only lacks any positive benefit but leads to all kinds of sins. They further believe that godliness is a means to financial gain, whereas Paul maintains that godliness with contentment is great gain in and of itself (6:3–6). Paul's appeal to Timothy to "pursue righteousness, godliness, faith, love, endurance, and gentleness" is set in opposition to the attitudes and actions of the false teachers from which he must flee (6:11).

There is proportionately less emphasis on godliness in 2 Timothy and Titus, each featuring only two uses of the word group. Second Timothy continues to focus on godliness in contrast to the false teachers. In a section where Paul encourages Timothy to present himself as an approved worker, useful vessel, and servant of the Lord (2 Tim 2:14–26), he writes that the irreverent and empty speech of the opponents produces "godlessness" (ἀσεβείας; 2:16). Shortly thereafter, Paul again exhorts Timothy to avoid the false teachers, who in addition to, or perhaps in culmination of, a list of other sins[457] are said to be "holding to the form of godliness but denying its power" (3:5; cf. Titus 1:15–16). It seems that the opponents connected godliness with knowledge apart from actual conduct, an idea Paul opposes as antithetical to a true knowledge of God (cf. 1 Tim 6:20).[458] As Paul continues to stress the difference between how true teachers are to live compared with false ones, he notes that those who pursue godliness will be persecuted, while "evil people and impostors will become worse, deceiving and being deceived" (2 Tim 3:12–13). He then enjoins Timothy to continue to pursue right teaching from the Scriptures, which leads to maturity and godly living (3:14–17). In 2 Timothy, then, true godliness leads to a life that is marked by righteous living and the suffering of persecution. Personal affirmations of spirituality and godliness are ultimately meaningless if a person's lifestyle fails to reflect God's character.

---

[457] Towner, *Letters to Timothy and Titus*, 559.

[458] Towner, *Goal of Our Instruction*, 148–49.

In Paul's instructions to Titus, there's a focus on godliness as one of the goals of the Christian life. Paul views his ministry as being for the edification of believers' faith and "their knowledge of the truth that leads to godliness" (Titus 1:1). This is not just characteristic of Paul's ministry but reflects God's purpose in sending Christ: "For the grace of God has appeared, bringing salvation for all people, instructing us to deny godlessness and worldly lusts and to live in a sensible, righteous, and godly way in the present age, while we wait for the blessed hope, the appearing of the glory of our great God and Savior, Jesus Christ" (2:11–13). Thus Christians are to live godly lives (2:1–10) because God's grace has appeared and taught them how to live (2:11–12) and because of their hope in Christ's return (2:13). Here, then, Paul draws a connection between ethics and eschatology (§6.3).

Paul also points again to the false teachers whose negative example serves to help Titus understand how he should shepherd. As Thielman notes, "The link between knowledge and conduct permeates [Titus] and explains the basic difference between the 'sound teaching' of the Pauline gospel and the deceptive message of the false teachers."[459] Thus knowledge of sound doctrine and God's work leads to godliness (Titus 1:1; 2:11–12), in contrast to the opponents, whose teaching leads to insubordination (1:10), greed (1:11), strife (3:9), and divisiveness (3:10). The false teachers weren't unconcerned with godliness. Quite the contrary, they believed they possessed it (2 Tim 3:5). But their lifestyle and teaching demonstrated that this wasn't the case. Godliness stems from a right knowledge of God, particularly demonstrated in Jesus Christ (1 Tim 3:16; Titus 2:11), that necessarily leads to a transformed life (Titus 2:12–13): "Implicit in the close relation between *eusebeia* and the knowledge of God is the understanding that this observable Christian lifestyle has become possible because of the historical Christ-event and salvation."[460] A life of godliness is a life lived in light of Christ's first and second comings, a life that not only professes knowledge of God but demonstrates that knowledge in godly, Christlike behavior.

---

[459] Thielman, *Theology of the New Testament*, 424.

[460] Towner, *Goal of Our Instruction*, 149; see Madsen, "Ethics of the Pastoral Epistles," 221–22; Thielman, *Theology of the New Testament*, 424.

§5.1.4 Self-control

Another important virtue Paul extols throughout the LTT is "self-control" (σώφρων).[461] Terms from this word group can be used to express correct reasoning and moderation and living life in a reasonable and sensible way, with proper decorum.[462] In classical Greek, *σωφροσύνη* was the virtue of rationality, having a sound mind, lacking ignorance. While the language is relatively uncommon in the LXX, as it lacks Hebrew equivalents, the author of 4 Maccabees states that self-control stems from being instructed by the law and results in being able to "master all pleasures and desires" (4 Macc. 5:23).[463] In the LTT, self-control is listed in a number of Paul's virtue lists, serving as an essential aspect of the Christian lifestyle.[464] It is to characterize godly women, both their dress in particular (1 Tim 2:9) and their way of life in general (1 Tim 2:15), and occurs as a requirement for elders in both of Paul's lists (1 Tim 3:2; Titus 1:8).

Significantly, when Paul encourages Timothy to minister boldly, he grounds his exhortation in the reality that God has not bestowed upon Timothy a spirit of fear but of power, love, and sound judgment (σωφρονισμοῦ; 2 Tim 1:7). In Titus, the older men, older women,[465] younger women, and younger men alike are all to display self-control (Titus 2:2, 4–5, 6). The repeated usage of the word in 2:2–10, where Paul is instructing Titus on *what* he should teach, is paralleled by its usage in 2:11–14, where Paul gives the foundation for *why* he can and should give these instructions: "For the grace of God has appeared, bringing salvation for all people" (2:11), and consequently we are instructed to right living, including living sensibly (σωφρόνως; 2:12). Marshall rightly concludes that Paul "has consciously adjusted the aspect of behavior expressed by

---

[461] The σωφρονέω word group occurs more frequently in the LTT (10x) than in the rest of the NT (6x).

[462] Spicq, "σωφρονέω, σωφρονίζω, σωφρονισμός, σωφρόνως, σωφροσύνη, σώφρων," *TLNT* 3:359–65; cf. Marshall, *Pastoral Epistles*, 182–91; M. Silva, "σωφροσύνη, κτλ.," *NIDNTTE* 4:443–45.

[463] Marshall, *Pastoral Epistles*, 182–83.

[464] Towner, *Letters to Timothy and Titus*, 206, as part of an excursus on self-control (pp. 206–8).

[465] Paul doesn't specifically call on older women to be self-controlled. Rather, in calling on older women to prudently instruct (σωφρονίζω) younger women to be self-controlled (σώφρων), he implies that they themselves possess this characteristic.

the σώφρων word-group by relating it to the Christ-event."[466] Paul hasn't radically altered the conception of "self-control," but neither has he simply taken Greek moral categories and applied them to the church.[467] While the culture at large was equally concerned with pursuing the virtue, Paul recognizes that true self-control is possible only because of what God has done in Christ.[468]

§5.2 Good Works

The emphasis on "good works" (ἔργον ἀγαθόν, καλόν ἔργον)[469] and proper conduct (ἀναστροφή, ἀναστρέφω) in keeping with the Pauline gospel of grace is a major distinctive of the LTT.[470] Good works are urged with regard to women (1 Tim 2:10; Titus 2:5), including widows (1 Tim 5:10; contrast v. 13), both slaves (1 Tim 6:2) and the wealthy (1 Tim 6:18), and the community of believers in general (e.g., Titus 2:14; 3:8, 14). Church leaders such as Timothy and Titus are to set an example of good works and godly conduct (1 Tim 4:12; 2 Tim 2:21; 3:17; Titus 2:7) and to teach believers "how people ought to conduct themselves in God's household" (1 Tim 3:15). Conversely, those who profess to know God but deny him by their actions are unfit for any good work (Titus 1:16). Those who reject the gospel don't practice right conduct but are characterized as having "departed" (ἀποστρέφω). This can be a general departure from the truth (2 Tim 4:4; Titus 1:14) or a personal departure from Paul (2 Tim 1:15). In addition, the false teachers' instructions can be said to lead to the ruin (καταστροφή) of their hearers (2 Tim 2:14), and divisive individuals can be described as "perverted" (Titus 3:11; ἐκστρέφω).

---

[466] Marshall, *Pastoral Epistles*, 184.

[467] See Silva, "σωφροσύνη," *NIDNTTE* 4:444–45.

[468] Mounce, *Pastoral Epistles*, 114; Towner, *Goal of Our Instruction*, 161.

[469] See Marshall, *Pastoral Epistles*, 227–28 for a discussion of these two expressions.

[470] See esp. Titus 3:5. For a helpful survey, see Young, *Theology*, 28–29. A rather large set of related vocabulary is used to discuss "good works" in the LTT. In addition to the words already mentioned, a number of words from the ἐργάζομαι word group are used: ἐργάτης, εὐεργεσία, ἀγαθοεργέω, κακοῦργος, οἰκουργός, περίεργος. See also Marshall, "Faith and Works in the Pastoral Epistles"; Marshall, *Pastoral Epistles*, 227–29 ("Goodness and Good Works in the Pastoral Epistles"); M. E. Sheldon, "The Apostle Paul's Theology of Good Works, with Special Emphasis on 1 Timothy 6:17–19" (Ph.D. diss., Southeastern Baptist Theological Seminary, 2012); and Towner, *Letters to Timothy and Titus*, 210–12 ("Good Deeds").

The LTT also connect good works and eschatology, as Paul notes that "some people's sins are obvious, preceding them to judgment, but the sins of others surface later. Likewise, good works are obvious, and those that are not obvious cannot remain hidden" (1 Tim 5:24–25), and Paul is convinced that God will repay those who have harmed him (2 Tim 4:14). He expects that his labor for the Lord will be rewarded (2 Tim 4:6–8) and views the return of Christ as a factor that will motivate Christians to live godly lives and fulfill their ministries (2 Tim 4:1–5; Titus 2:11–13). As Marshall sums up, "The concept of 'good works' is theologically determined. It is a way of characterizing the whole of the Christian life as a work of God's grace (the Christ-event) with visible results, the fruit produced by genuine faith."[471]

§5.2.1 Witness

As discussed above (§5.1.2.2), there is no basis in the LTT for suggesting that the emphasis on good works stands in contrast to Paul's earlier letters.[472] The LTT are just as opposed to works-righteousness as the rest of the NT.[473] Thus the LTT are clear that salvation is not based on works (2 Tim 1:9; Titus 3:5) but that works are evidence of salvation (Titus 1:16). The work of Christ instructs (Titus 2:11–14) and transforms believers (Titus 3:1–7) so that they can live new lives.[474] Some have suggested based on 1 Tim 2:2 that the LTT advocate a form of Christianity that is doing its best to get along with the culture in order not to be eradicated: "The author of the Pastorals seeks to build the possibility of a life in this world, although on the basis of Christian principles. He wishes to become a part of the world. Thus, for him, the peace of a secure life is a goal of the Christian."[475] But nothing could be further from the truth. To the contrary, Paul presents the Christian life as being "charged by something far more significant than the longing for 'the quiet and peaceful life.'"[476]

[471] Marshall, *Pastoral Epistles*, 229.

[472] For a thorough discussion of the topic, see Marshall, "Faith and Works," 203–18.

[473] Marshall, *Pastoral Epistles*, 216.

[474] Madsen, "Ethics of the Pastoral Epistles," 221–22.

[475] Dibelius and Conzelmann, *Pastoral Epistles*, 39.

[476] Towner, *Goal of Our Instruction*, 144.

Towner contends that Paul "endorses a lifestyle that is meant to facilitate the Church's mission by presenting a witness that is generally acceptable to the outsider. At the same time, by endorsing such an ethic he counters or corrects perversions of behavior introduced into the communities through the false teachers (whom the world would associate with the Church), and in so doing he protects the reputation of the Christian community in the world."[477] In other words, the goal of right living is being a witness, with the contrast between believers' and unbelievers' lives serving as intentional testimony, as "such behaviour provides an example for mission-minded Christians in all generations who, in a desire to win many, seek to make the doctrine of God more attractive (Titus 2:10)."[478] The concern that right living should form a part of God's people's witness to the nations is in harmony with the theology of the OT where Israel's witness was primarily focused on the testimony of their lives lived as God's chosen people.[479]

§5.2.2 Labor and Striving

Both ministry and the Christian life in general are presented in the LTT as involving concerted effort.[480] Paul commands Timothy to pursue godliness diligently, telling him to "train yourself in godliness" (1 Tim 4:7) because of its temporal and eternal value. This eternal value is also the basis for the labor and toil of Paul himself and his coworkers (1 Tim 4:10). In Paul's closing instructions in 1 Timothy, he tells his delegate to pursue virtues and labor hard for the faith (1 Tim 6:11–12; 2 Tim 2:22). Similarly, in his solemn charge in 2 Timothy, he tells Timothy to persist in proclaiming God's word, whether or not it is favorable to do so (2 Tim 4:1–2).

---

[477] Ibid., 255.

[478] Köstenberger and O'Brien, *Salvation to the Ends of the Earth*, 260n1.

[479] Ibid., 34–37, 40; Thielman, *Theology of the New Testament*, 429. The importance of a Christian lifestyle as a witness to the nations is powerfully developed in 1 Peter. See A. J. Köstenberger, "The Contribution of the General Epistles and Revelation to a Biblical Theology of Religions," in *Christianity and the Religions: A Biblical Theology of World Religions*, ed. E. Rommen and H. Netland (Pasadena, CA: William Carey Library, 1995), 121–24.

[480] Paul uses a wide range of vocabulary to highlight the labor of the Christian life. In addition to the language of "works" already discussed above, he uses more pointed words that stress concerted effort and particular care: ἀγών, ἀγωνίζομαι, γυμνάζω, διώκω, ἐφίστημι, ζηλωτής, κοπιάω, προΐστημι, and σπευδάζω. In addition, military imagery (discussed below) includes στρατεία, στρατεύω, and στρατολογέω.

The elders appointed by Timothy and Titus are also said to engage in their ministries by working hard (1 Tim 5:17).

Paul also uses metaphors that picture Christian ministry as involving diligent labor. He twice uses military imagery to encourage Timothy in his ministry, reminding him of the prophecies given about him "so that by recalling them you may fight the good fight" (στρατεύῃ ἐν αὐταῖς τὴν καλὴν στρατείαν, 1 Tim 1:18) and using the imagery of a dedicated soldier to help him understand the level of commitment and focus needed in pursuing ministry (2 Tim 2:4). He then immediately goes on to speak of the diligence of athletes and the hard work of farmers. The three pictures together serve to illustrate that there's a reward in view for believers, but diligent work is needed to obtain it.[481] Shortly after this, Paul again exhorts Timothy to the hard work of handling God's word, telling him to "be diligent to present yourself to God as one approved, a worker who doesn't need to be ashamed, correctly teaching the word of truth" (2 Tim 2:15). Paul uses both the athletic and military metaphors with reference to himself, saying that he has fought the good fight, finished the race, and is looking forward to God's reward (2 Tim 4:7–8).

The diligent labor of Timothy, Titus, and Paul would certainly have been a part of the example that the apostolic delegates were supposed to provide for believers in Ephesus and Crete (1 Tim 4:12; Titus 2:7). The salvation of Jesus Christ was accomplished "to redeem us from all lawlessness and to cleanse for himself a people for his own possession, eager to do good works" (Titus 2:14). Titus is told to remind believers to be ready for good works (Titus 3:1) and to be devoted to good works (Titus 3:8, 14).[482]

It's instructive to see how eschatology often goes hand in hand with a call to hard work (1 Tim 4:7–10; 2 Tim 2:4–7; 4:1–8; §6.6). Paul appears to view his own death as more imminent than Christ's return, but his eschatological hope and expectation have in no way dimmed in comparison with his earlier letters. The hope of eternal life and the seriousness of standing before Christ loom large throughout the LTT, serving as important motivation for engaging in the hard work of living the Christian life.

[481] Towner, *Letters to Timothy and Titus*, 495.

[482] Titus 2:8 makes this point even more explicitly, as believers are *to be careful to* devote themselves to good works.

§5.2.3 Endurance and Suffering

The LTT also don't shy away from the reality of suffering. In the LTT, the theme of suffering is largely confined to 2 Timothy, where the *πάσχω* word group occurs with a good deal of prominence, weaving its way throughout the book.[483] There is no tension between Paul's desire to "lead a tranquil and quiet life in all godliness and dignity" (1 Tim 2:2) and his affirmation that "all who want to live a godly life in Christ Jesus will be persecuted" (2 Tim 3:12). Paul doesn't here, or anywhere, advocate the pursuit of suffering but rather the solemn recognition that suffering for the gospel is a reality for Christians as they follow in Christ's footsteps (cf. 2 Cor 4:7–12; Col 1:24; 1 Pet 2:18–25).[484]

This was Paul's own experience (§1.2) as he suffered for the gospel, enduring all things in order to see the elect saved (2 Tim 1:12; 2:8–10). His ministry was apparent to Timothy and others, both the content of his teaching and his conduct, which included enduring suffering as he preached the gospel (3:10–11). He himself exhorted Timothy to pursue endurance (1 Tim 6:11) and teach with great patience (2 Tim 4:2), and Titus was to instruct older men to be sound in endurance (Titus 2:2). Paul encourages Timothy to share in his suffering for the sake of the gospel (2 Tim 1:8–12), as a soldier for Christ (2:3), as he carries out his ministry (4:5), and in the expectation of sharing in his reign (2:12). And Paul recognized that just as he suffered, and just as he called Timothy to share in his sufferings, "all who want to live a godly life in Christ Jesus will be persecuted" (3:12). This is in contradistinction to "evil people and impostors" who "will become worse, deceiving and being deceived" (3:13). Thus Paul connects suffering with godliness and again presents the false teachers as foils for what faithful shepherds and believers look like.

Interestingly, the suffering of Christ isn't directly mentioned in 2 Timothy (but cf. 1:8; 2:8–10), although Paul draws on the theme of the righteous sufferer in the Psalms to connect his own suffering

---

[483] Paul uses *κακοπαθέω*, *πάθημα*, *πάσχω*, and *συγκακοπαθέω*, as well as *διώκω* to express the idea of suffering. Endurance is indicated by *μακροθυμία*, *ὑπομένω*, and *ὑπομονή*.

[484] See Madsen, "Ethics of the Pastoral Epistles," 227.

with that of Christ.[485] Rather, the predominant focus is on Jesus's victory over the grave: he has abolished death and brought life and immortality to light (1:10); he has been raised from the dead (2:10); he reigns (2:12); and he is the judge of the living and the dead (4:1, 8). Paul's own experience is that while he has suffered, the Lord has always rescued him (3:11; 4:17). It is significant that it is the *Lord* who rescued Paul: the one who suffered and died but now lives and reigns is the one who stood with him and delivered him (4:17). What's more, Paul is confident Jesus will continue to rescue him and bring him "safely into his heavenly kingdom" (4:18).[486]

Here, at the end of the letter, Paul echoes his thoughts at the beginning that he can suffer without shame with "inflexible resistance" because "I am convinced that He is able to guard what I have entrusted to Him until that day" (2 Tim 1:12 NASB).[487] Thus Paul once again connects ethics with eschatology (§6.3–6). Suffering, even dying for the gospel, is not defeat when the one who defeated death is by our side. Rather, suffering is part of a Christian's expectation and should be viewed from the standpoint of mission, soteriology/Christology, and eschatology (§§1, 3, and 6): the LTT calls on believers to endure suffering for the sake of the gospel of Jesus Christ, the risen Lord. As we suffer for this message, we do so in order that the lost might be saved and in the hope of reigning with Christ who is coming to judge the living and the dead.

§5.3 Good Citizenship

Paul's ethical instructions, as observed repeatedly, bore some significant similarities to the surrounding culture. Consequently, a number of commentators have suggested that Paul's ethical instructions were focused on becoming a "part of the world."[488] But as I've noted and as has been argued elsewhere, this view largely depends on assuming that Paul was not the author of the LTT and

---

[485] Towner, "1–2 Timothy and Titus," 908–13, argues persuasively that in his references to suffering in 2 Tim 3:11; 4:16–18 Paul draws on the theme of the righteous sufferer, echoing Ps 34:17, 19 and Psalm 22, respectively.

[486] See G. A. Couser, "'The Testimony about the Lord,' 'Borne by the Lord,' or Both?," *TynBul* 55 (2004): 312.

[487] Quinn and Wacker, *Letters to Timothy*, 603. As noted in the commentary, Paul is most likely speaking of entrusting his life to God, not God entrusting the gospel to him (though of course he did that, too). See Mounce, *Pastoral Epistles*, 488.

[488] Dibelius and Conzelmann, *Pastoral Epistles*, 39.

on minimizing the eschatological and missional outlook of the letters (Introduction; §4).[489] It is far better to recognize that the LTT represent unique themes and emphases within the Pauline corpus that are in overall continuity with his theology elsewhere (§7.2). What, then, should we make of the similarities between Paul's description of the Christian life and the values of Greco-Roman literature? Even more particularly, what of those texts that appear to imply that Paul wants Christians simply to be "good citizens" of the empire?

In 1 Tim 2:1–2 Paul writes to Timothy, "First of all, then, I urge that petitions, prayers, intercessions, and thanksgivings be made for everyone, for kings and all those who are in authority, so that we may lead a tranquil and quiet life in all godliness and dignity." In a similar vein, he tells Titus that godly living is necessary because "the grace of God has appeared, bringing salvation for all people, instructing us to deny godlessness and worldly lusts and to live in a sensible, righteous, and godly way in the present age" (Titus 2:11–12) and then immediately goes on to say, "Remind them to submit to rulers and authorities, to obey, to be ready for every good work" (Titus 3:1).[490] These passages envision Christians living in an upright manner as good citizens. Indeed, Paul's ethical instructions in the LTT in general (not to mention his other letters and the rest of the NT) urge Christians to live as model members of society. Yet there are four significant points that lead to a different conclusion than that given by Dibelius, Conzelmann, and others: (1) Paul's ethical teaching is grounded in the two comings of Christ, not culture; (2) Paul's ethical teaching is often countercultural; (3) Paul's ethical teaching is aimed at mission, not accommodation to the culture; and (4) Paul's ethical teaching is pointedly eschatological.[491] As these items have been addressed in some detail elsewhere in this volume, a few brief comments on each point will suffice.

1. Whatever affinities Paul's language bears with the culture, he repeatedly connects his teaching and doctrine not with culture but with Christ. This is not to suggest that these are always at odds with each other, but there's no doubt that Paul in the LTT

[489] Towner, *Goal of Our Instruction*, 9–17.

[490] Ibid., 10.

[491] For a survey, see Madsen, "Ethics of the Pastoral Epistles."

derives his ethics first and foremost from the Hebrew Scriptures. Apostolic teaching is to be in accordance with sound doctrine, which is grounded in the OT and predicated on the Christian gospel (1 Tim 1:3, 10–11; 2 Tim 2:2; 3:15–17; Titus 1:3; 2:1), and a transformed lifestyle is rooted in the work of grace in a person's life (1 Tim 1:12–16; Titus 2:11–14), whereas false teachers oppose God's redemptive plan (1 Tim 1:4).

2. In addition, the application of these virtues is at times at odds with the prevailing culture. For example, by casting slaves in a role in which they were able to serve as benefactors to their masters (1 Tim 6:1–2), Paul went diametrically against cultural norms.[492] What's more, the expectation that the Christian life will inexorably lead to suffering (e.g., 2 Tim 3:12) indicates that Christian godliness will inevitably rub against the grain of the culture.

3. In the LTT, living a virtuous life forms part of a believer's witness to the world.[493] The goal of living a peaceful life (1 Tim 2:2) is predicated on God's desire to save the lost (1 Tim 2:3–7) rather than being an end in itself.[494] This is explicitly spelled out in Titus 2:1–10 where Paul gives two reasons for pursuing godly conduct: (1) it is in accordance with sound doctrine (2:1); and (2) it adorns the gospel before an unbelieving world (2:5, 8, 10).[495]

4. Finally, while Dibelius conceded that the LTT aren't totally devoid of eschatological expectation,[496] he didn't appreciate how keen that anticipation is. The LTT present life "between two epiphanies."[497] Jesus Christ is returning to save, reward, and judge, which brings great hope (1 Tim 1:1; 4:10; 2 Tim 2:12; 4:16–18; Titus 1:1–3; 2:11–14), motivation (1 Tim 4:7–8; 17–19; 2 Tim 2:3–13; 4:6–8; Titus 3:5–8), and solemnity (2 Tim 4:1–5) to Christians as they live their lives and engage in ministry.

§5.4 Conclusion

While Timothy and Titus were not pastors *per se*, the instructions given to them are nonetheless applicable to pastors as they

---

[492] See Towner, *Letters to Timothy and Titus*, 385–88.

[493] Ho, "Mission in the Pastoral Epistles," 242–43.

[494] Towner, *Goal of Our Instruction*, 168, 232.

[495] Knight, *Pastoral Epistles*, 316.

[496] Dibelius and Conzelmann, *Pastoral Epistles*, 40–41.

[497] Talbert, "Between Two Epiphanies."

lead and shepherd local churches. Consequently, our approach to mission and discipleship can be enriched by considering the unique contributions of the LTT. Perhaps we don't put enough emphasis on Christian virtues and the way in which they impact the totality of our lives. DeYoung suggests that many believers have "willingly embraced Christian freedom but without an equal pursuit of Christian virtue."[498] The LTT provide an important correction to this trend.

Virtue language is one of the unique features of these letters among the Pauline epistles, addressing an important aspect of the Christian life: the life of faith is the life of virtue. Holiness is more than avoidance of sin; it is the cultivation of particular character qualities, enabled by the transforming work of God through Jesus Christ that produces a people who are zealous for good works and who adorn the gospel of God.[499] A focus on virtues can help us guard against pharisaism, focusing merely on outward behavior, as it draws our attention not only to "the question of what we should do but also with *who we should be*."[500] The LTT remind us that we should cultivate virtue as part of our Christian lives and in our churches. Preaching and teaching these letters is a God-appointed means of achieving these goals.

§6 The Last Days

Paul identifies the period in which he writes as "the last days" (1 Tim 4:1; 2 Tim 3:1). At the same time, he refers forward to Jesus Christ's future "appearing" (the Second Coming) in conjunction with a final day of judgment (1 Tim 6:14; 2 Tim 4:1; Titus 2:13), though the term used in the LTT is ἐπιφάνεια rather than the more familiar παρουσία. In addition, Paul uses temporal phrases such as "his own time" (1 Tim 2:6; 6:15; Titus 1:3). According to Paul,

[498] K. DeYoung, *The Hole in Our Holiness: Finding the Gap between Gospel Passion and the Pursuit of Godliness* (Wheaton: Crossway, 2012), 18.

[499] See A. J. Köstenberger, *Excellence: The Character of God and the Pursuit of Scholarly Virtue* (Wheaton: Crossway, 2011), 46.

[500] M. Liederbach and A. Reid, *The Convergent Church: Missional Worshipers in an Engaging Culture* (Grand Rapids: Kregel, 2009), 186, who go on to note that "virtues describe the *quality* of the person, and indicate what ought to be the character and motive of the person. They do not, however, describe the *material content* of the behavior" (190, emphasis original).

therefore, his apostolic delegates and their congregations live and are embroiled in spiritual combat in the period between Jesus's first and second coming, conceived as the inauguration and consummation of the last days, respectively. This salvation-historical era is designated by temporal phrases such as "in his own time he has revealed" (in contrast with "before time began," 2 Tim 1:9–10; Titus 1:2–3), "this present world" (2 Tim 4:10), and "the proper time" (1 Tim 2:6). Notably, one aspect of this present period is God's concern with the salvation of the nations.[501]

Historical-critical scholarship has often assigned to the LTT the label "early Catholicism" and concluded that these letters belong to a phase when the delay of the παρουσία (Jesus's second coming) has moved the church from an emphasis on the exercise of spiritual gifts (χάρισμα) to increasing institutionalization. This, proponents argue, is evidenced by the emphasis in the LTT on qualifications for church officers and on the church's formal organization. Typically, these proponents assign to the LTT a date in the late first or early second century AD, and thus see them as having pseudonymous authorship. We've dealt with the "early Catholicism" hypothesis (advocated, among others, by R. Bultmann's student, E. Käsemann) in the Introduction.[502] Others, less stridently, have proposed that we find in the LTT evidence for a consolidation of Pauline authority or a church order facilitating further outreach to the Gentiles.[503] Here we address implications for our appraisal of the teaching on the end times in the LTT.

---

[501] Note the direct link between the temporal appearance of Christ and the preaching of Paul in 2 Tim 1:9–12 and Titus 1:1–3, preaching which had as a goal the salvation of the nations (cf. 1 Tim 2:5–7; 2 Tim 4:17).

[502] See, e.g., E. Käsemann, *Essays on New Testament Themes* (London: H. R. Allenson, 1964), esp. 100; Käsemann, *New Testament Questions of Today* (London: SCM, 1969), esp. 237, 242; Käsemann, "Paulus und der Frühkatholizismus," *ZTK* 60 (1963): 75–89. See also J. D. G. Dunn, *Unity and Diversity in the New Testament: An Inquiry into the Character of Earliest Christianity*, 3rd ed. (London: SCM, 2006), 372–400; and the critique by J. W. Drane, "Eschatology, Ecclesiology, and Catholicity in the New Testament," *ExpTim* 83, no. 6 (1972): 180–84.

[503] Cf., e.g., J. W. Aageson, "The Pastoral Epistles, Apostolic Authority, and the Development of the Pauline Scriptures," in *The Pauline Canon*, ed. S. E. Porter (Leiden: Brill, 2004), 5–26; R. W. Wall, "The Function of the Pastoral Letters within the Pauline Canon of the New Testament: A Canonical Approach," in *Pauline Canon*, 27–44. As M. Y. Emerson points out, reference to the eschatological context

It is undeniable that Paul, as he approached the end of his apostolic ministry, was increasingly concerned with providing his successors with relevant instructions for the leadership of the growing Christian movement and the respective local congregations. This includes both positive and negative types of instruction aimed at upholding standards and establishing criteria for discipline and even removal from church office. Thus the primary historical framework is the salvation-historical juncture at which we pass from the apostolic to the post-apostolic period (though not necessarily the delay of the παρουσία). This raises a series of questions: What about the teaching on the end times in the LTT? Has the expectation of Jesus's return faded from view entirely or almost completely? Do such expectations shine through occasionally? Should we understand the LTT's teaching in the context of an end-time framework such as Paul's inaugurated eschatology of the already/not yet?[504] Or do the LTT exhibit a thoroughgoing eschatological outlook that is central to their overall presentation rather than being marginal or sporadic?[505]

While final adjudication will have to await the presentation of the data below, the following evidence certainly seems to support the conclusion reached by F. Young: "The notion that the Pastorals have lost urgency because of a delay in the Parousia and a tendency to settle down in the world runs counter to the evidence in the texts."[506] In the following discussion we'll take a closer look at several interrelated eschatological themes, including Satan, demons, and angels; false teachers; virtues and vices; the need for perseverance; and the appearing of Christ in the final judgment and

of the LTT is absent from both essays ("Paul's Eschatological Outlook in the Pastoral Epistles," *CTR* NS 12, no. 2 [2015]: 85n9).

[504] P. H. Towner, "The Present Age in the Eschatology of the Pastoral Epistles," *NTS* 32 (1986): 427–48; Towner, *Goal of Our Instruction*, 61–74. As Emerson points out ("Eschatological Outlook," 84n5), however, Towner does not use eschatology as a unifying theme in his *Letters to Timothy and Titus*, 53–67. See also Young, *Theology*, 70–72.

[505] See esp. Emerson, "Eschatological Outlook," who speaks of a "full-throated eschatology in the Pastorals" (p. 86). See also Beale, *New Testament Biblical Theology*, esp. 141, 820–21.

[506] Young, *Theology*, 71, who adds that this point is well argued by R. M. Kidd, *Wealth and Beneficence in the Pastoral Epistles: A "Bourgeois" Form of Early Christianity?*, SBLDS 122 (Atlanta: Scholars Press, 1990), esp. chap. 4; and Towner, *Goal of Our Instruction*, esp. chap. 4.

salvation.[507] In this way we'll ensure that any relevant biblical-theological data emerge organically from the documents under consideration rather than being superimposed on them.[508] This means that while being sensitive to the overall biblical story line, and to the progressive unfolding of central themes throughout Scripture, we start with the classic book-by-book approach that seeks to understand a given piece or corpus of writings such as the LTT initially in their own right.[509]

§6.1 Satan, Demons, and Angels

Satan and his demons are portrayed in the LTT as standing behind the false teachers who threaten the church with their false teaching.[510] As Paul writes, "Among them are Hymenaeus and

---

[507] I inferred these categories inductively from the LTT. For a helpful survey, see Emerson, "Eschatological Outlook," 92–94, who discusses false teaching, time (e.g., phrases such as "proper time" or "present world"), and "mystery." See also B. Mutschler, "Eschatology in the Pastoral Epistles," in *Eschatology of the New Testament and Some Related Documents*, ed. J. G. van der Watt (Tübingen: Mohr-Siebeck, 2011), 362–402; Schnelle, *New Testament Theology*, 599; and various above-mentioned works by Towner.

[508] This is the danger of placing the LTT within a Pauline inaugurated eschatology (already-not yet) framework at the outset. It is also a weakness of the otherwise helpful essay by Emerson ("Eschatological Outlook"), who, speaking of "the eschatological shape of the Christian Bible" (p. 87), starts out with broader canonical assumptions (such as that Romans through Colossians emphasize the importance of Christ's first coming while 1 Thessalonians through Jude stress Christ's second coming [pp. 90–91] or that their placement in the NT canon between 1–2 Thessalonians and Hebrews signifies the eschatological character of the LTT [p. 91]). Not only is this distinction artificial and not borne out by the actual content of these letters (cf., e.g., the eschatological teaching of 1 Corinthians 15 or Romans 9–11 culminating in Rom 11:25–33), it unduly constrains these letters by larger assumptions about the canonical sequencing of the NT letters (and the LTT at the end of the Pauline portion) and their place in the larger biblical story line. This set of assumptions, in turn, unduly hampers the inductive process vital to an assessment of biblical-theological themes such as these letters' teaching on the end times.

[509] For a discussion of the four major approaches to biblical theology, see A. J. Köstenberger, "The Present and Future of Biblical Theology," *Them* 37, no. 3 (2012): 445–64.

[510] D. R. Brown, *The God of This Age: Satan in the Churches and Letters of the Apostle Paul*, WUNT 2/409 (Tübingen: Mohr-Siebeck, 2015), argues that although the LTT may sometimes reflect earlier Pauline references to Satan (cf. 1 Cor 5:5), the references to Satan in 1 and 2 Timothy seek to establish a link between false teaching and Satan intended to caution the readers against subscribing to teaching

Alexander, whom I have delivered to Satan, so that they may be taught not to blaspheme" (1 Tim 2:20). The only other reference to Satan in those terms is found in 1 Tim 5:14–15, again in conjunction with the false teachers but there over against the backdrop of Paul's concern with women as the victims of these opponents: "Therefore, I want younger women to marry, have children, manage their households, and give the adversary no opportunity to accuse us. For some have already turned away to follow Satan."

This latter passage, in turn, sustains a close connection with the earlier reference to Eve, "the woman," in 1 Tim 2:14, who "was deceived [i.e., by Satan in the Garden; cf. Gen 3:1–7] and transgressed." Paul adds, "But she will be preserved through childbearing, if they continue in faith, love, and holiness, with good sense" (v. 15; §3.8).[511] As in the garden, Paul fears that Satan is seeking to spiritually seduce women in his day, through the instrumentality of the false teachers. He urges them to devote themselves to their God-given roles as wives and mothers and to the domestic sphere so as not to succumb to the same temptation as Eve, who acted independently and led her husband into sin. The reference to "the teachings of demons" who, among other things, forbid marriage (1 Tim 4:1, 3) further underscores the way Satan seeks to use the false teachers to throw the churches and proper gender roles into disarray.[512]

In addition to specific references to Satan, there are several references to "the devil" in the LTT.[513] Two of these references are found in the list of qualifications for elders in 1 Timothy 3. This bears telling testimony to the fact that Paul's concern was supremely with the devil's corruption of church leaders and the intense spiritual warfare surrounding the leadership of the church. In 1 Tim 3:6 Paul instructs Timothy not to appoint a new convert,

---

separating them from the truth of the gospel and the community of believers. Regarding Satan/the Devil in Paul's writings (including the LTT), see also D. G. Reid, "Satan, Devil," *DPL* 862–67.

[511] I changed "saved" to "preserve" in the above translation, since this is the more likely meaning of the underlying Greek word here. Note the connection between "have children" in 1 Tim 5:14 and "childbearing" in 1 Tim 2:15.

[512] On the biblical teaching regarding gender roles, see esp. A. J. and M. E. Köstenberger, *God's Design for Man and Woman*.

[513] In addition, the word διάβολος is used twice with the meaning "slanderer" (1 Tim 3:11; 2 Tim 3:3).

"or he might become conceited and incur the same condemnation as the devil." In the following verse, Paul stipulates that the candidate "must have a good reputation among outsiders, so that he does not fall into disgrace and the devil's trap." Timothy's opponents have already fallen into "the trap of the devil" (2 Tim 2:26), and he must gently instruct them so that they may come to their senses and escape.[514]

Finally, the LTT feature two references to the unfallen angelic world. In the hymn at 1 Tim 3:16, we read that Jesus was "seen by angels," presumably subsequent to the resurrection. In 1 Tim 5:21 Paul writes, "I solemnly charge you before God and Christ Jesus and the elect angels to observe these things without prejudice, doing nothing out of favoritism." In context, this most likely refers to the public removal of sinning elders. In this, young Timothy must act in complete impartiality, recognizing his solemn and sacred responsibility to preserve the church pure and free from doctrinal and behavioral error by any church leaders who may have succumbed to the devil's schemes and fallen into his carefully laid trap (cf. 2 Tim 2:26). While, humanly speaking, removing elders may have been a terrifying prospect, even more terrifying was the expectation of standing before God and Christ Jesus and the elect angels.

All this reflects the larger biblical-theological perspective of spirit beings who populate the cosmos—on the one hand, angels who *serve* God and his people, and on the other hand, Satan and his minions who *stand against* God and his people[515]—and shows that the church is not merely operating on a horizontal plane. Rather, the church and its leaders are part of a cosmic battle between God and Jesus Christ on the one hand and Satan and his demons on the other. This cosmic conflict is one in which Paul and his apostolic delegates, and the elders they put in place, were fighting against evil supernatural forces who vehemently opposed the advancement of the gospel, which was the primary purpose of the apostolic mission and of the network of local congregations. Thus the expectation of the final judgment and the presence of the false teachers combine to form a supernatural end-time matrix which

[514] See commentary at 2 Tim 2:23–26.

[515] For a biblical-theological treatment of Satan, see, e.g., C. H. H. Scobie, *The Ways of Our God: An Approach to Biblical Theology* (Grand Rapids: Eerdmans, 2003), 243–45, 251–54. See also G. H. Twelftree, "Spiritual Powers," *NDBT* 796–802.

serves as a framework for local church administration and for the life of believers who ought to conduct themselves in holy fear in the light of the prospect of Jesus's return.

Satan	The Devil	Demons	Angels
1 Tim 1:20	1 Tim 3:6	1 Tim 4:1	1 Tim 3:16
1 Tim 2:14 [implied]	1 Tim 3:7		1 Tim 5:21
1 Tim 5:15	2 Tim 2:26		
	Titus 2:3		

§6.2 False Teachers and the Tribulation of the Last Days

We've already discussed the specific identities of the false teachers in view of the LTT in the general Introduction and the introductions to the individual LTT above. In this portion we'll focus on exploring the way the references to the false teachers in the LTT relate to the theology of the last days in these letters as a whole. Specifically, these references are an integral part of the background assumption that the presence of the false teachers is a sign that Paul and his apostolic delegates, as well as the churches under their jurisdiction, lived in the end times in which false teaching, in keeping with Jesus's prediction, was expected to proliferate.[516] Specifically, false teachers or those mentioned negatively in the LTT include the following:[517]

- Hymenaeus and Alexander (1 Tim 1:20)
- Phygelus and Hermogenes (2 Tim 1:15)
- Hymenaeus and Philetus (2 Tim 2:17)
- Demas (2 Tim 4:10)
- Alexander the coppersmith (2 Tim 4:14)

The presence of the false teachers and the proliferation of false teaching are signs that the tribulation of the end times has already come upon the church. As Beale notes, "The presence of tribulation in the form of false, deceptive teaching at the church of Ephesus is also one of the signs that the long-awaited latter days had finally come (1 Tim. 4:1; 2 Tim. 3:1)." Beale points out

[516] See esp. the Olivet Discourse in Mark 13 and Synoptic parallels.

[517] Paul doesn't typically name false teachers in his letters but may be doing so here because he's writing to his delegates.

that the reference to "the last days" (ἐν ἐσχάταις ἡμέραις) in 2 Tim 3:1 echoes repeated similar references to "the latter days" in the LXX.[518] He elaborates,

> That this idea in 1–2 Timothy is not a reference only to a distant, future time is evident in the recognition that the Ephesian church is already experiencing the latter-day tribulation of deceptive teaching and apostasy (see 1 Tim. 1:3–4, 6, 7, 19–20; 4:7; 5:13–15; 6:20–21; 2 Tim. 1:15; 2:16–19, 25–26; 3:2–9).[519]

According to Beale, "This understanding of a latter-day tribulation characterized by false teaching and unbelief is in line with the expectation that we observed in Dan. 7–12 and in early Judaism (especially the DSS and *Testaments of the Twelve Patriarchs*)."[520]

In addition, there are many generic references to those who "departed from the faith" (e.g., 1 Tim 6:21; cf. 2 Tim 2:18) or the like, in some cases with specific reference to them having been "delivered to Satan" (1 Tim 1:20; cf. 3:7; 5:15; 2 Tim 2:26). What's more, 2 Tim 3:1–9 connects the perilous times of the last days (v. 1) specifically with the false teachers of Ephesus (vv. 6–9):

> For among them are those who worm their way into households and deceive gullible women overwhelmed by sins and led astray by a variety of passions, always learning and never able to come to a knowledge of the truth. . . . [They] resist the truth. They are men who are corrupt in mind and worthless in regard to the faith. But they will not make further progress, for their foolishness will be clear to all.

Thus Timothy's Ephesian opponents are shown to engage in an attempt to infiltrate households, the proper center of instruction in the ancient world (§2), and to subvert proper learning by spreading their deviant doctrines. Their lack of understanding is shown to be rooted in their resistance to the truth due to the corruption of their minds. This, in turn, shows how the false

---

[518] Beale, *New Testament Biblical Theology*, 141.

[519] Ibid.

[520] Ibid. Though note that I don't endorse Beale's overall amillennial eschatological perspective.

teachers are rooted in the evil supernatural world and thus part of the cosmic battle into which the apostolic mission and the various Christian congregations are placed. Thus the preservation of believers in the faith and the defense of the faith over against the false teachers as motivated by Satan and his demons provides an important substructure of the entire ecclesiology of the LTT.

§6.3 Virtues and Vices

As discussed above (§5), virtues and vices play an important role in the LTT. One of the unique features of Paul's use of virtues and vices in comparison with their use in the Greco-Roman world at large is their connection with eschatology.[521] In 1 Timothy, Paul presents the Christian life as being pursued with an eschatological goal in mind. Correspondingly, he attests that virtues can have value that transcends their usefulness in this life: "Godliness is beneficial in every way, since it holds promise for the present life and also for the life to come" (1 Tim 4:8). The call to "fight the good fight of the faith" is intimately connected with the admonition to "take hold of eternal life to which you were called" (1 Tim 6:12; cf. 6:13–15). Again, Paul commands the rich to be generous not in hopes of increasing their social status in this world but in light of God's eternal rewards (1 Tim 6:17–19).

Similar themes are present in 2 Timothy. Paul himself endures suffering in order that the elect may be saved and in the hope of reigning with Christ (2 Tim 2:10–13; cf. 4:3–4). The vice list in 2 Tim 3:2–5 is a characterization of unbelievers "in the last days." With the arrival of Jesus, a new age has dawned. The appearance of wicked men such as are described in the list is a testimony to the truth that the last days have arrived.[522] Timothy's own ministry was to be carried out faithfully in view of Christ's coming judgment (2 Tim 4:1–5). Finally, Paul points ahead to the hope of eternal reward as the hope that lies at the end of a life of faithful labor for the Lord (2 Tim 4:6–8).

Titus contains similar injunctions. Paul's ministry is "for the faith of God's elect and their knowledge of the truth that leads to godliness, in the hope of eternal life that God, who cannot lie, promised before time began," connecting godliness and eternal life (Titus 1:1–2). The training of the Christian life toward virtue

[521] See N. J. McEleney, "Vice Lists of the Pastoral Epistles," 218.

[522] Towner, *Letters to Timothy and Titus*, 553–54.

in *this* age by a people who are zealous for good works is carried out in view of the coming age as we wait "for the blessed hope, the appearing of the glory of our great God and Savior, Jesus Christ" (Titus 2:13). All of this comports with the distinctive Christian eschatological outlook further discussed below. There is, therefore, a close connection between a virtuous life and the hope of eternal life. The eschatology of the LTT is not simply concerned with escaping this world but with faithful obedience, godly living, and patient endurance, recognizing that the inception of the new age finds people persisting in glaring ungodliness which will remain and increase until Christ appears to judge the living and the dead.

§6.4 The Need for Perseverance

In addition to overt references to "that day" (i.e., Christ's second coming, see below), there are more subtle indications in the LTT of a future expectation that requires perseverance in the here and now. This includes references to believers' preservation such as Paul's statement that women will be preserved by childbearing (1 Tim 2:15) and his exhortation to Timothy to watch his life and doctrine closely so that he will preserve both himself and his hearers (1 Tim 4:18). The importance of perseverance in light of Jesus's return is also reflected in Paul's expectation that the Lord will rescue him and bring him safely into his heavenly kingdom (2 Tim 4:18). In this way, then, the prospect of the final, eschatological judgment constitutes a "major warrant" for the ethical instruction in the LTT as believers live "between the times" of Christ's first and second coming.[523]

§6.5 The Resurrection of Believers

The LTT's teaching on the resurrection of believers takes on particular importance as the single doctrinal hallmark of the false teachers explicitly recorded in the LTT is that they taught that "the resurrection has already taken place" (2 Tim 2:18). G. K. Beale notes that the LTT speak of Christ's resurrection in 1 Tim 3:16 ("vindicated

[523] Young, *Theology*, 71, citing L. R. Donelson, *Pseudepigraphy and Ethical Argument in the Pastoral Epistles*, HUT 22 (Tübingen: Mohr-Siebeck, 1986), 148. One does not have to affirm pseudonymity, as Donelson does, to hold to this position. The phrase "between the times" in the above quote is Young's.

in the Spirit").[524] He connects the "(eternal) life" of the LTT with believers' resurrection (2 Tim 1:1: "the promise of life in Christ Jesus"; 2 Tim 2:11–12: "If we died with him, we shall also live with him; if we endure, we shall also reign with him"; Titus 1:2: "the hope of eternal life"). He also sees the "regeneration," or "re-enlivening," of Titus 3:5 as a precursor to the physical resurrection believers will experience: "The resurrection of the new creation . . . begins in this life spiritually and will be consummated in the full physical resurrection life of the age to come."[525] Thus the LTT clearly espouse an already-not yet position with regard to the resurrection of believers. While they have already experienced regeneration at conversion (Titus 3:5), the final resurrection is still future: it is a matter of hope (Titus 1:2), promise (2 Tim 1:1), and expectation, contingent on believers' perseverance in the faith (2 Tim 2:11–12).[526]

§6.6 The Appearing of Christ in Final Judgment and Salvation

References to Christ's future return in salvation and judgment are found repeatedly in the LTT.[527] Importantly, ἐπιφάνεια in the LTT refers to the abiding salvific presence of God's comprehensive activity in Christ.[528] The expectation of judgment undergirds Paul's comments in 1 Tim 5:24–25, "Some people's sins are obvious, preceding them to judgment, but the sins of others surface later. Likewise, good works are obvious, and those that are not obvious cannot remain hidden." Even more overt is the reference

---

[524] Note the section on "Resurrection in 1–2 Timothy and Titus" in Beale, *New Testament Biblical Theology*, 290–91. See also the section on the LTT in N. T. Wright, *The Resurrection of the Son of God*, Christian Origins and the Question of God 3 (Minneapolis: Fortress, 2003), 267–71.

[525] Beale, *New Testament Biblical Theology*, 291.

[526] Note also the affirmation of Jesus's resurrection and descent from David in 2 Tim 2:8 and see commentary there.

[527] On the terminological shift between Paul's earlier letters and the LTT see R. F. Collins, "From παρουσία to ἐπιφάνεια: The Transformation of a Pauline Motif." See also D. Lührmann, "*Epiphaneia*: Zur Bedeutungsgeschichte eines griechischen Wortes," in *Tradition und Glaube: Das frühe Christentum in seiner Umwelt. Festgabe für Karl Georg Kuhn zum 65. Geburtstag*, ed. G. Jeremias, H.-W. Kuhn, and H. Stegemann (Göttingen: Vandenhoeck & Ruprecht, 1971), 185–99.

[528] Jung, Σωτήρ, 330 ("bleibenden Heilsgegenwart des umfassend verstandenen göttlichen Tuns in Jesus Christus"), who notes the contrast with the pagan environment of the LTT where the term denoted a one-time intervention (with reference to Lührmann, "*Epiphaneia*").

to the final judgment in Paul's remarks in 2 Tim 1:12: "I know whom I have believed and am persuaded that he is able to guard what has been entrusted to me until that day." Similarly, in the context of his commendation of Onesiphorus, Paul writes, "May the Lord grant that he obtain mercy from [the Lord] on that day" (2 Tim 1:18).

Toward the end of 2 Timothy, Paul writes, "For I am already being poured out as a drink offering, and the time for my departure is close. I have fought the good fight, I have finished the race, I have kept the faith. There is reserved for me the crown of righteousness, which the Lord, the righteous Judge, will give me on that day, and not only to me, but to all those who have loved his appearing" (2 Tim 4:6–8). Similarly, in Titus 2:11–13 Paul writes, "For the grace of God has appeared, bringing salvation for all people, instructing us to deny godlessness and worldly lusts and to live in a sensible, righteous, and godly way in the present age, while we wait for the blessed hope, the appearing of the glory of our great God and Savior, Jesus Christ."

The above-cited passages add up to a robust expression of Paul's expectation of Jesus Christ's return in salvation and judgment. This expectation is fueling Paul's faithfulness in ministry until the end (see esp. 2 Tim 4:6–8; cf. 1 Cor 15:58). It is also presented as important motivation for believers to "deny godlessness" and live in "a godly way in the present age" (Titus 2:11–13). Another important motivation in this regard is that of receiving a reward (1 Tim 6:11–14; cf. 2 Tim 2:3–7). His expectation of a final day of judgment and accountability (regularly referred to as "that day," see 2 Tim 1:12, 18; 2 Tim 4:8) also forms the basis for his exhortation of Timothy's discipline of sinning elders (1 Tim 5:24–25).

§6.7 Conclusion

Eschatology is an often overlooked dimension of the LTT. As we've seen, Paul places the times in which he and his apostolic delegates perform their ministry within the eschatological scope of the "last days." These "last days," in turn, are characterized by the activity of false teachers who oppose their work by spreading false doctrine. This raises the question of the relationship between the LTT's eschatology and their ecclesiology. The assessment of this issue calls for balance, nuancing, and care. It would be easy to overreact against the rather extreme "early Catholicism" view in conjunction with the delay of the παρουσία that minimizes eschatology for the sake of ecclesiology. Such an overreaction might contend that the LTT exhibit a full-orbed eschatology almost akin to the book of Revelation.[529]

Most likely, however, the truth lies somewhere in between these two extremes. On the one hand, the church is shown to be the pillar and foundation of the truth in this life, and qualifications for church leaders are important because the church has an important function to play in the establishment of beachheads of truth in various urban centers such as Ephesus or the cities of the island of Crete, as well as other strategic locations. On the other hand, such strategic missional efforts are seen to be opposed by false teachers, instruments of Satan, who exhibit the tribulation characteristic of the end times inaugurated by Christ. At the same time, this is not to collapse the distinction completely between "the great tribulation," which immediately precedes the return of Christ and which witnesses the activity of the Antichrist and other distinctive end-time figures identified particularly in the book of Revelation.[530]

Thus one observes a certain amount of overlap between the church's being established and strategically put in place for

---

[529] See, e.g., Emerson, "Eschatological Outlook," 95, whose canonical hermeneutic leads him to collapse biblical-theological distinctions between the LTT and the rest of Scripture, the NT, and Paul's writings and who claims that false teaching in the LTT "is a sign of the tribulation, and as such ecclesial government is not a matter of preservation in perpetuity but of the church militant, defending herself against the gates of hell in the power of the Spirit" and who speaks of "Spirit empowered governance that allows the church to combat false teachers sent by the Deceiver" (apparently endorsing the amillennial eschatology of Beale, *New Testament Biblical Theology*, 820–22). Among other things, this unduly diminishes the demonstrable presence of a strong "preservation theology" that pervades the LTT. See A. J. Köstenberger, "Ascertaining Women's God-Ordained Roles: An Interpretation of 1 Timothy 2:15," *BBR* 7 (1997): 107–44 (here 130–32); A. J. Köstenberger, L. S. Kellum, and C. L. Quarles, *The Cradle, the Cross, and the Crown: An Introduction to the New Testament*, 2nd ed. (Nashville: B&H Academic, 2016), 752.

[530] Contra Emerson, "Eschatological Outlook," 95, following Beale, *New Testament Biblical Theology*, 187–227, 820–22. See also M. Harding, "'Apocalyptic Rhetoric' in the Pastoral Epistles" (paper presented at the annual meeting of the SBL, Atlanta, GA, November 2015), who detects in the LTT "apocalyptic rhetoric" (A. Y. Collins's term) not only in their eschatology but also in references to the mystery and revelation received and passed on by the author; and G. K. Beale and B. L. Gladd, "The Use of Mystery in 1 Timothy," in *Hidden but Now Revealed: A Biblical Theology of Mystery* (Downers Grove: InterVarsity, 2014), 237–59.

mission and the countervailing forces of the evil one seeking to subvert that mission. In this sense one may detect certain affinities with Paul's inaugurated, already-not yet eschatology, though it may be best not to completely submerge and identify the eschatology of the LTT with that of Paul's other letters (though there are certainly points of affinity; see, e.g., 2 Cor 13:5). The reason for this differentiation may be that the LTT present us with the apostle's more global outlook on the church and its mission within a larger eschatological context as over against some of his earlier correspondence in which he addresses concrete issues with which a given church or group of churches is confronted (e.g., 1 Corinthians, Galatians, Philippians).

We find thus in the LTT a unique conglomeration of ecclesiology and eschatology in the mature Pauline mission on the eve of its transition to the subapostolic period at which juncture we see his teaching on the church and on the last days coexist in a kind of balance in which both inform and legitimize the other. The great tribulation and the return of Christ are still future, perhaps even in the more distant future (though whether this is a result of the "delay of the παρουσία" is another question). This necessitates the establishment of the church as a bulwark of the truth on this earth as a mission center and outpost of the apostolic teaching regarding Christ, not unlike the function of local synagogues in the Second Temple period and the first-century Mediterranean world.

In this missional context Paul serves as overall apostle-at-large while his apostolic delegates serve as channels of life-giving teaching and remove any blocked arteries in the form of doctrinal and/or ethical error that threatens to suck the life out of the church's truth- and mission-pursuing fervor and propagating activity. The gospel, as the carefully guarded deposit of the true faith, is thus shown to be in need of vital and vibrant defense as it is handed on from apostle to apostolic delegates and by these to other faithful witnesses who continue the chain of careful transmission of the apostolic message regarding the Christ and his salvation.

In this way the Pauline mission, the gospel of salvation, the community of believers, and the backdrop of the "last days" exhibit a distinctive outlook that pervades the LTT in a way that casts the church's mission between Christ's first and second comings as a spiritual combat between the servants of Christ and the servants of Satan that places a given local congregation squarely within the crossfire of such spiritual conflict. This should jar and jolt any complacent church into vigilance and committed defense and propagation of the gospel. As a spiritual message of salvation, the gospel should expose the inadequacy of nominalism, traditionalism, or any other state in which the church has become part of the establishment in a culture that is blind to the spiritual dynamics which are in operation—not only behind the scenes but through real flesh-and-blood opponents of the true, apostolic gospel.

§7 The LTT and the Canon

Following the above investigation of significant themes in the LTT, it'll be helpful to conclude this study with a brief survey of the LTT in relation to other biblical corpora: the OT; Paul's other letters; the book of Acts; and other NT letters. Affinities between the LTT and the Gospels and the book of Revelation are significant at times as well, but space doesn't permit a full discussion here. We can only briefly note the following connections. With regard to the Gospels, one may note the apparent citation of Jesus's saying from Luke's Gospel in 1 Tim 5:18 (cf. Luke 10:7), not to mention other parallels between Luke's Gospel and Paul's first letter to Timothy.[531] The church discipline procedures in Matt 18:15–20 could be connected with the discipline occurring in the LTT toward the false teachers and (potentially) the elders as well (1 Tim 5:19–20; cf. Titus 3:10–11). In terms of mission, as mentioned, there are connections between Paul's conception of his apostolic mission in the LTT and the Great Commission grounded in God's promises to Abraham (Matt 28:18–20; cf. Gen 12:1–3; §1). With regard to the book of Revelation, we can only refer the reader to the above discussion of the LTT's eschatology (§6). While, as discussed, the LTT present the church age within the framework of the inauguration of the "last days," the NT Apocalypse depicts the final consummation, in particularly God's judgments on Satan, his demons, and the unbelieving world. The portrayal of Jesus's final "appearing" in the LTT, for its part, overlaps with the depiction of Christ's return

[531] See, e.g., Swinson, *What Is Scripture?*, 99–102. Cf. R. Riesner, "Once More: Luke-Acts and the Pastoral Epistles," in *History and Exegesis: New Testament Essays in Honor of Dr. E. Earle Ellis for His 80th Birthday*, ed. Sang-Won (Aaron) Son (New York: T&T Clark, 2006), 246–52.

as the triumphant, conquering king toward the end of Revelation (chap. 19).

§7.1 The LTT and the OT

Paul's use of the OT has already been discussed above (§2.7). While the LTT don't feature the kind of sustained engagement with Scripture that can be found in the book of Romans (esp. chaps. 9–11) or the letter to the Galatians (esp. chaps. 3–4), the OT does provide the substructure of Paul's argument in these letters. While a certain amount of overlap between our treatment here and the previous discussion will be inevitable, the grounding of the LTT in OT theology is too foundational and central to these letters to skip over them here. For this reason we will summarize some of the salient findings from the previous discussion and provide a substantive summary of the most relevant features of OT theology picked up in the LTT.

§7.1.1 The Pattern of Apostolic Mission: The Abrahamic Promise and Paul's Gentile Mission

One important instance where Paul grounds matters in OT realities is with regard to the apostolic mission. Particularly noteworthy is the intriguing connection between 1 Tim 2:8 and Mal 1:11. As mentioned above, Paul's command, "I want the men *in every place* to pray" (1 Tim 2:8), most likely harks back to Mal 1:11: "'My name will be great among the nations, from the rising of the sun to its setting. Incense and pure offerings will be presented in my name *in every place* because my name will be great among the nations,' says the LORD of Armies." Thus the prayers uttered in the churches Paul planted serve as a sign of the fulfillment of God's promise to extend the offer of salvation to all the nations. This comports with Paul's self-identification as "a herald, an apostle . . . and a teacher of the Gentiles" in the immediately preceding verse (1 Tim 2:7).

Similarly, Paul's language in 2 Tim 4:17 stands in continuity with the reference to "all the nations" in the Abrahamic promises (Gen 18:18; 22:18; 26:4), culminating in the Great Commission (Matt 28:19) and other teachings and instructions of Jesus (Mark 13:10; Luke 24:45–47). The phrase "all the nations/Gentiles" here and elsewhere in Paul's writings reflects his understanding that his mission constitutes the climactic fulfillment of God's ancient promises (cf., e.g., Rom

1:1–6). This is underscored by Paul's opening words in the letter to Titus, where he speaks of his apostolic mission as follows:

> Paul, a servant of God and an apostle of Jesus Christ, ... in the hope of eternal life that *God*, who cannot lie, *promised before time began. In his own time he has revealed his word in the preaching with which I was entrusted* by the command of God our Savior. (Titus 1:1–3, emphasis added)

§7.1.2 The Pattern of Righteous Apostolic Suffering: The Psalmist and Paul

The LTT are part of a complex web of connections in Scripture between the psalmist, Jesus, and Paul as righteous sufferers. The following points have been noted at some length above and will be briefly reiterated here in summary form:

1. Similar to the psalmist's (Ps 22:1) and Jesus's experience (Mark 15:34 par.), Paul's suffering was heightened by his sense of abandonment (2 Tim 4:16; cf. 1:15).

2. Just as the psalmist craved God's presence (Ps 22:19 [21:20]), so Paul was helped by the presence of the Lord in his sufferings (2 Tim 4:17).

3. Just as the psalmist (Ps 22:8) and Jesus (Matt 27:43) experienced eventual rescue, Paul was rescued from persecution both past and future (2 Tim 3:11; 4:17–18).

4. Just as the psalmist says his rescue "from the lion's mouth" (Ps 22:21) would effect that "all the ends of the earth will remember and turn to the Lord. All the families of the nations will bow down before you" (Ps 22:27), so Paul notes that God strengthened him to fully proclaim the gospel message to "all the Gentiles" and that it was *in conjunction with this universal gospel proclamation* that Paul was rescued "from the lion's mouth" (2 Tim 4:17).

These connections place Paul's suffering at the climax of a biblical trajectory of righteous suffering that encompasses David as well as Jesus Christ, the suffering Servant (cf. 1 Pet 2:21–25; cf. Isa 52:15–53:12).

In this way Paul's apostolic mission, reaching to the ends of the earth and including the Gentile nations, is shown to involve (vicarious) suffering that finds validating biblical-theological precedent in previous servants of the Lord such as David and, climactically, Jesus himself.

§7.1.3 The Pattern of Apostolic Succession: The Moses-Joshua and Paul-Timothy Relationship

There is in Paul's letters to Timothy a noticeable motif according to which the Paul-Timothy relationship is viewed as patterned after the Moses-Joshua relationship. This extends even to Timothy's opponents, who are shown to be prefigured in the antagonists of Moses at the time of the exodus. Again it will be helpful to briefly recapitulate the most salient points here:

- With regard to Korah's rebellion (Numbers 16), Alexander and Hymenaeus prefigure the false teachers, while Paul and Timothy parallel Moses and Aaron (2 Tim 2:19).
- The Egyptian magicians in Exodus 7 and 9, identified by name as Jannes and Jambres in later tradition, prefigure the false teachers (2 Tim 3:8–9).
- Moses's laying on of hands on Joshua (Num 27:18–23; Deut 34:9) serves as a precedent of the "laying on of . . . hands" on Timothy (2 Tim 1:6).
- Moses "the servant of the Lord" (Deut 34:5; cf. 2 Kgs 18:12) is shown to provide a pattern for Paul and Timothy (2 Tim 2:24; Titus 1:1).
- Moses "the man of God" (Deut 33:1) also serves as a precursor of Timothy (and others) as the "man of God" (2 Tim 3:17).
- Moses's exhortation to Israel and Joshua (Deut 31:6–7) to "be strong" finds its fulfillment in Paul's exhortation to Timothy to do the same (2 Tim 2:1).

Thus we see that the pattern of the apostolic mission is grounded in the Abrahamic promise; the pattern of righteous suffering is grounded in David, the righteous sufferer in the Psalms; and the pattern of apostolic succession is grounded in the Moses-Joshua relationship at the exodus and on the verge of entering the Promised Land. This constitutes a remarkable substructure of the conception of Paul's apostolic Gentile mission in the LTT.

§7.1.4 The Pattern of Human Relationships: Adam and Eve and Men and Women in the Church

In addressing the question of men's and women's roles in the church in general and roles of leadership in particular, Paul, too, grounds his apostolic directives in OT teaching.[532] Specifically, he appeals to the Genesis account of the creation of Adam and Eve (Genesis 2) and the scenario at the fall of humanity (Genesis 3) in instructing Timothy on what constitutes proper church leadership (1 Tim 2:13–15).

This connection shows that the apostle didn't see himself as providing innovative teaching on the issue of the roles of men and women in the church. Rather, he merely applied OT teaching regarding God's design for man and woman to God's "household," the church (cf. 1 Tim 3:15). According to Paul, women aren't permitted to teach or exercise authority over a man in the church because Adam was created first, not Eve (1 Tim 2:13); and it wasn't Adam, but Eve, who was deceived (1 Tim 2:14). Consistently throughout the LTT, Paul portrays qualified men (including himself and his apostolic delegates, as well as overseers/elders) in public roles of leadership while speaking of women as managers of households and involved in their families as wives and mothers (e.g., 1 Tim 2:15; 5:2–16, esp. v. 14; 2 Tim 2:5; Titus 2:3–5).

In this way God's design for man and woman is presented as part of Paul's conviction that God is good and that this good God created a good creation. This belief, in turn, also forms the basis for Paul's teaching in 1 Tim 4:1–5 opposing the false teachers' proscription of marriage and certain foods. To the contrary, Paul asserts, God created these "to be received with gratitude by those who believe and know the truth": "For everything created by God is good, and nothing is to be rejected if it is received with thanksgiving, since it is sanctified by the word of God and by prayer" (vv. 3–5).

§7.1.5 Conclusion

While explicit OT quotations are limited in the LTT, especially in the letter to Titus, we've seen that appearances can be deceiving. To conclude that the OT is of little significance in these letters based on the sparse direct citations of Scripture would be a demonstrable mistake. In fact, if one were to remove the Hebrew Scriptures as a substructure and foundation of the teaching of the LTT, the entire edifice would immediately begin to crumble and would soon collapse their interrelated theological emphases and distinctive themes.

[532] See esp. Köstenberger and Köstenberger, *God's Design for Man and Woman.*

As the above discussion has amply demonstrated, Paul consciously built the church on the foundation of OT teaching. This includes his consciousness of the apostolic mission being built on the divine promise to Abraham; his consciousness of the apostolic suffering being endured in continuity with the righteous suffering of David; his consciousness of the Mosaic leadership pattern with regard to Joshua being replicated in his succession by Timothy; and his consciousness of the divine design for Adam and Eve finding direct application in men's and women's roles in the church.

While other scriptural patterns and correspondence could be noted—such as the injunction to care for worthy widows (1 Tim 5:2–16; cf. Exod 20:12; cf., e.g., Lev 19:2, 9, 14; Deut 10:18) or the pattern of remuneration of elders, which finds their antecedents in OT stipulations (1 Tim 5:17–18; cf. Deut 10:15; 19:15–21; 25:4), among others—the close connection between the LTT and the OT is unmistakable. In fact, this apostolic grounding of the church and its mission in the authoritative, God-given Hebrew Scriptures constitutes a massive bulwark against the assaults of the false teachers. Indeed we find in 2 Tim 3:14–17 that while the opponents may deceive, the sacred writings of the OT are able to make one wise "for salvation through faith in Christ Jesus." What's more, it is by giving heed to "all Scripture," which includes the "sacred Scriptures" of the OT, that the "man of God"—Timothy specifically (cf. 1 Tim 6:11), but also those whom he will train (2 Tim 2:2)—will be able to teach, reprove, correct, and train in righteousness and will be equipped for every good work.

In this way the "church of the living God" serves as a "pillar and foundation of the truth" (1 Tim 3:15). Yet while some "have departed from the truth . . . and are ruining the faith of some," "God's solid foundation stands firm, bearing this inscription: The Lord knows those who are his, and let everyone who calls on the name of the Lord turn away from wickedness" (2 Tim 2:18–19; cf. Num 16:5). For the composition of the church, too, Paul is convinced, is known to the God who is the same in Moses's day and in his day. He is still the same God today.

§7.2 The LTT and Paul's Other Letters

As mentioned in the Introduction, the question of the relationship between the LTT and Paul's other, earlier letters features prominently in the pseudonymity debate. The question is often raised whether elements of the theology of the LTT such as the designation of God and Christ as Savior, the emphasis on godliness and other Christian virtues, the description of Christ's return in terms of "epiphany," and other theological distinctives are so distinct from the outlook of the undisputed letters of Paul that they constitute presumptive evidence for the pseudonymity of the LTT. We've discussed some of these issues already when dealing with pseudonymity in the Introduction above.

Another relevant historical issue is the relationship between Paul's opponents in some of his earlier letters and the opponents described in the LTT. On the assumption of the historicity of the LTT,[533] it appears that the opponents referred to in these letters don't match exactly Paul's previous opponents, though there are certain points of contact, in particular in 1 Corinthians (with regard to overrealized eschatology) and Colossians (with regard to asceticism). Some also detect similarities with Paul's opponents in 2 Thessalonians.[534] Again, we've dealt with this issue in some detail in the Introduction above. Most likely, the opponents in the LTT arose at a later time during Paul's apostolic mission, in the case of Ephesus perhaps even from within the circle of Ephesian elders (cf. Acts 20:30).

§7.2.1 The Need for Balance

The above commentary proceeded on the basis of the premise, argued at some length in the Introduction, that the apostle

---

[533] Cf. C. K. Barrett, "Pauline Controversies in the Post-Pauline Period," *NTS* 20 (1973–74): 229–45, who argues that the "heresy" of the LTT is, in essence, a "lumping together" of Judaism, legalism, mythology, and gnosis: "The author was concerned to omit no heresy he had heard of" (p. 240). C. Schaefer, "Judentum und Gnosis? Die Gegnerpolemik im Titusbrief als Element literarischer Konstruktion," in *Ein Meisterschüler: Titus und sein Brief. Festschrift M. Theobald*, ed. H.-U. Weidemann and W. Eisele, SBS 214 (Stuttgart: Katholisches Bibelwerk, 2008), 55–80, speaks of the polemic against the author's opponents in the letter to Titus in terms of "literary construction."

[534] W. Pratscher, "Die Auseinandersetzung mit Gegnern in den Pastoralbriefen," *SNTSU-A* 18 (1993): 133–50, who discusses affinities with 2 Thessalonians and Colossians. Pratscher concludes that while in 2 Thessalonians and Colossians Paul is primarily concerned with engaging his opponents in form of theological argument, his primary purpose with regard to the false teachers in the LTT is that of distancing the opponents from the addressees.

Paul did in fact write the LTT and that these letters conclude the Pauline corpus in the NT canon. In keeping with this conviction, the commentary has regularly highlighted parallel passages in the other ten canonical Pauline letters as well as other conceptual affinities between the LTT and the other Pauline writings. This is not to say that there aren't significant differences between the ten other Pauline letters and the LTT.

In fact, the depiction of the relationship between the LTT and the other Pauline letters calls for balance. On the one hand, differences between these corpora shouldn't be ignored or minimized. On the other hand, affinities should be noted as well (§7.2.3). As mentioned, the historical position of the LTT at the end of Paul's life sufficiently explains the different emphases. In addition, matters of contextualization are also relevant, such as the designation of God and Christ as Savior or the exhortations to pursue Christian virtues in the LTT.

§7.2.2 Congruence with the Pauline Mission

Most foundationally, as noted, the LTT evince congruence with the Pauline mission. This is seen particularly in Paul's focus on evangelizing major urban centers (see Acts), which is also evident in the LTT (cf. Titus 1:5). Also, Paul consistently relies on his network of coworkers and apostolic delegates (see, e.g., the references to Titus in 2 Corinthians) in order to follow up on churches he planted previously. Paul's concern to establish proper leadership in local congregations (particularly elders) is well documented from the earliest times in his mission.[535]

In other words, it's not true, as "early Catholicism" advocates maintain, that these writings reflect a concern with church leadership, structure, and organization that is substantially different from that found in Paul's earlier writings and missionary work. To the contrary, Paul's later writings are fully congruent with his approach attested from the beginning of his church-planting efforts and simply document the implementation of this approach in ever-expanding circles of geographical movement toward the ends of the then-known world.

In this regard, it's noteworthy that Paul seeks to evangelize an island such as Crete, which others might have considered to be of marginal significance. Yet in his methodical efforts to spread the gospel across the Mediterranean in a westward motion, Paul

---

[535] E.g., Acts 14:23; cf. Phil 1:1.

apparently believed that Crete occupied a strategic place, in part no doubt due to its two dozen or so cities. All this is consistent with Paul's words to the Romans, "But now I no longer have any work to do in these regions, and I have strongly desired for many years to come to you whenever I travel to Spain."[536]

§7.2.3 Similarities and Differences between the LTT and the Other Pauline Letters

As the chart below illustrates, there are a considerable number of both similarities and differences between the LTT and the other Pauline letters included in the canon. The list below is not comprehensive but merely illustrative. Other examples of affinities between the LTT and the remaining Pauline corpus and of distinctive features in the LTT are referenced in the commentary portions above.[537]

Similarities between LTT and Paul's Other Letters	*Distinctive Features of the LTT*
Letter openings follow standard format, including omission of thanksgiving due to a sense of urgency (1 Tim 1:3–4; cf. Gal 1:6)	Trustworthy sayings in all three LTT but nowhere else in the Pauline letter corpus (1 Tim 1:15; 3:1; 4:8; 2 Tim 2:11–13; Titus 3:4–7; see §2.6 above)
Paul's ministry as stewardship (οἰκονομία; 1 Tim 1:4; cf. 1 Cor 9:17; Eph 1:10; 3:2, 9; Col 1:25)*	Lists of qualifications for church leaders, both elders and deacons (1 Tim 3:1–13; Titus 1:5–9)
Practice of delivering a false teacher or offending person to Satan (1 Tim 1:18–20; cf. 1 Cor 5:5)	Exhortations to pursue virtues such as godliness (εὐσέβεια; 1 Tim 2:2; 3:16; 4:7–8; 6:3, 5–6, 11; 2 Tim 3:5; Titus 1:1)

[536] Rom 15:24; cf. v. 28. This, of course, doesn't necessarily imply that Paul ever made it to Spain, though this is certainly possible. See "Pauline Chronology" in the introduction and commentary at Titus 1:5.

[537] See also the similarities between 1 Timothy and Paul's other NT letters adduced by A. Schlatter in his commentary *Die Kirche der Griechen im Urteil des Paulus* as presented in R. W. Yarbrough, "Schlatter on the Pastorals: Mission in the Academy," in *New Testament Theology in Light of the Church's Mission. Essays in Honor of I. Howard Marshall*, ed. J. C. Laansma, G. R. Osborne, and R. F. Van Neste (Eugene, OR: Wipf & Stock, 2011), 302–6 (note that Schlatter shifted from affirming non-Pauline authorship of the LTT at the beginning of his career to accepting Pauline authorship in his later scholarship). According to Yarbrough, Schlatter identifies thirty-four parallels between Paul's ten-letter corpus and 1 Timothy, thirty-one with 2 Timothy, and nine with Titus (a total of seventy-four parallels). See also W. T. Wilson, *Pauline Parallels: A Comprehensive Guide* (Louisville: Westminster John Knox, 2009), 403–32, who identifies eighty parallels.

Similarities between LTT and Paul's Other Letters	*Distinctive Features of the LTT*
Teaching of submission to governing authorities (1 Tim 2:1–3; Titus 3:1–2; cf. Rom 13:1–7)	Intensely personal, testamentary nature (esp. 2 Timothy)
Solemn affirmation that Paul is telling the truth (ἀλήθειαν λέγω οὐ ψεύδομαι; 1 Tim 2:7; cf. Rom 9:1)	Rare use of distinctively Pauline terms such as *χάρις*, "grace" (except for 1 Tim 1:14; 2 Tim 1:9; 2:1; Titus 2:11; 3:7), *ἐλευθερία* ("freedom"), *σάρξ* ("flesh," in contrast to "Spirit," but see 1 Tim 3:16), *σταυρός* ("cross"), and *δικαιοσύνη θεοῦ* ("righteousness of God")**
Purpose of equipping and strengthening a church against its opponents (1 Timothy; cf., e.g., Galatians, Colossians)	Prominence of designation of both God and Jesus Christ as *σωτήρ* ("Savior"; 1 Tim 1:1; 2:3; 4:10; 2 Tim 1:10; Titus 1:3–4; 2:10, 13; 3:4, 6)
Virtue lists (1 Tim 4:12; 6:11; 2 Tim 2:22; 3:10; cf. 2 Cor 6:6–8; Gal 5:22–23; Eph 4:32; 5:9; Phil 4:8; Col 3:12) and vice lists (1 Tim 1:9–10; 2 Tim 3:2–5; Titus 3:3; cf. Rom 1:29–31; 13:13; 1 Cor 5:10–11; 6:9–10; 2 Cor 6:9–10; 12:20–21; Gal 5:19–21; Eph 4:31; 5:3–5; Col 3:5, 8)	Specific sets of instructions regarding caring for worthy widows and removing errant elders (1 Tim 5:3–16, 17–25)
Athletic metaphors (2 Tim 2:5; 4:7; cf. 1 Cor 9:24–26; Gal 2:2; 5:7; Phil 2:16; 3:13–14)***	Distinctive vocabulary related to the passing on of the apostolic tradition (e.g., *παραθήκη* in 1 Tim 6:20; 2 Tim 1:12, 14; *παράδοσις* in 1 Cor 11:2; 2 Thess 2:15; 3:6)
Verbal and conceptual parallels: (1) 1 Tim 1:12: ἐνδυναμώσαντί με; cf. Phil 4:13: ἐνδυναμοῦντί με; (2) 1 Tim 2:1–2 cf. Phil 4:6: prayer (*προσευχή*), petition (*δέησις*), thanksgiving (*εὐχαριστία*); (3) 2 Tim 1:8: not ashamed, gospel is power of God: cf. Rom 1:16; (4) 2 Tim 2:11: *εἰ γὰρ συναπεθάνομεν, καὶ συζήσομεν*; cf. Rom 6:8: *εἰ δὲ ἀπεθάνομεν σὺν Χριστῷ, πιστεύομεν ὅτι καὶ συζήσομεν αὐτῷ*; (5) Titus 3:5: saved not by works but justified by grace, and for works; cf. Eph 2:8–10	Other distinctive vocabulary, such as *εὐσέβεια* ("godliness"; see above), *σώφρων* ("self-controlled"; 1 Tim 3:2; Titus 1:8; 2:2, 5), and *ἐπιφάνεια* in the place of *παρουσία* ("coming," referring to Christ's return; 1 Tim 6:14; 2 Tim 1:10; 4:1, 8; Titus 2:13; but see 2 Thess 2:8)

Similarities between LTT and Paul's Other Letters	*Distinctive Features of the LTT*
Concern with local church leadership (1 Tim 3:1–13; Titus 1:5–9; cf. Phil 1:1; see also Acts 14:23)	Terminology not found elsewhere in the NT, e.g. ἀνδραποδιστής ("slave-trader/kidnapper"), ἐπίορκος ("perjurer"; 1 Tim 1:12); ἀφθορία ("integrity"; Titus 2:7)
Use of preformed tradition (e.g., 1 Tim 1:8–10, 15a–b, 17; 2:5–6a; 3:1, 16; 4:8, 9–10b; 5:24–25; 6:7, 10a, 11–16; cf. 1 Cor 15:3–8; Phil 2:6–11; Col 1:15–20)	Proportionately, more emphasis is placed on church offices and formal church structure and organization and less on spiritual gifts (1 Tim 3:1–13; cf. 1 Corinthians 12–14)****
Teaching on gender roles in the church being grounded in God's original creation design (1 Tim 2:13–15; cf. 1 Cor 11:8–9)	
Similar use of certain OT passages: Deut 25:4 in 1 Tim 5:18 and 1 Cor 9:9; Genesis 2–3 in 1 Tim 2:13–15 and 1 Cor 11:8–9; Deut 19:15 in 1 Tim 5:19 and 2 Cor 13:1	
Similarity between *Haustafeln* (house tables) in Ephesians and Colossians and household codes in LTT (e.g., 1 Tim 5:1–6:2; Titus 2:1–10)	

*See L. T. Johnson, "*Oikonomia Theou*: The Theological Voice of 1 Timothy from the Perspective of Pauline Authorship," *HorBT* 21 (1999): 87–104; and Tomlinson, "Purpose and Stewardship Theme," 52–83.

**But note that some of these terms are only found frequently in certain Pauline letters and not in others; see chart in Mounce, *Pastoral Epistles*, xc.

***See V. C. Pfitzner, "The *Agon* Motif in the Pastoral Epistles," in *Paul and the Agon Motif: Traditional Athletic Imagery in the Pauline Literature*, NovTSup 16 (Leiden: Brill, 1967), 164–86.

****See on this R. Y. K. Fung, "Charismatic versus Organized Ministry? An Examination of an Alleged Antithesis," *EvQ* 52 (1980): 195–214.

As the above chart illustrates, while there are differences between the LTT and the other Pauline epistles, there are certainly several significant affinities as well. These affinities include a broad range of similarities, from conceptual and thematic to specific verbal and terminological parallels. What's more, the differences are to be expected given the unique setting of the LTT (see the introduction).

§7.3 The LTT and Acts

Acts tells the story of the early church and its mission from Jerusalem to Judea, Samaria, and the ends of the earth, epitomized by Rome, the empire's capital, as spearheaded by the apostles Peter (Jewish focus) and Paul (Gentile focus).[538] It recounts Paul's persecution of the church, his conversion, and his three missionary journeys, as well as his arrest in Jerusalem and his subsequent interrogations before Roman government officials leading to his transport to Rome to stand trial. Timothy is first mentioned

[538] At times the theory is advanced that Luke himself wrote the LTT or that he at least served as an amanuensis or redactor. However, it is unlikely that Luke would write the statement, "Only Luke is with me" (2 Tim 4:11). What is more, all three letters overtly claim Pauline authorship (1 Tim 1:1; 2 Tim 1:1; Titus 1:1). If Luke served as an amanuensis, this would be an argument from silence; note that the amanuensis identifies himself explicitly in Romans (Tertius; Rom 16:22). Clearly Paul and Luke sustained a close partnership throughout Paul's missionary career, which may account for a certain amount of Lukan influence on Paul, but anything beyond this seems conjectural and unlikely, especially in light of the discussion of pseudonymity in the Introduction. See also the sharp rejection by Marshall (*Pastoral Epistles*, 87–88n14): "The hypothesis of a Lucan origin for the PE should be dropped from consideration."

For a history of scholarship and critique, see N. Brox, "Lukas als Verfasser der Pastoralbriefe?," JAC 15 (1970): 62–77; contra A. Feuillet, "La doctrine des Epitres Pastorales et leurs affinités aved l'oeuvre lucanienne," *Revue Thomiste* 78 (1978): 181–225; S. G. Wilson, *Luke and the Pastoral Epistles* (London: SCM, 1979). See also J.-D. Kaestli, "Luke-Acts and the Pastoral Epistles: The Thesis of a Common Authorship," in *Luke's Literary Achievement: Collected Essays*, ed. C. M. Tuckett, JSNTSup 116 (Sheffield: Sheffield Academic Press, 1995), 110–26, who concludes there's a family relationship and that both the LTT and Luke-Acts are part of the Pauline "trajectory" but demurs from positing a "fusional" relationship between these writings (p. 126).

For a rather daring argument that the LTT constitute the final volume of Luke-Acts, see J. D. Quinn, "The Last Volume of Luke: The Relation of Luke-Acts to the Pastoral Epistles," in *Perspectives on Luke-Acts*, Special Studies 5, ed. C. H. Talbert (Edinburgh: T&T Clark, 1978), 62–75. Riesner notes similarities such as widows, medical background, and Jesus traditions and argues that Luke served as redactor of the LTT. R. Riesner, "Once More: Luke-Acts and the Pastoral Epistles," in *History and Exegesis: New Testament Essays in Honor of Dr. E. Earle Ellis for His 80th Birthday*, ed. S.-W. Son (New York/London: T&T Clark, 2006), 239–58; cf. Riesner, "Paul's Trial and End," 397: "In my opinion, Luke expanded shorter letters addressed to co-workers of Paul to apostolic *mandata* (1 Timothy, Titus) and to an apostolic testament (2 Timothy), also making use of traditions from the Palestinian primitive church and his own memories after the death of the apostle. With Jerome D. Quinn, I hold the Pastoral Epistles to be something like the 'third part' of Luke's historical work."

in Acts 16 as a local disciple in Lystra where Paul selects him to accompany him on his travels and join him in ministry. Titus, on the other hand, is not mentioned in Acts at all.

It is highly likely that the LTT were written in the period after Acts ends, that is, after the year 60.[539] If so, there's no conflict between the data provided in Acts and the LTT; rather, these two sets of documents stand in a complementary relationship, with the LTT continuing parts of the story told in Acts.[540] In terms of the characterization of Paul, Acts focuses on his role in defending the integrity of the Christian movement and its innocence of the political and religious charges brought against it. The book also shows the irresistible movement of the gospel from Jerusalem to Rome, empowered by God, the risen Christ, and the Spirit. Focused on Paul in the second half of the book, in partial parallelism with the portrayal of Jesus in Luke's Gospel, Timothy is shown to be a valuable and integral part of the Pauline circle of coworkers (see, e.g., Acts 19:22; 20:4).

That said, the focus in Acts isn't on any one person, whether Peter or Paul, but on the gospel and on the Holy Spirit as empowering the church's witness. The main controversy featured in Acts is the Judaizing controversy, which is decisively addressed at the Jerusalem conference at the midpoint and pivot of the book (Acts 15). This development is corroborated by Paul's letter to the Galatians, which was most likely written just prior to the Jerusalem Council. Acts 19 shows Paul planting the church in Ephesus and engaging in a three-year ministry in that strategic city in the Roman province of Asia Minor (Acts 20:31; cf. 19:10). The following chapter records Paul's moving farewell to the Ephesian elders (Acts 20:17–38), including his prediction that dangerous opposition would soon arise from within the church (Acts 20:29–31). Apparently, in the interim between the meeting recounted in Acts 20 and Paul's first letter to Timothy, this prediction had come true,

[539] This is held by the majority of commentators, both those favoring pseudonymity and those holding to authenticity. The minority view, that 1 Timothy and Titus were written prior to the end of Acts, is represented by Riesner, "Once More: Luke-Acts and the Pastoral Epistles" (but see the brief critique in Marshall, "Pastoral Epistles in Recent Study," 290–91).

[540] Cf. Barrett, "Pauline Controversies," 229–45, who contends that Acts provides a sort of counterpart for the Pastorals Letters in that Acts "provides models for the minister who in the Pastorals is taught that it is his duty to preach." See also Riesner, "Once More: Luke-Acts and the Pastoral Epistles."

so that Paul must now urge Timothy, who had been dispatched to Ephesus, to deal with the false teachers, who may have included even some of the Ephesian elders (1 Tim 1:3–4, 18–20; 5:17–25).

At the same time, Paul also senses the need to turn his attention to the establishment of the church for the post-apostolic period. Some say that in this regard the LTT differ from some of Paul's earlier letters, which reflect his belief in Jesus's imminent return. The delay of the παρουσία, they argue, necessitated a change in approach from letters such as the Thessalonian correspondence to the LTT.[541] However, this difference in eschatological expectations is often exaggerated. More likely, as long as Paul was fully engaged in the ministry of planting and nurturing local congregations, his primary energy was devoted to addressing pertinent issues and providing doctrinal instruction. After Paul's release from his first Roman imprisonment, however, the situation may have changed, and the apostle sensed, perhaps in light of mounting Roman persecution of Christians, that his years of ministry were numbered. Also, in light of his imprisonment and advancing age, Paul must rely more significantly on apostolic delegates, with his LTT providing vital instructions.

This scenario is entirely plausible and shows the limitations of verbal and conceptual comparisons between Acts and Paul's earlier letters on the one hand and the LTT on the other. In fact, it would be surprising if Paul, toward the end of his life, had not felt a need to take this kind of course of action and if this were not reflected in letters to his subordinates. If Paul wrote such letters, in turn, it is clear that these would have been highly significant, valued and esteemed by the church, and included in the canon alongside Paul's other letters (see the esteem expressed for Paul and his letters in 2 Pet 3:15–16). The book of Acts and the LTT, therefore, sustain a complementary relationship, with Acts providing a narrative of the bulk of Paul's ministry from his conversion until his first Roman imprisonment and the LTT belonging to the phase toward the end of Paul's life at which the apostle cast his vision for the permanent shaping of the church in the

[541] See, e.g., J. C. Beker, *Heirs of Paul* (Philadelphia: Fortress, 1991), who holds to pseudonymity primarily because the παρουσία hope has receded in the LTT and because the author engages in polemic rather than engagement of the false teachers.

postapostolic period.[542] Just like Jesus appointed, trained, and commissioned the Twelve, so Paul assembled his circle of apostolic delegates that would be able to continue his mission—in fact, *God's* mission—subsequent to his martyrdom.

§7.4 The LTT and the Non-Pauline NT Letters

An intriguing connection between the LTT and Hebrews is provided by the reference in Heb 13:23, "Be aware that our brother Timothy has been released. If he comes soon enough, he will be with me when I see you." This shows that Timothy was well integrated in the NT circle and network of the early church's mission and sustained a close connection with the author of the letter to the Hebrews (whoever that was).[543] Also noteworthy is the reference to Jesus as mediator (μεσίτης) between God and humanity in 1 Tim 2:5, a theme which is developed in some detail in Hebrews, where Jesus is presented as mediator (μεσίτης) of a new covenant (see Heb 8:6; 9:15; 12:24).

A connection between the LTT and the book of James is found in the concern with dealing with wealthy members of the congregation (1 Tim 6:9–10, 17–19; Jas 1:9–11; 2:1–17; 5:1–6). Note also that James identifies caring for widows and orphans as the essence of true religion (Jas 1:27), a theme that is developed with regard to widows in great length in 1 Tim 5:3–16. Likewise, there is a clear connection between James's insistence on the need for works (Jas 2:18–26) and the emphasis on good works in the LTT (1 Tim 2:10; 5:10, 25; 6:18; 2 Tim 2:21; 3:17; Titus 2:7, 14; 3:1, 8, 14). Both James and the LTT also invoke the example of a farmer (Jas 5:7; 2 Tim 2:6). Finally, the phrase "wander/turn away from the truth" is shared

[542] Cf. J. Schröter, "Kirche im Anschluss an Paulus: Aspekte der Paulusrezeption in der Apostelgeschichte und in den Pastoralbriefen," *ZNW* 98 (2007): 77–104, who contends that the main differences between Acts and the LTT are the genres they employ and their range of coverage. Acts integrates Paul into an account of the history of early Christianity whereas the LTT focus on Paul's instructions for congregations under his jurisdiction toward the end of his life.

[543] It is all but certain that the Timothy mentioned in Heb 13:23 is Paul's apostolic delegate. Cf., e.g., Morris, who writes, "Timothy is no doubt the companion of Paul (no other Timothy is known to us from those times) and he seems to have had some ties with both the readers and the writer. Otherwise we would expect a general expression instead of 'our brother Timothy.'" L. Morris, *Hebrews*, EBC 12 (Grand Rapids: Zondervan, 1981), 157.

between James and the LTT (Jas 5:19; 1 Tim 6:5; 2 Tim 2:18; 4:4; Titus 1:14), though the verbs are different.

Affinities with Peter's letters, especially 1 Peter, should be noted as well. To begin with, both the LTT and 1 Peter emphasize the importance of good works as a witness to the surrounding unbelieving world (1 Tim 2:10; 5:10, 25; 6:18; 2 Tim 2:21; 3:17; Titus 2:7, 14; 3:1, 8, 14; 1 Pet 3:12, 15). Both the LTT and 1 Peter also urge believers' submission to the governing authorities (1 Tim 2:1–4; Titus 3:1; 1 Pet 2:13–17) and the submission of slaves to masters (1 Tim 6:1–2; Titus 2:9–10; 1 Pet 2:18–20). Both the LTT and 1 Peter also include instructions for wives to submit to their husbands (Titus 2:5; 1 Pet 3:1, 5–6) and for women to dress modestly and to focus on inner beauty (1 Tim 2:9–10; Titus 2:3–5; 1 Pet 3:2–5). Both the LTT and 1 Peter issue instructions regarding elders (1 Tim 3:1–7; 5:17–25; 1 Pet 5:1–4), and both caution against the devil (1 Tim 3:6–7; 2 Tim 2:26; 1 Pet 5:8–9). Both also refer to the church as "God's household" (1 Tim 3:15; cf. vv. 4–5; 1 Pet 4:17). Finally, both the LTT and 1 Peter speak of believers' good works silencing the unbelieving world (Titus 2:5, 8, 10; 1 Pet 2:13–3:7). In fact, the entire stance toward the world in terms of a witnessing mind-set is similar in Titus and 1 Peter. With 2 Peter, the LTT share a strong emphasis on the pursuit of Christian virtues (e.g., 1 Tim 4:6–16; 2 Pet 1:3–11).

The reference to testing the spirits in 1 John 4:1 in an end-time context is somewhat reminiscent of a similar reference introducing an end-time passage in 1 Tim 4:1 (cf. 2 Tim 3:1). The stern warning against false teachers in the book of Jude is fueled by a similar passion as corresponding warnings against opponents in the LTT, and the ethos behind the exhortation "to contend for the faith that was delivered to the saints once for all" in Jude 3 parallels the emphasis on the "deposit" of Paul's apostolic teaching and similar references in the LTT (e.g., 1 Tim 6:20; 2 Tim 1:14).

§7.5 Conclusion

The LTT are an integral part of the biblical and NT canon. They are firmly built on the substructure of OT theology, in particular with regard to the grounding of the early church's mission, the pattern of apostolic succession, the conception of righteous suffering, and their understanding of God's design for man and woman as it applies to the NT church. They display both similarities and distinctive differences in relation to the other ten letters in the Pauline corpus. Most likely written after the period covered in the book of Acts, the LTT provide an essential supplement to the Pauline chronology and account of his apostolic ministry. They also display a series of interesting connections with other NT letters, including the books of Hebrews, James, 1 and 2 Peter, 1 John, and Jude. Rather than belonging to the subapostolic period, the LTT are therefore best viewed as an integral part of the NT's depiction of the life and mission of the early church as spearheaded by apostles such as Paul.

Conclusion

The study of the biblical theology of the LTT has proved fascinating for several reasons. First, the LTT occupy a unique place literarily at the end of the Pauline letter canon and historically toward the end of the apostolic period. This means that, theologically, too, these letters exhibit a distinctive and highly relevant set of biblical-theological emphases that is not merely of antiquarian and academic interest but also has great potential to inform, instruct, and ground the contemporary church in the authoritative apostolic teaching found in these letters.

Second, a study of the LTT in their own right also has the potential to augment our understanding of the teachings found in Paul's earlier NT letters in a way that neither minimizes nor maximizes their historical, literary, and theological distance from them. As mentioned at the outset of this investigation, a certain amount of latitude is needed in analyzing the theology of the LTT that provides space for Paul to express himself in a way that best serves the needs of his apostolic mission at the particular salvation-historical juncture represented by these letters.

While the debate regarding the authorship of the LTT has often centered on their distinctive vocabulary or supposed "early Catholicism," it has been shown that within the larger context of the Pauline mission and the expansion of first-century Christianity, theology necessarily will evolve, not so much in terms of its essence but with regard to its contextualization, as the gospel increasingly became a universal message that resonated in varying cultural contexts with their respective belief systems, ethical understandings, and real-life applications.

In this context, what proved preeminent is the message of God's salvation in Christ, which set the church apart from other construals of deity, salvific notions, and related sets of beliefs in its day. This is not materially different from the challenges and opportunities the church faces in the twenty-first century as it finds itself placed in the context of a culture that is replete with a variety of modern forms of idolatry, ethical approaches, and notions of meaning, purpose, and salvation.

In the midst of such an increasingly cosmopolitan, pluralistic universe, where diversity is celebrated, the "new tolerance" extolled, and the notion of revealed truth is being increasingly marginalized, the church's abiding call stands in remarkable continuity to what we find expressed in the LTT. Two millennia after Paul planted his congregations the church continues to be called to proclaim the message of God's salvation in Christ as part of her end-time mission to the entire world.

This, in turn, places great value on preserving the purity of the gospel and on faithful service, as well as on careful selection of qualified leadership in local congregations. It also accentuates the need for committed discipleship, person-to-person mentoring, and discerning spiritual witness in a world ruled by the evil one. In this world the church can do no better than to heed the final words of Paul who at the end of his ministry told Timothy that his purpose was "that I might fully preach the word and all the Gentiles hear it" (2 Tim 4:17).

SELECT BIBLIOGRAPHY

Note: In keeping with the nature of this commentary and the primary target audience, this bibliography focuses primarily on scholarly works written in English; works written in other languages are included only if they make a particularly vital contribution to the field and if comparable English works do not exist. Special attention is given to works dealing with the major theological themes found in the Letters to Timothy and Titus. The bibliography generally does not include works that are limited to dealing with one particular passage. These works are cited at the appropriate location in the expository section of this commentary.

Commentaries

Brox, Norbert. *Die Pastoralbriefe*. RNT 7. 5th edition. Regensburg: Pustet, 1989.

Calvin, John. *1 & 2 Timothy & Titus*. 1556, 1549. Reprint, Wheaton: Crossway, 1998.

Collins, Raymond F. *1 and 2 Timothy and Titus: A Commentary*. NTL. Louisville: Westminster John Knox, 2002.

Dibelius, Martin, and Hans Conzelmann. *The Pastoral Epistles*. Translated by Philip Buttolph and Adela Yarbro. Hermeneia. Philadelphia: Fortress, 1972.

Fee, Gordon D. *1 and 2 Timothy, Titus*. NIBCNT 13. Peabody, MA: Hendrickson, 1984, 1988.

Fiore, Benjamin. *The Pastoral Epistles*. SP 17. Collegeville, MN: Liturgical Press, 2007.

Gorday, P. *Colossians, 1–2 Thessalonians, 1–2 Timothy, Titus, Philemon*. ACCS. Downers Grove: InterVarsity, 2000.

Gourgues, Michel. *Les deux lettres à Timothée. La lettre à Tite*. Commentaire biblique: Nouveau Testament 14. Paris: Cerf, 2009.

Guthrie, Donald. *The Pastoral Epistles*. Rev. ed. TNTC 14. Grand Rapids: Eerdmans, 1990.

Johnson, Luke Timothy. *The First and Second Letters to Timothy*. AB 35A. Garden City, NY: Doubleday, 2001.

________. *Letters to Paul's Delegates: 1 Timothy, 2 Timothy, Titus*. The NT in Context. Valley Forge, PA: Trinity Press International, 1996.

Kelly, J. N. D. *A Commentary on the Pastoral Epistles*. BNTC. London: Adam & Charles Black, 1963.

Knight, George W. *The Pastoral Epistles*. NIGTC. Grand Rapids: Eerdmans, 1992.

Köstenberger, Andreas J. "1 & 2 Timothy, Titus." Pages 487–625 in vol. 12 of *The Expositor's Bible Commentary*. Edited by Tremper Longman III and David E. Garland. Rev. ed. Grand Rapids: Zondervan, 2006.

Lea, Thomas D., and Hayne P. Griffin. *1, 2 Timothy, Titus*. NAC 34. Nashville: Broadman, 1992.

Marshall, I. Howard. *A Critical and Exegetical Commentary on the Pastoral Epistles*. In collaboration with Philip H. Towner. ICC. Edinburgh: T&T Clark, 1999.

Mounce, William D. *Pastoral Epistles*. WBC 46. Nashville: Nelson, 2000.

Oberlinner, Lorenz. *Die Pastoralbriefe*. 3 vols. HThKNT 11/2. Freiburg: Herder, 1994–96.

Quinn, Jerome D. *The Letter to Titus: A New Translation with Notes and Commentary, and an Introduction to Titus, I and II Timothy, the Pastoral Epistles*. AB 35. New York: Doubleday, 1990.

________, and William C. Wacker. *The First and Second Letters to Timothy*. ECC. Grand Rapids: Eerdmans, 2000.

Roloff, Jürgen. *Der erste Brief an Timotheus*. EKKNT 15. Zurich: Benziger, 1988.

Spicq, Ceslas. *Les épîtres pastorales*. 2 vols. 4th edition. Études bibliques 39. Paris: Gabalda, 1969.

Towner, Philip H. *The Letters to Timothy and Titus*. NICNT. Grand Rapids: Eerdmans, 2006.

Twomey, Jay. *The Pastoral Epistles through the Centuries*. Blackwell Bible Commentaries. Malden, MA: Wiley-Blackwell, 2009.

Wall, Robert W. *1 and 2 Timothy and Titus*. THNTC. Grand Rapids: Eerdmans, 2012.

Weiser, Alfons. *Der zweite Brief an Timotheus*. EKKNT 16/1. Düsseldorf: Benziger, 2003.

Witherington, Ben, III. *Letters and Homilies for Hellenized Christians*, vol. 1: *A Socio-Rhetorical Commentary on Titus, 1–2 Timothy and 1–3 John*. Downers Grove: InterVarsity, 2006.

Select Bibliography

Other Works

Aageson, James W. "Genesis in the Deutero-Pauline Epistles." Pages 117–29 in *Genesis in the New Testament*. Edited by Maarten J. J. Menken and Steve Moyise. LNTS 466. London: Bloomsbury T&T Clark, 2012.

________. "The Pastoral Epistles, Apostolic Authority, and the Development of the Pauline Scriptures." Pages 5–26 in *The Pauline Canon*. Edited by Stanley E. Porter. Pauline Studies 1. Leiden: Brill, 2004.

________. *Paul, the Pastoral Epistles, and the Early Church*. Peabody, MA: Hendrickson, 2008.

Adamczewski, B. *Heirs of the Reunited Church: The History of the Pauline Mission in Paul's Letters, in the So-Called Pastoral Letters, and in the Pseudo-Titus Narrative of Acts*. Frankfurt: Peter Lang, 2010.

Allen, J. A. "The 'In Christ' Formula in the Pastoral Epistles." *NTS* 10 (1963): 115–21.

Aune, David A. "The Pastoral Letters: 1 and 2 Timothy and Titus." Pages 551–69 in *The Blackwell Companion to the New Testament*. Chichester, UK: Wiley-Blackwell, 2010.

Barclay, John M. G. "There Is Neither Old Nor Young? Early Christianity and Ancient Ideologies of Age." *NTS* 53 (2007): 225–41.

Barentsen, Jack. *Emerging Leadership in the Pauline Mission: A Social Identity Perspective on Local Leadership Development in Corinth and Ephesus*. Princeton Theological Monograph Series 168. Eugene, OR: Wipf & Stock, 2011.

Bassler, Jouette M. "Epiphany Christology in the Pastoral Letters: Another Look." Pages 194–214 in *Pauline Conversations in Context: Essays in Honor of Calvin J. Roetzel*. Edited by Janice Capel Anderson, Philip Sellew, and Claudia Setzer. JSNTSup 221. Sheffield: Sheffield Academic Press, 2002.

________. "A Plethora of Epiphanies: Christology in the Pastoral Letters." *Princeton Seminary Bulletin* 17 (1996): 310–25.

Bauckham, Richard. "Pseudo-Apostolic Letters." *JBL* 107 (1988): 469–94.

Baum, Armin D. "Semantic Variation within the *Corpus Paulinum*: Linguistic Considerations Concerning the Richer Vocabulary of the Pastoral Epistles." *TynBul* 51 (2008): 271–92.

Beker, J. Christiaan. *Heirs of Paul. Their Legacy in the New Testament and the Church Today*. Philadelphia: Fortress, 1991.

Belleville, Linda L. "Christology, the Pastoral Epistles, and Commentaries." Pages 317–36 in *On the Writing of New Testament Commentaries. Festschrift for Grant R. Osborne on the Occasion of His 70th Birthday*. Edited by Stanley E. Porter and Eckhard J. Schnabel. Texts and Editions for NT Study 8. Leiden: Brill, 2012.

Bieringer, R., ed. *2 Timothy Revisited*. Colloquium Oecumenicum Paulinum 23. Leuven: Peeters, 2016.

Bjelland Kartzow, Marianne. *Gossip and Gender: Othering of Speech in the Pastoral Epistles*. BZNW 164. Berlin: Walter de Gruyter, 2009.

Blight, Richard C. *An Exegetical Summary of 1 Timothy*. Dallas: SIL International, 2009.

Brown, Raymond E. "The Pauline Heritage in the Pastorals: The Importance of Church Structure." Pages 31–46 in *The Churches the Apostles Left Behind*. New York: Paulist: 1984.

Campbell, R. Alastair. "Identifying the Faithful Sayings in the Pastoral Epistles." *JSNT* 54 (1994): 73–86.

Clark, Matthew. "The Pastoral Epistles." Pages 213–25 in *A Biblical Theology of the Holy Spirit*. Edited by Trevor J. Burke and Keith Warrington. Eugene, OR: Wipf & Stock, 2014.

Clarke, Andrew D. *A Pauline Theology of Church Leadership*. LNTS 362. London: T&T Clark, 2008.

Collins, Raymond F. "From παρουσία to ἐπιφάνεια: The Transformation of a Pauline Motif." Pages 273–99 in *Unity and Diversity in the Gospels and Paul: Essays in Honor of Frank J. Matera*. Edited by Christopher W. Skinner and Kelly R. Iverson. Early Christianity and Its Literature 7. Atlanta: SBL, 2012.

________. "The Image of Paul in the Pastorals." *LTP* 31 (1975): 147–73.

________. "The Theology of the Epistle to Titus." *ETL* 76 (2000): 56–72.

________. "Where Have All My Siblings Gone? A Reflection on the Use of Kinship Language in Pastoral Epistles." Pages 321–36 in *Celebrating Paul: Festschrift in Honor of Jerome Murphy-O'Connor, O.P., and Joseph A. Fitzmyer, S. J.* Edited by Peter Spitaler. Washington, DC: Catholic Biblical Association of America, 2011.

Couser, Greg A. "God and Christian Existence in the Pastoral Epistles: Toward Theological Method and Meaning." *NovT* 42 (2000): 262–83.

________. "'Prayer' and the Public Square: 1 Timothy 2:1–7 and Christian Political Engagement." Pages 277–94 in *New Testament Theology in Light of the Church's Mission: Essays in Honor of I. Howard Marshall.* Edited by Jon C. Laansma, Grant R. Osborne, and Ray F. Van Neste. Eugene, OR: Cascade: 2011.

D'Angelo, Mary Rose. "Εὐσέβεια: Roman Imperial Family Values and the Sexual Politics of 4 Maccabees and the Pastorals." *BibInt* 11 (2003): 139–65.

De Boer, Martinus C. "Images of Paul in the Post-Apostolic Period." *CBQ* 42 (1980): 359–80.

Dickson, J. *Mission-Commitment in Ancient Judaism and in the Pauline Communities: The Shape, Extent, and Background of Early Christian Mission*. WUNT 2/159. Tübingen: Mohr Siebeck, 2003.

Donelson, Lewis R. *Pseudepigraphy and Ethical Arguments in the Pastorals*. HUT 22. Tübingen: Mohr-Siebeck, 1986. Reprint, Eugene, OR: Wipf & Stock, 2015.

________. "The Structure of Ethical Argument in the Pastorals." *BTB* 18 (1988): 108–13.

Donfried, Karl Paul, ed. *1 Timothy Reconsidered*. Colloquium Oecumenicum Paulinum 18. Leuven: Peeters, 2008.

Downs, David J. "'Early Catholicism' and Apocalypticism in the Pastoral Epistles." *CBQ* 67 (2005): 641–61.

Duff, J. N. "A Reconsideration of Pseudepigraphy in Early Christianity." Ph.D. diss., University of Oxford, 1998.

Ehrman, Bart G. *Forgery and Counterforgery: The Use of Literary Deceit in Early Christian Polemics*. Oxford: Oxford University Press, 2013.

Ellis, E. Earle. "The Authorship of the Pastorals: A Resume and Assessment .of Recent Trends." Pages 49–57 in *Paul and His Recent Interpreters*. Grand Rapids: Eerdmans, 1961.

________. "The Origin and Composition of the Pastoral Epistles." Pages 65–84 in *History and Interpretation in New Testament Perspective*. BIS 54. Leiden: Brill, 2001.

________. "Pastoral Letters." Pages 658–66 in *Dictionary of Paul and His Letters*. Edited by Gerald F. Hawthorne, Ralph P. Martin, and Daniel G. Reid. Downers Grove: InterVarsity, 1993.

________. "Pseudonymity and Canonicity of New Testament Documents." Pages 212–24 in *Worship, Theology and Ministry in the Early Church: Essays in Honor of Ralph P. Martin*. Edited by Michael J. Wilkins and Terence Paige. JSNTSup 87. Sheffield: JSOT, 1992.

________. "Traditions in the Pastoral Epistles." Pages 237–53 in *Early Jewish and Christian Exegesis*. Edited by Craig A. Evans and William F. Stinespring. Atlanta: Scholars Press, 1987.

Ellis, Mark A. "Apostasy and Perseverance in the Pastoral Epistles." Th.M. thesis, Dallas Theological Seminary, 1988.

Fatum, Lone. "Christ Domesticated: The Household Theology of the Pastorals as Political Strategy." Pages 175–207 in *The Formation of the Early Church*. Edited by Jostein Ådna. WUNT 183. Tübingen: Mohr-Siebeck, 2005.

Fee, Gordon D. God's *Empowering Presence: The Holy Spirit in the Letters of Paul*. Peabody, MA: Hendrickson, 1994.

________. *Pauline Christology: An Exegetical-Theological Study*. Peabody, MA: Hendrickson, 2007.

Fiore, Benjamin. *The Function of Personal Example in the Socratic and Pastoral Epistles*. AnBib 105. Rome: Biblical Institute Press, 1986.

Fitzmyer, Joseph A. "The Savior God." Pages 181–96 in *The Forgotten God: Perspectives in Biblical Theology. Essays in Honor of Paul J. Achtemeier on the Occasion of His Seventy-Fifth Birthday*. Edited by A. Andrew Das and Frank J. Matera. Louisville: Westminster John Knox, 2002.

________. "The Structured Ministry of the Church in the Pastoral Epistles." *CBQ* 66 (2004): 582–96.

Gehring, Roger W. *House Church and Mission: The Importance of Household Structures in Early Christianity*. Peabody, MA: Hendrickson, 2004.

Glahn, Sandra L. "The First-Century Ephesian Artemis: Ramifications of Her Identity." *BSac* 172/688 (2015): 450–69.

________. "The Identity of Artemis in First-Century Ephesus." *BSac* 172/688 (2016): 316–34.

Goodrich, John K. "Overseers as Stewards and the Qualifications for Leadership in the Pastoral Epistles." *ZNW* 14 (2013): 77–97.

Greenlee, J. Harold. *An Exegetical Summary of Titus & Philemon*. 2nd ed. Dallas: SIL International, 2008.

Guthrie, Donald. *The Pastoral Epistles and the Mind of Paul*. London: Tyndale, 1955.

Häfner, Gerd. "Deuteronomy in the Pastoral Epistles." Pages 136–51 in *Deuteronomy in the New Testament*. Edited by Maarten J. J. Menken and Steve Moyise. LNTS 358. New York: T&T Clark, 2007.

Hagner, Donald A. *The New Testament: A Historical and Theological Introduction*. Grand Rapids: Baker, 2012.

________. "Titus as a Pauline Letter." Pages 546–58 in *Society of Biblical Literature* 1998 Seminar Papers, Part Two. SBLSP 37. Atlanta: Scholars Press, 1998.

Hanson, A. T. *Studies in the Pastoral Epistles*. London: S.P.C.K., 1968. Reprint, Eugene, OR: Wipf & Stock, 2015.

Harding, Mark. "The Pastoral Epistles." Pages 328–52 in *All Things to All Cultures: Paul among Jews, Greeks, and Romans*. Edited by Mark Harding and Alanna Nobbs. Grand Rapids: Eerdmans, 2013.

________. *Tradition and Rhetoric in the Pastoral Epistles*. StBibLit 3. New York: Peter Lang, 1998.

________. *What Are They Saying about the Pastoral Epistles?* Mahwah, NJ: Paulist, 2001.

Hasler, Victor. "Epiphanie und Christologie in den Pastoralbriefen." *TZ* 33 (1977): 193–209.

Haykin, Michael A. G. "The Fading Vision? The Spirit and Freedom in the Pastoral Epistles." *EvQ* 57 (1985): 291–305.

Herzer, Jens. "Rearranging the 'House of God': A New Perspective on the Pastoral Epistles." Pages 547–66 in *Empsychoi Logoi—Religious Innovations in Antiquity: Studies in Honour of Pieter Willem van der Horst*. Edited by Alberdina Houtman, Albert de Jong, and Magda Misset-van de Weg. Leiden: Brill, 2008.

Hetzler, Charles Oscar. "Our Savior and King: Theology Proper in 1 Timothy." Ph.D. diss., The Southern Baptist Theological Seminary, 2008.

Ho, C. E. "Do the Work of an Evangelist: The Missionary Outlook of the Pastoral Epistles." Ph.D. diss., University of Aberdeen, 2000.

Hoag, Gary G. *Wealth in Ancient Ephesus and the First Letter to Timothy: Fresh Insights from Ephesiaca by Xenophon of Ephesus*. BBRSup. Winona Lake, IN: Eisenbrauns, 2015.

Horrell, David G. "From ἀδελφοί to οἶκος θεοῦ: Social Transformation in Pauline Christianity." *JBL* 120 (2001): 293–311.

Huizenga, Annette Bourland. *Moral Education for Women in the Pastoral and Pythagorean Letters: Philosophers of the Household*. NovTSup 147. Leiden: Brill, 2013.

Hutson, Christopher R. "Ecclesiology in the Pastoral Epistles." Pages 164–88 in *The New Testament Church: The Challenge of Developing Ecclesiologies*. Edited by John Harrison and James D. Dvorak. McMaster Divinity College Biblical Studies 1. Eugene, OR: Pickwick, 2012.

________. "My True Child: The Rhetoric of Youth in the Pastoral Epistles." Ph.D. diss., Yale University, 1998.

Johnson, Luke Timothy. "II Timothy and the Polemic against False Teachers: A Reexamination." *JRS* 6–7 (1978): 1–26. Reprint, pages 331–62 in *Contested Issues in Christian Origins and the New Testament: Collected Essays*. Edited by Luke Timothy Johnson. NovTSup 146. Leiden: Brill, 2013.

________. "*Oikonomia Theou*: The Theological Voice of 1 Timothy from the Perspective of Pauline Authorship." *HorBT* 21 (1999): 87–104. Reprint, pages 383–403 in *Contested Issues in Christian Origins and the New Testament*. Edited by Luke Timothy Johnson. NovTSup 146. Leiden: Brill, 2013.

Karris, Robert J. "The Background and Significance of the Polemic of the Pastoral Epistles." *JBL* 92 (1973): 549–64.

Kidd, Reggie M. *Wealth and Beneficence in the Pastoral Epistles: A "Bourgeois" Form of Early Christianity?* SBLDS 122. Atlanta: Scholars Press, 1990.

Kirk, Alexander N. "Paul the Victor: Paul Approaches Death in 2 Timothy." Pages 217–38 in *The Departure of an Apostle: Paul's Death Anticipated and Remembered*. WUNT 2/406. Tübingen: Mohr Siebeck, 2015.

Klinker-De Klerck, Myriam. "The Pastoral Epistles: Authentic Pauline Writings." *EuroJTh* 17 (2008): 101–8.

Knight, George W., III. *The Faithful Sayings in the Pastoral Letters*. Kampen: Kok, 1968. Reprint, Baker Biblical Monographs. Grand Rapids: Baker, 1979.

Köstenberger, Andreas J., "Hermeneutical and Exegetical Challenges in Interpreting the Pastoral Epistles." *The Southern Baptist Journal of Theology* 7 (2003): 4–17.

________. "The Use of Scripture in the Pastoral and General Epistles and the Book of Revelation." Pages 230–54 in *Hearing the Old Testament in the New Testament*. Edited by Stanley E. Porter. Grand Rapids: Eerdmans, 2006.

________, and Thomas R. Schreiner, eds. *Women in the Church: An Analysis and Application of 1 Timothy 2:9–15.* 3rd ed. Grand Rapids: Baker, 2016.

________, and Terry L. Wilder, eds. *Entrusted with the Gospel: Paul's Theology in the Pastoral Epistles*. Nashville: B&H, 2010.

Lau, Andrew Y. *Manifest in the Flesh: The Epiphany Christology of the Pastoral Epistles.* Tübingen: Mohr-Siebeck, 1996.

MacDonald, Margaret Y. *The Pauline Churches: A Socio-Historical Study of Institutionalism in the Pauline and Deutero-Pauline Writings.* SNTSMS 60. Cambridge: Cambridge University Press, 1988.

Maier, Harry O. *Picturing Paul in Empire: Imperial Image, Text and Persuasion in Colossians, Ephesians and the Pastoral Epistles.* London: Bloomsbury/T&T Clark, 2013.

Malherbe, Abraham J. "'Christ Jesus Came into the World to Save Sinners': Soteriology in the Pastoral Epistles." Pages 331–58 in *Salvation in the New Testament: Perspectives on Soteriology.* Edited by Jan G. van der Watt. NovTSup 121. Leiden: Brill, 2005. Reprinted, pages 431–58 in *Light from the Gentiles: Hellenistic Philosophy and Early Christianity. Collected Essays, 1959–2012, by Abraham J. Malherbe.* Edited by Carl R. Holladay, John T. Fitzgerald, Gregory E. Sterling, and James W. Thompson. 2 volumes. NovTSup 150. Leiden: Brill, 2014.

________. "Godliness, Self-Sufficiency, Greed, and the Enjoyment of Wealth. 1 Timothy 6:3–19: Parts I and II." *NovT* 52–53 (2010–11): 376–405, 73–96. Reprinted, pages 535–58 in *Light from the Gentiles*, by Abraham J. Malherbe. Edited by Carl R. Holladay et al. NovTSup 150. Leiden: Brill, 2014.

________. "Medical Imagery in the Pastoral Epistles." Pages 19–35 in *Texts and Testaments: Critical Essays on the Bible and Early Church Fathers.* Edited by W. E. March. San Antonio: Trinity University Press, 1980. Reprint, pages 117–34 in *Light from the Gentiles, by Abraham J. Malherbe.* Edited by Carl R. Holladay et al. NovTSup 150. Leiden: Brill, 2014.

________. "Overseers as Household Managers in the Pastoral Epistles." Pages 72–88 in *Text, Image, and Christians in the Graeco-Roman World: A Festschrift in Honor of David Lee Balch.* Edited by Aliou Cissé Niang and Carolyn Osiek. Princeton Theological Monograph Series 176. Eugene, OR: Pickwick, 2012. Reprint, pages 559–74 in *Light from the Gentiles*, by Abraham J. Malherbe. Edited by Carl R. Holladay et al. NovTSup 150. Leiden: Brill, 2014.

________. "*Paulus Senex.*" *ResQ* 36 (1994): 197–207. Reprint, pages 277–88 in *Light from the Gentiles, by Abraham J. Malherbe.* Edited by Carl R. Holladay et al. NovTSup 150. Leiden: Brill, 2014.

Marshall, I. Howard. "The Christology of Luke-Acts and the Pastoral Epistles." Pages 167–82 in *Crossing the Boundaries: Essays in Biblical Literature in Honor of Michael D. Goulder.* Edited by Stanley E. Porter, P. Joyce, and D. E. Orton. BIS 8. Leiden: Brill, 1994.

________. "The Christology of the Pastoral Epistles." *SNTSU* A 13 (1988): 157–77.

________. "Congregation and Ministry in the Pastoral Epistles." Pages 105–25 in *Community Formation in the Early Church and the Church Today*. Edited by Richard N. Longenecker. Peabody, MA: Hendrickson, 2002.

________. "Faith and Works in the Pastoral Epistles." *SNTSU* A 9 (1984): 203–18.

________. "The Holy Spirit in the Pastoral Epistles and the Apostolic Fathers." Pages 257–69 in *The Holy Spirit and Christian Origins: Essays in Honor of James D. G. Dunn*. Grand Rapids: Eerdmans, 2004.

________. "Salvation, Grace, and Works in the Later Writings in the Pauline Corpus." *NTS* 42 (1996): 339–58.

________. "Salvation in the Pastoral Epistles." Pages 449–69 in *Geschichte—Tradition—Reflexion: Festschrift für Martin Hengel zum 70. Geburtstag*, vol. 3: *Frühes Christentum*. Edited by Hermann Lichtenberger. Tübingen: Mohr-Siebeck, 1996.

________. "'Sometimes Only Orthodox'—Is There More to the Pastoral Epistles?" *Epworth Review* 20 (1993): 12–24.

________. "Universal Grace and Atonement in the Pastoral Epistles." Pages 51–70 in *The Grace of God and the Will of Man*. Edited by Clark H. Pinnock. Minneapolis: Bethany House, 1989.

Martin, Séan Charles. *Pauli Testamentum: 2 Timothy and the Last Words of Moses*. Tesi gregoriana, serie teologia 18. Rome: Pontificia Università Gregoriana, 1999.

Matera, Frank J. "A Theology of the Pauline Tradition: The Pastoral Epistles." Pages 240–58 in *New Testament Theology: Exploring Diversity and Unity*. Louisville: Westminster John Knox, 2007.

McEleney, Neil J. "The Vice Lists of the Pastoral Epistles." *CBQ* 36 (1974): 203–19.

Meade, David G. *Pseudonymity and Canon. An Investigation into the Relationship of Authorship and Authority in Jewish and Earliest Christian Tradition*. WUNT 39. Tübingen: Mohr-Siebeck, 1986.

Merkle, Benjamin L. *The Elder and Overseer: One Office in the Early Church*. StBibLit 57. New York: Peter Lang, 2003.

Metzger, Bruce M. "Literary Forgeries and Canonical Pseudepigrapha." *JBL* 91 (1972): 3–24.

________. "A Reconsideration of Certain Arguments against the Pauline Authorship of the Pastoral Epistles." *ExpTim* 70 (1958–59): 91–94.

Miller, J. D. *The Pastoral Letters as Composite Documents*. SNTSMS 93. Cambridge: Cambridge University Press, 1997.

Minor, Eugene E. *An Exegetical Summary of 2 Timothy*. 2nd ed. Dallas: SIL International, 2008.

Mitchell, Margaret M. "New Testament Envoys in the Context of Greco-Roman Diplomatic and Epistolary Conventions: The Example of Timothy and Titus." *JBL* 111 (1992): 641–62.

Murphy-O'Connor, Jerome. "2 Timothy Contrasted with 1 Timothy and Titus." *RB* 98 (1991): 403–18.

Mutschler, Bernhard. "Eschatology in the Pastoral Epistles." Pages 362–402 in *Eschatology of the New Testament and Some Related Documents.* Edited by Jan G. van der Watt. WUNT 2/315. Tübingen: Mohr-Siebeck, 2011.

Ong, Hughson T. "Is There a Heresy in the Pastorals? A Sociolinguistic Analysis of 1 and 2 Timothy via the Ethnography of Communication Theory." Pages 119–38 in *Paul and Gnosis.* Edited by Stanley E. Porter and David I. Yoon. Pauline Studies 9. Leiden: Brill, 2016.

Oropeza, B. J. "1, 2 Timothy and Titus: The Influence of False Teachers in the Pastoral Letters." Pages 260–308 in *Jews, Gentiles, and the Opponents of Paul: The Pauline Letters.* Apostasy in the NT Communities 2. Eugene, OR: Cascade, 2012.

Page, Sydney. "Marital Expectations of Church Leaders in the Pastoral Epistles." *JSNT* 50 (1993): 105–20.

Pao, David W. "Let No One Despise Your Youth: Church and the World in the Pastoral Epistles," *JETS* 57 (2014): 743–44.

Pfitzner, Victor C. "The *Agon* Motif in the Pastoral Epistles." Pages 164–86 in *Paul and the Agon Motif: Traditional Athletic Imagery in the Pauline Literature.* NovTSup 16. Leiden: Brill, 1967.

Pietersen, Lloyd K. *The Polemic of the Pastorals: A Sociological Examination of the Development of Pauline Christianity.* JSNTSup 264. New York: T&T Clark, 2004.

Portefaix, Lilian. "'Good Citizenship' in the Household of God: Women's Position in the Pastorals Reconsidered in the Light of Roman Rule." Pages 147–58 in *A Feminist Companion to the Deutero-Pauline Epistles.* Feminist Companion to the NT and Early Christian Writings. Edited by Amy-Jill Levine with Marianne Blickenstaff. Cleveland: Pilgrim, 2003.

Porter, Stanley E. "Paul and the Pauline Letter Collection." Pages 19–36 in *Paul and the Second Century.* Edited by M. F. Bird and J. R. Dodson. Library of New Testament Studies 412. T&T Clark Library of Biblical Studies. New York: T&T Clark, 2011.

________. "Pauline Authorship and the Pastoral Epistles: Implications for Canon." *BBR* 5 (1995): 105–23.

________, and G. P. Fewster, eds. *Paul and Pseudepigraphy.* Pauline Studies 8. Leiden: Brill, 2013.

Prior, Michael. *Paul the Letter-Writer and the Second Letter to Timothy.* JSNTSup 23. Sheffield: JSOT, 1989.

Puig i Tàrrech, Armand, John M. G. Barclay, and Jörg Frey, eds. *The Last Years of Paul: Essays from the Tarragona Conference, June 2013.* WUNT 352. Tübingen: Mohr-Siebeck, 2015.

Quinn, Jerome D. "The Holy Spirit in the Pastoral Epistles." Pages 35–68 in *Sin, Salvation, and the Spirit.* Edited by D. Durken. Collegeville, MN: Liturgical Press, 1979.

________. "The Last Volume of Luke: The Relation of Luke-Acts to the Pastoral Epistles." Pages 62–75 in *Perspectives on Luke-Acts.* Edited by Charles H. Talbert. PRSt Special Studies Series 5. Macon, GA: Mercer University Press, 1978.

________. "On the Terminology for Faith, Truth, Teaching, and the Spirit in the Pastoral Epistles: A Summary." Pages 232–37 in *Teaching Authority and Infallibility in the Church.* Edited by Paul C. Empie, T. Austin Murphy, and Joseph A. Burgess. Lutherans and Catholics in Dialogue 6. Minneapolis: Augsburg, 1978.

________. "Timothy and Titus, Epistles to." Pages 560–57 in vol. 6 of *ABD.* Edited by David Noel Freedman. Doubleday: New York, 1992.

Riesner, Rainer. "Once More: Luke-Acts and the Pastoral Epistles." Pages 239–58 in *History and Exegesis: New Testament Essays in Honor of Dr. E. Earle Ellis for His 80th Birthday.* Edited by Sang-Won (Aaron) Son. New York: T&T Clark, 2006.

Schnabel, Eckhard J. "Paul, Timothy, and Titus: The Assumption of a Pseudonymous Author and of Pseudonymous Recipients in the Light of Literary, Theological, and Historical Evidence." Pages 383–403 in *Do Historical Matters Matter to Faith? A Critical Appraisal of Modern and Postmodern Approaches to Scripture.* Edited by James K. Hoffmeier and Dennis R. Magary. Wheaton: Crossway, 2012.

Schnelle, Udo. "The Pastoral Epistles: God's Philanthropy." Pages 578–601 in *Theology of the New Testament.* Translated by M. Eugene Boring. Grand Rapids: Baker, 2007.

Schreiner, Thomas R. "'Problematic Texts' for Definite Atonement in the Pastoral and General Epistles." Pages 375–97 in *He Came and Sought Her: Definite Atonement in Historical, Biblical, Theological, and Pastoral Perspective.* Edited by David Gibson and Jonathan Gibson. Wheaton: Crossway, 2013.

Skarsaune, Oskar. "Heresy and the Pastoral Epistles." *Them* 20 (1994): 9–14.

Smith, Claire. *Pauline Communities as "Scholastic Communities": A Study of the Vocabulary of "Teaching" in 1 Corinthians, 1 and 2 Timothy and Titus.* WUNT 2/335. Tübingen: Mohr-Siebeck, 2012.

Stepp, Perry L. *Leadership Succession in the World of the Pauline Circle.* NT Monographs 5. Sheffield: Sheffield Phoenix, 2005.

Strecker, G. "Sound Doctrine—the Pastoral Letters." Pages 576–94 in *Theology of the New Testament*. Edited by F. W. Horn. Translated by M. E. Boring. Berlin: de Gruyter, 2000.

Sumney, Jerry L. *'Servants of Satan,' 'False Brothers' and Other Opponents of Paul*. JSNTSup 188. Sheffield: Sheffield Academic Press, 1999.

________. "Studying Paul's Opponents: Advances and Challenges." Pages 7–58 in *Paul and His Opponents*. Edited by Stanley E. Porter. Pauline Studies 2. Leiden: Brill, 2005.

Swinson, L. Timothy. *What Is Scripture? Paul's Use of Graphe in the Letters to Timothy*. Eugene, OR: Wipf & Stock, 2014.

Talbert, Charles H. "Between Two Epiphanies: Clarifying One Aspect of Soteriology in the Pastoral Epistles." Pages 58–71 in *Getting "Saved": The Whole Story of Salvation in the New Testament*, by Charles H. Talbert and Jason A. Whitlark. Grand Rapids: Eerdmans, 2011.

Thornton, Dillon. *Hostility in the House of God: An Investigation of the Opponents in 1 and 2 Timothy*. BBRSup 15. Winona Lake, IN: Eisenbrauns, 2016.

Thurston, Bonnie. "The Theology of Titus." *HorBT* 21 (1999): 171–84.

Towner, Philip H. "1–2 Timothy and Titus." Pages 891–918 in *Commentary on the New Testament Use of the Old Testament*. Edited by D. A. Carson and G. K. Beale. Grand Rapids: Baker, 2007.

________. "Christology in the Letters to Timothy and Titus." Pages 219–44 in *Contours of Christology in the New Testament*. Edited by Richard N. Longenecker. Grand Rapids: Eerdmans, 2005.

________. "Gnosis and Realized Eschatology in Ephesus (of the Pastoral Epistles) and the Corinthian Enthusiasm." *JSNT* 31 (1987): 95–124.

________. *The Goal of Our Instruction: The Structure of Theology and Ethics in the Pastoral Epistles*. JSNTSup 34. Sheffield: Sheffield Academic Press, 1989.

________. "The Pastoral Epistles." Pages 330–36 in *NDBT*. Edited by T. D. Alexander, B. S. Rosner, D. A. Carson, and G. Goldsworthy. Leicester: InterVarsity, 2000.

________. "Pauline Theology or Pauline Tradition in the Pastoral Epistles: The Question of Method." *TynBul* 46 (1995): 287–314.

________. "The Portrait of Paul and the Theology of 2 Timothy: The Closing Chapter of the Pauline Story." *HorBT* 21 (1999): 151–70.

________. "The Present Age in the Eschatology of the Pastoral Epistles." *NTS* 32 (1986): 427–48.

Trebilco, Paul. *The Early Christians in Ephesus from Paul to Ignatius*. WUNT 166. Tübingen: Mohr-Siebeck, 2004.

________. "The Significance and Relevance of the Spirit in the Pastoral Epistles." Pages 241–56 in *The Holy Spirit and Christian Origins: Essays in Honor of James D. G. Dunn*. Edited by Graham N. Stanton, Bruce W. Longenecker, and Stephen C. Barton. Grand Rapids: Eerdmans, 2004.

________. “What Shall We Call Each Other? Part One: The Issue of Self-Designation in the Pastoral Epistles.” *TynBul* 53 (2002): 239–58.

Van Neste, Ray. *Cohesion and Structure in the Pastoral Epistles.* JSNTSup 280. London: T&T Clark, 2004

Verner, David C. *The Household of God: The Social World of the Pastoral Epistles.* SBLDS 71. Chico, CA: Scholars Press, 1983.

Wainwright, John J. “*Eusebeia*: Syncretism or Conservative Contextualization?” *EvQ* 65 (1993): 211–24.

Wall, Robert W. “The Function of the Pastoral Letters within the Pauline Canon of the New Testament: A Canonical Approach.” Pages 27–44 in *The Pauline Canon.* Edited by Stanley E. Porter. Pauline Studies 1. Leiden: Brill, 2004.

________. “Pauline Authorship and the Pastoral Epistles: A Response to S. E. Porter.” *BBR* 5 (1995): 125–28.

Westfall, Cynthia Long. “A Moral Dilemma? The Epistolary Body of 2 Timothy.” Pages 213–52 in *Paul and the Ancient Letter Form.* Edited by Stanley E. Porter and Sean A. Adams. Pauline Studies 6. Leiden: Brill, 2010.

Wieland, George M. “Roman Crete and the Letter to Titus.” *NTS* 55 (2009): 338–54.

________. *The Significance of Salvation: A Study of Salvation Language in the Pastoral Epistles.* Paternoster Biblical Monographs. Carlisle, PA: Paternoster, 2006.

Wilder, Terry L. “Does the Bible Contain Forgeries?” Pages 166–81 in *In Defense of the Bible: A Comprehensive Apologetic for the Authority of Scripture.* Edited by Steven B. Cowan and Terry L. Wilder. Nashville: B&H, 2013.

________. *Pseudonymity, the New Testament, and Deception: An Inquiry into Intention and Deception.* Lanham, MD: University Press of America, 2004.

Wilson, Steven G. *Luke and the Pastoral Epistles.* London: SPCK, 1979.

________. “The Portrait of Paul in Acts and the Pastorals.” Pages 397–411 in *SBL Seminar Papers.* Edited by George MacRae. Missoula, MT: Scholars Press, 1976.

Winter, Bruce W. *Roman Wives, Roman Widows: The Appearance of New Women and the Pauline Communities.* Grand Rapids: Eerdmans, 2003.

Wolfe, B. Paul. “The Place and Use of Scripture in the Pastoral Epistles.” Ph.D. diss., University of Aberdeen, 1990.

Yarbrough, Mark M. *Paul’s Utilization of Preformed Traditions in 1 Timothy: An Evaluation of the Apostle’s Literary, Rhetorical, and Theological Tactics.* LNTS 417. London: T&T Clark, 2009.

Yarbrough, Robert W. “Schlatter on the Pastorals: Mission in the Academy.” Pages 295–316 in *New Testament Theology in Light of the Church’s Mission: Essays in Honor of I. Howard Marshall.* Edited by Jon C. Laansma, Grant R. Osborne, and Ray F. Van Neste. Eugene, OR: Cascade: 2011.

Yarnell, Malcolm B. "*Oikos Theou*: A Theologically Neglected but Important Ecclesiological Metaphor." *Midwestern Journal of Theology* 2 (2003): 53–65.

Young, Frances. "On ἐπίσκοπος and πρεσβύτερος." *JTS* 45 (1994): 142–48.

________. "The Pastoral Epistles and the Ethics of Reading." *JSNT* 45 (1992): 105–20.

________. *The Theology of the Pastoral Letters*. Cambridge: Cambridge University Press, 1994.

Zamfir, Korinna. "Creation and Fall in 1 Timothy: A Contextual Approach." Pages 353–87 in *Theologies of Creation in Early Judaism and Ancient Christianity: In Honour of Hans Klein*. Deuterocanonical and Cognate Literature Studies 6. Berlin: de Gruyter, 2010.

________. "Is the *ekklēsia* a Household (of God)? Reassessing the Notion of οἶκος θεοῦ in 1 Tim 3.15." *NTS* 60 (2014): 511–28.

________. *Men and Women in the Household of God: A Contextual Approach to Roles and Ministries in the Pastoral Epistles*. NTOA/SUNT 103. Göttingen: Vandenhoeck & Ruprecht, 2013.

NAME INDEX

SUBJECT INDEX

SCRIPTURE INDEX

Luke

John

Ephesians

Scripture Index

Philemon

1–2 Timothy and Titus